Human Rights and Information Communication Technologies:

Trends and Consequences of Use

John Lannon
University of Limerick, Ireland

Edward F. Halpin
Leeds Metropolitan University, UK

Information Science
REFERENCE

Published in the United States of America by
Information Science Reference (an imprint of IGI Global)
701 E. Chocolate Avenue
Hershey PA 17033
Tel: 717-533-8845
Fax: 717-533-8661
E-mail: cust@igi-global.com
Web site: http://www.igi-global.com

Library of Congress Cataloging-in-Publication Data

Human rights and information communication technologies: trends and consequences of use / John Lannon and Edward F. Halpin, editors.
p. cm.
Includes bibliographical references and index.
Summary: "This book provides a current examination of policy, practice, and theory relating to human rights and information, communications and technology and offers a comprehensive review of the topic and the exponential changes that have occurred through the last decade"--Provided by publisher.
ISBN 978-1-4666-1918-0 (hbk.) -- ISBN 978-1-4666-1919-7 (ebook) -- ISBN 978-1-4666-1920-3 (print & perpetual access) 1. Human rights. 2. Information technology--Political aspects. 3. Information technology--Social aspects. I. Lannon, John M. II. Halpin, Edward F.
JC571.H768827 2013
323.44--dc23

2012005066

British Cataloguing in Publication Data
A Cataloguing in Publication record for this book is available from the British Library.

Table of Contents

Foreword xiii

Preface xv

Acknowledgment xxx

Section 1
Setting the Scene

Chapter 1
Human Rights and Technology: Lessons from Alice in Wonderland 1
Judith Dueck, The University of Winnipeg Global College, Canada
Michael Rempel, Software Architect, Canada

Chapter 2
ICT Policies Favouring Human Rights 21
Rolf H. Weber, University of Zurich, Switzerland

Chapter 3
Negotiating Boundaries between Control and Dissent: Free Speech, Business, and Repressitarian Governments 36
Brian J. Bowe, Grand Valley State University, USA
Robin Blom, Michigan State University, USA
Eric Freedman, Michigan State University, USA

Section 2
Case Studies from Around the World

Chapter 4
"In YouTube We Trust": Video Exchange and Arab Human Rights 57
Aziz Douai, University of Ontario Institute of Technology, Canada

Chapter 5
Truth-Seeking at a Distance: Engaging Diaspora Populations in Transitional Justice Processes 72
Eric Wiebelhaus-Brahm, Florida State University, USA

Chapter 6
ICT and Human Rights in Brazil: From Military to Digital Dictatorship 86
José Rodrigues Filho, Universidade Federal da Paraíba, Brazil

Chapter 7
Contingency and Hybridity in the Study of Digital Advocacy Networks: Implications of the Egyptian Protest Movement 100
Christopher Wilson, University of Oslo, Norway
Alexandra Dunn, University of Oslo, Norway

Section 3
Practitioner Perspectives

Chapter 8
Crowdsourcing for Human Rights Monitoring: Challenges and Opportunities for Information Collection and Verification 123
Jessica Heinzelman, The Fletcher School of Law & Diplomacy, USA
Patrick Meier, Stanford University and Ushahidi, USA

Chapter 9
Counting the Unknown Victims of Political Violence: The Work of the Human Rights Data Analysis Group 139
Ann Harrison, Benetech Human Rights Data Analysis Group, USA

Chapter 10
Human Rights Defenders and the Right to Digital Privacy and Security 157
Tanya Notley, Tactical Technology Collective, Germany
Stephanie Hankey, Tactical Technology Collective, Germany

Section 4
Economic and Social Rights

Chapter 11
Social Assistance via the Internet: The Case of Finland in the European Context 177
Minna Strömberg-Jakka, University of Turku, Finland

Chapter 12
Mental Health, Post-Secondary Education, and Information Communications Technology 196
Jenny Martin, RMIT University, Australia
Elspeth McKay, RMIT University, Australia

Chapter 13
ICTs and Gender-Based Rights 214
Ana-Cristina Ionescu, Chamber of Commerce and Industry of Romania - CCIR, Romania

Chapter 14
Health Information Technology and Human Rights 235
Shane O'Hanlon, University of Limerick, Ireland

Conclusion 247

Compilation of References 255

About the Contributors 284

Index 290

Detailed Table of Contents

Foreword xiii

Preface xv

Acknowledgment xxx

Section 1
Setting the Scene

Chapter 1
Human Rights and Technology: Lessons from Alice in Wonderland 1
Judith Dueck, The University of Winnipeg Global College, Canada
Michael Rempel, Software Architect, Canada

This chapter examines eleven technology issues faced by human rights organizations. These issues are critical if they are to use technology effectively. Although solutions are not proposed, the chapter highlights topics that increasingly require research and concrete solutions in order for human rights organizations to integrate technology tools into their work. The key issues addressed are: rapid technology changes; national security, personal information, and human rights; web security; data relationships; controlled vocabulary (a common language); Semantic Web and human interactivity; search - finding the information; assumptions and ease of use; trust; open source; and social media. These issues, chosen from the human rights and technology backgrounds of the authors, provide a frontier to human rights work that may seem daunting to the newly initiated. Human interaction must remain the key element. Technology must be a servant to the human rights needs and demands.

Chapter 2
ICT Policies Favouring Human Rights 21
Rolf H. Weber, University of Zurich, Switzerland

The tremendous developments in information and communication technologies (ICTs) over the last 20 years have substantially changed communication practices across the world. The Internet and mobile phones help to open new horizons for connections between people, leading to a global network for the sharing of information and ideas. In this new environment, human rights need to have a place, and traditional notions related to mass media need to be adapted to the needs of civil society. Freedom of expression has become much more individualistic, with information exchanges no longer relying on the traditional intermediaries (mass media) but on the exchange of ideas on social networking and other platforms. Civil society participation in the information world requires the necessary infrastructure however. And since states have an obligation to see to it that human rights are realized in practice, this may mean the facilitation of private investments to improve the ICT infrastructure. In this context, ICT policies favoring human rights must encompass a right to development.

Chapter 3
Negotiating Boundaries between Control and Dissent: Free Speech, Business, and Repressitarian Governments 36
Brian J. Bowe, Grand Valley State University, USA
Robin Blom, Michigan State University, USA
Eric Freedman, Michigan State University, USA

Increases in access to information and communication technologies (ICTs) have given citizens new tools to organize politically. This development has particular importance for those living under authoritarian regimes that rely on the repression of free speech to maintain power. These repressitarian elites resort to a variety of means to establish (or re-establish) control over citizen online communications. However, it is counterproductive for countries to crack down too tightly on Internet expression, because such actions can create negative economic consequences for countries hoping to engage in the 21st century's wired economy. The friction between online free expression and government repression is playing out with close interest of Western governments, human rights advocates, and citizens because it places many technology companies in the difficult position of either facilitating such government repression or finding themselves unable to compete in those markets. This chapter examines recent developments in Iran, Egypt, China, and Singapore. All four countries have been identified as having severe impediments to free expression. Iran and Egypt, however, have seen the rise of some organized opposition movements despite the controls on media expression, while China and Singapore offer useful case studies on the economic dimensions of the balance between participating in the global networked society and controlling citizen expression. This chapter considers how financial and economic factors lead to more moderate views of Internet use in those countries and examine the struggles between maintaining openness and crackdowns.

Section 2
Case Studies from Around the World

Chapter 4
"In YouTube We Trust": Video Exchange and Arab Human Rights 57
Aziz Douai, University of Ontario Institute of Technology, Canada

YouTube has enabled new forms of political dissent in Arab societies. This chapter examines the development and rise of YouTube in the Arab world. In particular, it looks at how this video exchange site is invigorating the online public sphere's vigorous demand for political reform and respect for human rights. Specifically, this investigation explores how social networking capabilities have made YouTube an effective asset in dissidents' arsenal among Arab activists. To examine the vibrancy of this fledgling online public sphere, the chapter scrutinizes how activists incorporated YouTube videos to shed light on human rights abuses, specifically police abuse, corruption, and brutality in two Arab countries, Egypt and Morocco. The chapter concludes with a discussion of the new campaigning modes that the Internet and YouTube have facilitated.

Chapter 5
Truth-Seeking at a Distance: Engaging Diaspora Populations in Transitional Justice Processes 72
Eric Wiebelhaus-Brahm, Florida State University, USA

The Liberian Truth and Reconciliation Commission (LTRC) was established by the Liberian government in 2005 to "promote national peace, security, unity, and reconciliation." The LTRC thought it essential to allow Liberians who had fled the conflict to participate in the truth and reconciliation process. As a result, it partnered with a US-based non-governmental organization, The Advocates for Human Rights, to conduct the Diaspora Project. This chapter provides an overview of the Diaspora Project, which enabled Liberians on three continents to give statements to the LTRC. Given the wide dispersion of the Liberian diaspora, the author of this chapter demonstrates how information communication technologies were essential in the success of the Diaspora Project.

Chapter 6
ICT and Human Rights in Brazil: From Military to Digital Dictatorship 86
José Rodrigues Filho, Universidade Federal da Paraíba, Brazil

Since the end of military government in Brazil, civilian governments have sought the accumulation and exercise of power to the detriment of the citizenry. They have done this with a kind of totalitarianism that takes the form of digital or bureaucratic dictatorship. Since the 1990s, they have started to implement information technology in the public sector to regulate and run the country in a command-and-control way through technological or bureaucratic dictatorship rather democratic process. While it is evident that there is a high level of investment in information technology in the public sector (e-government) in Brazil, there are also clear signs of the violation of human rights in terms of privacy. These occur, for instance, when the public administration exercises the power to engage in a process of electronic surveillance without the supervision of the judiciary. It is alleged that thousands of individual files have been accessed in the public administration in Brazil, despite the privacy protection offered by the national constitution. In addition, there is a proliferation of biometric identification using faces, eyes, fingerprints, and other body parts, especially in the e-voting system. This chapter shows how information technology (e-government) in Brazil could lead to violations of human rights because of the proliferation of biometric identification in the e-voting system as well as other sorts of invisible electronic surveillance that are affecting civil liberties and individual rights, including privacy.

Chapter 7
Contingency and Hybridity in the Study of Digital Advocacy Networks: Implications of the Egyptian Protest Movement 100
Christopher Wilson, University of Oslo, Norway
Alexandra Dunn, University of Oslo, Norway

This chapter proposes an analytic approach for the study of ICTs in contentious politics and human rights advocacy. By applying the analytical frames of contingency and hybridity to study design, this approach aims to promote empirical analyses, strengthen data comparability, and improve understanding into how human rights activists strategically combine digital and grounded communications to respond to complex and changing environments. The authors explore this analytic approach and its implications through a close analysis of the Front to Defend Egyptian Protesters (FDEP), a Cairo-based initiative utilizing multiple digital media to mobilize support teams for arrested protesters and work towards their release. Applying the analytical frames of contingency and hybridity to FDEP activities in 2010, prior to the uprisings now commonly referred to as the Arab Spring, the chapter observes a number of opportunities for targeted data collection. It closes by observing the challenges and opportunities this poses to the contemporary study of digital activism.

Section 3
Practitioner Perspectives

Chapter 8
Crowdsourcing for Human Rights Monitoring: Challenges and Opportunities for Information Collection and Verification 123
Jessica Heinzelman, The Fletcher School of Law & Diplomacy, USA
Patrick Meier, Stanford University and Ushahidi, USA

Accurate information is a foundational element of human rights work. Collecting and presenting factual evidence of violations is critical to the success of advocacy activities and the reputation of organizations reporting on abuses. To ensure credibility, human rights monitoring has historically been conducted through highly controlled organizational structures that face mounting challenges in terms of capacity, cost, and access. The proliferation of Information and Communication Technologies (ICTs) provide new opportunities to overcome some of these challenges through crowdsourcing. At the same time, however, crowdsourcing raises new challenges of verification and information overload that have made human rights professionals skeptical of their utility. This chapter explores whether the efficiencies gained through an open call for monitoring and reporting abuses provides a net gain for human rights monitoring and analyzes the opportunities and challenges that new and traditional methods pose for verifying crowdsourced human rights reporting.

Chapter 9
Counting the Unknown Victims of Political Violence: The Work of the Human Rights Data Analysis Group 139
Ann Harrison, Benetech Human Rights Data Analysis Group, USA

The Benetech Human Rights Data Analysis Group (HRDAG) (http://www.hrdag.org/) analyzes the patterns and magnitude of large-scale human rights violations. Together with local partners, HRDAG collects and preserves human rights data and helps NGOs and other human rights organizations accurately interpret quantitative findings. HRDAG statisticians, programmers, and data analysts develop methodologies to determine how many of those killed and disappeared have never been accounted for - and who is most responsible. This account illustrates how HRDAG pioneered the calculation of scientifically sound statistics about political violence from multiple data sources including the testimony of witnesses who come forward to tell their stories. It describes methodologies that HRDAG analysts have developed to ensure that statistical human rights claims are transparently, demonstrably, and undeniably true.

Chapter 10
Human Rights Defenders and the Right to Digital Privacy and Security 157
Tanya Notley, Tactical Technology Collective, Germany
Stephanie Hankey, Tactical Technology Collective, Germany

Digital technologies, such as mobile phones and the internet, provide new opportunities for Human Rights Defenders to mobilise people, coordinate activities, uncover and document abuses, publish findings, and engage new audiences. However, with these new opportunities come new risks as well. This chapter examines the right to and need for private digital communication as part of freedom of expression in the context of carrying out human rights work. Drawing on their experiences at Tactical Technology Collective, an international non-government organisation, the authors argue that the most effective means to address the digital privacy needs of people who are defending human rights is to provide a range of support including awareness raising media, how-to toolkits, and hands-on training that assist Human Rights Defenders to identify and then address digital risks by changing behaviours in in ways most appropriate to their local context.

Section 4
Economic and Social Rights

Chapter 11
Social Assistance via the Internet: The Case of Finland in the European Context............................ 177
Minna Strömberg-Jakka, University of Turku, Finland

This chapter examines the connection between social assistance and the use of information communication technologies to gain access to social rights as human rights. The research is based on data consisting of 594 online questions and answers related to social assistance. Of these, 160 analysis units were chosen for a detailed content analysis. The aim of the study was to determine what different positions and combinations of positions officials and service users found themselves in during online social service consultation and how service provision was affected by an official's educational background and the phase of the social assistance process that was in progress. The results show that there are several possible combinations of outcomes and that the educational background of an answering official, as well as the phase of the process for which answers are given, have an impact on the service received.

Chapter 12
Mental Health, Post-Secondary Education, and Information Communications Technology 196
Jenny Martin, RMIT University, Australia
Elspeth McKay, RMIT University, Australia

The primary aim of this chapter is to explore the use of information and communications technology (ICT) in post-secondary education to provide opportunities for students with mental health difficulties to remain engaged in their studies during times of mental illness. Higher incompletion rates are particularly concerning amongst this group. The authors discuss how improved outcomes can be achieved through effective use of ICT. This is particularly important from a human rights perspective so that people diagnosed with mental illness are afforded the same opportunities as other members of the community. Strategies afforded by ICT tools that are essential for supporting students with mental illness to optimise their chances of success in their post-secondary education outcomes are outlined. The authors combine mental health and human-computer interaction (HCI) to argue for the need to design appropriate instructional ICT strategies to support students experiencing mental illness to remain engaged with their studies. ICT has evolved with powerful and unique features, offering special applications such as educational software, eCommerce, and healthcare. Yet, very little is being said about how to streamline these applications as effective HCI environments to enhance mental health and wellbeing. The chapter explores the positive and negative impact of ICT tools on teaching and learning. In considering mental health and post-secondary education, it focuses on human rights issues of access and equity, disclosure, and stigma. Authors suggest that ICT can enable students to remain engaged with their learning in general, while at the same time promote a deep sense of community.

Chapter 13
ICTs and Gender-Based Rights.. 214
Ana-Cristina Ionescu, Chamber of Commerce and Industry of Romania - CCIR, Romania

In this new age, the Internet, the network of networks connected by a complex array of electronic, wireless, and optical technologies extending from the private to the public sector, and from academic to business and governmental organizations, is starting to have increasingly broad social implications, besides the technical ones. Nevertheless, as women and men enter and progress differently into employment and occupations, not all humankind benefits equally from information and communication technologies (ICTs). The question that this chapter addresses is whether women have equal rights and opportunities to access and use ICTs. In this chapter, the author aims to strengthen the idea that in this changing era, new ICTs represent a cardinal instrument for social transformation, enabling and empowering women to become controllers of information.

Chapter 14
Health Information Technology and Human Rights 235
Shane O'Hanlon, University of Limerick, Ireland

Information technology has the potential to transform healthcare and eradicate many of the inequities seen in the area. However, the use of electronic means to process sensitive health data poses significant risks. Electronic health records have been designed to be more secure than traditional paper records, but there have been notable cases where data has been lost, stolen, or viewed by unauthorised persons. Misuse of health information technology can result in severe violations of human rights. In particular, the right to privacy can be eroded by inappropriate protections, which still exist in some health systems. This chapter describes the rights framework in healthcare, analyses legal provisions for protection of health data, considers why such protections are necessary, outlines examples of rights violations, and proposes future directions.

Conclusion 247

Compilation of References 255

About the Contributors 284

Index 290

Foreword

In terms of my work as the Program Director at WITNESS (www.witness.org) where we support people to use video for human rights, I can say there has never been a year like 2011. Videos, social network updates, SMS, tweets, and many other forms of technology-enabled communications created by citizens on the ground are shared daily, directly, and "by the people" - from Tahrir Square, after Friday prayers in Homs, in Pearl Square in Bahrain, or the streets of Misurata. Meanwhile, around the world in far less-known and less publicized struggles, the tools of modern communication amplify and power-up existing grassroots activism for change.

For many participants, both near and far, as well as a broader global public, the events of the "Arab Spring" have brought to light the importance of ICTs as a tool for political mobilizing and organizing. This is true at a local level within small communities of activism, but also on a national and even worldwide scale.

Issues around ICTs reverberate at multiple levels of our societies. Policy and legal decisions are made at international and national level that affect the human rights of all to freedom of expression, privacy, and non-discrimination, as well as the ability for human rights defenders to use ICTs to defend and uphold all rights. At the same time, we are in the middle of a flowering in innovation in terms of ICTs being used to enhance and amplify the capacities of both grassroots networks and traditional non-governmental organizations. Innovation and tactical sharing occurs via the coordinated and organic efforts of empowered citizens, individually and collectively. It takes place in ad hoc networks, in organized coalitions, and via non-governmental organizations.

In this valuable book, the contributors provide a roadmap to the questions at a policy and legal level, as well as insights from both academic and practitioner perspectives into specific innovative uses of ICTs. They identify particularly knotty challenges and profile organizations engaged in developing new tools and approaches.

Strong data, well analyzed, is at the heart of most in-depth human rights work. In the activist organizations section, the generally unheralded work of data analysis and documentation utilizing ICTs is highlighted through the work of Benetech, who are pioneers and leaders in this field.

Participation is also integral to emergent human rights practice. In this volume it is explored through the work of Tactical Tech "turning information into action," and the thousands of individuals participating in the crowd-sourcing work of groups like Ushahidi.

Timely case studies illustrate high-profile examples of how ICTs are being used – for example, YouTube in Egypt and Morocco before the Arab Spring, and close analysis of the use of digital media by the Front to Defend Egyptian Protestors. They also present less well-known initiatives such as the use of digital media to engage diaspora Liberians in the Truth and Reconciliation process in that country, as well as the contradictions at a policy and individual level of ICT policy in Brazil.

Furthermore, in a year when many people's understanding of human rights has been framed by the violation of civil and political rights in the context of mass protest movements, the attention of this volume to economic and social rights – and how their realization and enjoyment is enhanced or compromised by ICTs – is an unusual and important contribution to understanding ICTs in a broader context, and in contexts that are less immediately dramatic or telegenic.

By understanding how ICTs work in such a range of contexts we can hopefully understand how to best ensure that the courage, commitment, and belief in human dignity that underlie all struggles for rights are not compromised or diminished but rather enhanced and fortified by new ICTs.

Sam Gregory
Program Director, WITNESS

Sam Gregory *helps people use the power of the moving image to create change. He is the Program Director at the human rights organization WITNESS (www.witness.org), where he supervises initiatives that partner on impactful campaigns with grassroots activists using video, and train and support the growing number of video activists to use video safely, effectively, and ethically. Within WITNESS 'Cameras Everywhere' Leadership Initiative, he identifies solutions to the challenges, and ways to capitalize on the opportunities, presented by increasingly ubiquitous video for human rights. Sam has created training tools and programs including the WITNESS Video Advocacy Institute, was lead editor on 'Video for Change' (Pluto Press, 2005) and teaches 'Human Rights Advocacy Using Video, Social Media, and Participatory Media' as an Adjunct Lecturer at the Harvard Kennedy School. Sam graduated from the University of Oxford and completed a Masters in Public Policy as a Kennedy Memorial Scholar at Harvard.*

Preface

Over a decade ago, The Honourable Lloyd Axworthy, the then Minister for Foreign Affairs for Canada, wrote in *Human Rights and the Internet* (Hick et al., 2000) that information and communications technology (ICT) had enormous potential to move the human rights agenda forward. He noted that the world had already glimpsed the possibilities and had begun to take some first, small steps, and that with further imagination and ingenuity the technology would be transformed into the new millennium's talking stick. The intervening years have seen plenty of the innovation that Lloyd Axworthy had hoped for, and as a result ICTs have helped enormously to move the promotion and protection of human rights forward. They have transformed the capacity of the human rights community to highlight human rights abuse and to advocate for causes and victims of oppression. They have made it easier to access and share information, to facilitate human rights data aggregation and analysis, to offer new tactical approaches to campaigning, and to precipitate real-world activities ranging from local demonstrations to intergovernmental agency lobbying. They have enabled global participation, and given local actors international visibility.

Human Rights and Information Communication Technologies: Trends and Consequences of Use provides a current examination of policy, practice, and theory relating to human rights and information, communications, and technology. The only previous comprehensive book on the topic, *Human Rights and the Internet*, is now more than 10 years old. Others have dealt with some elements of the subject matter, but have tended to focus on specific issues rather than the global picture. This volume provides the first comprehensive review of the topic and the exponential changes that have occurred through the last decade.

THE POTENTIAL OF ICTS FOR THE HUMAN RIGHTS COMMUNITY

In 2000 there was no YouTube for video sharing. Social networking with Facebook or Twitter was still half a decade away, blogging had not yet become mainstream, web mashups were non-existent, and wireless devices were still only emerging technologies. The World Wide Web was still relatively young at that time, and was all about read-only content and hyperlinked Web pages designed to be read by humans. The bursting of the dot com bubble in 2001 led many people to believe that this Web was overhyped, but organisations like O'Reilly Media (formerly O'Reilly & Associates) had a different view. They recognised that the Web was becoming more important than ever, with exciting new applications and sites popping up with surprising regularity (O'Reilly, 2005). To highlight these innovations they organised a conference in 2004 at which the term Web 2.0 was born (see Musser et al., 2006).

Web 2.0 applications that facilitate participatory online information sharing and collaboration have transformed the human rights community. Blogging in particular has become a vitally important tool for individuals and organisations that want to keep the public or the human rights community informed about human rights issues. Very often, the first people to present evidence of human rights violations publicly nowadays are "front-line" bloggers who are either witnessing and documenting the violations themselves or posting someone else's information. Aggregation bloggers like Global Voices Online (http://globalvoicesonline.org) amplify this information in a manner that makes it more accessible. International human rights NGOs and libraries also publish and translate selected blogs, and sometimes editorialise what they consider to be the "good sources" (Collins, 2007).

The value of Twitter, Facebook, YouTube, and other social media tools of the Web 2.0 era was demonstrated during the pro-democracy protests in Iran in June 2009 and in the Arab Spring uprisings in Tunisia and Egypt in January 2011. Real-time reports on what was happening on the streets went out on these social networks, as did calls to rally. Poignant images of suffering – a video recording of the death of Neda Agha-Soltan who was shot on her way to the election protests in Iran, or photographs of Mohamed Bouazizi, a street vendor who burned himself to death to protest at harassment by the Tunisian authorities - were seen by millions of people around the world.

Today the Web is used by large groups of people to create collective work whose value far exceeds that provided by any of the individual participants. In 2009, Tim O'Reilly and John Battelle wrote that it

... is no longer a collection of static pages of HTML that describe something in the world. Increasingly, the Web is the world—everything and everyone in the world casts an "information shadow," an aura of data which, when captured and processed intelligently, offers extraordinary opportunity and mind-bending implications (O'Reilly and Battelle, 2009).

We are now in the era of Web 3.0, which is all about personalisation, intelligent searching, and the Semantic Web. The latter links up information on a global scale and has the potential to provide powerful data organisation and query capabilities. These enable machines to understand the meaning of information on the Web through the addition of machine-readable metadata about pages and how they are related to each other. Resources can be aggregated, shared, and accessed from many different places, and users can choose the appropriate presentation for the tasks they need to accomplish (Hendler and Golbeck, 2008). As a result we are crossing into what Gruber (2008) calls a new learning paradigm which offers a qualitative change in the way people think of interacting on the web. With Web 2.0, interaction treats the Web as an information source and we learn by browsing, searching, and monitoring it. But with Web 3.0

"the web will be understood as an active human-computer system, and we will learn by telling it what we are interested in, asking it what we collectively know, and using it to apply our collective knowledge to address our collective needs." (Gruber, 2008, p.12)

An important factor in achieving this is to be able to draw on domain knowledge in areas where searches are difficult (Hendler and Golbeck, 2008). One of the key challenges, therefore, for the human rights community, is to bring human rights experts, information scientists, and technologists together in order to ensure that the necessary semantic linkages exists between the vast array of human rights-related information that is being published online.

THE OTHER SIDE OF THE COIN

In *The Net Delusion*, Evgeny Morozov argues that "Internet freedom" is an illusion and that technology has failed to help protect people's rights. He claims that new media will not bring democracy and freedom, but the entrenchment of authoritarian regimes (Morozov, 2011).

There are plenty of reasons why human rights workers and activists often struggle to take advantage of ICTs. For a start, some places are socially, economically or politically unfavourable for their usage. This may be a consequence of the digital divide, a concept that reflects inequalities derived from the digital environment but which is also linked to other socio-economic inequities (Barzilai-Nahon et al., 2009). It may also be because their government takes action to deny activists and human rights defenders, and even unhappy citizens, access to ICT-enabled communications channels. Take Burma in 2007 for example. The Internet was initially used to spread news of a revolt by Buddhist monks, and to inform the world about the brutal response by the ruling military junta. But because Burmese bloggers and citizen journalists were so effective in spreading news of the revolt internationally the government took drastic action. It controlled the only ISPs in the country and was therefore able to shut them down, thereby severing the flow of information in and out of the country via the Internet. Richard Hayman summarised the effect as follows:

At the beginning of the revolution, information communication technology (ICT) and Internet connections helped prevent abuses; once disconnected, images and documentation no longer escaped, and so the junta was able to continue its attack without international oversight. The revolution ended, and little has changed in the country (Hayman, 2009, p.50)

Inequalities exist throughout society on both global and local levels, and technologies like the Internet can amplify them rather than eliminate them (Manji et al., 2000; Agre, 2002). While people living in the Global North may feel they are part of a global networked society, with the ability to broadcast at any time to an ever-increasing audience, almost 70% of the world's population do not yet have access to the Internet (Internet World Stats, 2011). And of the 30% that do have access, not everybody can create their own content. This could be because of unreliable connectivity, inadequate fulfilment of the right to education, social stratifications and inequalities, language, or other barriers to Internet adoption and appropriation. For human rights defenders who draw attention to the illicit actions of a state there are additional difficulties. Political censorship and surveillance are commonplace across the world, as can be seen from the reports of international non-governmental organisations (NGOs) like Reporters without Borders and Human Rights Watch. As a result, human rights workers can put themselves or others at risk by posting information online. Human rights defenders generally take precautions, like using encryption and anonymous web surfing tools to prevent surveillance. But governmental efforts to control the Internet are becoming more subtle, flexible, and offensive in character (Deibert and Rohozinski, 2010). As a case in point, the Association for Women's Rights in Development (AWID) reported recently that it is becoming increasingly evident that women human rights defenders using ICTs for activism and advocacy are facing challenges in both their personal and public spaces (Tolmay, 2011). They say

The widespread use of ICTs to defend human and women's rights is cause for concern for repressive governments who are complicit in routinely violating these rights. Attempts by authorities to constrain WHRDs [women human rights defenders] from using ICTs to their full potential take a range of forms, including interference with Internet services, use of legal restrictions, email surveillance and monitoring, computer confiscation, virus and spyware attacks as well as harassment, intimidation and reprisals (Tolmay, 2011)

The political importance of new media is also reflected in the number of bloggers arrested around the world for exposing corruption or human rights violations, for posting comments about political figures or public policy, or for using online fora to organise or cover social protest. These arrests tend to increase during times of political uncertainty, such as around general elections or during large scale protests (Howard and World Information Access Project, 2008), and in many cases they can lead to lengthy prison sentences. At the end of 2010 Reporters Without Borders had records of 112 bloggers, webmasters, cyber-dissidents, and other netizens imprisoned around the world, some of which were sentenced to over ten years in prison (Reporters Without Borders, 2011). The majority of these were in China, but they also included cases from Vietnam, Iran, Syria, Saudi Arabia, Burma, Egypt, and other countries.

Governments are also pushing back through the development of techniques designed to control what people read, view, and discuss (Karlekar and Cook, 2009). China, for example, has a sophisticated system to restrict citizens' ability to disseminate and access information online but they are not alone in their efforts at censorship. Internet filtering takes place in at least forty states worldwide, with the offenders predominantly clustered in three regions: East Asia; the Middle East, and North Africa; and central Asia (Zittrain and Palfrey, 2008). In many of these countries, the Internet is under state control, with the authorities in places like Thailand, Saudi Arabia, and Uzbekistan proactively engaging in blocking websites and blogs, and in the surveillance of online expression (Reporters Without Borders, 2009). Even in democratic countries like the US, UK, Brazil, and Turkey, Internet freedom is increasingly undermined by content control mechanisms, opaque filtering procedures, and expanding surveillance (Deibert et al., 2008; Karlekar and Cook, 2009). In the UK and the US it is now permissible, for example, for the authorities to request all kinds of personal and private information, with anti-terrorism legislation being used to restrict the freedom of speech of people who question or oppose government policy. In the case of the US there are a number of laws that support Internet surveillance. There is the Communications Assistance for Law Enforcement Act (CALEA) which requires phone companies and Internet Service Providers (ISPs) to facilitate government wiretapping of telephone and Internet communications. There is also the Patriot Act, which in the wake of 9/11, broadened the scope of government surveillance of all types of electronic communications without requiring warrants (Chen, 2010). Several European countries are also working on steps to control the Internet. As a case in point, the French government approved a bill in 2010 that allowed police and security forces to use clandestinely installed software to spy on private computers (Simons, 2010). Although the government said the intention was to improve security for ordinary citizens by setting out a framework for the operations of law enforcement agencies working to combat illegal downloading and child pornography, civil rights activists saw it as an exercise in censorship and surveillance.

Jennifer Radloff, a senior project coordinator at the Association for Progressive Communications (APC)'s Women's Network Support Programme summed up the double-edged nature of ICTs for human rights quite well when she said, "The tools that we use to communicate, share and create change are the same tools that the state and anti-progressive forces can use to track, trace and target us" (Radloff in Tolmay, 2011).

ICTS' ROLE IN HUMAN RIGHTS ABUSE

As Radloff noted, the features that make ICTs an effective tool for the promotion and protection of human rights also make them useful in the exploitation of people and the violation of human rights. One area in particular that has been adversely affected by their proliferation is personal information privacy. This started to become one of the most critical issues in the emerging information society as far back as the mid 1990s (Milberg et al., 1995). Since then, online social networking – an environment in which "gossip, harassment, hacking, phishing, data mining, and (ab)use of personal data by third parties are a reality" (Debatin et al., 2009) - has significantly increased the threats to users, particularly those that are young or not computer literate. So too has the use of biometrically enabled identity cards. With these, information may be gathered without permission or knowledge or without explicitly defining the purpose for which it is required. It can be used for a variety of purposes other than that which it was originally acquired; it can be shared without explicit permission. It can even be used to track people across multiple databases to amalgamate information for surveillance or social control (Smith, 2011).

The ways in which ICTs now contribute directly and indirectly to the abuse of children is an area of major concern. The prevalence of child pornography (or child abuse images as advocacy organisations like Save the Children prefer to call it) has increased massively over the last decade as a result of the emergence of the Internet as a mass consumer technology. This makes it easier to access, disseminate, and sell the material (Calcetas-Santos, 2001). As a result there has been a shift from small scale 'amateur' production of images, exchanged by and between collectors, to the distribution of images on a huge scale by members of organised crime for financial benefit (Carr & Hilton, 2010). New technologies also increase the opportunities available to predators by allowing them to stalk, recruit, and exploit children anywhere in the world through chat rooms, blogs, and other online applications (Human Rights Council, 2009), and even to organise into communities.

Identifying and locating the children who are abused for the production of child pornography is a major challenge for law enforcement and other child protection agencies. Painstaking assessment of the information within an image can lead to the identification of an abused child (Save the Children, 2006), but this takes time and technical expertise. Protective legal measures are also required, and as Dillon (2008) notes in her discussion of child sex trafficking, this has implications for culture and education as well as regulation of Internet pornography.

Indeed the role of the Internet in human trafficking in general is quite troubling. In 2008 the UN estimated that about 2.5 million people from 127 countries were trafficked to 137 countries for purposes such as forced labour, sexual exploitation, the removal of organs or body parts, forced marriage, child adoption, and begging (United Nations, 2008). The vast majority of trafficking victims (around 80%) are women and girls, and of these, the majority are trafficked for purposes of sexual exploitation (Jones, 2010). For traffickers, the Internet provides a convenient and anonymous way to contact and recruit victims, to communicate with other traffickers, to advertise trafficked women, and to identify markets (Maltzahn, 2005; Sykiotou, 2007). Online employment agencies, particularly those ostensibly seeking fashion or artists' models, as well as marriage agencies, can be used to lure victims, as can publically accessible chat-rooms and other seemingly innocent websites (Jones, 2010). Websites are also used to advertise brothels and other services, sometimes with pictures of women displayed without their knowledge or consent. This is a violation of the women's right to privacy and is exploitative, as are other practices of distributing and selling of female images online.

On the positive side, it is worth remembering that the Internet is also a useful tool in the prevention of trafficking and the protection of trafficked victims. The Internet has been used by NGOs to provide education, information, and support to women going abroad, and to policymakers and others trying to combat trafficking. And in many cases the rapid transfer of information between groups has helped find women and children who have disappeared abroad.

The distribution of material that is hostile to racial and religious groups over the Internet is another area for concern. Even though this has been sent by mail and distributed on streets all over the world for years, the advent of the Internet has made it accessible to people who would previously not have come in contact with it. Just as information from human rights organisations can be distributed to millions of people at the push of a button, so can racist and xenophobic propaganda. The Internet is a powerful tool for extremist groups seeking an international audience or wishing to link up with other extremist groups. But research conducted by Joseph A. Schafer in 2002 indicated that although the Internet is likely to increase the efficiency of these groups by providing faster and more reliable modes of internal communication, it may not be a more effective means of recruiting new followers (Schafer, 2002). The Internet does little to increase the size of extremist groups, although it may be a powerful tool to increase the allegiance of those who are already committed to their ideologies.

It is important to note here that the issue of freedom of opinion and expression in relation to hate speech is disputed. Cyber-libertarians such as Starr (2004) and advocates of free speech argue against censorship, claiming that more speech is the best antidote. However human rights advocates would argue that since hate speech is racist, endangers minorities (ethnic groups, homosexuals, and others), and violates international human rights principles, it should be eliminated. Europe has tended towards prohibiting Internet hate speech over the years. When the Council of Europe was adopting a measure to criminalise it in 2002 it noted that

The emergence of international communication networks like the Internet provide certain persons with modern and powerful means to support racism and xenophobia and enables them to disseminate easily and widely expressions containing such ideas (Council of Europe, 2002)

Hate speech is generally protected as free speech in the United States however, with measures to restrict it seen as dangerous trends in censorship or ineffective action against elusive agents of hate.

ABOUT THIS BOOK

In the last decade, the human rights agenda has been broadened to encompass areas such as corporate accountability, development and climate change. Human rights based approaches have been widely adopted in the development field, with increased attention being given to poverty as a human right. Furthermore, human rights advocates and activists all over the world have embraced economic, social, and cultural rights and have worked towards their fulfilment by governments. Meanwhile, efforts to ensure the protection of civil and political rights around the world are still ongoing - Amnesty International's 2011 report documented restrictions on free speech in at least 89 countries, cases of prisoners of conscience in at least 48 countries, torture and other ill-treatment in at least 98 countries, unfair trials in at least 54 countries, and thousands of human rights defenders around the world who were threatened, imprisoned, tortured, and killed (Amnesty International, 2011).

There has also been an increased globalisation of the international human rights norms and standards that help to protect people from abuse and injustice in recent times. Communication, facilitated by ICTs, has catalyzed and intensified this globalisation by combining an increase in technical capacity and volume, a shift in the distribution of capabilities, a diversification of channels, and an expansion of content (Brysk, 2002).

In this context it is difficult to give adequate coverage to the trends and consequences of ICT usage on human rights in one book. Our approach, therefore, is to bring together a range of perspectives from practitioners and academics in order to provide a diverse set of insights into the application and use of ICTs in the world of human rights. It is divided into four sections, each of which contains informative and thought provoking chapters from contributors.

The first section of the book sets the scene by addressing a number of key trends and issues relating to ICTs and human rights. In Chapter 1, Judith Dueck and Michael Rempel examine current technological issues faced by human rights organisations including web security, the Semantic Web and social media. Given the extent to which intergovernmental agencies, governments, and NGOs are now using ICTs to collect, organise, and disseminate human rights information, this is an area of vital importance. Dueck and Rempel show us that today's technological wonderland is filled with promises, delights and dangers and that the human rights community must continue to proactively explore it for solutions that help the human rights cause.

One issue discussed by Dueck and Rempel which is of particular importance to human rights advocacy organisations is that of metadata or "data about data." This is a set of structured data or content types that characterise an information object – for example a human rights violation, video testimony from a witness, or a report outlining the situation in a particular country. Metadata can be used to compile data from multiple databases, thus creating a more complete picture. Developing a useful metadata system for the human rights community could have tremendous impact, as it would enable the use of different data sets to discover and report patterns of abuse.

Freedom of expression and the right to privacy need to be balanced in an open society, according to Rolf H. Weber in Chapter 2. He takes a historical look at the frameworks adopted to support global civil society's participation in the information society, and looks at the current potential of ICT policies to enable it to use digital communications in ways that lead to better realisation of human rights. Weber suggests a number of interesting ways in which policies could be used to achieve this, including measures to improve the enjoyment of economic and social rights, the removal of trade barriers, and the realisation of an enforceable right to development.

The right to development has been controversial since its adoption by the UN General Assembly in 1986 (Greenstein & Esterhuysen, 2006), and its normative content remains relatively opaque (Green & Randolph, 2010). As a result there is a lack of clarity relating to the specific duties incumbent on states and other actors. Nonetheless there is widespread agreement that the systematic integration of ICTs into all aspects of development policy is required. As Green and Randolph note,

Without giving priority at the national and global levels to the need to integrate information and communication considerations in development, we run the risk of missing out on the important contribution these can make to the development process (Green & Randolph, 2006, p.299)

Weber notes that ICTs allow civil society to more actively participate in discourses by exchanging information, which in turn strengthens freedom of expression and other fundamental rights. He suggests that if private companies are not able or willing to offer services (for example in sparsely populated geographical areas), the state might have to consider granting subsidies to the private sector. However in Chapter 3 Brian J. Bowe, Robin Blom, and Eric Freedman show how states and Western technology companies often straddle the border between free information dissemination and censorship. They consider recent events in Iran, Egypt, Singapore, and China to discuss how information and social network corporations facilitate dissent. All four countries have been identified as having severe impediments to freedom of expression, but Iran and Egypt have seen the rise of some organised opposition movements despite the controls on media expression. On the other hand, China and Singapore offer useful case studies on the economic dimensions of the balance between participating in the global networked society and controlling citizen expression. Bowe et al.'s well researched contribution considers how financial and economic factors lead to more moderate views of Internet use in those countries, and examines the ongoing struggles between maintaining openness and crackdowns.

The second section of the book presents four case studies that explore different consequences of ICT usage for human rights. The first of these from Aziz Douai examines the development and rise of the popular video-sharing website, YouTube, in Arab societies, and describes how video exchange is invigorating the online public sphere's demand for political reform and respect for human rights. Douai looks at videos that succeeded in publicising police corruption and brutality in Egypt and Morocco, and uses these to highlight two strategic roles that YouTube has played in the struggle for democracy and political reform in the Arab world. The first is the re-energising of (cyber) activists demands for political reform and respect for international human rights norms as a result of the global attention that was drawn to their regimes' oppressive practices. The second is the invigorating of public concern and debate regarding human rights issues.

Douai's case studies show that not only have computer users turned to social media services to circumvent government controls on free expression in countries like Egypt (as described by Bowe et al.), they are also using these services to work towards greater respect for human rights and for democratic reform.

Chapter 5 describes a project designed to enable Liberians on three continents to give statements to the Liberian Truth and Reconciliation Commission (LTRC). Eric Wiebelhaus-Brahm describes how the Commission was set up to examine gross human rights violations that occurred during the fourteen years of brutality and violence in Liberia from 1979 to 2003. ICTs proved instrumental in attempts to include the Liberian diaspora in the truth and reconciliation process, and Web 2.0 technologies allowed Liberians to interact with each other and to provide statements to the Commission. However Wiebelhaus-Brahm warns that ICTs are not a panacea for transitional justice processes. While they may increase the efficiency and level of participation, there are still challenges to be overcome in areas like trust, the facilitation of reconciliation between victims and perpetrators, and the acknowledgement of suffering.

José Rodrigues Filho raises some potential negative consequences for human rights in what would typically be seen as a positive area of development, namely e-government in Brazil. He looks at concerns in relation to tax collection and e-voting, and in particular at the misuse of collected information for surveillance purposes. His contribution questions the extent to which ICTs have benefited the democratic process, and highlights ways in which ordinary citizens' right to privacy could be compromised.

While many of the human rights community's concerns in relation to surveillance have been noted already, Rodrigues Filho provides an important reminder that today's surveillance is "a peculiarly ambiguous process in which digital technologies and personal data are fundamentally implicated and meet in software coding that classifies yet more groups in different ways" (Lyon, 2007, p.5). This is not just a privacy issue; it is also a human rights issue and is recognised as such by the UN Declaration of Human Rights, the International Covenant on Civil and Political Rights and many other international and regional human rights mechanisms.

Chapter 7, by Christopher Wilson and Alexandra Dunn, uses an analysis of a digital activism initiative to examine a proposed approach for the study of ICTs in contentious politics and human rights advocacy. The initiative is the Cairo-based Front to Defend Egyptian Protestors (FDEP), which uses mobile phone and online applications to mobilise support teams for arrested protestors and work towards their release. The research gives us another important insight into the much touted role of ICTs and social media before and during the Arab Spring revolutions. It also helps to advance theoretical and practical understandings of digital activism by proposing an analytical approach to research study design. The approach which applies frames of contingency and hybridity, can improve understanding into how human rights activists strategically combine digital and grounded communications to respond to complex, changing environments.

The process of strategically and systematically gathering quantitative or qualitative human rights data builds a strong platform for advocacy, as it provides evidence with which to challenge governments' human rights reporting and performance. This documentation process includes several steps: (i) determining what information is needed and establishing means for acquiring it; (ii) recording the discovered information and storing it in appropriate containers, or collecting already-existing documents containing the needed information; (iii) organising the documents to make them more accessible; and (iv) providing the documents to users who need the information. There are many types of human rights data that can be collected. These include reports of human rights violations; testimonies, monitoring indicators (which are particularly helpful for discrimination and ongoing oppression); legal investigations and government data; archives of repressive regimes that may contain important information; newspapers; documented human rights interventions; anthropological research data; ecological studies; and real-time data (New Tactics in Human Rights, 2010).

The third section of the book presents three different perspectives on how ICTs can help the human rights community to collect, record, and make effective use of this human rights data. In the first of these, Jessica Heinzelman and Patrick Meier look at how ICTs provide new opportunities for crowdsourcing as a means of human rights monitoring (defined by Guzman & Verstappen (2003) as the close observation of a situation or case). They note that to ensure credibility, human rights monitoring has historically been conducted through highly controlled organisational structures that face mounting challenges in terms of capacity, cost, and access. ICTs provide new opportunities to overcome some of these challenges through crowdsourcing. However this technique raises new challenges of verification and information overload that have made some human rights professionals sceptical of their utility. Heinzelman and Meier explore whether the efficiencies gained through an open call for monitoring and reporting human rights abuses provides a net gain for human rights monitoring, and they analyze the opportunities and challenges that new and traditional methods pose for verifying crowdsourced human rights reporting.

In Chapter 9, Ann Harrison of the Benetech Human Rights Data Analysis Group (HRDAG) looks at the use of statistics about political violence from multiple data sources, and describes methodologies that HRDAG analysts have developed to ensure that statistical human rights claims are transparently and demonstrably true. HRDAG collects and preserves human rights data, together with local partners, and helps NGOs and other human rights organisations to accurately interpret quantitative findings. As

Harrison's contribution demonstrates, the collection and analysis of data can be based on the coding of existing qualitative data on human rights abuses and their subsequent analysis via multiple systems estimation or random sample surveys.

Qualitative information – like the recorded testimony of a survivor of torture – is a very rich and important source of information in relation to patterns of human rights abuse. Asher et al. (2008) explain that

The history of the analysis of qualitative human rights violations begins with the local NGO within their own countries. Traditionally ... these stories would then be passed on to international NGOs, which would make them available to governmental organisations such as the United Nations, who would then exert pressure on that country's government to improve the situation. At the onset of the Truth and Reconciliation Commissions, such qualitative data was deemed one of the more useful of the truth-seeking tools available, and many TRCs sponsored data collection efforts of their own (Asher et al., 2008, p.18)

While Wiebelhaus-Brahm provided an assessment of how ICTs were used to collect qualitative statements directly by the Liberian Truth and Reconciliation Commission, Harrison's contribution provides a valuable insight into how, in an effort to defend the accuracy of human rights data and account for mass atrocities witnessed by thousands or tens of thousands of people, truth commissions and other groups have turned to scientists to clarify history.

Tanya Notley and Stephanie Hankey of Tactical Technology Collective take us back to the start of the human rights documentation chain to examine digital privacy threats and the implications for human rights defenders in greater depth. They note that it is not possible to remove digital risks completely or perhaps even substantially, even with the support of digital security experts from the private and NGO sectors. The best strategy for protection, they say, is to educate human rights defenders about the kinds of risks that exist so as to enable them to better manage and reduce these risks. In this way human rights defenders can develop creative approaches to make the most of the digital tools and resources available to them, given the limits and constraints that surround them.

While many of the traditional approaches to documenting human rights violations have been used primarily in relation to civil and political rights, the human rights community is now strengthening its focus on the documentation of economic, social, and cultural (ESC) rights. There are three broad categories of violations of these rights (New Tactics in Human Rights, 2010). These are state violations resulting from government actions, policies, and legislation; violations related to patterns of discrimination; and violations related to the state's failure to fulfill minimum core obligations of enumerated rights.

As Weber notes in Chapter 2, the impact that ICTs have on the enjoyment of economic and social rights is highly context specific, with regulatory frameworks and market competitiveness having a substantial influence. Even more crucially, being on the wrong side of one of the many digital divides that exist globally precludes billions of people from taking advantage of the opportunities the Internet and other ICTs present. Inequalities relating to ICT access and use can only be understood in combination with other socio-economic inequalities. Nonetheless, the lack of access to ICTs implies the existence of discrimination, and can be seen as adding to human rights violations such as discrimination against vulnerable groups (Zarrehparver, 2006).

It is important, therefore, to critically examine contexts in which the use of ICT impacts on the enjoyment of ESC rights. Consequently, the fourth and final section of the book focuses on these and on the implications of ICT usage for potentially vulnerable groups in society. In the first chapter of the section, Minna Strömberg-Jakka examines the use of ICTs to gain access to social rights as human rights in Finland, a country with one of the highest Internet penetration rates in the world (Internet World Stats, 2011). Her research, which looks at online social service consultation, indicates that inequalities can be created between service users, and highlights how issues such as officials' education, linguistic matters, and cultural habits need to be taken into account.

According to the World Health Organisation there exists a hidden burden of stigma and discrimination faced by people with mental disorders. In both low- and high-income countries, stigmatisation of people with mental disorders has persisted throughout history, manifested by stereotyping, fear, embarrassment, anger, and rejection or avoidance (World Health Organisation, 2005). They say that violations of basic human rights and freedoms, and denial of civil, political, economic, social, and cultural rights to those suffering from mental disorders, are a common occurrence around the world, both within institutions and in the community. In terms of human rights, this is therefore an area of growing concern. Mental illness ranks fourth of the 10 leading causes of disability in the world and is expected to approach second place by 2020 (Zolnierek, 2008). In this context Jenny Martin and Elspeth McKay's contribution exploring the use of ICTs in post-secondary education to provide opportunities for students with mental health difficulties is important. They outline strategies afforded by ICT tools for helping students with mental illness to optimise their chances of success, and argue for the need to design appropriate instructional ICT strategies to support students experiencing mental illness to remain engaged with their studies.

Women all over the world strive to have access to information and to engage in communication that will improve their livelihoods and help them to achieve their human rights. This can be a difficult challenge for them however, especially in developing countries. Odame (2005) says there are systemic gender biases in ICTs and their applications, and as a result women are far more likely than men to experience discrimination in the information society. Nonetheless

Women are not giving up on ICTs. On the contrary, even resource-poor and non-literate women and their organizations are aware of the power of information technologies and communication processes and, if given the opportunity to do so, will use them to advance their basic needs and strategic interests. (Odame, 2005, p.13)

Cristina Ionescu takes up this issue in Chapter 13, asking whether women have equal rights and opportunities to access and use ICTs. She concludes that in this changing era, new ICTs in fact represent a cardinal instrument for social transformation, enabling and empowering women to become controllers of information.

In the final chapter, Shane O'Hanlon looks at the impact of ICT usage on the right to access to healthcare. He says that misuse of health information technology - which is generally viewed as improving the overall quality, safety, and efficiency of a health delivery system (Chaudhury et al., 2006) - can result in violations of human rights. In particular, the right to privacy can be eroded by inappropriate protections which still exist in some health systems. In his contribution he describes the rights framework in healthcare, analyses legal provisions for protection of health data, considers why such protections are necessary, and outlines examples of rights violations.

The chapters in this final section show that the consequences of ICT usage for economic and social rights are varied. On the one hand they can empower women, and support people with mental illnesses to continue to enjoy access to education. On the other, they raise concerns over the security of personal health data, and equitable access to social assistance services. Together with the other contributions to *Human Rights and Information Communication Technologies: Trends and Consequences of Use* they demonstrate that the ubiquitous nature of ICTs means that government policies, private sector investment, and civil society innovation can all impact on human rights. This trend will continue, with both positive and negative consequences.

John Lannon
University of Limerick, Ireland

Edward F. Halpin
Leeds Metropolitan University, UK

REFERENCES

Agre, P. E. (2002). Real-time politics: The internet and the political process. *The Information Society, 18*(5), 311–331. doi:10.1080/01972240290075174

Amnesty International. (2011). *Amnesty International report 2011: The state of the world's human rights*. Retrieved December 11, 2011, from http://www.amnesty.org/en/annual-report/2011

Asher, J., Banks, D. L., & Scheuren, F. (2008). *Statistical methods for human rights*. Springer. doi:10.1007/978-0-387-72837-7

Barzilai-Nahon, K., Gomez, R., & Ambikar, R. (2009). Conceptualizing a contextual measurement for digital divide/s: Using an integrated narrative. In Ferro, E., Dwivendi, Y., Ramon, G., & Williams, M. (Eds.), *Overcoming digital divides: Constructing an equitable and competitive information society*. Hershey, PA: Idea Group Inc. doi:10.4018/978-1-60566-699-0.ch034

Brysk, A. (Ed.). (2002). *Globalization and human rights*. Berkeley, CA: University of California Press.

Calcetas-Santos, O. (2001). Child pornography on the Internet. In Arnaldo, C. A. (Ed.), *Child abuse on the Internet: Ending the silence* (pp. 57–60). Paris, France: UNESCO Publishing/Berghahn Books.

Carr, J., & Hilton, Z. (2010). Combating child abuse images on the Internet: International perspectives. In Davidson, J., & Gottschalk, P. (Eds.), *Internet child abuse: Current research and policy* (pp. 52–78). Taylor & Francis.

Chaudhry, B., Wang, J., Wu, S., Maglione, M., Mojica, W., & Roth, E. (2006). Systematic review: Impact of health information technology on quality, efficiency, and costs of medical care. *Annals of Internal Medicine, 144*(10), 742–752.

Collins, C. (2007). Disseminating truth to power - Human rights, information and the Internet as court of last/only resort. *Information for Social Change, 25*. Retrieved August 26, 2011, from http://libr.org/isc/issues/ISC25/articles/DISSEMINATING%20TRUTH%20TO%20POWER.pdf

Council of Europe. (2002). *Additional protocol to the Convention on cybercrime, concerning the criminalisation of acts of a racist and xenophobic nature committed through computer systems*. CETS No, 189. Retrieved October 9, 2009, from http://www.conventions.coe.int/Treaty/Commun/QueVoulezVous.asp?NT=189&CM=8&DF=06/10/2009&CL=ENG

Debatin, B., Lovejoy, J. P., Horn, A.-K., & Hughes, B. N. (2009). Facebook and online privacy: Attitudes, behaviors, and unintended consequences. *Journal of Computer-Mediated Communication, 15*, 83–108. doi:10.1111/j.1083-6101.2009.01494.x

Deibert, R., Palfrey, J., & Rohozinski, R. (Eds.). (2008). *Access denied: The practice and policy of global internet filtering*. Cambridge, MA: MIT Press.

Deibert, R. J., & Rohozinski, R. (2010). Beyond denial: Introducing next-generation information access controls. In Deibert, R. J., Palfrey, J., & Rohozinski, R. (Eds.), *Access controlled: The shaping of power, rights, and rule in cyberspace* (pp. 3–13). Cambridge, MA: MIT Press.

Dillon, S. (2008). What human rights law obscures: Global sex trafficking and the demand for children. *UCLA Women's Law Journal, 17*, 121–149.

Green, M., & Randolph, S. (2010). *Bringing theory into practice: Operational criteria for assessing implementation of the international right to development*. Human Rights Council A/HRC/15/WG.2/TF/CRP.5

Greenstein, R., & Esterhuysen, A. (2006). The right to development in the information society. In Jorgenson, R. F. (Ed.), *Human rights in the information society* (pp. 281–302). Cambridge: MIT Press.

Gruber, T. (2008). Collective knowledge systems: Where the social Web meets the Semantic Web. *Web Semantics Science Services and Agents on the World Wide Web, 6*(1), 4–13. doi:10.1016/j.websem.2007.11.011

Guzman, M., & Verstappen, B. (2003). *Human rights monitoring and documentation series, Volume 1: What is monitoring?* Versoix, Switzerland: Human Rights Information and Documentation Systems, International (HURIDOCS).

Hayman, R. (2009). Human rights software: Information support solutions for social justice. *Information for Social Change, Special Issue on Science & Technology for Utopias, 29,* 44-67. Retrieved September 1, 2010, from http://www.libr.org/isc/issues/ISC29/Issue%2029.pdf

Hendler, J., & Golbeck, J. (2008). Metcalfe's law, Web 2.0, and the Semantic Web. *Journal of Web Semantics, 6*(1). doi:10.1016/j.websem.2007.11.008

Hick, S., Halpin, E. F., & Hoskins, E. (Eds.). (2000). *Human rights and the Internet*. Houndmills, UK: MacMillan Press Ltd.

Howard, P. N., & World Information Access Project. (2008). *World information access report - 2008*. Seattle, WA: University of Washington.

Human Rights Council. (2009). *Promotion and protection of all human rights, civil, political, economic, social and cultural rights, including the right to development: Report of the Special Rapporteur on the sale of children, child prostitution and child pornography, Najat M'jid Maalla*. United Nations. Retrieved December 11, 2011, from http://www.crin.org/docs/A.HRC.12.23.pdf

Internet World Stats. (2011). *Internet usage statistics- The Internet big picture: World Internet users and population stats*. Retrieved December 8, 2011, from http://www.internetworldstats.com/stats.htm

Jones, J. (2010). *Human trafficking in Wales 2010*. Working Paper. University of the West of England. Retrieved December 12, 2011 from http://eprints.uwe.ac.uk/14615/

Karlekar, K. D., & Cook, S. G. (2009). *Access and control: A growing diversity of threats to internet freedom*. Special Reports Section, Freedom House. Retrieved December 8, 2011, from http://freedomhouse.org/template.cfm?page=384&key=194&parent=19&report=79

Lyon, D. (2007). *Surveillance studies: An overview*. Polity.

Maltzahn, K. (2005). *Digital dangers: Information & communication technologies and trafficking in women*. AWID and APC Women's Networking Support Programme.

Manji, F., Jaffer, M., & Njuguna, E. N. (2000). *Strengthening human rights organisations in Africa: challenges of the new technologies*. Canada: International Development Research Centre (IDRC).

Milberg, S. J., Burke, S. J., Smith, H. J., & Kallman, E. A. (1995). Values, personal information, privacy and regulatory approaches. *Communications of the ACM, 38*(12), 65–74. doi:10.1145/219663.219683

Morozov, E. (2011). *The Net delusion: How not to liberate the world*. Allen Lane.

Musser, J., O'Reilly, T., & The O'Reilly Radar Team. (2006). *Web 2.0: Principles and best practices*. Sebastopol, CA: O'Reilly Media, Inc.

New Tactics in Human Rights. (2010). *Documenting violations: Choosing the right approach - Online dialogue*. Retrieved December 12, 2011, from http://www.newtactics.org/en/blog/new-tactics/documenting-violations-choosing-right-approach

O'Reilly, T. (2005). *What is Web 2.0? Design patterns and business models for the next generation of software*. O'Reilly Media. Retrieved December 7, 2011, from www.oreillynet.com/pub/a/oreilly/tim/news/2005/09/30/what-is-web-20.html

O'Reilly, T., & Battelle, J. (2009). *Web squared: Web 2.0 five years on*. Special Report for the Web 2.0 Summit, 20-22 October, San Francisco CA. Retrieved December 7, 2011, from http://assets.en.oreilly.com/1/event/28/web2009_websquared-whitepaper.pdf

Odame, H. H. (2005). Introduction: Gender and ICTs for development: Setting the context. In Valk, M., Cummings, S. J. R., & Van Dam, H. (Eds.), *Gender and ICTs for development: A global sourcebook* (pp. 13–34).

Reporters without Borders. (2009). *Wars and disputed elections: The most dangerous stories for journalists*. Retrieved January 31, 2011, from http://www.rsf.org/Wars-and-disputed-elections-The.html

Reporters without Borders. (2011). *Press freedom barometer 2010*. Retrieved May 22, 2011, from http://en.rsf.org/press-freedom-barometer-netizens-imprisoned.html?annee=2010

Save the Children. (2006). *Visible evidence – Forgotten children*. Save the Children. Retrieved December 10, 2011 from http://www.savethechildren.net/alliance/resources/reports/VisibleEvidence.pdf

Schafer, J. A. (2002). Spinning the Web of hate: Web-based hate propagation by extremist organizations. *Journal of Criminal Justice and Popular Culture*, *9*(2), 69–88.

Simons, S. (2010). France moves closer to unprecedented internet regulation. *Spiegel Online*. Retrieved February 11, 2011 from http://www.spiegel.de/international/europe/0,1518,678508,00.html

Smith, R. G. (2011). Human rights in the digital age. In Jaishankar, K. (Ed.), *Cyber criminology: Exploring Internet crimes and criminal behaviour* (pp. 393–410). London, UK: CRC Press. doi:10.1201/b10718-27

Sykiotou, A. P. (2007). *Trafficking in human beings: Internet recruitment*. Council of Europe.

Tolmay, S. (2011). *ICTs – A double-edged sword for women human rights defenders*. Association for Women's Rights in Development (AWID). Retrieved December 8, 2011, from http://www.awid.org/News-Analysis/Friday-Files/ICTs-A-double-edged-sword-for-Women-Human-Rights-Defenders

United Nations. (2008). *UN-backed container exhibit spotlights plight of sex trafficking victims*. UN News Centre. Retrieved December 11, 2011, from http://www.un.org/apps/news/story.asp?NewsID=25524

World Health Organisation. (2005). *WHO resource book on mental health, human rights and legislation*. World Health Organisation. Retrieved December 14, 2011, from http://www.who.int/mental_health/policy/resource_book_MHLeg.pdf

Zarrehparver, M. (2006). A nondiscriminatory information society. In Jorgenson, R. F. (Ed.), *Human rights in the information society* (pp. 221–234). Cambridge, MA: MIT Press.

Zittrain, J., & Palfrey, J. (2008). Introduction. In Deibert, R. J., Palfrey, J., & Rohozinski, R. (Eds.), *Access denied: The practice and policy of global internet filtering* (pp. 1–4). Cambridge, MA: MIT Press.

Zolnierek, C. D. (2008). Mental health policy and integrated care: Global perspectives. *Journal of Psychiatric and Mental Health Nursing*, *15*(8), 562–568. doi:10.1111/j.1365-2850.2008.01267.x

Acknowledgment

The editors would like to acknowledge the help of all those involved in the drafting and review process of this book. Without their input and support it could not have been completed.

We are grateful to Myla Harty in the Development Division of IGI Global for her advice, encouragement, and patience along the way. We would also like to thank everybody who offered constructive review feedback for the different chapters. These were Liam Bannon, Robin Blom, Tony Bryant, Lakshman Dissanayake, Alexandra Dunn, David Griffin, Cristina Ionescu, Sheila Killian, Nehal Mahtab, Jenny Martin, Fergal McGrath, Shane O'Hanlon, José Rodrigues Filho, John Walsh, John Willott, and Christopher Wilson.

Finally we would like to thank all the authors for their excellent contributions to this book. Without their insights and expertise it would not have been possible to adequately cover the ever-changing worlds of human rights and information and communication technologies.

John Lannon
University of Limerick, Ireland

Edward F. Halpin
Leeds Metropolitan University, UK

December 2011

Section 1
Setting the Scene

Chapter 1
Human Rights and Technology:
Lessons from Alice in Wonderland

Judith Dueck
The University of Winnipeg Global College, Canada

Michael Rempel
Software Architect, Canada

ABSTRACT

This chapter examines eleven technology issues faced by human rights organizations. These issues are critical if they are to use technology effectively. Although solutions are not proposed, the chapter highlights topics that increasingly require research and concrete solutions in order for human rights organizations to integrate technology tools into their work. The key issues addressed are: rapid technology changes; national security, personal information, and human rights; web security; data relationships; controlled vocabulary (a common language); Semantic Web and human interactivity; search - finding the information; assumptions and ease of use; trust; open source; and social media. These issues, chosen from the human rights and technology backgrounds of the authors, provide a frontier to human rights work that may seem daunting to the newly initiated. Human interaction must remain the key element. Technology must be a servant to the human rights needs and demands.

INTRODUCTION

The wonderland of information communication technologies is upon the human rights community. The Oxford Dictionary of Phrase and Fable (Knowles, 2006) defines wonderland as:

> *a land or place full of wonderful things, a fairyland; the term is recorded from the late 18th century, but is most frequently used with reference to the country which Alice found down a rabbit-hole in Lewis Carroll's Alice's Adventures in Wonderland. (Knowles, 2006)*

DOI: 10.4018/978-1-4666-1918-0.ch001

One could suggest with little levity that perhaps Alice's wonderland is similar to the technology wonderland today – a wonderland with promises, delights and dangers. *Alice's Adventures in Wonderland*, a classic fantasy novel written in 1865 under the pseudonym Lewis Carroll, is about a girl who falls down a rabbit hole into a fantasy world (Wonderland). The quotations used in this chapter are from this book, as well as *Through the Looking Glass* which was a sequel to *Alice's Adventures in Wonderland.* Alice's wonderland in some ways parallels the "wonderland" of technology with its complexities, mystery and unknown future.

The following quote sets the stage:

Alice started to her feet, for it flashed across her mind that she had never before seen a rabbit with either a waistcoat-pocket, or a watch to take out of it, and burning with curiosity, she ran across the field after it, and fortunately was just in time to see it pop down a large rabbit-hole under the hedge.

In another moment down went Alice after it, never once considering how in the world she was to get out again.

The rabbit-hole went straight on like a tunnel for some way, and then dipped suddenly down, so suddenly that Alice had not a moment to think about stopping herself before she found herself falling down a very deep well.

Either the well was very deep, or she fell very slowly, for she had plenty of time as she went down to look about her and to wonder what was going to happen next (Carroll, 1865, Chapter 1).

On contemplating the curious world of technology that everyone seems to have fallen into, one must admit that many once impossible processes are now not only possible but have been implemented. This advancement in technology has many advantages but also some inherent dangers - dangers that may be critical in a field as sensitive as human rights. Alice rushes down the rabbit hole without consideration of any repercussions. Organizations, on the other hand, must ensure a holistic approach considering the technical, organizational, ethical, communication, human rights and other implications before they jump into the alluring rabbit hole of technology.

BACKGROUND

Looking back one can see many trendsetters – those who led the way into wonderland. For example, in the mid-80s only a few human rights organizations used email. Examples include Al Haq, the West Bank branch of the International Commission of Jurists and Amnesty International. They had the foresight to see the potential of the new communications technology.

Trendsetters in human rights documentation in the 1980s included non-governmental organizations (NGOs) such as the Centre for Legal and Social Studies (CELS) in Argentina. In 1986 the Argentinian government passed the "Ley Punto Final", a law that created a 60 day time limit for prosecution of crimes committed during the military dictatorship (Jelin, 1994). Human rights NGOs such as CELS turned to manual documentation systems in order to proceed with prosecutions as quickly as possible. In 2005 the "Ley Punto Final" was overturned and once again the documentation systems of human rights NGOs were invaluable. These documentation systems identified perpetrators, times of events, reported incidents, places, roles of persons involved, and other details. The CELS system was one of several which were examined carefully as useful examples in the development of electronic human rights documentation systems. Organizations began to create methods of documenting violations using discrete pieces of information and relational databases. Some of the discussions around these processes can be found in Guinchat & Minou

(1983), Chaves (1989), Ball et al (1994), Ball (1996), Metzl (1996, 1997), Ball et al (1997), Guzman & Verstappen (1998), Frontalini (1990), Ball et al (2000), and Cross & Jarvis (2000).

In the 1980s and 1990s, Human Rights Information and Documentation Systems International (HURIDOCS) explored and began to develop systems of electronic documentation with a focus on tracking cases, analysis and communication possibilities (HURIDOCS, 1990; Dueck et al, 1993). They referenced the systems developed by CELS, Task Force Detainees in the Philippines, Asociación Pro Derechos Humanos (APRODEH - Association for Human Rights in Peru) and other NGOs, in order to build electronic documentation tools for use by a wide range of organizations.

Other early attempts to make information accessible include the development of thesauri and controlled vocabulary lists. Examples include those thesauri, controlled vocabulary and simple lists developed by Stormoken and Zwaak (1988), Dueck & Noval (1993), Caccia (1993), UNESCO (1995), Aitchison (1996), Organization for Economic Co-operation and Development (1998), Amnesty International (2000), Hansen (2000) and Dueck et al (1993, 2001a). Some of these early lists are still relevant today for use in meta-tagging and Dublin Core indexing as discussed later in this chapter, particularly in the sections on controlled vocabulary and Semantic Web. Newer lists are being developed by organizations such as WITNESS (Lile & Ng, 2011) and some older ones are in a constant state of development.

Today there is a complex wonderland of technological options that serves a variety of purposes, both good and ill. What are the issues human rights organizations should address as they find their way through Alice's wonderland maze? Eleven such issues, chosen from the technology and human rights backgrounds of the authors are presented below. Considering these issues as even more technology options present themselves is critical.

ISSUES

Issue 1: Rapid Technology Changes

It is not merely the pace, but the acceleration of the pace that is somewhat impossible. Things once thought impossible are regularly asserted as true so that nothing seems impossible any more. The ability to apply new knowledge, but more importantly to analyze its impact, is where the impossibility may lie. Here the Queen has a relevant comment:

Alice laughed. "There's no use trying," she said: "one can't believe impossible things."

"I daresay you haven't had much practice," said the Queen. "When I was your age, I always did it for half-an-hour a day. Why, sometimes I've believed as many as six impossible things before breakfast" (Carroll, 1871, Chapter 5).

In this world, many arguments are so convoluted that the ways things look are completely unfamiliar, making all the logical conclusions of the past seem unreasonable. If examined carefully in due course, and before it can be solved, the subject simply disappears. This is a world where technology is used for both good and evil; for both control of information and access to information; for both justice and oppression. Some specifics include:

- The "global war on terror" suggests that even so-called information documentation and security come at a high price – perhaps too high (Office of the United Nations High Commissioner for Human Rights, 2008)
- Important information and documentation is regularly lost or confiscated at tremendous cost (for example Syal, 2009).
- Personal information is accidently or intentionally disclosed, violating the right to privacy and sometimes leading to other se-

rious human rights abuses (Privacy Rights Clearinghouse, 2011)

All this is found in a world that labels itself with the enigmatic idiom of Web 2.0. What is the world coming to? If one looks forward and runs as fast as possible is it then even possible to remain in place? Web 3.0, the Semantic Web, promises to be an even greater challenge. How will human rights organizations – both small and large - cope with these challenges?

Perhaps the computer industry suffers from excessive positivism and endless faith - somehow someone else will solve the huge problems created by the latest technologies. There is often a very real tension between the user with valid, practical and critical objectives, and the developer who wishes to explore the possible or limit the very difficult into something manageable. It is imperative to critically evaluate technologies that can create emerging social realities, influence and at times control the standards that will develop.

Issue 2: National Security, Personal Information, and Human Rights

"Off with his head" utters the Queen of Hearts at the slightest provocation in *Alice's Adventures in Wonderland*. At one point the Queen orders the Cheshire Cat to be beheaded, only to have her executioner complain that this is impossible since the head is all that can be seen of him.

In wonderland it is increasingly important for people to read the smoke signals that use of technology creates. Will the lure of technology leave some organizations with compromised or lost information? A false sense of security is an easy illusion for masters of the digital domain. From pin numbers embedded in debit cards, video surveillance and Radio Frequency Identifier tags (RFID) in passports, people are duped and pacified by self-serving privacy invasion technology sold to us as being used for one purpose, but useful for another. In 2009, 57% of all passports issued globally have the chip (RFIDWorld.ca, 2010). Adam Laurie, a British security researcher had this to say:

You can buy a fake passport anywhere and adding the chip, for someone producing these in volume, is going to add $10 cost to what he needs to do," said Laurie. "The chip is actually the easiest bit (Laurie, cited in Pilieci, 2010).

What remains likely is that the security guard at the border will be lulled into a false sense of security by the digital photograph. The $10 cost mentioned is probably a bit high. Security remains an intractable problem and data gathering is a favorite bureaucratic hobby. When assessing the real purpose behind innovations like full body scans and invasive body searches, it is important to examine the real impact of its use. Does it pacify? Does it regulate? Is the 'solution' a pretext? How transparent and connected are the procedures and the use of the data?

Issue 3: Web Security

"Why is a raven like a writing desk?"

'Have you guessed the riddle yet?' the Hatter said, turning to Alice again.

'No, I give it up,' Alice replied: 'what's the answer?'

'I haven't the slightest idea,' said the Hatter.

'Nor I,' said the March Hare.

Alice sighed wearily. 'I think you might do something better with the time,' she said, 'than waste it in asking riddles that have no answers' (Carroll, 1865, Chapter 7).

Is technology a riddle with no answers? Take password cracking software, which has been around for a long time, as a case in point. With Microsoft Windows XP, an operating system that is still in widespread use, for example, it is fairly easy to find password cracking tools that can reveal the administrator password, which allows access to anything on a computer. What is new is that a method called rainbow tables (http://www.freerainbowtables.com/) can do it in a matter of minutes even with the best of passwords. Old encryption and password technology is obsolete and not safe.

Even well-known web security problems have been ignored for a long time:

When logging into a website you usually start by submitting your username and password. The server then checks to see if an account matching this information exists and if so, replies back to you with a "cookie" which is used by your browser for all subsequent requests.

It is extremely common for websites to protect your password by encrypting the initial login, but surprisingly uncommon for websites to encrypt everything else. This leaves the cookie (and the user) vulnerable. HTTP session hijacking (sometimes called "sidejacking") is when an attacker gets a hold of a user's cookie, allowing them to do anything the user can do on a particular website. On an open wireless network, cookies are basically shouted through the air, making these attacks extremely easy (Butler, 2010).

Open wireless networking and this side-jacking problem go hand in hand to produce a security nightmare for the vulnerable public. The hack that exposes this problem, ironically, is a good thing because it makes finding a solution to the problem an unavoidable immediate concern.

The world's largest educational and scientific computing society and leading publisher of computer science research and scholarship is the Association for Computing Machinery (ACM - http://www.acm.org/). A few examples from a single issue of the Risks Digest published by their Committee on Computers and Public Policy illustrate that the scope of the problem is huge and multi-faceted (ACM Committee on Computers and Public Policy, 2011):

"Computer screens in Sweden faded to black in October 2009 when the entire country lost its Internet connection due to a missing period (in ".se"). It took almost 24 hours to get things working again."

"A federal judge ruled on 31 Mar 2010 that the National Security Agency's program of surveillance without warrants was illegal, rejecting the Obama administration's effort to keep shrouded in secrecy one of the most disputed counterterrorism policies of former President George W. Bush."

"April 4, 2010 1:54:42 PM EDT: It appears the iPad has been jail broken... in something like 24 hours."

"There is a serious bug with YouTube and Flash Player that is affecting many users. This has been reported on the many YouTube Forums for over a year.Google is well aware of the problem. It is also well aware of the angst of its users. Yet [to date, March 2011] it refuses to 1/ acknowledge the problem, and 2/ do anything about it."

Wired Magazine offered some of its readers a surprise recently in order to illustrate lack of privacy and the impact of modern technologies. A few of its selected readers received an ultra-personalized cover on their issue of Wired UK in order to show how much personal data could be easily found about them from publicly available sources (Rowan, 2011).

All of this is in the domain of the traditional web. When these security problems are applied to human rights as a whole, the issue of web security becomes extraordinary – especially for small human rights organizations that may not have the expertise or funds to deal with it but need to use the web for at least a portion of their work. What are the answers to these riddles?

Issue 4: Data Relationships

I almost wish I hadn't gone down that rabbit-hole — and yet — and yet — it's rather curious, you know, this sort of life! I do wonder what can have happened to me! When I used to read fairy-tales, I fancied that kind of thing never happened, and now here I am in the middle of one! There ought to be a book written about me, that there ought! (Carroll, 1865, Chapter 4)

It is well known that semantic technology is an attempt to create a more intelligent web. Is this equivalent to Alice's rabbit-hole? The goal has been substantially reached in several disciplines already but there is not a general understanding of semantic data systems, and how they essentially differ from other kinds of information systems.

One example of work on semantic data relationships is Dublin Core which provides metadata vocabularies that support interoperable solutions for discovering and managing online resources. It contains a vocabulary of fifteen properties used in resource description. These elements are broad and generic, usable for describing a wide range of resources (http://dublincore.org/documents/dces/). Another example, WonderWeb (http://wonderweb.semanticweb.org/), which is an ontological infrastructure, also established the idea of the Semantic Web as an emerging and important area of investigation. This was linked to the U.S. Defense Advanced Research Projects Agency (DARPA)'s Agent Markup Language (DAML) program which is beyond the scope of this book.

The Semantic Web came into being as an abstract method for handling meanings because the single point of view taken by traditional databases was insufficient. A look at medical database development and specifically the OpenGALEN model (http://www.opengalen.org/index.html) may serve as an example of some of the issues which could face those working in human rights. The traditional medical database was strongly goal oriented, looking to classify and define treatments. Management of healthcare resources concerns itself with the resource allocation for treatment, which these databases do not cover. In the medical field the use of systematically recorded medical information has proliferated to the point where large numbers of complex detailed descriptions abound. Language and culture need to be transcended quickly in medical emergencies, and there is a need to extend definitions for local uses everywhere.

This management usage reversed assumptions that formed the traditional treatment databases. A more objective, ontological approach was required that could separate diagnosis, treatment, cost reduction measures and many other perspectives, while retaining a coherent case by case story. Traditional databases can handle one or even several of these well but all of them together often stretch resources beyond capacity. Every attempt to constrain this growth limits the ability of the systems in question to respond to new situations or even provide responses to existing situations. Semantic Web technology suggests that the data is a universal context resource able to embrace any purpose through the use of relationships.

In traditional software the logic is encapsulated for a single purpose, but it is not coherent enough to make other purposes tractable. Synchronization of many expert systems used for many purposes in such a complex domain is intractable. A unified approach that covers any possible knowledge use would be harder, requiring a strangely ontological but manageable rule set. But once created, the rule set could possibly be applied to any knowledge use scenario.

Often an apparently modest desire to increase the expressiveness of a traditional scheme can produce a large increase in terms and relationships. When the goal is to make the relationships viable for purpose-driven decision making, this combinatorial explosion needs to be accounted for in detail and purposefully constrained. When the core knowledge base is large and complex, the representation of its knowledge will be commensurately large and complex. It is difficult in the extreme with traditional schemes when they rely on human effort to enumerate and interpret all of the possible terms and their relationships.

The world of human rights is not merely equal in complexity to the medical example above, but rather it is vastly larger. It covers the entire scope of potential human meaning. Human rights organizations are already being pushed into a new kind of meaning-making, and down a strangely ontological rabbit-hole. In this rabbit-hole, clarity in data relationships will be essential. Distinctions of identity, time, place, affiliation, and other similar factors have often produced content with contradictions or unobvious connections for certain groups and with entirely different and often conflicting meanings for other groups. Meaning-making in this sense is a much harder problem than the attempt at clear, concise, repetitive meaning in scientific endeavors. Emotion, culture, religion and every form of worldview can play into these meanings in ways not yet captured in software.

Issue 5: Controlled Vocabulary: A Common Language

'Curiouser and curiouser!' cried Alice (she was so much surprised, that for the moment she quite forgot how to speak good English); 'now I'm opening out like the largest telescope that ever was! (Carroll, 1865, Chapter 2).

Many human rights organizations use controlled vocabularies to define and index information. One difficulty is that enumerative vocabularies (pick lists, hierarchies, thesauri, etc.) are often designed for a single purpose or single point of view that has a small group of closely related purposes. Re-use in other contexts, or in independent applications, is difficult and complex. Enumerative vocabularies always require a choice to be made in advance. Organizations and professionals need to decide which concepts to include, and at what detail level. As a result, vocabulary systems often use only a simple hierarchy and have a fixed depth of hierarchy. Often only one layer is available, a simple alphabetical pick list. As a result there is a fixed limit on the concepts. Terms are often mixed, with the reason for an action and the nature of the decision in the same hierarchy. In each situation the mixture is usually valid for the purpose it was intended for, but it restricts the usefulness of the information for other purposes. Preferences for the strangely ontological nature of Semantic Web information are an attempt at making universally valid data. It works quite well for medical information but we already know it has some limitations when it comes to the social sciences.

In multi-lingual vocabularies, the precise language used for concepts, terms, synonyms and lexical variants are not the same or parallel from one language to the next or even from one group to the next. Such a revelation might be shocking to a computer, but humans understand this. The nature of oral traditions and meanings associated with language adds yet another layer of complexity. It is like opening Alice's telescope. Glossaries, cross-references and traditional thesauri can help with this, but even these have not solved the issues.

In examining the various human rights vocabulary lists whether hierarchical, alphabetical or otherwise arranged, a series of complex issues come to the fore. The fact that such detailed and comprehensive work continues to go into building these vocabularies indicates a clear need which includes common understandings of terminologies. Forty-eight lists of human rights terms along with a discussion on establishing such lists, whether hierarchical or alphabetical, can be found in the HURIDOCS *Microthesaurus* (Dueck et al, 2001b). The work and complexity of maintaining and building these vocabularies is expensive, complex and subjective – and yet clarity of language is essential for both medicine and human rights.

Issue 6: Semantic Web and Human Interactivity

'What I was going to say,' said the Dodo in an offended tone, 'was, that the best thing to get us dry would be a Caucus-race.'

'What is a Caucus-race?' said Alice; not that she wanted much to know, but the Dodo had paused as if it thought that somebody ought to speak, and no one else seemed inclined to say anything. (Carroll, 1865, Chapter 3).

As noted above, a combination of data with clear relationships and clear terminology is needed. The Semantic Web notion of data pushes issues further than traditional databases. The subtle complexities involved in the concepts humans discuss normally from day to day must be carefully considered. Computers lack deep intellect or wisdom. Their substitute is deeply detailed and carefully modeled formality. The current Semantic Web approach sometimes leaves an imprecision when very precise vocabulary or definition of relationship is needed, perhaps something like the Dodo's pause. The Semantic Web has the tools to express data relationships quite well. However, sufficiently clear methodologies to adequately address the implied requirements are currently lacking. There ought to be a way to assemble data, validate it for a large number of purposes, and articulate which uses have been thus vetted. Semantic Web implementations are typically just as naively optimistic about the veracity and universal usefulness of data as traditional databases. The ability to mashup data and make inferences at will is not yet mature but is clearly growing. The initiatives are strongly influenced by Google, Yahoo and other web vendors. Mashups have been used mainly to create new and innovative data visualizations. The desire for individual expression, education and other motivations drive the initiatives, but the relevance for databases and information sharing is highly important (Horizon Report, 2008; Robinson, 2010; Grabowiz, 2011).

The solution to this problem must be practical for human developers and be computationally tractable. It is of little value to propose a solution that requires evaluation of a computationally huge or nearly infinite set of possibilities. Changing these references requires new effort from the developers. Developers and users do not always share semantic meanings sufficiently to make formal verification of the effect of changes possible. It is a paradox of software that flexibility in use requires formal rigidity in structure, which in turn offers the chance to verify the consequences of change.

Perhaps the Semantic Web offers a means to begin to capture knowledge and meaning. However there are severe limitations to its ability to do so in the field of human rights although it works reasonably well in the world of medicine because medical fields provide relatively static, structured, environments of meanings. Human rights covers a broad, sometimes vague, and emotionally charged field with many differing definitions, opinions, perspectives, cultures and languages. Semantic Web, at this point, cannot reflexively determine when the context has been compromised nor does it currently offer a solution that can deal effectively with this. It is an emerging tool which should be monitored as it develops.

The project that embraces the need for human interactive reality the most so far is work done by CycCorp (http://www.cyc.com/). It has several thousand micro-theories that are a bundle of assertions and assumptions about particular domains of knowledge, at a particular level of detail, a particular interval of time, etc. It can maintain independent assertions that are contradictory, and is focused on the inferencing process. At the moment it is able to parse hanging negation, modals and nested qualifiers. However it suffers from needing to be expressed in its own language, CycL, and not English or some other natural human language. It also cannot express human language directly yet. It has no capacity to validate, verify, or discern anything beyond what it is fed, which is an unacceptable situation if it is to be useful for human rights organizations.

Issue 7: Search - Finding the Information

'The Duchess! The Duchess! Oh my dear paws! Oh my fur and whiskers! She'll get me executed, as sure as ferrets are ferrets! Where can I have dropped them, I wonder?' Alice guessed in a moment that it was looking for the fan and the pair of white kid gloves, and she very good-naturedly began hunting about for them, but they were nowhere to be seen (Carroll, 1865, Chapter 4).

Finding white kid gloves is much easier than finding information, although perhaps not if one was looking for size small in a mountain of size medium and large. Early search technologies in the 1990s included Excite, WebCrawler, Lycos, Alta Vista and Ask Jeeves to name a few. Metasearch technologies such as Dogpile and Infospace followed. For now most Internet users would agree that Google dominates searching on the web, but specialized engines abound as well. Current search engines have a plethora of approaches and features including answering services. Specialized search engines such as HURISEARCH (www.hurisearch.org) which search more than 5000 human rights websites also exist.

Semantic technology changes everything about how search is done, and consequently the results that are found. The Semantic Web makes searching for ideas or meanings rather than key words somewhat tractable. To illustrate this, Feigenbaum (2009), a leader of the Semantic Web technology, asks the following question of search engines: "Find me genes involved in signal transduction that are related to pyramidal neurons". The traditional web cannot deal with his complex medical question at all, as demonstrated by the fact that 223,000 hits showed with no relevant answers. PubMed, a medical domain search tool shows 2580 potential results. These results are interesting because they require integration of many disparate databases, each holding only a partial clue to the answers. Despite this, the Semantic Web search implemented by PubMed finds precisely relevant articles.

Contextual collaborations like this to find search results is new and has an exceptionally powerful capacity. The process depends on agreement around common terms and relationships, a flexible data structure, good enough modeling, and a query interface tailored to the data model. Can this be done in the Social Sciences? The answer is not directly at present, although the Semantic Web does represent human knowledge, and assertions can be made to cover any topic. However the meta-language of human conversation and perceptions with varying degrees of assertion and contextualization are not easily represented in Semantic Web terms. Such language is vital, and the Semantic Web is sufficiently extendable that the definition's beginnings are already being created.

In fact once created and put in place, the hegemony of that reality will likely be very strong, regardless of how distorted and unplanned it is. The cautious and careful do well to engage deeply now, while the metaphorical cement is still not set. While it is definitely not magic, the new 'intelligence' of search engines and Semantic Web technologies have a tendency to feel a bit magical because it is often hard to trace where and how inferences are made. Over a decade ago, MIT professor Tim Berners-Lee, creator of the World Wide Web, and Semantic Web concept, suggested:

At this point it is important to clarify that the Semantic Web is not a kind of magical artificial intelligence; rather it is a solution that allows a machine to solve a well-defined problem by performing well-defined operations on existing well-defined data (Berners-Lee, 1998).

Search engines are tools designed to be smart. They are tools designed to magically find things people are interested in. The Berners-Lee denial here is a strong caution and perhaps wishful thinking. This is a new tool that needs exploration. If the only tool you are holding is a hammer, then everything looks like a nail, according to an old English saying. This is especially true in an era where nations express deep anxiety over security. National data processing centers with deep processing capacity, almost limitless storage capacity, unknown and unproven correlation engines, theories that remain unscrutinized, Semantic Web data, and significant budgets devoted to 'finding the enemy within' all point to a huge potential for human rights abuse.

That said there are many advantages to this data model. The most salient is perhaps that it is applicable to many programming languages. It presumes that the world of data is wide open and not created for the singular purpose of feeding a particular piece of software its data.

It is useful to draw out some pragmatic observations here. But where does one get started? Without knowing it, many people already are part of the Semantic Web. Anyone who blogs with popular software like phpBB or WordPress is part of the Semantic Interlinking of Online Communities, SIOC (http://sioc-project.org/). Anyone's Google search results can influence the actual search engine since the user search itself has an impact on result lists. More frequently searched items appear higher on Google result lists. This can be problematic for small human rights organizations who often have the information but whose websites don't appear near the top of a Google result list. Hence the need for specialized search engines such as HURISEARCH.

Autonomy (www.autonomy.com) recently released its IDOL (Intelligent Data Operating Layer) engine software platform, which has the potential to push meaning based search to a new level. It is not yet clear how deep the impact of this will be, but it may lead to the capabilities of data engines to comprehend complex meanings at a deeper levels. Monitoring and developing ways to make, hold and share meanings is critical. Ignoring this process can result in grave dangers to human rights organizations.

There is no doubt that semantic technology has arrived. Has the profession of social scientists been co-opted by computer scientists in some measure? How should the human rights community react to this complex and possibly dangerous search technology? Is it time to make the explicit and deep commitment to understanding this technology, both to use it in their Search mechanisms, and to protect people from the deep and profound abuses it enables?

Issue 8: Assumptions and Ease of Use

'Digging for apples, indeed!' said the Rabbit angrily. 'Here! Come and help me out of this!' (Sounds of more broken glass.)

'Now tell me, Pat, what's that in the window?'

'Sure, it's an arm, yer honour!' (He pronounced it 'arrum.')

'An arm, you goose! Who ever saw one that size? Why, it fills the whole window!'

'Sure, it does, yer honour: but it's an arm for all that.'

'Well, it's got no business there, at any rate: go and take it away!' (Carroll, 1865, Chapter 4).

How do the assumptions of some computer scientists operate? This might seem tangential, but in fact it is a core concern. It may be instructive to look at the Digital Bibliography & Library

Project (DBLP), Computer Science Bibliography (http://dblp.uni-trier.de/) as a salient example of the Semantic Web. After all, what computer science does for itself is illustrative of the kind of things it will likely provide by default for others, including the human rights community.

DBLP started life as a small experimental Web server. The design decisions and details of the XML- records behind DBLP were never well documented. Computer scientists are notorious for gaining knowledge through direct experience of the domain, reflexively adapting as they go. When the direct experience of the software is tractable and useful in terms they are accustomed to, then it just evolves to become the de-facto standard. The decision is not made - it emerges. Like bees migrating to a new nest, new standards are collectively discovered by community consensus.

The first observation is that computer scientists invent all kinds of reasons to play with their data. It is easy to derive graphs of the data, like person-publication graphs, co-author graphs and other social network visualizations. Another surprise with this data is that it often lacks citation information. This may be seen as very attractive but abandoned as too costly to be done manually. The socially desirable attribute most expressive of this mindset is 'viral'- highly replicating, and requiring little or no work on the part of the progenitor. This goes both for the designer and for the user. In this paradigm, making unnecessary rules about usage is seen as problematic, bad data is preferred over no data. This is, of course, incorrect since bad data leads to bad conclusions – a critical problem for human rights organizations.

Another factor that encourages viral adoption is stability even in the face of obvious problems. The author Michael Ley admits "DBLP isn't a well-designed project... our policy is to keep DBLP as stable as possible. Data formats, URLs etc. are only changed if they prevent important functionality, and not if they are simply unaesthetic." (Ley, 2009). Presumably this stability is maintained so that software written against the data is not broken. The most important technology difference for this database is that it does recognize authors quite well. This is a fairly typical computer science attitude borne of a care for pragmatic sufficiency. The hegemony of software design is a pervasive if often understated controlling fact of life. Another word for this pervasive controlling hegemony is algorithm. Programmers are tacitly if quietly aware that the software they write will become (one hopes) a benevolent dictator.

The DBLP web server lists all known papers published by a person on her/his "person page". This simple mapping becomes tricky, as soon as a person has several names (synonyms) or if there are several persons with the same name (homonyms). The main obstacles are the bad habit to abbreviate (given) names beyond recognition and spelling errors. The main algorithmic idea we use to identify names we should check more precisely, is to look at person pairs which have the distance two in the coauthor graph and have a "similar" name (Ley, 2009).

This is a typical Semantic Web notion. It is imperfect and relies on a mostly correct heuristic to do the work, rather than human interpreters who are able to understand and interpret variance. This is highly problematic when the assumptions of an index like this are forgotten and the information is trusted.

The coding effort for this index is substantially the work of one person. The index covers most of the journals in computer science. They do understand the nature of changing information landscape; however heuristic standards have not emerged to deal with the problem of slowly changing data and meta-data.

The DBLP key namespace layout is coarse and sometimes fuzzy: periodicals or conference series often are renamed, sometimes they are split or they are joined. The world of publications does not form a hierarchy, the mapping into the DBLP namespace often is a very helpful sub-categorization, but sometimes it may be wrong or controversial. A typical problem is the decision when to treat a satellite workshop as a self-contained event or as a part of the hosting conference (Ley, 2009).

This index is popular among computer scientists because it requires little work. It is tractable in computer science terms, and it is where people go to find computer science journal articles. The formatting has rules which are commonly understood in the computer science domain, but are not accepted in general academia, being seen as far too casual. A further explanation:

We fear that a "perfect" data model becomes very complex and makes data acquisition too expensive. In DBLP we use plain hypertext pages to describe situations not covered by our data model (Ley, 2009).

This fairly accurate description may indeed be worrisome – a chaotic solution. As the saying goes, "automating chaos just produces faster chaos". In order to understand how to create good standards the building blocks of the Semantic Web must be examined. The core premise is that linked data is better. However this might not always be true.

The message learned from Alice's rabbit is that organizations that think they have an arm need to be sure they indeed do have an arm. The assumptions need to be checked. The ease of use must be balanced against critical accuracy. It is fairly common for the data needs of users to outgrow their software. Planning for large comprehensive and well represented information architecture is both expensive and essential for the long term. This is a significant challenge for human rights organizations.

Issue 9: Trust

'If everybody minded their own business,' the Duchess said in a hoarse growl, 'the world would go round a deal faster than it does.'

'Which would not be an advantage,' said Alice, who felt very glad to get an opportunity of showing off a little of her knowledge. 'Just think of what work it would make with the day and night! You see the earth takes twenty-four hours to turn round on its axis —'

'Talking of axes,' said the Duchess, 'chop off her head!' (Carroll, 1865, Chapter 6)

Another Berners-Lee (1997) related idea now getting some deserved research attention is the Web of Trust (Lunn, 2010). This impacts human rights deeply. It intends to express the identity of different people online, knowing whether they are honest, authoritative, or whatever. The term "whatever" is troubling in this context; but as noted earlier, it is used by computer scientists to mean exactly that. The feedback structure used in eBay and Facebook (as two examples) will become more universal. Expectation is that digital signatures and security certificates, aided by or encoded in metadata, will provide some mechanism to assert various kinds of competency. Privacy and personal information standards are needed now to put limits on how pervasively this web of hegemony is allowed to prevail. Appropriately, work is being done on the topic. The Office of the Privacy Commission of Canada has extensive resources on this topic including cases, consultations and research (see (http://www.priv.gc.ca/information/pub/pipeda_h_s_04_e.cfm). Other bibliographies related to privacy, technology and human rights include Concordia University President's Conference Series (2009) and Raynes-Goldie (2011).

The current presumption that unrestrained physical access to any device implies a security breach is valid, and is likely to remain so. While some efforts have been undertaken to protect privacy in the public sector of many countries, it is not enough. Political pressure to apply legislation like Canada's Privacy Act (Office of the Privacy Commissioner of Canada, 2010) more universally is very appropriate. Corporations and private individuals will likely not volunteer for this. At present most of the world has little or no effective control over what information can be stored, what purposes it can be used for, or how long it can be retained.

In the world of human rights, the debate over sharing data is still not resolved. It is clear that sharing information indiscriminately is foolish. Many data collectors seem blissfully unaware that their data may be shared more widely than they expect. Recent news over Wikileaks should give everyone in the community enough reason to be concerned. The surveillance capacity of nations has not been widely understood.What are the circumstances requiring secrecy? How much trust is deserved? For whom? Nobody is truly above self-interest. In practical terms, nothing can be achieved without trust. The fundamental technology of trust is the database. The database and its web of relationships is the hub of meaning in computer software. And this meaning has grown vast. Often hundreds of sophisticated servers crawl over personal intimate data; even the smallest details of personal habits and patterns of behavior are recorded.Who should receive access?

Issue 10: Open Source

This time there could be no mistake about it: it was neither more nor less than a pig, and she felt that it would be quite absurd for her to carry it further.

So she set the little creature down, and felt quite relieved to see it trot away quietly into the wood.

'If it had grown up,' she said to herself, 'it would have made a dreadfully ugly child: but it makes rather a handsome pig, I think.' And she began thinking over other children she knew, who might do very well as pigs, and was just saying to herself, 'if one only knew the right way to change them —' (Carroll, 1865, Chapter 6).

To start a project in the open source world that semantic technology lives in is not trivial. The culture of open source software is well established, but is human rights work particularly compatible with solutions from the voluntary open source community? Some will no doubt try to use open source software hoping that eventually standards will improve and some of the difficulties will be overcome.

What does 'ownership' mean when property is infinitely reduplicable, highly malleable, and the surrounding culture has neither coercive power relationships nor material scarcity economics?

Actually, in the case of the open-source culture this is an easy question to answer. The owner of a software project is the person who has the exclusive right, recognized by the community at large, to distribute modified versions (Raymond, 2000).

Is this a true assumption? What happens to unmet expectations if the "owner" is no longer available, loses interest, lacks time, or is for whatever reason unable to continue to develop the project?

Open source code is only as good as the platform on which it is delivered when it comes to the deep needs of security and privacy. The problem has proven to be just too hard for simplistic approaches, and even some sophisticated approaches have fared no better recently. Open source efforts are sometimes substantial copies of core functionality from various commercial offerings. These efforts may carve a niche by incorporating one or more of the international standards in data or protocols. Good standards can offer robust meaningful cross-functionality between software systems. Sometimes these distinctions are vital and open source provides a handsome solution to a difficult problem. Sometimes open source is a half-hearted solution to a subset of the problem. Even if open source's missing or badly designed pieces are easily identified, the economics of the situation may mean that the community finds itself unable to change them.

In the world of security it is also important to presume that data has been accessed when it is available to a technically savvy person or organization - especially a laptop, thumb drive, CD, DVD, or network connected computer with that data on it. Military security demands for physically and electronically locked down computer access are not viable for most real situations. So being aware of such deep losses and anticipating them is vital to the trust mechanism. Physical security is extremely important. Data encryption is still vital in dangerous situations because cracking the encryption that hides the data takes time, and that time can be well used to flee or organize resistance. More information on cryptography is well outlined by Kessler (2011). The oldest standards are no longer good enough because they can be cracked too quickly and too easily. It is vital that the community understands what kind of animal their particular software really is, and treats it accordingly.

Issue 11: Social Media

'I don't think they play at all fairly,' Alice began, in rather a complaining tone, 'and they all quarrel so dreadfully one can't hear oneself speak — and they don't seem to have any rules in particular; at least, if there are, nobody attends to them — and you've no idea how confusing it is all the things being alive; for instance, there's the arch I've got to go through next walking about at the other end of the ground — and I should have croqueted the Queen's hedgehog just now, only it ran away when it saw mine coming!' (Carroll, 1865, Chapter 8).

People experience social media in different ways. For some, it is unfair, especially when untruths or misleading personal information are out there for the world to see. For others it is confusing in how it works, how it is used and its impact. For some like the hedgehog, it is dangerous. For still others it feels like everything is constantly moving, like Alice's arch – a somewhat unknown future.

Human rights organizations use social media techniques to communicate with advocates, the public, government, perpetrators, researchers and others interested or even those not so interested in current human rights issues and actions. According to Amnesty International, "examples of human rights abuses against activists using social media as a tool of communication continue to climb" (Jones, 2011).

At the same time, some "governments try to silence the messenger because they do not want the message heard," Human Rights Watch noted in its 2010 report (Roth, 2010). Facebook, twitter, blogging and other forms of social media played a strong role in the Arab spring uprisings with varying results. According to a Reporters without Borders study (Morillon & Julliard, 2010), over 60 countries used some form of web censorship even in 2009. The Reporters without Borders 2010 "Enemies of the Internet" list includes Saudi Arabia, Burma, China, North Korea, Cuba, Egypt, Iran, Uzbekistan, Syria, Tunisia, Turkmenistan, and Vietnam. According to the report, governments are attacking increasing numbers of websites and bloggers are finding themselves behind bars, particularly in China, Vietnam and Iran. The report also states that as of March 18, 2010, China had detained over seventy bloggers.

The tension between protection and privacy on the one hand and activism and advocacy on the other is heightened with social media. Human rights organizations must protect their information. It is about people – real people whose lives can be endangered if information about them is circulated – information about their family, their whereabouts, their activities, their cases. While social media provides access to information, sometimes confidential and sensitive information, it also can endanger individuals and organizations. On the other hand, it is the job of activists and advocacy groups to use information to make change. Social media has demonstrated its effectiveness in communication and gathering people together. Indeed social media has remarkable potential both for the human rights community as well as for those who would use the information for less honorable purposes. The ethics of privacy, personal information, protection, power, along with human and financial costs must be examined.

Social media is not the end in itself. It is the means to the end. The end objective is not thousands or millions of people engaged in social media. Rather the goal is the realization of an articulated and desired change. That may involve policies, practices or other change related to government, paramilitary, drug wars, legal matters, revolutions, or specific human rights issues. Adam Elkus writes

networked social movements are still in an immature stage. But as information campaigners grow more experienced, skilled, and above all else pragmatic, the quality of digital campaigns is sure to improve. But until then, we should take a realistic view of networked social movements' mobilizing power. Social media adds another dimension to political conflicts and activism, but not a necessarily decisive one. (Elkus, 2011)

Clearly social media is a fast evolving technology. Research on best practices, standards, and impact must be undertaken.

The challenge is to find the most effective and ethical ways to use social media without being mesmerized by its power. As Sam Gregory states,

We live, work, and create in a world of purposeful witnesses, of casual producers, documentary producers and advocacy producers, of governmental, corporate and non-governmental promoters of technology as panacea, of curators and aggregators, of citizen participants in projects of collective voice, and of re-mixers, re-purposeful witnesses and casual sharers of the spreadable and viral. As ... participants in this new technological topography, we need to move beyond machines and images and into a collaborative, on-going discussion about ethics. (Gregory, 2011)

A FEW EXISTING SOLUTIONS

'What do you know about this business?' the King said to Alice.

'Nothing,' said Alice.

'Nothing whatever ?' persisted the King.

'Nothing whatever,' said Alice.

'That's very important,' the King said, turning to the jury. They were just beginning to write this down on their slates, when the White Rabbit interrupted: 'Un important, your Majesty means, of course,' he said in a very respectful tone, but frowning and making faces at him as he spoke (Carroll, 1865, Chapter 12).

In the human rights world there are several human rights documentation solutions. One example is the HURIDOCS relational database, OpenEvsys (http://www.huridocs.org/openevsys/), built in Sri Lanka on PHP and MySQL. Another database application is Martus (http://www.martus.org/). They are designed to assist NGOs and others to build human rights violation cases, providing necessary and sufficient data in an accepted structured manner.

Whatever systems are used security must be a key factor in the considering its use. Once a 'crack' has been figured out by one programmer and published, that security mechanism is breached everywhere. Modern security software is written so that the core algorithms can be changed as needed. Many older implementations use only a single algorithm, or do not implement the ability to change algorithms easily.

At this point, free human rights software developers simply do not have the resources to constantly fight security battles that never end. There are a number of problems with this implementation that go beyond the old encryption standards. If encryption is used, keys should be changed regularly and safely. A carefully arranged and closely guarded secret protocol that must be followed exactly with pretended acceptance for situations where the protocol is compromised is recommended. Further research and development need to be done to enable re-securing a hacked database, regardless of whether the hack is internal, or external, known or unknown. Several approaches are documented in the research of the Association for Computing Machinery (http://www.acm.org/).

For the sake of everyone wanting to trust such software, larger organizations should be monitoring the software in use to report on its integrity as part of any data capturing agreement. Updates should be tested and vetted by competent local technology workers. After all, updates could become a source for new unanticipated problems, or even intentional leaks introduced by motivated parties known or unknown to the software vendors. The scope of this depends on the local circumstances, but caution is always best. Staying off the Internet altogether is advisable for sensitive data. Alternatives like thumb drives, DVDs, and other physical media might be considered. Other creative solutions that do not involve the Internet can be implemented as well.

Organizations need to make considered technology choices – whether that be on the basis of elegant programming, ease of use, ethical considerations, privacy, procedural requirements or specific organizational needs or other factors. The implications are too important to be left to political preference or ideological alignment. The systems chosen need to be as tough and resilient as the people they serve and they must remain a servant to the human objectives and intentions.

FUTURE RESEARCH DIRECTIONS

The executioner's argument was that you couldn't cut off a head unless there was a body to cut it off from: that he had never had to do such a thing before, and he wasn't going to begin at his time of life.

The King's argument was, that anything that had a head could be beheaded, and that you weren't to talk nonsense.

The Queen's argument was, that if something wasn't done about it in less than no time she'd have everybody executed, all round (Carroll, 1865, Chapter 8).

Technology is never going to be the solution to all of this mayhem. In fact technology creates many problems, and solves few in and of itself. Automated chaos just produces faster chaos and carelessness is common among inventive people. For the inventor it is hard enough to come up with something new. It is essential to take the time to consider technology issues, to allow insights to emerge and to consider the problems the new creations will create. Regrettably some inventors seem to see the difficulty and proceed regardless. Organizations must be involved in the technology they develop or use. Testers and protesters are the skeptics that keep the developers focused. Better testers are needed. Ethics belong to all of us. Skepticism is healthy but sometimes uncommon. In both politics and technology, sometimes the best allies are a loyal informed and vocal opposition. At the very least, organizations and their leaders must proceed with caution in this technology wonderland.

Computers and other technologies change the power structure of society dramatically. The real power is not in large dramatic gestures, but in the small integrated communities of care that are developing around the globe. The question remains: How can technology best serve these dedicated communities? Researching and finding effective and inventive ways to deal with the issues noted above is critical.

CONCLUSION

'And how many hours a day did you do lessons?' said Alice, in a hurry to change the subject.

'Ten hours the first day,' said the Mock Turtle: 'nine the next, and so on.'

'What a curious plan!' exclaimed Alice.

'That's the reason they're called lessons,' the Gryphon remarked: 'because they lessen from day to day.' (Carroll, 1865, Chapter 9)

When people invent and invest in technology, sometimes the easiest path is taken to get at the desired goals. Human beings, with all their creativity, curiosity and intelligence sometimes fail to understand what purpose these efforts serve or to notice obvious contradictions and problems. That is what community is for. The debates will rage, technologies will change, and the very mechanisms of knowledge representation itself will be part of that change.

Wonderland is amazing, inspiring and fascinating, but the purpose of it, the amazement of it and the joy of it must all be founded on the needs, desires, and understanding of its most amazing, inspiring and fascinating inhabitants. Not the Queen, not the Cheshire Cat, not the Mad Hatter, not the Mock Turtle with his curious plans. No, the most amazing, wonderful and fascinating inhabitant is Alice. Alice is the human element. Without her, all is lost.

REFERENCES

ACM Committee on Computers and Public Policy. (2011). *The risks digest: Forum on the risks to the public in computers and related systems*. Retrieved from October 20, 2011 from http://catless.ncl.ac.uk/Risks/

Aitchison, J. (1996). *International thesaurus of refugee terminology*. New York, NY: United Nations.

Amnesty International. (2000).*Updated list of Amnesty International keywords*. London, UK: Amnesty International. AI Index: DOC 20/01/00. Internal document.

Ball, P. (1996). *Who did what to whom? Planning and implementing a large scale human rights data project*. Washington, DC: American Association for the Advancement of Science.

Ball, P., Cifuentes, R., Dueck, J., Gregory, R., Salcedo, D., & Saldarriago, C. (1994). *A definition of database design standards for human rights agencies*. Washington, DC: American Association for the Advancement of Science.

Ball, P., Girouard, M., & Chapman, A. (1997). Information Technology, information management, and human rights: A response to Metzl. *Human Rights Quarterly*, *19*(4), 836–859. doi:10.1353/hrq.1997.0035

Ball, P., Spirer, H., & Spirer, L. (Eds.). (2000). *Making the case: Investigating large scale human rights violations using information systems and data analysis*. Washington, DC: American Association for the Advancement of Science.

Berners-Lee, T. (1997). *Realising the full potential of the Web*. Retrieved October 11, 2011, from http://www.w3.org/1998/02/Potential.html

Berners-Lee, T. (1998). *What the semantic web can represent.* Retrieved October 20, 2011, from http://www.w3.org/DesignIssues/RDFnot.html

Butler, E. (2010). *Firesheep.* Retrieved October 20, 2011, from http://codebutler.com/firesheep

Caccia, I. (1993). *Human rights thesaurus*. Ottawa, Canada: Human Rights Research and Education Centre and Human Rights Internet.

Carroll, L. (1865). *Alice's adventures in Wonderland.* Retrieved October 20, 2011, from Project Gutenberg http://www.gutenberg.org/files/11/11-h/11-h.htm

Carroll, L. (1871). *Through the looking glass, and what Alice found there.* Retrieved October 20, 2011, from Project Gutenberg http://www.gutenberg.org/ebooks/12

Chaves, H. (1989) *Confidentiality of information*. Paper presented at the Conference Human Rights Violations and Standard Formats: Towards Compatibility in Recording and Transferring Information, Utrecht, Netherlands.

Concordia University President's Conference Series. (2009). *Bibliography*. Retrieved October 11, 2011, from http://www.concordia.ca/presidentsconferences/every-breath-you-take/bibliography/

Cross, N., & Jarvis, H. (2000). *New information technology applied to genocide research: The Cambodian genocide program*. Graduate School of Library and Information Science, Simmons College. Retrieved December 10, 2010, from http://web.simmons.edu/~chen/nit/NIT'98/98-019-Cross_Jarvis.html

Dueck, J., Guzman, M., & Verstappen, B. (1993). *HURIDOCS events standard formats: A tool for documenting human rights violations*. Oslo, Norway: HURIDOCS.

Dueck, J., Guzman, M., & Verstappen, B. (2001a). *Micro-thesauri: A tool for documenting human rights violations*. Versoix, Switzerland: HURIDOCS.

Dueck, J., Guzman, M., & Verstappen, B. (2001b). *HURIDOCS events standard formats: A tool for documenting human rights violations*. Versoix, Switzerland: HURIDOCS.

Dueck, J., & Noval, A. M. (1993). *HURIDOCS events standard formats: Supporting documents*. Oslo, Norway: HURIDOCS.

Elkus, A. (November, 2009). Reflecting on Iran, social media, and change. *Huff Post World*. Retrieved October 4, 2011, from http://www.huffingtonpost.com/adam-elkus/reflecting-on-iran-social_b_355448.html

Feigenbaum, L. (2009). *The 2009 Semantic Web landscape.* Retrieved October 20, 2011, from http://www.slideshare.net/LeeFeigenbaum/semantic-web-landscape-2009

Frontalini, J. (1990). Advantages of using standard formats. *HURIDOCS News*, *9*, 20–25.

Grabowicz, P. (2011). *Databases, data visualizations and map mashups: The Transition to digital journalism.* Retrieved November 1, 2011, from http://multimedia.journalism.berkeley.edu/tutorials/digital-transform/databases/

Gregory, S. (2011). *The ethical engagements of human rights social media*. Retrieved May 11, 2011, from http://blog.witness.org/2010/11/the-ethical-engagements-of-human-rights-social-media/

Guinchat, C., & Minou, M. (1983). *General introduction to the techniques of information and documentation work*. Paris, France: United Nations Educational, Scientific and Cultural Organization.

Guzman, M., & Verstappen, B. (1998). International Conference on Computerised Documentation of Human Rights Events: Mexico City, 11-13 November, 1998. *HURIDOCS News, 22*, 11-17.

Hansen, S. A. (2000). *Thesaurus of economic, social, and cultural rights: Terminology and potential violations*. Washington, DC: American Association for the Advancement of Science and HURIDOCS.

HURIDOCS. (1990). Human rights violations and standard formats: towards compatibility in recording and transferring information. *HURIDOCS News, 9*, 38.

Jelin, E. (1994). The politics of memory: The human rights movement and the construction of democracy in Argentina. *Latin American Perspectives, 81*(4:2), 38-58. Retrieved October 1, 2011 from http://www.latinamericanstudies.org/argentina/human-rights.pdf

Jones, M. (2011). *The human cost of the social media revolution.* Amnesty International. Retrieved May 11, 2011, from http://www.amnesty.org.au/features/comments/25268/

Kessler, G. (2011, October 16). *An overview of cryptography*. Retrieved October 20, 2011, from http://www.garykessler.net/library/crypto.html

Knowles, E. (Ed.). (2006). *A dictionary of phrase and fable*. Oxford University Press. Retrieved October 1, 2011, from http://www.oxfordreference.com/views/ENTRY.html?subview=Main&entry=t214.e7762

Ley, M. (2009). DBLP - Some lessons learned. *Proceedings of the VLDB Endowment,* Vol. 2, (pp. 1493-1500). Retrieved October 20, 2011 from http://www.vldb.org/pvldb/2/vldb09-98.pdf.

Lunn, B. (2010, April 27). *Does Facebook Open Graph help or hinder the Web of trust?* Retrieved October 20, 2010, from http://semanticweb.com/does-facebook-open-graph-help-or-hinder-the-web-of-trust_b595

Lyle, G., & Ng, Y. (2011). *WITNESS media archive cataloging manual section 1.* Retreived October 1, 2011, from http://www.witness.org/sites/default/files/downloads/witness_catalogingmanual_2011aug_sect1.pdf

Metzl, J. F. (1996). Information technology and human rights. *Human Rights Quarterly, 18*(4), 705–746. doi:10.1353/hrq.1996.0045

Metzl, J. F. (1997). Metzl response to Ball, Girouard, and Chapman. *Human Rights Quarterly, 19*(4), 860–863. doi:10.1353/hrq.1997.0041

Morillon, L., & Julliard, J. (2010). *Web 2.0 versus Control 2.0.* Reporters Without Borders. Retrieved October 4, 2011, from http://en.rsf.org/web-2-0-versus-control-2-0-18-03-2010,36697

Office of the Privacy Commissioner of Canada. (2010). *Information related to the Privacy Act.* Retrieved December 4, 2011, from http://www.priv.gc.ca/legislation/02_07_01_01_e.cfm

Office of the United Nations High Commissioner for Human Rights. (2008). *Human rights, terrorism and counter-terrorism, fact sheet No. 32*. Retrieved October 21, 2011, from http://www.ohchr.org/Documents/Publications/Factsheet32EN.pdf

Organisation for Economic Co-operation and Development. (1998). *Macrothesaurus for information processing in the field of economic and social development*. Paris, France: Organisation for Economic Co-operation and Development.

Pilieci, V. (2010). *New ePassports flawed, security expert warns; ID chips easily copied, researcher says. The Ottawa Citizen,* A1. Retrieved October 20, 2011 from http://search.proquest.com/docview/241360594?accountid=32724

Privacy Rights Clearinghouse. (2011). *Chronology of data breaches: Security breaches 2005 – present*. Retrieved December 4, 2011, from https://www.privacyrights.org/data-breach

Raymond, E. S. (2000). *Homesteading the Noosphere*. Retrieved October 20, 2011, from http://catb.org/~esr/writings/homesteading/homesteading/

Raynes-Goldie, K. (2011). *Digitally mediated surveillance, privacy and social network sites*. Retrieved October 11, 2011, from http://www.digitallymediatedsurveillance.ca/wp-content/uploads/2011/04/Raynes-Goldie-Digitally_mediated_surveillance_privacy_and_social_network_sites.pdf

Report, H. (2008). *Two to three years: Data mashups*. The New Media Consortium. Retrieved November 1, 2011, from http://wp.nmc.org/horizon2008/chapters/data-mashups/

RFIDWorld.ca. (2010). IT expert in Britain warns that Canadian RFID E-passports not secure enough. *RFIDWorld Canada*. Retrieved on October 11, 2011, from http://www.rfidworld.ca/it-expert-in-britain-warns-that-canadian-rfid-e-passports-not-secure-enough/116

Robinson, B. (2010). Web mashups put transparency to the test. *Federal Computer Week*. Retrieved November 1, 2011, from http://fcw.com/articles/2010/01/11/feat-mashups-test-transparency.aspx

Roth, K. (2010). The abusers' reaction: Intensifying attacks on human rights defenders, organizations, and institutions. *Human Rights Watch World Report 2010*. Retrieved May 11, 2011, from http://www.hrw.org/en/node/87544

Rowan, D. (2011). Behind the scenes of wired UK magazine's personalized covers. *Wired Magazine*. Retrieved October 21, 2011, from http://www.wired.com/epicenter/2011/02/behind-the-scenes-of-wired-uk-magazines-personalized-covers/

Stormorken, B., & Zwaak, L. (1998). *Human rights terminology in international law: A thesaurus*. Dordrecht, The Netherlands: Martinus Nijhoff Publishers.

Syal, R. (2009, February 1). 17,000 asylum seekers' files lost. *The Guardian*. Retrieved October 22, 2011, from http://www.guardian.co.uk/uk/2009/feb/01/refugees-asylum

United Nations Educational, Scientific and Cultural Organization. (1995). *UNESCO thesaurus: A structured list of descriptors for indexing and retrieving literature in the fields of education, science, social and human science, culture, communication and information*. Paris, France: UNESCO Publishing.

Chapter 2
ICT Policies Favouring Human Rights

Rolf H. Weber
University of Zurich, Switzerland

ABSTRACT

The tremendous developments in information and communication technologies (ICTs) over the last 20 years have substantially changed communication practices across the world. The Internet and mobile phones help to open new horizons for connections between people, leading to a global network for the sharing of information and ideas. In this new environment, human rights need to have a place, and traditional notions related to mass media need to be adapted to the needs of civil society. Freedom of expression has become much more individualistic, with information exchanges no longer relying on the traditional intermediaries (mass media) but on the exchange of ideas on social networking and other platforms. Civil society participation in the information world requires the necessary infrastructure however. And since states have an obligation to see to it that human rights are realized in practice, this may mean the facilitation of private investments to improve the ICT infrastructure. In this context, ICT policies favoring human rights must encompass a right to development.

INTRODUCTION

This chapter begins with a few general remarks on technological developments relating to the Internet and mobile phones. These are followed by a historical (political-legal) review of how the approach to extending ICT rights globally has moved from the New World Information and Communication Order (NWICO) to the World Summit of the Information Society (WSIS). After that, the chapter examines the current legal framework for human rights, and the new opportunities presented by digital communications (particularly in relation to freedom of expression as a key hu-

DOI: 10.4018/978-1-4666-1918-0.ch002

man right) and the risks related to their realization (censorship, storage of data/surveillance as threats, acknowledgement of indirect effects of human rights). The analysis shows that the traditional human rights are still apt to comply with the new needs, however, the scope of interpretation might have to be extended to updated understandings. Subsequently the targets for successful enjoyment of human rights, such as the enlarged scope of economic and social rights, the removal of trade barriers, the achievement of diversity, and the establishment of community media are discussed in detail. Finally the chapter concludes with a proposal to strengthen the (enforceable) right to development.

TECHNOLOGICAL DEVELOPMENTS

Recent technological developments in the field of information and communication technologies have been tremendous. These developments encompass aspects of fixed and mobile infrastructure. In respect of the fixed networks the provision of broadband is at the forefront, allowing the transmission of much more information and images at a higher speed. The mobile infrastructure is becoming more significant in terms of information exchanges and the execution of business transactions. According to the International Telecommunication Union (ITU), the number of mobile cellular subscriptions globally reached 5 billion at the end of 2010, and the use of mobile phones is likely to continue to increase significantly in the near future.

The explosion in access to digital communications over the last 20 years has been remarkable. 15 years ago only 0.4% of the world's population had access to the Internet, but by the end of 2009 an estimated 26% of the world's population were using it (corresponding to 1.7 billion people) (ITU, 2010). This development has been supported by the fact that the costs of Internet services fell on average by 15% during the last 3 years. Nevertheless Internet usage is still concentrated in the West, with Internet penetration in developed countries estimated at 64%, as compared with 18% in developing countries.

The steep growth in mobile cellular subscriptions is at least in part driven by an increased take-up and advancement of mobile business services around the world. However the growth of these mobile business services does not only depend on technological advances, but also on consumer confidence in the services provided. In industrialized countries, the additive model applies, meaning that mobile business services constitute a further (suitable) channel for consumers already demanding the respective services. In the developing world, the transformative model aims at offering these services to customers that have not previously been involved in business services transactions.

POLITICAL DEVELOPMENTS

The realization of a global communications order is not a new objective. For almost 40 years politicians have debated how a reasonable legal framework supporting the participation of global civil society could be institutionalized. For the present discussions it is worthwhile to reflect upon the historical milestones.

New World Information and Communication Order

The attempt to introduce principles of governance in relation to information services is not completely new as the issue of information flow has been a discussion topic for many decades. The Internet is a new medium, but traditional media also facilitate cross border information services which have called for an applicable legal framework.

After decolonization became wide-spread (in the 1950s and 1960s many former colonies attained their independence), the world was divided along

East-West and North-South axes in the 1970s (Padovani & Nordenstreng, 2005). Since global flows of news and information were already the subject of intense debates in international fora in the early 1970s, a group of block-free countries discussed the idea of a "New World Information and Communication Order" (NWICO) (Weber, 2004) that grew out of the International Economic Order of 1974 (Carlsson, 2003). After its launch at the non-aligned Summit of 1973 in Algier, calling for united action in the field of mass communication (Padovani & Nordenstreng, 2005), it soon became obvious that the NWICO would have to be incorporated into a broader concept of a third world development policy as stated in the United Nation General Assembly Resolution 37/94 of December 10, 1982 (Hedebro, 1982). Being built on a mainly political approach, the New World Information and Communication Order implied far-reaching reforms of the existing order, including all kinds of information (political, social, economic and technical information), all media (including press, radio, TV, film, data banks, etc.), and all forms of communications technologies (Carlsson, 2003).

At the same time, the Soviet Union proposed to release a "Mass Media Declaration" under the auspices of the United Nations Educational, Scientific and Cultural Organization (UNESCO, Doc. COM-74/CONF. 6/6/3). This was aimed at the development of globally acceptable guidelines for the role of mass media in the international system (UNESCO Res. 4/9.3/2; Carlsson, 2003). This attempt provoked opposition from Western and Northern countries that were afraid the principle of "free flow of information" could be jeopardized (Sussman, 1989).

MacBride Report

In December 1977 an International Commission for the study of information and communication problems, appointed by UNESCO and chaired by Nobel laureate Sean MacBride, began its work on compiling an impressive report under the title "Many Voices One World" (United Nations Educational, Scientific and Cultural Organization, 1980). During the inquiry process of the MacBride Commission, the participants of the UNESCO General Conference agreed on November 28, 1978 on the "Declaration on the Fundamental Principles Concerning the Contribution of the Mass Media to Strengthening Peace and International Understanding, to the Promotion of Human Rights and to Countering Racialism, Apartheid and Incitement to War". Agreement on the Mass Media Declaration was achieved in relatively short time due to the fact that the developed countries offered infrastructure help to developing countries for agreeing to weaken some of their substantive requests. However the resulting publication led to the USA and UK condemning the report, and leaving UNESCO in 1984 and 1985 respectively.

Mansell and Nordenstrang (2006) suggest that the MacBride Report strongly emphasized the social aspect and the potential contribution of the media and communication to forces of democratization. Its authors expressed their hope for the emergence of societies in which there would be "the diffusion of power through broader access to and participation in the communication process; . . . the benefits of communication used as an educational and socializing force; . . . the reduction of inequalities through democratization; [and] . . . the abolition of the vestiges of domination as full national liberation becomes a reality" (United Nations Educational, Scientific and Cultural Organization, 1980, p.6).

The MacBride report addressed a large number of matters, and in particular the following topics: (i) strengthening independence and self-reliance; (ii) social consequences of a new information order and new tasks; (iii) professional integrity and standards; (iv) democratization of communication; (v) fostering international co-operation; and (vi) provision of more extensive financial resources in favour of less developed countries. However after its publication, only a fairly limited discussion took place within UNESCO. Without having funds to subsidize the communication infrastructure of less developed countries, the information and communication order subsequently disappeared from the political agenda.

World Summit on the Information Society

With the advancement of the Internet in the 1990s, more and more actors felt a need for regulation. Taking up the discussion of a global information and communication order, the International Telecommunications Union (ITU) passed a resolution in 1998 proposing the idea of a World Summit on the Information Society (WSIS) under the auspices of the United Nations. In 2001, the ITU Council endorsed the approach of holding the Summit in two phases, the first one in Geneva in 2003, the second one in Tunis two years later.

In the first phase, the December 2003 Geneva Conference enacted the Geneva Declaration of Principles and the Geneva Action Plan. These defined the common vision and a framework for measures to be taken in order to realize an inclusive information society. The key principles encompassed the following lines of action:

1. The role of governments and all stakeholders in the promotion of ICT for development is becoming increasingly important and requires joint efforts.
2. Information and communication infrastructure is an essential foundation for an inclusive information society.
3. The provision of access to information and knowledge for the whole population must become a mandatory target for regulators.
4. The capacity to acquire the necessary skills and knowledge in information technologies including continuous education should be strengthened.
5. The building of confidence and security in the use of ICT is becoming crucial (trust framework).
6. An enabling environment at national and international levels is an important tool for good governance (incl. intellectual property protection and standardization).
7. An improvement of ICT applications can bring benefits in all aspects of life.
8. The promotion of cultural diversity and identity, linguistic diversity and local content serves the common heritage of humankind.
9. The freedom of the media and the freedom of information should be guaranteed.
10. The promotion of the ethical dimensions of the information society (incl. solidarity, tolerance) is of essence.
11. International and regional co-operation should be improved.

In 2005 the Tunis Summit adopted the Tunis Commitment and the Tunis Agenda. These outlined a medium-term future for global Internet governance. In addition, the international community agreed in Tunis that an Internet Governance Forum (IGF), a multi-stakeholder platform for the discussion of public policy issues related to the Internet, should be created and that a "process of enhanced co-operation" with the full involvement of all stakeholders should be established.

Lessons from History

The history of global communications shows that technical developments in ICTs have drastically changed information flows and thereby also the legal framework relating to them. In the 1970s and 1980s, traditional media (including radio and television) were the intermediaries of communications (one-to-many voices). Since then platforms have emerged which allow a system of many-to-many communications. While a dense penetration of access points to these networks is now possible, the legal framework has to see to it that participation in the exchange of communications remains feasible for the whole of society.

PRESENT LEGAL FRAMEWORK FOR HUMAN RIGHTS

Freedom of Expression as Key Human Right

In elaborating a legal framework specifically for the needs of the new information society, common standards that adequately protect human rights must become a basis for discussion. In particular the different human rights - for example freedom of expression and the right to privacy - need to be balanced in order to reach an adequate level of protection in an open society (Dutton et al. 2010).

New technologies enabling a fuller realization of human rights are particularly relevant for the right to freedom of expression, with ICTs enhancing the ability to not only receive information, but also to actively seek and impart it. Digital communications are spurring the development of empowering spaces for the exchange of ideas, collaboration and participation (EU Parliament, 2010). Furthermore, ICTs enable human rights activists to apply new tools in the defence of human rights. Internet access via mobile phones, for example, gives civil society the power to communicate rights violations in real time to global audiences, while networking tools connect human rights defenders across the world.

In contrast, ICTs also encompass threats to freedom of expression. Increasingly sophisticated censorship and surveillance mechanisms endanger the unrestricted exploitation of human rights. Notwithstanding this, however, ICTs empower people to express themselves more directly in public arenas without having to go through the traditional media gatekeepers. In opening up these opportunities, digital communications are helping to more fully realize not only freedom of expression, but also other human rights such as the participation in public affairs (Jøergensen, 2006).

The importance of the right to freedom of expression is reflected by its protection in all significant international and regional human rights treaties. These protections include Article 19 of the International Covenant on Civil and Political Rights (ICCPR), Article 13 of the American Convention on Human Rights (ACHR), Article 11 of the European Convention on Human Rights (ECHR) and Article 9 of the African Charter (Banjul Charter of October 2002). However, as in the non-virtual world, human rights in digital communications need to be carefully balanced since there are different rights and responsibilities of individuals at stake. Human rights jurisprudence provides guidance on how to balance rights (Human Rights Committee, 2010; Murphy & Ó Cuinn, 2010). The human rights community is called upon to take the lead in examining how to get the balance between human rights and social goods right in digital environments (EU Parliament, 2010).

With the advent of the Internet more than ten years ago, the new technical possibilities were expected to lead to a knowledge-based society, allowing all members of civil society to enjoy a right to information and participation in relevant information exchanges (Banisar, 2006). A knowledge-based society must take into account the human rights constituting the basic framework for society, namely freedom of expression as the right to communicate and freedom of information as the right of access to information. The realization of freedom of expression requires the making available of sufficient and adequate distribution channels and reception devices. The realization of freedom of information requires the establishment of access possibilities, not only to the technical infrastructure, but also to the content, i.e. to the substantive material.

New Digital Communications' Opportunities

Appropriate ICT policies have the potential to create new opportunities for civil society to use digital communications in ways that lead to better realization of human rights as follows (EU Parliament, 2010):

1. ICTs can effectively democratize expression and empower people across the world to communicate directly with each other in the public sphere without having to go through communication gatekeepers such as the traditional media.
2. The framework for the right to privacy (which is beyond the scope of this chapter) must be strengthened in response to the potential for ICTs to be misused, for example by governments across the world applying them to monitor the behaviour of citizens in increasingly sophisticated and hidden ways. Such actions constitute non-compliance with generally accepted data protection principles, and the misappropriation of technical devices.
3. The right of people to take part in cultural life, to benefit from scientific progress and to access knowledge and information becomes more important. The higher the ICT penetration is in a given area, the more achievable this is.
4. Further opportunities and challenges relate to the right to development insofar as ICTs provide new tools for individuals and governments to improve access to income, employment, public services, and the overall economic environment.

The evolution of digital communications is changing the ways in which opportunities and challenges need to be conceptualized and addressed. In this context it is useful to think of communications' environments as being made up of a number of broad, overlapping conceptual 'layers' (EU Parliament, 2010):

1. Physical infrastructure encompassing the basic cables, wireless towers, and hardware that carry and route digital material;
2. Connectivity, including protocols and codes that allow digital material to be transported across networks, and devices to receive and interpret digital data into words, sounds, and pictures;
3. Applications, being the platforms and tools used to create, view, manipulate, and navigate digital content (web browsers, search engines, blogging platforms, etc.);
4. Content, being the material of the communications which can be seen, heard and watched by civil society.

As far as the infrastructure layer is concerned, the geographical reach of networks and hardware is at the core of the debate and the uneven availability in developed and less developed countries must be overcome. In respect of the connectivity layer, the aspect of an open network is of utmost importance. With regard to the applications layer, the dependence on intermediary companies (media in the large sense) could cause problems. Finally the content layer has the closest relation to human rights since the differences in notions and interpretations of expressions and culture are to be taken into account.

The importance of ICT infrastructure for human rights has also been re-affirmed in the context of the WSIS-Principles which can be crystallized around the following goals for an open society:

1. Everyone should be able to acquire basic information and electronic education, in order to master social transformations in all their practical and civic aspects.
2. Access to public data without charge is a necessary condition enabling everyone to exercise his/her civil rights.

3. Access to infrastructure under adequate economic conditions must be guaranteed by supporting the possibility of being a provider as well as a consumer of information.
4. The respect of intellectual property should be interpreted in view of the right to education and knowledge. Furthermore, intellectual work and the ideas, including programming methods and algorithms, should not be monopolized through legal or technical measures.

SPECIFIC RISKS FOR THE REALIZATION OF HUMAN RIGHTS

The enjoyment of human rights can be jeopardized by state action. The best known example is censorship. But other governmental measures also interfere with individual rights. In particular the storage of data allows close surveillance of members of civil society by government authorities. However, there are other risks, too. For example a telecommunications provider could deny access to a specific individual in a discriminatory way. Traditionally, human rights do not apply horizontally amongst private actors, but the newer legal doctrine has acknowledged the notion of the indirect effect of human rights to tackle such a situation.

Censorship as Threat

Mobile phones and Internet-based communications like email, online chat, and voice over Internet are making it easier for people to connect to each other for personal, business and political reasons (EU Parliament, 2010). Indeed, in the public domain, ICTs are playing an increasingly significant role in enhancing expression and association. The ability of people to hold their leaders to account is a key tenet of liberal democracy. Nevertheless, looking around the globe it is obvious that content is censored for a wide variety of reasons, some of which are legitimate under human rights law, the vast majority of which are not.

Censorship can occur as a result of political considerations, for social/cultural reasons, for the promotion of security, or for the purpose of restricting the use of Internet tools for what might be deemed inappropriate or improper activity. Censorship mechanisms are often divided into several categories. Certain content or online services can be blocked or filtered so that users trying to access them are prevented from doing so. Content can also be taken down from the Internet or can effectively be hidden from users so that they do not know that it is available. Finally, there is evidence of some states working to build a pervasive culture of self-censorship preventing 'unsuitable' content from being created and published online.

From a technical point of view, there are a range of filtering mechanisms and processes for blocking an Internet user from visiting certain websites. These include DNS tempering, URL filtering, IP address filtering, deep packet inspection, HTTP proxy filtering, geolocation filtering, content filtering software, and denial of service attacks (Dutton et al. 2010). A further significant problem is the fact that technologies developed for legitimate purposes can easily be used to violate human rights. For example hardware features designed to manage day-to-day Internet traffic are often suitable to be misused by repressive governments to censor traffic and monitor use.

The roles and responsibilities of corporate actors in all this should not be underestimated. There are numerous ways in which businesses can be complicit in censorship (EU Parliament, 2010). If services providers and application companies are required to obtain a license in order to operate in a specific country, this can be used to make the business conditional upon adherence to specific requirements such as blocking access to certain kinds of content (Deibert et al., 2008).

Storage of Data/ Surveillance as Threat

Following increased international efforts to enhance security during the last ten years, human rights advocates point to a 'dramatic increase of [sic] the storage and exchange of personal data in relation to activities of the police and justice sector' (Article 29 Data Protection Working Party, 2009). The respective trends encompass the increased use of surveillance, more elaborate data sharing between governments across borders, and the retention of data for extended periods of time (Human Rights Council, 2009). At least partly, the responses to tackling the misuse of communications networks have been driven by moral panic and have been disproportionate to the threat. From a human rights perspective, individuals should be enabled to decide where the line is to be drawn between the use of their personal data to improve their online experience and their right to limit such use as part of their right to privacy.

The privacy rights of individuals have been threatened by states and corporate activities throughout history. However, ICT developments are making the risks and dangers far more pronounced. During the last ten years, digital communications have revolutionized society, but on the flip side the evolution has also made it easier, cheaper and more efficient to monitor an unlimited number of members of civil society (EU Parliament, 2010). The fact that the collection and storage of huge volumes of data can be undertaken without major problems and that the efficient consolidation and analysis of this information is possible, means that protection for individuals in respect of their personal data has become increasingly difficult. Furthermore access to data collections is cumbersome from a practical point of view (even if access would be legally possible) since individuals often do not know who is collecting the data.

Indirect Effects of Human Rights

The traditional approach applied in relation to human rights adheres to the principle of non-interference by states into the exercise of human rights by private persons. This traditional approach is only looking from a vertical perspective, however. Human rights of individuals can also be jeopardized by the exercise of human rights by other individuals. Therefore a more modern approach is required, taking into consideration horizontal and indirect effects of human rights. State legislators on an international and a national level should work to avoid restriction on freedom of expression or freedom of information which should be guaranteed to all individuals (Cheung & Weber, 2008).

The typical wordings of international law provisions are centred around the formulation 'everyone has the right to ...'. Consequently, the human rights are directed against state interventions into a protected sphere of individuals. However, this notion does not exclude the notion that human rights obligations can also concern non-state actors.

A further consideration concerns the question of whether states are (also) obliged to protect human rights from violations committed by non-state actors. Article 2 of the ICCPR, Article 1 of the ECHR, and Article 1 of the ACHR acknowledge the principle that the implementation of human rights is a domestic matter. In particular, the ECHR obliges states 'to secure everyone within their jurisdiction the rights and freedoms defined in ... the Convention'. Similar provisions are contained in the ICCPR and the ACHR holding that each state party 'undertakes to respect and to ensure' to all individuals the rights and the freedoms recognized in the Covenant and the Convention, respectively (Cheung & Weber, 2008).

From these provisions the conclusion can be drawn that states have to actively secure the protection of human rights as well as refraining from violating them. To this extent, the classical "negative" perception of human rights and freedoms must be complemented by positive obligations, i.e. a state is obliged to balance legally protected interests. Concretely, private censors blocking information flow should also be subject to legal challenge by affected individuals in court.

TARGETS FOR A SUCCESSFUL ENJOYMENT OF HUMAN RIGHTS

Since there is potential for an improvement of the present situation, scientific research should be intensified in respect of several targets for a successful enjoyment of human rights by civil society (see also Dutton et al. 2010). A number of examples are now discussed. These are the enlarged scope of economic and social rights of individuals, the removal of trade barriers, the achievement of cultural/linguistic diversity including capacity building, the establishment of electronic community media, as well as the realization of an enforceable right to development.

Enlarged Scope of Economic and Social Rights

As outlined already, states have certain obligations to provide the technological environment to enable civil society to participate in the exchanges of ideas and communications. Consequently, states are responsible for putting measures in place that will spur the realization of economic and social rights to the maximum of their available resources (Gatto, 2011). In line with Article 2 of the International Convention on Economic, Social, and Cultural Rights (ICESCR), states are obliged to create an environment which enables civil society to make participative decisions, provide basic public services and infrastructure to support development, and not undermine the ability of other states to work towards the realization of human rights through international relations (EU Parliament, 2010). Furthermore, the impact that ICTs have on social, economic and cultural dynamics should be evaluated under a context-specific approach. The following examples of mobile services show the type of creative solutions that civil society should be free to develop:

1. Community telecenters offer rural communities special access to information and communication tools, for example by providing access to ICT workshops and remote training courses (Mali, Colombia).
2. A Dutch NGO, Text to Change, is helping to communicate knowledge about HIV/AIDS via mobile phones to over 60,000 people in Uganda using text messages.
3. In Bangladesh, the Palliathya Helpline Project provides access to virtually any information needed by women who visit rural households by enabling them to dial a central help and information centre with mobile phones.
4. In Ghana, the Text Me! Flash Me! helpline allows phone users to "flash" help centres to signal that they would like to be phoned back by an HIV councillor.
5. The Jalin Merapi Project in central Java, Indonesia, connects community radios, an interactive website and SMS reporting to provide communities living in the vicinity of the Merapi volcano with an early warning system in the event of volcanic activity. This became particularly relevant in late 2010.
6. Mobile Active (http://mobileactive.org) is a network of NGOs, activities and service providers who are dedicated to using mobile technology for social change.
7. Skype and the United Nations High Commissioner for Refugees (UNHCR) have developed new software enabling communications (voice and video calls) for humanitarian workers in remote areas. The service has been successfully tested in Iraq, Sudan and Afghanistan, to be followed by

Algeria, Bangladesh, Chad, Congo, Kenya, Kyrgyzstan and Nepal.

Ensuring equal access to ICTs for all who want to have access is an area in which the principle of non-discrimination should be applied. The realization of economic and social rights can be achieved at individual and community levels by providing civil society with hardware and software tools to help improve the quality and standard of living. At the community and state levels ICTs can improve the delivery of public services and social security systems such as health and education (EU Parliament, 2010). As already mentioned, mobile devices and networks are cheaper and faster to implement than fixed networks. Furthermore, the use of mobile devices is also easier for less educated members of civil society. For this reason improvement of the human rights situation can benefit from implementation of an efficient mobile communications infrastructure.

Apart from governments, private actors can also play an important role in the realization of economic and social rights. ICTs have enabled the establishment of many initiatives providing services structures in less developed areas and supporting remote communities' access to aspects of health and social rights (EU Parliament, 2010).

Removal of Trade Barriers

Traditionally, the legal framework of the World Trade Organization (WTO) has been directed to the cross-border trade of goods. The exchange of (information) services has gained importance meaning that a further liberalization of WTO rules in this field seems to be required, in particular in light of the fact that digital products and digital services cannot always be easily identified.

Notwithstanding the fact that WTO negotiations on a further liberalization of trade in the field of digital products and services have not advanced during the last 5 years, legal doctrine is available on guidelines for the interpretation of the WTO rules dealing with virtual goods (Weber, 2010b). Furthermore, trade in digital products will continue in the coming years, meaning that developments in practice are going to put pressure on the legal framework to adapt to the real needs of businesses and civil society.

Achievement of Cultural/Linguistic Diversity and Capacity Building

The globalization of ICT technology does not mean that substantive standards must also be globalized. Moreover, a good mobile communications infrastructure helps to preserve cultural and linguistic diversity since members of civil society can use the respective networks in order to exchange information in line with their culture and language.

In particular, Article 15 paragraph 1 (a) of the ICESCR on the right to take part in cultural life puts obligations on states. These are in the form of an obligation to respect, protect and fulfil cultural diversity. Therefore states are obliged to take specific measures aimed at achieving respect for the right of everyone to freely choose his/her own cultural identity, to enjoy freedom of opinion and expression, to have access to his/her own cultural and linguistic heritage and to freely take part in any decision-making process (United Nations Economic and Social Council, 2009).

Education is an important aspect of the exploitation of ICT goods and services as a basis for the actual realization of human rights. Soft factors such as capacity building for young and old should be high on the political agenda. ICTs can be used to contribute to the realization of the corresponding rights objectives (Spence & Smith, 2009). As already noted, hardware and software elements can be developed in ways that provide people with tools to help them improve their quality and standard of living, while at the community and state level they can be used to more effectively deliver public services and social security systems such as health and education.

For example, mobile banking services can be used by people at the 'bottom of the pyramid', or who are considerd socially or economically disadvantaged or excluded, for money transfers and other financial or banking services.

ICTs offer further potential through improving the capacity of individuals and communities to realise their rights and/or claims in the social and political sphere. Better access to network infrastructures, easier flow of information, and improved knowledge about the merits of ICTs facilitate the enjoyment of the rights to free expression and information. Digital communications can help empower individuals and communities by giving them access to the knowledge and tools that they need to hold power to account. Consequently, new technological means enable civil society to take advantage of improved political participation (Klein, 2006). Insofar as they bring this about, ICT policies favour human rights.

Establishment of Electronic Community Media

While traditional press and broadcast media are directed towards the general public, mobile infrastructure allows media to become more individual since personal communications can be disseminated through the networks (Dutton et al. 2010). If private enterprises are not able or willing to offer services (for example in sparsely populated geographical areas), the state might have to consider granting subsidies to the private sector.

Private initiatives are often more efficient than state interventions. However in areas that are not densely populated - for example in rural or mountainous regions - the costs associated with ICT investments cannot be borne by private enterprises alone. In the interest of society states should therefore subsidize the provision of the respective services. But if a government prefers not to be directly involved in the construction of the necessary infrastructure, the alternative is to support private actors that are willing to invest in the infrastructure.

For obvious reasons, subsidies need to be controlled and private activities should be subject to oversight. In particular, in less developed countries the situation whereby the subsidies granted by a government mainly lead to an increase in profit of private businesses has to be avoided. Nevertheless, in addition to specific provisions in the WTO legal framework, general principles have also been developed to ensure transparency and accountability in the context of subsidies (Weber & Grosz, 2009).

Recent experiences have shown that mobile communications infrastructure can also be used for community media services by providing journalists with the possibility of offering their information services through mobile networks. However, the implementation of the necessary infrastructure could once again be too costly for the private sector. In this situation the government might have to consider applying direct investments. Since this can be costly, financial mechanisms have to be put in place that provide governments in less developed countries with the means needed for the building of the infrastructure. It is widely acknowledged that this need for increased financial resources for ICT development can only be met with more engaged international cooperation (Weber & Menoud, 2008).

ICTs allow civil society to more actively participate in discourses by exchanging information. This not only strengthens the classical freedom of expression and freedom of information, but also other fundamental rights such as democratic participation.

Realization of an Enforceable Right to Development

On the basis of general human rights' understanding, a right to development must be acknowledged. Article 2 paragraph 1 of the ICESCR sets out the following legal obligation:

Each state party to the present Covenant undertakes to take steps, individually and through international assistance and co-operation, especially economic and technical, to the maximum of its available resources, with a view to achieving progressively the full realization of the rights recognized in the present Covenant by all appropriate means, including particularly the adoption of legislative measures.

Notwithstanding questions as to whether this provision can impose obligations on states that are immediately justiciable, the general meaning is well accepted and the provision is undoubtedly directly applicable.

For the last 50 years or so there has been a growing body of thought from developing countries in favour of the establishment of a legal right to development. These attempts culminated in the UN Declaration on the Right to Development (RTD) of 1986 (Resolution 4/128) which states in Article 1 that the right to development is a human right. Despite being in place for more than 20 years, the Declaration, not being a legally binding instrument, is suffering from a lack of implementation and the political will required for international co-operation. In particular in the field of information and communication technologies, the right to development merits more support from developed countries, based on a human and cultural-centred approach.

The realization of a right to development needs financing. But finding the financial means that would provide sufficient resources to achieve global access and to realise a fair and equitable information and communication order appears to be a daunting task. Leveraging and mobilizing the necessary instruments requires a focussed and strong international consensus that is not always present (Weber/Menoud, 2008). However, there are many financial mechanisms in place, which could, with few amendments and improvements, make a substantial flow of funds available to invest in ICT projects. No instrument alone is able to contribute sufficient resources; however, several mechanisms combined could together supply the necessary funding and address developing countries' needs with respect to ICT infrastructure and services development. If such financing instruments were in place, the chances of the present digital divide being overcome would increase, as would the possibility for global civil society to take advantage of an adequate information and communication order.

The right to development plays an important role in respect of mobile financial services; their development depends on the economic circumstances as well as on the suitability of the legal framework regulating the services' application. The user-friendliness of the offered services is certainly a key aspect of the success of mobile financial services[1].

CONCLUSION

ICT developments have the potential to extend the enjoyment of human rights to a larger part of society. Not only do they make the exchange of information easier, but they also help to make the democratic participation of all possible. However the provision of the respective (mobile) infrastructure is a prerequisite for the realization of many human rights. ICT policies should do more than encompass the notion of fundamental rights in theory; state undertakings need to be designed in ways that directly or indirectly support the establishment of this necessary infrastructure.

Digital communications environments are not apolitical spaces. The same power relationship and inequalities that pervade in the offline world also affect people's use of ICT and their experiences online. ICT can be used as tools to help empower minorities and groups that are discriminated against in specific ways. For this reason, the international community should draw on lessons learnt over the past decade to build innovative programmes that have significant and sustainable impact (EU Parliament, 2010). In particular, states should have a clear understanding of their responsibility to put measures in place that will spur the realisation of economic and social rights to the maximum of their availability resources. Since the impact that ICT have on social, economic and cultural dynamic is highly context specific, regulatory frameworks and market competiveness have a substantial influence. And finally since it is impossible to predict what creative solutions society will come up with when they have the capacity and tools with which to innovate, building the capacity of poor communities to empower its members through ICTs is a key objective.

The potential for ICTs to deliver development is obviously hampered by the persistent digital divide. Therefore, economic inequalities must be overcome in order to allow the individuals to effectively take advantage of the opportunities of ICT.

REFERENCES

Article 29 Data Protection Working Party. (2009, December 1). *The future of privacy: Joint contribution to the consultation of the European Commission on the legal framework for the fundamental right to protection of personal data*. Retrieved from http://ec.europa.eu/justice/policies/privacy/news/docs/pr_01_12_09_en.pdf

Banisar, D. (2006). The right to information in the age of information. In Jørgensen, R. F. (Ed.), *Human rights in the global information society* (pp. 73–89). Cambridge, MA: The MIT Press.

Carlsson, U. (2003). *The rise and fall of NWICO – And then? From a vision of international regulation to a reality of multilevel governance*. Paper presented at the EURICOM Colloquium, Information Society: Visions and Governance, 5-7 May 2003, Venice, Italy. Retrieved from http://www.bfsf.it/wsis/cosa%20dietro%20al%20nuovo %20ordine.pdf

Cheung, A., & Weber, R. H. (2008). Internet governance and the responsibility of ISPs. *Wisconsin International Law Journal*, *26*, 403–477.

Deibert, R. J., Palfrey, J. G., Rohozinski, R., & Zittrain, J. (Eds.). (2008). *Access denied: The practice and policy of global internet filtering*. Cambridge, MA: The MIT Press.

Dutton, W. H., Dopatka, A., Hills, M., Law, G., & Nash, V. (2010). *Freedom of connection – Freedom of expression: The changing legal and regulatory ecology shaping the Internet*. Report prepared for UNESCO's Division for Freedom of Expression, Democracy and Peace.

European Parliament. (2010). *Information and Communications Technologies and Human Rights. Directorate-General for External Policies of the Union. (EXPO/B/DROI/2009/24, PE 410.207, June 2010)*. Brussels, Belgium: European Parliament.

Gatto, A. (2011). *Multinational enterprises and human rights: Obligations under EU law and international law*. Cheltenham, UK: Edward Elgar Publishing Limited.

Geneva Declaration of Principles. (2003, December 12). *WSIS-03/GENEVA/DOC/4-E*. Retrieved from http://www.itu.int/wsis/docs/geneva/official/dop.html

Geneva Plan of Action. (2003, December 12). *WSIS-03/GENEVA/DOC/5-E*. Retrieved from http://www.itu.int/wsis/docs/geneva/official/poa.html

Hedebro, G. (1982). *Communication and social change in developing nations – A critical view*. Iowa State University Press.

Human Rights Committee. (2010). *Draft general comment No. 34* (Upon completion of the first reading by the Human Rights Community). (CCPR/C/GC/34/CRP.5). Retrieved from http://www.aidh.org/ONU_GE/Comite_DH/Images/Projet.pdf

Human Rights Council. (2009, March 20). *Promotion and protection of all human rights, civil, political, economic, social and cultural rights, including the right to development*. Retrieved from http://www.un.org/disabilities/ default.asp?id=1477

International Telecommunications Union (ITU). (2010). *Measuring the information society*. Retrieved from http://www.itu.int/ITU-D/ict/publications/idi/2010/Material/MIS_2010_without%20annex%204-e.pdf

Jørgensen, R. F. (2006). The right to express oneself and to seek information. In Jørgensen, R. F. (Ed.), *Human rights in the global information society* (pp. 53–72). Cambridge, MA: The MIT Press.

Klein, H. (2006). The right to participation and the information society. In Jørgensen, R. F. (Ed.), *Human rights in the global information society* (pp. 185–196). Cambridge, MA: The MIT Press.

Mansell, R., & Nordenstreng, K. (2006). Great media and communication debates: WSIS and the MacBride report. *Information Technologies and International Development*, *3*(4), 15–36. doi:10.1162/itid.2007.3.4.15

Murphy, T., & Cuinn, Ó, G. (2010). Works in progress: New technologies and the European Court of Human Rights. *Human Rights Law Review*, *10*, 601–638. doi:10.1093/hrlr/ngq038

Padovani, C., & Nordenstreng, K. (2005, December). From NWICO to WSIS: Another world information and communication order? *Global Media and Communication*, *1*(3), 264–272. Retrieved from http//www.ufa.fi/jour/laitos/From_NWICO_to_WSIS.pdf doi:10.1177/1742766505058123

Spence, R., & Smith, M. (2009). *Information and communication technologies, human development, growth and poverty reduction: A background paper*. Retrieved from http://www.idrc.ca/uploads/user-S/12412058391HF2_Background_Paper_28-04-09.pdf

Sussman, L. R. (1989, October). What the North wants from UNESCO: Mediator and catalyst. *Sources*, *8*, 13.

Tunis Agenda for the Information Society. (2005, November 18). *WSIS-05/TUNIS/DOC/6*(Rev. 1)-E. Retrieved from http://www.itu.int/wsis/docs2/tunis/off/6rev1.html

Tunis Commitment. (2005, November 18). *WSIS-05/TUNIS/DOC/7-E*. Retrieved from http://www.itu.int/wsis/docs2/tunis/off/7.html

United Nations Economic and Social Council. (2009, December 21). *Committee on Economic, Social and Cultural Rights, Forty-third Session, General comment No. 21* (E/C.12/GC/21).

United Nations Educational, Scientific and Cultural Organization. (1980). *Many voices one world*. Report of the MacBride Commission. Paris, France: Author. Retrieved from http://unesdoc.unesco.org/images/0004/000400/040066eb.pdf

Weber, R. H. (2004). From "many voices one world" to "information society". *Computer und Recht International*, 97-104.

Weber, R. H. (2010a). *Regulatory framework for mobile financial services*. In National Forum on Mobile Applications for Inclusive Growth and Sustainable Development. Delhi. Retrieved from http://www.mgovworld.org/libra/mbanking/papers

Weber, R. H. (2010b). Digital trade in WTO-law – Taking stock and looking ahead. *Asian Journal of WTO & International Health Law and Policy*, *5*, 1–25.

Weber, R. H., & Grosz, M. (2009). Governments' interventions into the real economy under WTO law revisited: New tendencies of governmental support of the automobile industry. *Journal of World Trade*, *43*, 969–1013.

Weber, R. H., & Menoud, V. (2008). *The information society and the digital divide – Legal strategies to finance global access*. Zurich, Switzerland: Schulthess.

ENDNOTE

1 Mobile financial services encompass two main types of business activities, namely mobile payment and mobile banking (Weber, 2010a).

Services providers engaged in the mobile payment business fulfil an intermediary function between buyers and sellers (often in e-commerce or m-commerce transactions), by facilitating the purchase of goods or services with the help of mobile devices. In the developing world, mobile-money schemes have emerged, which offer their services in various fields and for multi-faceted purposes. For example, Safaricom – Kenya's largest mobile operator – launched the money transfer service 'M-PESA' in 2007; apart from its primary use to transfer money, the service allows customers to execute daily payments for everything from school fees to taxi rides; more recent applications also concern health insurance premiums and similar kinds of payments. M-PESA's concept enjoys great popularity in Kenya: In 2009, it had already seven billion subscribers out of a 38 million population.

Mobile banking includes the whole range of services in which a banking activity is involved, including mobile accounting, mobile brokerage, and the complementary service of mobile financial information. Mobile banking is gaining momentum in the developing world. For example, MTN – a South-Africa-based telecommunications company – launched a mobile accounting service in Uganda in March 2009 that allows the execution of transactions through text messages and the storage of money on mobile devices. Mobile brokerage, in contrast, refers to intermediary services in both capital markets and markets for goods and services. For example, the Danish Saxo Bank provides through the 'SaxoMobileTrader' a flexible trading platform, enabling customers to trade in various financial markets. 'Google Trader' is a marketplace application which allows customers to buy and sell goods and services through their mobile phones via text messages. Further examples of mobile brokerage providers are 'TradeNet' in Ghana and 'CellBazaar' in Bangladesh. Lastly, mobile financial information, as a complementary service, helps customers to execute mobile financial transactions more smoothly. For example, 'First Direct', with headquarters in the United Kingdom but branches around the world, sends mini-statements as text messages alerting customers to keep their accounts up-to-date (Weber 2010a).

Chapter 3
Negotiating Boundaries between Control and Dissent:
Free Speech, Business, and Repressitarian Governments

Brian J. Bowe
Grand Valley State University, USA

Robin Blom
Michigan State University, USA

Eric Freedman
Michigan State University, USA

ABSTRACT

Increases in access to information and communication technologies (ICTs) have given citizens new tools to organize politically. This development has particular importance for those living under authoritarian regimes that rely on the repression of free speech to maintain power. These repressitarian elites resort to a variety of means to establish (or re-establish) control over citizen online communications. However, it is counterproductive for countries to crack down too tightly on Internet expression, because such actions can create negative economic consequences for countries hoping to engage in the 21st century's wired economy. The friction between online free expression and government repression is playing out with close interest of Western governments, human rights advocates, and citizens because it places many technology companies in the difficult position of either facilitating such government repression or finding themselves unable to compete in those markets. This chapter examines recent developments in Iran, Egypt, China, and Singapore. All four countries have been identified as having severe impediments to free expression. Iran and Egypt, however, have seen the rise of some organized opposition movements despite the controls on media expression, while China and Singapore offer useful case studies on the economic dimensions of the balance between participating in the global networked society and controlling citizen expression. This chapter considers how financial and economic factors lead to more moderate views of Internet use in those countries and examine the struggles between maintaining openness and crackdowns.

DOI: 10.4018/978-1-4666-1918-0.ch003

INTRODUCTION

Increased public access to the means of media production has opened new questions related to freedom of the press and expression in countries such as Iran and China, whose governments could be classified as repressitarian. They are both repressive in terms of human rights practices and authoritarian in terms of governance (Freedman, Shafer & Antonova, 2010). Information and communication technology (ICT) provides oppositional groups new opportunities to spread information in countries where free speech is normally curtailed, although those regimes continuously undertake exhaustive efforts to block or remove such critical messages from the World Wide Web.

Those crackdowns reveal the harsh consequences of online dissent. In the past few years, among the targets of criminal action in Iran were bloggers Hossein Derakhshan—nicknamed Iran's *blogfather*—sentenced to 19½ years, and Hossein Maleki Ronaghi, sentenced to 15 years. Web designer Saeed Malekpour received a death sentence for purportedly designing and moderating adult sites, "agitation against the regime," and "insulting the sanctity of Islam." Blogger Omid Reza Mirsayafi, serving a sentence for propaganda against the state and criticism of Iran's supreme leader, died in Evin Prison, although the cause of death is disputed. Some sentences include flogging, such as those of bloggers Omid Memarian, Roozbeh Mirebrahimi, Shahram Rafizadeh, and Javad Gholamtamimi, who were sentenced in 2009 to up to three years in prison (U.S. State Department, 2011).

The situation elsewhere reflects many similar obstacles for users of the Internet and social media across the globe. These examples from 2010 are illustrative, as drawn from international media reports and human rights advocacy groups: The Ukrainian Security Service questioned a blogger for purportedly insulting and threatening the country's president and removed some of his Live Journal posts. The administrator of "Troktiko," Greece's most popular social and political blog, was fatally shot in front of his home. Turkmenistan authorities hacked the website of a Europe-based Turkmen-language human rights organization. Acting under court order, Turkey banned YouTube for three years. Kuwait sentenced a blogger to one year for criminal defamation based on an article criticizing the prime minister. After finishing a 30-month term on trumped-up tax evasion charges, a Vietnamese blogger remained in custody pending investigation of a new charge of carrying out propaganda against the government. And the Palestinian Authority detained a man for supposedly criticizing Islam and other religions on Facebook and in blogs.

In contrast to such human rights violations stands immense progress in regards to free speech through computer-mediated communication. Consistent with Prensky's (2001) digital natives concept, the generations of users who have grown up in the Internet age seem to be increasingly skilled at finding ways to circumvent government controls. Young, tech-savvy protestors throughout the world avoid censorship by creating proxy websites and servers to access illegal information (Iran Proxy, 2007; Samin, 2008). Additionally, youthful protestors try to outwit detectors in censoring software by replacing "forbidden" words with symbols and characters (Shuguang, 2008).

Social media users in countries such as Iran and Egypt have used such tools to organize mass protests outside of government scrutiny, while in China and Singapore they have been able to bypass the official gatekeepers at news media organizations handcuffed by government control. Groundbreaking news reports ignored by the mainstream press outlets have made their way to the public through the Internet in Indonesia, Myanmar, and Moldova, among many other nations under authoritarian rule. For instance, in Kyrgyzstan, an advocacy blog provided a temporary alternative to official information and a shuttered independent newspaper in the run-up to the 2005 "Tulip

Revolution" that ousted an authoritarian president (Kulikova & Perlmutter, 2011). A few years later, even Myanmar's military government was unable to stop information about the violent crackdown of Buddhist monk protests from leaking out at the hands of bloggers (Deibert et al., 2010).

Sometimes, however, even the most overt government repression is unable to restrain social movements from organizing to bring about social change. In early 2011, the Egyptian government of Hosni Mubarak attempted to shut down the Internet within that country as a way of quelling a popular uprising. However, social media were still considered powerful weapons in the arsenal that helped bring about the eventual toppling of the Mubarak regime. (Ishani, 2011; Khakis & Vaughn, 2011).

OVERALL OBJECTIVES OF THE CHAPTER

The techniques deployed by regimes to maintain supremacy over Internet expression include governmental controls, legal controls, and technological controls. Those techniques range from subtle and cunning to overt and blunt. Nonetheless, it is counterproductive for countries to completely shut down all Internet connections because cracking down too tightly on Internet expressions can create negative economic consequences for countries hoping to engage in the 21st century's wired economy. For that reason, some countries with poor human rights records have adopted cautiously moderate views of the Internet, even when this leads to opportunities for protestors to influence the direction of public deliberations (Handy, 2009). The friction between online free expression and government repression is playing out with close interest of Western governments, human rights advocates, and citizens. Abdel Dayem (2009) contends that the blogosphere is the frontier where the limits of free expression are tested, writing that governments are "involved in a constantly evolving engagement with bloggers to define the boundaries of what can be said" (p. 44).

This is the political and economic climate in which many nations and Western technology conglomerates operate—straddling the border between free information dissemination and censorship. Consequently, the increase in access to ICT raises economic and ethical questions. In this chapter, we will consider recent events in Iran, Egypt, Singapore, and China to discuss how Western information and social network corporations facilitate dissent. All four of those countries have been identified as having severe impediments to free expression (see Table 1). Iran and Egypt, however, have seen the rise of some organized opposition movements despite the controls on media expression. In the former, the regime was successful in quelling protests following a contested 2009 election; in the latter, a largely peaceful movement was successful in bringing about change in 2011.

We will consider how financial and economic factors lead to more moderate views of Internet use in those countries and examine the struggles between maintaining openness and crackdowns. China and Singapore offer useful case studies on the economic dimensions of the balance between participating in the global networked society and controlling citizen expression.

The software that dissidents use is often produced by companies based in Western countries without excessive government repression. Programs, such as Instant Messenger (AOL), MSN Live (Microsoft), Talk (Google), and Skype are unambiguously intended for people to communicate with each other privately. And blogging software has been developed for people to express their opinions and share stories about their personal lives without explicit intrusion by others. Yet some of those manufacturers (e.g., Yahoo!) have sometimes adjusted their products to be allowed to enter the financial markets of repressitarian countries. Those modifications have enabled such governments to censor, spy on, track down, and prosecute dissidents (Dann & Haddow, 2008).

In the last section of this chapter we examine the ethical implications of software development that facilitates oppression and discuss the risks to the communities at the receiving end of these business deals. For instance, to win access to the Chinese market, Skype allowed administrators to secretly store chat conversations when certain words forbidden by the government were used (Charny, 2006). In another example, a teenage blogger was not allowed to use words such as *human rights* and *democracy* in her blog title on the Chinese-language version of MSN Spaces. The program automatically responded that titles were not to contain prohibited language, such as profanity. Yet in other versions of MSN Spaces outside China, such an error message would not pop up (MacKinnon, 2005).

DIGITAL ARMS RACE

Deibert et al. (2010) maintained that control over the Internet is not limited to a few countries with spotty human rights records. Many nations have recently made attempts to regulate certain kinds of content, among them Germany, France, Japan, South Korea, and other economic superpowers. Internet censorship is seemingly becoming a troubling global norm. Telecom companies in almost every country are ordered to store some personal information about senders and recipients of messages online. Many Western countries are trying to combat large-scale copyright infringement and anti-Semitic or Holocaust-denying publications online. In other occasions, legislatures attempt to prevent online gambling and close websites with sexually explicit content.

Despite these "good" intentions, the same governments also operate security programs that are increasingly obtrusive and nontransparent. European countries collect Internet Service Providers (ISP) data and monitor e-mail traffic, not necessarily with a warrant. Especially after the 11 September 2001 terrorist attacks in New York City and Washington, sophisticated Internet surveillance programs have been assembled without complete legislative and judicial oversight, including strict security measures by the United States. For instance, Australia has one of the most restrictive Internet policies among Western countries. This most notably includes filtering of websites hosted abroad and whose content the government deems offensive. When an URL is prohibited, officials notify certified web-filter firms to adjust their products. For example, a few pages from the WikiLeaks website about Internet safety measures were banned in 2009. Two years earlier, several states banned YouTube over school networks because of violent content involving Australian teenagers (Colley, 2007).

Countries that seek to control the Internet with ill intent to oppose free speech can do so by citing examples from countries that are usually considered favorable to this essential human right. Often disguised as measures against terrorism, child pornography, and cyber security, repressive regimes easily gain control over the web. "States no longer fear pariah status by openly declaring their intent to regulate and control cyberspace" (Deibert et al., 2010, p. 4). In fact, some scholars caution that an increasingly wired populace is actually a boon for dictators, offering opportunities to conduct surveillance more efficiently than secret police agencies (Mozorov, 2011).

It is plausible that countries will increasingly invest in Internet security, especially after a nuclear power plant in Iran was attacked with a highly sophisticated computer worm called Stuxnet. There are indications that the malware was hidden for months in the plant's computer system and destroyed about one-tenth of all centrifuges. The complexity of the attack displays the potential for cyber attacks between nations, but also on specific individuals or companies (Barns, 2010; Nasseri, 2010; Clayton, 2011).

Table 1. Press freedom

	China	Egypt	Iran	Singapore
Media Sustainability Index^*				
Unsustainable Anti-Free Press	N/A	—	1 of 5 criteria	N/A
Unsustainable Mixed System	N/A	1 of 5 criteria	4 of 5 criteria	N/A
Near Sustainability	N/A	4 of 5 criteria	—	N/A
Press Freedom Index**				
Ranking (Out of 178 Countries)	171	127	175	136
Internet Enemy Classification	Internet enemy	Internet enemy	Internet enemy	—
Freedom of the Press***				
Status of Press Freedom	Not free	Partly free	Not free	Not free

^ Criteria: 1) Free Speech; 2) Professional Journalism; 3) Plurality of News Sources; 4) Business Management; 5) Supporting Institutions

* International Research & Exchanges Board, *Media Sustainability Index 2008*

** Reporters Without Borders, *Press Freedom Index 2010*

*** Freedom House, *Freedom of the Press Report 2010*

N/A = Not available

Nations have been able to monitor computer networks domestically and abroad for years through botnets. As available technology becomes more sophisticated, it will be important for governments to defend themselves and their citizens online (Shiels, 2011). Deibert et al. (2010), therefore, expect "an arms race in cyberspace" (p. 8). Regardless of the measures taken, it can be foreseen that such actions, at least to a certain extent, will curb free speech, infringe on press freedom, and intrude on personal privacy protections.

MEANS OF CONTROL

The power of the Internet is globally understood, especially by those despots who fear it as a revolutionary tool. Even though the regime of Myanmar notoriously limits access to the web to a few government, military, and business leaders while hindering access for ordinary citizens, its own website distributes propaganda worldwide to counterattack claims by citizens in exile. Myanmar is not the only country with such a policy; several also block access to most web pages except, perhaps, those published by the regime (e.g., North Korea and Turkmenistan).

Other countries do not create complete blackouts but try to maintain control of online discourse by different means (e.g., China, Egypt, Saudi Arabia, Tunisia, Uzbekistan, and Vietnam). The interference level varies by country and type of content, with most attention directed to political and religious speech (Hachigian and Wu, 2003; Morillon and Julliard, 2010).

Governments take a variety of actions to circumvent access to specific content from within their territory, such as (1) blocking servers, domains, keywords, and IP addresses; (2) compelling Internet sites to register with authorities or establishing a licensing system; (3) setting strict criteria for what content is considered acceptable and unacceptable; (4) expanding libel laws to deter and punish posting of critical material; and (5) surveillance of individual Internet accounts. This includes formal and informal information government directives to remove information, technical shutdowns, and policing of cybercafés.

One of the most effective ways to hinder online communication has been distributed denial of service (DDos) attacks, which are concerted efforts to prevent Internet sites from functioning temporarily or indefinitely. This is possible when someone purposely sends an exorbitant number of communications requests to a page host to consume all the resources, leaving it unable to respond to legitimate requests to access the website. The attacks are an effective tool to block communication to and from certain websites for short periods of time. For example, this has happened during the 2005 elections in Kyrgyzstan (OpenNet Initiative, 2005) and when the Russian and Georgian armies squared off in a conflict about the disputed territory of Ossetia (Swaine, 2008).

Nations differ as to the extent to which these censorship tactics are overt and legally established, such as the severity of slander and defamation laws that impose moderate-to-extreme penalties for dissenters critical of those in power. Bloggers also have been arrested on charges of overthrowing the constitution, which is possible when laws are overly broad, ambiguous, and interpreted in ways that allow authorities to intervene on their own terms whenever it suits them. Moreover, many of these actions are conducted in secrecy without judicial review (Deibert and Rohozinski, 2010a).

OVERALL MEDIA ENVIRONMENTS

A government's attitude toward the web and social media generally reflects its attitude toward the press at large. Thus a constrained environment for traditional print and broadcast outlets is usually mirrored in the country's environment for new media, demonstrated by the realities in Egypt, Iran, China, and Singapore. Despite constitutional and statutory assurances about freedom of speech and the press, all four countries rate poorly in their respect for press rights (see Table 1). The U.S. NGO Freedom House classified the Mubarak-era press system in Egypt as "partly free" and that of Iran, Singapore, and China as "not free." Other media rights organizations, including Reporters sans Frontieres (RSF), also classify them as hostile to press freedom. This section provides an overview of the media setting in each country and examples of how these governments apply their media policies. Information is drawn from reports by national and multinational agencies, human rights and press rights advocacy groups, and media accounts.

Even though these nations are similar in terms of their hostility toward press freedom, they differ in other regards (see Table 2). For example, Singapore has a much higher GDP per capita than the other three; likewise, on the Freedom House index, Egypt is classified as "partly free," while the other three are "not free." It is valuable to consider such distinctions, dispelling a possible misperception that only poorest or the most authoritarian countries impose such controls.

The following country-by-country overviews are drawn from international press reports and accounts by foreign governments, multinational agencies, and human rights and press rights monitoring and advocacy NGOs.[1]

Iran

In Iran, the constitution's free-expression provision exempts speech considered "detrimental to the fundamental principles of Islam or the rights of the public." Freedom of the press is highly constrained, with independent media outlets subject to arbitrarily enforced censorship. Journalists face imprisonment and work under self-censorship; the Press Supervisory Board revokes press licenses; the government monopolizes broadcasting facilities through its Voice and Vision Organization; and foreign correspondents are closely monitored. Criminal complaints by public officials against reformist newspapers have gone to the media court for hearings in front of a jury of appointed clerics, with the possibility of fines and closure.

Table 2. Exploratory matrix of variables for predicting press freedom

	China	Egypt	Iran	Singapore
Government Type	Communist State	Republic	Theocratic Republic	Parliamentary Republic
Population	1,330,141,295	80,471,869	76,923,300	4,701,069
Median Age	35.2	24	26.3	39.6
GDP Per Capita	$6,600	$6,000	$12,500	$52,200
Official Language(s)	Chinese	Arabic	None	Mandarin, English, Malay, Tamil
Literacy Rate	91.6%	71.4%	77.0%	92.5%
Percentage of Education Expenditures (of GDP)	1.9%	3.8%	4.8%	3.2%
Annual Net Migration Rate per 1,000	-0.34	-0.21	-0.04	4.79
Percentage of Urban Population	43.0%	43.0%	68.0%	100.0%
Plurality Religion	Daoist (Taoist)	Muslim	Muslim	Buddhist
Percentage of Plurality Religion (of Population)	N/A	99.6%	98.0%	42.5%
Internet Penetration Rate*	31.6%	21.2%	43.2%	77.8%

Primary source: U.S. Central Intelligence Agency, *The World Factbook* (2010)

* Internet World Stats (2010)

N/A = Not available

Representative incidents include the shutdown of two business newspapers for reporting about student protests; closure of the daily *Kargozaran* for downplaying Israeli military actions in Gaza; and banning the reformist newspaper *Etemad Melli* after publishing an article critical of Iran's detention centers. The Ministry of Culture and Islamic Guidance has prohibited stories about a cleric critical of the regime in a country where the government arrests, imprisons, fines, or tortures traditional and Internet journalists because of their reporting. An Iranian-Canadian reporter for Newsweek was kept in solitary confinement and compelled to confess on television that Western journalists were spies. Iran held 43 journalists in detention at the end of 2009.

Similarly, bloggers, cyber-dissidents, and ordinary Internet users face tightened controls over the web. The government monitors social networking sites such as Twitter, Facebook, and YouTube and threatens and arrests users whose posts criticize the regime. Some citizens returning on international flights have been ordered to log into their Facebook and YouTube accounts and required to delete information.

The Ministry of Culture and Islamic Guidance, which approves all ISPs, has used filtering software to block domestic blogs and Western news media and NGO websites and to delete material. In some instances, ISPs redirected users from opposition to pro-government news sites. In the run-up to the 2009 presidential election, for example, Facebook, YouTube, Twitter, and other social networking sites were blocked. In addition, Iran has limited Internet speed to impede downloads and reduce access to blocked sites.

RSF called Iran "one of cyber-censorship's record-holding countries," noting that new media are demonized as "serving foreign interests" and noting that users contend with content filtering, intimidation, detention, and even torture (Morillon & Julliard, 2010, p. 18). The government claimed to have censored five million sites in 2008 — a number that increased 49% in 2009 (Farokhina, 2010). Blogs the government considers immoral are filtered, as are opposition blogs and blogs about women's rights and journalism, among others (Esfandiari, 2010c).

Technological controls include both filtering and closure of sites. In the first situation, users are greeted with a screen with a message that the site has been blocked; in the second situation, users are greeted with nothing at all. The closure of a site is considered a more strict punishment (Farokhnia 2010).

Yet against that backdrop, there remains a vibrant blogging scene in Iran. Kelly and Etling (2008), researchers for the Berkman Center for Internet and Society at Harvard University, estimated that in early 2008 there were about 60,000 routinely updated blogs. Abdel Dayem (2009) attributed the popularity of blogging in Iran to a highly literate and very young population. The prevalence of blogging in Iran offers those users tools for identity formation that might not be available in unmediated space; as Kia (2008) noted, young Iranians "gravitate towards the Internet to avoid cultural and political obstacles in their lives and expectations to follow social norms" in ways that influence lifestyle choices. (p. 29).

Egypt

Prior to the 2011 uprising that brought down the 30-year reign of President Mubarak, arrests, censorship, harassment, and detentions illustrated the Egyptian government's partial constriction of press rights, as did its use of criminal, mass media, and emergency laws. For example, an *Al Fagr* journalist who reported about coercion and other police abuses was convicted and fined for insulting a police officer, while four independent newspaper editors were fined for articles "insulting" senior officials of the ruling party. Other limitations affect licensing and license revocations for media outlets, government ownership of domestic broadcast stations, blockage of foreign broadcasts, and libel suits by private individuals. The government seized publications by Islamists. Its satellite transmission company halted broadcasts of the privately owned London-based channel Al-Hiwar, which aired talk shows with government critics as guests. The Supreme Press Council revoked a weekly newspaper's license in retaliation for a story about a police investigation of a gay prostitution ring. Despite such events, the U.S. State Department (2010a) wrote, "Citizens and journalists openly expressed their views on a wide range of political and social issues, including vigorous criticism of senior government officials and policies and direct criticism of the president in the independent press, on satellite television, and on blogs."

In Egypt, like Iran, computer users have turned to social media services to circumvent government controls on expression (Ishani, 2011). Although website blocking remains limited, authorities are striving to regain control over bloggers who are more and more organized, despite harassment and arrests.

Blogging is widespread in Egypt, predominantly in Arabic, where an estimated 20 percent of blogs deal with politics, 15 percent with culture and arts, 7 percent with religion, 6 percent with personal matters, 4 percent with technology and science, and 2 percent with social issues. The government has ordered Internet cafes to collect names, e-mail addresses, and telephone numbers of their customers. Bloggers and web activists have been arrested and detained. Among them were Tamer Mabrouk, fined for libeling a chemical company by accusing it of polluting a lake; Dia Eddin Gad, placed in solitary confinement for insulting the president for being a "Zionist, an agent for Israel, and a loser;" and Hany Nazir, arrested for blogging about religious issues.

Kareem Amer, the first Egyptian blogger to be convicted based on his writings, finished a four-year sentence in November 2010 for "inciting strife and defaming Muslims on the Internet" and for defaming the president, whom he described as "a symbol of tyranny;" Amer claimed that security officers beat and abused him in custody. The first blogger to face a military tribunal for a blog posting, Ahmed Mostafa, was released in March 2010; he was charged with publishing military secrets for a post alleging nepotism in the military. Another blogger, Bedouin rights activist Musaad Abu Fagr, was detained without trial for nearly three years before his release in July 2010.

RSF called the Internet in Egypt "a mobilization and dissension platform," adding that: "Although website blocking remains limited, authorities are striving to regain control over bloggers who are more and more organized, despite all the harassment and arrests" (Morillon & Julliard, 2010, p. 15). Egyptian protesters were able to use Facebook to launch forbidden protests critical of the ruling regime on 6 April 2008. Government forces responded with arrests and other crackdowns.

According to the *New York Times*, Facebook is the third most-visited website in Egypt. Shapiro (2009) noted that Facebook "allows users to speak freely to one another and encourages them to form groups," which makes it "irresistible as a platform not only for social interaction but also for dissent." Yet those protests were not without danger; the organizers were arrested, as were other Egyptian bloggers. "Although later released, their detention is yet another example of the authorities' usual heavy-handed response to unknown manifestations of evolving new media platforms" (Hamdy, 2009, p. 99).

The groundwork laid by the 6 April Movement blossomed into a popular uprising in 2011. As the protests began to gain momentum near the end of January, the Mubarak government shut down most Internet access for a week. The shutdown was believed to be the first attempt by a government to engage in such a wide-ranging blockage of Internet access, effectively shutting down business and public institutions across the country (with the exception of the stock exchange) (Cowie, 2011; Gillmor, 2011; Johnson, 2011). Activsts swiftly established clandestine FTP servers to share large files with Internet users outside the country (Ishani, 2011).

However, even though the protestors successfully brought about the end of Mubarak's rule, they were unable to ensure full freedom of expression for online activists. In April 2011, blogger Maikel Nabil Sanad received a three-year prison sentence for insulting the military, whose officials replaced Mubarak in an interim government (CPJ 2011).

Singapore

The constitutional guarantee of free expression is subject to official restrictions in Singapore, as well as self-censorship, governmental pressure, and defamation lawsuits against media outlets. The government has authority to restrict publications that incite violence, endanger national security, or arouse racial and ethnic tensions. Singapore Press Holdings Limited (SPH) and MediaCorp hold a monopoly on all general-circulation newspapers in English, Chinese, Malay, and Tamil, the four official languages; a government investment company owns MediaCorp, while SPH is a private holding company closely tied to the government. Only one radio station is fully independent; the rest are controlled by government-connected companies and organizations, as are all television channels.

Evidence of constraints include censorship by the Media Development Authority of broadcast media and websites, a ban on some political and religious publications, and authority to restrict foreign broadcasts and limit the circulation of foreign publications. The editor and publisher of the *Far Eastern Economic Review* paid $282,000 to settle a defamation suit filed by the prime minister and another official stemming from a published interview with an opposition politician. A senior editor of the *Wall Street Journal Asia* and the newspaper were fined for contempt of court for publishing three items, including a letter to the editor doubting the independence of courts from the government. Also, a British author was sentenced to jail and fined for contempt of court based on his book alleging judicial misconduct in death penalty cases.

As the U.S. State Department (2010b) reported of Singapore, "Although residents generally had unrestricted access to the Internet, the government subjected all Internet content to the same rules and standards as traditional news media." The Media Development Authority licenses and regulates ISPs and registers religious and political websites, while the government monitors blogs and podcasts and blocks some websites as pornographic. Even so, the U.S. State Department (2010b) did acknowledge a "moderate level of debate in newspapers and on the Internet on some public issues such as income inequality, immigration policy, and the role of religion in public life." It also said that "columnists' opinions and letters to the editor" in newspapers owned by Singapore Press Holdings and MediaCorp "expressed a moderate range of opinions on public issues."

The government of Singapore learned the lesson that restrictive media policies can hurt a nation financially. In the early 1990s, financial institutions were not fully informed about failing negotiations between the United States and Iraq because of a ban on satellite dishes. While international competitors reacted accordingly to CNN's news coverage about a looming war, businesses in Singapore were slow to respond. This lag damaged the country's economy (George, 2003, 2009).

Eventually this led to more moderate media policies, not only for satellite dishes, but also for the Internet. Singapore was the first country to regulate the web to create a balance between regulating speech and access to information. This allowed the ruling People's Action Party to maintain its dominance—a battery of proxy servers were used as a first line of defense—but still opened the door for citizens to discuss human rights openly without obtrusive gatekeepers at government-controlled news media. Even so, government censors and law enforcement still looked over their virtual shoulders (Lai, 2004; Lee, 2004).

Other countries comparable to Singapore in size and economic prospects, such as Bahrain, Kuwait, Malaysia, and Qatar, have adopted similar stances towards the Internet. Regulations were intended to stimulate economic prosperity, especially because they wish to position themselves in the global economy as frontrunners of information technology development, but still allow thorough safeguards to protect the power positions of the elite. In fact, because of its economic strategy, Singapore encouraged wide Internet penetration among its citizens for educational purposes.

China

The government does not generally respect laws that nominally provide for press freedom. Rather, it interprets the Communist Party's constitutional role as trumping such rights and uses its control of electronic, broadcast, and print media and its power to censor and manipulate the press to advance party ideology mandated in the constitution. Other constraints include disseminating lists of politically sensitive issues such as corruption, industrial accidents, and environmental problems that domestic news media cannot cover and denying travel permits for foreign journalists to report from Tibet and the largely Muslim Xinjiang Uighur Autonomous Region in Western China. Self-censorship is widespread. Foreign journalists have been detained, attacked, intimidated, had photographs seized and prohibited from filming in Tiananmen Square, the site of 1989 pro-democracy protests.

"In the hands of a regime obsessed with maintaining stability – censorship has developed into a tool

for political control," reported RSF (Morillon & Julliard, 2010, p. 8).

Representative incidents include assaults on reporters from the *Beijing Times* and *Nangfang People's Weekly* while researching a corruption-related story and the jamming of broadcasts from the British Broadcasting Corporation, Radio France International, Deutsche Welle, and Voice of America. Thirty-four journalists were imprisoned at the end of 2009, including an employee of a state-run radio station in Xinjiang for advocating "splittism" stemming from articles critical of the government she posted on foreign websites.

In terms of Internet controls, the seven Internet Access Providers in China are under state control, making it a monopoly for the state (Li, 2010). Initially, as Endeshaw (2004) noted, the expectation was that it would be simple to keep dissent off the Chinese web, but "[g]radually, the usual Chinese pragmatism prevailed and institutional and legal means of taming the Internet started to take over" (p. 41). As a result, controls are much tighter in China than in Singapore. For example, the government blocks distribution of podcasts and streaming radio news from foreign broadcasters, and it has thousands of employees who monitor electronic communications. Officials have reportedly shut thousands of illegal websites, blocked blogs of political activists and academics, and deleted millions of items of information because of their "harmful" content. One result is self-censorship by blog-hosting services and web portal operators. Following government orders, news portals have required users to register with their real names and identification numbers if they want to comment on news articles; Internet users at public libraries must use their national identity cards to register. Software installed at Internet cafes enables officials to monitor customers' use, and authorities subject some users to surveillance. The Ministry of Industry and Information Technology has directed schools and cybercafés to use "Green Dam" software to censor objectionable content based on a centralized database.

Among the most commonly blocked websites are those that discuss Taiwan and Tibetan independence, pro-democracy movements, underground religious and spiritual groups, and the violent suppression of demonstrations at Tiananmen Square during the 1989 crackdown. Automatic censorship of e-mail and web chats is triggered by such key words as "Falun Gong." Also blocked have been social networking sites and search engines that enable users to quickly communication or organize, as well as those of major international press outlets and foreign governments. Restraints tighten during tumultuous events, such as the summer 2009 inter-ethnic violence and resulting military response in the Xinjiang Province city of Urumqi; the government shut all text messaging, web access, and international telephone calls from the region.

Although there is software accessible to bypass official censorship, self-censorship remains the dominant means of limiting online speech. Through the Internet Society of China—sponsored by state and private Internet companies, government offices, and universities—the China Internet Illegal Information Reporting Centre solicits public reports of purportedly illicit online activity ranging from fraud and pornography to "attacks on the party and government."

Internet writers, bloggers, and cyber-dissidents have landed in prison. Among them have been Wu Baoquan, sentenced to 18 months for posting articles criticizing local government in postings about land rights in Inner Mongolia; Tibetan independence website editor Kunchok Tsephel, sentenced to 15 years for "divulging state secrets;" and writer-environmental activist Chen Daojun, sentenced to three years for "inciting subversion." Several writers associated with Uighur-language web forums in Xinjiang region have been convicted, including Gulmire Imin, who received a life term for revealing state secrets, separatism and organizing an illegal protest; Diliziati

Paerhati, sentenced to five years for endangering state security; and Nureli, sentenced to ten years for endangering state security. Authorities freed blogger Guo Baofeng after a public letter-writing campaign sparked by his Twitter announcement of his own arrest.

China has shown that it recognizes the value of being interconnected with other countries and, therefore, must grapple with cyberspace as it seeks to achieve economic dominance in the technology sector. This has resulted in investments of billions of dollars in a vast expansion of its broadband capabilities and information technology infrastructure to sustain the e-commerce sector (Bi, 2001).

Congruent with those goals, Winfield and Peng (2005) view the Chinese media system as moving away from totalitarianism toward market authoritarianism, while Weber and Jia (2007) see China putting more emphasis on the commercial aspects of state media rather than using them as pure propaganda tools. But tight official control of the Internet allows the government to maintain a much stricter policy to keep dissent messages offline compared to other countries, while at the same time trying to minimize economic disadvantages (Chan, Lee and Pan, 2006).

RESPONSE BY COMPANIES

The fight between the government and oppositional forces resembles a cat-and-mouse game. The regimes expend tremendous resources to protect their informational and communications territory from intruders, but—ironically—also deliberately allow holes in their security. These countries could certainly block complete Internet access if they desired. But there are large incentives not to do so. In interconnected global financial markets, it is essential for large corporations to have fast and direct access to all available economic news and information that enables them to respond quickly when markets fluctuate. Furthermore, with its wealth of information for educational purposes, instant Internet access for people in all layers of societies is important.

Losing some control over political expression was a price the governments were willing to pay in expectation that benefits would outweigh the potential harm done by oppositional forces (George, 2003; Baber, 2005). Furthermore, the authorities still employ people who monitor the online environment, and they do not hesitate to prosecute with fines and prison time when it suits them.

To do so, those regimes usually rely on Western companies to facilitate the monitoring practices. Those corporations are not necessarily in the business of censorship but must compromise with oppressive regimes to be permitted access to their markets (Fry, 2006). Because of this reliance, China occasionally cedes control over its own infrastructural fate to companies opposed to government controls. But because of China's tremendous amount of human capital sought by technology companies, it has great leverage to maintain this position when negotiating with Western firms (Dann & Haddow, 2008). The government can effectively shut out companies that refuse to make concessions regarding the censorship models as spelled out by the Communist Party, thereby cutting those companies out of the lucrative Chinese market (Endeshaw, 2004; Human Rights Watch, 2006).

Twitter was claimed to have played an important part in protests following contested 2009 Iranian elections. Some commentators credited the micro-blogging service with helping to organize protests in the wake of a disputed presidential election that June (Quirk, 2009; Sullivan, 2009; Washington Times, 2009). Harsh restrictions were imposed on foreign journalists following the voting, so in many ways social media provided the most effective way to rapidly get news out of the country. BBC editor Stephan Herrmann noted that "there's a huge ongoing, informed and informative discussion in Iran between people who care deeply about what is happening there and who are themselves monitoring everything they can, then circulating the most useful information and links" (Herrmann, 2009).

Both YouTube and Twitter played a major role in disseminating the video of the fatal shooting of protester Neda Agha-Soltan — a story that took on international importance (Fathi, 2009). Twitter (2009) seemed to acknowledge a sense of responsibility during the height of the situation when it re-scheduled a routine maintenance shutdown to "recognize the role Twitter is [...] playing as an important communication tool in Iran." However, the company moved to postpone the maintenance at the request of the U.S. State Department (Landler and Stelter, 2009).

Esfandiari (2010a) wrote that the importance of Twitter to the organization of protests within Iran was overblown, noting that some of the major Twitter users posting on the events were posting far from Iran. Instead, he wrote, "good old-fashioned word of mouth was by far the most influential medium used to shape the postelection opposition activity." Rather, he suggested, Twitter proved more effective in spreading news about Iran to the wider world.

Regardless of whether Twitter was used to spread news within Iran or internationally, the regime tightened its grip on social networks after the protests. Twitter, Facebook, Flickr, and YouTube were all blocked and inaccessible, and there were reports of cell phone seizures and possible arrests of people taking photos or filming events with their phones (Morillon and Julliard, 2010, p. 19). In fact, Esfandiari (2010b) asserted that Facebook and YouTube deserve more credit than Twitter. Overall, the reformists were so successful in using the Internet to mount protests that hardliners referred to it as a "cyberwar" against the government (Esfandiari, 2010c).

Numerous governments, including China, Pakistan, India, Indonesia, and Bangladesh, have temporarily blocked YouTube because parent company Google resisted pressures to remove political videos deemed offensive to government officials and religious leaders (Deibert et al., 2010). Google's confrontation with the Chinese government is perhaps the most salient example of the tense competition between openness and control. For four years, Google offered a government-filtered version of its search engine after it negotiated access restrictions with the government. Those restrictions result in selective exposure to government-approved material. The arrangement provided Google access to the massive Chinese market, but also allowed the regime a measure of control it wouldn't have had if Google located its servers offshore (Garvie, 2007). That arrangement broke down in early 2010, when Google announced it would stop filtering its search engine results and would host its site in Singapore instead (Drummond, 2010; Global Network Initiative, 2010). In response, China's state-owned mobile telephone provider and state-run news service announced that they would join forces to create an alternative search engine (Barboza, 2010).

On the heels of Google's announcement that it would cease operations in China, U.S. Secretary of State Hillary Clinton unveiled an official American policy of encouraging world governments to ensure freedom of expression on the Internet. "We stand for a single Internet, where all of humanity has equal access to knowledge and ideas," she said. Referring to the Google announcement, she added: "Censorship should not be accepted by any company from anywhere. American companies need to make a principled stand" (Krazit & McCullagh, 2010).

The State Department position marked a change from four years earlier, when during a U.S. congressional hearing on Internet censorship in China, representatives of both Microsoft and Google argued that withdrawal from markets in oppressive countries would make things worse for citizens. They also contended that even with some government censorship, their companies provided additional options for citizens to access information (Baker, 2010). Other observers feared that stance would give authoritarian countries too much leverage to demand additional changes in the future, sparking a "race to the bottom" (Maclay, 2010, p. 89).

SOLUTIONS AND RECOMMENDATIONS

One attempt to strike a balance between business interests and the protection of free expression was launched in 2008 following Yahoo!'s decision to provide Chinese authorities information on dissidents that led to the jailing of journalist Shi Tao and the arrests of other activists and journalists (Dann & Haddow, 2008; Wan, 2009). The company has since then made a diligent effort to better protect its users. For instance, it established two academic fellowships at Stanford University and Georgetown University to study the advancement of freedom of expression through technology (Global Network Initiative, 2010).

More important, the backlash against ICT-corporations that facilitated repressitarian regimes sparked the founding of the Global Network Initiative (GNI), by Yahoo!, Microsoft, Google, nine human rights and press freedom organizations, five investment corporations, and representatives from four universities and think tanks. The organization aims to develop a "corporate commitment to meaningfully integrate the protection of freedom of expression and privacy into both business practice and corporate culture" (Maclay, 2010, pp. 87-88).

This organization offers guidance to ICT companies on good practices with a goal of "reducing human rights risks and promoting an Internet that is safe, thriving, and protective of free expression and privacy" (Global Network Initiative, 2010, p. 6). The main goal is to ensure that participating companies are making systematic efforts to change their decision-making processes to investigate each potential business deal as to whether freedom of expression and privacy of users could be jeopardized. Because the member organizations are often negotiating in similar circumstances and dealing with the same government restrictions and regulations, they hope to learn from each others' experiences.

Additionally, they seek to foster accountability for their actions. The corporate members ought to be publicly pronouncing their decisions to remove content or restrict access to information. For instance, Google (2010) put its Transparency Report online with an overview of all the government requests for eliminating information from certain websites, although it is still developing features to present all the information. The company claims that it cannot show the removal requests from the Chinese government because it considers censorship a state secret, while that information would be of most interest of human rights activists.

The three multimedia companies committed about $200,000 to the organization since it was founded in 2008 (Figliola et al., 2010). Two years after its start-up, the Global Network Initiative appointed its first executive director and board of directors. In its inaugural status report, delivered towards the end of 2010, the organization emphasized the direction it wants to take in the next few years:

The first step will be a review process to examine members' progress in creating internal policies to protect the human rights and privacy of their users. As presented in the inaugural report, "The goal of examining specific responses is not to audit whether the company made the 'right' choice in a given experience, but to assess whether the processes and systems established earlier work in the context of actual practice" (p. 11). The organization also wants to increase its membership to bundle know-how from privacy and technology experts, representing the most influential ICT-business and human rights groups.

Organizations such Amnesty International and RSF were initially involved in the development of GNI, but eventually decided not to participate as full members. They had pressed for more stringent measures against repressitarian regimes and remain skeptical about the effectiveness of the new association (Figliola et al., 2010). More troubling is the refusal of two social media giants — Twitter and Facebook — to sign on to the GNI. Morozov (2011) suggests "that an American company does not need to make many ethical commitments to be friends with the U.S. government, at least as long as it is instrumental to Washington's foreign policy agenda" (p. 23).

The progress of the Global Network Initiative is followed closely among academics and politicians who hope that the cooperation, indeed, leads to increased human rights protection. Secretary of State Clinton (2010) was encouraged by the members' augmented efforts to protect free speech, saying, "The initiative goes beyond mere statements of principles and establishes mechanisms to promote real accountability and transparency."

So far it is too early to judge whether the organization will reach its goals, because the "effectiveness of such self-regulation is untested and still questionable" (Deibert & Rohozinski, 2010b, p. 26). This is seconded by Nolan: "Voluntary codes of conduct that aim to delineate corporate responsibility for human rights can aid protection of such rights but cannot alone ensure uniform protection" (p. 24). Without a mechanism in place to force technology companies to comply with their commitments, the GNI runs the risk of becoming merely a publicity stunt (Mozorov, 2011). It may be up to governments to enact such policies.

FUTURE RESEARCH DIRECTIONS

This chapter has examined countries with well-known poor human rights records. Yet even countries with a great degree of freedom for speech and the press curtail access in certain situations, claiming to protect public safety, national security, or moral values. Researchers should look at the line between suppression of dissent and legitimate government controls in the online world and the interplay of variables such as GDP, literacy, and Internet penetration rates as predictors of online freedom.

Undergirding part of the argument of this chapter is the notion that exposure to ICT will increase freedom in societies where it previously was absent. However, it could possibly work in the opposite direction where traditionally free governments find it irresistibly easy to increase surveillance of their citizens online. Researchers should, continue to examine this topic in the context of other nations.

Finally, researchers should continue to scrutinize the efforts of ICT companies to regulate themselves. More work needs to be done to determine the effects of government control over Internet information. The largest of these companies possess a tremendous amount of leverage in negotiating with repressetarian regimes, and if they choose to exercise that leverage they could have a positive impact on Internet freedom. However, there is a danger that those efforts could become mere window-dressing.

CONCLUSION

The tools of ICT continue to offer opportunities for users to circumvent government controls to fulfill the role of journalists, which is to provide citizens with the information required to be free and self-governing (Kovach & Rosenstiel, 2007). Yet repressitarian regimes do not cede control easily. Thus by instituting invasive technology to prevent dissemination of "objectionable" messages and imposing legal controls to persecute those who engage in unauthorized political organizing, citizens who dare seize these opportunities may ultimately be less free.

These ethical implications for social media companies are of even more significance, especially because youths—the targeted demographic that makes business for ICT-corporations in every country attractive and perhaps lucrative—put themselves in potential harm by disseminating oppositional voices online. Of the countries discussed here, many have populations that are relatively young, especially Egypt and Iran where the median age is 24 and 26.6, respectively. Egypt's average is almost half the median age of that of economic superpowers, such as Germany (44.3) and Japan (44.6) (CIA World Factbook, 2011). Therefore, whatever harsh consequences are meted out to online political dissidents seem more likely to fall on young computer users.

Western companies have an ethical role to play in this conflict as they confront the choice between providing the tools of repression or foregoing lucrative business opportunities. In a corporate world in which shareholders determine the ultimate course of business, the feasibility of upholding such a high ethical standard may be questionable.

Attempts at corporate self-regulation through programs like the Global Network Initiative are promising, but their effectiveness is still in question. Its success will also be determined by the velocity of their undertakings. The organization has allowed itself two years to review all the internal Internet policies of its members. That may or may not be an adequate time period. Meanwhile the freedom and privacy of many human rights activists will remain in jeopardy as long as corporations cannot find ways to exercise leverage over the repressitarian governments they are negotiating with.

Furthermore, its success will also be a test of flexibility to change course when unexpected developments in international politics require such effort—and oppositional forces most need support in their battles against government elites. Ongoing tensions regarding Iran's potential nuclear capability demonstrate that ICT-companies must be prepared for essential roles in disseminating news around the globe in the short-term, because social media may be the only vehicle for delivering impartial information from areas where independent journalism is non-existent.

Finally, Morozov (2011) criticized what he calls Western "cyber-utopians" whose early theorizing about the potential of the Internet to foster democracy "failed to make any space for the state, let alone a brutal authoritarian state with no tolerance for the rule of law or dissenting opinions" (p. xiv). Instead, he recommends a sober assessment of both the opportunities and risks posed by political organizing via the Internet in repressetarian countries. This approach eschews technological determinism and supports actions that originate "not in what technology allows but in what a certain geopolitical environment requires" (p. xvii). That is a caution that activists and supporters of technology might do well to heed.

REFERENCES

Abdel Dayem, M. (2009, Summer). Attempting to silence Iran's 'Weblogistan.' *Nieman Reports,* 42-44.

Baber, Z. (2005). The unintended consequences of technological policy: The Internet and civil society in Singapore. In Baber, Z. (Ed.), *Cyberasia: The Internet and society in Asia* (pp. 57–74). Leiden, The Netherlands: Brill.

Barboza, D. (2010, August 13). New China search engine will be state-controlled. *New York Times*. Retrieved from http://www.nytimes.com/2010/08/14/technology/internet/14search.html

Barns, E. (2010, November 26). Mystery surrounds cyber missile that crippled Iran's nuclear weapons ambitions. *Fox News*. Retrieved from http://www.foxnews.com/scitech/2010/11/26/secret-agent-crippled-irans-nuclear-ambitions/

Becker, L. B., Vlad, T., & Nusser, N. (2007). An evaluation of press freedom indicators. *International Communication Gazette*, *69*, 5–28. doi:10.1177/1748048507072774

Bi, J. (2001). The Internet revolution in China: The significance for traditional forms of communist control. *International Journal (Toronto, Ont.)*, *56*, 421–441. doi:10.2307/40203576

Castells, M. (1997). An introduction to the information age. *City*, *7*, 6–16. doi:10.1080/13604819708900050

Charny, N. (2006, April 20). Chinese partner censors Skype text messages. *PCmag.com*. Retrieved from http://www.pcmag.com/article2/0,2817,1951637,00.asp

CIA World Factbook. (2011). Retrieved from https://www.cia.gov/library/publications/the-world-factbook/

Clayton, M. (2011, January 3). Stuxnet attack on Iran nuclear program came about a year ago, report says. *Christian Science Monitor*. Retrieved from http://www.csmonitor.com/USA/2011/0103/Stuxnet-attack-on-Iran-nuclear-program-came-about-a-year-ago-report-says

Clinton, H. R. (2010, January 21). *Speech on Internet freedom*. Retrieved from http://www.state.gov/secretary/rm/2010/01/135519.htm

Colley, A. (2007, March 6). States still hold out on YouTube. *Australian*. Retrieved from http://www.theaustralian.com.au/australian-it/states-still-hold-out-on-youtube/story-e6frgamx-1111113102808

Committee to Protect Journalists. (2011, April 11). *More journalists held in Libya; blogger jailed in Egypt*. Retrieved from http://www.cpj.org/2011/04/more-journalists-held-in-libya-blogger-jailed-in-e.php

Cowie, J. (2011). Egypt leaves the Internet. *Renesys Blog*. Retrieved from http://www.renesys.com/blog/2011/01/egypt-leaves-the-internet.shtml

Dann, G. E., & Haddow, N. (2008). Just doing business or doing just business: Google, Microsoft, Yahoo! And the business of censoring China's Internet. *Journal of Business Ethics*, *79*, 219–234. doi:10.1007/s10551-007-9373-9

Deibert, R., Palfrey, J., Rohozinski, R., & Zittrain, J. (Eds.). (2010). *Access controlled: The shaping of power, rights, and rule in cyberspace*. Cambridge, MA: MIT Press.

Deibert, R., & Rohozinski, R. (2010b). Risking security: Policies and paradoxes of cyberspace security. *International Political Sociology*, *4*, 15–32. doi:10.1111/j.1749-5687.2009.00088.x

Drummond, D. (January 12, 2010). A new approach to China. *Official Google Blog*. Retrieved from http://googleblog.blogspot.com/2010/01/new-approach-to-china.html

Endeshaw, A. (2004). Internet regulation in China: The never-ending cat and mouse game. *Information & Communications Technology Law*, *13*, 41–57. doi:10.1080/1360083042000190634

Eng, P. (1998, September/October). A new kind of cyberwar. *Columbia Journalism Review*, 20–21.

Fathi, M. (2009, June 23). In a death seen around the world, a symbol of Iranian protests. *New York Times*. Retrieved from http://www.nytimes.com/2009/06/23/world/middleeast/23neda.html

Figliola, P. M., Nakamura, K. H., Addis, C. L., & Lum, T. (2010). *U.S. initiatives to promote global Internet freedom: Issues, policy, and technology*. Washington, DC: Congressional Research Service.

Freedman, E., Shafer, R., & Antonova, A. (2010). Two decades of repression: The persistence of authoritarian controls on the mass media in Central Asia. *Central Asia and the Caucasus*, *11*(4), 94–110.

Garvie, J. (2007). Trading free speech. *Index on Censorship*, 42–50.

George, C. (2003). The Internet and the narrow tailoring dilemma for "Asian" democracies. *Communication Review*, *6*, 247–268. doi:10.1080/10714420390226270.002

George, C. (2009). *Coercion unmasked: The counter-hegemonic impact of new media activism in Singapore.* Paper presented at the annual meeting of the International Communication Association, Chicago, IL.

Gillmor, D. (2011) Egypt's communications "kill switch." *Salon*. Retrieved from http://www.salon.com/technology/dan_gillmor/2011/01/28/egypt_kill_switch

Global Network Initiative. (2010). *Inaugural report 2010.* Retrieved from http://www.globalnetworkinitiative.org/cms/uploads/1/GNI_annual_report_2010.pdf

Google. (2010). *Google transparency report.* Retrieved from http://www.google.com/transparencyreport/governmentrequests/

Hachigian, N., & Wu, L. (2003). *The information revolution in Asia*. Santa Monica, CA: RAND.

Hamdy, N. (2008). Building capabilities of Egyptian journalist in preparation for media in transition. *Journal of Arab and Muslim Media Research*, *1*, 215–243. doi:10.1386/jammr.1.3.215_1

Hamdy, N. (2009). Arab citizen journalism in action: Challenging mainstream media, authorities and media laws. *Westminster Papers in Communication and Culture*, *6*, 92–112.

Herrmann, S. (2009, June 16), Social media in Iran. *BBC News*. Retrieved from http://www.bbc.co.uk/blogs/theeditors/2009/06/social_media_in_iran.html

Human Rights Watch. (2006). *China report.* Retrieved from http://www.hrw.org/english/docs/2006/01/18/china12270.htm

Ishani, M. (2011). The hopeful network. *Foreign Policy.* Retrieved from http://www.foreignpolicy.com/articles/2011/02/07/the_hopeful_network

Jardin, X. (2007). Future web: Exporting censorship. *Index on Censorship*, *4*(88), 80 doi:10.1080/03064220701741515.

Jiang, S. (2010). China blanks Nobel Peace Prize searches. *CNN*. Retrieved from http://www.cnn.com/2010/WORLD/asiapcf/10/08/china.internet/index.html.

Johnson, B. (2011) How Egypt switched off the internet. *GigaOm*. Retrieved from http://gigaom.com/2011/01/28/how-egypt-switched-off-the-internet/

Kelly, J., & Etling, B. (2008). *Mapping Iran's online public: Politics and culture in the Persian blogosphere.* Retrieved from http://cyber.law.harvard.edu/publications/2008/Mapping_Irans_Online_Public

Khamis, S., & Vaughn, K. (2011). Cyberactivism in the Egyptian revolution: How civic engagement and citizen journalism tilted the balance. *Arab Media & Society, 13*. Retrieved from http://www.arabmediasociety.com/?article=769

Kia, A. A. (2008). Iranian youth online: Identity between traditional and modern lifestyles. *3CM. Journal of Community, Citizen's and Third Sector Media and Communication*, *4*, 28–36.

Kovach, B., & Rosenstiel, T. (2007). *The elements of journalism*. New York, NY: Three Rivers Press.

Kulikova, S. V., & Perlmutter, D. D. (2011). Blogging down the dictator? The Kyrgyz revolution and *Samizdat* websites. In Freedman, E., & Shafer, R. (Eds.), *After the czars and Commissars: Journalism in authoritarian post-Soviet Central Asia* (pp. 263–286). East Lansing, MI: Michigan State University Press. doi:10.1177/1748048507072777

Lai, O. K. (2004). Differential e-mobilization and cyberspace in East Asian economies: Contours of emerging cyber-activism and (anti)democratic regimes in the information society. In Abbott, J. P. (Ed.), *The political economy of the Internet in Asia and the Pacific: Digital divides, economic competiveness, and security challenges* (pp. 33–56). Westport, CT: Praeger.

Landler, M., & Stelter, B. (2009, June 16). Washington taps into a potent new force in diplomacy. *New York Times.* Retrieved from http://www.nytimes.com/2009/06/17/world/middleeast/17media.html

Lee, T. (2004). Emulating Singapore: Towards a model for Internet regulation in Asia. In Gan, S., Gomez, J., & Johannen, U. (Eds.), *Asian cyberactivism: Freedom of expression and media censorship* (pp. 162–199). Bangkok, Thailand: Friedrich Naumann Foundation.

Li, S. (2010). The online public space and popular ethos in China. *Media Culture & Society, 32*, 63–83. doi:10.1177/0163443709350098

MacKinnon, R. (2005, June 17). Screenshots of Censorship. *RConversation Blog*. Retrieved from http://rconversation.blogs.com/rconversation/2005/06/screenshots_of_.html

Maclay, C. M. (2010). Protecting privacy and expression online: Can the Global Network Initiative embrace the character of the Net? In Deibert, R., Palfrey, J., Rohozinski, R., & Zittrain, J. (Eds.), *Access controlled: The shaping of power, rights, and rule in cyberspace* (pp. 87–108). Cambridge, MA: MIT Press.

Morillon, L., & Julliard, J. (2010). *Enemies of the Internet: Web 2.0 versus control 2.0*. Reporters Without Borders. Retrieved from http://www.rsf.org/ennemis.html

Morozov, E. (2011). *The net delusion: The dark side of Internet freedom*. Philadelphia, PA: PublicAffairs.

Nasseri, L. (2010, November 29). Ahmadinejad confirms several Iran centrifuges affected by computer virus. *Bloomberg*. Retrieved from http://www.bloomberg.com/news/2010-11-29/ahmadinejad-confirms-several-iran-centrifuges-affected-by-computer-virus.html

Nolan, J. M. (2009). The China dilemma: Internet censorship and corporate responsibility. *Asian Journal of Comparative Law, 4*, 1–28. doi:10.2202/1932-0205.1160

OpenNet Initiative. (2005, April 15). *Special report: Kyrgyzstan, election monitoring in Kyrgyzstan.* Retrieved from http://opennet.net/special/kg/

Prensky, M. (2001). Digital natives, digital immigrants. *Horizon*, 9.

Quirk, P. W. (2009, June 17). Iran's Twitter revolution. *Foreign Policy in Focus*. Retrieved from http://www.fpif.org/articles/irans_twitter_revolution

Sakr, N. (2010). News, transparency and the effectiveness of reporting from inside Arab dictatorships. *International Communication Gazette, 72*, 35–50. doi:10.1177/1748048509350337

Shapiro, S. M. (2009, January 22). Revolution, Facebook-style. *New York Times*. Retrieved from http://www.nytimes.com/2009/01/25/magazine/25bloggers-t.html

Shiels, M. (2010, December 30). Cyber-sabotage and espionage top 2011 security fears. *BBC*. Retrieved from http://www.bbc.co.uk/news/technology-12056594

Shuguang, Z. (2008). Notes on the net. *Index on Censorship*, 90–96.

Stanyer, J., & Davidson, S. (2009). *The internet and the visibility of oppression in non-democratic states: The online exposure of human rights violations and the other repressive acts*. Paper presented at the annual meeting of the International Communication Association, Chicago.

Sullivan, A. (2009, June 13). The revolution will be twittered. *The Atlantic*. Retrieved from http://www.theatlantic.com/daily-dish/archive/2009/06/the-revolution-will-be-twittered/200478/

Swaine, J. (2008, August 11). Georgia: Russia 'conducting cyber war.' *The Telegraph*. Retrieved from http://www.telegraph.co.uk/news/worldnews/europe/georgia/2539157/Georgia-Russia-conducting-cyber-war.html

Times, W. (2009, June 16). *Iran's Twitter revolution*. Retrieved from http://www.washingtontimes.com/news/2009/jun/16/irans-twitter-revolution/

Twitter (June, 2009). *Down time rescheduled*. Retrieved from http://blog.twitter.com/2009/06/down-time-rescheduled.html

U.S. State Department. (2010a). *2009 human rights report: Egypt*. Retrieved from http://www.state.gov/g/drl/rls/hrrpt/2009/nea/136067.htm

U.S. State Department. (2010b). *2009 human rights report: Singapore*. Retrieved from http://www.state.gov/g/drl/rls/hrrpt/2009/eap/136008.htm

U.S. State Department. (2011). *2010 human rights report: Iran*. Retrieved from http://www.state.gov/g/drl/rls/hrrpt/2010/nea/154461.htm

Van Dijk, J., & Hacker, K. (2000). *The digital divide as a complex and dynamic phenomenon*. Paper presented at the Annual Conference of the International Communication Association, Acapulco, Mexico.

Wan, C. D. (2009). The Shi Tao case: Its development in mainland China. *Journal of Contemporary China*, *18*, 517–539. doi:10.1080/10670560903033836

Weber, I., & Jia, L. (2007). Internet and self-regulation in China: The cultural logic of controlled commodification. *Media Culture & Society*, *29*, 772–789. doi:10.1177/0163443707080536

Winfield, B. H., & Peng, Z. (2005). Market or party controls? Chinese media in transition. *International Journal for Communication Studies*, *67*, 255–270.

KEY TERMS AND DEFINITIONS

Botnet: A network of small Internet applications (or "bots") that run automated tasks. Botnets are frequently used in Distributed Denial of Service attacks.

Distributed Denial of Service Attack: An attack on a computer network that typically involves crippling the network with a high volume of automated traffic, so that legitimate requests are unable to get through.

Malware: Harmful computer software.

Repressitarian: A government that is both authoritarian in governance and repressive in human rights practices.

ENDNOTE

1 These reports were culled from sources including: Reporters sans Frontieres, U.S. State Department, Freedom House, International Research & Exchanges Board, Committee to Protect Journalists, *New York Times*, *Washington Post*, Human Rights Watch, Radio Free Europe/Radio Liberty, Organization for Security and Co-operation in Europe Representative on Freedom of the Media, Open Society Foundations, and British Broadcasting Corporation.

Section 2

Case Studies from Around the World

Chapter 4
"In YouTube We Trust": Video Exchange and Arab Human Rights

Aziz Douai
University of Ontario Institute of Technology, Canada

ABSTRACT

YouTube has enabled new forms of political dissent in Arab societies. This chapter examines the development and rise of YouTube in the Arab world. In particular, it looks at how this video exchange site is invigorating the online public sphere's vigorous demand for political reform and respect for human rights. Specifically, this investigation explores how social networking capabilities have made YouTube an effective asset in dissidents' arsenal among Arab activists. To examine the vibrancy of this fledgling online public sphere, the chapter scrutinizes how activists incorporated YouTube videos to shed light on human rights abuses, specifically police abuse, corruption, and brutality in two Arab countries, Egypt and Morocco. The chapter concludes with a discussion of the new campaigning modes that the Internet and YouTube have facilitated.

INTRODUCTION

The "Arab Democracy Spring" has promised to end the entrenched history of human rights violations in Egypt, Libya, Syria, and Tunisia, among other Arab authoritarian states. However, the long fight against these abuses commenced years prior to the 2011 mass protests as an unprecedented era of virtual politics and activism took shape within Arab societies. At the forefront of these shifts, the Internet and other new communication technologies have been central forces for change (e.g. Seib, 2007; Lynch, 2007; Ibahrine, 2008;Douai, 2009). A few years after its inception, YouTube soon became an important tool for publicizing Arab regime's human rights abuses both locally and globally. This chapter seeks to understand the strategic role that YouTube has

DOI: 10.4018/978-1-4666-1918-0.ch004

carved in those human rights advocacy campaigns and political reform struggles in Arab societies. Preliminary evidence suggests that YouTube has been effective in highlighting police abuse cases and prosecuting perpetrators. This work thus contributes to a growing body of research that underscores the vital role of communication and information technologies in promoting human rights worldwide (Metzl, 1996; Brophy&Halpin, 1999; Weyker, 2002; Hick, Halpin, & Hoskins, 2000; Ron, Ramos, & Rodgers, 2005).

Within the above framework, Arab citizens have similarly harnessed the site's video exchange capabilities to expose political corruption, police brutality, and demand political reform in the same way bloggers have countered official narratives and/or media blackouts on local events (Al Malky, 2007; Douai, 2009). YouTube and the new breed of social media have grown more effective as favourite political instruments for several reasons. Some reasons include high levels of anonymity, global reach, technical simplicity, absence of professional pre-requisites, and local/global organizing tool capabilities. Significantly, YouTube is hosting and abetting a new political discourse in which readers vent their frustrations and heap their scorn online before moving offline. The first tremors of this movement toward harnessing YouTube's social networking and video exchange capabilities appeared in 2007, as videos of police brutality and corruption in Egypt and Morocco were posted online.

YouTube in the Arab world has emboldened an emerging online public sphere and bolstered its demands for political reform. Arab citizens are appropriating the new forms of mediated communication to call attention to the abuse of the state (Azimi, 2007), invigorating the Arab "public sphere" debate (Lynch, 2007; Douai, 2009). This investigation explores how these social networking capabilities have made YouTube an effective asset in dissidents' arsenal. To comprehend the vibrancy of this fledgling online public sphere, the study examines how YouTube has helped shed light on human rights abuses, specifically police abuse, corruption, and brutality in the region. The main question this chapter addresses is: How have activists incorporated YouTube in their campaigns for political and democratic reform in Arab societies? To answer this question, it analyzes the reach and implications of four videos publicizing corruption and police abuse cases in Egypt and Morocco. Specific attention is paid to the videos' political impact and global implications on the struggle for political reform in Arab societies. After reviewing the political impact and history of YouTube, the chapter analyzes how this communication technology has become an effective platform against Arab authoritarianism.

YOUTUBE POLITICS: A BRIEF REVIEW

The story of how new media have assumed a reformist, if not a "liberationist," mantle in the Arab world may be well-worn (Seib, 2007; Ibahrine, 2008), but it deserves to be re-told. Authoritarian rulers have long co-opted traditional mass media and used these outlets to strengthen their grip on power and subdue political adversaries (Pintak, 2008). International non-governmental organizations have documented this state of affairs and accumulated an oppressive record of infringements on political and individual liberties. Human Rights Watch, Amnesty International, Reporters without Borders, and Freedom House have routinely placed the region among the ranks of states that regularly violate universal human rights, the right to free expression and the right to communicate (Human Rights Watch [HRW], 2010). State owned mass media were effectively used to "gloss" over these violations, or dismiss these international reports as politically motivated and grossly misinformed (Dayem& Mahoney, 2010). "New" media, particularly the rise of web-enabled social media, have opened a ray of hope for activists and alternative voices to break up the strangling arm of the state, tell the story in their own voices, and construct alternative narratives that refute the dominant line (Ibahrine, 2008).

The evolving nature of social media may be behind why video exchange sites have largely been under-researched in new media studies on the Arab world. While many studies have looked at new media's potential, whether from a utopia-centered vision or through sceptical lens (e.g. Kalathil& Boas, 2003; McLaughlin, 2003), studies that shed light on the potential roles YouTube could play in transforming the political sphere and contributing to the ongoing discussion taking place on the World Wide Web are rare. Behind this lack of research lie a host of reasons that include inherent difficulties surrounding the study of new media, how new are the new media, the shifting landscape of social media, and the treacherous paths linking offline and online politics. It does not help that social networking sites (SNS) are constantly shifting their outlook, policies, and updating their technical capabilities. For instance, Facebook's privacy policies have been updated and changed more than four times within three months in 2010 (Paul, 2010). YouTube has similarly experienced shifts and updates regarding privacy protections and copyrights regime. For instance, in 2006-2007 alone, YouTube had to take down more than 250.000 videos from its site because of lawsuits from media giants including Viacom and News Corporation, as well as other international organizations (Driscoll, 2007).

YouTube's bottom-up structure of content creation and video information exchange facilitates interaction among the social network's members. The bottom-up structure, a hallmark feature of Web 2.0, enhances user participation. In their analysis of this participatory culture, Green and Burgess (2009) argue that YouTube signals a larger societal trend with shifting attitudes toward the structure of authority and power. Cultural production and consumption, historically dominated by large corporations (Bagdikian, 1992), become subject to challenges from web surfers. With interactive features including "most responded" and "commented" categories, YouTube constantly redefines the realm of the popular without abiding by traditional standards of mass markets and mass consumers. As Zoonen, Vis, and Mihelj (2010) conclude after examining YouTube videos in response to the inflammatory Dutch documentary, *Fitna,* YouTube transforms the traditional notions of citizenship and identity.

Like other social media, YouTube's user-centered and participatory architecture has been amenable to politics. For activists in the Arab world, as this chapter argues, YouTube has offered a unique platform for documenting and publicizing state oppression incarnated in police corruption and abuse. As stated above, the study's objective is to understand the strategic role that YouTube has carved in advocacy campaigns and the struggle for political reform in Arab societies. Focusing on how and why netactivists are harnessing the power of YouTube, this study addresses the following broad research question:

How have activists employed YouTube in their campaigns for human rights reform in Arab societies? Specifically, how did these YouTube videos present police abuse and corruption and with what impact?

In addressing this broad question, the study presents and analyzes some YouTube videos that publicize police abuse, corruption, and brutality in Egypt and Morocco. High Internet access has certainly enabled the creation of vibrant net activist communities in these two Arab countries. A closer examination of the selected videos will focus on 1) the "YouTube effects," 2) the target audiences, and 3) the new campaigning modes which YouTube enables.

METHOD AND RATIONALE

Political videos laying claim to exposing political corruption and abuse in the Arab world abound on YouTube. This study selects four YouTube videos that succeeded in publicizing police corruption and brutality in two Arab countries: Egypt and Morocco (see Table 1). The study's selection criteria were based on the level of public and media salience that the YouTube videos gained from 2005-2010. This period coincides with the birth and prominence of YouTube as the world's pre-eminent video exchange site. As stated above, the 2005-2010 period witnessed strident calls for more political reform and accountability in the Arab world with the ascendancy of mass movements like Kefaya ("The Egyptian Movement for Change") in 2004 and Lebanon's Cedar Revolution (after the assassination of Prime Minister Rafik Hariri) in February 2005, which finally culminated in mass uprisings in 2011.

In this time frame, two stories about police corruption and brutality had garnered wide media attention in Morocco: the so-called "Targuist Sniper" about police bribery, and YouTube coverage of police intervention in a local "uprising" in Sidi Ifni, a city in the south of the country. The "Targuist Sniper" is the chosen moniker of the person (or people) who had secretly taped members of the gendarme and police force taking bribes in 2007 (Abdo, 2007). In 2008, police forces and army-militia used a heavy force to quell public demonstrations against the authorities in the southern Moroccan city, Sidi Ifni (Transparency Maroc, 2009). As traditional mass media were barred from freely reporting and accessing the scene, YouTube videos of police brutality against the locals became the main outlet. Interdependence is another rationale for selecting these videos: YouTube coverage of Sidi Ifni was inspired in part by the public success and media attention that the "Targuist Sniper" had achieved (Abdo, 2007). This was explicit in many YouTube videos using the same moniker, for instance "Sidi Ifni Sniper."

The next two YouTube videos on Egyptian police brutality were selected following a similar rationale. They were retrieved from the YouTube site using the key words of "police torture in Egypt" and "police brutality in Egypt" and were found to correspond to news reports about police abuse in Egypt. Incidents of Egyptian police human rights violations have gained unprecedented publicity in the last few years both in domestic and international media. In 2007, a leaked video of Egyptian police officers sodomizing a citizen inside a police station became widely circulated on the web (Anderson, 2007). Human rights organizations took notice of the video and used it as evidence of the Egyptian government's deteriorating human rights record. The Middle East Director of Human Rights Watch publicly pressured the Egyptian government as she stated that "The people responsible for this disgusting crime must face justice. The government should send the message that it won't tolerate torture by police or any other officials" (HRW, 2006, n.p.). In countries far from Egypt, such as Canada, the video was discussed as a flagrant case of Egyptian police brutality (Urquhart, 2007).

Table 1. YouTube videos included in the study

	Title	YouTube Address
Video 1	"Gendarme"	http://www.youtube.com/watch?v=Z8RgWRmRtUc&feature=player_embedded
Video 2	"bol3lam sidiifni 19 08 2008"	http://www.youtube.com/watch?v=VHby7HarMzo
Video 3	"Police Torture in Egypt"	http://www.youtube.com/watch?v=BKLiGZyY4HQ
Video 4	"Police Brutality In Egypt"	http://www.youtube.com/watch?v=iCHM6LYiBsY&feature=related

Further, these particular videos received a high number of viewer counts and comments in comparison to similar versions (see Table 2). A qualitative-based descriptive analysis of this small YouTube video sample is conducted. The descriptive analysis underscores the main themes and visual messages employed in this "exposé" of human rights abuses. Finally, statistical and viewing data retrieved from YouTube will be used to support and illuminate the observations drawn in the discussion section.

FINDINGS: A CONTENT DESCRIPTION

In addition to traditional mass media attention, the selected videos have garnered significant following and user interest on YouTube (see Table 2). Viewer count had reached more than half a million for the YouTube video entitled "Gendarme" (Video 1) by June 23, 2010 (a random date during which this study was being conducted). The other three YouTube videos obtained viewer counts of more than 70,000 by the same date. User comments ranged between a low of 53 for a video exposing police brutality in Morocco (Video 2 "bol3lam sidiifni 19 08 2008") to a high of 260 for a YouTube video exposing torture in Egypt (Video 3 "Police Torture in Egypt"). Table 2 provides more information on the selected videos, web addresses, uploading dates, users, and other uploading data. It reveals that these videos' categories span from News & Politics, Nonprofits& Activism, and People & Blogs to Entertainment, making search for such videos by categories elusive and unreliable. The "Tags" information is more helpful because it ties the videos to the actual events and/or related themes.

The visual content in all these YouTube videos provides evidence of human rights violations, working as documentation and publicity tools at the same time. These videos range from documentation of human rights abuses to campaign style videos. They range from secretly taped evidence of police abuse to trophy-like videos leaked on YouTube. The video editing also varies widely from the professional to the amateurish, and from tacky to smooth visuals and transitions, as the description below indicates.

The following descriptions sum up the four YouTube videos included in the study.

Table 2. Raw YouTube video data

	Video 1	Video 2	Video 3	Video 4
Title	Gendarme	Bol3lam sidiifni 19 08 2008	Police Torture in Egypt	Police Brutality In Egypt
Country	Morocco	Morocco	Egypt	Egypt
Uploading Date	July 08, 2007	August 22, 2008	September 14, 2006	April 17, 2007
User	TarSniper	ItoubeMaroc	Cairogem	Hairman180
# Viewer Counts	586,171	74,968	84,832	93,894
# Comments	191	53	260	175
Category	News & Politics	Nonprofits& Activism	People & Blogs	Entertainment
Tags	police gendrames Targuist	bola3lam Sidi Ifni 19 08 2008 Maroc Morocco	Egypt police human rights mubarak politics brutality prison jail gamal democracy masr	Police Brutality In Egypt barbaric Barbaric Inhumane inhumane cruel egypt torture beating up innocent people

Video 1: Police Corruption in Morocco ("Gendarme")

The first YouTube video shows members of the Royal Moroccan Gendarmerie, a special highway patrol force, taking bribes from drivers. Posted on July 8, 2007, the video has gone viral amassing more than half a million views. The YouTube user explicitly states the purpose of the video: exposing a culture of corruption rife among these police forces, calling it "the phenomenon of highway bribery" in the northern Moroccan city of Targuist. The opening title stresses this mission: "The Sniper of Targuist Presents: The True Promise." Ominous machine gunfire punctuates the amateurish video as it cuts to a green van moving along the road. Then some bird chirping noises are heard although it is not clear whether these are some special effects or random noises caught by the camera. In this 6:38 minute long video, the two gendarmes stop more than 20 vehicles, furtively pocketing what motorists hand out to them. In those short encounters, bribe money is apparently exchanged and the officers' furtive actions point to their culpability.

Video 2: Police Abuse in Morocco ("bol3lam sidiifni 19 08 2008")

The second YouTube video selected for the analysis is a 1:43 minute secret video recording of Moroccan police officers beating protesters in Sidi Ifni, a southern Moroccan city. In addition to the title's implication that this event took place on August 19, 2008, the date is boldly inserted in the video recording. For the first seven seconds, the recording shows a still photo of Morocco's Minister of Interior speaking at a press conference. As the video shows officers beating three male protesters, a female voice is overheard repeatedly directing another female to hide the camera. The video then zooms on several police officers kicking and beating one male protester. The protester loudly shrieks and writhes in apparent pain, as the same female voice is heard cursing the officers for their savagery and abuse. Crowd jeers and taunts mingle with shrieks when the police drag and beat the man. The video's final seconds get more tumultuous with police sirens growing louder, and officers chasing demonstrators.

Video 3: "Police Torture in Egypt"

The third video purportedly takes place inside an Egyptian police station. In a 00:55 second video, a police officer first feigns to slap a man who stands still, apparently scared. Loud cheers from unseen fellow officers exhort the officer to hit the man. The officer turns to the camera and asks another officer to beat the man. Briskly entering the scene, a burly officer with a cigarette in his mouth begins slapping the man hard and fast, as laughs and loud cheers grow in the background. Despite the man's attempts to parry the officer's slaps, the beating continues on until he finally collapses. The scene ends with the victim collapsing on the ground. There is no indication that the video was secretly taped. In fact, the video closes with the officers' loud laughs and celebratory cheers.

Video 4: "Police Brutality in Egypt"

A 2:35 minute long video montage, this YouTube video compiles different photos and audio material documenting Egyptian police abuse of citizens. The montage highlights several incidents of police abuse, including a video of police officers sodomizing a prisoner in a police station. As fast paced and ominous background music plays, the first scene shows two police officers in civilian dress abusing another man. In the same scene, one police officer is seen slapping the man while the other officer tries to hold him still. Two more scenes of police officers beating and slapping prisoners are shown before the video reveals police officers sodomizing a prisoner with a stick. In a crescendo, the sodomized man's cries mix with the background music. The video cuts to dramatic scenes of mass protests and police scuffling with protesters, punctuated with some special effects.

DISCUSSION AND IMPLICATIONS

The videos described above provide enough data to answer the research question posed earlier in the chapter. Highlighting police torture and abuse in Arab societies, these YouTube videos are emblematic of a developing, strategic role of a new platform in the fight for respect of human rights. YouTube video exchange has become a force for political change as activists strategically deploy videos in their campaigns for political and democratic reform in Arab societies. In turning the camera on cases of abuse and political corruption in the region, the four videos loudly denounce the political culture of oppression. These YouTube videos do not necessarily bring new information to the public consciousness, however. Their purpose revolves more around exposing and documenting what ordinary citizens in their societies already know: police corruption, brutality, and abuse are commonplace. The videos create a shocking emotional impact and visceral reactions among viewers, as the viewer counts and comments attest.

Several factors may explain the popularity of YouTube as a site of online activism and demands for political reform in Arab societies. Chief of these is the ability to avoid the stranglehold of Arab governments on the flow of information, flagrantly exercised on "mainstream" media, enabling a mass form of "citizen journalism." In addition to evading government censorship, online media offers higher levels of anonymity and interactivity. These net activists have seized another main advantage of social networking, specifically the ability to publicize local grievances to a wider, global audience. For these activists, YouTube does not make publicizing government officials' criminal and oppressive records merely possible. YouTube preserves that record for posterity and keeps their cause alive for a longer time on the web (Stanyer& Davidson, 2009). It helps construct some sort of "historical memory" that is more accessible than traditional human rights violations archives (Block, 2001). Moreover, YouTube facilitates net activists' goal of creating some sort of "permanent" campaign to lobby global audiences for the cause of human rights in Arab societies. YouTube and the Internet have made authoritarian states' violation of international human rights norms costly in the court of world public opinion (Rosneau, 2002). So, what sort of impact have these videos had? And how do these YouTube videos illustrate the above arguments?

The YouTube Effect

No reliable opinion surveys exist to gauge the influence and impact of these YouTube videos on the cause of democratic reform and the ongoing fight against police brutality, torture and corruption. Anecdotal evidence gleaned from press accounts suggests that these YouTube videos have galvanized the public, leading to frequent copy-cats which compelled Moroccan authorities to re-assess their approaches and policies. According to Abdo (2007),

The Moroccan authorities have allegedly copied the sniper's tactics, and have dispatched their own 'video sniper teams': plainclothes policemen in anonymous cars who try to catch their corrupt colleagues red-handed.

The corrupt policemen themselves have become wary of 'citizen journalists'; Moroccan citizens report that in some regions, the gendarmes have started to scan their surroundings suspiciously looking for hidden 'video snipers.'

Police corruption and abuse became a "hot" topic for discussion among Moroccan citizens, as the press began following the video instalments exposing corruption of the gendarme (YouTube

Video 2). The person behind the video became a mystery, sometimes described as a new "Robin Hood" who had eluded police attempts to uncover his identity and arrest him. Finally, the uproar generated by these YouTube videos forced the authorities to investigate and indict the gendarmes caught red-handed taking bribes.

The videos shattered the police's sense of impunity. The videos of the gendarme and police corruption captivated the national imagination, especially their sense of cynicism. Further embarrassment and public awkwardness made the headlines as Moroccan authorities' failed attempts to apprehend the person who had secretly recorded the videos. Public pressure from Transparency International and other non-government organizations compelled the authorities to arrest and eventually try the officers involved in the corruption cases. Videos showing police brutality in Morocco's southern city (as in Video 2) have been used to counter the official narrative that the violence was an isolated case. As international rights organizations condemned the violence, the web videos finally led to a parliamentary commission that investigated the allegations of indiscriminate police brutality and abuse.

Similarly, the large political impact of the videos is apparent in Egypt. For the Egyptian government, the YouTube videos proved to be embarrassing, self-incriminating evidence of state torture. As international pressure mounted, the Egyptian government successfully prosecuted the officers involved in the torture crime. Using the YouTube video as evidence, an Egyptian court sentenced the officers to three years in prison. Human rights organizations continued to criticize Egyptian police methods, particularly their over-reliance on forced confessions as means of obtaining evidence in the criminal justice system (BBC, 2007). Sand Monkey, a well-known Egyptian blogger, captured the sense of the moment and activists' success at bringing the police to justice:

The Impossible took place today. Justice was served! The Police Officer who sodomized Emad El Kebeer by sticking a broomstick up his ass and videotaped him on his cellphone and was put on trial for it just got a sentence today: 3 years in an Egyptian prison. This, as far as I remember, is a first. A Police Officer held accountable (Global Voices Online, 2007).

Later, a rash of web videos showing Egyptian police's brutality and abuse were posted. Such videos have heralded a new found sense of empowerment among net activists, if not the wider public.

While YouTube had made possible a new breed of "citizen journalists" who exposed and shamed authoritarian states, its impact on traditional media was more palpable. In fact, news coverage widely used the videos as an excuse to expose and discuss other corrupt practices in the system. Among others, Al Jazeera television devoted several of its shows to the topic. A 2009 episode of "The Opposite Direction," a signature Al Jazeera talk show, delved into the history of torture and abuse practices in Arab prisons (August 9, 2009). Another Al Jazeera show was more specific in discussing the role of police in society, and how Arab citizens were afraid to visit police stations. Also, several Moroccan print media reports followed a similar path in investigating police corruption. That this YouTube effect has strengthened independent media in the long term is impossible to tell from available data.

The "YouTube effect" may further be gauged from the comments posted on the videos. Users' commentsoffer some insights into the "impact" of these YouTube videos on web users and net activists, particularly at the emotional level. Outrage, embarrassment, and shame remain dominant and common feelings across users' comments and reactions posted on the videos' pages. Combing these reactions, outright calls for violent retribution mingle with reasoned, thoughtful political analysis. In reacting to the video showing police abuse (Video 4), some users go as far as issue death threats, as the "GazaNewsChannel" user's post put it: "Kill Husni Mubarak!!!" Other users seek to place the abuse Video 3 shows within the geopolitical context of the Egyptian's regime relationship with the U.S., as "AfroCanadian89" user explains:

There is a place for men like Husni Mubarak. Its [sic] six feet under the soil and eventually the hell fire that awaits him.

……

America gives Husni Mubarak the leader of Egypt at this moment. They give him 3.2 billion dollars a year. If America truly was out to spread freedom. Ask yourself why they support such a man and his oppressive reign.

A similar mix of responses is found in reactions to videos showing Moroccan police corruption and abuse (Video 1&2). In Arabic, a user by the name "aufir" twists a police motto in a sarcastic, rhetorical question: "Who says the police aren't in the service of the people?" Sarcastic comments and insults pepper reactions to the police officers who were shown taking bribes from motorists in Video 1, praising the self-described "sniper" who posted the videos on YouTube. In very rare instances criticism of the "sniper" is found. One such instance is found in the angry reaction of a poster who identified him/herself as a police officer, heaping slurs and threats at the "sniper." User comments on Video 2, in which Moroccan police officers violently arrest and abuse protesters, were rarely in disagreement that police brutality was a shameful act "…against humanity," as a YouTube user, "DaBulldog4LYF," puts it.

Global Audiences

As YouTube videos go viral, the potential of reaching a global audience, or an audience spread over different continents, has become real. In publicizing police abuse and brutality in Arab countries, the videos in this analysis actively seek this global audience and prominence. YouTube statistics provide some clues about how global audiences and the geographical popularity of the uploaded videos. Of these YouTube videos, the third video about Egyptian police brutality and torture of ordinary citizens gained the greatest global coverage. Uploaded on September 14, 2006, "Police Torture in Egypt" video has achieved unparalleled levels of popularity in four different continents. As the YouTube statistics map (Figure 1) indicates, the video has been very popular in Egypt, portrayed by the darkest shade of green on the African continent. The United States and the United Kingdom represent the second most popular area the video receives. Following Pakistan in popularity are Canada, Australia, Western Europe (Spain and France) and North Africa (Morocco and Algeria).

Within this sprawling reach, the video raises very little interest in other Arab countries, with the notable exceptions of Algeria and Morocco where its popularity still ranks well below Pakistan, Australia, Canada, the UK and the US. The largest number of hits the video receives comes from Egypt. This can be explained by the fact that Egyptian activists and ordinary citizens with access to the Internet are more concerned with Egyptian police brutality than other nations. The video is thus more likely to generate a buzz more among Egyptians than abroad. The video generates a similar buzz in countries that host a large Egyptian expatriate community, a possible reason for the popularity of the video in the US, UK, Canada, and Australia. An additional reason for the global popularity of the video outside Egypt can be due to human rights and net activists' interest in the issue. The latter reason explains the video's popularity in Morocco and Algeria, with many young people accessing the web to voice their dissent. While Arab countries in the Gulf also host a significant Egyptian migrant workers community, those countries did not generate the

Figure 1. "Police Torture in Egypt" video: YouTube video popularity by country

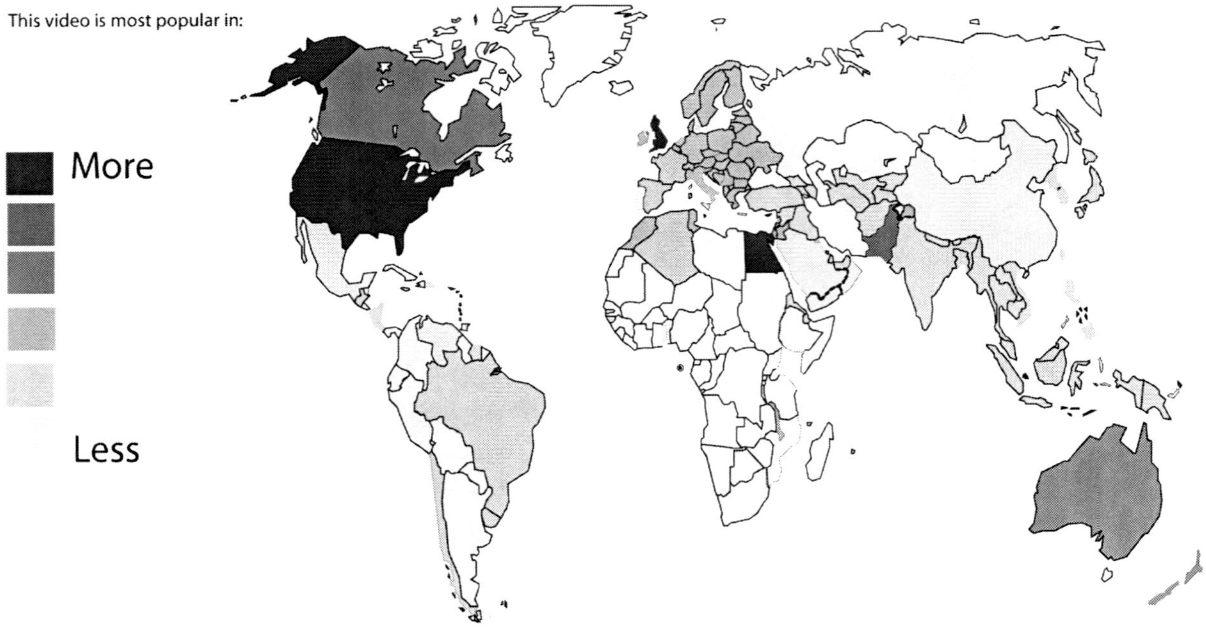

same buzz. Media and public salience of the video might have helped raise awareness of the issue as well. If rising education and Internet access issues are considered, a combination of these reasons should be used to understand the popularity of the videos however.

Publishing on YouTube does not guarantee instant global audiences and popularity. Uploaded in July 2007, the "Gendarme" YouTube video shows two Moroccan patrol officers taking bribes from motorists on the highway. Despite reaching more than half a million views, the video exposing Moroccan police force corruption did not raise the same interest globally. The YouTube statistical map (Figure 2) reveals that the video gained most popularity in Morocco, with Algeria and some parts of Western Europe showing some interest in the video as well. Rather than being globally widespread, the attention this YouTube video gained is rather regional. In addition to geographical proximity, the presence of a large Moroccan expatriate community in Western Europe explains this popularity. Even the argument that this video does not cover something as explosive as police abuse in the Egyptian YouTube video case does not sufficiently justify this discrepancy in global attention. Similarly, the other video exposing Moroccan police brutality against demonstrators gained much popularity only in Morocco.

The "Permanent" Campaign

In exposing police corruption and brutality, these videos do more than just create an audio-visual record of potential crimes and infringements of human rights (Block, 2001). They usher what can be termed as a "permanent" campaign to fight government abuse in their countries. As long as YouTube keeps hosting those videos, local and global activists have access to this "permanent" record. The record of police corruption, brutality, and abuse can be used to lobby international organizations and mobilize local public opinion. Unlike traditional mass media's short-lived memory, YouTube videos could become global sensations for a longer period. For instance, while

Figure 2. "Moroccan Police Corruption" video: YouTube video popularity by country

media coverage of the Iraqi journalist throwing his shoes at former US President George W. Bush has long receded from the airwaves (Douai, 2009), a mouse click retrieves the video from YouTube and the web at large.

The availability of this long record has the unprecedented advantage of keeping the causes of these cyber activists alive longer than before (Stanyer& Davidson, 2009). Examining YouTube statistics for these selected videos (Figure 3 "Egypt", and Figure 4 "Gendarme") shows that the popularity of these videos on YouTube as indicated by view counts accumulates gradually. In fact, Figure 3 illustrates clearly that viewer counts of the YouTube video on Egyptian police torture hit their highest approximately two years (2008) after the original video was uploaded (2006). By 2008, viewer counts more than tripled, reaching almost 60, 000. Figure 4 tells a similar story about the YouTube video exposing Moroccan police brutality. While this video was uploaded in 2008, it reached 20 thousand views in 2009 and about 80 thousand in 2010. The gradual accumulation of viewer counts and YouTube popularity of these videos manifest levels of influence and penetration markedly different from traditional mass media.

In addition to the "permanence" of human rights violations' records, the "permanent" cam-

Figure 3. "Police Torture in Egypt" video: Total views between 09/13/2006 – 06/23/2010

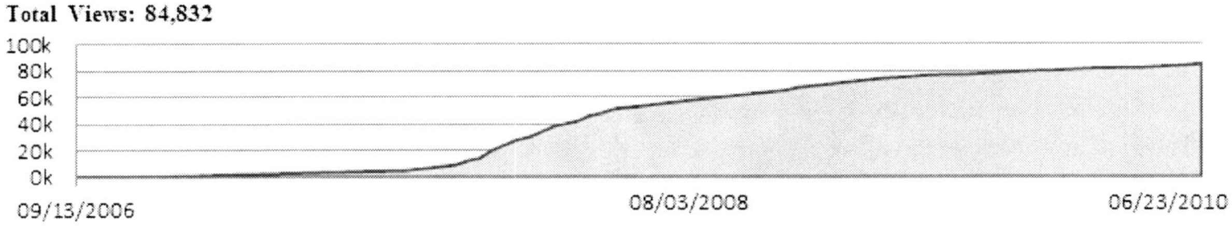

Figure 4. "Moroccan Police Corruption" video: Total views between 08/21/2008 – 06/23/2010

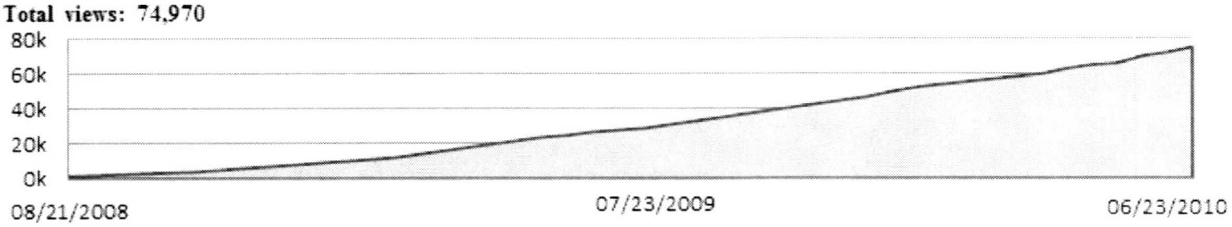

paigning mode also refers to "long-running communication campaigns to organize protests and publicize issues" (Bennet, 2003, p. 150). This brand of global activism is not actually new, but these Internet campaigns are more likely to be "protracted" and sustained. Further, they lack a hierarchical structure with centralized command and control to coordinate their activities. As Bennet (2003, p.150) describes them:

They are less likely to be run by central command and coordinating organizations such as unions or environmental NGOs, making them less centrally controlled, and more difficult to turn on and off. The networking and mobilizing capacities of these ongoing campaigns makes campaigns, themselves, political organizations that sustain activist networks in the absence of leadership by central organizations.

In facilitating this mode of campaigning, authoritarian states have to reckon with the challenge of having their violations of human rights being under a constant, global microscope. As international human rights organizations are likely to pick up evidence of abuse from YouTube and the Internet (Stanyer& Davidson, 2009), the ever-present threat of sanctions and denunciations may serve as an outside pressure mechanism that pushes for more respect of international human rights norms. As effective "technologies of freedom," YouTube and the Internet have a real potential to work as a deterring force in these global human rights campaigns.

CONCLUSION

Rosneau (2003) argued that the twin forces of globalization of communication technologies mean that "the misdeeds of human rights violators no longer pass from human kind's conscience" (2002, p. 149). This chapter's focus on YouTube videos in publicizing police abuse, corruption, and other human rights violations in Egypt and Morocco illuminates how those "misdeeds" are publicized. Summarily put, the YouTube effects include 1) bringing awareness of human rights violations to a greater audience from several Arab countries, 2) providing evidence that human rights organizations can use to demand accountability and more respect for international norms, and 3) changing in authoritarian regimes' behavior through prosecution of perpetrators. While the four YouTube videos do not constitute enough data to draw sweeping generalizations, the observations and insights gained from this analysis are in synch with similar research studies of the Internet and human rights campaigns (e.g. Stanyer& Davidson, 2009).

In scrutinizing the role of new media in the campaign for human rights, I do not seek to ascribe extraordinary or transformational powers to YouTube. Instead, this article underscores two strategic roles YouTube has played in the struggle for democracy and political reform in the Arab world. First, drawing global attention to the oppressive practices of Arab regimes has energized (cyber)activists' demands for political reform and respect for international norms. For these activists,

YouTube's repository and exchange capabilities provide audio-visual evidence for the excesses of the state. The more shocking the video evidence is, the louder the public and global outcry against those excesses will be. Also, the "permanent campaign" implies that the more "permanent" the record is, the more salient and constant the fight becomes. Permanent campaigning means constant surveillance of authoritarian's violations. Internationalization of human rights abuses builds on a well-proven record of transnational solidarity movements, similar to the movements behind publicizing human rights abuses in Latin America (Keck &Sikkink, 1998). In their campaign, these "activists without borders" are wielding cameras and low tech skills whether they post amateurish videos showing police abuse or they construct highly edited videos.

The second strategic role of YouTube and the Internet lies in invigorating "public arguments," strengthening the public concern and debate regarding human rights issues. As viewers' comments illustrate in the YouTube videos selected for this study, citizens decry the heavy handedness of the state apparatus in dealing with protests. YouTube videos elevate the discussion to the public agenda making it more salient and widely available. It is this public salience that encourages independent voices from mainstream media to cover human rights abuses, as the Committee to Protect Journalists observed in 2009. That is why mainstream media and journalists in Egypt, Morocco, Bahrain, and elsewhere in the Arab world used existing YouTube videos as a political cover and excuse to publicly debate and expose police corruption and human rights abuse in their countries. Mainstreaming media coverage and public debate of human rights abuses becomes indeed a strategic milestone in the fight for democratic reform in Arab societies.

NOTE

Due to the low resolution quality of YouTube generated figures, the author has reproduced the YouTube statistics in this chapter for printing purposes. While the figures' data approximate YouTube's own data, the author has kept the original figures and can share these with interested readers upon their request.

REFERENCES

Abdo, L. (2007, November 12). *Morocco's 'video sniper' sparks a new trend.* Mennassat.com. Retrieved October 30, 2009, from http://www.menassat.com/?q=en/news-articles/2107-moroccos-video-sniper-sparks-new-trend

Al-Malky, R. (2007). Blogging for reform: The case of Egypt. *Arab Media and Society, 1*. Retrieved May 10, 2009, from http://www.arabmediasociety.com/articles/downloads/20070312143716_AMS1_Rania_Al_Malky.pdf

Anderson, K. (2007, January 12). YouTube exposes torture in Egypt. *The Guardian*. Retrieved June 5, 2010, from http://www.guardian.co.uk/news/blog/2007/jan/12/youtubeexposes1

Azimi, N. (2007, February 19). Blogging against torture. *The Nation*. Retrieved June 12, 2010, from http://www.thenation.com/article/bloggers-against-torture?page=0,2

Bagdikian, B. H. (1992). *The media monopoly*. Boston, MA: Beacon Press.

Bennett, W. L. (2003). Communicating global activism: Strengths and vulnerabilities of networked politics. *Information Communication and Society*, *6*(2), 143–168. doi:10.1080/1369118032000093860a

Block, D. (2001). *Broadcast and archive: Human rights documentation in the early digital age*. A paper presented at the Florida State University Conference on Human Rights, November, 1-3.

British Broadcasting Corporation (BBC). (2007, January 10). *"Torture" victim jailed in Egypt*. Retrieved July 5, 2010, from http://news.bbc.co.uk/2/hi/6249027.stm

Brophy, P., & Halpin, E. (1999). Through the net to freedom: Information, the Internet and human rights. *Journal of Information Science*, *25*(5), 351–364. doi:10.1177/016555159902500502

Burgess, J., & Green, J. (2009). *YouTube: Online video and participatory culture*. Cambridge, UK: Polity Press.

Dayem, M. A., & Mahoney, R. (2010, February 16). *Human rights coverage spreads, despite government pushback*. The Committee to Protect Journalists, February 16, 2010. Retrieved June 10, 2010, from http://cpj.org/2010/02/human-rights-coverage-spreads.php

Douai, A. (2009). Offline politics in the Arab blogosphere: Trends and prospects in Morocco. In Russell, A., & Echchaibi, N. (Eds.), *International blogging: Identity, politics, and networked publics*. New York, NY: Peter Lang.

Driscoll, M. (2007). Comment: Will YouTube sail into the DMCA's safe harbor or sink for Internet piracy? *The John Marshall Review of Intellectual Property Law*, 550. Retrieved June 2, 2010, from http://www.jmripl.com/Publications/Vol6/Issue3/Driscoll.pdf

El-Naggar, M. (2010, June 25). Beating death in Egypt ignites protests over police brutality. *McClatchy Newspapers*. Retrieved June 30, 2010, from http://www.mcclatchydc.com/2010/06/25/96572/beating-death-in-egypt-ignites.html

Global Voices Online. (2007, November 6). Egypt: Final chapter of a torture case. *Global Voices Online*. Retrieved June 2, 2010, from http://globalvoicesonline.org/2007/11/06/egypt-final-chapter-of-a-torture-case/

Hick, S., Halpin, E. F., & Hoskins, E. (Eds.). (2000). *Human rights and Internet*. Basingstoke, UK: Macmillan.

Human Rights Watch (HRW). (2006, December 22). *Egypt: Hold police accountable for torture*. Human Rights Watch. Retrieved May 12, 2010 from http://www.hrw.org/english/docs/2006/12/23/egypt14924.htm

Human Rights Watch (HRW). (2010, January 24). *World report 2010: Abusers target human rights messengers*. Human Rights Watch. Retrieved August 12, 2010, from http://www.hrw.org/en/news/2010/01/24/world-report-2010-abusers-target-human-rights-messengers

Ibahrine, M. (2008). Mobile communication and sociopolitical change in the Arab world. In Katz, J. (Ed.), *Handbook of mobile communication studies*. Cambridge, MA: The MIT Press.

Kalathil, S., & Boas, T. (2003). Open networks, closed regimes: The impact of the Internet on authoritarian rule. *First Monday*, *8*(1). Retrieved May 12, 2010, from http://firstmonday.org/htbin/cgiwrap/bin/ojs/index.php/fm/article/view/1027/948

Keck, M. E., & Sikkink, K. (1998). *Activists beyond borders: Advocacy networks in international politics*. Ithaca, NY: Cornell University Press.

Lynch, M. (2007). Blogging the new Arab public. *Arab Media & Society*, *1*, 1–30. Retrieved May 10, 2009, from http://www.arabmediasociety.com/?article=10

McLaughlin, S. M. (2003). The use of the Internet for political action by non-state dissident actors in the Middle East. *First Monday, 8*(11). Retrieved October 10, 2009, from http://131.193.153.231/www/issues/issue8_11/mclaughlin/index.html

Metzl, J. F. (1996). Information technology and human rights. *Human Rights Quarterly, 18*(4), 705–746. doi:10.1353/hrq.1996.0045

Paul, I. (2010, May 6). Facebook privacy complaint: A complete breakdown. *PC World*. Retrieved June 10, 2010, from http://www.pcworld.com/article/195756/facebook_privacy_complaint_a_complete_breakdown.html

Pintak, L. (2008). *The role of the media as watch-dogs, agenda-setters and gatekeepers in Arab states*. Paper presented in "The Role of the News Media in the Governance Reform Agenda," Harvard-World Bank Workshop, 29-31st May 2008. Retrieved May 5, 2010, from http://www.hks.harvard.edu/fs/pnorris/Conference/Conference%20papers/Pintak%20Arab%20Media.pdf

Ron, J., Ramos, H., & Rodgers, K. (2005). Transnational information politics: NGO human rights reporting, 1986–2000. *International Studies Quarterly, 49*(3), 557–588. doi:10.1111/j.1468-2478.2005.00377.x

Rosneau, J. M. (2002). The drama of human rights in a turbulent, globalized world. In Brysk, A. (Ed.), *Globalization and human rights*. Berkley, CA: University of California Press.

Seib, P. (Ed.). (2007). *New media and the new Middle East*. New York, NY: Palgrave Macmillan. doi:10.1057/9780230605602

Stanyer, J., & Davidson, S. (2009). *The Internet and the visibility of oppression in non-democratic states: The online exposure of human rights violations and other repressive acts*. Paper prepared for the 2009 Annual Meeting of the International Communication Association Conference, Chicago, IL, May 20-25, 2009.

Transparency Maroc. (2009). *Revue de presseh-ebdomadaire n°56. Transparency Maroc: Observatoire de la Corruption*, January 2009. Retrieved June 10, 2010, from http://transparencymaroc.ma/uploads/revue/42.pdf

Urquhart, C. (2007, March 4).Why torture is routine in Egypt. *The Toronto Star*. Retrieved July 5, 2010, from http://www.thestar.com/news/article/188036

van Zoonen, L., Vis, F., & Mihelj, S. (2010). Performing citizenship on YouTube: Activism, satire and online debate around the anti-Islam video *Fitna*. *Critical Discourse Studies, 7*(4), 249–262. doi:10.1080/17405904.2010.511831

Weyker, S. (2002). The ironies of information technology. In Brysk, A. (Ed.), *Globalization and human rights*. Berkley, CA: University of California Press.

Ziraoui, Y., & Alaoui, M. S. (2009, October 14). Sur la piste du sniper de Targuist. *TelQuel*. Retrieved June 12, 2010, from http://www.telquel-online.com/292/couverture_292.shtml

Chapter 5
Truth-Seeking at a Distance:
Engaging Diaspora Populations in Transitional Justice Processes

Eric Wiebelhaus-Brahm
Florida State University, USA

ABSTRACT

The Liberian Truth and Reconciliation Commission (LTRC) was established by the Liberian government in 2005 to "promote national peace, security, unity, and reconciliation." The LTRC thought it essential to allow Liberians who had fled the conflict to participate in the truth and reconciliation process. As a result, it partnered with a US-based non-governmental organization, The Advocates for Human Rights, to conduct the Diaspora Project. This chapter provides an overview of the Diaspora Project, which enabled Liberians on three continents to give statements to the LTRC. Given the wide dispersion of the Liberian diaspora, the author of this chapter demonstrates how information communication technologies were essential in the success of the Diaspora Project.

INTRODUCTION

The Liberian Truth and Reconciliation Commission (LTRC) Diaspora Project was a path-breaking attempt to consciously incorporate a diaspora community into a transitional justice process. Diaspora populations had contributed to some previous truth commission investigations, but earlier commissions had not made concerted systematic efforts to engage diasporas in their truth-seeking exercise. With displacement such a common feature of the Liberian conflict, the LTRC deemed it essential to involve the diaspora in its work. Hundreds of thousands of Liberians had fled the country during

DOI: 10.4018/978-1-4666-1918-0.ch005

the country's fourteen-year civil war.[1] Through a partnership with The Advocates for Human Rights (The Advocates), a Minneapolis, Minnesota, USA-based non-government organization, the Diaspora Project was undertaken. Over a three-year period between mid-2006 and mid-2009, the Diaspora Project collected statements from over 1,600 Liberians in the United States, the United Kingdom, and at the Buduburam refugee camp in Ghana. Information communication technologies were instrumental in making this possible.

This chapter examines the role of information communication technologies in giving Liberians around the world an opportunity to contribute to their native country's reconciliation process. I begin by providing an overview of Liberia's civil war and the decision to establish the LTRC to address the numerous human rights violations that occurred during the conflict. After providing a brief overview of the LTRC and its relationship with other truth commissions around the world, I examine the Diaspora Project and its attempts to incorporate Liberians in the United States and elsewhere into the truth and reconciliation process. I focus in particular on how information communication technologies enabled the Diaspora Project to train volunteers, raise awareness and collect statements from the far-flung Liberian population. I conclude by offering suggestions on how future truth commissions can learn from Liberia's experiment in engaging its diaspora.

THE ORIGINS OF THE DIASPORA PROJECT

The LTRC was established to examine fourteen years of Liberian history, from 1979 to 2003, that were characterized by violence and brutality. Although more proximate causes were important, the origins of the conflict can be traced back to the origins of Liberia itself. Returned slaves and free African Americans founded the country in the early 1800s. This group, known as Americo-Liberians, economically and politically dominated the indigenous populations who were living in the area since Liberia's founding. Although tensions existed for much of Liberia's history, they reached their peak in the 1970s as Liberians became increasingly desperate in the face of a deteriorating economy. In 1979, Rice Riots broke out in Monrovia, Liberia's capital, when rumors spread that President William Tolbert was going to raise the price of rice to feather his own pocket. Events culminated in the 1980 military coup, which resulted in the murder of President Tolbert and brought army master sergeant Samuel Doe to power. Thirteen government ministers were summarily executed shortly afterward.

Doe ruled Liberia for the next decade, a period in which government brutality escalated. Doe's regime was known for murdering, imprisoning, and suppressing opposition (The Advocates for Human Rights, 2009: 9-10). Other groups in Liberia perceived the government's policies as favoring Doe's own tribe, the Krahn, and the Mandingo, which created further tensions. Unsurprisingly, an anti-government resistance soon emerged. Thomas Quiwonkpa led a failed coup against Doe in 1985. Four years later, Charles Taylor's National Patriotic Front of Liberia (NPFL) invaded from Côte d'Ivoire. When the conflict began in December 1989, many Liberians initially saw Taylor as a savior. However, Taylor set off a period of civil war that lasted for more than a decade and embroiled the entire West African region.

Historians often distinguish the First Liberian Civil War (1989-1997) and the Second Liberian Civil War (1997-2003). After Doe made tribe a salient division in Liberia, subsequent fighting occurred largely along tribal lines. Although Taylor was himself Americo-Liberian, he played upon tribal tensions, particularly feelings of victimization among the Gio-Mano. The NPFL fought its way across the country to surround Monrovia. As the NPFL disintegrated and other groups formed to resist it, the fighting dissolved into a chaotic contest among several warring factions, all fighting for control of the government and exploitable natural resources. Fighters on all sides committed widespread violations of international humanitarian and human rights law. The Economic Community of West African States (ECOWAS) first intervened in the conflict in 1990. Eventually, it was able to broker a ceasefire in 1996 that permitted elections in 1997. Charles Taylor, who employed threats and intimidation during the campaign, won the election. After only a brief respite, continued government brutality quickly led to a resumption of the civil war. Finally, the parties returned to the negotiating table in 2003 following more decisive intervention by the international community, including ECOWAS and the United States.

Over the period from 1979 to 2003, the human scale of the conflict was terrible. The Diaspora Project's final report estimates that one in twelve Liberians were killed in the conflict (The Advocates for Human Rights, 2009: 3). Furthermore, the fighting displaced approximately half of Liberia's pre-war population of three million. The war provided opportunities for looting and mayhem in which countless Liberians engaged (Ellis, 2006: 110-149). Of the Liberians displaced by the conflict, tens of thousands fled the country to other West African countries; many refugees were uprooted multiple times as instability spread across the region. Given Liberia's historical ties to the United States, it was a popular destination for the Liberians who were able to flee West Africa. Although estimates of the size of the Liberian population in the United States vary widely from the tens of thousands to a half million (Steinberg, 2010b: 7; Young and Park, 2009: 342-343), the numbers grew dramatically as a direct result of the conflict. As illustrated by Figure 1, the United States was the destination of the largest number of Liberian refugees after neighboring West African countries.

LIBERIAN TRUTH AND RECONCILIATION COMMISSION AS A FORM OF TRANSITIONAL JUSTICE

Since the early 1980s, more than two dozen countries have established truth commissions in an attempt to transition from periods of violence and repression.

A truth commission (1) is focused on past, rather than ongoing, events; (2) investigates a pattern of events that took place over a period of time; (3) engages directly and broadly with the affected population, gathering information on their experiences; (4) is a temporary body, with the aim of concluding with a final report; and (5) is officially authorized or empowered by the state under review. (Hayner, 2011: 11-12)

Truth commissions may be established by executive order or an act of parliament; they may have been agreed to in a peace accord. They are intended to produce an authoritative history of a period in which widespread human rights violations occurred. The experience of telling one's story and having one's suffering acknowledged by an official body can be empowering for victims, especially given that human rights abuses were often officially denied in the past. Investigations also may uncover information regarding the fate of loved ones. Truth commission final reports summarize the investigation's findings regarding past human rights abuses and put forward recommendations that are designed to provide further redress, such as reparations, and to promote reforms that will make human rights abuses less likely in the future. As such, victims may gain several potential benefits from participation.

The LTRC's origins are in the peace accord that ended the fighting in Liberia. The August 2003 Accra Comprehensive Peace Agreement included provision for the LTRC. Warring factions dominated the peace talks. Despite the fact that

Figure 1. Total number of Liberian refugees (1988-2003). Source: United Nations High Commissioner for Refugees.*

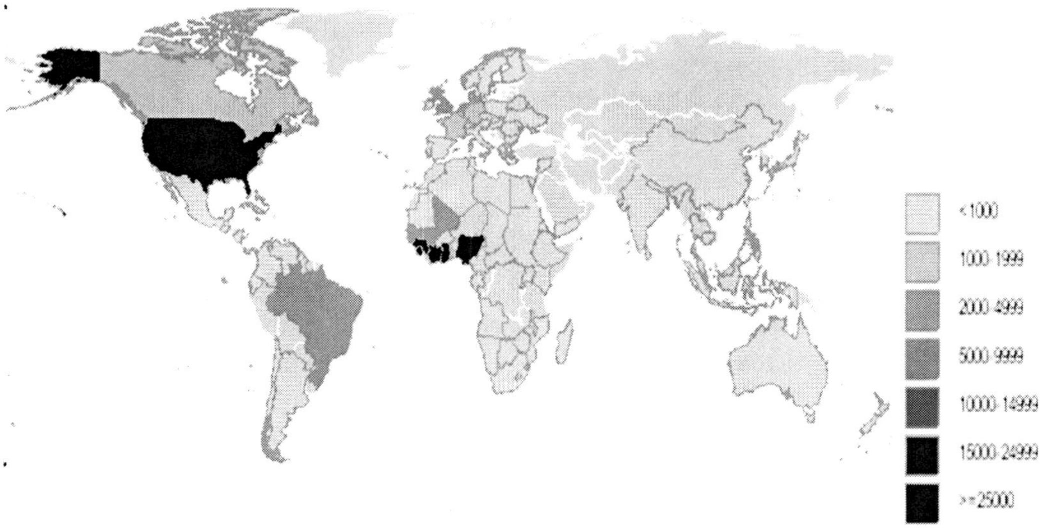

* Earliest data available.

Taylor resigned the presidency and went into exile in Nigeria after the Special Court for Sierra Leone indicted him during the talks, other faction leaders appear to have had little fear that transitional justice would affect them or their future political and economic prospects. As Steinberg (2010a: 138) describes the talks, "[i]n the parlance that developed between negotiators, 'truth commission' was considered shorthand for 'amnesty', or, at any rate, for '*not* a tribunal'." (emphasis in original) There was an assumption of amnesty, but, because no one wanted to raise the issue of human rights abuses and draw the attention of civil society groups, the Accra accord did not contain a formal amnesty (Hayner, 2007: 16; Steinberg, 2010a: 138). As a result, a truth commission became the mode of transitional justice seemingly by accident. Further negotiations took place for more than a year on the structure of the commission before the Truth and Reconciliation Commission Act was approved by the Liberian Transitional Legislative Assembly in 2005. The Act mandated the LTRC to 1) investigate gross human rights violations that occurred between January 1979 and October 2003 and their causes; 2) collect statements privately and in public hearings; 3) identify individuals and organizations involved in human rights violations; 4) restore the human dignity of victims and promote reconciliation by allowing victims and perpetrators to tell their stories; and 5) produce a report summarizing the LTRC's findings and outlining recommendations for measures to provide further redress and to prevent future human rights abuses.

Given the centrality of displacement to Liberians' experiences during the civil war, the LTRC believed it was critical to include refugees in the truth-seeking process. Earlier truth commissions had not systematically sought the involvement of diaspora populations. Although a few Latin American truth commissions had accepted statements at the country's embassies abroad, this required significant affirmative action on the part of would-be statement-givers. The LTRC Diaspora Project argued that participation had several potential benefits for participants and for Liberia (Young and Park, 2009: 349-360). First, given the large number of Liberians who had fled the country, the LTRC could produce a more complete picture of the conflict by reaching out to the diaspora. Second, the diaspora was accused of fueling the conflict. Moreover, some perpetrators were known to be living in the diaspora community. At the same time, neither the LTRC nor the Diaspora Project did much to cajole the participation of alleged perpetrators (Steinberg, 2010b: 8). Third, many Liberians in the diaspora were victims of human rights abuses. It was morally appropriate to treat them in the same manner as victims who remained in Liberia. Finally, the LTRC hoped that engaging the diaspora would encourage individuals to contribute to Liberia's rebuilding process.

INFORMATION COMMUNICATION TECHNOLOGIES AND THE DIASPORA PROJECT

The Advocates for Human Rights and the Origins of the Diaspora Project

The LTRC asked The Advocates to coordinate its work among the diaspora. For more than 25 years, The Advocates has worked on social justice issues. It conducts research and advocacy on behalf of refugees, minorities, women, children, and other marginalized populations. Headquartered in Minneapolis, Minnesota, it has worked on human rights and rule of law promotion projects across the United States and in countries around the world.

In many respects, the organization was ideally suited for the Diaspora Project (The Advocates for Human Rights, 2009: 36). The organization has provided pro bono legal services to Liberian asylum seekers for decades. The Advocates are based in Minnesota, the US state with the largest Liberian population. Some estimates put Minnesota's Liberian population at upwards of 30,000. As such, it has intimate knowledge of the Liberian diaspora's experience and needs. Furthermore, The Advocates had experience with this form of transitional justice from working with earlier truth commissions in Peru and Sierra Leone. The Advocates' long history of human rights work enabled it to tap into an extensive network of partners, without which the Diaspora Project would not have been possible. In total, the Diaspora Project estimates that volunteers donated more than USD 10 million in in-kind services and pro bono hours to its work (The Advocates for Human Rights, 2009: 4).

Although the Diaspora Project formally began its work in January 2007, the groundwork was being laid several months earlier. Liberians in the diaspora provided input on the Diaspora Project by serving on a national advisory committee and by volunteering. Outreach and volunteer training began in Minnesota as early as mid-2006. Liberians in Minnesota tend to live in dense concentrations so going door-to-door to raise awareness was an effective strategy. However, throughout the year, organized statement-taking expanded to Atlanta, Chicago, New York, Newark, Philadelphia, Providence, and Washington DC where there were significant Liberian populations. Eventually, through the efforts of The Advocates, the opportunity to participate in the truth commission process was extended to Liberians in the United Kingdom and at the Buduburam refugee settlement in Ghana. For reasons related to either the capacity of the LTRC and The Advocates or a lack of demand from Liberians elsewhere, the Diaspora Project was not extended to Liberians who had fled elsewhere.

As opportunities for participation expanded to encompass a growing swath of the diaspora, information communication technologies played an increasingly important role. First, technology was important in raising awareness of the LTRC's work in the diaspora. The Diaspora Project's outreach efforts endeavored to explain and demystify the truth commission process. By explaining the LTRC and its goals, the Diaspora

Project hoped to encourage participation among the diaspora. Information communication technologies also allowed the diaspora to stay abreast of the LTRC's activities in Liberia and among the diaspora. Second, technology was instrumental in collecting statements. Information communication technologies enabled the Diaspora Project to train a widely disbursed group of volunteers. Over the Diaspora Project's lifetime, over 800 individuals donated their time to the effort (Young and Park, 2009: 344). Furthermore, technology made it possible for the LTRC to collect statements that had been taken from Liberians around the world in one centralized location.

Outreach

Once the Diaspora Project's work expanded beyond Minnesota, face-to-face outreach was more challenging. Volunteers conducted door-to-door outreach in some cities. Several cities held launch events that included food and cultural performances to raise awareness. In many other municipal areas, however, Liberians do not live in as dense concentrations (or in as large of numbers).[2] The Diaspora Project also wanted to ensure Liberians who did not live in the handful of major cities where organized LTRC activities would take place were aware of their work and had the opportunity to contribute to the process. Given the relatively small, widely dispersed nature of the United States' Liberian population, engaging national media was not feasible. Nonetheless, local media in several cities where the Diaspora Project conducted organized statement-taking, including outlets with a national profile like *The New York Times*, did provide some coverage. On its own, however, this coverage was not sufficiently consistent or targeted to suit the LTRC's outreach needs. In the end, the Diaspora Project developed several innovative strategies, all of which were approved by the LTRC prior to their use, which were designed to raise awareness among the diaspora.

To reach the far-flung diaspora, many outreach strategies made extensive use of information communication technologies. For example, the Diaspora Project produced a video entitled *A Quest for Justice* that explained the statement-taking process and encouraged participation. The Advocates made the video available on YouTube in July 2007. As of February 2011, it had logged over 7,900 views.[3] The Advocates also created an electronic brochure to explain the process.[4]In addition, The Advocates employed online messaging and developed PowerPoint presentations, videos of Commissioners, and the TRC Peace Song among other things to raise awareness.[5]Furthermore, the Diaspora Project's *pro bono* partners set up and staffed toll-free telephone numbers to provide Liberians with information about the LTRC and the Diaspora Project and to arrange appointments to give a statement.

The LTRC also worked with a team at the Georgia Institute of Technology (Georgia Tech) to harness the benefits of information communication technologies. The centerpiece of the strategy was the LTRC's website (www.trcofliberia.org). Current World Bank data estimate less than 1% of Liberians are Internet users and nearly 40% are illiterate (Pelsinger, 2010: 745). Given the low levels of Internet access in Liberia, the Georgia Tech-designed website was largely geared toward the diaspora. The Georgia Tech team designed the site in collaboration with Liberians in the diaspora; the final product was the result of a series of focus groups involving members of Atlanta's Liberian community, LTRC representatives, and Liberian government officials. The nature of the diaspora facilitated a stronger final product; "feedback from longer-time residents of the U.S. included suggestions for site features such as multimedia galleries, while more recent immigrants were less tech savvy, but could offer more accurate advice on cultural considerations" (Best et al., 2009: 12). The website provides basic information on the LTRC, including its legal mandate, profiles of the commissioners, quarterly reports, the LTRC and Diaspora Project's final reports, and other documents on the commission's functioning. The focus groups were instrumental in producing a website that employs multimedia and focuses on themes of reconciliation and national unity. The website is innovative for providing a platform that was able to accept formal sealed statements and amnesty applications on behalf of the LTRC. It did so using 2048 bit encryption. In addition, the website provides LTRC news, a venue for user-generated audio and video storybooks, and live and archived video of LTRC and Diaspora Project public hearings (over 600 videos from public hearings in total). Georgia Tech's focus groups also expressed a desire to use the website's multimedia capabilities to produce virtual memorials to the conflict (Best et al., 2009: 6). According to LTRC Chairman Jerome J. Verdier, videos were included on the LTRC's website in a conscious effort to engage Liberians all around the world in the truth commission process (Balancing Act, 2008).

During the week of June 9-14, 2008, the Diaspora Project held public hearings at Hamline University in St. Paul, Minnesota, USA. This marked the first time that a foreign truth commission had conducted a public hearing in the United States. All of the LTRC Commissioners came to Minnesota for the event. During the week, the Commissioners heard from 29 witnesses from ten US states. The witnesses told of their experiences in Liberia that led them to leave the country, during their displacement, and since their resettlement in the United States. Liberians anywhere could watch the proceedings online; the content of the hearings remains available on the LTRC's website.[6]

The LTRC's website has succeeded in attracting visitors. As of early 2009, the website was receiving several hundred unique visitors each day (Best et al., 2009: 14). According to the LTRC, during the commission's existence, an average of over 3,700 visitors per month came to the site and averaged more than six page views per visit (The Truth and Reconciliation Commission of Liberia, 2009: 91). Given the low Internet penetration in Liberia, the vast majority of the traffic on the LTRC's website has been from outside the country. As of the LTRC final report's publication in mid-2009, the majority of visitors were in the United States, followed by the United Kingdom, Canada, the Netherlands, Spain, Sweden, Belgium, and Lebanon. It is impossible to determine what proportion of visitors were members of the Liberian diaspora and what proportion were non-Liberian academics or activists. Videos of LTRC public hearings were the most popular pages on the LTRC's website.

In some respects, information communication technologies also served as an impediment to the Diaspora Project's outreach efforts. Liberians in the diaspora make significant use of listservs, blogs, and online news media to stay connected with each other and events in Liberia. The LTRC was a popular topic of discussion in the Liberian diaspora's corner of cyberspace. The Diaspora Project attempted to engage these outlets to inform Liberians in the diaspora of their opportunity to participate. However, online sentiment toward the LTRC was generally negative (Minikon and Shepler, 2009: 150). As such, volunteers had to confront this obstacle in trying to generate interest in the Diaspora Project's work and to encourage Liberians to give statements regarding their experiences during the conflict.

Perceptions of the Diaspora Project also were inevitably tied to perceptions of the LTRC's activities in Liberia. Throughout its existence, the LTRC struggled with its ambiguous position in Liberia (Steinberg, 2010b: 4-5). The Act establishing the LTRC gave it more significant powers than the warlords who had negotiated the Accra accords had anticipated. Many of those at the negotiating table were now politicians or civil servants; most were openly dismissive of the LTRC. It did not help that the LTRC's Commissioners did not have high profiles within Liberia. In this ambiguous position, commissioners disagreed on how to conduct the investigation. Liberians in the diaspora were keenly aware of the LTRC's actions and the reactions to it within Liberia. As the Diaspora Project's final report highlights, "the TRC's decision not to call major perpetrators to public hearings until late in the process, the reluctance of key actos, including the president, to appear before the TRC, and media coverage of internal conflicts at the TRC all had dampening effects on participation in the diaspora." (The Advocates for Human Rights, 2009: 39) Given that the Diaspora Project was inevitably tied to the LTRC, the weaknesses of the latter were tied to the former in the minds of many Liberians in the diaspora.

Statement-Taking

Not only did the Diaspora Project need to reach tens of thousands of Liberians spread across the globe, but it also had to train volunteers to take their statements. The Diaspora Project's *pro bono* affiliates provided space for in-person training and produced DVDs and print versions of training materials. However, information communication technologies allowed volunteers to train from virtually anywhere. With the help of volunteers, The Advocates produced a series of training videos and an approximately 400-page training manual.[7] The training materials provided volunteers with a comprehensive overview of the Liberian conflict, the LTRC, and the statement-taking process. Specifically, they "received training on the mandate of the [L]TRC, the history of Liberia and the conflict, international human rights and humanitarian law, statement taking protocols and policies, interviewing survivors of torture and war trauma, avoiding vicarious trauma, and cultural considerations for working with Liberians." (The Advocates for Human Rights, 2009: 42)

Volunteers also used information communication technologies at the local level to coordinate their work. In Chicago, where the author worked with the Diaspora Project, volunteers set up a wiki site to organize their efforts. Volunteers used the wiki to keep everyone informed of individual volunteers' activities. It provided a calendar of upcoming events and a checklist of outreach ideas. It was a venue to brainstorm outreach strategies and to match up volunteers with potential statement-givers. For a small group of volunteers in a sprawling metropolitan area, the site was indispensible.

The LTRC and the Diaspora Project also required a means of aggregating statements that volunteers would collect around the world. To accomplish the task, a web-based data management system was created. The LTRC asked Benetech to provide technical assistance and database management. Benetech is the leading provider of database expertise in the transitional justice field. It has worked with truth commissions in such diverse locations as Ghana, Guatemala, Haiti, Peru, Sierra Leone, South Africa, and Timor-Leste. Benetech consulted with the LTRC on "establishing analytical objectives, collecting data, designing and implementing an information management system…" (The Truth and Reconciliation Commission of Liberia, 2009: 86). It provided advice on collecting, coding, and analyzing the data. Benetech also conducted the statistical analysis of the data collected by the LTRC and the Diaspora Project.

As part of their training, volunteers were introduced to the data management system. Upon completion of the training, volunteers received an individual password to access the Diaspora Project's secure on-line statement database. The database only permitted volunteers to view statements that they had individually entered into the system. The Diaspora Project was sensitive to concerns regarding the security of statements. Nonetheless, as part of the arrangement with the LTRC, the statements were turned over to the LTRC to be housed in its archive after the completion of the Diaspora Project. Liberians in the diaspora were more skeptical of the Liberian government's ability and willingness to maintain the security of statements in the longer term (Wiebelhaus-Brahm, 2010: 397-398).

In total, the Diaspora Project collected 1,631 statements. Two hundred thirty-seven statements were taken in the United States and 15 in the United Kingdom; the remainder of the statements were taken at Buduburam (The Advocates for Human Rights, 2009: Appendix H). Infrastructure provided by the Diaspora Project's *pro bono* partners enabled Liberians who did not live in areas where organized statement-taking was conducted to participate in the process. In addition to face-to-face meetings, Liberians were able to give statements over the phone, by mail, or online.[8] Georgia Tech's focus groups approved of the LTRC's website and felt that the design would make Liberians comfortable providing statements online (Best et al., 2009: 7). However, although the Diaspora Project's final report, *A House With Two Rooms*, does not provide precise data, few Liberians appear to have given statements online (Young and Park, 2009: 355).

FUTURE RESEARCH DIRECTIONS

The LTRC and the Diaspora Project were path breaking in their use of information communication technologies. It seems likely that future truth commissions will attempt to emulate the use of technology to increase participation in truth-telling processes. The LTRC was able to leverage its partnerships with developed country organizations like The Advocates, Georgia Tech, and Benetech to develop technological capacity at minimal cost. Technology has the potential to enable truth commissions to collect more information without sorely taxing their limited resources. Given the modest budgets of most truth commissions, technology is attractive. Nonetheless, the limits of technology's benefits also must be recognized. Information communication technologies remain beyond the reach of many in most poverty-stricken, post-conflict societies. Moreover, information communication technologies may alter the nature of truth produced and reinforce the very isolation and alienation that truth commissions hope to overcome.

Pelsinger (2010), for example, argues that Web 2.0 technologies have the potential to provide a tremendous boost to transitional justice processes by providing a cost-effective way of collecting and disseminating knowledge of past human rights abuses. Information communication technologies might enable truth commissions to produce a more complete picture of past violence. Such tools enabled the Liberian diaspora to participate in the truth commission. Information communication technologies also create opportunities for expanding participation within the country. Georgia Tech developed the MObile Story Exchange System (MOSES) for use in Liberia to increase the LTRC's penetration of rural, isolated parts of the country (Smyth et al., 2010; The Truth and Reconciliation Commission of Liberia, 2009: 90-91). MOSES is an SUV-mounted, interactive computer system that allows users to learn about the LTRCs and to contribute to the truth-telling process by recording their own video statement. The MOSES team worked with Liberians in Atlanta and in Liberia to design an interface that would be intuitive for users regardless of technological sophistication, level of education, or language capability (Best et al., 2009; Smyth et al., 2010). The potential benefits of the technology are clear; if it "were to decrease the costs of interviewing rural Liberians such that it became as cheap as interviewing Liberians located in Monrovia, the LTRC would no longer have to choose between interviewing rural and local Liberians." (Pelsinger, 2010: 738) In the future, wireless and mobile technologies have the potential to expand access to truth commission participation even further.

Information communication technologies appear to have allowed the LTRC to do more with less. Pelsinger (2010: 738-739) also argues that technology is an important factor in explaining how the LTRC was able to collect statements from a larger proportion of Liberia's population than

South Africa's Truth and Reconciliation Commission (TRC) did with a much smaller budget. Performing a similar comparison with only the Liberian diaspora is complicated by the wildly divergent estimates of the diaspora's size. Yet, even in Chicago, where we only collected eight statements, the ratio of statements to population compares favorably with South Africa's TRC (Wiebelhaus-Brahm, 2010: 390). However, although it makes intuitive sense the technology contributed to the LTRC being able to engage a wider portion of the population than the South African TRC, there is little empirical evidence to support the contention that technology has made truth commissions more efficient. While these correlations suggest a relationship, there is a need for studies to examine the causal connection. Overall, assessing the effectiveness of outreach is difficult for several reasons, not least of which being that one cannot distinguish whether non-participation was a result of ignorance or conscious choice.

Nevertheless, there are reasons to be cautious about the ability of technology to expand participation in truth commission processes dramatically. It is a deeply personal experience to provide testimony regarding human rights abuses that one has witnessed or suffered. Experience in the Diaspora Project indicated that Liberians needed time to build up a level of interpersonal trust with the statement-taker. For that reason, it was often most effective for statement-givers to work with the same individual from outreach through giving a statement in order to build trust (Minikon and Shepler, 2009: 152). Providing testimony via a computer terminal is a much more impersonal experience. Such an interface would likely dissuade some would-be statement givers from testifying. Others may alter the tone or content of their statement. Text or video chat technology may help to personalize the experience for statement-givers. A more general point is that we should be cognizant of the fact that the nature of the truth that is produced will inevitably be shaped by the medium in which information is collected. Commissioners and staff should be cognizant of this in their data analysis and, where possible, provide different options to statement-givers to allow them to contribute in the way they find most comfortable.

Liberians in the diaspora were reluctant to give statements for three major reasons (Wiebelhaus-Brahm, 2010: 396-398). First, many were concerned about how giving a statement would affect their immigration status. The Diaspora Project could not guarantee that their testimony would be protected from a subpoena for an immigration hearing. Given that many feared it was not yet safe to return to Liberia, this was a major concern. Second, some Liberians feared retribution toward themselves or relatives for giving a statement. Third, some did not trust the security of their statements. Most did not express misgivings about the adequacy of the Diaspora Project or LTRC's security measures. Rather, they were skeptical of the Liberian government's willingness or ability to store statements securely. After the end of the LTRC, the Liberian government took possession of the LTRC's records.

These concerns are common in transitional situations and future attempts to engage diaspora populations are likely to encounter them. There is reason to suspect that these issues might be magnified for potential statement-givers contemplating participation via information communication technologies. Once testimony is posted online, whether in textual, audio, or video form, it enters the public domain and is nearly impossible to control. As such, individuals' statements are likely to be more readily available. Inconsistencies between truth commission statements and testimony in immigration proceedings might be more easily identifiable. Victims and witnesses who testify may be targeted by individuals they have accused of wrongdoing in order to silence them. At the same time, the ease of placing testimonies online potentially violates the due process rights of individuals accused of human rights violations. Given that truth commissions do not possess the same legal protections for the accused that courts provide, alleged perpetrators do not have the ability to respond to allegations immediately. Once posted on a website, the accusations may gain an air of credibility regardless of their strength and may expose the accused to vigilante justice. In principle, the accusations could permanently remain in the digital universe regardless of the findings of any subsequent investigation. Truth commissions have always faced a tension between protecting those who provide them with information and the desire for transparency and openness that increase the likelihood that the investigation will have a more significant impact. The greater use of information communication technologies amplified these concerns.

Information communication technologies have the potential to transform the practice of conducting truth commissions much more fundamentally than by simply expanding visibility and participation. It could radically change the very nature of truth commissions. The LTRC celebrated the potential of technology in truth-telling processes, arguing that "anyone who has actively participated in dynamic online communities, or who has found new avenues of creation and expression online, knows that these environments can be deeply transformative. Thus, modern information and communication systems can play a critical role in a nation's post-conflict truth-seeking and reconciliation." (The Truth and Reconciliation Commission of Liberia, 2009: 91)In practice, this was more a reality for the diaspora than for Liberians in Liberia.

At the same time, there is a potential dark side. Many truth commission proponents see truth commission hearings as opportunities to bring people and communities together. Yet, technology can be isolating. Imagine how different a truth commission experience would be "[if] uploading a photograph or an amnesty application has become just as official as showing up at a truth commission to provide testimony" (Pelsinger, 2010: 745). Pelsinger (2010: 742-743) rightly cautions that technology has the potential to hamper the potential healing and reconciliatory benefits of truth commissions. One risk is that information communication technologies may dehumanize truth commission processes. Since South Africa's iconic TRC, truth commissions have increasingly employed public hearings and attempted to bring individual perpetrators and victims together to facilitate reconciliation. Communication technologies, however, makes it easier to avoid face-to-face encounters. If technology enables victims to choose not to attend truth commission events due to inconvenient or fear, it "undercut[s] exactly what is so intimate, personal and effective about a truth commission." (Pelsinger, 2010: 743)

One potential way of addressing some of these concerns might be to pursue a strategy similar to that of South Africa's TRC. It collected thousands of testimonies around the country and then selected several hundred statement-givers to appear during the commission's public hearings. This would allow technology to cast a wider net for statements. Yet, the public hearings might provide opportunities for face-to-face encounters for some statement-givers. Community-level conflict resolution and reconciliation processes might give statement-givers not selected for public hearings with the same personal experience.

CONCLUSION

The LTRC's Diaspora Project provides important lessons for other societies emerging from periods of conflict and repression. Somalia and Sri Lanka, where long, brutal conflicts have produced sizeable diaspora populations, are but two countries that could benefit from Liberia's example. Information communication technologies proved instrumental in the LTRC's attempt to include the Liberian diaspora in the truth and reconciliation process. Liberians around the world learned of the LTRC's work via the Internet. The Diaspora

Project used cyberspace to inform Liberians in the diaspora of their opportunity to participate in the truth-telling process and to counter misconceptions and negative sentiment in virtual diaspora communities. It enabled hundreds of volunteers to receive uniform training to prepare themselves to take statements on behalf of the LTRC. Moreover, Web 2.0 technologies allowed Liberians to interact with each other and to provide statements to the LTRC.

Nonetheless, information communication technologies are not a panacea for transitional justice processes. They cannot obviate the fear and insecurity that potential statement-givers might feel. In addition, they magnify the challenges of unsubstantiated accusations. Finally, they risk depersonalizing what should be an intimate experience. Eliminating the physicality of truth-telling potentially undermines some of the main justifications for truth commissions. Face-to-face encounters seem central to attempts to facilitate reconciliation between individual victims and perpetrators and the potential healing benefits victims might receive from having their suffering officially acknowledged. Future truth commissions will have to carefully consider how they can use information communication technologies to increase their efficiency and expand opportunities for participation without losing the aspects of truth-telling that have made truth commissions such an attractive and popular transitional justice option. The use of text and video chat mentioned above is one technology that could be used to allow statement-giver and statement-taker to develop a rapport. Over several interactions, a level of trust could be developed that would make individuals more comfortable revealing such intimate details.

REFERENCES

Balancing Act. (2008). Web2.0 technology to help the Truth and Reconciliation Commission in Liberia. *Balancing Act, 398*. Retrieved February 9, 2011, from http://www.balancingact-africa.com/news/en/issue-no-398/web-and-mobile-data/web20-technology-to/en

Best, M. L., Smyth, T. N., & Serrano-Baquero, D. (2009). *Designing for and with diaspora: A case study of work for the Truth and Reconciliation Commission of Liberia*. Paper presented in the Extended Abstracts of the ACM Conference on Human Factors in Computing Systems (CHI 2009), April 4-9, Boston, MA.

Ellis, S. (2006). *The mask of anarchy: The destruction of Liberia and the religious dimension of an African civil war*. New York, NY: New York University Press.

Hayner, P. (2007). *Negotiating peace in Liberia: Preserving the possibility of justice*. Geneva, Switzerland: Centre for Humanitarian Dialogue.

Hayner, P. (2011). *Unspeakable truths: Transitional justice and the challenge of truth commissions*. New York, NY: Routledge.

Minikon, P., & Shepler, S. (2009). Documenting human rights abuses among the diaspora: Lessons learned from the Liberian Truth and Reconciliation Commission. In Shawki, N., & Cox, M. (Eds.), *Negotiating sovereignty and human rights: Actors and issues in contemporary human rights politics* (pp. 141–158). Farnham, UK: Ashgate Publishing.

Pelsinger, S. (2010). Liberia's long tail: How Web 2.0 is changing and challenging truth commissions. *Human Rights Law Review*, *10*(4), 730–748. doi:10.1093/hrlr/ngq036

Smyth, T. N., Etherton, J., & Best, M. L. (2010). *MOSES: Exploring new ground in media and post-conflict reconciliation*. Paper presented at the ACM Conference on Human Factors in Computing Systems (CHI 2010), April 10-15, Atlanta, GA.

Steinberg, J. (2010a). Liberia's experiment with transitional justice. *African Affairs*, *109*(434), 135–144. doi:10.1093/afraf/adp085

Steinberg, J. (2010b). A truth commission goes abroad: Liberian transitional justice in New York. *African Affairs*, *110*(439), 1–19.

The Advocates for Human Rights. (2009). *A house with two rooms: Final report of the Truth and Reconciliation Commission of Liberia Diaspora Project*. Retrieved February 9, 2011, from http://www.theadvocatesforhumanrights.org/Final_Report.html

The Truth and Reconciliation Commission of Liberia. (2009). *Volume II: Consolidated final report*. Retrieved February 9, 2011, from http://www.trcofliberia.org/reports/final/volume-two_layout-1.pdf

Wiebelhaus-Brahm, E. (2010). A volunteer's perspective on the Liberian Truth and Reconciliation Commission Diaspora Project. *Journal of Human Rights Practice*, *2*(3), 386–400. doi:10.1093/jhuman/huq010

Young, L. A., & Park, R. (2009). Engaging diasporas in truth commissions: Lessons from the Liberia Truth and Reconciliation Commission Diaspora Project. *International Journal of Transitional Justice*, *3*(3), 341–361. doi:10.1093/ijtj/ijp021

KEY TERMS AND DEFINITIONS

Diaspora: A group that has been dispersed outside of its traditional homeland.

Outreach: Attempts to make individuals aware of opportunities or events.

Reconciliation: The repair of relationships that have been ruptured by violence, abuse, and mistrust.

Statement: Testimony individuals provide regarding human rights abuses they experienced, witnessed, or perpetrated.

Transitional Justice: Collective term for mechanisms such as trials and truth commissions through which societies attempt to address histories of violence and repression.

Truth Commission: A temporary body established by a government to investigate a period of violence or repression that finishes its work by preparing a report that documents its findings and outlines recommendations for further redress and the prevention of future human rights abuses.

ENDNOTES

1 The United Nations High Commissioner for Refugees' (UNHCR) estimates of Liberia's refugee population varies considerably over the course of the civil war from 30 in 1988 (the first year data is available) to a maximum of 797,835 in 1994. Between 1990 and 2003, the average size of the Liberian refugee population was approximately 518,000 based on UNHCR data.

2 Chicago, for example, has an estimated Liberian population of between 3,000 and 5,000, spread around the city and in several far-flung suburbs. See Wiebelhaus-Brahm 2010.

3 Retrieved February 9, 2011, from http://www.youtube.com/watch?v=kC5ubo_T4Cg.

4 Retrieved February 9, 2011, from http://www.theadvocatesforhumanrights.org/uploads/4-fold+brochure%2c+with+JP+photo_2.pdf.

5 An example of a Powerpoint presentationwas retrieved February 9, 2011, from http://www.theadvocatesforhumanrights.org/uploads/General+TRC+Diaspora+ppt_2.ppt.

6 Video footage was retrieved February 9, 2011, from http://www.trcofliberia.org/hearings. Transcripts of the hearings were

retrieved February 9, 2011, from http://www.theadvocatesforhumanrights.org/US_Hearing_Transcripts.html.

7 Training materials were retrieved February 9, 2011, from http://www.theadvocatesforhumanrights.org/Materials_Trainings_Archive.html. Specific statement-taking instructions were retrieved February 9, 2011, from http://www.theadvocatesforhumanrights.org/uploads/Statement-taking+instructions+National+03.30.07.pdf.

8 Forms for submitting a statement were retrieved February 9, 2011, from http://www.theadvocatesforhumanrights.org/uploads/Submit+Your+Own+Statement+Form++04.30.07.pdf.

Chapter 6
ICT and Human Rights in Brazil:
From Military to Digital Dictatorship

José Rodrigues Filho
Universidade Federal da Paraíba, Brazil

ABSTRACT

Since the end of military government in Brazil, civilian governments have sought the accumulation and exercise of power to the detriment of the citizenry. They have done this with a kind of totalitarianism that takes the form of digital or bureaucratic dictatorship. Since the 1990s, they have started to implement information technology in the public sector to regulate and run the country in a command-and-control way through technological or bureaucratic dictatorship rather democratic process. While it is evident that there is a high level of investment in information technology in the public sector (e-government) in Brazil, there are also clear signs of the violation of human rights in terms of privacy. These occur, for instance, when the public administration exercises the power to engage in a process of electronic surveillance without the supervision of the judiciary. It is alleged that thousands of individual files have been accessed in the public administration in Brazil, despite the privacy protection offered by the national constitution. In addition, there is a proliferation of biometric identification using faces, eyes, fingerprints, and other body parts, especially in the e-voting system. This chapter shows how information technology (e-government) in Brazil could lead to violations of human rights because of the proliferation of biometric identification in the e-voting system as well as other sorts of invisible electronic surveillance that are affecting civil liberties and individual rights, including privacy.

INTRODUCTION

During the last few years the connection between information technology and human rights has been recognized and discussed by scholars and practitioners, particularly in areas such as privacy, political participation, freedom of expression and gender equality. While in most discussions the opportunities presented by information technology are deemed to advance human rights, in some cases the challenges and threats to human rights are emphasized (Jorgensen, 2006; Metzl, 1996).

In this chapter I argue that there is a need to rethink the concepts or assumptions of information and communication technology (ICT) and human rights in current discussions about the "Informa-

DOI: 10.4018/978-1-4666-1918-0.ch006

tion Society", which are based largely in the "developed North" and influenced by neo-liberal economic reforms. In short, the ICT assumptions based on market-led values have to be replaced by an emphasis on ICT and well-being in terms of health, education and human needs or the association between ICT, development and human rights, avoiding the dominance and legitimate role of dominant international organizations in democratizing the global governance process.

Furthermore, it is recognized that the influence of private interests in human rights organizations (Sparks, 2005) has resulted in national ICT policy "where 'pro-poor' interventions could only be justified through 'pro-market' solutions" (Chakravartty, 2007, p. 310). Besides, how do we make the connection between new assumptions of ICT and human rights and the historical context of each country with regard to its democratic regime? How do we make the connection between the historical context of each country and the agenda of international organizations? Is ICT improving or reducing human rights? By challenging the dominant and mainstream assumptions of ICT, human rights can be examined as the most powerful instrument for human emancipation and participation to improve the condition of people's lives.

Despite the potential of ICT to strengthen human rights, it seems that it is not improving human rights in Brazil as expected. Since the end of military government in Brazil, civilian governments have sought the accumulation and exercise of power to the detriment of the citizenry with a kind of totalitarianism that takes the form of digital or bureaucratic dictatorship.

The same critique made of the US government (Gingrich, 2009) seems to be applied to the Brazilian government when the desire for power led the executive branch of the government to mobilize the National Congress to change the national Constitution late in the 1990s and to allow President Fernando Henrique Cardoso to run for reelection. By creating a kind of imperial executive branch of government, the National Congress seems to be nullified and no longer serves its purpose of representing the Brazilian people.

It was with this kind of totalitarian arrogance that information technology started to be implemented in the public sector to regulate and run the country in a command-and-control way through technological and bureaucratic dictatorship rather than democratic process (Gingrich, 2009). While it is evident that there has been a high level of investment in information technology in the public sector (e-government) in Brazil, there are clear signs of violation of human rights in terms of privacy when the public administration exercises the power to engage in a process of electronic surveillance without court-issued warrants.

According to the Brazilian press thousands of individual files have been accessed in the public administration in Brazil, despite the privacy protection offered by the national Constitution. In addition, there is a proliferation of biometric identification using faces, eyes, fingerprints and other body parts, especially in the e-voting system.

A political scandal arose recently, in the 2010 presidential election, over the alleged creation of a dossier against the daughter of a candidate running for the presidency and members of his political party, who were under covert surveillance. This scandal, named "Receitagate" in reference to the American Watergate case, is described in a later section. In the media/political scandal in Brazil, reported by the Brazilian press (Lima, 2010), it became clear how information technology in the public administration may simply endanger the lives of the population as a whole. In this chapter an attempt will be made to show how information technology (e-government) in Brazil is violating human rights, especially in terms of the proliferation of biometric identification in the e-voting system, and other sorts of invisible electronic surveillance that is affecting civil liberties and individual rights, including privacy.

ICT, DEVELOPMENT, AND HUMAN RIGHTS

If initiatives in information and communication technology for development (ICTD/ICT4D) do not have regard for human rights and basic human needs, there will be a tendency towards a widening of the inequality gap within and between countries, considering that up to now it is unclear what benefits will accrue to less developed countries (LDCs) from these technologies.

Along with many other works in this field, I have found the absence of empirical evidence makes it hard to examine the connection between ICT, human rights and socio-economic development, and the utility of ICT in development projects, especially in LDCs where ICT is very much in the hands of the private sector.

As Akpan suggested, while "ICT can indeed be used as tools for socio-economic development, their success in this endeavour will depend on how they are applied such that their positive effects can spread to the larger population rather than concentrate in a few hands and further perpetuate the existing wide income disparities in many LDCs" (Akpan, 2003, p. 272). A recent study has shown that, despite the predominance of professionals from the field of computer science, there was a dramatic rise in the number of ICTD projects, but development areas "such as sustainable environment and eradication of hunger were comparatively seen as outside the scope of ICTD". What is more, in the opinion of 20% of the respondents in the study, ICTD had an overall negative impact on poverty alleviation (Patra, Pal & Nedevschi, 2009, p. 363).

This pessimistic view is well documented in the literature, despite the recognition that more access to information and knowledge plays a crucial role in advancing political, economic and social well-being. However, as the use of ICT is predominantly limited to the high-income countries, and the élite in low-income countries, its largest impact has occurred in the already industrialized societies (Fors & Moreno, 2002, p. 198). The use of ICT "to enhance human development is increasingly possible, but needs to be done with awareness of their potential downsides and tradeoffs, and the need for significant financial resources. People-centred strategies and technologies are needed to make ICT4D a model for people-centred development." (Hamed, 2010, p.60).

The discourse of ICT and human rights has to focus on people and not on technology in order to make ICT4D a model for people-centered development, because what we can see is the "people-centred framework being reversed in favour of a technology centred-approach" (Fors & Moreno, 2002, p.199). This approach is severely affecting those in need in developing countries, when scarce resources are shifted away from basic and traditional social development programs (health, education, shelter, clean water, sanitation, etc.) towards those programs that encompass a central ICT-based proposition, serving the interests of big corporations (Brown & Grant, 2008; Rodrigues Filho, 2010).

The incorporation of ICT in development studies tends to use a top-down approach "developed for Western use with little concern for the user-needs existing outside this cultural and economic context" (Fors & Moreno, 2002, p. 200). The United Nations definition of development puts people at its center:

Development is a comprehensive economic, social, cultural and political process, which aims at the constant improvement of the wellbeing of the entire population and of all individuals on the basis of their active, free, and meaningful participation in development and in the fair distribution of benefits resulting therefrom. (United Nations, 1986).

Some studies have found that this is not always the case in ICTD/ICT4D, which sometimes is not clear about the development theory used. If knowledge and information are basic needs in themselves, human rights are the essence to empower people to develop ICT strategies that are not only relevant but also important for people-based development. In this case, a bottom-up approach to both ICT development and development in itself, taking countries' political, historical, cultural and social context into consideration, is necessary.

ICT may not be the most important technology for developing countries (Arocena & Senker, 2003). E-mail, for instance, is less important than vaccines and clean water, especially in developing countries. In Brazil, spending in ICT has been increasing substantially during the last few years, while investments in many social programs have decreased, despite their importance in improving the population's quality of life and human development. While ICT investments seem to be a top priority in the agenda of international organizations, as will be seen in the next section, reinforcing the quasi-monopolistic power of providers in the developed world, it hides and blurs the distinction between these and all sort of inequalities that have risen at highest rates, even in the developed world.

Surprisingly social programs developed in Brazil during the last few years, designed to end hunger and starvation, despite their limitations, have had the power to advance human development. Programs such as Bolsa Família and Fome Zero (Zero Starvation) rather than ICT programs are propelling the country into the First World (Moore, 2010).

ICT AND THE INTERNATIONAL ORGANIZATIONS' AGENDA

International organizations (e.g. the World Bank, the United Nations and the OECD) have strongly emphasized in their basic agendas the link between ICT and economic development and growth, but arguably based on a simplistic and narrow economic theory, although for them ICT is identified as a requirement for economic growth and social gains. Unfortunately, the above-mentioned organizations do not suggest a radical shift in policy, clearly indicating the framework of prevailing development paradigms that offer no space for a different conceptualization of development as a process of empowerment that enables people to participate in the governance of their own lives (Amoretti, 2007).

At present, the disparities in access to ICT-related development or the future are remarkable and are likely to become greater, at the current rate of technological advancement... The new paradigm of development requires a review of the way countries consider ICTs and e-government. It needs innovative approaches to government and the public sector; business and the citizen; and culture and society; in other words, a holistic approach which fully exploits the centrality of ICT for the vision of a future knowledge society. (United Nations, 2004)

Similarly, the World Bank (1997) and the Organization for Economic Co-operation and Development (OECD, 2001, 2003)

have adapted their strategies in the direction of a state-friendly and holistic approach: ICTs are considered not just another factor of production, but rather a unique opportunity for achieving higher standards of living and greater economic and social empowerment for millions of citizens around the world. (Amoretti, 2007).

To quote from "Information and Communication Technologies: A World Bank Group Strategy":

Information and communication technologies are opening new opportunities for emerging markets. The World Bank Group aims to stimulate sustainable economic growth, increase productivity, improve public services, promote transparency, and reduce poverty through the reach of the technologies in the developing world. (World Bank 2002).

There is no doubt that ICTs hold the potential to improve the provision of services and the democratic process, but they also have the ability to perpetuate and reinforce existing social and economic inequalities, as is always the case in developing countries. In the same way that ICTs can be used to empower the people, there are numerous examples of cases in which they are actively disempowering (Stahl, 2008).

In addition, some observers are not convinced that high levels of investment in ICTs "have provided the expected outcomes in terms of increased efficiency in the administrative procedure and improvement in the quality of services actually delivered" (Cordela, 2007, p. 269). Furthermore, the figures are quite alarming in terms of ICT failures, when it is argued "that approximately 85% of government information technology projects worldwide have been failures" (Cordela, 2007). It has been estimated that in the developed world (the UK, for instance), only 30% of technology-based projects are a success (Cordela, 2007, p. 268).

Therefore, many of the ICT applications can be seen as a set of market-driven reforms in line with the narrow discourse of the New Public Management (NPM) initiated in the early 1980s (Dunleavey & Hood, 1994; Hood, 1995), based very much on a technological issue that is related to lean government that promises "to put your tax dollars to work more efficiently". In this "service-first-and-democracy later" approach, the relationship between ICTs and human and economic development should be analysed in depth, especially since ICTs are seen as tools for the generation of profits in the developed world. Unfortunately, in many cases the roots of and conflicts caused by ICTs are masked, hidden and concealed "by the ideological effects of these institutions" (Amoretti, 2007).

According to Chakravartty (2007, p. 309), giant corporations like Microsoft and Cisco,

along with their Southern corporate counterparts in Asia and Latin America, are playing a growing role in setting the development agenda at the national, regional and local levels, often coordinating their efforts directly with NGOs who provide research and implementation assistance.

This is done through an intense collaboration with other civil society organizations including "community groups, NGOs, labor unions, faith-based organizations, professional associations, and universities" (Chakravartty, 2007, p. 309).

In practice, the dominant role and the agenda of major international organizations is oriented towards the globalization of international markets or the creation of the global marketplace as an integrated system that benefits Western suppliers disproportionately through the utilization of ICTs (Amoretti, 2007), in an infrastructure built through contracts with the private sector (Rodrigues Filho, 2010). While the advantages offered by computers and information technology in many parts of the world are recognized, these technologies are always introduced with little democratic debate over whether they will benefit society or harm it.

The next section describes briefly the e-government and ICT agenda in Brazil. As in many other countries, this is characterized as privatized, in the sense that its infrastructure is built through contracts with the private sector. It is also politicized, as the government awards large contracts to private sector companies, especially from the developed world, that always enjoy high profit gains, even in times of financial crisis (Rodrigues Filho, 2010).

THE CASE: BRAZILIAN GOVERNMENT

Formerly a Portuguese colony, Brazil became independent in 1822, and has been a republic since 1889. The period from 1889 to 1930, called the Old Republic (*República Velha*) ended in 1930 with a military coup that installed a dictator. The current Constitution defines Brazil as a federal republic, and the federation is formed by the union of the Federal District, the 26 states, and more than 5,000 municipalities. From 1964 to 1988, Brazil experienced a second period of military dictatorship, referred to as the military regime. After more than two decades of this military dictatorship, Brazil held its first democratic presidential elections in 1989 to elect a democratic government with universal suffrage by direct and secret ballot, supported by the Brazilian Constitution, enacted in 1988. This short historical description shows that the Brazilian society has had quite long periods of living under a military dictatorship.

The later period was a time of hardship and fear, with many victims of gross human rights abuses and violations. Human Rights Watch (2009) reported 1,918 accounts of torture from 1964 to 1979 and noted that its source material "excluded an 'incalculable' number of other cases". In addition, it was reported by Human Rights Watch that the military regime in Brazil from 1964 to 1985

was responsible for systematic human rights violations, including extrajudicial killings, forced disappearances, torture, arbitrary detention, and the curtailment of free expression. According to official estimates, around 50,000 persons were detained just in the first months of the dictatorship and roughly 10,000 went into exile at some point during that period (Human Rights Watch, 2009).

However, the move from the military regime to a civilian government does not mean that democracy came to be established in Brazil. The more stable democracies all over the world are the result of a long struggle between many opposing parties, aided by resourceful individuals, influential thinkers and the population in general. Therefore, a so-called "constitutional democracy" is never simply invented, but is the result of a long power struggle to keep the equilibrium and the separation of powers (legislature, executive and judiciary). In this *trias politica* established by the rule of law, or the system of balancing of powers, the basic idea is to limit the power of the state by spreading it over different competencies to work together through a system of mutual control or checks and balances. For Hildebrandt (2008, p. 61), a "sustainable democracy presumes and maintains the rule of law. The rule of law is often defined in reference to the protection of human rights and limited government.". In other words,

the rule of law establishes constitutional protection of citizens' rights and liberties over and against their government, safeguarded by an independent judiciary that shares the authority of the state. This is called the paradox of the Rechtsstaat: the state gives its authority to those that judge citizens who contest the way the state uses its authority in a given case. (Hildebrandt, 2008, p.61).

While human rights violations in the military regime in Brazil were both physical and mental, involving killings, torture, arbitrary detention and so on, in the information society the violation of human rights is done by the use of sophisticated technological apparatus, in an invisible way, with potential threats against democracy and the rule of law. "A state that does not provide its citizens with a minimum of security is qualified as what we call a failed state, incapable of protecting citizens against each other and against abusive state officials" (Hildebrandt, 2008, p. 62). In the process of international economic globalization, however, "the enforcement mechanisms for human rights have lagged", and "you cannot have a functioning global economy with a dysfunctional global legal system" (Brannagan, 2009, p.2).

Methodology

Researchers who study e-government implementation usually come from the field of information systems, and tend to take a techno-centric view of e-government (Sorrentino, 2010). As result of this, the linearity of the dominant approach to e-government does not shed much light on the social interaction that is necessary in the evaluation of e-government.

Further to this, the dominant and mainstream research approach does not always accept different approaches or hear the voices of researchers from developing countries. In some cases they are even excluded from academic journals and conferences because of their critical or pessimistic view of the way ICTs have been developed and promoted in both developed and developing countries (Stahl, 2008). As result of this, critical voices have often been seen as backward and obstructive, especially when they try to explore the social and political consequences of technological choices.

It would be most helpful if the academic community worldwide could look not only at the technicalities of ICTs in general, and e-government in particular, but much more to its social and political issues in order to design these technologies in ways that could reflect our best understanding of freedom and social justice, emphasizing the source of inequality and injustice worldwide.

While the interpretivist or qualitative research approach is well recognized in the field of information systems (Orlikowski & Baroudi, 1991; Klein & Myers, 1999), this approach is rarely used in e-government research. Therefore there is a need not only for more interpretivist research in e-government but for critical studies to investigate its implementation and its effects on surveillance from a critical theory perspective. Because the critical research approach is also rarely used in the field of e-government in general and surveillance in particular, it is unlikely that the traditional positivist approach can reveal how power structures and dominant discourses shape consciousness. A critical approach that can avoid acculturation to feeling comfortable with regard to domination and subordination is needed.

Cecez-Kecmanovic (2001, p. 1451) argues that critical researchers should "provide an explanation of historical, socio-cultural, political and economic conditions and structural sources of identified ailments, such as increasing control, dominations and alienation". In addition, she has also argued that the critical research approach does not have a clear methodological identity of research methods of its own, especially with regard to the implementation of information technology.

This research on e-government and human rights in Brazil is divided into three phases, with findings from the first phase presented here. In this first phase, historical data from several sources in Brazil, including the national and international press, were reviewed. In addition, data on investments in ICTs and social programs designed to improve human living conditions were compiled from national budgets. For the second phase, politicians, taxpayers, and civil servants will be interviewed in order to gain their views on digital surveillance, invisibly accessed files, and the use of biometric technologies in voting. In the second phase, the interpretivist approach will be used to examine the effects of e-government on human rights. Finally, in the third phase, the critical research perspective will be used for a deeper examination of the problem, relying methodologically on the interpretivist approach (Cecez-Kecmanovic, 2001).

E-Government and Human Rights in Brazil

There are many e-government initiatives in Brazil, starting with the creation and promotion of websites in the infrastructure of e-government marketing so that the population has access to many online transactions, such as online forms, e-voting, e-health, and the well known submission of tax declarations. There is no doubt about the potential and benefits of some online services. However, caution is required concerning the logic of the citizen/state relationship, in the attempt to transform the former into a satisfied customer or end-user, and not a citizen who needs to participate actively in government decisions. Under this approach it is hard to combine the interests of the existing political and bureaucratic elite with a real process of democratization.

The increasing levels of investment in and adoption of ICTs in Brazil is recognized by the recent Gartner Report as follows:

As a percentage of GDP, IT spending in Brazil is increasing faster than in Russia, India, and China because IT is pervasive among large organizations, small and midsize enterprises, government and all segments of consumers ... [this] is different from other BRIC countries, such as India, where IT spending is primarily concentrated on IT services, and in China, where IT spending is focused on large central government IT projects. (Gartner, 2010).

It is estimated that in 2010 IT end-user spending in Brazil will have reached more than US$ 100 billion, making the country the tenth largest global economy and second-largest IT market among the BRIC countries after China (Gartner, 2010). These investments are made in the public and financial sectors, healthcare, telecommunications, utilities and SMEs that are seen as the ones with the most growth potential.

It is worth mentioning how investments in ICTs in Brazil have shifted during the last decade. In the years 2000 and 2001 the highest investments were made by the Ministry of Defense in the US$ 1.4 billion project named SIVAM (The Amazon Monitoring System). Although the relationship between this project and the military regime is not clear, it is probable that it was influenced by the military government. SIVAM is a military project that emerged in the late 1990s "amidst allegations of corruption and trafficking of influence in the contract process", although it was cleared by a Congressional inquiry. The official information is that SIVAM was fully implemented in 2005, as a project to control air safety, monitor weather forecasts and assist in the prevention and control of diseases, especially in the Amazon Region. However, it is hard to find information about this project, even in the official documents.

Since 2005 investments have been oriented towards the command and control of the economy, with the Ministry of Finance making the highest investment in ICTs up to the end of the decade. Therefore, in the second half of the last decade, due to the influence of international organizations and the neo-liberal discourse of economic globalization, high investments were made to attend to administrative activities, especially at the federal government level, in the public banking system and financial management. The online tax collection system is well known and is used by more than 10% of the population for paying or receiving back some sort of income tax.

Another information technology in which quite high investments have been made since 2000 is e-voting technology. During the whole decade more investments were made in e-voting than in e-health technology (Rodrigues Filho & Gomes, 2010). Investment in e-voting technology was acknowledged in a news release by the Diebold corporation, the supplier of the hardware: "For Diebold this is the largest single order in the company's 141-year history" (BlackBoxVorting. Org, 2007).

Table 1, for instance, shows that spending in some ICT projects is higher than that in other social projects that could have a greater impact on the population's human rights and well-being. While investments in e-voting technology were quite high, especially during the years in which elections were held, investments in social programmes such as cancer prevention and treatment and mass vaccinations were low, and decreasing in recent years. In some years of the last decade, for instance, the Brazilian government spent more money on the e-voting technology than on all the teaching hospitals in the country (Rodrigues Filho & Gomes, 2010).

In spite of this, there are many concerns related to e-voting technology security and a worldwide consensus that the existing technology does not attend sufficiently to the principles of computer security (Rodrigues Filho & Gomes, 2008).

Table 1. Expenditures on e-voting versus other social programs, 2001–2005 (Value in Million US$). Source: SIAFI/TCU

Expenditure Nature	2001	2002	2003	2004	2005
Electoral Justice (Electronic Voting)	25,235.4	71,346.7	1,641.5	64,375.3	7,742.3
Cancer Prevention/Treatment	10,587.9	9,756.6	9,278.0	N/A	N/A
Vaccination Of Population	14,430.6	9,617.7	5,152.0	2,664.6	3,080.4

Note: Conversion of the Brazilian currency, real (R$), into US$: the Annual Average was calculated based on the daily official rate as registered by the Brazilian Central Bank. 2001 = 2.3522; 2002 = 2.9285; 2003 = 3.0715; 2004 = 2.9257; 2005 = 2.4341.

Because of this, the security of electronic voting is susceptible to failures and frauds according to Brazilian experts that have questioned our e-voting system and its security through internet sites, forums, articles and books (Maneschy, 2000; Brunazo Filho & Cortiz, 2006). According to them, the Electoral Court in Brazil has opened the doors for new and sophisticated frauds that are much more serious than the traditional ones (Maneschy, 2000).

Similarly, international reports have questioned the security and risks of this kind of system in the United States (Caltech/MIT Study, 2001; Norden et al. 2006). It seems that e-voting technology has alienated the voter from the electoral process and his own vote, turning democracy into an illusory exercise during elections (Rodrigues Filho & Gomes, 2008). In many countries people need democracy between elections and not just during election time, especially when it requires a sophisticated technological apparatus to be used without an adequate justification, just to count votes.

To complicate matters further, with claims about the lack of security of e-voting, the e-voting technology in Brazil became more sophisticated in the 2010 presidential election with the use of biometric identification that can scan the thumbprint of registered voters. Therefore, biometrics technology was tested in the country for the first time with the participation of voters in 60 municipalities of 23 states. The concerns about the use of biometrics technology are well known (Gutwirth, 2007; Lodge, 2007). It is stated that "Biometrics *per se* are not the problem. The central question has to be control over their use: who's controlling 'big brother'"? (Lodge, 2007, p.24). Academics and computer experts in Brazil are worried about the gross violation of human rights after the introduction of biometrics voting in the country.

Ironically the two presidential candidates with most votes in the last year's election are familiar with the evils of a dictatorial regime and with human rights issues. The elected president, Dilma Rousseff, as the nation's first woman to hold the office, was a left-wing guerrilla fighter during the military dictatorship, who claims that she was barbarically tortured. In her victory speech she has mentioned that she is going to fight against inequality and poverty, and promote human rights. Her opponent, Jose Serra, also suffered persecution during Brazil's military dictatorship and was forced into exile during the 1960s.

It was during the elections in 2010 that a political scandal emerged in Brazil when the tax collection system came into discussion. As it is compulsory to submit income tax declarations over the Internet, taxpayers have to use the government's online tax system for this purpose. More recently, the agency responsible for the use of the system (*Secretaria da Receita Federal*) has been heavily criticized because of its use as a surveillance system.

The scandal named "Receitagate" arose during the 2010 presidential election, when the opposition candidate from the Social Democratic Party (PSDB) accused the government candidate and her leftist Workers' Party (PT) of having illegally accessed the tax records of his daughter and of other members of the PSDB in search of potentially damaging information. This so-called mini-Watergate scandal, in allusion to the Watergate political scandal in the United States in the early 1970s, rumbled on for weeks, but it did not have a negative impact, as expected, on polls. It was mentioned that "a key reason why the mudslinging over tax records is not having an impact on polls may be that only about 15 percent of Brazilians pay income tax and therefore have little understanding of the scandal" (Grudgings, 2010).

At the same time, it emerged that thousands of taxpayers had had their private tax information accessed illegally. In order to avoid damage to the government candidate, measures to restrict access to private tax information were taken by the Ministry of Finance. However, it was mentioned that total protection was impossible, and the challenge was to increase taxpayers' security without hurting the system's operation (Soliani & Galvao, 2010).

Despite the nefarious intent of the government to use citizens' data abusively, violating their privacy and human rights, as in the abovementioned case, there were clear intentions to hide it. In short, along with many of my compatriots, as a taxpayer and Brazilian citizen I feel completely unprotected and insecure in the absence of legislation to face this sort of human rights abuse. It may be necessary to seek international human rights instruments or some other sort of jurisprudence to deal with gross human rights abuses, once it is acknowledged that the "law and justice system are servants of society, not the reverse" (Brannagan, 2007).

There is no doubt that with this sophisticated tax collection system taxpayers in Brazil can be under widespread surveillance by a public institution, where the priority does not seem to be to adapt the system to taxpayers' needs, but the other way round. In short, what the Minister of Finance said was that security should be achieved, but without hurting the system's operation. How can one envisage the realization of citizenship in a scenario like that?

The human rights appeal to the participatory design approach for the development of information technology in general, and information systems in particular, is more than necessary, moving from the top-down or tool approach to the bottom-up and democratic approach (Rodrigues Filho & Gomes, 2008). In other words, the development of these technologies will require substantial cooperation between social scientists, computer engineers, lawyers, and policy makers with a clear understanding of the democratic process and the rule of law.

CONCLUSION

There is a need to rethink the assumptions on ICTs and human rights towards human development based on the rule of law that should be required by a democratic state. In a dictatorial or failed state, ICTs by themselves do not offer protection and security to citizens. The preliminary results from the second phase of this research work are indicating that citizens seem to be as frightened as they were before, when living under a military dictatorial regime.

Unfortunately, the technological determinism continues to be reinforced and promoted by corporate managers, intellectuals, academia, and the whole community of mythmakers. All seem to weigh the 'digital opportunities' and 'possibilities' before the heavy inequalities and one-sided market powers and economic exclusion of the extremely poor, especially in developing countries. While computerization is to increase central control and surveillance, we need new approaches to ICTs that can have the ability to realistically capture social and political dimensions in its development.

The use of e-voting technology in Brazil has not increased turn-out, which seems to be decreasing over the years, despite the fact that voting is mandatory. In addition, people have not stopped selling their votes in a corrupt and corrupting system. In short, e-voting technology is very expensive and there is no sign that it has improved the democratic process in the country. The introduction of biometrics in voting makes the system more expensive, while privacy, civil liberty and democracy are in serious crisis.

It is has been mentioned that it is depressing to use the most modern technology to elect candidates that do not seem to be qualified for their mandate (H.J. 2010). In last year's election, for instance, a famous Brazilian clown, named Tiririca, was the most popular federal deputy candidate, elected with more than one million votes. The basic political platform of Tiririca was the following slogan: "What does a federal deputy do? To tell the truth, I don't know. But vote for me and I will tell you". I think there is nothing wrong with electing Tiririca, as a clown, to represent the Brazilian people and his profession. What is more frustrating is when it is mentioned that the National Congress is full of cheats or thieves. A former president, Lula da Silva, said in the early 1990s that the Brazilian National Congress had more than 300 fraudsters (*picaretas*). Now a columnist writing in *The Economist* has confirmed that a candidate in Brazil can be elected with the most modern technology, and "may go on to be a thief in office". (H.J. 2010).The question is: Do we need such sophisticated technologies to elect this sort of politicians?

The illegal access to taxpayer files through the tax collection system in Brazil, one of the most sophisticated in the world, is a cause of concern, because taxpayers may be under an invisible process of surveillance. However, the reports of tax data being used dishonestly for political gain, and the reports that thousands of taxpayers have had their files accessed, may not mean that ICT is used for surveillance purpose in Brazil. Further research is under way and is required for this discussion, when it seems that now anyone not in favor of the government may be under suspicion and guilty by default.

Most of the e-government initiatives in Brazil are top-down without participation and discussion. More research work is required not only to point out the advantages of e-government, but also its disadvantages, especially because it has a fundamental role in the surveillance-oriented society that can affect privacy, basic human rights, and democracy (Ogura, 2006). If surveillance is seen as the law beyond the state and is here to stay, and the use of its methods can develop a level of control approaching totalitarianism (Giddens, 1985), it is time to understand that its "complexities, manipulability, and regulatory effects should not be underestimated" (Backer, 2002).

REFERENCES

Akpan, P. I. (2003). Basic-needs to globalization: Are ICTs the missing link? *Information Technology for Development*, *10*, 261–274. doi:10.1002/itdj.1590100405

Amoretti, F. (2007). International organizations' ICTs policies: E-democracy and e-government for political development. *Review of Policy Research*, *24*(4), 331–344. doi:10.1111/j.1541-1338.2007.00286.x

Arocena, R., & Senker, P. (2003). Technology, inequality, and underdevelopment: The case of Latin America. *Science, Technology & Human Values*, *28*(15), 15–33. doi:10.1177/0162243902238493

Backer, L. C. (2002). Global panopticism: States, corporations and the governance of monitoring regimes. *Indiana Journal of Global Legal Studies*, *15*(1). Retrieved October 11, 2010, from http://papers.ssrn.com/sol3/papers.cfm?abstract_id=1081242

BlackBoxVoting.Org. (2007). Diebold's *PRO-COMP subsidiary awarded largest order in Diebold history.* Retrieved October 11, 2010, from http://www.bbvforums.org/cgi-bin/forums/board-profile.cgi?action=rate&topic=70328&page=46799&post=33641

Brannagan, C. A. (2009). Corporate complicity in international humans rights violations: The tort of negligence as a civil remedy in Canadian courts. *Peace and Conflict Review, 3*(2), 1–23.

Brown, A., & Grant, G. (2008). *Is it ICT "for development" or "in developing countries"? Exposing the duality of the ICT and development research agenda.* First Annual Workshop, ESCP-EAP University, Paris (13 October 2008).

Brunazo, F., & Cortiz, M. A. (2006). *Fraudes e defesas no voto eletronico.* São Paulo, Brazil: All-Print-Editora.

Caltech/MIT Study. (2001). *Residual votes attributable to technology – An assessment of the reliability of existing voting equipment.* Caltech/MIT Voting Technology Project. Retrieved from http://www.hss.caltech.edu/~voting/CalTech_MIT_Report_Version2.pdf

Cecez-Kecmanovic, D. (2001). *Critical research in information systems: The question of methodology.* Retrieved from http://is2.lse.ac.uk/asp/aspecis/20070023.pdf

Chakravartty, P. (2007). Governance without politics: Civil society, development and the postcolonial state. *International Journal of Communication, 1*, 297–317.

Cordela, A. (2007). E-government: Towards the e-bureaucratic form? *Journal of Information Technology, 22*, 265–274. doi:10.1057/palgrave.jit.2000105

Dunleavy, P., & Hood, C. (1994). From old public administration to new public management. *Public Public Money and Management, 14*(3), 9–16.

Fors, M., & Moreno, A. (2002). The benefits and obstacles of implementing ICTs strategies for development from bottom-up approach. *Aslib Proceedings, 54*(3), 198–206. doi:10.1108/00012530210441746

Gartner. (2010). *Gartner says IT end-user spending in Brazil will reach $ 101.3 billion in 2010.* Press release. Retrieved October 10, 2010, from http://www.gartner.com/it/page.jsp?id=1435720

Giddens, A. (1985). *The nation-state and violence.* Cambridge, UK: Polity Press.

Gingrich, N. (2009). *Has bureaucratic dictatorship arrived?* Retrieved October 11, 2010, from http://www.washingtonexaminer.com/opinion/columns/Has-bureaucratic-dictatorship-arrived_-8648572-79001702.html

Grudgings, S. (2010). *Scandals dominate Brazil campaign as votes nears.* Retrieved September 14, 2010, from http://af.reuters.com/article/worldNews/idAFTRE68D5LJ20100914

Gutwirth, S. (2007). Biometrics between opacity and transparency. *Annali dell'Istituto Superiore di Sanita, 43*(1), 61–65.

Hamed, J.-Y. (2010). *ICT4D and human development and capabilities approach: The potentials of information and communication technology.* Retrieved October 20, 2010, from http://mpr4a.ub.uni-muenchen.de/25561/MPRA Paper No 25561

Hildebrandt, M. (2009). Profiling and the rule of law. *Identity in the Information Society, 1*(1), 55–70. doi:10.1007/s12394-008-0003-1

Hood, C. (1995). The "new public management" in the 1980s: Variations on a theme. *Accounting, Organizations and Society, 20*(2/3), 93–109. doi:10.1016/0361-3682(93)E0001-W

Human Rights Watch. (2009). *Brazil: Prosecute dictatorship-era abuses. Landmark international decision provides powerful push for accountability*. Retrieved October 25, 2010, from http://www.hrw.org/en/news/2009/04/14/brazil-prosecute-dictatorship-era-abuses

Jorgensen, R. F. (2006). *Human rights in the global information society*. Cambridge, MA: The MIT Press.

Klein, H. K., & Myers, M. D. (1999). A set of principles for conducting and evaluating interpretive field studies in information systems. *Management Information Systems Quarterly*, *23*(1), 67–94. doi:10.2307/249410

Lima, V. A. (2010). *Os escândulos políticos midiáticos*. Observatório da Imprensa. Retrieved from http://www.observatoriodaimprensa.com.br/artigos.asp?cod=607JDB002

Lodge, J. (2007). Freedom, security and justice: The thin end of the wedge for biometrics? *Annali dell'Istituto Superiore di Sanita*, *43*(1), 20–26.

Maneschy, O. (2000). Fraude eletronica nas eleições. *Jus Navigandi, Teresina*, *5*(45). Retrieved from http://jus.uol.com.br/revista/texto/1552/fraude-eletronica-nas-eleicoes

Metzl, J. F. (1996). Information technology and human rights. *Human Rights Quarterly*, *18*, 705. doi:10.1353/hrq.1996.0045

Moore, A. (1998). Intangible property: Privacy, power, and information control. *American Philosophical Quarterly*, *35*, 365–378.

Moore, M. (2010, April 29). The world's most influential leaders (Luiz Inacio Lula da Silva. The 2010 Time 100). *Time*. Retrieved April 29, 2010, from http://www.time.com/time/specials/packages/article/0,28804,1984685_1984864_1984866,00.html

Norden, L. (2006). *The machinery of democracy: Protecting elections in an electronic world*. New York, NY: The Brennan Center of the NYU School of Law.

OECD. (2001). *The new economy – Beyond the hype*. Retrieved from http://www.oecd.org/dataoecd/2/26/2380634.pdf

OECD. (2003). *ICT and economic growth – Evidence from OECD countries, industries and firms*. Retrieved from http://www.labs-associados.org/docs/OCDE_TIC.PDF

Ogura, T. (2006). Electronic government and surveillance-oriented society. In Lyon, D. (Ed.), *Theorizing surveillance – The panopticon and beyond*. Devon, UK: Willan Publishing.

Orlikowski, W. J., & Baroudi, J. J. (1991). Studying information technology in organizations. Research approaches and assumptions. *Information Systems Research*, *2*(1), 1–28. doi:10.1287/isre.2.1.1

Patra, R., Pal, J., & Nedevschi, S. (2009). ICTD State of the Union: Where have we reached and where are we headed? *ICTD'09, Proceedings of the Third International Conference on Information and Communication Technologies and Development*, (pp. 357-365). Piscataway, NJ: IEEE Press.

Rodrigues Filho, J. (2010). E-government in Brazil – Reinforcing dominant institutions or reducing citizenship? In Reddick, C. (Ed.), *Politics, democracy and e-government: Participation and service delivery*. Hershey, PA: IGI Global. doi:10.4018/978-1-61520-933-0.ch021

Rodrigues Filho, J., & Gomes, N. P. (2008). E-voting in Brazil – Exacerbating alienation and the digital divide. In Santap, S. M. (Ed.), *E-democracy – Concepts and practices*. India: IFCAI Books.

Rodrigues Filho, J., & Gomes, N. P. (2010). E-health in Brazil: Less care for the poor? In Pease, C., Cooper, M., & Gururajan, R. (Eds.), *Biomedical knowledge management: Infrastructures and processes for e-health systems*. Hershey, PA: IGI Global. doi:10.4018/978-1-60566-266-4.ch017

Soliani, A., & Galvao, A. (2010). Brazil to boost security at tax agency after leaks. *Bloomberg Businessweek*. Retrieved November 12, 2010, from http://www.businessweek.com/news/2010-09-14/brazil-to-boost-security-at-tax-agency-after-leaks.html

Sorrentino, M. (2010). The challenges of e-government evaluation. In D'Atri, A., & Saccà, D. (Eds.), *Information systems: People, organizations, institutions, and technologies*. Berlin, Germany: Springer Physica-Verlag.

Sorrentino, M., Naggi, R., & Agostini, P. L. (2009). In Wimmer, M. A. (Eds.). Lecture Notes in Computer Science: *Vol. 5693. E-government implementation evaluation: Opening the black box*. Berlin, Germany: Springer-Verlag.

Sparks, C. (2005). Civil society as contested concept: Media and political transformation in Eastern Central Europe. In Hackett, R., & Shao, Y. (Eds.), *Democratizing global media: One world, many struggles* (pp. 37–56). Boulder, CO: Rowan & Littlefield.

Stahl, B. C. (2008). *Information systems – Critical perspectives*. London, UK: Routledge Taylor and Francis Group.

The Economist. (2010, October 3). Grumpy on the stump: America's views. *The Economist.*

UN. (2004). *UN global e-government readiness report. Towards access for opportunity*. Publication No: UNPAN/200/11.

United Nations. (1986). *Declaration on the right to development*, Res. 41/128, Retrieved from http://www.un.org/documents/ga/res/41/a41r128.htm

World Bank. (1997). *World development report 1997: The state in a changing world*. Washington, DC: World Bank.

World Bank. (2002). *Information and communication technologies: A World Bank group strategy*. Washington, DC: World Bank.

Chapter 7
Contingency and Hybridity in the Study of Digital Advocacy Networks:
Implications of the Egyptian Protest Movement

Christopher Wilson
University of Oslo, Norway

Alexandra Dunn
University of Oslo, Norway

ABSTRACT

This chapter proposes an analytic approach for the study of ICTs in contentious politics and human rights advocacy. By applying the analytical frames of contingency and hybridity to study design, this approach aims to promote empirical analyses, strengthen data comparability, and improve understanding into how human rights activists strategically combine digital and grounded communications to respond to complex and changing environments. The authors explore this analytic approach and its implications through a close analysis of the Front to Defend Egyptian Protesters (FDEP), a Cairo-based initiative utilizing multiple digital media to mobilize support teams for arrested protesters and work towards their release. Applying the analytical frames of contingency and hybridity to FDEP activities in 2010, prior to the uprisings now commonly referred to as the Arab Spring, the chapter observes a number of opportunities for targeted data collection. It closes by observing the challenges and opportunities this poses to the contemporary study of digital activism.

DOI: 10.4018/978-1-4666-1918-0.ch007

INTRODUCTION[1]

Research exploring the relationship between human rights and information and communication technologies (ICTs) has developed significantly in the last decade. Following early optimism about the role of digital media in promoting freedom (Brophy and Halpin 1999), careful study has attended to the role of ICTs in monitoring human rights (Lannon, 2009); the role of ICTs in instrumentally promoting human rights by generally strengthening individuals' capacities (Hamel, 2010); and the role of ICTs in specific relation to the freedoms of expression and access to information (Dutton et al, 2010).

Within this context, increasing attention has also been paid to the role of ICTs in contentious politics, and how access to information and digital media influences power struggles over human rights and processes of democratization. Driven largely by the challenges innovative advocacy and communication practices pose to traditional theoretical models, the resulting body of research enjoys contributions from a variety of disciplines, and is as eclectic as it is dynamic. The application of multiple and divergent analytical methods to novel empirical phenomenon has resulted in a variety of new concepts and subfields, each with their own insights and assumptions. As objects of study, "digital activism," "new new social movements," "dot-causes," "liberation technologies" and "cyber movements" (to name a few) represent significantly distinct analytical approaches and traditions (Breindl, 2010; Clark and Nuno, 2006; Scott & Street, 2001; Custard, 2008; Van Laer & Van Aelst, 2009; Boyle and Schmierbach, 2009; Diamond, 2010; Fleming, 2002; Joyce, 2010), yet often attempt to account for the same empirical phenomena, with each exploring phenomena as dramatically different as Chinese web journalism and citizen election observation in Africa (to take just two of the many example in Diamond's (2010) sweeping account).

This eclecticism may prove to be theoretically productive, insofar as it represents convergence on a common and clearly delineated object of study. In our attempt to approach that object, and notwithstanding the rich diversity of activities of which it is composed, we follow Joyce in using the term "digital activism," "because it is exhaustive and exclusive—the best term to discuss all instances of social and political campaigning practice that use digital network infrastructure" (2010, pp ix).

The broad and heterogeneous collection of phenomena to which "digital activism" refers may benefit from a broad and heterogeneous collection of analytical approaches. And while there is significant potential for cross-disciplinary collaboration and insight, there is also a great need for methodological refinement, both at the level of individual research initiatives and at the broader level of a common research agenda.

Firstly, and at the register of individual research initiatives, there is a need for more empirical analysis and more rigorous study design to move the digital activism research beyond anecdotal evidence and inspirational case studies. As articulated by prominent scholars in the recent report "Blogs and Bullets: New Media in Contentious Politics," produced by U.S. Institute of Peace and George Washington University:

Research design matters. Many claims currently made about the effects of new media are blind to hidden variables, confuse output with impact, or assume causal relationships that may be spurious. The first step must therefore be to get the research design right. The lack of data, a problem that is addressed later in this report, can be overcome (i.e., through better processing of online information in multiple languages), but data will only help if used in the right ways, with careful attention to which questions they can help answer. (Aday et al, 2010, p. 6).

The report goes on to propose seven guidelines for rigorous study design (regarding case selection, counter factuals, hidden variables, causal mechanisms, system effects, new media outlet selection and strategic interaction) and five levels of analysis for identifying and distinguishing the "political effects of new media" (individual transformation, intergroup relations, collective action, regime policies and external attention) (Aday et al, 2010,pp. 6-7, 9-12). These are strong heuristics that will serve digital activism research well, if commonly observed. But we find that the authors do not go far enough in exploring problems of data paucity and anecdote. The issue of case selection is especially critical in this regard, and intimately related to the other six guideline areas.

As the report notes, the rhetorical appeal of documenting "heroic accounts of scrappy activists" (Aday et al, 2010, p. 6) risks a bias toward prominent and apparently successful initiatives. In order to avoid this type of selection bias, the authors suggest link tracking, content tracking and meme tracking as methods for collecting large amounts of online data (Aday et al, 2010, p. 9). These techniques can provide important information about how information travels and how behavior changes on the web, but are unable to provide equally important information on activist motivations and strategic contexts. Nor should the inability to automate the collection of such "grounded" data diminish its priority and importance in strengthening research practices in case selection and study design.

Offline data on grounded social contexts is rather a necessary compliment to web-based data sets, both because it grounds analysis of digital behavior in real-world social and strategic contexts in which that behavior is shaped, and because it is the only way to document important social factors underpinning digital activism initiatives (especially in highly contentious politics where security concerns limit the amount of information individuals release online). These considerations are critical in order to accurately diagnose the five levels of analysis proposed by Aday et al. (2010), and mentioned above, in individual studies. This also has important implications for the development of digital activism research in aggregate, about which more below.

Secondly, and regarding the conglomerate body of digital activism research, the relationship between case studies, empirical data paucity and study design has an important role to play in further developing the emergent field. The broad and heterogeneous body of contemporary digital activism research is dominated by case studies, with a smattering of conceptually sound theoretical treatises that are only loosely linked to empirical phenomenon (Moody et al, 2008; Raffl et al, 2008; Neumayer et al 2009). The predominance of case studies is understandable given the novel character of phenomena at study. But this predominance is also problematic, as it is largely driven by the inspirational quality of cases, which, when coupled with conceptual and practical obstacles to data collection, has resulted in widespread reliance on anecdotal evidence,[2] "shaky data" and the often spurious claims referenced above (Aday et al, 2010, 6).

This has brought scholars to question the field's reliance on case studies, and propose more comparative analyses, as was suggested above. Yet case studies remain our most important safeguard against theoretical bubbles, and our only window into a rapidly evolving set of phenomena. From a meta-perspective, case studies are also an essential element in the inductive process of establishing common research methodologies and shared analytical models. This makes empirical data and individual study design all the more important for the development of the field.

Joyce (2010) does a good job of sketching the larger implications, describing what she calls the field's "two-part data problem":

Scholars have questioned the reliance on case studies, yet they are still central to our understanding of digital activism practice because the field

> *is beset with a two-part data problem. First, there simply is not enough data available to scholars, both because data have not been collected and because digital activism is a relatively new practice and its instances are still limited. Second, data that do exist (such as usage patterns from social media platforms) have not yet been rigorously analyzed. The field needs to create foundational knowledge by using rigorous quantitative analysis to test theories based on case studies and qualitative information. The first step in creating such knowledge is to analyze digital actions in the aggregate, rather than focus on an endless number of individual cases (2010, 8-9).*

Such analysis is, of course, not possible without comparative data on all five levels of analysis proposed above, which in turn requires something approximating a common research agenda, or at the very least, a set of commonly applied analytical principles for study design.

In an effort to contribute to the development of such an agenda, this chapter proposes two analytical frames for study design and data collection on individual case studies. These frames are intended to focus analysis on the interaction of online network activity and "real world" political economies in digital activism case studies, and to strengthen the quality and comparability of data collected. We illustrate this approach and explore its consequences for further study, through analysis of an initiative to protect the human rights of participants in Egyptian protest demonstrations.

BACKGROUND

Digital media have played an important role in Egyptian social and political activism in recent years. The Egyptian blogosphere has been widely lauded for its vibrancy and reach in a media environment otherwise tightly controlled by the state. As of April 2008, there were an estimated 160,000 active Egyptian blogs, half of which were published in Egypt, and 8,000 of which were read by more than 50,000 people. This explosion of activity and the hard-hitting political subject matter of many blogs in a repressive media environment have led to characterizations of Egyptian bloggers as a new political vanguard (Mehanna 2008; Hardaker 2008; Fahmi, 2009; Khaled, 2009; Rakha, 2009; Etling, et al, 2009). Facebook has also warranted significant attention for its role in disseminating political information and organizing protest movements.[3]

As with digital activism studies more generally, the majority of these analyses tend to hyperbolize either the impact or failure of new media (Faris, 2009; Bimber, 1998). Interestingly, each tendency also appears to adhere to its own rhetorical focus: online network expansion consistently grounding assertions of new media's political potential, and persistent "real world" power structures consistently advanced as evidence of their failure.[4]

Assertions of digital media's potential tend to revolve around the phenomenon of broadening political engagement and online network expansion. Whether in the context of blog readership or social media coordination, academic analyses in this vein examine online behavior, often with only abstract hypotheses about its consequences for offline behavior or tangible impact. Though content, and not relational networks, is arguably the determinate element in such dynamics – whether as a coordinating factor on Facebook or political information blogged – we are aware of no studies documenting the role of content in expanding networks (either in the Egyptian context or in digital activism studies more generally). This is presumably due to the inherent difficulties in tracking online content to measure relationships between online communication and "real world" activities (though increased and demographically diverse protest participation are compelling evidence of effective communication, this indicator tells us nothing about how protesters relate to media). This inability to document causality, or even correlation, between online and offline practices surrounding political engagement in Egypt is also the primary reference point for analyses that decry the failure of digital activism in Egypt.

This analytical gap between online and offline behavior is not unique to the Egyptian context, and constitutes an important element in the developing research agenda for digital activism per se. It is perhaps only by compiling correlational and comparable data on the strategic interaction between activity online and offline that we can begin to intuit a more heuristic understanding of what compels digital activism and what conditions its success. This would demand loosely standardized data collection across a multitude of factors impacting contextualized media-use (including social mappings and power analyses, relationships between content and media types and survey data on incentives and cost perceptions of media engagement to name a few), and would be ambitious. Indeed, a daunting amount of data would be necessary to make even the most passing of inferences about even a single strategic initiative. How many such studies would be necessary to draw conclusions about a national context is impossible to say, and it should be clear that we are a long way from uncovering digital media's political heuristics.

THEORETICAL PREMISES

We believe that such a research agenda is practically viable through loose coordination of researchers, and that analytical alignment is a useful point of departure. The primary aim of this chapter is to begin defining an analytical model towards this end by identifying conceptual frames and premises for collecting data from individual initiatives without discussing specific research methodologies. This section will sketch these analytical frames and premises in general terms before discussing how they may be observed in a specific case study.

Autopoiesis

The concept of *network* is recurrent throughout this chapter, and is understood as a web of communicative paths that are ordered as the result of collective awareness. Networks are thus understood as autopoietic systems, which "exist by specifying the topological domain of its realization as such a network" (Maturana and Varela, 1980, 89). The appearance and disappearance of networks are thus a function of their alignment towards communicative potential rather than the kind or degree of communication. Similarly, *initiative* is here intended to include instances of activism that are loosely structured, without either identifiable leadership structures or identical motivations among participants, and *strategy* indicates the strategic functioning of tactics and activities without implying or requiring the identification of central authorities to perform strategic planning. As such, this analysis will implicitly assume the premise of autopoietic initiatives as loosely coordinated and polycentric network systems, whose rational self-structuring and response to stimuli constitute de facto strategy.

Contingency

The concept of *contingency* is proposed here as a key frame for analysis, and is meant to refer to the strategic tailoring of activities and organization to developments in concrete power struggles. Simply put, an instance of activism is strategically contingent to the extent that its structure and media are selected and mobilized to address specific aspects of any given power struggle, and amended in response to changes of that context.

Degrees of contingency will thus tend to increase with the specificity of campaign goals, such that the Facebook campaign "Un Millon de Voces Contra las *FARC*" ("One Million Voices against the *FARC*") in Columbia was designed and deployed to meet concrete needs in a specific context and can be said to be strategically contingent, while Amnesty International's Facebook page is not (but is best considered a strategically non-specific public relations component). Degrees of contingency are thus closely related to, but not synonymous with questions of effectiveness and measurable metrics. While the success of digital activism with broad objectives is generally more difficult to measure, and will often be less contingent, the relationship between complexity, success and measurability is complicated by a multitude of contextual factors. In fact, we expect that increased contingency will improve data quality independent of an initiative's (measurable) success, and high contingency may be a key entry point to identifying dynamics of failure or pinpointing identifiable metrics. There is relatively little literature documenting highly contingent digital activism strategies, but a superficial comparison of the well-known examples of Twitter mobilization in Moldova and Iran are suggestive.

The failed Moldovan revolution of 2009 was immediately and enthusiastically heralded by mass media as a success for digital activism, and appears at first blush contingent – in as far as a specific digital media was (arguably) well-positioned to meet coordination challenges posed by a repressive media environment. Yet, a closer look at contingent activities on the ground quickly prompted debate among the tech community, and continues to illustrate how little we know about the initiative beyond the hype. Pending further research that might provide concrete information – who was responsible for the (micro-) blogging, to what degree phone service was jammed by authorities, the influence and motivation of transnational actors, what communications prefaced the daily inflation of protesters, and how these factors motivated one another – there is little that can be said about this as an instance of digital activism, except that it produced a lot of tweets.

Enthusiastic description of Twitter-use surrounding the Iranian elections in 2009 was both more sustained and widespread. As with the Moldovan case, we know little about what motivated and defined Twitter-use on the ground, or how the informal and ad hoc network of users following relevant hashtags grew. What we do know is that while the phenomenon began as mildly contingent technology adaption similar to the Moldovan example, a series of events introduced new uses and responses, demonstrating strong strategic contingency in the process. Twitter was used to alert citizens to security movements and relay information to all individuals following the unfolding events. As the hashtags attracted international attention, people in other countries began to switch their home to Iran, in order to both indicate solidarity with protests and to frustrate efforts to shut down Iranian Twitter accounts. This activity in turn generated a flurry of international media attention and official statements in sympathy with the protesters. The US state department went so far as to request that Twitter postpone a service upgrade so that the site's use would not be interrupted during the protest. This shows that not only was the US government stirred to action but it also (justifiably or not) identified Twitter as a key component in the Iranian protests. Though the so-called "Twitter revolution" did not ultimately provoke an Iranian revolution, strategic contingency effectively activated dormant support networks. These interactions provide important entry points for the analysis of norm mobilization, transnational networks, and social movement incentive structures in the context of digital activism.

Hybridity

Though intuitively of great importance, there has been little study of the joint mobilization of digital and traditional media, or communication bridging digital and grounded networks, and what consequences this might have for how we understand the interaction between online and offline activity in digital advocacy[5]. The characteristic of hybridity is an attempt to counteract this inattention, by identifying objects of analysis in which online and offline activity interact per se, in which that interaction is measurable and comparable, and in which that interaction is meaningful. In the first instance, hybridity most obviously describes the complementary utilization of digital and traditional strategies, and initiatives that are hybrid in this most basic sense. This phenomenon is expected to be most measurable and yield comparable data when it occurs at registers of high specificity, preferably between individuals that may be identified in multiple interactions over time and interactions that are repeated by other actors. Thus, while contingency is considered an attribute of strategic action in sum, hybridity is identified as specific instances of information mobilization across the digital boundary. These instances are expected to be most meaningful when they are conducted at strategically critical points in an overall activism strategy. Hybridity will therefore also tend towards complexity in deployment, and we propose that the characteristics of contingency and hybridity be identified and analyzed together.

We expect such an analysis to be generally useful both for identifying illustrative initiatives, and for identifying those moments of strategic mobilization at which interaction between the grounded and the digital will prove illustrative. While the insights gained here will of course be most relevant in the immediate and grounded context from which they are retrieved, we hope that at a comparative register, they are also likely to indicate the types of data worth collecting from individual case studies. To explore the limits and potential of such an analysis, we will now turn to a close examination of an initiative that exemplifies the characteristics of contingency and hybridity.

THE FRONT TO DEFEND EGYPTIAN PROTESTERS

The growing notoriety of political Facebooking and blogging in Egypt has provoked an increasingly sophisticated state response. Targeted detention and torture of bloggers have been facilitated by online surveillance and engagement via avatar operatives working "undercover" in opposition social media groups, online propaganda in support of the ruling National Democratic Party (NDP), and the development of an Internet task force of 45 state intelligence officers charged with monitoring Facebook to identify and monitor popular movements and influential online actors. (Raoof, 2009; Raoof, 2010) These countermeasures indicate that, if nothing else, the hype surrounding digital advocacy has attracted the attention of the Egyptian government. They have also motivated a number of novel and more sophisticated uses of digital media in advocacy.

The Front to Defend Egyptian Protesters (FDEP) is prominent among these. Founded by an informal coalition of activist groups and national NGOs, the FDEP mobilizes information via a variety of technologies and network strategies in order to protect peaceful demonstrators against human rights abuses. The small group of activists who originally conceived of the FDEP was technologically savvy and extremely well connected within the activist community nationwide. Employed at human rights NGOs and regularly participating in protests, this group recognized the role that public information could play in protecting protesters. The narrative below outlines the FDEP's first deployment in 2010.

Work on the FDEP began with a multi-faceted outreach program, including a formal invitation to every NGO in Egypt, and encouragement for them to distribute information through their professional and personal networks, both online and off. Responses to this outreach afforded the FDEP an opportunity to assess the potential contribution of NGOs across a variety of fields. Within 48 hours, the official NGO network reached 31 organizations. In 48 hours the FDEP also had the contact information of, and commitments of support from, 55 lawyers. This explicit network made it possible for the organizers to host a large meeting with

NGO representatives, where NGOs could share information about the resources available to them through professional and personal contacts. This resource assessment then informed the design and development of the initiative's strategy. After the establishment of the FDEP website and hotline, organizers used offline social networks with potent online presences to widely distribute the FDEP url and hotline numbers nationally. FDEP email lists were used to inform international media and NGOs about the initiative and where developments could be followed online.

To maximize the effectiveness and safety of protestors on the ground, the FDEP hosted two trainings for a total of 170 demonstrators. These trainings covered a variety of basic issues, ranging from physical security to documentation tactics, and were tailored to the skills and hardware of individual participants. To prepare for the demonstrations, participants were encouraged to ensure that their cell phones were fully charged with both batteries and credit; that all relevant phone numbers were saved in the individual's phone and written down in case the phone was confiscated; and that a draft SMS containing the demonstrators' name and the word "arrested" was saved so that it could be sent quickly to FDEP in the event of arrest.

Documentation tactics covered by the trainings included techniques for uploading documentation content to multiple media platforms, as well as the comparative advantages and disadvantages of multiple technologies for individual skills and hardware. Trainings focused largely on mobile phone use for documentation, but systems were also developed to support the relay of documentation to key members in the FDEP for upload, in the event that protesters felt that anonymity was necessary. Trainings also included development of practical documentation skills, including how to take a photograph or video with a phone while appearing to be talking on it to protect against the Egyptian law that criminalizes photography of security forces. This tactic was also designed to protect protestors from police seizure of phones and cameras during demonstrations, a common practice of Egyptian security forces.

To prepare trainees for the eventuality of arrest, the trainers provided a list of protestor rights in the context of search, seizure, and interrogation. Though the Egyptian police do not consistently respect individual rights, experienced activists note a change in police attitude when individuals demonstrate legal knowledge. All of the information presented at the trainings, excepting that which was particularly vulnerable to state interference, was compiled into a manual and distributed online.

On the day of the demonstration, the FDEP set up a communications office near the protest site, where a small team could respond to information from on-the-ground protestors, relay pertinent information to the legal and medical teams, and disseminate documentation and details about police movements. Activists continually updated the FDEP with police movements, photos of the protests and police response, and reports of arrests through the SMS hotline, email, and phone calls. This information was shared on the FDEP website, multiple blogs and social media platforms, providing an online audience with real-time information about the crackdowns on protests, as they unfolded.

Demonstrators came to the FDEP's communications office to drop off memory cards and recount events so that data could be collected and posted online. Several content platforms were indexed and tagged in creative ways. For example Flickr, the social photo platform, was used to host Piggipedia[6], which profiles security officials linked to allegations of torture. Links to Piggipedia were in turn distributed via blogging and microblogging sites. This type of broad cross-posting and link circulation led to a vibrant, cross-platform dissemination of documentation – ultimately supporting a network of followers that closely tracked the day's events as they unfolded.

A forceful crackdown initiated two hours after the demonstrations began halted all protests and resulted in the arrest of 106 demonstrators. Each of these 106 either sent an SMS alerting FDEP to their arrest, or their arrest was documented by a third party. Often this happened concurrently. Within three hours of the arrests, the FDEP had made a list of all detained activists publically available, and with the help of the detainees' family and friends, the FDEP compiled an accurate list of all of the detainees' names and addresses. The names and addresses made it possible for the FDEP to track their processing in police stations and direct support teams to the proper police precinct.

The FDEP's efforts to support and release detained protesters were largely successful. On at least one occasion, knowledge of FDEP activities prompted direct contact from the police, who communicated that they would be promptly releasing detained protesters in anticipation of the legal and medical teams' imminent arrival, to discourage the teams appearance at the precinct (the support team was sent despite this assurance, and the detainees were promptly released). Within the first 24 hours, 33 detainees were released; within 48 hours, 53 more individuals were released; and within 7 days all of those arrested were freed.

For this analysis, however, the most striking element of the FDEP is the interdependent composition of online and offline activities. The interplay of elements is elaborate, as shown in Figure 1.

Despite this complex interplay of elements, the initiative is surprisingly lean. Each element of protest support was specifically targeted and necessary to achieve the overarching aim. The hype cycle of cutting-edge technologies was virtually circumvented, as all technology in the FDEP was selected and tailored to specific ends in a specific context.

Figure 1. A diagram designed by the FDEP to show the interplay between the different components of the network (© 2011, Ramy Raoof, used with permission)

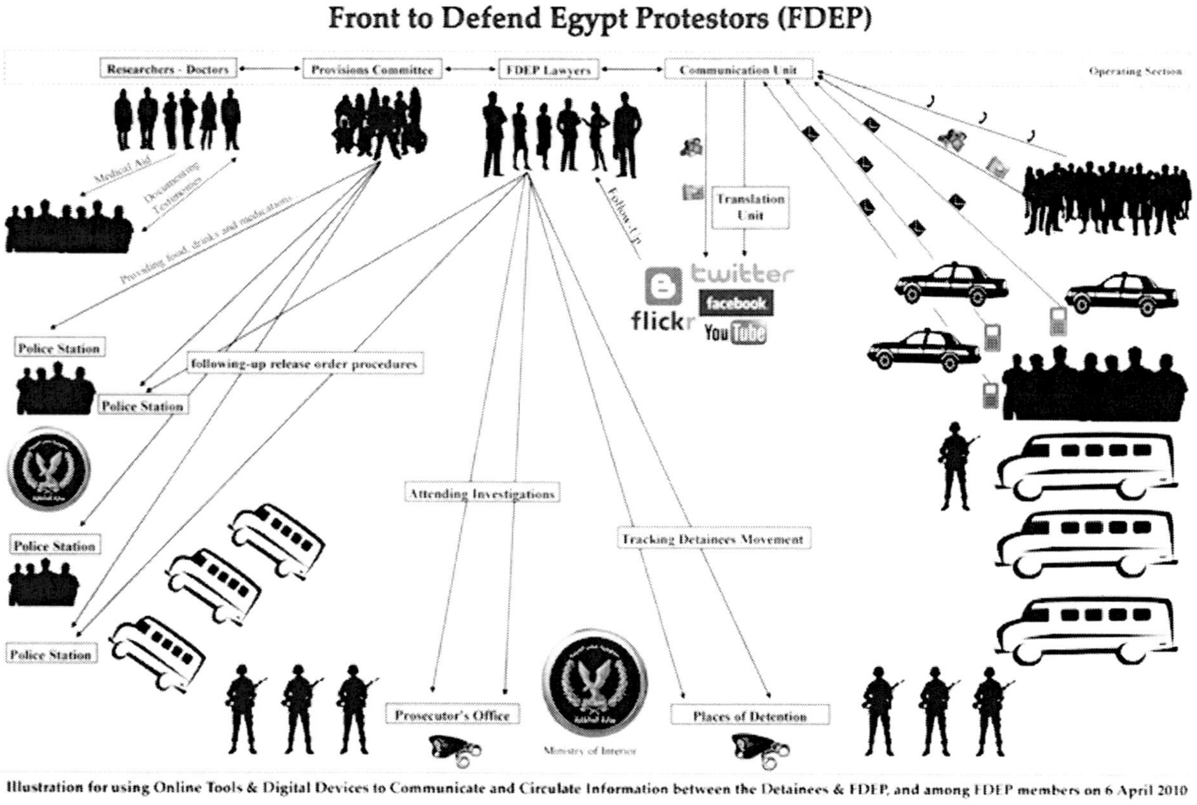

ANALYSIS

The "complexly lean" nature of the FDEP underscores its contingency, and a closer look towards hybridity in FDEP's strategic design suggests four distinct movements. These movements are characterized by their location in a context of ecological challenge and strategic engagement, as well as the mobilization of information across digital and traditional network structures. The four movements are outlined below as *recruitment and awareness*, *dissemination and capacity building*, *protest documentation*, and *detention response*.

Identifying these contingent moments of hybridity allows for a more detailed mapping of network formations, network activities, digital communications and traditional communications, and helps to clarify the interplay of digital networks and real world power structures in the evolution of the FDEP towards its goals. Plotting these moments along a causal progression – during which strategic communications enable the development of novel network structures, specifically adapted to context – results in Figure 2.

The following section will explore each movement by discussing: (i) the nature of the communicative act and its context, (ii) it's strategic consequences, (iii) potential insights regarding incentive, coordination and efficacy structures, and (iv) the types of data desirable to investigate these implications.

1. Recruitment and Awareness-Raising

Though there is a strong tradition for public demonstrations in Egypt and protests tend to be initially tolerated before police crackdown, Egyptian law criminalizes the unauthorized public gathering of more than five people, and authorities work actively to discourage assembly. The Internet has proved a popular tool for organizing protests in this context. Since 2006, Facebook has been the social media of choice for coordinating protest movements among the young, and notable for the rigid hierarchies employed by ostensibly egalitarian groups in technically "open" spaces (Dunn, 2010). Egyptian authorities have been quick to respond, however, with targeted detention of online activists and covert engagement within online networks. It is in this context that the FDEP engaged in the recruitment and awareness-raising activities of grounded networks via digital media.

Figure 2. A diagram chronologically outlining the progressive network development of the FDEP and the multiple media and individuals used for the networks (© 2011, The Engine Room, used with permission)

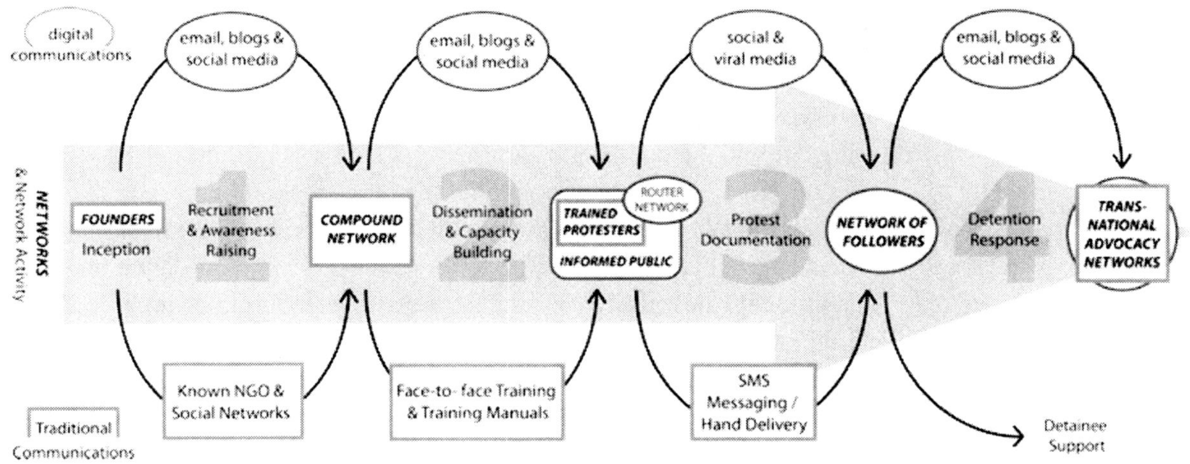

Doing so had a number of important strategic consequences. The most obvious of these lies in the capacity of digital media to effortlessly relay information beyond known networks. This indeterminate network extension is likely to have quickly and effectively cast a much wider net than had been possible either for traditional network communication, which would later be important for maximizing engagement. Simultaneously, basing digital amplification on known grounded network structures enabled communications to capitalize on the common (and in the FDEP context, constitutive) conviction that a protest support initiative was necessary. In assembling a grounded conglomerate network for core initiative activities, this hybrid approach also seems to have performed a filtration function in as far as the organizations joining the FDEP subsequent to these communications were represented by individuals strategically well positioned to utilize hybrid tools. Though lacking demonstrative data, we suggest that this was due not only to the initiative's technological focus, but also the media tools used in recruitment, as the individuals within an organization best suited to drive hybrid communicative activities would also likely those to first be receive and relay digitally broadcast information detailing the initiative.

Recruitment and awareness-raising activities thus had two immediate effects. Indeterminate amplification through digital networks traced the contours of communicative pathways with potential for future increases in engagement. A compound network was also convened to drive key FDEP activities. This network was in effect a conglomerate of disparate grounded and digital networks, aligned by a common incentive structure. This group was also notable for the fact that membership was already predicated on hybrid network activity per se, and individuals tended to represent extant but indeterminate networks already thematically engaged both online and off. This also greatly facilitated a rapid assessment and allocation of previously scattered resources.

Lastly, the strategy of amplifying grounded network structures with digital broadcast brought important security advantages. In as far as the broadcasting function of digital amplification was "one-way" – i.e.: other than "rebroadcasts," the broadcasters of information did not receive information from the "public" – there was no online activity or coordination in which authorities could interfere. One-way broadcast of non-sensitive information relegated all recipients of information to the same role of passive recipient, and the only modes of interference available to authorities were to fully block media that were widely used by non-participating Egyptians, such as Facebook, or to interfere with publicized grounded activities. Though blanket censorship was considered unlikely because it would risk agitating a broader segment of the public, interference in trainings was considered a necessary risk.

This analysis of hybridity in context prompts a number of observations. In terms of incentives, it is clear that digital broadcast dramatically lowered engagement costs for receiving relevant information. By making information publicly available and non-sensitive, the initiative also dramatically lowered the risks for receivers of that information in relaying it to other networks. The increased scope of digital broadcast also appears to have directly increased communicative efficacy and indirectly facilitated coordination by enabling the composition of a grounded network that represented broader networks and scattered resources. These are assumptions and implications in the absence of solid data. A thorough mapping of recruitment and awareness activities across digital and grounded networks would more definitively support these claims, given that such a mapping would enable characterization of nodal associations to extant, grounded networks.

2. Dissemination and Capacity-Building

In the second phase of information mobilization, FDEP trained protesters and publicized the tools that would be used to crowdsource protest documentation. The strategy of digitally amplifying known networks was employed to broadcast web addresses for digital media platforms, a summary of non-sensitive information covered in the face-to-face trainings, and the SMS hotline number through which the FDEP could receive alerts. This information was accompanied by an appeal for individuals to report violence or mass arrests, and lay the communicative pathways for a broad, indeterminate and loosely constituted network, linked solely by common attention to a single grounded event as represented through a variety of digital media and audience members, which we have termed the "informed public."

Again, the one-way broadcast quality of hybrid communication was notable for excluding modes of state interference. Though authorities were able to overtly act on the public information disseminated, they were unable to pose as opposition figures either online (because online broadcast was "one-way") or in physical events (as the compound network established and responsible for trainings in this phase was operating at a register of face-to-face trust and tight-knit cooperation). The security this implied for grounded events was especially important as it allowed the compound network a forum in which to disseminate highly sensitive skills, tools and information that were excluded from broader digital broadcast.

Face-to-face trainings were based on previous experience with violent police and detention, and were structured to focus on the individualized development of protesters' safety and documentation skills. The highly contingent strategy of tailoring trainings to individuals' hardware and expertise produced an environment highly conducive to building solidarity and trust among trainees. This, in turn, may suggest that developing networks through hybrid communications holds significant potential for recruitment at a more general level[7].

The second phase of contingent hybridity was thus composed of two parallel processes: the broadcast of information on documentation media, and the face-to-face training in using documentation media. Together, these communicative activities enabled the constitution of a distinct system of networks operating during the protests. The hybrid broadcast strategy allowed the constitution of an informed public, capable of following the protest online, and contributing documentation to digital networks. Individuals with specific skill-sets manned the communications center and constituted a router network responsible for channelling communications across a variety of media.

These processes prompt a number of considerations. Again, the tandem deployment of digital broadcast and grounded network communication engenders shifts in incentive structures. The dynamics of *no-cost for receipt* and *low-cost for rebroadcast* are again present in the development of an informed public. For engagement in the grounded network of trained protesters, we note that the ubiquity of attention promised by digitally broadcast documentation appears to reduce the perceived risks of participation, while grounded solidarity may function as an abstract social reward. Entrance and exit surveys could be designed to measure trainees' perceptions in this regard, and a longitudinal study might capture the role of such recruitment methods in promoting long-term engagement with protest movements. An extension of the network mapping described above could also apply similar surveys to determine the efficacy of hybrid broadcast, both by indicating the extent to which hybridity qualitatively and quantitatively impacted the development of the informed public, and testing the thesis that the latent network paths established through digital broadcast facilitate node activation in later communications.

Lastly, we note the customization of hybrid tools and media to individual capacities and incentives in this phase, and that this performed a coordinating function. The individualization of skills, roles and technologies to be used in documentation (and in correspondence with individuals' aversion to risk) actualizes a division of labor among participants, maximizing both media use and participation. This dynamic is especially clear in the trained protester network, but we believe it also to be present in the informed public network, where the individualization of skills and media occurs independently, but may have a similar consequence at lower levels of engagement.

3. Protest Documentation

Protest documentation is by far the most dynamic and complex of these four hybrid acts. This phase involves at least three distinct network groupings and variety of communications across network structures and diverse media. These roles were largely distinct and complementary: trained protesters were the prime source of documentation, the informed public acted as a recognized audience, and a router network managed information flow. This clean division of labor collapses under closer investigation, however, revealing both the complexity of network interaction, and the highly contingent facilitation of individual engagement provided by strategic hybridity.

This is most obvious in processes of documentation production. The raw content of documentation – including live video, pictures, social media posts; each conveying information on movements of protesters, police and detention vehicles, flashes of violence, official communications and arrests – originated primarily from trained protesters, but a significant amount was also provided by citizens and bystanders in the broader, informed public. While some of this documentation was posted directly to digital media platforms, the majority was channelled by the FDEP router network which received alerts sent to the SMS hotline, and memory cards delivered by individuals who did not wish to be directly linked to their digital documentation. This information was then relayed by the FDEP to a variety of online platforms, which they also monitored for direct uploads. When any of this information was relevant for protester safety, it was also broadcast back to protesters via SMS.

This control over information flow and matching of information with media was an essential component of FDEP network interaction during protest documentation. That the router network was composed largely of members of the founders' network, but did not solicit or produce content or execute any other authoritative functions, indicates the degree to which the system was automated – by clear procedures and technical compatibility in some instances, by individual incentives in others, and more generally by the polycentric production of information posted to a highly fragmented but fully transparent array of media platforms. As a grounded network, the router network cultivated the trust necessary to engage risk-averse individuals, who could deliver documentation in person and receive encouragement before returning to protests. As a digital network, the majority of information posted by the FDEP router network was not targeted to individual audiences, but broadcast to multiple media platforms for the widest possible dissemination. Together with the direct uploads of protesters, this manifest a running digital narrative and real-time mapping of protest activities, distributed across a variety of online media platforms, and interconnected via hyperlinks.

Without clear statistics on traffic or postings to these sites, we posit that they together constituted a wide and loosely knit digital network defined by its passive membership. This network of followers is a (transnational) group whose engagement cannot be explained or predicted according to the traditional tropes of tie strength and coordination except in the most abstract sense (Somma, 2009). We argue that this loose network structure uniquely facilitates increased engagement in the informed public by minimizing risks associated with engagement. Thus, a member of the informed public watching the demonstration may be compelled by solidarity or other factors to report an event to the SMS hotline. This act alone does not have any concrete effect on her grounded network position, but will likely increase her interest in events surrounding the protest, thus strengthening her position within that network. Simultaneously, the nature of digital media places individuals with other strong network ties on digitally equal footing with other members of the informed public, yet allows for instant increased engagement when incentives structures change. This was most apparent when family members of arrested protesters contacted the router network to correct inaccuracies in arrest documentation, inaccuracies that would have otherwise frustrated release efforts.

We propose that actions of engagement – from direct contact with the FDEP to reposting a hyperlink on a social media site – are all motivated by contingent changes in personal incentive structures, and to a large degree enabled by this peculiar structure of hybrid communications. This observation begs for workable data, and at least two avenues immediately suggest themselves. Mapping documentation by its source in network structures, its media type and its channel (direct upload or via the router network) would do a great deal to clarify how directly hybrid structures facilitated increased engagement, and to what degree this affected network development. Extended exit and entrance surveys could also be used in this context to explore how levels of trust and commitment developed during the course of the protest and how this related to media use.

Secondly, mapping the spread of links and hashtags would shed light on how the network of followers developed, as would tracking hits to relevant websites and social media platforms. Together, these data might help in assessing the role that the contingent deployment of hybrid structures plays in crowdsourcing coordination, in crowdsourcing documentation activities, and in gathering popular support.

4. Detention Response

In the final communicative phase, detainee information aggregated through hybrid communicative structures was posted online and used to mobilize support teams. The deployment of support teams to detention centers, and subsequent release of detainees, is the most striking aspect of the FDEP, yet the least informative for this analysis. An argument for FDEP impact, even if supported by comparative data on FDEP-supported and non-supported protests, would beg an impossible distinction between the impact of support team pressure and the impact of publicized information. Without access to the black box of officials' motivations and rationale, this phase can tell us little that is concrete about the interaction of digital media and real world power structures.

Before concluding this analysis, however, it is worth noting what happens in the shadow of such an elegantly evolved initiative, when virtually no intention or effort is expended. Transnational actors were contacted in initial efforts to raise awareness for the FDEP, and subsequently followed developments online, likely relaying information. The scope of digital broadcast takes on a different shade here, as it facilitates engagement of individuals and organizations not at all engaged with the issues areas of the actual protest, or even national politics per se. When the information at hand becomes relevant to individual incentive structures, however – as detainee information qua documentation of violations of the freedom to assemble is relevant to human rights organizations – this information is easily mobilized as norms, and fits well within an argumentative understanding of transnational activist networks (Risse, 2002; Keck, 1998).

In our case study, this made little actual difference. Egyptian authorities are seemingly impervious to international normative pressure, and international organization's appeals were met with predictable indifference. The FDEP representative that we interviewed was frank about why they alerted international actors to the possibility of following online media in the first place:

Nothing that international networks or media do affect our activities on the ground [but] you have to tell them our world is shit and everyone is lying so whenever I have a chance to show how the government is really working I just send it to everyone.

Transnational network contact was made not because it is worth the effort, but because it is effortless. It is also compelling that this contact motivated transnational actors such as Human Rights Watch and Amnesty International to expend energy and resources, and raises interesting questions about the contextual preconditions for effective transnational activism. For this analysis, the most immediate suggestion is that transnational activist network efforts forged outside the kiln of contingency are poorly equipped to effect social change.

PROGRESSIVE NETWORK DEVELOPMENT

Observing these four hybrid instances in isolation and synchronically, we are struck by the way in which each successive communicative phase allows for the development of novel network structures. This analysis has employed an autopoeietic understanding of networks as collections of communicative relationships that are actualized by an alignment of intentions, and thus does not understand communicative acts to produce network formations (which would in any case neglect the highly contingent and thematic contexts in which networks are formed), but as laying communicative pathways which support the alignment and self-recognition that actualize networks. We see this occurring in digital landscapes such as those supporting the loose constitution of a network of followers, and in more grounded contexts of high contingency, like protest training. Though structurally distinct, both are predicated on hybrid communications in contexts of contingency and are distinctly structured to support further strategic communications. Viewed together, in fact, these dynamics suggest a teleological progression towards strategic network objectives. We find this progression evident in the increased scope, complexity and automation of network activities towards the point at which they reach their explicit goals of detainee release.

Scope is the most obvious example of this progression, as digital broadcasts repeatedly amplify the reach of known communicative structures. The indeterminate nature of this continual expansion (the fact that it can never be exhaustively mapped) poses challenges for data collection, but has compelling implications. Practical individual anonymity results directly from passive membership in a large network defined by one-way digital broadcast, where the majority of members do not distinguish themselves within that network. This practical anonymity is far from absolute, but has a concrete impact on incentive structures, and merits close analysis. The perception of individual anonymity increases with the scope and indeterminacy of compound network structures, as does the power of public transparency. As complexity increases and information published becomes more contingent, the advantages of transparent broadcast move from broadly structural (such as limiting opportunity for state duplicity online) to affecting individual incentive structures.

High visibility and network scope may very well have mobilized incentives at the early stages of network development, but this phenomenon is most clear during detainee support, when the publication of detention information traditionally subject to exclusive state control was likely relevant to officials' decisions. It is not possible to speculate on this impact without data on official perceptions. In the absence of such data, we can only suggest that the perceived exposure of information that was previously private and controlled may have impacted decision-makers' incentive structures to some degree, and that this degree is likely related to a perception of how many are included in that observing public – namely, the scope and indeterminacy of networks.

As network structures expand through instances of hybridity, we also observe a progressive tendency towards *complexity* in network development. This is apparent in the evolution from the founders' network – which was both simple and obvious from a strategic perspective – to the sophisticated interplay of networks manifest during protest documentation, which would have been difficult, if not impossible to achieve without previous contingent and hybrid activity. This (increasingly contingent) complexity carries the specific strategic advantages of facilitated node activation and content actionability.

Complex network structures appear to be particularly relevant for facilitating the activation of nodes in compounded network structures. Network expansion engenders increased perceptions of anonymity, which mitigate the perceived risk of engagement for nodes that are distanced from the initiative in grounded networks. As expansion through both digital and grounded communicative structures increases access to these nodes, increased complexity and interplay between network structures may increase modalities for network engagement. It is in this sense that those contacted during the initial recruitment and awareness-raising efforts had a limited set of options (ignore, follow, share or join), while followers of protest activity and documentation could choose to engage in a variety of ways, from providing documentation, offering support, to bringing sandwiches or starting a campaign. We anticipate that longitudinal data on the motivations and intentions of individuals who increased their level of engagement during FDEP activities would demonstrate "activation" independent of grounded network position, indicating an essential role for digital broadcast in altering incentive structures, and a decisive role for content in motivating heightened engagement.

The actionability of content is also a key and recurring theme in this analysis. As content becomes more accessible and less risk-laden, it is more readily circulated, and we see increases both in the amount of content distributed and in the type of content that is relevant and actionable.

This phenomenon also supports node activation, as complex network structures and the dissociation of content from its production further bolsters practical anonymity between networks. Thus, digital relay of a four digit hotline supports, yet is dissociated from, the production of Piggipedia content – whose distribution would in any case have been both meaningless and dangerous in a traditional media and grounded network context. Already observable in the individualization and dissemination of training materials, the camouflage complex hybridity provides to grounded activity becomes more concrete as network complexity increases, until multiple individual actions (such as a bystander sending an SMS, a protester delivering a memory card to the FDEP, and later "liking" the FDEP's Facebook page) coherently but independently support a broad strategic aim, without revealing grounded network activity. This camouflage provided by complex network structures is also a good entry point for observing the FDEP's progressive trend towards automation.

As hybrid communicative acts enable the expansion of network structures that are increasingly indeterminate and complex, we have also observed an increase in perceived anonymity and public observation, and in the potential for independent engagement and content re-appropriation. These phenomena contribute significantly to increased *automation*, which we identify as the third trend in FDEP's progressive development.

Though clearly implied in broadcast indeterminacy, we see automation most clearly evidenced in late FDEP communications, particularly the complex interplay of structures and media during protest documentation. Here, media type is the determining factor for how (and if) information is mobilized; and legitimacy is the determinant factor for how information impacts behavior. This also matches a general and steady diffusion of authority, from the initial activity of the founders network, to subsequent phases in which autonomy was ceded to individuals. Communications that influenced group behavior during protest activity (which hashtag to follow online, which way to run from advancing police, which spelling of a detained protester's name to publish), did so by virtue of legitimacy in a fragmented informational landscape. The source of these communications was grounded solidly in the immediate context of individuals, their access to information and immediate needs (actual and perceived). This messy landscape of fragmented media and complementary network structures poses questions about coordination and hierarchy that will not be addressed here. It is clear, however, that the FDEP communicated strategically in the service of its objectives, did so in a context of increasingly diffuse authority, and that this trend is relevant to the overall development of the initiative.

CONCLUSION

We have assumed in this chapter that theoretical and practical understandings of digital activism would be advanced by a broad research agenda attentive to how and why individuals engage with digital media in contexts of social advocacy, and that this research agenda would be strengthened by common principles for study design in order to strengthen the quality and comparability of empirical data. This chapter aims to contribute to this agenda by proposing an analytical approach to study design that emphasizes the relationship between digital communication and real-world power structures in case selection and data collection.

Prominent in this approach are the analytical frames of contingency and hybridity, which we define as the dynamic, dependent and reactionary relationship of advocacy strategies to real world power contexts, and the praxis of mobilizing information across complementary digital and grounded network structures and media platforms, respectively. In order to illustrate the theoretical contours of these concepts and how they can support analysis, we have applied them to a concrete case study of digital activism.

Applying these analytical frames to the Front to Defend Egyptian Protesters (FDEP), we find that they enable the identification of specific communicative acts on which to map network engagement with digital and tradition media. This mapping (represented in Figure 2) suggests that digital media and digital network engagement provide a number of strategic advantages to the FDEP.

Firstly, we note that the *increased scope*, or communicative reach enabled by digital media in this instance engenders anonymity for individuals, while providing a broadly transparent public profile that is capable of motivating engagement and impacting official decision-making processes. Secondly, we note that coordination tasks were streamlined by the *increased complexity* of network structures and media strategies employed by the FDEP, which also provided strategic camouflage to individuals' grounded activity and network relationships. Thirdly, we note that the first two factors constitute *increased automation* of FDEP activities, highlighting digital media's strategic potential for content re-appropriation and the increased engagement of passive network nodes independent of network tie strength or proximity.

Importantly, each of these strategic advantages may also be identified as concrete interactions between specific individuals, repeated over time and thus amenable to targeted data collection. We would expect such data to demonstrate digital technology's concrete impact on individual incentive structures, as well as concrete contributions to the FDEP's coordination and efficiency.

Lastly, we note that these three strategic phenomena appear to intensify as the FDEP evolves towards its strategic aims, which has led us to identify digital technology as a key factor in supporting the development of strategically specific network structures. This progressive tendency is exciting, both because it supports assertions of technologies' demonstrable and attributable impact, and also because it implies the potential of strong comparative data sets to be drawn from individual initiatives where this progressive character is present.

Though it was not within the scope of this chapter to document the impact of digital technologies in FDEP activities, nor to identify hallmarks of successful digital activism writ large, we believe that our analysis demonstrates the analytic utility of hybridity and contingency for investigating how underlying social structures impact engagement with digital media. We hope that these insights contribute to the development of a broad and collaborative research agenda, spanning social movement theory, network analysis, strategic action fields and transnational actors, and aimed towards better understanding the way digital media engage with real world power structures and movements for social change.

We also hope that this can have a positive impact on how contemporary debates about digital activism (both academic and popular) are structured and engaged. Indeed, even our superficial (and admittedly anecdotal) analysis poses a number of challenges to how digital activism is currently argued. Especially suspect are the reigning tropes of hierarchy and coordination in popular discourse, given the interplay of anonymity and automation displayed by complex network structures in the FDEP. Similarly, the powerful role of information in latent networks suggests a paradigm shift for network theory's habitual reference to tie strength as a determinant factor for political engagement. Finally this case study illustrates the powerful effect "just information" can have on argumentative and normative structures when propelled by digital technology, and may merit revisiting the 20th century's literature on transnational advocacy networks. We expect that collecting data within these frames and as indicated above, would produce strong arguments to this effect

We also expect that applying the analytical frames of contingency and hybridity in study design more generally will produce rich data sets capable of comparison across genres and fields, and which are bound to productively complicate the discursive paradigms described above. Ultimately, we believe that this will contribute to a better understanding of how and why individuals grounded in real world contexts of power and power struggle engage with digital media for social change.

REFERENCES

Aday, S., Farrell, H., Lynch, M., Sides, J., Kelly, J., & Zuckerman, E. (2010). *Blogs and bullets: New media in contentious politics*. Report from an event at US Institute of Peace and George Washington University's Institute for Public Diplomacy and Global Communication. Retrieved August 11, 2011, from http://www.usip.org/events/blogs-and-bullets-evaluating-the-impact-new-media-conflict

Alfaro, V. (2009). Digital activism in the virtual public sphere, from silence and disruption to cyberactivisms 2.0. In *Proceedings of the WebSci '09: Society On-Line*, 18-20 March 2009, Athens, Greece. Retrieved August 21, 2011, from http://journal.webscience.org/174/

Bimber, B. (1998). The internet and political transformation: populism, community, and accelerated pluralism. *Polity*, *31*(1), 133–160. doi:10.2307/3235370

Boyle, M., & Schmierbach, M. (2009). Media use and protest: The role of mainstream and alternative media use in predicting traditional and protest participation. *Communication Quarterly*, *57*(1), 1–17. doi:10.1080/01463370802662424

Breindl, Y. (2010). Internet-based protest in European policymaking: The case of digital activism. *International Journal of E-Politics*, *1*(1), 57–72. doi:10.4018/jep.2010102204

Brophy, P., & Halpin, E. (1999). Through the Net to freedom: Information, the Internet and human rights. *Journal of Information Science*, *25*, 351–364. doi:10.1177/016555159902500502

Clark, J. D., & Nuno, S. T. (2006). Linking the Web and the street: Internet-based 'dotcauses' and the 'anti-globalization' movement. *World Development*, *34*(1), 50–74. doi:10.1016/j.worlddev.2005.09.001

Custard, H. A. (2008). The Internet and global civil society: Communication and representation within transnational advocacy networks. *Global Media Journal: Mediterranean Edition*, *3*(2), 1–11.

Diamond, L. (2010). Liberation technology. *Journal of Democracy*, *21*(3), 69–83. doi:10.1353/jod.0.0190

Dunn, A. (2010). *Public as politician? The improvised hierarchies of participatory influence of the April 6th Youth Movement Facebook group*. Presented at the New Media/Alternative Politics Conference, Centre for Research in Arts, Social Sciences, and History, University of Cambridge.

Dutton, W. H., Dopatka, A., Hills, M., Law, G., & Nash, V. (2010). *Freedom of connection - Freedom of expression: The changing legal and regulatory ecology shaping the Internet*. Paper presented at the Internet Governance Forum. September, Vilnius. Retrieved August 11, 2011, from http://papers.ssrn.com/sol3/papers.cfm?abstract_id=1654464

Etling, B., Kelly, J., Faris, R., & Palfrey, J. (2009). *Mapping the Arabic blogosphere: Politics, culture, and dissent*. Published by the Berkman Center for Internet and Society at Harvard University.

Fahmi, W. S. (2009). Bloggers' street movement and the right to the city. (Re)claiming Cairo's real and virtual 'spaces of freedom.'. *Environment and Urbanization*, *21*(1), 89–107. doi:10.1177/0956247809103006

Faris, D. (2009). The end of the beginning: The failure of April 6th and the future of electronic activism in Egypt. *Arab Media & Society, 9.*

Fleming, S. (2002). Information and communication technologies (ICTs) and democracy development in the South: Potential and current reality. *The Electronic Journal of Information Systems in Developing Countries*, *10*(3), 1–10.

Foth, M., & Hearn, G. N. (2007). Networked individualism of urban residents: Discovering the communicative ecology in inner-city apartment buildings. *Information Communication and Society*, *10*(5), 749–772. doi:10.1080/13691180701658095

Hamel, J. (2010). ICT4D and the human development and capabilities approach: The potentials of information and communication technology. *Human Development Research Paper Series, 37,* 1-77. Retrieved August 11, 2011, from http://ideas.repec.org/p/hdr/papers/hdrp-2010-37.html

Hardaker, D. (2008). *Putting the genie back in the bottle: Ruling regimes and the new media in the Arab world*. Lowy Institute for International Policy.

Isherwood, T. (2008). A new direction or more of the same? Political blogging in Egypt. *Arab Media and Society, 6*.

Joyce, M. (2010). *Digital activism decoded: The new mechanics of change*. International Debate Education Association. Retrieved from http://www.meta-activism.org/book/

Keck, M. E. (1998). *Activists beyond borders: Advocacy networks in international politics*. Cornell University Press.

Khaled, M. (2009). *An Egyptian blogger crosses red lines*. Committee for the Protection of Journalists. Retrieved August 11, 2011, from http://www.cpj.org/blog/2009/10/an-egyptian-blogger-crosses-red-lines.php

Lannon, J. (2010). The role of information and communications technologies in human rights monitoring and advocacy. In Martin, J., & Hawkins, L. (Eds.), *Information communication technologies for human services education and delivery: Concepts and cases* (pp. 184–200). doi:10.4018/978-1-60566-735-5.ch012

Maturana, H., & Varela, F. (1980). *Autopoiesis and cognition: The realization of the living*. Dordrecht, The Netherlands: Reidel Publishing Company.

Mehanna, O. (2008). *Internet and the Egyptian public sphere*. Presented at CODESRIA General Assembly.

Moody, R., Bekkers, V., Edwards, A., & Beunders, H. (2008). *Micro-mobilization, political resonance and the role of new and old media: Towards a conceptual framework*. Paper presented at the PSA Conference 2008. Retrieved August 11, 2011, from http://www.psa.ac.uk/journals/pdf/5/2008/Moody1.pdf

Neumayer, C., & Raffl, C. (2011). *Facebook for protest? The value of social software for political activism in the anti-FARC rallies*. In DigiActive Research Series, December 2008. Retrieved August 11, 2011, from http://www.digiactive.org/research/facebook-for-protest-the-value-of-social-software-for-political-activism-in-the-anti-farc-rallies/

Neumayer, C., Raffl, C., & Bichler, R. (2009). Politics and social software: Recommendations for inclusive ICTs. In Riha, D., & Maj, A. (Eds.), *The real and the virtual: Critical issues in cybercultures* (pp. 183–191). Oxford, UK: Interdisciplinary Press.

Raffl, C., Fuchs, C., Hofkirchner, W., & Schafranek, M. (2008). The Web as techno-social system. The emergence of Web 3.0. In Trappl, R. (Ed.), *Cybernetics and Systems 2008* (pp. 604–609). Vienna: Austrian Society for Cybernetic Studies.

Rakha, M. (2009). *Egypt: Bad boys who do not moderate blog comments*. Global Voices Online. Retrieved August 11, 2011, from from http://globalvoicesonline.org/2009/09/09/egypt-bad-boys-who-do-not-moderate-blog-comments/

Raoof, R. (2009). *Egypt: Egyptian government utilizes electronic media*. Global Voices Online. Retrieved August 11, 2011, from http://advocacy.globalvoicesonline.org/2009/08/12/egyptian-government-utilizes-electronic-media/

Raoof, R. (Creator). (2010). *Illustration for using online tools & digital devices between detainees & FDEP on 6 April 2010* (Image). Retrieved December 12, 2010, from http://www.flickr.com/photos/ramyraoof/4537322405/

Raoof, R. (2010). *Egypt security department to monitor Facebook and support government*. Global Voices Online. Retrieved August 11, 2011, from http://advocacy.globalvoicesonline.org/2010/08/29/egypt-security-department-to-monito-facebook-and-support-the-government/

Risse, T. (2000). Let's argue! Communicative action in world politics. *International Organization*, *54*(1). doi:10.1162/002081800551109

Rutherford, R. (2000). Internet activism: NGOs and the Mine Ban Treaty. *International Journal on Grey Literature*, *1*(3), 99–106. doi:10.1108/14666180010345528

Scott, A., & Street, J. (2001). From media politics to e-protest? The use of popular culture and new media in parties and social movements. In Webster, F. (Ed.), *Culture and politics in the information age: A new politics?* London, UK: Routledge.

Somma, N. M. (2009). How strong are strong ties? The conditional effectiveness of strong ties in protest recruitment attempts. *Sociological Perspectives*, *52*(3), 289–308. doi:10.1525/sop.2009.52.3.289

Van Laer, J., & Van Aelst, P. (2009). Cyberprotest and civil society: The Internet and action repertoires in social movements. In Jewkes, Y., & Yar, M. (Eds.), *Handbook on Internet crime* (pp. 230–254). Willan Publishing.

ENDNOTES

1 **AUTHORS' NOTE:** This chapter was finalized at the end of January 2010, when seismic shifts in Tunisia were just beginning to resonate in the streets of Cairo. The 18 days and presidential ouster that followed were not anticipated by this chapter, but well illustrate some of its core assumptions and arguments.

Most obviously, the Egyptian uprising underscored the necessary relationship between digital communication and grounded realities. From international Facebook advice on how to handle teargas, to tweets asking for medicine and blankets in Tahrir square, social media behavior consistently responded to threats, exigencies and opportunities in the offline world.

Just as clearly, and closely related, was the predominance of hybrid information paths that crossed the boundaries of geography and media and acted as the battleground in the struggle to control information. In the days preceding January 25th, Egyptian security agents were reported to be touring Cairo cafes, changing the channels of televisions away from Al Jazeera broadcasts of citizen video that had been smuggled out of Tunisia. When the full internet blackout finally came, activists broke through by physically transporting citizen video on hard drives and word-of-mouth messages to one of the last nodes of activist controlled access to the world wide web. These complementary examples well illustrate the interplay of contingency and hybridity described in this chapter. It is also worth noting that the latter activity was directly influenced by the iterative practice of the FDEP described below, and reinforces this chapter's conception of iterative learning processes and embeddedness in autopoeitic networks.

As this chapter goes to press in the early fall of 2011, Egypt's future remains largely uncertain. Also uncertain is whether the prominence of digital media in the Arab Spring has done anything to improve our understanding of digital activism. Academic debate continues to entertain the question of whether or not the Egyptian uprising was "a Facebook revolution," which illustrates just how much we need a more sophisticated analytical model. This chapter suggests two analytical frames with which to develop such a model.

2 The polemics this has produced among prominent commentators and more rigorous social scientists are well known in the field. See, for example, the exchange between Stanford's Patrick Phillip Meyer and Evgeny Morozov, summarized in Meyer's blogpost *Digital Activism and the Puffy Clouds of Anecdote Heaven* (2009)

3 Particular examples of Facebook as a powerful platform for organizing outside of traditional political spaces include the April 6th Youth Movement, the Mohamed ElBaradei constitutional reform campaign, and the collective response to the torture and death of Khaled Said in 2010.

4 Ironically, the notable exception here seems to be what Joyce terms the "pessimists," who argue that new technologies are at least as useful for dictators as they are for activists, and who can readily document how surveillance of online activity regularly leads directly and speedily to real life detention, or worse (Joyce, 2010, 12).

5 With the notable exception of the Zapatista movement's use of multiple platforms to circulate revolutionary materials in Mexico.

6 Piggipedia (http://www.flickr.com/groups/piggipedia/pool/) is hosted on Flicker and provides a platform where citizens can upload photographs of police and security officers that were witnessed committing rights violations. The aim of Piggipedia – with the subtitle "Profiling Hosni Mubarak's pigs" – is to identify offending officers by triangulation and crowdsourced identification. Subjected to naming and shaming, officers are perhaps less likely to repeat abuses.

7 While there are a large number of demonstrations in Egypt, it is a small collective of activists that stage protests and face police crackdowns. This one-on-one training provided for close quarters encouragement and capacity building, and key FDEP members noted trainings' potential for increasing the number of these core, experienced, protestors that participate repeatedly in protest events.

Section 3
Practitioner Perspectives

Chapter 8
Crowdsourcing for Human Rights Monitoring:
Challenges and Opportunities for Information Collection and Verification

Jessica Heinzelman
The Fletcher School of Law & Diplomacy, USA

Patrick Meier
Stanford University and Ushahidi, USA

ABSTRACT

Accurate information is a foundational element of human rights work. Collecting and presenting factual evidence of violations is critical to the success of advocacy activities and the reputation of organizations reporting on abuses. To ensure credibility, human rights monitoring has historically been conducted through highly controlled organizational structures that face mounting challenges in terms of capacity, cost, and access. The proliferation of Information and Communication Technologies (ICTs) provide new opportunities to overcome some of these challenges through crowdsourcing. At the same time, however, crowdsourcing raises new challenges of verification and information overload that have made human rights professionals skeptical of their utility. This chapter explores whether the efficiencies gained through an open call for monitoring and reporting abuses provides a net gain for human rights monitoring and analyzes the opportunities and challenges that new and traditional methods pose for verifying crowd-sourced human rights reporting.

INTRODUCTION

Accurate information is a foundational element of human rights work. Collecting and presenting factual evidence of violations is critical to the success of advocacy activities and the reputation of organizations reporting on abuses. To ensure credibility, human rights monitoring has historically been conducted through highly controlled organizational structures that face mounting challenges in terms of capacity, cost and access.

The proliferation of Information and Communication Technologies (ICTs) may provide new opportunities to overcome some of these

DOI: 10.4018/978-1-4666-1918-0.ch008

challenges. For example, ICTs make it easier to engage large networks of unofficial volunteer monitors to crowdsource the monitoring of human rights abuses. Jeff Howe coined the term "crowdsourcing" in 2006, defining it as "the act of taking a job traditionally performed by a designated agent and outsourcing it to an undefined, generally large group of people in the form of an open call" (Howe, 2009). Applying this concept to human rights monitoring, Molly Land (2009) asserts that, "given the limited resources available to fund human rights advocacy...amateur involvement in human rights activities has the potential to have a significant impact on the field" (p. 2). That said, she warns that professionalization in human rights monitoring "has arisen not because of an inherent desire to control the process, but rather as a practical response to the demands of reporting - namely, the need to ensure the accuracy of the information contained in the report" (Land, 2009, p. 3).

Because "accuracy is the human rights monitor's ultimate weapon" and the advocate's "ability to influence governments and public opinion is based on the accuracy of their information," the risk of inaccurate information may trump any advantages gained through crowdsourcing (Codesria & Amnesty International, 2000, p. 32). To this end, the question facing human rights organizations that wish to leverage the power of the crowd is "whether [crowdsourced reports] can accomplish the same [accurate] result without a centralized hierarchy" (Land, 2009). The answer to this question depends on whether reliable verification techniques exist so organizations can use crowdsourced information in a way that does not jeopardize their credibility or compromise established standards. While many human rights practitioners (and indeed humanitarians) still seem to be allergic to the term crowdsourcing, further investigation reveals that established human rights organizations already use crowdsourcing *and* verification techniques to validate crowdsourced information and that there is great potential in the field for new methods of information collection and verification.

This chapter analyzes the opportunities and challenges that new and traditional methods pose for verifying crowdsourced human rights reporting. The first section reviews current methods for verification in human rights monitoring. The second section outlines existing methods used to collect and validate crowdsourced human rights information. Section three explores the practical opportunities that crowdsourcing offers relative to traditional methods. The fourth section outlines critiques and solutions for crowdsourcing reliable information. The final section proposes areas for future research.

TRADITIONAL METHODS OF HUMAN RIGHTS MONITORING

Human rights organizations traditionally operate through highly trained groups of professionals who gather and verify information under a demanding burden of proof. Researchers visit sites where human rights abuses are suspected to be taking place and conduct detailed interviews with witnesses, look for environmental clues and seek to gain a greater understanding of the dynamics at play. The role of the professional researcher becomes to collect, verify and pull information into a cohesive story that is based in fact.

The follow-up conducted by human rights researchers is extensive and significantly more involved than what is realistic to expect from untrained amateurs. Professionals are taught to systematically assess the usefulness and accuracy of information they collect before incorporating applicable and accurate information into official reports. The veracity of each individual report is extensively evaluated before it can be used. Researchers investigate sources in order to discern the previous record of an individual or organization and identify any biases or agendas that might shape the way in which information was framed.

Above and beyond judgment of verification, they provide judgment on what information can be shared and how while protecting victims and witnesses and interpret information, putting reports in context for a consumer (Beutz Land, personal communication, January 30, 2011). When human rights information is crowdsourced, the qualitative analysis of researchers may still be required depending on the use of the reports and sensitivity of the situation.

Reports are also assessed based on existing information that is known to human rights researchers and compared against other reports related to the issue. A handbook distributed by Amnesty International instructs monitors to "Compare the allegation with other cases and country patterns" and "Cross-check the information with other contacts or sources" (Codesria & Amnesty International, 2000, p. 33). According to the handbook, "Monitoring the country over time systematically allows you to build a picture of the country's record and of typical forms of violations. You can assess the particular allegation with what you know about this type of violation" and "Allegations of violations, whether originating from one contact, the media, the victim or family members should be verified with other contacts or sources" (Ibid).

When information cannot be confirmed but is of significant concern, human rights organizations may choose to publicize the purported evidence despite a lack of definitive verification. In such cases, credibility is safeguarded through the strategic use of language and transparent disclaimers. Amnesty International's handbook advises human rights monitors that "there are ways to get around cases where absolute confirmation of every fact is impossible...by rely[ing] on careful use of language, carefully-worded conclusions, such as 'it appears that' or 'the evidence suggests that' (Codesria;Amnesty International, 2000). This tactic, however, is used sparingly so as not to erode the reputation through over-reliance on unverified information. That said, one should not confuse the idea of how human rights monitoring *should* work with the reality of how it *actually* works. (Spagat, 2011) The handbook described above presents best practices for an ideal case. In reality, human rights monitoring is not necessarily as solid or as cross-checked as the handbook requires. It is important that the use of crowdsourcing for human rights monitoring be evaluated based on the reality of the field rather than the best case scenarios possible.

No matter what strategies are used for assessing information, triangulation of evidence is fundamental to the verification process. Different approaches to data collection complement one another. The more reference points that human rights researchers have to contextualize the overall situation, the higher confidence there will be in its accuracy.

CURRENT APPLICATIONS

Human rights researchers and reporters are *already* using crowdsourced information as another point for information collection and triangulation, and are finding innovative approaches to verifying and using reports including: 1) traditional follow-up, 2) comparing and cross-referencing, 3) forensic assessment, and 4) language and disclaimers. This section discusses some current applications of crowdsourcing human rights monitoring and how verification is being dealt with.

Traditional Follow-Up

Some professional human rights researchers are integrating the use of ICTs and crowdsourcing into traditional verification methods as a way to gather tips and prioritize in-person investigations. Crowdsourcing is not significantly different from traditional methods when used to collect and validate *initial* information. According to Anna Neistat, Associate Director of the Emergencies Division for Human Rights Watch (HRW), "getting information is crucial, especially in areas where [HRW does] not have an extensive human rights network" and crowdsourcing can be a useful "tool for evidence collection" (Neistat, 2010). For example, HRW benefited from the use of crowdsourcing in their investigations of the Kyrgyz ethnic violence that took place during the summer of 2010 and the Sri Lankan conflict in 2009 in which researchers employed mobile phones to assist with information collection to prioritize resources and overcome access issues respectively (Neistat, 2010).

Immediately following the outbreak of violence in Kyrgyzstan, HRW sent a team of two researchers to monitor the human rights situation. With flare-ups dispersed throughout the southern region, researchers had to move rapidly from one area to the next gathering information through traditional face-to-face interviews with witnesses. Concerned about the security of those who had provided reports, they left their mobile phone numbers and encouraged interviewees to call if they were victims of retribution as a result of reporting information. Originally not intended as a mechanism for collecting status updates or new incident reports, the Kyrgyz contacts began calling in news of arrests, security operations and other information regarding the rapidly changing conflict environment. In some cases they passed the phone numbers on to others in the community who also contributed information. With limited time and capacity, the researchers used the information to set their itinerary based on where the greatest abuses were taking place.

Human Rights Watch also used crowdsourcing techniques to gather information during the high-intensity fighting between the Sri Lankan Government and Tamil Tiger forces in 2009 when researchers barred from entering the conflict area and the populations' movement was highly restricted. Human Rights Watch was able to interview dozens of people fleeing and being evacuated from the conflict zone, as has been historically practiced in the face of access issues. However, with the use of ICTs researchers were able to get ongoing reports from a small group of unknown doctors with satellite phones. Without the ability to conduct visits, traditional in-person follow-up investigations were impossible. The research team instead relied on detailed interviews conducted over the phone with the unverified sources, compared testimonies against one another as well as against limited reports from the Red Cross, other international organizations, and satellite imagery that confirmed physical evidence of shelling. In the end, HRW was confident enough about the information to publish a report on the situation in Sri Lanka.

Neistat underscored that while the use of crowdsourced information in both of these cases helped inform the work of researchers, HRW still needed to conduct due diligence investigation. Crowdsourcing provided a useful source of information with which they used to inform additional investigation and analysis through available means.

Compare and Cross-Reference

Much of verification is comparing and contrasting information analytically. The large volume of reports that is made possible by crowdsourcing can provide a wealth of information from which to draw methodical conclusions. Mark Colvin, a respected Australian journalist who has covered international issues for more than 35 years and host's the Australian Broadcasting Corporation Radio's daily current affairs program commented on his approach to verifying the crowdsourcing information following the 2009 Iran elections:

"There was what the intelligence people call a lot of static or chatter - a vast amount of miscellaneous material coming out of Iran on Twitter, with no way of verifying it absolutely. But if you had a sharp eye for detail, you could pick up indications of whether someone was reliable or not. If it referred to protest action in a particular

square, were other people saying the same thing? Quite often I would find three twitter sources, all apparently in different parts of the crowd, reporting on the same event, though from a different perspective. Time came into the judgment as well. Was this someone whose tweets yesterday and the day before had been proved to be true by other reports later? One twitter user, Change_for_Iran, reported in a series of messages being under siege in a dormitory. Another Twitterer, from another part of the campus, reported seeing the same thing from another angle. A day later, pictures started coming through of the damage done in the attack. It starts to add up to something like credibility"(Colvin, 2010).

As highlighted by Colvin, crowdsourced information can hold many clues that provide information about veracity if approached like a puzzle. Subtle differences in detail can help evaluators differentiate between supporting reports and self-reinforcing rumors. The language and patterns of proliferation provide hints as to whether information is original or a retelling of another unverified report. In cases in which information is being gathered from Twitter, Facebook, Flickr or other social networking sites, one can determine relationships and whether there may be a chance that the information being reported is a result of sharing between "followers" or "friends."

Recall also the importance of pictures and video footage shared online during the uprising in Iran. As Philip Howard (2010) noted, "Specialty Persian news channels in Los Angeles received hundreds of digital videos daily, and YouTube became the repository for the digitally captured, lived experiences of the chaotic streets of Tehran." And on June 20, when Neda Agha-Soltan was shot dead, "her death was caught on several mobile phone cameras" (Howard, 2010).

Additionally, electronic records create histories that can be scoured for additional information. These can help contextualize information and provide helpful clues about the source. This extends beyond the individual's "track-record" for accuracy, but other useful information can be gleaned. For instance, what topics have other reports been about? Has the account been created solely to propagate information on a particular issue? Much can be determined about biases, location and other important details through online investigation.

While the remote nature of most crowdsourced information may prohibit the collection of certain types of clues such as physical and interpersonal observations, data collected through ICTs provide different and similarly useful evidence that can be used in assessing veracity.

Forensic Assessment of Multimedia

The increasing availability of camera phones, inexpensive video recorders and other electronic documentation tools has already had a profound impact on the ability of communities to document and report human rights abuses in a manner that is both compelling and provides contextual clues that can help with forensic verification. Sam Gregory, Program Director at WITNESS, a non-profit organization that provides training to human rights advocates on the strategic use of video, comments, "[S]eeing is believing," but warns that "Activists often approach photographs and moving images and transparent mirrors of reality and conflate them with proof; this despite the fact that images always demand interpretation" (S. Gregory, 2006, p. 192). The way technology is used simply reflects our motivations and values as human beings. In this way, technology may be considered neutral a priori but not a posteriori. Consumers of human rights information cannot simply take visual "proof" at face value, but need to view it with an equally critical eye within the larger context of the issue.

Video documentation of human rights abuses has been successfully used and often aided by a professional forensic assessment to establish the veracity. Audiovisual reports provide additional details to help experts judge the credibility of material by looking for evidence of tampering and physical details that are difficult to fake. In 2009 a video of an execution of Tamils by Sri Lankan soldiers provided by an anonymous individual came under scrutiny. The Sri Lankan Government responded by hiring four expert nationals who supported government claims that the footage had been falsified. Assessment by an expert hired by the Times UK, however, called the Sri Lankan experts' findings into question and further investigation by the United Nation determined that the video was, in fact, authentic. The Times and UN experts defended their assessment based on details such as visible recoil from the weapon, audio/video synchronization, the physical movement of victims after being shot, consistency between visual and audio details such as the presence of wind and evidence that the type of recording device was a mobile phone as reported, (UN Human Rights Council, 2010). The footage from an unknown and unconfirmed source brought international attention to the issues has led to the formation of a United Nations commission of experts charged with determining if an international investigation should take place. The commission is currently ongoing.

Gregory (2010) contends that crowdsourcing lends itself to gathering numerous multimedia reports and that multiple viewpoints of the same incident increase can significantly increase the credibility of documentation. Falsification at a grand scale is possible, but may require a significant amount of organization and resources that raise barriers to staging false events (Meier, 2010a). Unfortunately, the multi-viewpoint approach is only a possibility for cases in which human rights abuses take place at public events, such as rallies or riots, where multiple parties can capture the event. It is not as useful in verifying closed-door abuses or those more structural in nature (Sam Gregory, 2010).

Unverified material has been successfully used as the basis for calls for investigation into human rights abuses and for raising awareness. Because visual images hold a powerful emotional immediacy, they, more than verbal or written human rights reports, can "play a central role in determining which violences are redeemed and which remain unrecognized [sic]" (McLagan, 2006, p. 191). In a 2010 case, a trophy video taken by Indonesian soldiers and was picked up by trusted international human rights organizations and media. The video, featuring the torture of a Papua man, led to an internal investigation and recognition of abuses by the central Indonesian Government, followed by disciplinary action (Survival International, 2010). The advocacy organization, B'Tselem, has successfully raised awareness about human rights issues in the Palestinian Territories by distributing over 150 digital video cameras through the Palestinian Territories and posted hundreds of videos online. Their YouTube views average over 80,000 per month and footage appears multiple times a month on Israeli television and radio and is shown regularly on international networks such as CNN, BBC, Al-Jazeera and more ("B'Tselem Activity Report," 2008).

Multimedia reports can be powerful and provide contextual evidence for the trained eye. While seeing must not be conflated with believing, the medium is ripe for analysis and holds significant details when dissected into various parts.

Phrasing and Disclaimers

Numerous news organizations covering human rights issues have reported unverified information gathered through crowdsourcing, protecting their credibility through the carefully worded disclaimers. For example, during Iran's "Twitter Revolution," CNN's David Mattingly stated in one news cast, "Because Western journalists are not allowed to cover these events, we are looking at the social networking sites and seeing what's posted on there" and another news anchor introduced coverage warning the audience, "Because of these new restrictions, what we are doing at CNN is relaxing our usual vetting process a bit" ("Irandecision 2009 - CNN's Unverified Material," 2009). A graphic was also place prominently next to the "CNN Live" icon reading "Unverified Material" whenever reporting contained unverified crowdsourced information. This allowed CNN and (as well as other media organizations using similar tactics) to provide what information they had access to as was demanded by international viewers, while also protecting their credibility had information been challenged or later proved to be false.

The use of unverified crowdsourced information must be used judiciously, but can have a significant impact in bringing attention to issues that cannot be confirmed yet for which there is significant evidence of abuse.

THE POTENTIAL OF CROWDSOURCING

The current "light weight" use of crowdsourced information in human rights monitoring demonstrates the burgeoning potential for the incorporation of population-generated information into traditional methodology. Crowdsourcing represents an opportunity for human rights organizations to increase the number of eyes-on-the-ground through locally embedded volunteer monitors. An increase in communications technologies, likewise, has empowered "Local human rights activists [who] are...truly 'embedded,' living and reporting on the context of rights violation on a long-term basis" to monitor and report on human rights abuses as they bare witness (S. Gregory, 2006, p. 202).

The ability to crowdsource human rights monitoring through ICTs promises to significantly expand the documentation of abuses worldwide. This shift presents a benefit to communities not previously prioritized by human rights organizations as well as a benefit to the field as a whole. As James Surowiecki writes, "We don't always know where good information is...That's why, in general, it's smarter to cast as wide a net as possible, rather than wasting time figuring out who should be in the group and who should not" (Surowiecki, 2005, p. 276). The mass proliferation of ICTs represents an important shift in the field of human rights in that the traditional capacity constraints no longer apply: there is no longer a limit to the number of issues that human rights advocates can follow as long as there are amateur monitors willing to report.

A worldwide network of volunteer monitors can perform many of the same functions as formalized human rights organizations, but engaging this resource creates new challenges. As Shirky observes of transitions to collaborative systems of production, organizations "shed the institutional cost[s]" but "lose the right to shape people's work" (*Clay Shirky on institutions vs. collaboration on TED*, 2005). In monitoring human rights, the shift from traditional professionalized models to crowdsourcing results in a trade-off between maintaining control over verification methods that ensure accuracy and an expanded information gathering capacity, a dilemma that is the basis for many of the current fears and critiques of crowdsourcing in a human rights context.

CRITIQUES OF VERIFICATION AND CROWDSOURCING

The feared loss of control around issues of verification has given criticisms of crowdsourcing human rights monitoring including: 1) the potential for bias or misinformation, 2) assumptions regarding statistical validity of information, and 3) capacity constraints for analyzing large quantities of incoming reports. This section discusses each, highlighting challenges and providing solutions.

Bias and Misinformation

There is some concern among many human rights experts that opening human rights reporting to the general population will allow bias and misinformation to color the information that is received and will degrade the accuracy of reports. Patrick Ball, lead of the Human Rights Data Analysis Group at Benetech and a critic of using crowdsourcing for human rights monitoring, likens the approach to that of crowdsourcing public tips about security threats. Ball concludes that asking amateurs to help with security produces amateur security, so it follows that "Crowdsourcing in the human rights context creates more rumor and contradiction than clear signals" (Ball, 2010). Similar critiques have been made of Wikipedia,1 the free online encyclopedia of over 17 million entries that has been created (and is continually improved upon) through the aggregation of amateur knowledge. Critics of the crowdsourced encyclopedia, claim "that the principle of being open for editing by everyone makes Wikipedia unauthoritative and unreliable, that it exhibits systemic bias, and that its group dynamics hinder its goals" ("Wikipedia - Wikipedia, the free encyclopedia," n.d.).

What Ball, critics of Wikipedia and others forget is that in all of these cases, crowdsourcing is working. In reference to the security analogy, emergency phone numbers like 999 in the UK and 911 in the US are examples of crowdsourcing *par excellence* in which the population as a whole alerts emergency responders to issues that need attention (Meier, 2010c). Social norms and systems have been put in place to ensure that individuals take reporting seriously and only report incidents that meet certain criteria for veracity. Crowdsourced information use in this way has been found particularly helpful in tracking "events that are spatially diffuse...[in which] sources of information from multiple eyes-on-the-ground can be more helpful than official…sources because the information can provide a more local context and rapid updates" (Palen, Vieweg, Liu, & Hughes, 2009, p. 2). Compared to *Encyclopedia Britannica*, Wikipedia covers approximately thirty-four times as many topics and has done so for relatively little cost compared to the $32 million price tag of *Britannica's* 15th edition produced by 4,000 expert authors in 1974 (the most recent edition) ("Encyclopaedia Britannica -- Britannica Online Encyclopedia," n.d.). The significant amount of free labor and aggregate expertise has made Wikipedia's crowdsourced model far superior to *Britannica* in its ability cover a broad spectrum of information at relatively low cost. Comparative studies have found that the overall accuracy of entries is of equivalent quality to traditional encyclopedias (Giles, 2005,Thomas, 2006, Bragues, 2007).

This is not to suggest that crowdsourcing human rights information is not without its challenges. Crowdsourcing cannot be applied blindly, but requires safeguards to be in place that set social expectations for accurate reporting and include mechanisms to discipline or correct for misinformation. These mechanisms as best applied to human rights monitoring have yet to be defined, but those looking to crowdsourcing monitoring can look to similar examples for guidance.

For example, Wikipedia provides a relevant case study that addresses issues of bias or purposeful misinformation. While the *overall* accuracy of Wikipedia entries is comparable to traditional encyclopedias, there are notable exceptions among entries on controversial or highly contested topics (like human rights issues). One example, the Arab-Israeli conflict, has been the subject of much arbitration in which site administrators and a trusted group of administrators must intervene. Some of the edits are ad hoc, but some attempts to shape the prevailing narrative are highly organized. One right-wing Israeli group offers a workshop called "Zionist Editing for Wikipedia" aimed to educate and enable an 'army' of editors of Wikipedia with the skills to write and edit content "in a manner which defends and promotes Israel's image" (Ezra & Kempinski, 2010). The Palestinian Journalists Syndicate responded with a commitment to counter efforts through building their own editing forces, threatening to create Wikipedia into an information war zone rather than a reliable research resource (YNET, 2010). Wikipedia has responded to these issues through institutional mechanisms such as an arbitration board that can investigate individual edits as well as by creating as "self-conscious social-norms-based dedication to objective writing" that is played out in a transparent fashion through an archived histories of edits as well as "Discussion" pages for each topical entry where disagreements can be played out (Benkler, 2006, p. 72). Through this mechanism, it can be argued that an even more complete picture of the issue can be found.

In other cases it has also been shown that establishing an accepted standard of proof can lead participants to self-censor information that is not confirmed *prior* to submission. A study of the social dynamics of ad hoc online groups that collectively compiled a list of 32 victims of the Virginia Tech shooting in 2007 found that victims names listed on social networking sites were *never incorrect* and that "Participants in the list-building activities self-policed, and they knew that adding a name to the list was a serious statement. Accuracy, verification, credentialing, and gravitas ruled the interaction" (Palen et al., 2009, p. 9). Those reporting names without some description of how the information was obtained were often asked to substantiate their source before a name would be added to the online list.

Despite the potential to create social standards and norms, the *perception* of accuracy may still present issues for the mainstreaming of crowdsourced human rights monitoring. As previously discussed, the perception of accuracy is as important (if not more so) than the accuracy itself. For instance, academics still hesitate to cite Wikipedia because it "doesn't have the right credentials" (Beutz Land, personal communication, June 30, 2011). Similarly, major advocacy organizations, legal institutions, governments and other actors with a reputation to uphold may continue to have reservations about adopting crowdsourced models as a primary means of monitoring – perhaps based more on the perception it creates rather than a judgment on its accuracy.

The Wikipedia, emergency hotline or Virginia Tech examples do not translate exactly to human rights issues, but present a solid case that systems can be set up to mitigate misinformation and bias. The challenge remains to shift perceptions of bias and accuracy among consumers before the potential of crowdsourced monitoring can be fully realized.

Statistical Representation

Concern has been raised that because of the potential for a large volume of human rights reports made possible through crowdsourcing, information will be misused for statistical analysis without the appropriate verification or scientific sampling. Such concerns are unjustifiable. First, the most common form of human rights investigation focuses on documenting patterns of human rights abuses and is not dependent on statistically valid data collection. Second, aggregated crowdsourced data has been shown to closely mirror on-the-ground realities. It may not be any less credible that currently accepted analysis methods.

As Neistat noted regarding the work of HRW, human rights researchers seek out information that can be connected together to establish a history of abuse. Uncovering human rights abuses does not require sources to be statistically representative and therefore need not meet the criteria of strict scientific sampling (Neistat, 2010). Yet strong reservations about statistical relevance continue. Ball (2010), who leads Benetech's work with the statistically-driven "multiple systems estimation" (MSE) method, states that "crowdsourced information is not statistically meaningful." Ball's MSE approach attempts to approximate the total number of human rights violations when evidence is incomplete using "two separately collected but incomplete lists of a population to estimate the total population size" and data on abuses validated in the field according to the particular context of the project.2 Benetech holds that, "this information is vital to producing a complete accurate historical record of the violations and to provide evidence at the trial of the architects of large-scale human rights abuses." However, the technique itself has hardly been evaluated and is not easily verifiable.

As Michael Spagat from Royal Holloway College notes, these "established" methods remain "unvalidated just like crowdsourcing" (Spagat). Furthermore, the assumptions that need to be imposed for MSE to theoretically work for statistical inference are "really strong and far from being satisfied in almost all the cases it has been applied to" (Spagat). This means that conclusions derived from statistical analysis using MSE may be misleading and likely no more trustworthy than crowdsourced information that is analyzed judiciously. Finally, the point in a court of law might be to demonstrate convincingly that some perpetrator has killed a number of individuals. In this case, "getting an unbiased estimate of how many people this person has killed is not useful—it is better to document well 10 deaths than to estimate 10 thousand deaths" (Spagat, 2010). Hence the importance of documentation over estimation in many cases. Of course, statistical validity is valuable for some human rights work, but certainly not for all human rights analysis.

As discussed by Colvin (2010), crowdsourced information needs to be assessed before it can be used whether qualitatively *or* quantitatively. Information cannot be taken at face value and the frequency of a report cannot be interpreted as evidence of its truth. During the 2008 post-election violence in Kenya, for instance, rumors were often conflated as truth among the population. While the media dismissed most as propaganda, the proliferation of ICTs allowed for alternative methods of information sharing through social networks that lead to the mass propagation of rumor as fact. The end result as described by a study of the proliferation of rumors during the violence, "Where rumours were once local, taking time to percolate outwards and onwards to a broader, national audience, the use of high-tech communication, such as mobile phones, email, internet websites and weblogs, has transformed the pace and range of rumour. Kenya's local rumours now go national in minutes" (Osborn, 2008, p. 316). The population of Kibera, Nairobi's largest informal settlement, took one rumor so seriously that they closed all bars for the four days leading up to the elections after it had been suggested that an opposition party was poisoning the community's beer supply (Osborn, 2008). The level of concern surrounding such rumors and their ability to inspire action ensures that they will emerge repeatedly in crowdsourced data.

Crowdsourced data sets offer value in identifying non-statistical patters and can also be used for statistical purposes if paired with verification processes that fit the environment. In controversial settings, crowdsourced human rights monitoring will likely need to be analyzed and culled, but with the appropriate process may still be helpful in statistical analysis of comparable reliability to current methods.

Information Overload

More than the veracity of information itself, it is the capacity to verify that presents the greatest challenge to crowdsourcing human rights information. Criticisms of misinformation or statistical analysis, in fact, often stem from underlying concerns of limited capacity of human rights organizations to deal with large volumes of user-generated data rather than the actual process of crowdsourcing. As Ball (2010) noted in his critique of statistical validity, "Adding lots of amateur tips stresses the follow-up mechanism by adding too many false positives." And Neistat (2010) remarked that many of her colleagues would view her team's use of mobile phones in Kyrgystan as a distraction from traditional research tasks and an unnecessary burden. Seeing as though human rights organizations are already struggling with issues of capacity, the additional hiring of staff to process reports is unlikely. However, there may be other ways to address information overload by harnessing crowdsourcing in a different role – peer verification.

The previous sections have discussed crowdsourcing as a mechanism for the *reporting* of information. However, information can also be *reviewed* by the crowd as a means of evaluating large flows of information. Crowdsourcing traces its roots back to the open source software movement in which volunteer programmers collaborate to improve upon software and fix bugs. Capturing the power of bottom-up program design relative to top-down institutional systems, Raymond introduced Linus's Law in his groundbreaking work *The Cathedral & The Bazaar*. Linus' law states: "given enough eyeballs, all bugs are shallow," or in laymen's terms, the more people looking at a problem, the easier it is to fix (Raymond, 2001). Initially used to explain why bugs in corporate software took years to fix, with small staffs working on extensive code, and open source programs were repaired rapidly with thousands of volunteers working collaboratively, a similar principle has been applied to other types of peer production products such as qualitative reviews and veracity. Peer verification has yet to be applied to human rights reports in a systematic way. But lessons can be taken from other peer verification models capitalizing on the creation of social norms and verification protocols.

Multi-layered review systems that limit participation to small judgments and reward positive contributions can be effective in channeling positive peer review. Slashdot, a news aggregation site, offers one of the most complex, but effective relevance and accreditation systems that could be used as a model for assessing human rights reports. First, the crowd suggests articles as useful or interesting reads. Second, users of the site post comments that often challenge or endorse the article. These initial stages are quite common forms of peer review that form the basis of rankings and rating systems on sites such as Amazon, YouTube, and other user-driven websites. Slashdot, takes the implementation of peer review beyond these initial steps in order to better appraise content. Using an automated system, the website selects moderators that are registered regular users who have participated on the site for an extended period and have earned positive ratings on their previous comments from other moderators. Each moderator then gets a limited number of reviews they can make (in the case of Slashdot, five). A final step allows for "metamoderation" in which moderators can rate their peers. Those with consistently poor feedback on their judgments risk being demoted from moderator. As Benkler assesses, Slashdot is able to moderate individual bias because it is "designed to give many users a small amount of power…[and] decreases the effect of users with an ax to grind or with poor judgment" (Benkler, 2006, p. 61).

Peer verification is certainly not an infallible solution, but if implemented strategically, has the potential to greatly reduce the likelihood of inaccurate information from rising to the top of crowdsourced reports. Casual inaccuracies resulting from human error will likely be detected through peer review. Coordinated intentional misinformation campaigns may still arise, but will require an increasing amount of resources and organization as the size of the peer review community grows.

Perhaps the most challenging obstacle to the implementation of an effective peer verification system is access to the level of technology required for participation. Peer verification, to work properly, requires broad involvement of individuals who have some frame of reference to know whether or not a report is true. Currently the technologies that are widely available in the field are best suited for data collection rather than dissemination (e.g. basic mobile phones). Community, discourse and rating systems rely heavily on access to the Internet, making them a problematic solution in low-tech settings as well as highly repressive political environments in which technology is often in the hands of the repressor rather than the repressed.

Until there is better connectivity at a local level, some narrow verification tasks might be conducted by international human rights advocates to expedite information processing. While individuals looking through reports from remote locations might not have adequate knowledge to make informed judgments, breaking down the complex analysis process into smaller independent modules might allow for a networked community to assist professional analysts in filtering through information (Benkler, 2006). For instance, reports with similar content, as identified by computerized natural language processing3, could be presented to volunteers to make judgments about whether reports are "in agreement" or "contradict" one another. Information could begin to be organized by engaging the crowd in categorization or geolocation of reports, essentially creating a searchable database for use by professional human rights researchers. Quality could be controlled through redundancy and automated averaging of responses.

All these observations are informing the development of a technology called SwiftRiver that will help organize professional and amateur analysis. The free and open source platform developed by the African technology group Ushahidi seeks to help users crowdsource, cluster and verify information in near real-time by drawing on many of the traditional methods that already exist in the field of human rights (Meier, 2009).4 Indeed, SwiftRiver combines crowdsourcing, comparison and cross-checking, assesses multimedia content, includes peer verification and trusted networks. SwiftRiver combs and cross-checks events reported via email, Twitter, SMS, smartphone app, online news, blogs, Facebook, Flickr and soon YouTube to generate veracity scores, i.e., probability scores with respect to the reliability of the information collected. In other words, SwiftRiver simply automates some of the intuitive, manual steps outlined by Colvin (2010) to answer the following question: what is the probability that this event being reported by several different sources over time and across different media has actually happened?

Several media groups including the BBC, UK Guardian and Australian Broadcasting Corporation have tested SwiftRiver. A number of humanitarian groups such as the UN are also piloting the platform, most recently to monitor social media content relating to the Sudanese Referendum of January 2011. SwiftRiver is for sure no silver bullet and should only be considered as one tool to use in combination with more manual methods. The platform is also a work in progress and the Ushahidi team invites interested groups to test the free tool and provide feedback so that the software can be improved and provide direct added value to information collection and verification in the field of human rights. It is also worth noting that collecting and verifying information in near real-time opens up new possibilities for early response and prevention in a way that retroactive human rights assessments can't.

Whether through SwiftRiver or other emerging technologies, what is needed to compliment human labor is a more automated method of information analysis that draws on natural language processing to collect, cluster and cross-check reports from diverse sources that relay information on similar or identical events. While some manual efforts require that 80% of resources be allocated to information collection and cross-checking, leaving 20% to analysis, existing parsing technologies can reverse this ratio, allowing 80% of human resources to be focused on what humans do best, analysis. In other words, the informal method developed by Colvin (2010) should be considered for automation.

As the automation of certain tasks is designed it must incorporate a multimedia approach to compare reports across different media as well. An automated method for information collection and cross-checking should not be limited to text based evidence but ought to include visual evidence in the form of photographs and video footage, e.g., potential evidence uploaded to Flickr and YouTube. Recall the role of these technologies in the Iran protests of 2009. Moreover, the use of crowdsourcing to analyze and cross-check photographic evidence has already been used successfully in other sectors (Tapscott & Williams, 2010).

There is considerable evidence that the challenges of verifying crowdsourced information are not insurmountable. These challenges should not be the enemy of innovation, but rather ought to encourage human rights organizations and advocates to develop ways to overcome some of the constraints that come with loosened control. Local populations, now with greater access to communication technologies, have a shared incentive for expose human rights abuses and can be effective partners in research and reporting. Despite the challenges outlined above, crowdsourcing can provide a net benefit to human rights monitoring. The manner in which the crowd is engaged and the verification technologies employed will ultimately determine how valuable crowdsourced human rights monitoring will be in the coming decade.

FUTURE RESEARCH DIRECTIONS

As this chapter outlines, crowdsourcing is already being integrated into human rights monitoring and has great potential for increased use in the field. However, the tactic is still largely untested and has not been systematically evaluated to determine the extent to which the opportunities and challenges weigh against traditional methods. The field of human rights needs a new research agenda that seeks to answer pressing questions with respect to the role of new methodologies like crowdsourcing as they compare to and can compliment industry standards.

This research agenda should also seek to shed more transparency on the validity of crowdsourcing as well as traditional methods for the collection and validation of human rights data. Traditional methods may have more a theoretical case in the literature, but the empirical evidence is as thin as what exists in terms of crowdsourcing (Spagat, 2010). As argued, some of these methods are accepted as valid without much in the way of empirical evidence in contrast to extensive theoretical explanations as to why they should or do work. There appear to be little to no literature that empirically validates the actual methods (Spagat, 2010). For example, most scholars and practitioners simply assume that respondents to human rights surveys (based on representative sampling) are giving truthful answers. "Too often, survey work is carried out with insufficient care to ensure that the results are reliable, let alone generalizable" (Barahona & Levy, 2003). In other words, while validating human rights information is obviously central to the work of human rights practitioners, more research is needed to evaluate the effectiveness of the methods used to accomplish this core task.

Human rights advocates therefore need be more transparent and objective about the weaknesses of the traditional methods that have been used in the field and not discount the potential added value of crowdsourcing. New methodologies and technical tools need to be tested with the same level of rigor under various conditions. Greater research needs to be conducted to determine which methods are more effective than others, why and under what circumstances.

CONCLUSION

As demonstrated in this chapter there is great potential for the use of crowdsourcing in gathering and verifying human rights information. Existing methods used for the collection and verification of human rights information face issues of capacity. They are limited by availability of professional staff, the time and staggering costs of some retroactive human rights assessments, and access to areas that have (and continue to be) the site of mass atrocities. As more individuals around the world participate in documenting human rights abuses thanks to easy and cheap access to ICTs, there is an increasing resource for human rights organizations and advocates to use these technologies for initial gathering and triangulation of information.

Hybrid methodologies that combine the benefits of crowdsourcing with the professionalized or centralized analysis and verification offered by traditional methods present a promising opportunity for expanding human rights monitoring. For now, data collected through crowdsourcing will likely still be assessed for accuracy using traditional methods even though they offer no silver bullets. Like any methodologies in the social and hard sciences, they have strengths and weaknesses. In any case, some of the traditional methods used for information collection already employ some forms of crowdsourcing successfully and there are opportunities for growth while continuing to rely on researchers to provide analysis, context and interpretation.

All of the current uses of crowdsourcing have the capability to increasingly advance human rights monitoring, but must be more fully incorporated and supported by the development of new tools in order to realize their full potential. The need for traditional follow-up may become less acute as more sophisticated methods for collecting and aggregating multimedia information, and comparing and cross-referencing this information with other data collected in more traditional ways. As Amnesty International's handbook on monitoring human rights advocates for the use of different sources, crowdsourcing information can greatly increase the pool of reports against which to compare. At the same time, the significant increase in user-generated multi-media content means that keeping up with larger volumes poses new challenges.

Dealing with a significantly larger volume of information that needs to be codified and verified, however, is unlikely to scale at this point. The human resources required for cross-checking a large influx of data quickly becomes a laborious and time-intensive process that requires a sharp eye for detail beyond what human rights organizations can currently handle (Colvin, 2010). Peer verification represents an untapped resource for organizing and analyzing human rights reporting in a systematic way. The potential for automated systems should also be explored, as when details multiply, adding more "manual" eyes may not be sufficient to handle the added complexity. Improvements that increase the capacity and ease of analysis will have a tremendous impact on the ability and willingness of organizations to use new technologies to leverage ICTs for both the data collection and verification of human rights reports and reduce the current obstacles that are the foundation of most criticism.

As the challenges associated with crowdsourcing and verifying large amounts of information are addressed, crowdsourcing will provide an increasing benefit to in the field of human rights. The integration of amateurs into the data collection infrastructure will become a useful input for the holistic analysis and triangulation necessary in ensuring accuracy in human rights monitoring.

REFERENCES

B'Tselem. (2008). *Activity report*. Retrieved from http://www.btselem.org/english/about_btselem/2008_Activity_Report.asp

Barahona, C., & Levy, S. (2003). *How to generate statistics and influence policy using participatory methods in research: Reflections on work in Malawi 1999-2002*. Institute of Development Studies.

Benkler, Y. (2006). *The wealth of networks: How social production transforms markets and freedom*. Yale University Press.

Bragues, G. (2007). *Wiki-philosophizing in a marketplace of ideas: Evaluating Wikipedia's entries on seven great minds*. SSRN eLibrary. Retrieved from http://papers.ssrn.com/sol3/papers.cfm?abstract_id=978177

Clay Shirky on institutions vs. collaboration on TED. (2005). Retrieved from http://www.ted.com/talks/clay_shirky_on_institutions_versus_collaboration.html

Codesria, & Amnesty International. (2000). *Ukweli: Monitoring and documenting human rights violations in Africa: A handbook*. Amsterdam, the Netherlands: Council for the Development of Social Science Research in Africa, Amnesty International, African Books Collective (distributor).

Colvin, M. (2010, September 30). Taking the twit out of Twitter and finding value. *The Punch: Australia's Best Conversation*. Retrieved December 14, 2010, from http://www.thepunch.com.au/articles/taking-the-twit-out-of-twitter-and-finding-value/

Encyclopaedia Britannica. (n.d.). *Britannica online encyclopedia*. Retrieved December 17, 2010, from http://www.britannica.com/EBchecked/topic/186618/Encyclopaedia-Britannica

Ezra, H., & Kempinski, Y. (2010, August 18). *First ever: Zionist Wikipedia editing course*. Israel National News. Retrieved November 18, 2010, from http://www.israelnationalnews.com/News/News.aspx/139189

Giles, J. (2005). Internet encyclopaedias go head to head. *Nature*, *438*(7070), 900–901. doi:10.1038/438900a

Gregory, S. (2006). Transnational storytelling: Human rights, WITNESS, and video advocacy. *American Anthropologist*, *108*(1), 195–204. doi:10.1525/aa.2006.108.1.195

Gregory, S. personal communication, December 18, 2010

Howard, P. N. (2010). *The digital origins of dictatorship and democracy: Information Technology and political Islam*. Oxford University Press. doi:10.1093/acprof:oso/9780199736416.001.0001

Howe, J. (2009). *Crowdsourcing: Why the power of the crowd is driving the future of business*. New York, NY: Three Rivers Press.

Kushner, A. (n.d.). *Crowdsourcing: The trailer*. Retrieved from http://crowdsourcing.typepad.com/cs/2008/07/crowdsourcing-t.html

Land, M. B. (2009). Peer producing human rights. *New York Law School Legal Studies, Research Paper Series 09/10 #12*, 1-25.

McLagan, M. (2006). Introduction: Making human rights claims public. *American Anthropologist*, *108*(1), 191–195. doi:10.1525/aa.2006.108.1.191

Meier, P. (2010a, April 8). *Wag the dog, or how falsifying crowdsourced data can be a pain*. Retrieved December 20, 2010, from http://irevolution.wordpress.com/2010/04/08/wag-the-dog/

Meier, P. (2010b, September 19). Analyzing the veracity of tweets during a major crisis. *iRevolution*. Retrieved January 12, 2011, from http://irevolution.wordpress.com/2010/09/19/veracity-of-tweets-during-a-major-crisis/

Meier, P. (2010c, September 22). *Calling 911: What humanitarians can learn from 50 years of crowdsourcing*. Retrieved January 12, 2011, from http://irevolution.wordpress.com/2010/09/22/911-system/

Neistat, A. personal communication, December 7, 2010

Osborn, M. (2008). Fuelling the flames: Rumour and politics in Kibera. *Journal of Eastern African Studies*, *2*(2), 315–327. doi:10.1080/17531050802094836

Palen, L., Vieweg, S., Liu, S. B., & Hughes, A. L. (2009). Crisis in a networked world. *Social Science Computer Review*, *27*(4), 467. doi:10.1177/0894439309332302

Raymond, E. (2001). *The cathedral and the bazaar: Musings on Linux and open source by an accidental revolutionary* (Rev. ed.). Sebastopol, CA: O'Reilly.

Surowiecki, J. (2005). *The wisdom of crowds* (1st ed.). New York, NY: Anchor Books.

Survival International. (2010, October 22). *Indonesian government admits its soldiers tortured Papuans*. Retrieved December 21, 2010, from http://www.survivalinternational.org/news/6610

Tapscott, D., & Williams, A. D. (2010). *Macrowikinomics: Rebooting business and the world*. Portfolio Hardcover.

The Daily Show with Jon Stewart. (2009, June 16). *Irandecision 2009 - CNN's unverified material*. Retrieved from http://www.thedailyshow.com/watch/tue-june-16-2009/irandecision-2009---cnn-s-unverified-material

Thomas, C. (2006). An empirical examination of Wikipedia's credibility. *First Monday*, *11*(11).

UN Human Rights Council. (2010, January 7). *UN expert concludes that Sri Lankan video is authentic, calls for an independent war crimes investigation*. Retrieved from http://www.reliefweb.int/rw/rwb.nsf/db900SID/EGUA-7ZGQCB?OpenDocument

Wikipedia. (n.d.). *Wikipedia, the free encyclopedia*. Retrieved November 16, 2010, from http://en.wikipedia.org/wiki/Wikipedia

YNET. (2010, August 28). The battle for Wikipedia: Palestinians counter Israeli editing group. *Ynetnews*. Retrieved November 18, 2010, from http://www.ynetnews.com/articles/0,7340,L-3944937,00.html

ENDNOTES

1. In 2010, Jeff Howe suggested the "cocktail party" definition for his groundbreaking concept as: "Crowdsourcing is Wikipedia, with everything" (Kushner, n.d.).
2. http://www.hrdag.org/resources/mult_systems_est.shtml
3. Natural language processing combines linguistics and computer science to process and analyze large amounts of text.
4. Disclaimer: co-author Patrick Meier is directly involved in the development of this tool. See http://www.swiftly.org and also http://www.ushahidi.com

Chapter 9
Counting the Unknown Victims of Political Violence: The Work of the Human Rights Data Analysis Group

Ann Harrison
Benetech Human Rights Data Analysis Group, USA

ABSTRACT

The Benetech Human Rights Data Analysis Group (HRDAG) (http://www.hrdag.org/) analyzes the patterns and magnitude of large-scale human rights violations. Together with local partners, HRDAG collects and preserves human rights data and helps NGOs and other human rights organizations accurately interpret quantitative findings. HRDAG statisticians, programmers, and data analysts develop methodologies to determine how many of those killed and disappeared have never been accounted for - and who is most responsible. This account illustrates how HRDAG pioneered the calculation of scientifically sound statistics about political violence from multiple data sources including the testimony of witnesses who come forward to tell their stories. It describes methodologies that HRDAG analysts have developed to ensure that statistical human rights claims are transparently, demonstrably, and undeniably true.

INTRODUCTION: DOES THE TRUTH MATTER?

We see their pictures in news reports from conflict zones around the world. Frightened people, forced out of their homes, abducted, imprisoned, abused and sometimes killed by assailants who assume they will never be held accountable for their actions. Stories of mass human rights violations stir our moral outrage. We feel compelled to act, to document the violence. How many atrocities have been committed? How many displaced into refugee camps? How many people have simply disappeared?

DOI: 10.4018/978-1-4666-1918-0.ch009

Data gathering is the cornerstone of human rights efforts. Information about the scope and patterns of violence is needed to support legal action, political sanctions, and humanitarian intervention. Yet this vital information is often clouded by biases or inaccurate data collection. These errors produce more than a distorted view of the facts. Inflated claims or false accounts that exclude key events can embolden critics and undermine well-intentioned efforts to prosecute perpetrators.

Consider the case of Kosovo. In March 1999, NATO allies launched air strikes against the Yugoslav army based on information from the U.S. State Department that 100,000 Kosovo Albanians were missing and feared dead. Members of the UN Security Council backed this decision arguing that the number of deaths justified action to halt further atrocities. After the bombing campaign and subsequent invasion of Kosovo by NATO, it was found that Yugoslav forces were responsible for about 10,000 deaths. Opponents of the action seized on the ten-fold inflation of possible deaths to dispute that mass violations occurred. Was there sufficient violence to justify war on humanitarian grounds? Do the numbers matter?

In an effort to defend the accuracy of human rights data – and account for mass atrocities witnessed by thousands or tens of thousands of people - truth commissions and other groups have turned to scientists to clarify history. Since 1991, members of the Human Rights Data Analysis Group (HRDAG) have developed relational data bases and statistical techniques to analyze not only how many victims and violations have been *documented* during a conflict – but also how many of the killed and disappeared have never been accounted for. HRDAG helps NGOs and human rights organizations accurately interpret quantitative findings that support historical clarification and the prosecution of perpetrators.

The HRDAG team currently includes two dozen statisticians, programmers, demographers and data analysts who passionately believe that scientific arguments can help clarify the past and end impunity. HRDAG is part of the Human Rights Program at Benetech, a nonprofit technology organization based in Palo Alto, California. The HRDAG team is led by Dr. Patrick Ball, a statistician who has worked with dozens of human rights organizations to build databases that provide a quantitative understanding of human rights violations. HRDAG investigators focus on large-scale violations of civil and political rights. They have pioneered scientific methods for collecting and interpreting information about state-sanctioned violence that can be used to identify those responsible. The scientists of HRDAG have been called on to help clarify patterns of violence under difficult conditions in some of the world's most troubled nations. Over the past twenty years, HRDAG investigators have analyzed human rights data for official truth commissions in South Africa, Haiti, Guatemala, Perú, Ghana, Sierra Leone, Timor-Leste and Liberia. They provided critical information to the International Criminal Tribunal for the Former Yugoslavia that was used to prosecute former Serbian president Slobodan Milošević for crimes committed in Kosovo. (Ball, Asher, 2002) In 2010, HRDAG analysis of the Guatemalan National Police Archive was used to support the successful prosecution of two former Guatemalan police officers for the 1984 disappearance of a labor activist - one of the few examples of accountability in that troubled country. HRDAG has also analyzed information about human rights violations for the International Criminal Court and United Nations Field Missions in Timor-Leste, Guatemala, and the Democratic Republic of Congo, as well as numerous non-governmental human rights groups.

The methodologies that HRDAG has developed over the last twenty years are now being rediscovered and adapted by social scientists throughout the world. HRDAG analysts created these methodologies by carefully examining a wide variety of data in countries where political conflicts created chaotic descriptions of violence.

This chapter will illustrate how HRDAG investigators worked through the technical challenges of how to examine a wide range of information sources in which the obvious data is not a reliable narrator of the true pattern of violence. Each source of information must be carefully examined to ensure that its inherent biases do not skew an accurate historical clarification of events. As scientists, members of the HRDAG team remain non-partisan. They do not take sides in military or political disputes and they do not support the advocacy of any particular government or policy. HRDAG is not neutral, however. Members of the group are always in favor of human rights and support the promotion of the Universal Declaration of Human Rights and the International Covenant on Civil and Political Rights.

The scientific process seeks to remove researchers' prejudices from their findings. Using mathematics, relational databases and statistical analysis, the scientists of HRDAG can determine, with a high degree of certainly, which individuals are most responsible for crimes against civilians in a given conflict. But these efforts are based on the acknowledgement that observed events only offer a partial version of the truth. Scientists believe that statements can be made about occurrences that are true based on available evidence within a range of known probability. They base these findings on reproducible techniques that account for possible error and bias. HRDAG argues that scientific analysis of human rights violations can move arguments about history past political polarization and support policy initiatives that help heal troubled counties.

The diversity of conflicts in counties where HRDAG scientists work has required that they develop a range of solutions to carefully interrogate human rights data. HRDAG's investigations in Perú, Ghana, Sierra Leone, the Democratic Republic of Congo and other conflict zones has shown that by itself, large amounts of data shed only limited light on the truth of human rights conflicts. This chapter chronicles how HRDAG has approached the analysis of complex of human rights information by coding narrative testimony and developing innovative surveys and statistical models to uncover obscured facts. It will illustrate how HRDAG creates complex relational databases to compare data sources and uses the statistical technique of multiple systems estimation to present accurate and defensible human rights data that can be used as the basis for policy decisions.

BACKGROUND: WHY IS HUMAN RIGHTS DATA SO DIFFICULT TO ANALYZE?

HRDAG researchers rely on information from many different sources. They examine individual testimonies, legal depositions, administrative records from morgues and cemeteries, exhumation reports, operational records from prisons, career information on military and police officers, historical police archives, eyewitness interviews and official customs and immigration records. After locating these records, the HRDAG team designs statistical methods to analyze the information and find patterns in the violence.

An important part of HRDAG's mission is to point out to the human rights community why it's so difficult to accurately collect, structure and analyze this information. For instance, testimony by witnesses about assassinations may also include information about detentions or torture that victims experienced before they were killed. If detentions, torture and assassinations are all of interest to researchers, then all three types of violations must be represented in the researcher's database. Collecting information about only the "most important" violation will obscure instances of the other violations, creating significant biases in the analysis. Researchers must also consider both violations that were directly observed, and violations that were not witnessed but estimated based on the available information. (Ball, 2001)

Selection Bias

In addition to under-counting incidents, many human rights data projects are vulnerable to selection bias. Every group collecting human rights data will have better access to some victims than others. This creates distortions in the statistical analysis of violations. The most frequent source of bias in human rights projects occurs because some victims or witnesses will trust or have access to the organization collecting data, while others will not. For instance, if victims in the southern part of a country trust investigators while those in the north do not, investigators will likely gather more testimonies in the south. This bias could result in a false finding that violence is primary based in the southern region. This kind of bias can also arise from limited access to unreachable or dangerous areas. If those analyzing human rights violations in a given country are basing their analysis on press accounts, and reporters avoid areas that they perceive as more dangerous, then the data about violence in those areas will be skewed.

Due to the nature of how human rights violations are witnessed, duplicate reporting of the same incident, victim or perpetrator also becomes a major problem for researchers. A human rights group may collect several accounts of one incident because multiple witnesses may report the same event. For example, the testimony describing an especially notorious assassination may be reported hundreds of times by different witnesses. This phenomenon was illustrated in witness testimony about the killing of former Liberian president Samuel K. Doe which HRDAG analyzed for the Liberian Truth and Reconciliation Commission (Cibelli, Hoover & Krüger, 2009). A good information system needs to identify which records describe the same events and participants in order not to double or triple count them.

Counting Errors

Several sources recounting the same human rights violation may also provide slightly different versions of the same event. The interpretation of the actions or organizational affiliation of perpetrators, the location of a crime scene or the nature of a violation, as understood by a witness, may be different than the interpretation of these details provided by the organization that is collecting and analyzing the information. Different numbers of perpetrators may also have committed each violation. Consequently, no count of perpetrators from one organization can be combined with the number of perpetrators from other groups unless the perpetrators are combined in categories. Since any given violation may have been committed by one or more perpetrators who were not identified – perhaps by one, two, or many identified perpetrators - researchers must combine categories of perpetrators to analyze how actual violations were committed. Even when researchers consider these complexities, counts of perpetrators are still limited only to events that are directly observed.

Finally, it is difficult for researchers to accurately analyze data when witnesses offer contradictory views of the same event. HRDAG uses data analysis techniques to assess the underlying uncertainty about the incident in social memory. This allows analysts to recalculate statistics that describe a human rights violation using contradictory views of the same incident. If the results remain stable, investigators know that their data analysis can take into account possible variations on the same story.

The wide range of conflicts in which HRDAG analysts are asked to analyze human rights data compelled members of the research team to find scientific techniques that can address many different types of violence. Of the 19 counties where HRDAG has analyzed large-scale human rights violations, the most critical development of its methodologies took place in four troubled places, El Salvador, Guatemala, Kosovo and Timor-Leste.

EL SALVADOR 1991: WHO DID WHAT TO WHOM?

In an effort to capture and accurately reflect the complex relationships between different people and events, Ball created a model for examining human rights data that he named "Who Did What To Whom" (WDWTW). Ball, who was originally trained as a sociologist, began analyzing human rights data in 1991.The initial focus of his study was the cauldron of state-sponsored terror carried out against the citizens of El Salvador. Ball looked for ways to analyze a large collection of human rights testimonies and determine who was most responsible for these crimes. It was an extraordinary challenge under difficult circumstances. In the early 1990's, a 12-year civil war in El Salvador was coming to a close. The conflict between the military-led government and the Farabundo Martí National Liberation Front (FMLN), a coalition of left-wing militias, was sparked by the infamous assassination in March 1980 of Catholic Archbishop Óscar Romero. The Archbishop was shot while conducting mass, a month after publicly asking the U.S. Government to stop military aid to the Salvadoran government. At his funeral, bombers and snipers massacred forty-two mourners.

In the years that followed, tens of thousands of Salvadorans were killed, many by right-wing death squads dressed in civilian clothes and traveling in anonymous vehicles. The death squads conducted torture and disfigured bodies. They published death lists of intended targets, delivered coffins to future victims and sent them invitations to their own funerals. By the mid-1980's state sponsored terror against civilians included indiscriminate bombing, mining and the harassment of medical personnel. Members of the security forces tortured and killed *campesinos* (rural peasants), shot at their houses and burned their crops. Refugees from the countryside poured into the capital city. Fighting continued through 1991 and peace accords were signed in late December of that year.

In an effort to understand the nature and scope of the conflict, the Salvadoran Human Rights Commission, founded in 1977 by Archbishop Romero, launched one of the earliest and most ambitious large-scale human rights information projects. Known in Spanish as the Comisión de Derechos Humanos de El Salvador no gubernamental (CDHES), the Commission collected over 9,000 testimonies from people who witnessed the violence. The testimonies helped begin to clarify what happened during the years of conflict. But individual stories were not enough to hold those who had ordered killings accountable for their actions. Ball, who had never before examined human rights data, was then living in El Salvador working for a peace organization. One day, he was approached by his human rights colleagues who asked him if it would be possible to organize their information in a database.

As a social scientist and database designer, Ball knew that he had to find some method to create units of analysis out of the unstructured narrative of the thousands of testimonies. Ball realized that the raw information generated from the testimonies would be complex. A single person could be identified as a witness, a victim and/or a perpetrator within a sequence of events. He knew that he needed a way to model the data that could accurately reconstruct which victims suffered which violations committed by which perpetrators. Ball worried that simplifying information about the violations could lead to distorted statistical results that could be attacked by opponents of the process. To capture and maintain these complex relationships between different people and events, Ball began creating a model for examining human rights data that he would later name, "Who Did What To Whom (WDWTM)."

Computer models are efficient, but they depend on carefully structured information. Before analyzing the patterns of the violations committed in El Salvador, Ball first created a structured, relational database of violations reported in the testimonies. Relational databases were first used in the early 1970's on mainframe computers. By the early 1980s, PC users were building their own small relational databases that described complex relationships between different pieces of information. These types of databases are well-suited to counting and tabulating human rights violations and then creating statistics based on these counts. Turning to available commercial software, Ball began building his database of violations using commercial FoxPro database software.

Human rights groups started using databases in the mid-1980s. Some organizations built unstructured databases to keep track of individual cases. Other groups created text databases to gain easy access to documents. But these databases have limitations. A researcher using an unstructured text database to search for cases involving "electric shock," for example, will need to search for many different words or phrases that describe "electric shock." Many documents and case files are likely to emerge in this broad search and important references are missed. A structured database is different in that it describes violations using a controlled vocabulary. Any violation that is classified as an "electric shock" fits within the organization's definition of this kind of violation. A search in the database for "electric shock" can be absolutely specific and yield all of those cases - and only those cases - in which electric shocks are used. By framing the search differently, a researcher using a structured relational database can, for instance, list all those people who suffered electric shock torture, organized by names or by profession. Or the researcher can list all the police stations in which instances of this kind of torture have been alleged. If a researcher is searching for cases that occurred in a particular time, or at a particular place, a structured database can yield precisely these cases. Structured databases can generate simple or complex statistics that can be useful to human right groups examining thousands, or tens of thousands of individual testimonies. However, these statistics were subject to a key flaw that did not become obvious until the late 1990s.

In El Salvador, Ball used his WDWTW system to begin methodically building a structured, relational database using 200 cases from the 9,000 available testimonies to the Salvadoran Human Rights Commission. While Ball was working on this database, others in his human rights group began creating an index to the 9,000 testimonies using a table feature in WorldPerfect 5.1 DOS word processing software. Ball wrote a program to read the WordPerfect files and transform the tables into database records. But creating one database and an index was not enough to determine who was most responsible for twelve years of savage human rights violations in El Salvador. To address this question, Ball began creating another structured database that showed the career history of the 400 most senior military officers. This database held information describing when each officer graduated from military academy, what jobs they held, and which units they commanded. Much of the information was gleaned from newspaper accounts and declassified U.S. government documents.

While Ball was compiling these service records, another Los Angeles-based human rights organization named El Rescate, began creating their own database of Salvadoran military officers. El Rescate monitors human rights conditions in El Salvador and in 1985, began publishing reports on the country's human rights situation. The group developed a theoretical foundation for combating institutionalized impunity, established a legal basis for prosecuting past human rights violations and defined ways to utilize command responsibility to hold senior officers accountable for systematic human rights abuses (Howland, 2008).

In 1987, El Rescate began collaborating with El Salvador-based NGOs to petition international bodies such as the Inter-American Commission on Human Rights (IACHR) and the International Labour Organization (ILO). El Rescate also pushed for structural changes in the Salvadoran police and military and for the creation of entities that had the power to remove active security officers for human rights abuses - and identify specific abuses and responsibility for them. This effort was successful due to a unique political moment created by the UN-brokered Salvadoran Peace Accords, signed in the closing minutes of 1991. The Accords mandated structural reforms, created a quasi-judicial Ad Hoc Commission to remove those implicated in human rights violations from military service, and formed a Truth Commission to compile an official public accounting of human rights abuses.

El Rescate shared their database of Salvadoran military officers with CDHES. Ball compared El Rescate's information with the officer data collected by the CDHES. The El Rescate database was one of first examples of "found data" that the HRDAG research team now routinely seeks in the countries where they work. This data comes from a wide variety of sources including cemetery or morgue records, border crossings, church groups or labor unions. Any group that collects data on human rights violations is a potential source of information.

After completing the two CDHES databases describing witness testimony and information about the Salvadoran military officers, Ball linked the data sets together. He then compared the dates in which individual officers lead specific military units with the dates of documented human rights violations. El Rescate also compared their officer data with a different database of violations acquired from the Salvadoran Catholic Church. Both sets of analysis identified 100 Salvadoran military officers who led units involved in the worst human rights violations. (Howland, 2008)

The results of this analysis were delivered to the Ad Hoc Commission which was empowered by the Peace Accords to force the named officers to resign. While the Salvadoran Peace Accords did not support legal trials, the names of the officers were reported in the press. Posters displaying their photographs and listing their crimes were displayed on the streets in the capital city of San Salvador. This information sparked a public uproar and the officers were forced into retirement. The ultimate test of Ball's new WDWTW system took place when officers responsible for many of the killings and incidents of torture sued CDHES for defamation in Salvadoran court. A guilty verdict would have resulted in criminal penalties. Staff lawyers for the CDHES responded by bringing to court boxes of documents containing all 9,000 testimonies – plus the FoxPro software and the database which Ball offered to demonstrate for the judges. The officers withdrew their case.

GUATEMALA 1993 – 1999: USING MULTIPLE SYSTEMS ESTIMATION TO ANALYZE HUMAN RIGHTS DATA

Inspired by the success of his human rights data analysis in El Salvador, Ball began to apply his Who-Did What-To-Whom (WDWTW) model to human rights information in other countries. Over the next six years, Ball was asked to analyze large-scale human rights violations in Ethiopia, South Africa, Haiti and Guatemala. Working in Washington, D.C, where he was a senior program associate for the Science and Human Rights Program at the American Association for the Advancement of Science (AAAS), Ball developed new methods for analyzing state-sanctioned violence. He was assisted by senior scientific colleagues including statistician Dr. Herb Spirer. This work helped Ball and his fellow researchers build on their experience in El Salvador and better understand the complexities of human rights data.

In 1992, a group of non-governmental organizations in Guatemala asked the scientific community to gather and analyze information on human rights violations. Ball advised the International Center for Human Rights Research in Guatemala (CIIDH) as they collected evidence of more than 43,000 human rights violations during the country's 36-years of conflict which ended in 1996. The descriptions of this violence that Ball gathered for the CIIDH were collected from press reports, NGOs and testimonies from victims of the violence. From 1992 to 1998, Ball assembled this data into one large database and protected the information by encrypting it with PGP encryption software.

In 1996, peace accords brokered by the United Nations ended the armed conflict in Guatemala. Ball's data gathering project for the CIIDH provided a valuable source of information for the Commission for Historical Clarification (CEH) which was formed by the United Nations after the peace accords. The CEH sought to objectively clarify human rights violations and acts of violence in Guatemala by investigating a portion of the deaths and disappearances reported during the conflict. In 1998, the CEH asked the American Association for the Advancement of Science (AAAS) to answer the following question: How many people were killed in Guatemala from 1960 to 1996? Ball was asked to set up an information management system to analyze the large numbers of reported human rights violations and undertake the analytical study requested by the Commission.

When Ball began analyzing data about patterns of violence in Guatemala, he developed methods to overcome one of the basic complexities of counting human rights violations – removing duplicate reports of the same incident. A truthful accounting of human rights violations demands that every violation counts once and only once. Ball and other researchers began refining a process of de-duplication in which they could identify multiply reported incidents and assure themselves that each violation is counted only once. This de-duplication process, together with methods that control for bias in groups collecting human rights data, allowed Ball to use a statistical technique called multiple systems estimation (MSE). Dating back to at least the nineteenth century where it was first used to count fish, MSE was later extended to estimate both wildlife and human populations. MSE allows researchers to use separately collected but incomplete lists of a given population to estimate the total size of that group. It uses the identification of multiply-reported incidents – essentially overlapping accounts - to estimate the number of events that are never reported.

When Ball was asked to analyze mass human rights violations in Guatemala, statistician Fritz Scheuren of the American Statistical Association, suggested that MSE could be used to project how many total violations took place, including those that were never documented. In a human rights calamity in which many thousands of people are killed or disappeared over many years, information about the uncounted victims is vital to producing a complete and accurate historical record and provided the evidence needed to document years of violations. This was especially necessary in Guatemala where violence had been ongoing for many years.

To answer the question of how many people died during the violence in Guatemala, Ball compared information from three available three databases of human rights information. Because state-supported violence in Guatemala was so extreme and had continued for so long, a number of different groups collected data on killings and disappearances. This allowed Ball to compare different collections of information and use MSE to determine how many victims had never been counted. The databases Ball used included the data set that he created for the (CIIDH). The second data set was generated by the CEH and the third was gathered by the REMHI (Recovery of Historical Memory) project which originated at the Human Rights Office of the Archbishop of Guatemala. Since Ball had three sources of data, he attempted to determine how many unduplicated killings were documented by the three projects and then calculate how many total killings occurred during the conflict. Ball completed a rudimentary de-duplication on the CIIDH data in August and September of 1998. He then conducted tests using the CEH, CIIDH and REMHI data in the fall of that year and completed the multiple systems estimation in January of 1999. (Chapman & Ball, 2001)

Duplicated reporting of deaths in more than one database is called "overlap." To estimate the total number of victims reported by the three databases, the overlap between databases must be estimated to reduce the contribution of each database by its overlap rate. If none of the victims in any database appear in any other database, then the total number of victims of killing and disappearance is equal to the sum of the number of victims in the three databases - which in this case was 54,643 victims. This is the upper limit to the number of observed victims. The lower limit can be found in the extreme possibility that the largest of the three databases, the CEH database, contains all the cases reported in the other REMHI and CIIDH databases. In this case, the total number of killings is simply the number of killings reported in the largest database which was 24,910. The true number of unique victims in the three databases must fall within these two limits, that is, between 24,910 and 54,643. The purpose of Ball's analyses to estimate the total number of documented killings was to narrow this range of possible victims.

Ball also knew that many killings that took place in Guatemala were not reported to any of the three projects collecting information. During the data gathering process, there were problems in the coverage of violations over time and location. None of the three projects provided good coverage of violations that took place from 1960 to 1977 and thus no estimation of this period was possible. The most important complication for the estimation of more recent violations was that the data gathering projects did not cover all the regions with the same intensity. In order to calculate the total number of killings with multiple systems estimation (MSE) Ball needed to generate estimates of the overlap between the three databases that collected data in the same areas.

Using MSE, Ball was able to calculate the probability of any given killing being documented by each database. It was then possible to estimate the number of killings excluded by two of the databases. With the same logic, Ball could then derive an estimation for the number of killings that were not documented by any of the three projects. Using these techniques, Ball was able to calculate the total number of killings in Guatemala from 1979 to 1996 by region. Over all regions in Guatemala, Ball determined that there were approximately 47,706 documented killings. He was also able to calculate that there were approximately 84,468 killings that were not reported to the CEH, to the CIIDH, or to the REMHI project. Ball's final estimate, which was published as part of the CEH report in 1999, was that 132,174 killings took place in Guatemala between 1978 and 1996 with a standard error of 6,568. This number of deaths due to violence dwarfed the number of those killed in the publicized political conflicts in El Salvador, South Africa, Haiti and Perú. In the final analysis, the CEH also found that acts of genocide were committed against Guatemala's indigenous Mayan communities. MSE allowed Ball and his fellow analysts to account for those Guatemalans whose deaths had never been recorded (Ball et al., 2000, especially chapters 8-12).

KOSOVO 1999: USING MULTIPLE SYSTEMS ESTIMATION TO ANALYZE A VERY DIFFERENT CONFLICT

After the first use of MSE to account for undocumented deaths in Guatemala, Ball then applied these techniques to clarify the history of a very different conflict in Kosovo. The turmoil began in 1989 when Serbian President Slobodan Milošević revoked Kosovo's autonomous status within the Republic of Serbia and sparked a violent confrontation between the Kosovar Albanians and the Yugoslav government. Allegations of widespread and systematic human rights violations were made against Serbian forces including deportations, destruction of homes and property, murder and rape. Ultimately NATO intervened to repel Serb forces from Kosovo. (Ball, Tabeau, Verwimp, 2007)

With support from members of the American Association for the Advancement of Science (AAAS), Ball gathered information in the field and wrote several reports on the conflict in Kosovo. First Ball, then Scheuren traveled to Albania in 1999, gathering data from border crossings and other sources. They then used this information to examine the claim by the Yugoslav government that the activities of both NATO and the Kosovo Liberation Army opposition force displaced the population and created a refugee crisis. During his analysis, Ball used MSE to examine the exodus of the refugees and compare this data with information about the scope of the conflict over time. (Ball, 1999)

The first report on migration in Kosovo was released in March 2000 by AAAS (Ball, 2000), and a second report on the killings was released a few months later with partners from the American Bar Association/Central European and Eurasian Law Initiative (AAAS & ABA CEELI, 2000). A third report was used in the prosecution of former Yugoslav president Slobodan Milošević at the International Criminal Tribunal for the Former Yugoslavia (ICTY) at The Hague.

The report given to the ICTY, "Policy or Panic? The Flight of Ethnic Albanians From Kosovo. March-May 1999," (Ball, Betts, Scheuren, Dudukovich & Asher, 2000) looked at possible reasons for the mass exodus of refugees from Kosovo. It examined the claim by Yugoslav authorities that military actions undertaken by NATO and the Kosovo Liberation Army (KLA) were responsible for the mass migration of Albanian refugees from Kosovo. The report found that killings and refugee flows occurred in a regular pattern characterized by three phrases. In each phase, a high volume of killings and refugee flow was followed by a much lower level of killings and flow of refugees. The analysts used these findings to evaluate three possible explanations for the pattern. The first potential explanation is that military actions by the KLA forced Kosovars to leave their homes. The second possible answer was that NATO air attacks created local conditions that led to Kosovars being killed and leaving their homes. The third potential reason for the pattern is that a systematic campaign by Yugoslav forces expelled Kosovar Albanians from their homes.

The study concluded that the pattern of both refugee flow and killings exhibit characteristics that are consistent with the presence of an external cause for these events. It found that the flow of refugees and the killings occurred in the same places at the same times. This implies that there was a common cause for both phenomena. The study found that two of the hypotheses that analysts considered to explain the pattern, the military activities of the KLA and bombardment by NATO forces, are inconsistent with the observed patterns of refugee flow and the killing of refugees. In their final analysis, the researchers concluded that the statistical evidence was consistent with the hypothesis that Yugoslav forces conducted a systematic campaign of killings and expulsions in Kosovo.

TIMOR-LESTE 2006: CREATING SURVEYS TO UNCOVER THE TRUTH

In some countries where HRDAG analyzes human rights information, the available data is threatened or too incomplete for accurate historical clarification. In the small south Asian nation of Timor-Leste, HRDAG scientists took steps to preserve critical human rights information during civil unrest – and found new ways to combine found data and surveys to measure the impact of violence on civilian populations. Large-scale human rights violations in Timor-Leste stretch back to 1975 when the Indonesian government invaded the eastern part of the small, divided island. The resulting Indonesian occupation of Timor-Leste resulted in a series of abuses against the local resistance movement and the broader civilian population that lasted until the Timorese independence vote in August 1999. Disappearances, torture, forced displacement and extra-judicial killings were documented during this period. The Timorese people also suffered a severe famine between 1978 and 1983. Qualitative historical accounts estimating the total death toll during the Indonesian occupation varied widely from a conservative 50,000 fatalities to more than 200,000 deaths. (Klingner & Silva, 2011, forthcoming) note how each individual data source, such as grave marker inscriptions, reflect only a fraction of the entire number of the dead. Such information is one kind of "found data" or records that were originally created or gathered for some purpose besides counting casualties.

In their paper, Silva and Klinger describe how the biases inherent in a single data source can be overcome by combining found data with surveys and other intentionally gathered data. This strategy allows analysts to more accurately estimate the magnitude and patterns of deaths. This methodology was tested when the Commission for Reception, Truth and Reconciliation in East Timor (CAVR) was established by the UN Transitional Authority in July 2001. The CAVR was tasked with investigating human rights abuses committed by all sides between April 1974 and December 1999, but it had little information at its disposal. HRDAG began advising the group on its information management processes and guided the development of the Commission's statistical findings.

The partnership between the CAVR and HRDAG resulted in the creation of three data sets that integrated quantitative methods into CAVR's broader truth seeking activities. These data sets included a database created by Ball, CAVR consultant Ken Ward and HRDAG demographer Romesh Silva. This database collected almost 8,000 narrative testimonies from people throughout the country who participated in the commission's statement-taking process. Silva also conducted a census of all public graveyards in the country that encompassed approximately 319,000 gravestones. The third data set was comprised of a retrospective mortality survey drawing on a probability sample of approximately 1,400 households throughout the thirteen districts of Timor-Leste (Silva & Ball, 2006).

To create these data sets, CAVR and HRDAG pioneered techniques for gathering human rights data. No previous truth commission had ever undertaken a survey to ask the population about deaths that occurred in the past. While historical demographers have used gravestone information to estimate deaths, this was the first time that a human rights project employed such methods. Each of the data sets independently produced valuable empirical results. Comparative analysis among the data sets corroborated the findings of each individual set of information. After matching deaths reported across all three sets of data, HRDAG analysts conducted multiple systems estimation to estimate the pattern and extent of conflict-related deaths and ultimately create a substantial body of documentary evidence to support the human rights findings of the CAVR. HRDAG also developed survey-based estimates of the extent and pattern of total conflict-related displacement between 1974 and 1999. The combined analysis of deaths and displacement complemented the Commission's historical, legal and qualitative findings about famine and displacement in Timor-Leste. Finally, HRDAG developed an array of statistical data that profiled the form, pattern and structure of torture, ill-treatment, arbitrary detention and sexually-based violations which were reported to the CAVR.

These statistical and demographic findings, developed jointly by the CAVR and HRDAG, were presented in CAVR's 2,500-page final report titled "Chega!" (Portuguese for 'no more, that's enough'). In February 2006, HRDAG co-published with CAVR a chapter of the report and accompanying mortality data (Silva & Ball, 2006). The report estimated that at least 102,800 (+/- 11,000) Timorese died as a result of human rights violations in Timor-Leste from a year prior to the Indonesian army's invasion in 1975, to the country's 1999 independence referendum that formally ended the occupation. HRDAG researchers estimated that that 18,600 people were murdered or disappeared, and approximately 84,200 citizens died due to hunger and illness in excess of what would be expected during peacetime.

HRDAG's analysis revealed the surprising truth that far more people died in Timore-Leste as a result of the famine which followed the conflict than in the fighting itself. (Silva & Ball, 2007) The actions that followed the release of the report were also unexpected. In July 2006, armed gangs broke into the offices of the CAVR in the capital city of Dili and stole their motorbikes. HRDAG scientists and other human rights observers were concerned that the mobs would soon return to loot the irreplaceable paper records used by the CAVR to compile the "Chega!" report. In case electronic records were destroyed or stolen, the CAVR and HRDAG created back-up copies of the CAVR's interview data and moved the information to secure servers. Other critical human rights data in UN offices was lost forever in the looting.

SOLUTIONS AND RECOMMENDATIONS

Without combining data sources and estimation methods in Timor-Leste, a full understanding of deaths due to the conflict would have been incomplete. The number of people who died due to direct violence ultimately accounted for about 20% of deaths during the Indonesian occupation. By incorporating survey-based methods, HRDAG analysts were able to obtain more precise estimates of the full range of conflict-related deaths and gain new insight into deaths related to famine that were not as obvious.

After the damage caused by the riots in the Timor-Leste capital of Dili, HRDAG researchers released a statement calling for all current and future United Nations field missions deployed to Timor-Leste to avoid past mistakes and take steps to secure and back up their human rights data outside of Timor-Leste. Despite the importance of information to their mission, many human rights organizations lack the resources to preserve their data securely. Much of their information is stored in a single hard disk, and often in unencrypted form. Critical documentation is often subject to viruses, computer theft, accidents, neglect and staff turnover. If files containing sensitive identifying information about victims and perpetrators are compromised, witnesses can be put at serious risk. HRDAG urges human rights groups to develop information management systems that store data electronically, in multiple copies and in multiple locations to prevent loss due to physical destruction. The analysts of HRDAG encourage their partners to encrypt data with Martus (www.martus.org) or other software tools, and allow only authorized users to access the information.

HRDAG also cautions human rights organizations, and those who use their data, to be alert for bias in both information collection and analysis. Single sources of information offer only a limited view of what occurs during human rights violations and cannot be relied upon for unbiased analysis. Human rights analysts examining multiple sources of information should also take steps to correct for biases that result in the collection of only the "most important" violations. While this error can obscure the instances of other violations, even aggregated databases can contain significant bias. The who-did-what-to-whom (WDWTW) system that that Ball developed in El Salvador beginning in 1991, addresses the creation of structured databases of human rights information. But directly reported information is always limited because only certain people chose to report the violence.

During their analysis of patterns of violence in Guatemala, HRDAG researchers also sought more efficient ways to remove duplicate accounts of violations. Much of the de-duplication of violations in Guatemala was done by hand, meaning that identifying overlaps required individual human expertise applied to each and every potential match. But this process poses a number of problems. The number of people, the time and concentration this requires makes it impossible to analyze some large collections of data. In addition, criteria for hand-matching are necessarily subjective and inconsistently applied. It is impossible to eliminate the different judgments people use in evaluating data, even over the course of a single person's work. Most importantly, hand-matching is not auditable or repeatable. Those reviewing the analysis cannot do the matching themselves to validate the results, and researchers cannot review the prior matches when incorporating new or updated data. For researchers on the HRDAG team, improving the de-duplication process has been the key to expanding their analysis of human rights data. Over the years, they have developed a usable, reproducible large-scale system for automatically matching duplicated records of the same violation, victim or perpetrator.

While the scientists of HRDAG have focused on developing data analysis techniques that stand up to scrutiny, their findings and methods have been questioned in legal cases. One legal body that struggled with HRDAG's data is the International Criminal Tribunal for the Former Yugoslavia (ICTY) where Ball served as an expert witness for the prosecution in the trials of Slobodan Milosevic (ICTY IT-02-54) and Milan Milutinovic et al (ICTY IT-02-57) (Ball et al. 2002a, 2002b). In a report published in 2000 by the American Association for the Advancement of Science (AAAS), Ball analyzed four incomplete data sources on killings and forced migration during the conflict in Kosovo to estimate the pattern of deaths from March to May 1999. Ball's analysis identified 4,400 deaths from March to May 1999. He used this data to estimate that approximately 10,000 Kosovar Albanians had been killed during the March-May period.

After the 2000 AAAS report, Ball conducted another study for the ICTY (Ball et al. 2002a, 2002b) where he looked at other sources, including border-crossing records, to estimate patterns of migration during the March-May period. He determined that the estimated patterns of deaths and migration were consistent with the hypothesis that Serbian forces had carried out these crimes. Milosevic died during his trial and the defendants were found guilty of most of the charges against them, but the ICTY were not convinced by Ball's statistical evidence. In her paper entitled, Learning the Hard Way at the ICTY: Statistical Evidence of Human Rights Violations in and Adversarial Information Environment, Amelia Hoover Green, notes that statisticians need to be sensitive to the overwhelming amount of information that judges must contend with during trials (Hoover, 2010). As the judges in these cases tried to determine the defendant's responsibility for large scale killings and migration of Kosovo Albanians during the March to June time period, Hoover suggests that statisticians may have made their findings clearer if they presented background data vital to the judge's understanding, conducted redundant and exhaustive hypothesis testing, focused on causation rather than description when possible, privileged simple, familiar or traditional modes of statistical investigation, pursued total transparency in data analysis process and trained to present their work in court.

HRDAG scientists have carefully considered Hoover's analysis of their work in these cases, and taken other steps to make the findings accessible and credible. In order to develop findings that stand up to scrutiny, all the software tools that HRDAG uses to analyze human rights data are open for review and critique. HRDAG employs open source software, such as the R statistical software, and also creates free software that uses open data standards. Over time, HRDAG has worked to publish the data used in its analysis, and the group is now working on publishing more of the software it uses to conduct its calculations. HRDAG researchers believe that transparency helps generate trust in the scientific process. All of HRDAG's findings are publicly available, and whenever possible, the results are presented in reviewed scholarly journals. This is the way HRDAG believes that the science of human rights data analysis should be conducted.

FUTURE RESEARCH DIRECTIONS: ANALYZING A LARGE POLICE ARCHIVE

HRDAG is currently involved in an unusual data project analyzing a sample of the estimated 31.7 million papers, books, photographs and floppy disks in the Guatemalan National Police Archive (Guzman, Guberek, Shapiro, Zador, 2009). The archive was discovered by chance in a military munitions storehouse near Guatemala City in 2005. The Guatemalan National Police were disbanded after the country's 1996 Peace Accords which ended 36 years of internal armed conflict. In March 2006, a coalition of Guatemalan NGO and government groups invited Ball to evaluate the documents in the collection. After inspecting the archive, Ball recommended that analysts collect a multi-stage random sample of the documents and secure the sample data with the *Martus* software for later analysis (Price, Guberek, Zador, Shapiro, 2009). With advisors from the American Statistical Association and Westat, HRDAG statisticians Romesh Silva and Daniel Guzmán designed a sampling strategy that is now being used to create a clearer picture of archive contents. Together with other HRDAG statisticians, Guzmán has been analyzing a sample of the documents in the archive generated from 1960 to 1996 during Guatemala's years of conflict.

Expert testimony by Guzmán provided key evidence in the October 2010 conviction of two former police officers who were found guilty of the 1984 forced disappearance of Guatemalan student and union leader Edgar Fernando García. The Recovery of Historical Memory (REMHI) Project led by the Catholic Church estimated that approximately 40,000 Guatemalans disappeared during the years of violence. Documents discovered in the archive may help determine what happened to García who vanished in 1984 while in police custody. During the García trial, Guatemalan and international experts testified about National Police policies to "control and clean" suspected insurgents and their blurring of "insurgents" and political opponents. The analysis that Guzmán presented in his testimony was based on three years of coding key variables from random probabilistic samples of documents drawn from the archive. Since the contents of the archive were too large to directly observe, HRDAG statisticians developed a plan to create a physical map of the archive and sample randomly from different groupings of documents inside the building. Using this methodology, analysts were able to extrapolate from what was known about the sampled documents and make estimates about the contents of all the documents in the collection.

The García trial is the first case in the Guatemalan judicial system based primarily on archive documents. The guilty verdicts in this case have paved the way for judges to trust these records as evidence in future trials and accept statistical evidence which is rarely used in Guatemalan legal cases. Through his analysis, Guzmán was able to calculate the percentage of documents about García known by different police units and support the prosecution's argument that high-level officers were involved in his disappearance. This analysis continues to generate quantitative results that can answer further questions about command responsibility and human rights abuses. Analysis of police documents by Guzmán provided critical information used to support the June 2011 arrest of the former chief of the Guatemalan National Police who is accused of complicity in García's disappearance. The arrest of Hector Bol de la Cruz, 70, at his home in Jutiapa southwest of Guatemala City on June 9, is the latest step in an ongoing investigation of former police officials accused of disappearing and murdering García and other political activists.

By determining which documents were known by police command structures, HRDAG analysts can also make findings about relationships among security forces and communications between the army and police. This evidence is critical because historical data has shown that the Guatemalan army was the force most involved in human rights violations against civilians. The guilty verdict against the former National Police officers provides a critical legal precedent needed to prosecute others for forced disappearance. Judges in the García trial determined that Guzmán's analysis of archive records was relevant in building the case and removing reasonable doubt about the authenticity and reliability of the documents. Prosecutors have stated that HRDAG's statistical estimations regarding the content of archive documents will play a key role in future investigations. In particular, judges highlighted the role of this data in corroborating information about the disproportionate urban focus of the National Police, their practice of disappearing opponents, and the estimated number of documents in the archive related to disappearances. The judges in the case have announced that prosecutors will continue to investigate responsibility for García's disappearance further up the National Police chain of command.

CONCLUSION

The scientists of HRDAG believe that the legitimacy of the human rights community comes from presenting uncomfortable facts to those in power. But demands for accountability after violent conflicts are often denied or dismissed. In the absence of firm evidence, these debates are paralyzed by competing claims of historical accuracy. In order to prosecute perpetrators of human rights violations, the courts rightly demand evidence. In crimes against humanity, researchers must show that these actions follow a pattern. Carefully crafted human rights arguments offer the greatest opportunities to halt the cycle of violence and create lasting social change during difficult-to-foresee periods of political transition. Unless the human rights community is ready with unimpeachable information about past abuses, opportunities for official acknowledgment, accountability or reform are lost.

HRDAG data analysts have worked through an arc of technical issues to analyze human rights data which a new generation of statisticians are now reinventing and rediscovering. The development of these structures is important to chronicle because of how diverse and heterogeneous the problems have been and the scope of their solutions. In their quest to accurately measure mass human rights violations, HRDAG has discovered that human rights violations or events are complex and rarely straightforward. Nevertheless, NGOs and government groups have used available technology (even spreadsheets) to tell stories with data. The researchers of HRDAG keep reminding the human rights community and their supporters that data can be an unreliable narrator, a trickster. The data may sometimes reveal the truth. But if researchers rely on only a single source, such as press accounts or testimonies given to a single organization, they cannot be exactly sure when data is consistent with reality, and when it provides a reflection distorted by selection bias. As in the post-modern literary tradition, seemingly obvious information must be carefully interrogated. Investigators can examine data in complex ways, but larger quantities of information do not necessarily shed greater light on reality.

Careful analysis of human rights data can provide clues to the fates of people who disappear during conflicts and provide an opportunity to understand the role of political policies in disappearances, kidnappings and assassinations. This analysis can offer a view of the perpetrators' perspective on human rights violations and help researchers understand how a national leader, or their security forces, can turn against their own citizens. Researchers can defend these findings by showing that their analysis is calculated from a consistent application of a scientific classification criteria applied to raw data. These scientifically defensible techniques can be used by prosecutors, as they were in the García case in Guatemala, to determine chain of command and responsibility for crimes of policy.

The scientific methods developed by HRDAG analysts over the last twenty years have set standards of scientific rigor that can help overcome political arguments about the content of human rights records. Together with its local partners, who often take great risks to do this work, HRDAG has established scientific paradigms for examining large collections of human rights data. These techniques have enabled scientists to transform emotional debates about politics, policies and history into evidence-based discussions about science and methodology. The researchers of HRDAG have shown that careful, accurate data analysis can help fight impunity, bring perpetrators to justice and strengthen the rule of law.

REFERENCES

American Association for the Advancement of Science. (2000). *Political killings in Kosova/Kosovo, March-June 1999: A cooperative report by the Central and East European Law Initiative at the American Bar Association and the Science and Human Rights Program of the American Association for the Advancement of Science*. Washington, DC: Author.

Ball, P. (1999). *Policy or panic? The flight of ethnic Albanians from Kosovo*. Washington, DC: American Association for the Advancement of Science.

Ball, P. (2000). *Refugee flow patterns in Kosovo, March-May 1999. American Association for the Advancement of Science, Science and Human Rights Program*. Washington, DC: American Association for the Advancement of Science.

Ball, P. (2001). Making the case: The role of statistics in human rights reporting. *Statistical Journal of the United Nations Economic Commission for Europe*, *18*(2-3), 163–174.

Ball, P., & Asher, J. (2002). Statistics and Slobodan. *Chance*, *15*(4), 17–25.

Ball, P., Tabeau, E., & Verwimp, P. (2007). *The Bosnian book of the dead: Assessment of the database (Full Report). Households in Conflict Network Research Design Note 5*. Brighton, UK: Institute of Development Studies, University of Sussex.

Chapman, A. R., & Ball, P. (2001). The truth of truth commissions: Comparative lessons from Haiti, South Africa, and Guatemala. *Human Rights Quarterly*, *23*(4), 1–42. doi:10.1353/hrq.2001.0005

Cibelli, K., Hoover, A., & Krüger, J. (2009). *Descriptive statistics from statements to the Liberian truth and reconciliation commission. A Report by the Human Rights Data Analysis Group at Benetech and Annex to the Final Report of the Truth and Reconciliation Commission of Liberia*. Palo Alto, CA: Benetech.

Guzman, D. R., Guberek, T., Shapiro, G. M., & Zador, P. (2009). *Studying millions of rescued documents: Sampling plan at the Guatemalan National Police Archive (GNPA). JSM Proceedings, Survey Research Methods Section*. Alexandria, VA: American Statistical Association.

Hoover, A. G. (2010). Learning the hard way at the ICTY: Statistical evidence of human rights violations in an adversarial information environment. In Smeulers, A. (Ed.), *Collective violence and international criminal justice: An interdisciplinary approach*. Antwerp, Belgium: Intersentia.

Howland, T. (2008). How El Rescate, a small nongovernmental organization, contributed to the transformation of the human rights situation in El Salvador. *Human Rights Quarterly*, *30*(3), 703–705. doi:10.1353/hrq.0.0019

Klinger, J., & Silva, R. (2010). *Combining found data and surveys to measure casualties. Human rights data analysis group*. Palo Alto, CA: Benetech.

Price, M. E., Guberek, T., Guzman, D. R., Zador, P., & Shapiro, G. M. (2009). A statistical analysis of the Guatemalan National Police archive: Searching for documentation of human rights abuses. In Proceedings, J. S. M. (Ed.), *Survey Research Methods Section*. Alexandria, VA: American Statistical Association.

Shapiro, G. M., Guzman, D. R., Zador, P., Guberek, T., Price, M. E., & Lum, K. (2009). Weighting for the Guatemalan National Police Archive Sample: Unusual Challenges and Problems. In Proceedings, J. S. M. (Ed.), *Survey Research Methods Section*. Alexandria, VA: American Statistical Association.

Silva, R., & Ball, P. (2005). On the use of sample surveys and multiple systems estimations in assessing large-scale human rights violations: Recent experiences from Timor-Leste. *Proceedings of the Social Statistics Section – Joint Statistical Meetings*. Alexandria, VA: American Statistical Association.

Silva, R., & Ball, P. (2006). *The demography of large-scale human rights atrocities: Integrating demographic and statistical analysis into post-conflict historical clarification in Timor-Leste*. Paper presented at the 2006 meetings of the Population Association of America. Silver Spring, MD: Population Association of America.

Silva, R., & Ball, P. (2006). *The profile of human rights violations in Timor-Leste, 1974-1999. A report by the Benetech Human Rights Data Analysis Group to the Commission on Reception, Truth and Reconciliation*. Palo Alto, CA: Benetech.

Silva, R., & Ball, P. (2007). The demography of conflict-related mortality in Timor-Leste (1974-1999): Empirical quantitative measurement of civilian killings, disappearances & famine-related deaths. In Asher, J., Banks, D., & Scheuren, F. (Eds.), *Statistical methods for human rights*. New York, NY: Springer. doi:10.1007/978-0-387-72837-7_6

ADDITIONAL READING

Ball, P. (2005). On the quantification of horror: Field notes on statistical analysis of human rights violations. In Davenport, C., Johnston, H., & Mueller, C. (Eds.), *Repression and mobilization*. Minneapolis, MN: University of Minnesota.

Davenport, C., & Ball, P. (2002). Views to a kill: Exploring the implications of source selection in the case of Guatemalan state terror, 1977-1996. *The Journal of Conflict Resolution*, *46*(3), 427–450. doi:10.1177/0022002702046003005

Gohdes, A. (2010). *Different convenience samples, different stories: The case of Sierra Leone*. Palo Alto, CA: Benetech.

Guberek, T., Guzmán, D., Price, M., Lum, K., & Ball, P. (2010). *To count the uncounted: An estimation of lethal violence in Casanare. A Report by the Benetech Human Rights Program*. Palo Alto, CA: Benetech.

Guzmán, D., Guberek, T., Hoover, A., & Ball, P. (2007). *Missing people in Casanare (Los Desaparecidos de Casanare)*. Palo Alto, CA: Benetech.

Lum, K., Price, M., Guberek, T., & Ball, P. (2010). *Measuring elusive populations with Bayesian model averaging for multiple systems estimation: A case study on lethal violations in Casanare, 1998-2007*. Palo Alto, CA: Benetech.

Price, M., & Guzmán, D. (2010). Comments to the article. In D. Mejia & M. J. Uribe (Eds.), *Is violence against union members in Colombia systematic and targeted?* Bogota, Colombia: Universidad de los Andes.

Silva, R., Klingner, J., & Weikart, S. (2010). Measuring lethal counterinsurgency violence in Amritsar District, India using a referral-based sampling technique. In Proceedings, J. S. M. (Ed.), *Social Statistics Section*. Alexandria, VA: American Statistical Association.

Silva, R., Klingner, J., & Weikart, S. (2010). *State coordinated violence in Chad under Hissene Habre: A statistical analysis of reported prison mortality in Chad's DDS prisons and command responsibility of Hissene Habre, 1982-1990. A Report by Benetech's Human Rights Data Analysis Group to Human Rights Watch and the Chadian Association of Victims of Political Repression and Crimes*. Palo Alto, CA: Benetech.

Silva, R., Marwaha, J., & Klingner, J. (2009). *Violent deaths and enforced disappearances during the counterinsurgency in Punjab, India: A preliminary quantitative analysis. A Joint Report by Benetech's Human Rights Data Analysis Group & Ensaaf, Inc*. Palo Alto, CA: Benetech.

KEY WORDS AND DEFINITIONS

Human Rights Data Analysis Group (HRDAG): A group of two-dozen statisticians, programmers, demographers and data analysts. HRDAG is part of the Human Rights Program at Benetech, a nonprofit technology organization based in Palo Alto, California.

Multiple Systems Estimation (MSE): A statistical method that allows researchers to use separately collected but incomplete lists of a given population to estimate the total size of that group. MSE uses the identification of multiply-reported incidents – essentially overlapping accounts - to estimate the number of events that are never reported.

Who Did What To Whom (WDWTM): A model for examining human rights data created by HRDAG founder Dr. Patrick Ball.

Chapter 10
Human Rights Defenders and the Right to Digital Privacy and Security

Tanya Notley
Tactical Technology Collective, Germany

Stephanie Hankey
Tactical Technology Collective, Germany

ABSTRACT

Digital technologies, such as mobile phones and the internet, provide new opportunities for Human Rights Defenders to mobilise people, coordinate activities, uncover and document abuses, publish findings, and engage new audiences. However, with these new opportunities come new risks as well. This chapter examines the right to and need for private digital communication as part of freedom of expression in the context of carrying out human rights work. Drawing on their experiences at Tactical Technology Collective, an international non-government organisation, the authors argue that the most effective means to address the digital privacy needs of people who are defending human rights is to provide a range of support – including awareness raising media, how-to toolkits, and hands-on training – that assist Human Rights Defenders to identify and then address digital risks by changing behaviours in ways most appropriate to their local context.

RIGHT TO PRIVACY WHEN USING DIGITAL TOOLS

In *The History of Human Rights* Micheline Ishay points out that state justifications for using surveillance are not new (Ishay, 2008). The British utilitarian philosopher, Jeremy Bentham (1748-1832), argued that the right act or policy was that which would cause "the greatest good for the greatest number of people." Perhaps most famously, this perspective led him to develop the idea of a 'panopticon' to gaze over the walls of prisons to provide a constant watch on the prisoners kept inside (ibid., p352). While his idea was not taken up by the government of the

DOI: 10.4018/978-1-4666-1918-0.ch010

time, Bentham's argument that the more people believe they are being watched, the more likely they are to decide to not engage in behaviour they believe they may be punished for, is one which remains pervasive among governmental and corporate policies around the world. This same rationale, for example, is applied to justify the use of surveillance cameras – placed in streets, airports, hotels, homes, schools and shops – by governments, citizens and private companies. However, while the widespread use of video surveillance is often controversial in terms of privacy rights, in this chapter we will illustrate that internet and mobile telephony surveillance is something quite different. This is because new methods of internet and mobile telephony surveillance can and are being used to track our behaviour and communication in spaces we often believe are private; this usually happens without our knowledge or consent.

Changes to our right to and ability to control privacy can be understood as part of what Ishay refers to as the rise "of a more bureaucratized, cyber-controlled society" (Ishay 2008, p352). At the root of these changes, she contends, are the expansion of counter-terrorist activities (particularly post September the 2011 terrorist attacks in the United States), paralleled with increases in access to and use of digital technologies. Within this context she asks if we need new human rights laws and mechanisms to protect digitally-mediated spaces that support both freedom of thought and freedom of expression. To debate what changes are needed in order to catch up with technological change, she suggests that we may need to look not only to new human rights treaties, but also toward greater coordination and campaigning among civil society regarding the implications of new forms of control that can be exerted when we use digital technologies to communicate (Ishay, 2008, pp. 354-5).

There are many factors that can be used to explain why we are now seeing increasing levels of and types of digital surveillance activities. Diebert and Rohozinski (2010) contend that the risks to governments posed by what they call 'dark networks' (which they define as networks carrying out or promoting criminal activities which might range from paedophilia networks to copyright infringements to credit card fraud) and also 'resistance networks' (referring to those who legitimately oppose governments or challenge their actions and effectiveness) have contributed to a "massive expansion of electronic surveillance among all countries, a significant portion of it carried out through extra-legal means and / or downloaded to private companies" (ibid. p28). More specifically, the September 2011 attacks, they state, led the United States to quickly implement wide-ranging legislation, in the form of the PATRIOT Act, which expanded the scope for electronic surveillance. Many countries were quick to follow in the footsteps of the U.S., requiring lawful access provisions for law enforcement to the files and records kept by private Internet Service Providers (ISPs) (ibid.).

Today we are seeing significant changes to privacy laws rights in a number of countries alongside changes to media and communication regulatory structures, policies and laws that can also impact on our privacy. For example, in the United States, the proposed 'Commercial Bill of Privacy Rights' would clarify and in some cases significantly extend the rights of governments and companies to obtain, keep and share private digital communications (Electronic Frontier Foundation, 2011; Kerry, 2011; Ramonas, 2011). In India, the government is in the process of drafting a Privacy Bill (Gupta, 2011), while 2011 rules to the IT Act (amended in 2008) increase the ability of companies and states to carry out a range of surveillance activities (Abraham, 2011a, 2011b).

Some countries have a dedicated 'Privacy Ombudsmen' or Commissioner to oversee and protect privacy rights including those in the digital realm. One exceptional example that illustrates the potential for country-level privacy regulations and laws to impact upon global digital platforms and networks emerged recently from Canada. In 2009 the Privacy Commissioner of Canada investigated a series of allegations about the social networking site, Facebook, in the context of Canada's Personal Information Protection and Electronic Documents Act. The Commissioner found Facebook's privacy information to be confusing: Facebook's 'account settings', for example, described how to deactivate a Facebook account but did not explain how to delete an account to allow a user personal to remove their data from Facebook's servers. The Commissioner also found problems with over-sharing of users' personal information with third-party developers who create Facebook applications. Facebook complied with all of the Commissioner's requests for changes to their platform – the subsequent changes they made now apply to all Facebook users, not only those living in Canada (Crawford & Lumby, 2011; Denham, 2009). This example is not only important as a general trend, but also has particular significance in the context of Human Rights Defenders increasingly using popular social media tools for coordinating and organising.

In relation to international agreements that promote the free flow of information and rights to privacy and freedom of expression, Article 19 of the Universal Declaration of Human Rights states that, "Everyone has the right to freedom of opinion and expression; this right includes freedom to hold opinions without interference and to seek, receive and impart information and ideas through any media and regardless of frontiers" (United Nations, 1948). This article is one of 30 that define what is meant by human rights in the United Nations (UN) Charter, which is a binding agreement for all member states.[1] However, while this article is frequently used to provide moral justification and financial support for activities which promote media reforms that support freedom of expression and plurality, it is yet to be made a useful and meaningful agreement for protecting Human Rights Defenders from state spying and other kinds of digital communication privacy abuses. Far less cited in relation to debates regarding our communication rights is Article 12 of the Declaration. In this article the right to privacy is made explicit: "No one shall be subjected to arbitrary interference with his privacy, family, home or correspondence, nor to attacks upon his honour and reputation" (ibid.).

Certainly the issue of freedom of expression on the internet is, at the time of writing, being made a more prominent issue within the UN. The 'Joint Statement from the UN Special Rapporteurs on Freedom of Opinion and Expression', released in June 2011, appears at least in part to be a response to the 'Arab Spring' uprisings that have taken place in 2011, during which time a number of governments including those in Egypt, Tunisia and Syria acted to censor or entirely block internet and mobile phone access in order to suppress the ability of citizens to coordinate and communicate (LaRue, Mijatoviæ, Marino, & Tlakula, 2011). But while censorship remains a pressing issue for Human Rights Defenders in terms of freedom of expression, this is a subject that has received far more policy and academic attention when compared with the issue of digital privacy rights[2]. In fact in the 21 recommendations included in the Joint Statement's 'Declaration on Freedom of Expression and the Internet', which the UN Special Rapporteurs on Freedom of Opinion and Expression have recommended member states adopt, digital privacy issues, whether in relation to limiting the powers of states or private companies to track and monitor private communications, receives no mention at all other than a clause relating to the information management practices of 'Internet intermediaries' (ibid.).

While diplomatic efforts are very occasionally applied in support of freedom of expression and even privacy rights online, accusations of hypocrisy, alongside suggestions of ulterior motives, are quick to be made when this takes place – and one could argue this is with good reason. For example, in January 2010, when Google announced it would no longer comply with censorship agreements it had made with the Chinese government and simultaneously made allegations that two email accounts of activists using their services had been breached, the US government publicly condemned this alleged behaviour by the Chinese government. Yet their criticisms appeared to have had no real impact, with the Chinese government responding with an assertion that the U.S. had no right to interfere with long-standing laws in their country (Landler & Wong, 2011). Given that our own research (detailed later in this chapter) finds that Human Rights Defenders know their emails are routinely hacked and monitored by governments, it is unclear why the U.S. government responded so assertively to this single, alleged hack of two activists' email accounts.[3] Without knowing the true motivation for the U.S. State Department's response, a more cynical conclusion might be that it could be in their interest to make assertions that suggest they have some moral authority over China by being seen to take actions that protect freedom of expression; another could be that they acted to protect the interests of Google, a large and profitable U.S. company which had much to gain financially from their Chinese operations. In any case, the U.S. government's intervention to criticise another governments' email hacking activities was an exceptional case.

While it is difficult in a fast-changing technological environment to fully understand the implications of existing, emerging and proposed privacy laws and no analysis has been carried out regarding how these changes will play out across countries[4] any changes made to privacy laws are likely to have consequences for citizens who use digital technologies to communicate. For those who are working on sensitive issues – uncovering corruption, human rights abuses and serious injustices – the ability of companies and the state to monitor private communications has specific and additional implications.

DIGITAL PRIVACY THREATS AND THE IMPLICATIONS FOR HUMAN RIGHTS DEFENDERS

"Human Rights Defender" is a term used to describe people who, individually or with others, act to promote and/or protect human rights. Human Rights Defenders may address any human rights concern ranging from summary executions and torture, arbitrary arrest and detention, employment issues, forced evictions, state corruption, access to health care and the impact of toxic waste on the environment. The term "Human Rights Defender" has become more widely used since the adoption of the *Declaration on Human Rights Defenders* in 1998 by the United Nations. Until then, terms such as human rights "activist", "professional", "worker" or "monitor" had been most common. The term "Human Rights Defender" was seen to be a more cohesive, relevant and useful term (ONHCR, no date).

In 2010 Tactical Tech carried out a study that reviewed existing research, case studies and media reports relating to the digital security and privacy of Human Rights Defenders. These research initiatives were complemented by in-depth interviews with 20 people who work within, or closely with, different Human Rights Defender network organisations around the world (Tactical Technology Collective, 2010, unpublished). This study sought to understand the perspectives and concerns of Human Rights Defender networks operating at the grassroots and across all the regions, as well as the views and experiences of the journalists and lawyers who work with these networks. The research also built upon experience from Tactical Tech's ongoing evaluation research carried out around the more than 80 trainings we have provided in digital privacy and security for Human Rights Defenders during the period 2000 to 2011.

Through this research we identified multiple cases where Human Rights Defenders' email accounts had been compromised (with emails being read, forwarded, modified and deleted); mobile phones confiscated and therefore networks and meetings infiltrated (with SIM cards being destroyed, copied or cloned[5]); computers and other hardware remotely accessed or physically confiscated (with files copied, deleted or altered). In addition we found instances where the Human Rights Defenders we interviewed had been interrogated by state authorities and forced to reveal passwords or they were able to relay stories when colleagues found the computers they were using had software installed that recorded their passwords, allowing their computer files and emails to be read and copied by others. The study concluded that while censorship of online content is pervasive and problematic for many Human Rights Defenders, the day-to-day compromising of human rights-related information and communications, including personally targeted forms of physical and digital surveillance and harassment, was the most significant and pressing concern for most of those we interviewed. These issues rarely receive media attention and almost never gain diplomatic or international support or redress; however, they directly contribute to the repression, isolation and intimidation of Human Rights Defenders and often negatively impact on the effectiveness of their work. The following examples of breaches of privacy are taken from interviews we carried out with Human Rights Defenders (Tactical Technology Collective, 2010, unpublished).

"It's not uncommon now for a fake gmail screen to be left up on the screen in an internet cafe. Someone comes in and types in their name and password and then that's it, the [state] have it... Sometimes the owner of the internet cafe they use might not even know this has happened. But we know, it is happening." Human Rights Defender 1

"I've had my email hacked and it was used to send out to all my contacts what it said was a New Year's greeting. That attached file had a virus spyware embedded. When things like this happen, we can't be sure the [state] did this, but we think it is likely." Human Rights Defender 2

"It's the physical threats that are our biggest concern. It's very common for the offices of civil society organisations are broken into. Our hard-drives are stolen, our files are searched. It happened to us just a few weeks ago. These are targeted attacks initiated by people whose wrong-doings we are working to uncover." Human Rights Defender 3

"While investigating alleged human rights abuses by security forces, X came across a paramilitary patrol, who confiscated his mobile phone for about an hour. After the officials returned his mobile phone, X noticed that the back of the phone was half opened and the card misplaced. X believed his SIM card had been cloned, which is a very easy thing to do in his opinion...In another instance he was staying in a small hotel in the city while carrying out investigations and while he was gone someone broke in to the hotel room, stole his computer and reformatted it... He lost files, copies of text messages, research, files and contact details for people." Interviewer's notes with Human Rights Defender 4

Overall, the problem of digital security and safety for Human Rights Defenders can be framed as a problem of success. It is usually when an individual or organisation is successful in uncovering misconduct and abuses that they attract significant attention from the media or other influential players, in turn making them a target of the rights abusers they have identified. While this may be true of Human Rights Defenders, regardless of the tools they use to collect and share information, there are some unique challenges that uses of digital information and communications technologies introduce.

Digital technologies present an unparalleled opportunity for individuals to expose and broadcast abuses of power. Consider, for example, Noha Atef's blog, *Torture in Egypt*, which documented cases of police brutality and abuses and in one case lead to the release of a man who had been wrongly imprisoned for 14 years; or a case in Morocco where an anonymous person uploaded videos showing police collecting bribes from motorists, which ultimately led to the introduction of new state surveillance practices to observe and monitor the behaviour of traffic police (Tactical Technology Collective, 2009).

The digital technologies and tools people tend to use to expose rights abuses, however, are designed with unprecedented tracking and archiving abilities. This leaves an increasingly long trail of evidence behind individuals' digital activities which ultimately means that Human Rights Defenders, and those that they associate with, are potentially exposed when using digital technologies and tools, including popular online services and applications. Through this potential exposure, they can be more precisely targeted by perpetrators of rights abuses who have access to people skilled in using digital technologies for investigative purposes.

To provide some indication of the extent of potential exposure, we can consider the website, dictionary.com, which the Wall Street Journal found installed 234 tracker files onto a computer when it was visited. Of these, 133 files collected information that could be kept indefinitely, while 143 could be used to share this information with others (Wall Street Journal, 2010). This example provides some indication of the many 'hidden layers' that operate on websites that may appear innocuous, but have ulterior motives. Similarly, if we consider the traces that may be left behind by an individual who uses YouTube to upload a video exposing human right abuses, we can see a digital trail is likely to be created, unless specific security measures are taken. On YouTube, a person uploading content will need to be aware that the Internet Protocol address (IP address), a unique number assigned to each device connected to the internet, is logged when they post content. This IP number can be traced back to their Internet Service Provider (ISP) and ultimately to the user who has registered for internet connectivity via this provider. Further the ISP is able to or is often required to record all user activities, including posts to YouTube, and may choose to, or be requested to, pass this information on to the state.

An additional risk of using digital technologies for documenting and exposing human rights abuses is the exposure of individuals featured in public posts. In some cases, even the individuals featured within images and videos posted online have been targeted. This was the case during the Iranian uprising in 2009 and the 'Saffron Revolution' people's uprising in Burma in 2008 (Gregory, 2010). In both cases, despite tight controls on the media and journalists, individuals were able to get photographs and videos from protests out of the country and then posted on to websites. These images were essential for informing the world about what was happening in a situation where international media could not gain access; but they were also later used by authorities to identify individuals who were then arrested, tortured or who disappeared (ibid.) Due to the viral and open nature of online media, this is extremely difficult to control. It ultimately means, those who post content online need to take responsibility to consider the privacy and safety of those they are exposing. Yet, enforcing or even widely encouraging this, is extremely difficult.

STATE SURVEILLANCE OF HUMAN RIGHTS DEFENDERS

There is some evidence to suggest that state surveillance and monitoring of internet user behaviour is increasing and diversifying, though no wide-scale studies have been carried out to assess this. Most evidence that would support this claim is anecdotal since surveillance activities are usually carried out by highly trained, skilled and secretive bodies and therefore are difficult to systematically monitor.

In one example, from July 2010, authorities in the United Arab Emirates (UAE) began harassing and arresting young Blackberry users who had forwarded or received information on their handsets about a planned protest. This planned protest sought to challenge an increase in the price of gasoline (one of the highest in the Arab world). Any demonstration in the UAE requires a special permit from the security forces, which is extremely difficult to obtain. However, the protest was called off before it took place after the organiser, 18-year-old Badr Ali Saiwad Al Dhohori, learnt that it would probably result in problems with the authorities. Despite this, Badr was arrested after authorities identified him as a key organiser because his BlackBerry Personal Identification Number (PIN) was included in a message he sent calling for the protest, meaning authorities were able to track him down. He was held for a week and interrogated in order to trace those he had been messaging; a number of young people who forwarded or received the message then lost their jobs or were threatened by the authorities (Front Line, 2010; Tactical Technology Collective, 2010, unpublished).

This example is one of many that has emerged in recent years that demonstrates that states are increasingly aware of the open channels that digital technologies can provide for concerned citizens and rights advocates and it provides evidence that they are steadily asserting their influence over these spaces. The full extent of state surveillance of online and mobile communications, however, remains largely hidden from the public, making raising awareness about this issue very difficult. Perhaps the fullest account we have of the extent of digital surveillance of rights activists comes out of the 2011 people's uprising against the Mubarak regime in Egypt. Following the popular Egyptian uprising that began on 25 January 2011 and led to the President Mubarak stepping down 16 days later, activists raided the headquarters of Amn Al Dowla, the state security agency, uncovering secret memos and personal dossiers that showed the many ways their online communications were being monitored. In June 2011, the Wall Street Journal reported that after participating in this raid, 26-year-old activist Basem Fathi claimed he found files describing his love life and trips to the beach, apparently gleaned from intercepted emails and phone calls, including conversations he had using the online telephony platform, Skype. Although many activists knew their digital communications were being tracked, they were surprised that communications platforms they thought were secure, had not been. Fathi said: "We were using Skype for a long time thinking that it was protected and secure." (Stecklow, Sonne, & Bradley, 2011).

In other revelations relating to digital surveillance techniques by states, we have learnt that the United States government, who were quick to make public pronunciations about the rights of activists and citizen demonstrators in Egypt, have also acted to secretly monitor the private digital communication of people who had not been charged with committing any crimes. For example, in 2010 in the United States, investigations by the Electronic Frontier Foundation, a non-profit civil liberties group, found that the Department of Homeland Security had been mining online social networking sites to detect citizenship fraud (Lynch, 2010; Weinberger, 2010) while a review of a legal database by news agency, Reuters, shows that since 2008, federal judges have authorised at least two dozen warrants to search individuals' Facebook accounts (Roberts, 2011). Also, in perhaps what is the most widely reported case relating to digital privacy issues in the U.S., prosecutors investigating the disclosure of thousands of classified government documents by the whistle-blowing and pro-transparency group, WikiLeaks, went to court to demand the Twitter account information of several people linked to the organisation, including two non-U.S. citizens and one U.S. citizen, Jacob Appelbaum, despite the fact that there were no criminal charges against any of them[6] (Scott & Burns, 2010). This wasn't the first time user details had been requested by the U.S. government from an internet company: during the first six months of 2010, for example, the U.S. government asked Google for information about website owners 4,287 times. To date, neither Google nor the U.S. government have clarified what these requests were for (BBC, 2010a; Google, 2010).

How surveillance by authorities is carried out varies greatly from country to country. However, it is the more widespread surveillance carried out under repressive regimes that has received far more attention in the mainstream media and by vocal analysts such as the Belarusian internet critic and journalist, Evgeny Morozov. In his book, *The Net Delusion*, Morozov (2011) frames the use of digital technologies as a significant hazard to Human Rights Defenders. In particular, he is both wary and critical of the use of social media tools (such as Facebook and Twitter) by activists which he sees as essentially 'doing the job of the security forces for them' as they document and expose networks, their actions and connections – citing the Iranian government's use of social media to track down and intimidate its opponents as one example of this (his information might Morozov, 2009; 2011).

While the more sensational and revolutionary potential of digital technologies are extremely important for human rights, it is also critical to see these examples in the context in which they occur – within extremely oppressive regimes at moments of threatened uprising, revolt or revolution. Our own research with Human Rights Defenders who work to address a diverse range of rights violations, corrupt activities and miscarriages of justice found that it is everyday privacy risks – those known and those they are unsure about – that provide the greatest concern in relation to the use of digital technologies. Many of these concerns relate directly to the way new technologies have been configured.

DIGITAL FREEDOMS AND PRIVACY RIGHTS AND THE CONFIGURATION OF NEW TECHNOLOGIES

When Human Rights Defenders working in high-risk contexts used landline telephones in the past, they knew that it was likely that the phone would be tapped, and they would tailor their activities accordingly. Depending on their situation and level of risk, they would not use the phone, speak in code, or just go ahead and take the risk. The biggest challenge that activists face now in using new information and communications technologies, is that in such a dynamic and fast changing digital technology landscape they have lost their ability to understand and therefore control their communication risks. The level of technical knowledge necessary to carefully assess digital security risks is increasingly beyond the reach of most Human Rights Defenders. Much of the current debate related to information and communications technology and the communication rights of Human Rights Defenders centres on issues related to the freedom of the internet, particularly in relation to freedom of speech and censorship. There are, however, broader trends that relate to the configuration of information and communications technologies that should be considered in order to understand how the development and use of information and communications technologies might affect human rights in the future.

As information and communications technologies become easier to use, they also become more opaque. Questions relating to who owns data, default settings on hardware and software applications, and a lack of understanding about how to control traces of information that we leave behind, raises serious concerns for technology users working with sensitive information. Online service providers that make it extremely easy for users to publish their content in increasingly sophisticated forms – images, videos, visualisations, daily online journals (blogs) – at the same time retain, and in some cases own, the data that is uploaded.

As Sunil Abraham, from the Centre for Internet Society in India, points out in criticising proposed legal changes to India's IT Act, "surveillance capabilities are not a necessary feature of information systems. They have to be engineered into these systems" (Abraham, 2011a). Surveillance functionality, when built into and hidden within digital tools, are a considerable issue for those working with sensitive information who want to benefit from new distribution channels. Even online services and applications used solely for accessing content, such as internet browsers, store significant data about their users. Websites, online platforms and online or mobile applications are designed with default settings that store detailed information about a user's activities, and in many cases, about their connections with others. These features can be useful in some circumstances. For example, online tracking of our behaviour can support the customisation of a browser or website so that it is more relevant and useful to an individual user, or it can allow market analysis to be carried out so that a company can understand it's website audience better and deliver them content they are likely to find more interesting. But when Human Rights Defenders are using the internet to share and collect sensitive information and they are not informed that tracking is taking place and have no ability to control this, these actions can be extremely dangerous since they can expose where they have been online and where they are located offline.

The owners and developers of online services are consistently experimenting with how they utilise their users' information with or without user permissions. As boundaries are pushed companies can be restricted from violating privacy (as was the case with Facebook and the Canadian Privacy Commissioner) or they can be forced to impede on privacy by government requirements. The example cited earlier, where the UAE government tracked private communications using Blackberrys that were used by citizens to plan a protest, is linked to an issue that emerged a few months before this incident, when a number of governments objected to the way Blackberry functions as a communication technology. By sending all messages in an encrypted form to servers, which may be located outside of the countries in which they originated, authorities would be unable to gain access to information about calls made or text messages sent using Blackberrys, should they demand access to a user's account from telecommunications service providers. This led to at least three governments threatening to ban the use of Blackberrys in 2010, claiming that not having access to citizen's mobile phone calls and text message records posed a national security threat; the UAE was one of these three countries. The UAE government eventually agreed to lift their proposed ban after they had engaged in private negotiations with Blackberry's Canadian owner, Research in Motion (BBC, 2010b). But as is usually the case with closed-room government-corporate negotiations, the public were not made privy to the details of these discussions or the compromises that were made.

This example highlights the privacy and censorship risks that Human Rights Defenders face when they use digital technologies to communicate. In this instance, digital technologies enabled a group of young people to respond immediately to a situation they saw as unjust (the rise of oil prices in an oil-rich nation) and it would have supported people who agreed with them to protest against this. However, because one organiser did not fully understand the risk of his digital communications – and since the company who developed the technology he used appears to have not protected his identity – he ultimately put himself and others at risk by *exposing his identity because of the digital traces he left behind*. The response of the UAE authorities in turn highlights an ongoing tension between citizen needs for private communication and authorities demands for traceable communication, which they argue is required to protect societies from terrorism and to uphold national laws. Although it is not clear what measures the owners of Blackberry agreed to take to appease the UAE government, it seems very likely they did make some concessions to the authorities relating to the provision of access to Blackberry user information – ultimately putting the young person who called for the protest at risk as well as any Human Rights Defender who uses this technology and is not aware of the risks they may be taking in doing so (BBC, 2010b; Srinivasa, 2010; Tactical Technology Collective, 2010, unpublished).

As companies add features to hardware devices – whether to help popularise them or make them easier to use by facilitating synergies between different applications and services – it becomes increasingly difficult for users to limit and control what information they provide about themselves and their activities in different online environments. For example, as online services detect new content added to computers, offline and online devices synchronise, and as users upgrade from one hardware device to another, technology users can find themselves unable to control settings and to be clear on where data about them is being stored and who has access to that data. For Human Rights Defenders this raises the barrier to using digital technologies safely and securely.

Many online services are used for distributing human rights related content because of their ability to reach and connect with so many people. There is an inherent contradiction in this; services designed to connect also expose. Many users don't think through the potential misuse of the content they willingly contribute and don't look ahead to the profile they are building of themselves when services and networks become inter-linked.

An analysis of social networking websites carried out by security experts from Cambridge University for the *2009 International Conference on Advances in Social Network Analysis and Mining*, highlights what they refer to as the 'social graph' and how this makes users particularly vulnerable.

> *A broader threat is extraction of the social graph, that is, the graph consisting of users and their friendship links... While the commonly considered graph is of friendship links, the graph connecting users through common group membership can also be sensitive... The greatest problem, however, may be the lack of user understanding of the limited amount of privacy which can actually be enforced by today's sites (Bonneau & Anderson, 2009, pp. 4-6).*

As reinforced by Evgeny Morozov (2011), Human Rights Defenders using the internet are sometimes making the work of the intelligence services easier by leaving traces behind them online that show where they have been and provide evidence of their connections. Intelligence gathering can now be carried out as desk research that would have previously taken more resources and time to gather. In our research, many Human Rights Defenders told us that intelligence gathering is also being carried out by their adversaries, including staff at private companies, who have a vested interest in hiding the rights abuses they are uncovering and trying to address. Increasingly this investigative desk research will have a long history due to the lifespan of online data, while it can easily be passed on to or intercepted by others.

If current trends continue, the problems that arise for human rights through the prevalence and abuse of private information online are likely to increase over time. Online services and applications are trending towards 'hubs' that act like platforms through which users can engage with multiple services and applications, owned by many different companies, all offering very different end-user license agreements, often based on what is permissible under the law in the country the company is registered. These services and applications are usually made for commercial purposes, leaving activists engaged in politically or culturally sensitive activities trapped between making decisions about using technology to broaden outreach and needing to protect their own and others privacy.

The example cited earlier in this chapter, of WikiLeaks members' Twitter accounts being infiltrated by the U.S. government, has also become a test case for how online services choose to deal with controversial content. While Twitter opted to challenge a court order that forced it to hand over the information of users without their knowledge, other online services went in a completely different direction, taking extra measures they were not legally required to do: Amazon refused to allows Wikileaks to host its website on their servers; Paypal refused to allow Wikileaks to use their services for accepting donations; while a small data visualisation service, Tableau Public, took down content created by others using WikiLeaks data on their free online services (De Waal, 2010; New York Times, 2010; Paypal, 2010; Singel, 2011a; Svensson, 2010; Tableu Software, 2010). This is significant when we consider providers of services can exercise their own powers of censorship and surveillance. As one observer, Mary De Waal, noted: "What the WikiLeaks case is telling us is that we may treat the Internet as a public space, but that it is held by private players and these players may make the decision to constrain speech based on business criteria" (De Waal, 2010).

Many of the most popular online services have been designed by commercial organisations, located in the United States. These commercial entities work from their own specific view of democracy, ethics and rights. Creators and the users of these systems are now seeing how the design of these technologies impacts upon their use in different environments including repressive societies, where there are serious limits to freedom of expression and a lack for respect for fundamental human rights. Activists are testing the limits of systems designed for activities very different to their own and in doing so they are forcing new debates around freedom of expression and digital privacy and content ownership rights. Through this work they are discovering that online services and hubs will often say 'no' to upholding their right to expression at times, even sometimes without any explanation, and there is little to no recourse when this happens. As the WikiLeaks case shows, privacy boundaries within these new online services are being challenged even within democracies that promote themselves as being defenders of freedom of expression. The question here for Human Rights Defenders, and those seeking to support their work, is: how best to deal with this? One option is to counter new digital vulnerabilities and threats by developing new software tools.

THE PROBLEM WITH SOFTWARE SOLUTIONS

There is a range of software and applications that can be utilised to help uphold the privacy of those using digital technologies and working with sensitive information[7]. These tools only cover a small area of digital privacy needs though, ranging from the back-up of files and virus protection to prevent data loss, to rendering tracking activities on a website visible so as to alert a user of potential risks, to encryption of files and passwords and encrypted access to online platforms and services to protect sensitive content and information[8]. Our own research (Tactical Tech, unpublished, 2010) found that, unfortunately, Human Rights Defenders and those who work with them, including independent journalists, often don't use any digital security software applications available to them until it is too late – that is, until something has already happened to them or their colleagues. In other cases where they had been using digital security software, they cited examples of where colleagues had failed to do so, and this resulted in their private communications being intercepted.

For many of the more widely used tools and services, such as mobile phones and online services like Facebook or YouTube, there are no one-size-fits-all, simple, consequence-free software solutions or technical fixes. When there are available tools, there are issues relating to their implementation. The use of some tools might raise flags if users are being monitored and this could potentially direct more attention to their activities and therefore increase risks. In other cases, software tools need to be promoted with caution, depending on context and risks; for example, although it is technically possible to password protect a computer or an online web account from easy access, it is not advisable if it increases the chances that the owner will be tortured to reveal that password. In these cases, other measures should be taken. In some cases though, Human Rights Defenders simply don't want to use extra software tools that are cumbersome to use, slow down their machines and restrict their online access and user experience.

Other problems with the development of software solutions that claim to uphold privacy and freedom of expression rights have also arisen in recent years. One example, often referred to as the 'Haystack debacle,' involved software developed by a U.S.-based organisation, Censorship Research Centre. The software was designed to allow people in Iran to bypass censorship restrictions; however, the developers of this software openly admitted that they had no credentials in terms of understanding the risks and local context of Human Rights Defenders. The U.S. Government granted an export license to and promoted this software, helping it to receive a great deal of international attention as well as some development funding. When the software was finally tested independently, it was found to compromise the identity and thus the safety of users[9] (Evgeny Morozov, 2010; O'Brien, 2010).

While it may be technically possible to create a secure digital information sharing and communications security environment, our own research with Human Rights Defenders and our experience in providing training in digital security has informed an approach that is not solely reliant on promoting the use of security software. We feel this is not the solution that activists or those who support them should be looking for since technologies and software will continue to change rapidly, making these solutions defunct and potentially dangerous over time. Instead, activists need to be able to make better self-assessments, so they have the awareness and knowledge to ascertain their privacy needs and to establish how to best manage everyday risks as they emerge. There is also a role for lobbying and holding to account the companies who create and promote digital technologies, tools and services and the governments and international bodies who have national and international obligations to uphold human rights laws and treaties, including those relating to privacy and freedom of speech.

SUPPORTING THE DIGITAL PRIVACY OF HUMAN RIGHTS DEFENDERS

Attempts to stifle and control the free flow of information and abuses of privacy rights will continue to be carried out by states, companies and other players with a vested interest in doing so. At the same time it is important to remember that because digital technologies are playing an important role in uncovering and addressing rights abuses around the world, Human Rights Defenders are finding ways to mitigate the risks these technologies introduce, by skilfully adapting their use of these tools to work within their known limitations.

Included in our research with Human Rights Defenders and Independent Journalists was a story involving an activist who was arrested and beaten by police. Just before his phone was confiscated he was able to send an SMS to his colleagues alerting them of his whereabouts so they were able to immediately appeal for his release. In another case, a group working on recording corruption cases, refused to hand over their computers to authorities on request. In the few days between the refusal of the request and a 'break-in' to their offices and theft of all their computers, the group was able to replace all the names of individuals who had reported instances of corruption with a number based code system. Activists from one organisation who were documenting human rights abuses by the state told us that they do not store any data at all on their computers and instead use small portable devices, which they never connect to the computer when they are online, and which they know how to destroy quickly, if need be (Tactical Technology Collective, 2010). These three examples highlight that, despite the risks individuals take in utilising information and communications technologies in their quest to defend human rights, they can still be used to expose atrocities when Human Rights Defenders find their own 'smart' strategies to protect themselves, and those they are working to support.

It is important to look at the trends outlined in this chapter, considering what they mean in a range of situations; from vibrant democracies, in which government's claim to uphold freedom of expression principles and fundamental human rights, to repressive states that have scant respect for the Universal Declaration of Human Rights and other binding UN charters and are without laws and legal systems that protect basic human rights. In addition, there needs to be very different levels of concern for different types of individuals – ranging from high-profile Human Rights Defenders, to marginalised or occasionally politically active individuals – who use new technologies to promote human rights. In each case, the strategies for action need to be unique and the level of understanding and technical know-how needed varies greatly.

Strategies may range from a desire to achieve and maintain complete anonymity, to the decision to intentionally create a carefully crafted public profile. The strategy each Human Rights Defender takes needs to be directly linked to the ultimate objective of their actions and their overall approach to security and risk taking. For example, an individual from a marginalised community expressing their opinion on a highly controversial human rights issue in a repressive society may want to maintain complete anonymity so as not to raise unnecessary attention. This may involve careful consideration about when and how they access the internet, what services they are utilising, what public profile they adopt, what kind of connections they have to others and conscious decisions about a range of other behavioural patterns that may expose their identity. However, an established human rights organisation operating in the same country, working on the same issue, may intentionally carry out a series of high-profile online activities which can be easily linked back to them in order to raise awareness of an issue. At the same time this organisation may need to operate a strict approach to the security and identity of their sources, concealing the path they took to find this information, to ensure there is no incriminating metadata in their evidence and to cover their traces of interactions with third parties related to their action. In this scenario, the human rights organisation has to undertake a carefully planned hybrid approach, differentiating between the safety of private data while creating public data, being unconcerned about privacy in one area while being meticulous about the security of privacy in another.

Our own approach to digital privacy and security at Tactical Tech is built on the premise that individuals, organisations and communities who advocate for rights will and should take risks; the main danger is when actors are not aware of the risks they are taking. Our work to support the digital privacy and security of Human Rights Defenders, implemented in partnership with Front Line Defenders (http://www.frontlinedefenders.org), involves four different but connected activities that help human rights defenders build their own strategies for handling their digital security and privacy. Firstly, we aim to reach broad audiences, including non-activist communities who may become active suddenly, in response to changing circumstances. To achieve this we produce awareness-raising materials such as a series of animations that outline, in an engaging way, the different digital privacy and security risks that exist (see http://onorobot.org/). These materials are circulated virally and are screened offline by activists at their own events and within their own communities. Secondly, we have produced and continue to update a digital privacy and security toolkit for those rights advocates who may want to learn more deeply about and then implement different options to address their risks (see http://security.ngoinabox.org/). Our third activity involves the more targeted training of trainers and direct training of Human Rights Defenders to ensure they have the skills required to identify and address the specific risks and threats they face in their own context. Finally, we provide ongoing support and mentoring for a much smaller group, through ongoing communication with Human Rights Defenders to ensure they are able to receive timely and context specific information that will help them address their ever-changing privacy and security needs. In all of these activities our approach to giving advice and support is never didactic and prescriptive: in the end Human Rights Defenders need to continually assess their own risks and respond to the situation around them; strictly adhering to the advice of people outside of their work environment, country and community is always going to be dangerous.

The work of organisations and activists who are focused on deploying different approaches to Tactical Tech in pushing for digital privacy rights – including lobbying governments and international bodies as well as the private companies who produce and promote the use of digital tools and services – is vital for supporting future uses of digital technologies for human rights. Recent lobbying successes in this area provide some indication of how important and potentially influential this work can be. For example, it was a complaint lodged by the not-for-profit Canadian Internet Policy and Public Interest Clinic that led to the Privacy Commissioner in Canada objecting to a number of Facebook's policies and practices, which ultimately resulted in increased privacy rights for all Facebook users (Denham, 2009). Similarly, the actions of Christopher Soghoian, an academic and privacy activist, including published research and freedom of information requests, have pushed U.S. companies including Yahoo! and Dropbox to be more honest and transparent about the digital security risks involved in using their services (Singel, 2011b; Zetter, 2009). Soghoian was also one of 37 privacy and security experts who published a public letter to Google, which successfully urged the company to offer SSL encryption[10] by default to users of its services including Google Mail, Google Calender and Google Docs (Soghoian, 2009). These examples illustrate that it is possible to force change by using existing privacy laws and by threatening the credibility and integrity of private companies.

THE FUTURE OF PRIVACY AND THE USE OF DIGITAL TECHNOLOGIES TO SUPPORT HUMAN RIGHTS

This chapter has outlined three approaches that can be deployed to support the digital privacy and security of Human Rights Defenders. Firstly, technologies, applications and services can be made more transparent and flexible, allowing users to understand what data is being collected about them and giving them control to conceal the data, communications and media they have created, shared or uploaded. Secondly, Human Rights Defenders can be trained and supported to both understand and mitigate digital privacy and security threats – this is the approach Tactical Tech is currently focused on addressing. Thirdly, governments, international regulatory bodies and private companies can be lobbied to uphold, strengthen and protect the digital privacy rights of individuals, including Human Rights Defenders.

As an organisation working to support Human Rights Defenders to use digital technologies effectively and securely, we are acutely aware at Tactical Tech that the future of digital privacy and security is dependent on a future still unwritten in terms of how governments and commercial companies will be legally permitted to utilise their central role and increasing power over the free flow of information. This issue may dominate future uses of information and communications technologies and their impact on human rights, in particular, freedom of expression. It is clear that much needs to be done if UN Charters or governmental policies are to play a role through new legal, policy or diplomatic measures in supporting Human Rights Defenders to effectively and safely use digital technologies. In the meantime, as privacy laws continue to change and both states and companies continue to push the boundaries of what is permissible in terms of tracking and monitoring online behaviours, Human Rights Defenders and the organisations, researchers and activists that want to support their work, can not afford to either ignore the digital privacy and security risks that exist or rely solely on technical solutions to address these.

Through our own experiences at Tactical Tech, training and supporting advocates to address digital security over an eight-year period, we have come to the conclusion that if Human Rights Defender Networks are to make use of a wide range of digital technologies to advance their work, even with the support of digital security experts from the private and NGO sectors, it is not possible to remove digital risks completely or perhaps even substantially. The best strategy for protection is to educate Human Rights Defenders about the kinds of risks that exist so as to enable them to better manage and reduce them, as part of their overall communications and security strategies and to help them find ways to utilise online technologies that advance their work yet decrease their risk of accidental exposure. Through this approach Human Rights Defenders are able to develop creative approaches to work with and make the most of the digital tools and resources available to them, while being agile and innovative in working within the limits and constraints that surround them.

ACKNOWLEDGMENT

We would like to thank our colleagues at Tactical Tech, especially Marek Tuszynski and Bobby Soriano, for contributing to this paper. Thanks also to Sunil Abraham from the Centre for Internet and Society in India for providing useful very feedback on an early draft and thanks also to our two anonymous reviewers.

*Tactical Technology Collective (*http://www.tacticaltech.org*) is an international NGO that supports rights advocates to use information, communications and digital technologies to maximise the impact of their work. In collaboration with Front Line Defenders (*http://www.frontlinedefenders.org/*), Tactical Tech has produced a number of digital privacy and security support materials and has trained more than 1500 advocates and journalists to understand their digital security and privacy risks and manage their vulnerabilities.*

REFERENCES

Abraham, S. (2011a, 30th June). *Do you want to be watched?* Retrieved July 4, 2011, from http://www.cis-india.org/advocacy/igov/blog/want-to-be-watched/

Abraham, S. (2011b, 16th June). *Privacy and security can co-exist*. Retrieved July 4, 2011, from http://indiatoday.intoday.in/site/story/privacy-and-security-can-co-exist/1/142179.html/

BBC. (2010a). *Google releases censorship tools*. Retrieved July 1, 2011, from http://www.bbc.co.uk/news/technology-11380677/

BBC. (2010b, 8 October 2010). *United Arab Emirates will not ban Blackberries*. Retrieved June 16, 2011, from http://www.bbc.co.uk/news/technology-11499755/

Bonneau, J., & Anderson, J. (2009, 20-22nd July, 2009). *Prying data out of a social network*. Paper presented at the 2009 Conference on Advances in Social Network Analysis and Mining, Athens, Greece. Retrieved June 1, 2011, from http://www.cl.cam.ac.uk/~jra40/publications/2009-ASONAM-prying-data.pdf/

Crawford, K., & Lumby, C. (2011). *The adaptive moment: A fresh approach to convergent media in Australia*. The University of New South Wales. Retrieved July 1, 2011, from http://www.apo.org.au/node/24734/

De Waal, M. (2010, December 10th 2010). The WikiLeaks effect - An end to free speech that radically offends? Retrieved June 1, 2011, from http://www.thedailymaverick.co.za/article/2010-12-10-the-wikileaks-effect-an-end-to-free-speech-that-radically-offends/

Deibert, R., Palfrey, J., Rohozinski, R., & Zittrain, J. (Eds.). (2008). *Access denied: The practice and policy of global internet filtering*. Cambridge, MA: MIT Press.

Deibert, R. J., & Rohozinski, R. (2010). Risking security: Policies and paradoxes of cyberspace security. *International Political Sociology*, *4*, 15–32. doi:10.1111/j.1749-5687.2009.00088.x

Denham, E. (2009). *Report of findings into the complaint filed by the Canadian Internet Policy and Public Interest Clinic (CIPPIC) against Facebook Inc. under the Personal Information Protection and Electronic Documents Act*. Privacy Commissioner of Canada. Retrieved October 1, 2011, from http://www.priv.gc.ca/cf-dc/2009/2009_2008_0716_e.cfm/

Electronic Frontier Foundation. (2011). *Well-meaning "Privacy Bill of Rights" wouldn't stop online tracking*. Retrieved June 1, 2011, from https://www.eff.org/deeplinks/2011/04/well-meaning-privacy-bill-rights-could-codify/

Google. (2010). *Transparency report*. Retrieved June 1, 2011, from http://www.google.com/transparencyreport/governmentrequests/

Gregory, S. (2010). Cameras everywhere: Ubiquitous video documentation of human rights, new forms of video advocacy, and considerations of safety, security, dignity and consent. *Journal of Human Rights Practice*, *2*(2), 191–207. doi:10.1093/jhuman/huq002

Gupta, A. (2011, June 30th). *Analysis of the Privacy Bill, 2011*. Retrieved July 1, 2011, from http://www.iltb.net/2011/06/analysis-of-the-privacy-bill-2011/

Ishay, R. M. (2008). *The history of human rights: From ancient times to the globalization era* (2nd ed.). Berkeley, CA: University of California Press.

Kerry, J. (2011). *Proposed Commercial Bill of Privacy Rights*. Retrieved July 1, 2011, from http://kerry.senate.gov/work/issues/issue/?id=74638d00-002c-4f5e-9709-1cb51c6759e6&CFID=79733731&CFTOKEN=26547080/

Line, F. (2010). *United Arab Emirates: Young activists arrested for organising peaceful protest via BlackBerry*. Retrieved December 10th, 2010, from http://www.frontlinedefenders.org/node/12818/

Lynch, J. (2010). *Applying for citizenship? U.S. Citizenship and Immigration Wants to Be Your "friend*." Retrieved January 10th, 2011, from https://www.eff.org/deeplinks/2010/10/applying-citizenship-u-s-citizenship-and/

Morozov, E. (2009). *From the "told you so" department*. Retrieved June 1, 2011, from http://neteffect.foreignpolicy.com/posts/2009/12/03/from_the_told_you_so_department/

Morozov, E. (September 16th, 2010). The Great Internet Freedom Fraud: How Haystack endangered the Iranian dissidents it was supposed to protect. *Slate*. Retrieved June 1, 2011, from http://www.slate.com/id/2267262/

Morozov, E. (2011). *The Net delusion: The dark side of Internet freedom*. New York, NY: Public Affairs.

O'Brien, D. (2010, January 15th). *Haystack vs how the internet works*. Retrieved June 1, 2011, from http://www.oblomovka.com/wp/2010/09/14/haystack-vs-how-the-internet-works/

ONHCR. (n.d.). *Special Rapporteur on the situation of Human Rights Defenders*. Office for the United Nations High Commissioner for Human Rights. Retrieved July 14, 2011, from http://www2.ohchr.org/english/issues/defenders/who.htm

PayPal. (2010, 28th June). *PayPal statement regarding WikiLeaks*. Retrieved June 1, 2011, from https://www.thepaypalblog.com/2010/12/paypal-statement-regarding-wikileaks/

Quinn, A. (2010, 6th February, 2011). US weighs security after 'serious' Google allegation *Reuters*. Retrieved June 1, 2011, from http://www.msnbc.msn.com/id/43253703/ns/technology_and_science-security/t/us-weighs-security-after-serious-google-allegation/

Ramonas, A. (2011). Leahy introduces bill to update digital privacy law. Retrieved May 20th, 2011, Retrieved June 1, 2011, from http://www.mainjustice.com/2011/05/17/leahy-introduces-bill-to-update-digital-privacy-law/

Roberts, J. J. (2011, 12th July, 2011). A new law-enforcement tool: Facebook searches. *Reuters*. Retrieved June 1, 2011, from http://newsandinsight.thomsonreuters.com/Legal/News/2011/07_-_July/A_new_law-enforcement_tool__Facebook_searches/

Scott, S., & Burns, J. F. (2010, January 8th, 2011). U.S. subpoenas Twitter over WikiLeaks supporters. *New York Times*. Retrieved January 1, 2011, from https://www.nytimes.com/2011/01/09/world/ 09wiki.html?_r=1/

Singel, R. (2011a, January 10th, 2011). Twitter's response to WikiLeaks subpoena should be the industry standard. *Wired Magazine*. Retrieved March 1, from http://www.wired.com/threatlevel/2011/01/twitter/

Singel, R. (2011b, 13th May, 2011). Dropbox lied to users about data security, complaint to FTC alleges. *Wired Magazine*. Retrieved October 1, from http://wired.com/threatlevel/2011/05/dropbox-ftp

Soghoian, C. (2009). *An open letter to Google's CEO, Eric Schidt.* Retrieved October 1, 2011, from http://cloudprivacy.net/letter

Srinivasa, S. (July 29, 2010). *BlackBerry agrees to address India's security concerns, says ministry.* Retrieved May 1, 2011, from http://www.ibtimes.com/articles/39418/20100729/blackberry-security-india-india-concerns-on-blackberry.htm/

Svensson, P. (2010). WikiLeaks website kicked off Amazon's servers. *Yahoo Finance, 2011*. Retrieved from http://finance.yahoo.com/news/WikiLeaks-website-kicked-off-apf-2762807500.html?x=0/

Tableu Software. (2010, December 2nd 2010). *Why we removed the WikiLeaks visualizations*. Retrieved February 1, 2011, from http://www.tableausoftware.com/about/blog/2010/12/why-we-removed-wikileaks-visualizations?page=7/

Tactical Technology Collective. (2009). *10 tactics for turning information into action*. India: Tactical Technology Collective. Retrieved June 1, 2011, from http://www.informationactivism.org/

Tactical Technology Collective. (2010, unpublished). *Digital security at the grassroots; Vulnerabilities of rights advocates and independent journalists through using information and communications technologies.*

Times, N. Y. (2010, December 26th, 2010). Banks and WikiLeaks. *New York Times*. Retrieved 01st June 2011, from https://www.nytimes.com/2010/12/26/opinion/26sun3.html?_r=1

United Nations. (1948). *Universal declaration of human rights.* Retrieved June 1, 2011, from http://www.un.org/en/documents/udhr/

Wall Street Journal. (2010). *What they know.* Retrieved June 1, 2011, from http://online.wsj.com/public/page/what-they-know-digital-privacy.html

Wall Street Journal. (2010). *Dictionary.com.* Retrieved May 12th, 2011, from http://blogs.wsj.com/wtk/2010/07/30/dictionaryreferencecom/

Weinberger, S. (October 15, 2010). US government monitoring social networking sites. *AOL News*. Retrieved June 1, 2011, from http://www.aolnews.com/2010/10/15/homeland-security-monitoring-social-networking-sites/

Zetter, K. (2009, 1st December, 2009). Yahoo, Verizon: Our spy capabilities would 'shock', 'confuse' consumers. *Wired.* Retrieved October 1, 2001, from http://wired.com/thratlevel/2009/12/wiretap-prices

ENDNOTES

1. For a list of UN member states (currently there are 192) see: http://www.un.org/en/members/.
2. For example see Deibert, R., Palfrey, J., Rohozinski, R., & Zittrain, J. (Eds.). (2008). *Access Denied: The Practice and Policy of Global Internet Filtering*. Cambridge: MIT Press.
3. The US government appeared to be more cautious about making a statement or raising the issue with China when new allegations arose the following year from Google of more extensive email hacking involving the email accounts of U.S. officials. At the time of writing the U.S government have said only that they are still investigating this incident with Google (Quinn, 2010).
4. However, it is worth noting that Privacy International (https://www.privacyinternational.org/) is carrying out ongoing research around changes to privacy laws.

5 SIM card refers to a circuit technology that is used to provide a unique identity to each mobile telephony subscriber. There are a number of ways to clone a SIM card so that can receive and make calls from a mobile registered to someone else. The most precise way to do this is to buy specific hardware for this (for example see: http://www.imserba.com/forum/sim-card-cloning-basics-all-you-wanted-know-t139291/).

6 The request covered addresses, screen names, telephone numbers and credit card and bank account numbers, but it did not ask for the content of private messages sent using Twitter.

7 Tactical Tech and Front Line Defenders' toolkit, Security in-a-box, details many of the tools that can be used for digital privacy and security in the context of rights advocacy (http://security.ngoinabox.org/).

8 It is worth mentioning here that this software was rigorously tested by Jacob Appelbaum, the aforementioned American citizen whose Twitter account was the subject of a subpoena by the U.S. government. Within our own organisation and among many of those we are affiliated with, Appelbaum is considered to be significantly skilled in encryption and programming and he has worked closely with Human Rights Defenders in support of their work.

9 SSL adds a layer of encryption that, when used on these services, would make surveillance and tampering much more difficult to carry out.

Section 4
Economic and Social Rights

Chapter 11
Social Assistance via the Internet:
The Case of Finland in the European Context

Minna Strömberg-Jakka
University of Turku, Finland

ABSTRACT

This chapter examines the connection between social assistance and the use of information communication technologies to gain access to social rights as human rights. The research is based on data consisting of 594 online questions and answers related to social assistance. Of these, 160 analysis units were chosen for a detailed content analysis. The aim of the study was to determine what different positions and combinations of positions officials and service users found themselves in during online social service consultation and how service provision was affected by an official's educational background and the phase of the social assistance process that was in progress. The results show that there are several possible combinations of outcomes and that the educational background of an answering official, as well as the phase of the process for which answers are given, have an impact on the service received.

INTRODUCTION

The use of information and communications technologies (ICT) is increasing in the service sector. In the coming 10 to 20 years there will be mounting pressure to develop electronic services (e-services) particularly in the public sector due to the fact that the population is aging, and this will see an increase in demand for services. The availability of a labor force and the recruitment of personnel will also be key issues in the future particularly in the Finnish context, as Finland is already experiencing a shortage of social workers. Increasing the share of e-services is also aimed

DOI: 10.4018/978-1-4666-1918-0.ch011

at reducing costs in public sector services. This transition towards e-services also applies to the social and health care sectors, which will be introducing more and more new information and communication technologies.

The emergence of e-services has seen a reduction in personal, face-to-face interaction. Service structures must be reformed so that equal and adequate services can be ensured for everyone. Today, one of the challenges the service sector is already faced with is that many service users have insufficient knowledge of different services, not to mention which of these services are available online. As not everyone has access to e-services, online services may place different population groups on uneven footing with regard to one another, thus creating inequality. According to a report from the Human Rights Council of the United Nations General Assembly (La Rue, 2011), Internet access is a human right. Internet access not only allows people to exercise their right to freedom of opinion and expression, but also enables and facilitates the realization of other rights, such as social rights.

The introduction of e-services has become increasingly important in sparsely populated areas, like the ones chosen for this study. Six towns in Lapland, in northern Finland, have introduced online consultation for issues that involve social services such as social assistance, daycare, and services for families with children and the handicapped. However, the content of the service varies between towns. In the Finnish system, KELA (The Social Insurance Institution of Finland) provides social security benefits targeted at situations that may cause a risk to human life, such as unemployment, sickness or disability. In addition to these, people may as a last resort receive social assistance, which is financial assistance provided by the municipality. The aspects of inequality are particularly important as everyone should have the opportunity to apply for social assistance, regardless of external factors such as their place of residence. For example, in Lapland people may find it difficult to visit their social office, due to long distances. Their possibility to access the Internet in order to obtain services also varies. The Constitution of Finland, (731/1999) guarantees the right to social security, which includes social assistance. In order to access the online social service consultation, service users log into an encrypted connection identifying themselves with their Internet bank access codes. A respondent group consisting of social workers and other professionals working at the social office prepare a response to the service user, who then receives a notification of the response either to their e-mail or cell phone. The response can then be read on a special "response account" produced by this online service. Service users should receive a response within five days.

The data for this study consists of 594 online questions and answers related to social assistance. These questions were asked and answered between 2005 and 2009 in three towns (Rovaniemi, Tornio and Kemijärvi). According to statistics from population censuses by the Centre of Municipality Information (31.12.2009), Rovaniemi is the largest of these towns with a population of 59,848, followed by Tornio (22,426) and Kemijärvi (8,519). The possibility of using services via the Internet is important for these towns as they are situated in sparsely populated areas in northern Finland with long distances to services.

The study first explains the connection between ICT, social rights and social assistance. Second, it discusses the character of social assistance in Finland and other European countries. Next, it gives the theoretical background for the analysis, after which the data is analyzed. In the next part the study presents results relating to the research questions; what position or combinations of positions do officials take and social assistance service users can find themselves in during and after an online consultation event, how is service provision affected by an official´s educational background or the phase of the social assistance process being carried out? The final section of the study includes a summary of characteristic features of good and bad online service for social assistance, based on the data. The end of the study includes suggestions for future research directions.

BACKGROUND

eEurope is a political initiative that originally aimed to ensure that the EU benefitted from the changes in the information society, ensuring the EU´s interests with regard to employment, growth and productivity. During the 2000s, a range of initiatives, action plans and evaluations have been initiated in the eEurope scheme. One of the most central issues in eEurope has been making public and administrative information more available online, and for EU citizens to have better interaction with administrative services. This is called eGovernment (European Commission, 1999; 2002a, 2002b; 2003; 2006b; 2008).

eGovernment aims at improving the quality and accessibility of public services via ICT (European Commission, 2006a). If eGovernment is government or governing through the use of ICT, eService could be described similarly, as service via ICT. Goldkuhl (2007) has examined public e-services and stated that citizens should be able to reach or contact governmental agencies around the clock. Statistics on the use of the Internet for interaction with public authorities (European Commission, 2010a) and the number of people using eGovernment services for returning filled out forms (European Commission, 2010b) show that Finland is placed above the EU27 average, but is the weakest within the Nordic countries.

An important aspect concerning this study, is the statement presented at the Vienna "E-Inclusion" Ministerial Conference (European Commission, 2008), that it is important to develop the ability of social services personnel to use and utilize ICT effectively. Social services must be arranged in a way that ensures that the use of ICT does not lead to further marginalization of certain user groups, and attention must be paid to the quality of services.

Social and economic rights are part of human rights. According to Baehr (1999), Articles 23, 25 and 26 of the Universal Declaration of Human Rights are defined as such rights because they guarantee the right to work, to an education and to an adequate standard of living: including food, clothing, housing and medical care. Article 25 continues with the right "to necessary social services" by listing various social risks. Article 22 mentions the right to social security in general. This study focuses on last resort social assistance that can be tracked to the Universal Declaration of Human Rights (1948), in which "everyone has the right to a standard of living adequate for the health and wellbeing of himself and of his family, including food, clothing, housing and medical care".

Social rights guarantee among other things economic security in the event of various risks in life such as unemployment, sickness, old age or motherhood. The concept of social rights is originally based on Marshall´s (1950) ideas about how citizens´ rights have expanded from civil rights to political rights and then to social rights. Today, the EU has come to the decision that social policies are policy areas in which responsibility is left to member states (de Witte, 2005). There are a number of treaties that concern social rights throughout Europe. The principles of social rights have been included in the constitutional laws of many countries. Fábre (2005) has examined the role of social rights in European constitutions. According to her, one major difference between the constitutions is how explicitly and in how much detail social rights are described, and whether a discourse of "rights" has even been used. Not all European constitutions allow constitutional social rights-related conflicts in court proceedings.

According to Kuivalainen (2004), the Finnish model of providing social assistance is in many ways ideal with regard to social rights. The generosity (the actual level of social assistance) is at a high level and the model helps alleviate poverty well. These two features can be described as the realization of the social right for social assistance as financial support. The current Finnish Social Assistance Act (1412/1997) is a form of last resort assistance that aims to ensure minimum subsistence for an individual or a family. The applicant´s municipality of residence is responsible for the payment of these benefits. The amount of social assistance varies based on the composition of the family and the municipal rating in costs and expenses. An applicant must apply for social assistance monthly. The right to social assistance is a subjective right. A subjective right is a concept that mean that the law does not only obligate a public authority in an objective manner, but rather this is an individual right. In Finland, anyone in need of social assistance can apply for it by citing the Constitution (Tuori & Kotkas, 2008). In spite of this, social assistance is a means-tested benefit. The payment of social assistance is based on a calculation of the applicant´s income, all easily realizable movable assets and acceptable expenses. All income received by the person or the household is taken into account with a few exceptions. There are also forms of supplementary and preventive social assistance.

The requirements stipulated for each applicant to take steps to support themselves and to engage in job searches are in line with legislation and practices in the other EU-countries. In addition, recipients must participate in various activating programs. For example, in Luxembourg, social assistance has two benefit categories of which the inclusion benefit is directed to people under the age of 60, who are capable of taking on employment. In order to receive this benefit individuals must sign an integration contract in which they commit to working at integrating themselves into society both occupationally and socially by participating in integration activities (Kerchen, 2009). Requirements for how applicants must co-operate with social workers during the social assistance application process and how applicants are assessed vary throughout Europe. For example, in Latvia recipients of social assistance must co-operate with social workers by fulfilling social duties such as accepting medical examinations or by taking part in medical and social rehabilitation processes. In Germany, an applicant´s personal life and the need for social assistance is assessed by an external service. However, in other parts of Europe the assessment process is for the most part in the hands of local authorities although not necessarily social services. In the Czech Republic, the connection to social work is obvious because social departments in each municipality are responsible for carrying out assessments by investigating and conducting home visits. In Cyprus, the application process is also closely tied to social work, because social service officers conduct home visits in order to perform a socio-economic analysis of the family´s situation (MISSOC, 2010).

In recent years one of the biggest changes to Finland's social assistance has been related to service culture. The relationship between social assistance and social work has been controversial. During the recession of the 1990s, the number of social assistance service users began to grow, and it was therefore necessary for a wider range of personnel to share the task of the assessment process. Social workers were no longer the only ones appointed to this task, as other personnel also took part in the work. In practice, this meant that the task of assessment was transferred primarily to office secretaries with no social work education to speak of. Service users were transferred to office secretaries in cases where their situation was considered stable and unproblematic or where they were just in need of financial support (Karjalainen, Hiilamo & Raivio, 2003). However, decisions requiring professional discretion were still, in most cases, processed by social workers. This change in the tasks of social office personnel also led to a situation whereby today most social assistance applications are assessed and decisions are made on the basis of a written application process that has become extremely important, particularly in larger towns. According to Karjalainen and his colleagues (2003), service users experience a number of problems including difficulty with filling out social assistance applications. Social workers are also difficult to reach because during call times their phone lines are congested, and it may take weeks to get an appointment with a social worker.

From the service users' perspective, the duration of the handling process for social assistance applications is unreasonable (Muuri, 2006). Kauppinen & Raivio (2007) have studied the stream of new social assistance applicants and the queuing time the service users are forced to wait through for either the processing of their applications or a personal appointment with a worker at the social office. The longest waiting times were in urban municipalities. Due to these long waiting times, a section concerning the handling process was added to Finland's Social Assistance Act (originated in 1997) in 2007. According to the new regulations, a decision on social assistance must be given within seven workdays after the application is received, with a few exceptions. In cases where service users request a personal conversation with a social worker, the opportunity must be arranged within seven workdays from the time the request is made. With these new time limits, Finland now has the fastest application turnarounds of the EU-countries. For example in the Netherlands, a decision must be reached within eight weeks (MISSOC, 2010). Two recent studies (Muuri, 2008; Kaskisaari et al., 2010) on the opinions and experiences of social assistance service users show that there are still huge problems in the Finnish social assistance system. The studies show that not all people entitled to social assistance apply for it or want to apply for it or dare to trust they will receive it. Also, social assistance is perceived as stigmatizing. The level of social assistance is considered to be too low i.e. it is not sufficient to support an individual in a specific life situation nor is it a suitable rapid response to varying life crisis situations. Many feel that the authorities making decisions on social assistance do not have sufficient information available, that the terms for receiving social assistance are not sufficiently clear, that the processes are too complex and inflexible, and finally, that decisions on social assistance are made using the wrong criteria.

To summarize, social rights are human rights. Social rights, included in constitutions of many countries, enable the possibility for economical support in different contents and variations in different countries. In Finland, this last resort financial support is called social assistance.

When the service system expands into new service channels such as the Internet, it is necessary to ensure that the system functions properly, as social assistance is a constitutional right for all of Finland's citizens. It is possible that some service users are asking for advice on social assistance for the first time via online consultation, and it is their only contact channel. For this reason, the kind of service they receive online is not insignificant.

ONLINE CONSULTATION OF SOCIAL ASSISTANCE VIA THE INTERNET

A Theoretical Framework for the Analysis

As this article examines what is a new phenomenon as online consultation there are no relevant previous studies on the subject. In formulating the theoretical framework for this study, I have used studies and other material that are close to the topic, which I thought would be of use. From these, I have gained inspiration to study my own data from different viewpoints. In this section I will present the material I have drawn from.

There has been an ideological shift in the ways of thinking about how services are produced. This has been driven by global influences. A split in service providers' to different sectors such as public or private has caused the boundaries between them to blur. For example, in health services, there are doctors that work in the public sector, who also run private clinics. Services, including social services, are also produced under different administrative models. According to Newman (2000), this development is in part related to public service modernization efforts, a discourse that began in the 1980′s and 1990′s. These modernization requirements were associated with market mechanisms that were being introduced to the public sector.

This development has also changed the perception of persons in need of services; these persons can be referred to as clients, consumers or service users. However, the Finnish language does not have different terms to convey different meanings for those in need of services, depending on the type of relationship they have with the service providers or institutions. For example Finnish lacks different positions of power included in the variation of English words. Therefore, this article aims to systematically use the term service user. The shift described above has meant that those in need of services have had to take on a variety of roles, and also go through role changes. Role changes can be seen as a continuum, a service user as, in this case, an object and not as an active citizen at one end. At the other end the earlier service user has been transformed into a consumer who has a variety of choices to make between different services and different service providers. Newman & Vidler (2006) describe this "consumerism" within the health care sector in the UK and call it choice-oriented service. According to Niiranen (2002) there are three different roles for persons in need of services: target customers, consumers and democratic citizenship (service customers). Target customers are objects, they follow the instructions given, agree with the objectives set by the social worker, for example, do not self-assess their problems nor are they otherwise active. Consumers are active and make choices after having adequate information and the ability to make comparisons between services. Finally, customers representing democratic citizenship are more active than target customers. They feel like members of the community and actively participate, for example, in the development of the social services. It should be noted that all the persons in need of services should be aware of the perspectives professionals assess their situation and problems from.

This discourse on restructuring social services and changes in service users′ roles has concerned Finland too. Finland has initiated a project (PARAS) in order to reform the country's municipal and service structure, with the aim of improving healthcare and welfare services as well as social security. The project is based on legislation (The Act on the Restructuring of Local Government and Services, 169/2007), which was instated in 2007 and is to be completed in 2012. The project aims to strengthen municipal structures, rearrange services for a broader population base, create new working practices and increase collaboration between municipalities.

According to Virkki (2010), this reform can ensure that social services become more diverse and they can form service chains, but on the other hand, the service system can also splinter so that some services are totally eliminated. The service user′s role in these scenarios is an interesting one. In diversified services, the role of the service user is to be a rational active party who makes choices between services (see "consumer" in Niiranen, 2002). If they are determined to be a good recipient for services, and the social office employee has an important role, because he or she must have the skills and competence to enable him or her to help and guide the service user. The customer therefore has a passive role in this option (see "target customer" in Niiranen, 2002). If the service system is very fragmented, the service user′s role is characterized by self-help, self-direction and activity. In a way, implementation of the whole service is the responsibility of the service user. For example, if there is an application to fill out in order to receive some financial benefit, the service user must fill out the application independently without help no matter how many questions they have concerning the application. The last group is excluded from the service. This group consists of service users who may not have the ability to act in their own case and have no resources. They are left without service. Applying this to social assistance service users, my hypothesis was that service users may hold any of these roles, except that of a rational consumer. This is because in the Finnish welfare service system, the municipality has the exclusive right to grant social assistance, i.e. it is a municipal task and cannot be transferred to the private sector so the service user also does not have the option of choosing between different service providers.

Wilding (1994) has written about maintaining quality in human services. He states that accessibility, acceptability, effectiveness and openness are the key elements in quality service. Accessibility refers to such things as easy geographical and physical access. Psychological access means that users are not stigmatized due to the use of a specific service. Acceptability means that forms of interaction are acceptable from the users´ viewpoint, not just from the employees´. The interaction should be supportive, empowering and personal. The service should also be flexible, reliable and satisfy any given needs, i.e. be effective. And finally, there are demands for openness: the organization should reveal its aims, objectives, and standards as well as show self-criticism in how it manages to achieve these goals. It should also recognize situations in which it is unable to offer service and be prepared to receive criticism.

To date, five separate studies have been carried out, which have focused on face-to-face contacts and telephone consultation at KELA, The Social Insurance Institution of Finland. These studies are important to the extent that KELA is also an organization that grants financial benefits on the basis of an application process. In addition, these studies cover various forms of contact (application, phone or face-to-face) that KELA uses instead of consultation via the Internet. According to Laaksonen (2006), service users feel that the use of application forms hinders communication between service users and authorities as application forms are considered too long, too complicated to fill out, and often illegible. Sorjonen and his colleagues (Sorjonen, 2006a, 2006b; Sorjonen & Raevaara, 2006) have studied ways in which to initiate conversation at KELA offices, as well as how service users express feelings of dissatisfaction and annoyance, and how officials then respond to these behaviors. Sorjonen (2006b) has also examined how officials deal with situations in which service users clearly seem to demand understanding and empathy. All of these studies refer to face-to-face situations. It is important for officials to formulate a reaction to a service user´s annoyance. One way to respond to these situations is to react minimally and to maintain a professional demeanor (Sorjonen, 2006a). The minimum response technique that officials use also encompasses displays of empathy as well as identification and acknowledgment of the service user´s situation (Sorjonen, 2006b).

According to a telephone service study by Heinonen (2009), there are several ways in which officials display either a willingness to serve service users or act in a bureaucratic manner towards them. In their bureaucratic roles, officials refused to connect phone calls, relied heavily on law sections, remained distant when service users sought understanding and help, avoided referring to the service user directly, and refused to look at the situation from the service user´s perspective. On the other hand, a different attitude was also possible when officials responded to service users kindly and helpfully, took initiative and an active role and made the service feel personal. The officials gave the best service when they formed an alliance with the service user and showed advocacy when trying to solve the service user´s problems.

These bureaucratic or service oriented roles that officials took on (Heinonen, 2009) were approaching the concept of accountability, or the duty to report one's activities to someone else. Juhila

(2009) gives an example of this: when a service user needed to arrange an appointment with their social worker and the first possible time for this was after an unreasonably long period, it was the duty of the social worker to explain the situation to the service user. Social workers cannot act arbitrarily, but are accountable to various parties such as service users, the organization including their employer and colleagues, the municipalities, as well as the law and their own professional ethical principles and finally, society as a whole and its citizens with regard to prevailing cultural values. As Hall, Slembrouck & Sarangi (2006) state, language practices are central in social work because social workers justify their actions through speech and writing.

Analyzing the Data

A study is reliable when the same results are reached each time research is carried out in a certain way, no matter who the examiner carrying out the research is (Rubin & Babbie, 2008). Therefore, to provide greater consistency it is important to go through the analysis process in detail. In this study, quantification has been used throughout the data. According to George (2009), it is a natural part of content analysis, because it offers the possibility to obtain systematically counted descriptive information about the content of the data. The studies reviewed in the previous section offer a kind of hypothetical background for this research. As George´s study showed, this is a content analysis of hypothesis-testing. As he points out, using hypotheses also facilitates the coding process, because it is easier to concentrate on the actual substance neglecting irrelevant information.

The data consists of a total of 594 questions and answers, and was received in a de-identified form, i.e. without references to service users´ identities such as social security numbers. After this information was received the data was analyzed. The data showed only the gender and the age of the service user and the date and time of the day a question was asked. As only the age and the gender of a questioner were known, it was not possible to determine how many different questioners were included in the data. This is why it was important to carefully read through message chains, in order to determine all the questions and answers belonging to the same chain; questioners may have continued or supplemented earlier questions after an interval of several days. The gender and the educational background of the workers responding to questions were known.

The questions posed by service users were considered as narratives or stories, noting that there were three types. First, there were stories with a multitude of details concerning living situations and various social problems such as unemployment or substance abuse. Other questions concerned the process of applying for and receiving social assistance. And finally, there were questions consisting of both of these elements. Of these 594 questions and answers a set of 378 analysis units were shaped. An analysis unit consists of one or more question-answer pairs, which the same questioner posed, with regard to the same situation, even when a considerably long time period had passed between the times the questions were posed. However, this article does not include the social work aspect but focuses on a close examination of 160 of the original 378 analysis units that dealt with receiving social assistance and its process, as social assistance represents the realization of social rights as a last resort for financial support.

During the next step of the analysis, the questions included in these 160 analysis units were divided into phases according to how the social assistance process progresses in the Finnish system. These start with the application phase and the principles of social assistance and continue through to the processing phase resulting in payment of social assistance and receiving an official decision. Issues closely related to the process such as obtaining an appointment with the social worker or way in which a social assistance service user is treated at the social office are also included in the analysis. Service user behavior refers to the ways in which service users try to advance the processing of their applications or the way they behave at the social office in general.

After that, subcategories were established for these main categories (see Table 1). The number in the column refers to the number of contacts falling into that specific group of questions. For example, processing social assistance applications consists of subcategories and as we can see, this category has the most questions, followed by applying and decision.

It is possible to increase the reliability of the study by, for example, using reliable indicators addressed already in other studies, or by using more than one coder at the analysis stage. Coding is the key process in analyzing the data. The coder classifies and categorizes individual pieces of data and defines coding units that are intended to be utilized for interpreting the data. If the study demands that judgments be made by more than one coder, it is important that coders come to an agreement or find consistency in their findings (Rubin & Babbie, 2008). In this study, this approach was applied by presenting relevant questions of the data that emerged from the literature introduced earlier in the theoretical framework, and by making notes of the online consultation situation separately for answerers and questioners. Although a number of coders were not used, due to the notes, it was easy to later go back to check the overall picture of the communication situation between the answerer and the questioner. In addition, by utilizing several steps of the analysis process, it was possible to check whether the interpretation of the final result of the online consultation situation changed at these different steps. The original interpretation changed only a few times and in cases of inconsistency, all the

Table 1. Summarizing the main categories and subcategories of questions asked about the social assistance procedure in online consultation

Applying (51): Possibility of receiving social assistance or receiving it retroactively, availability and practices of the application form, filling out the form or clarifying a detail on it, appendixes, doubts and fears about the loss of application forms or appendixes, doubts about the application getting through the long queue, addressing the application to the correct person, canceling the application, the correct time when to apply
Principles (19): Principles of social assistance and discretionary social assistance, changes in principles, effect of income, expenses taken into account, the effects of living arrangements and the General Housing Allowance granted by the Social Insurance Institution of Finland
Process (77): Timing, the phase or duration of processing time, general questions about the process, the person responsible for processing the application, adding extra clarification to the application
Payment (38): Vouchers, paying the bills, the sum of the basic social assistance, reclaiming of social assistance, unclearness of payment arrangements, delays in payments
Decision (48): Content of the decision, dissatisfaction with the content, general questions, ambiguity in the decision, notification of the decision
Appointments (5): Requests for meetings with social workers, changing the date of a set up appointment, lack of clarity regarding whether it is necessary to meet with a social worker or not
Service user behavior (13): Demanding contact information of the officials or demanding that officials contact the service users, demanding that officials handle everything on a service user's behalf, call times to the office
Treatment (11): Reprimanding an official due to a broken promise, criticizing an official and the decision or decision duration times that were too long, delay in processing the application, criticizing the officials' behavior, being discontent with the received answers, criticism of practices, service users are unable to contact officials by phone
Others (6): New service users, obtaining personal information or making a correction to personal information stored to the database at the social office, unclearness of the responsible unit taking care of the application, inquiries about the change of the person making the decision, questions posed by someone else on a service user's behalf

analysis units in question were collected and reanalyzed. In other words, the data went through several different coding steps and was read several times before the final analysis.

Payment of social assistance might not always be made in the form of money. Alternately service users may receive vouchers with which they can get medication or groceries. Sometimes social assistance can be targeted to bills. In such cases money may be directly paid to an electricity company or a dentist. Such situations might cause ambiguity as to whether bills have been paid and to whom. Social assistance might also be reclaimed. This might happen for example in a situation where the service user has the right to another benefit and social assistance is granted because the service user cannot make use of that benefit at that time, but will receive it at a later date (see Social Assistance Act, 1997; MISSOC 2010).

Various Roles in Online Consultation for Social Assistance

The following section presents the types of alliances used by officials and the position service users find themselves in. The most common situation was that in which the service user received service, with the situations in which service users did not receive service being rare. Compared with the literature used, a complementary position of alliance with both the service user and the organization was found. "The intermediate state" is characterized by features such as the service user expected to act autonomously in ascertaining information, he is forced to be an active participant or must fill out application forms alone. The service user remains in a kind of "floating" situation, in which he does not get answers to his questions or the situation otherwise remains unsolved.

A good example of an alliance with the service user is a situation in which the service user wanted to know about the processing time of their application. The official not only gave them the name of the person responsible for processing the application, but showed initiative and found the exact date on which the application was processed. In this kind of a situation the service user gets answers and receives service.

Online communication is not always as smooth. A service user asked questions regarding three matters and the official neglected two of them by responding that the application was in the queue and will be processed as soon as possible. Next, the service user wished to be informed about these matters by text message, or by email. Because of the neglected questions in the first stage, the service user had to contact online consultation a second time. This time, the official responded that the decision would be posted by mail, without justifying the procedure. Finally, the service user had to return a third time with the same questions. The official´s responses were not service user-oriented because some of the questions were neglected and the procedure was not fully

Table 2. The number of different positions officials may take and those service users can find themselves in social assistance online consultation

Official	alliance with the service user	99
Official	alliance with the organization	42
Official	alliance with both the service user and the organization	48
Official	alliance with the organization and the law	2
Service user	receives service	107
Service user	remains without service	20
Service user	remains in the intermediate state	73

explained or justified. This can be considered quite organization-oriented. The service user was forced to return again and again with neglected or unanswered questions. In this study, this service user position is referred to as "an intermediate state". This means, that the service user has to remain active in order to receive answers to questions. Here, the service user returned with questions inherently, or, so to say, of their own initiative. However, it is also possible that the service user will be asked to contact social services in order to fill out an application form or to meet someone.

Personnel can create alliances with the organization in many ways, thus indicating that service users do not always receive the required service. This may happen for example when the service user asks several questions and some of the questions are overlooked and not answered. It seems that there is one very embarrassing issue within the organization that is rarely acknowledged – the question of the statutory time limit within which applications should be processed. Officials prefer to not comment when time limits have been surpassed. Another typical situation, in which service users may have been left without an answer, are cases in which they have posed questions on behalf of someone else. These situations are difficult because of the legislation guaranteeing privacy for service users in social services, but even in such cases, it would be possible to answer in general terms. An example where the service user does not get an answer to the question comes from the situation when the service user wanted to know about the principles of social assistance; what amount of money was considered adequate for living and the basic amount of social assistance. The official gave a response summarizing the law, using vague expressions, feigning incomprehension on what is meant by "living", and making moral statements on what "one's own choices are thought to be in connection to the adequate amount of money".

In some of the situations, officials seem to have an alliance with both the service user and the organization. For example, the service user criticized an official who had made the decision and voiced an opinion that the amount of social assistance he received should have been larger. The official answering online did not get provoked by this, but did not want to comment on the content of the decision. The answerer then claimed that responsibility for the issue lay with their colleague that has made the decision and was away on holiday at that time. This side of the behavior can be interpreted as making an alliance with the organization. But then, the official promised to relay a message and ask their colleague to phone the service user after their holiday so that the service user no longer had to be an active player in the matter. This side of the official´s behavior can, on the contrary, be interpreted as making an alliance with the service user.

Fourteen Possible Combinations of the Outcome

What happens when the various positions taken by officials and those that service users can find themselves in as presented above are linked together? Does the official always need to be in an alliance with the service user for the service user to receive an experience of service? What actions by officials leave the service user in the intermediate state? There are diverse combinations (14 altogether) of possible situations the service users and the officials could be left in. The most common situation (n times) was one in which the official was in an alliance with the service user and the service user received service. However, the second and third most common situations were those in which the official formed an alliance with either the organization or with the organization and the service user, leaving the service user in the intermediate state.

Sometimes an official seems to have an alliance or a good co-operative relationship with the service user with the end assumption that the service user will receive the service they require.

Table 3. Possible combinations of positions officials may take and those service users can find themselves in during and after a social assistance online consultation event

	The official has an alliance with			
	Service user	**Organization**	**Service user, organization**	**Organization, law**
Service user receives service	87	1	16	-
Service user remains in the intermediate state	15	29	26	-
Service user remains without service	-	7	2	-
Service user partially receives service and partially remains without service	1	-	4	-
Service user partially remains without service and partially remains in the intermediate state	-	1	-	2
Service user partially receives service and partially remains in the intermediate state	-	-	2	-
Service user partially receives service, partially remains without service and partially remains in the intermediate state	-	-	2	-

Interestingly, this may not always be the case. For example, in one instance a service user needed to pay the rent on time but had yet to receive a decision to the application she had sent, although the statutory time limit had been exceeded by quite some time. The official voiced his regrets about the situation, admitted that the complaint was a valid one, convinced the service user that everything was being done for the service user´s best, but the service user remained in a state of uncertainty about whether a decision would be made on time, and whether she would be able to pay her rent. This example shows that no matter how much the official has tried to make an alliance with, or to be helpful for the service user, the result may sometimes be incomplete.

In situations where service users have several questions, some of them might not be answered, particularly if they have been presented as a chain of individual questions over a long period. Then any one of the outcomes (partially receives service, partially does not receive service, or partially remains in the intermediate state) might be possible. However, it can be stated that situations in which the service user is left completely without answers are rare. Naturally, the combinations in which online questioners receive responses to their questions and receive service are the best ones. This situation can be produced either by the official having an alliance with the service user or an alliance with both the service user and the organization. Here, however, it is important to note that the official´s compromise to have an alliance with both the service user and the organization might also produce a positive result from the service user´s perspective.

The Success of the Social Assistance Process from Phase to Phase

The following table shows the phases of the social assistance application process from filling out an application to receiving a decision as well as some of the questions service users have about meetings, treatment and other matters. The number in the first column means the number of contacts falling into that group of questions. Within these groups, the duration of the process, application appendixes, processing stage of the application, the content of the decision and the expenses taken into account raise the most questions, in this order of magnitude. Often these seem be those questions that are ignored online. Commenting on the content of decisions creates inequality between service users because some are told the content of a decision in detail while the others are told nothing.

In these three categories of service users, it is evident what happens to service users at each phase of the social assistance process. Here, the service user receiving service represents a successful service event, while the other two options represent unsuccessful service events. Finally, the number and percentage of successful online consultation service events for each phase of the application process were calculated. According to this, online consultation for social assistance succeeds the best in questions concerning the applying phase (70%). On the other hand, online consultation succeeds the most poorly in such responses when a service user feels they have been poorly served and need justification for their experience (20%).

Does the educational background of officials affect the service they produce? In this data, there were 59 answers from social workers with a university level education, 56 from persons with a polytechnic degree in the field of social services, 83 from persons with an office secretary background or equivalent, and one in-office comment seen only by other personnel from the superior of the social office. In one of the towns, the structure of the personnel working at the social office was not diverse enough, i.e. there were only social workers responding online. In addition, one particular social worker produced 70% of all the responses given online and as this would have distorted the outcome of this case that town was dropped from this article. The data gathered regarding the educational background is therefore from the two remaining towns.

It seems that persons with all the mentioned educational backgrounds are able to make an alliance with the service user, but this is where the differences begin. Social workers seem to very seldom make an alliance with either the organization or with both the organization and the service user. This means that other personnel working at social offices prefer using other strategies than forming an alliance with the service user. The situation becomes even more evident when looking at it from the service user´s perspective. The multitude of varying positions that service users can find themselves in is striking when service users are at their weakest, namely in a position in which they do not receive service, or remain in the intermediate state. In 77% of the situations

Table 4. The success of online consultation in each phase of the social assistance process from the service user´s perspective

	Service user receives service (n times/ %)	Service user remains without service (n times)	Service user remains in the intermediate state (n times)
Applying (50)	35 (70.0)	6	9
Principles (30)	17 (56.7)	5	8
Process (72)	37 (51.4)	9	26
Payment (38)	21 (55.3)	7	10
Decision (68)	37 (54.4)	14	17
Time appointment (5)	3 (60.0)	0	2
Service user behavior (11)	5 (45.5)	0	6
Treatment (15)	3 (20.0)	6	6
Others (11)	5 (45.5)	4	2

where the service user remained without service, their questions were handled by someone who was not a social worker. In 95% of the cases where the service user remained in the intermediate state, the person handling their questions did not have the educational background of a social worker. Based on these results, it would be easy to draw the conclusion that the educational background of officials has an effect on the quality of the service the service user receives from online consultation. However, this question would demand further research, with more diverse data than that of just two towns.

Good Service versus Bad Service

What elements make up good service in online consultation for social assistance? Which factors leave service users with the impression that they are not served at all, or leave them feeling that they have been left alone to find their way through the maze of application forms, thus forcing them to be active participants in communication with officials in order to obtain service?

To put it simply, and this is apparent most often in the data as well, good service requires that the service user´s questions are all answered. In the event that not all the questions asked by an individual can be answered, this can be compensated for by giving a wider range of answers to the questions, answering questions the service user did not actually ask. Also, if a service user receives extra information on their matter and particularly if an official shows initiative in the matter, the service experience will be a positive one. Service users seem to feel it is important that officials advise them spontaneously, find out things on their behalf, clarify and explain things and give concrete examples. They also wish for officials to take their wishes into account when possible, inconvenience themselves on the service user´s behalf, relay messages from service users to some other person working at the social office and justify parts of the process. Officials should also express apologies in situations which may have caused harm to the service user irrespective of whether the issue in question was due to the official´s own actions or those of another.

Additionally, the language used in answers is not irrelevant either, as officials seem to use a certain formula with which to appease overheated and angry service users. Some examples of this language are; responding with a greeting of "good morning" or "have a good week", and using the phrase "sincerely" at the end of their answers. Other linguistic tactics seem to make online conversations resemble a face-to-face conversation like happens in a situation where the communication on the Internet is about to come to an end and both the official and the service user wish each other a good summer. Smileys are very rarely used in the service users´ online messages, but the official has a possibility to affect the atmosphere of the online conversation by choosing whether to react to the service user´s smiley or not.

When it comes to bad service, it is noteworthy that from the service user´s perspective, it might be a risk, when the person answering online questions changes in the middle of a dialogue that begun earlier. There are examples of this where the entire communication turns into a vicious cycle and does not end well from the service user´s perspective. Sometimes in these situations, service users have even received different answers from different persons in regard to the same matter. Situations in which the questioner was someone other than the service user, such as a relative, were quite interesting. In these cases, the official may have meant to guard the privacy of the service user, but mistakenly revealed the details of the decision-making process or the content of the decision. Another interesting point was that sometimes service users were clearly forced to use other service channels than online consultation. This happened when service users were advised to fill out an application form, asked to seek additional information on the Internet by themselves, or asked to make phone calls to other officials within the social services or other agencies.

Using certain language may also cause negative service experiences. The official might use passive or vague expressions, such as the application will be processed “soon”. The choice of words may be harsh, if it lacks an apology even when one is called for. Questions are not always answered in an intelligible way or may be answered in a way that does not offer any added value or concrete information. The answer may also be something entirely different from what the service user asked. It is noteworthy that this tactic works in a positive sense when having a compensating nature, if all the service users´ questions cannot be answered for one reason or another. However, this tactic does not work here, if all the service users´ real issues are skipped and ignored.

Officials may transfer or dodge responsibility, and give false information by using incorrect terms. The official might avoid justifying his own conduct completely and keep referring to the difficult queue situation or someone else’s holiday, particularly when it comes to the length of processing times. Sometimes officials do not seem to listen to service users´ wishes, they deny service users´ arguments immediately or moralize. One way in which a service experience becomes a negative one seems to be when officials do not take any position on issues and avoid commenting on them, or when they explain and justify things too bureaucratically.

FUTURE RESEARCH DIRECTIONS

In the future, it would be important to reach the opinions and experiences of service users as they themselves describe it. This information could be acquired through an Internet survey. It would be useful to study the opinions of those in need of social assistance or the social office’s other services, but who do not have a possibility to use the Internet as a service channel. This would be important particularly from the perspective of the so-called digital divide and equal possibilities.

It would also be important to find out whether the picture of online consultation for social assistance will change when questions concerning social problems that have now been left out of the article are included. This is important when considering whether, how, and in what kind of form social work could be carried out online. Examining the effect of the educational background of officials could be taken further in this study as well.

Without a doubt today´s situation in which social workers and other personnel share responsibility for those service users who do not have serious problems or have less complex life situations, represents client selection. For example, in Sweden, a study by Minas & Stenberg (2000) found that some service users are rejected or turned away even on the basis of their very first contact to the social office, which usually took place over the phone. At a theoretical level, this probably means that they are using categorization (see Hall et al. 2006). It would be important to find out, what kind of client selection is used in online consultation. Does this vary depending on the official´s educational background, and how for example does it differ from client selection that takes place over the phone.

CONCLUSION

In conclusion, if online consultation is to be implemented in other countries, the problems brought up in this study should be taken into account. The different practices or answering styles used by officials at social offices affect the position that service users find themselves in and the quality of the service they receive, creating different combinations of the final outcome. There is also a strong message that the educational background of officials answering online questions is relevant in regard to the responses service users receive via online consultation. From the service users´ perspective this means that online consultation can create inequality between service users. Good and bad characteristics of the service are also universal. However, for example linguistic matters and cultural habits should be taken into account. When online consultation and its technical solutions are implemented somewhere the country´s legislation must be tailored with regard to confidentiality and protection of service user privacy.

It can be argued that Finland has recently had some problems with social assistance with regard to fulfillment of social rights, as the duration of the application process has been far too long. Therefore, a new time limit has been added to Finnish social assistance legislation. Bearing this in mind, some answers given in online consultation violate not only this new legislation but also service users´ social rights. This has occurred sometimes, when the legal processing time had already been surpassed. Social assistance payment delays affect the actual materialization of social rights. Practices varied whether service users were told the exact sums of the social assistance that was to be paid to their bank accounts. This also creates inequality between service users.

Finland, which is known as Nokia-land, has a reputation worldwide of having a high ICT-profile. In addition to this, Finland is known for having the ideal model for social assistance with respect to social rights. This picture of a successful social assistance system and the good condition of social rights is however shaken by bringing a new element to the picture, namely technology and its new application: online consultation or social assistance.

REFERENCES

Baehr, P. R. (1999). *Human rights: Universality in practice*. Basingstoke, UK: Palgrave Macmillan.

Centre of Municipality Information. (2009). *Population censuses*. Retrieved from www.kunnat.net/attachment.asp?path=1;29;374;36984;148786;149482;150319.

de Witte, B. (2005). The trajectory of fundamental social rights in the European Union. In de Búrca, G., & de Witte, B. (Eds.), *Social rights in Europe* (pp. 153–168). New York, NY: Oxford University Press. doi:10.1093/acprof:oso/9780199287994.003.0008

European Commission. (1999). *eEurope: An information society for all: A communication on a commission initiative for the special European Council of Lisbon, 23 and 24 March 2000*. Retrieved from http://www.support-eam.org/waec/docs/mod01/COM(1999)_687_eEurope_initiative_en.pdf

European Commission. (2002a). *eEurope 2005: An information society for all: An action plan to be presented in view of the Sevilla European Council, 21/22 June 2002*. Retrieved from http://eur-lex.europa.eu/LexUriServ/LexUriServ.do?uri=COM:2002:0263:FIN:EN:PDF

European Commission. (2002b). *eEurope 2005: Executive summary*. Retrieved from http://ec.europa.eu/information_society/eeurope/2002/news_library/documents/eeurope2005/execsum_en.pdf

European Commission. (2003). *eEurope 2002 final report*. Retrieved from http://eurlex.europa.eu/LexUriServ/site/en/com/2003/com2003_0066en01.pdf

European Commission. (2006a). *i2010 eGovernment action plan – Accelerating eGovernment in Europe for the benefit of all*. Retrieved from http://europa.eu/legislation_summaries/information_society/l24226j_en.htm

European Commission. (2008). *Vienna "e-inclusion" Ministerial Conference conclusion*. Retrieved from http://ec.europa.eu/information_society/events/e-inclusion/2008/doc/conclusions.pdf

European Commission. (2010a). *E-government usage by individuals by gender*.

European Commission. (2010b). *Europe's digital competitiveness report*. Retrieved from http://ec.europa.eu/digital-agenda

European Commisson. (2006b). *The Riga Ministerial Declaration on eInclusion*. Retrieved from http://ec.europa.eu/information_society/events/ict_riga_2006/doc/declaration_riga.pdf

Fabre, C. (2005). Social rights in European constitutions. In de Búrca, G., & de Witte, B. (Eds.), *Social rights in Europe* (pp. 15–28). New York, NY: Oxford University Press. doi:10.1093/acprof:oso/9780199287994.003.0002

George, A. L. (2009). Quantitative and qualitative approaches to content analysis. In Krippendorff, K., & Bock, M. A. (Eds.), *The content analysis reader* (pp. 144–155). Los Angeles, CA: Sage.

Goldkuhl, G. (2007). What does it mean to serve the citizen in e-services? *International Journal of Public Information Systems*, *3*(3), 135–159.

Hall, C., Slembrouck, S., & Sarangi, S. (2006). *Language practices in social work: Categorisation and accountability in child welfare*. London, UK: Routledge.

Heinonen, H.-M. (2009). *Byrokraatti vai asiakaspalvelija?: Kelan virkailijan toimintatavat ja roolit Yhteyskeskuksessa palvelukulttuurin muutosten keskellä* [Bureaucrat of customer servant?: The role and conduct of officials in Kela's customer contact centre over the course of a transition in the service culture]. Helsinki, Finland: Kela.

Juhila, K. (2009). Sosiaalityön selontekovelvollisuus. [Accountability in social work]. *Janus*, *17*(4), 296–312.

Karjalainen, J., Hiilamo, H., & Raivio, H. (2003). *Harkinta toimeentulotuessa: Toimeentulotuen muutosten arvioinnin väliraportti* [Discretion in social assistance: The interim report of the evaluation of the changes in social assistance]. Helsinki, Finland: Stakes.

Kaskisaari, M., Tammelin, M., Hirvonen, J., Hämeenaho, P., Ilmarinen, K., & Vartiainen, A. (2010). *Kuntalaisten arvioita sosiaalipalveluista: ParasSos-tutkimus Keski-Suomen yhdeksän kunnan alueella. [Residents' assessments of social services: ParasSos study in Central Finland, of nine municipalities in the region]*. Helsinki, Finland: Terveyden ja hyvinvoinnin laitos.

Kauppinen, T. M., & Raivio, H. (2007). *Toimeentulotuen uusien asiakkaiden jonotilanne 2007* [The queues of new applicants in social assistance 2007]. Helsinki, Finland: Stakes.

Kerchen, N. (2009). The welfare system of Luxembourg. From past dependency to the European approach. In Schubert, K., Hegelich, S., & Bazant, U. (Eds.), *The handbook of European welfare systems* (pp. 310–327). London, UK: Routledge.

Kuivalainen, S. (2004). *A comparative study on last resort social assistance schemes in six European Countries*. Helsinki, Finland: Stakes.

La Rue, F. (2011). *Report of the Special Rapporteur on the promotion and protection of the right to freedom of opinion and expression*. Retrieved from http://www2.ohchr.org/english/bodies/hrcouncil/docs/17session/A.HRC.17.27_en.pdf

Laaksonen, K. (2006). Mitä mieltä asiakkaat ovat Kelan lomakkeista? [What do the service users think about the application forms of The Social Insurance Institution of Finland?]. In M-L Sorjonen & L. Raevaara (Eds.), *Arjen asiointia. Keskusteluja Kelan tiskin äärellä* (pp. 35-47). Helsinki, Finland: Kotimaisten kielten tutkimuskeskus.

Marshall, T. H. (1950). *Citizenship and social class*. Cambridge, MA: The University Press.

Minas, R., & Stenberg, S.-T. (2000). Telefonmottagningen – Socialtjänstens dörrvakt. [Telephone Reception – Social Services´ Gatekeepers]. In A. Puide (Ed.), *Socialbidrag i forskning och praktik* (pp. 205-223). Göteborg, Sweden: Centrum för utvärdering av socialt arbete och Förlagshuset Gothia AB.

MISSOC. EU's Mutual Information System on Social Protection. (2010). *Guaranteed minimum resources*. Retrieved December 5, 2010, from http://ec.europa.eu/employment_social/missoc/db/public/compareTables.do?lang=en

Muuri, A. (2006). Sosiaalipalvelut 2004 – Väestön mielipiteitä ja asiakkaiden palvelukokemuksia. [Social services 2004 – Public opinions and service experiences] In Kautto, M. (Ed.), *Suomalaisten hyvinvointi 2006* (pp. 204–235). Helsinki, Finland: Stakes.

Muuri, A. (2008). *Sosiaalipalveluja kaikille ja kaiken ikää?: Tutkimus suomalaisten mielipiteistä ja kokemuksista sosiaalipalveluista sekä niiden suhteesta legitimiteettiin* [Social welfare services for all, at every age?: Opinions of the Finnish public on, and its experiences of, social welfare services, and their relation to legitimacy]. Helsinki, Finland: Stakes.

Newman, J. (2000). Beyond new public management: Modernizing public services. In Clarke, J., Gewirtz, S., & Mclaughlin, E. (Eds.), *New managerialism, new welfare?* (pp. 45–61). London, UK: Sage Publications.

Newman, J., & Vidler, E. (2006). Discriminating customers, responsible patients, empowered users: Consumerism and the modernisation of health care. *Journal of Social Policy*, *35*(2), 193–209. doi:10.1017/S0047279405009487

Niiranen, V. (2002). Asiakkaan osallistuminen tukee kansalaisuutta sosiaalityössäkin. [Service user's participation supports citizenship in social work] In Juhila, K., Forsberg, H., & Roivainen, I. (Eds.), *Marginaalit ja sosiaalityö* (pp. 63–80). Jyväskylä, Finland: Sophi.

Rubin, A., & Babbie, E. R. (2008). *Research methods for social work* (6th ed.). Belmont, CA: Wadsworth/Thomson Learning.

Social Assistance Act [Laki toimeentulotuesta]. (1412/1997).

Sorjonen, M.-L. (2006a). Tunteet pinnassa: Affektista puhetta Kelan asioinneista [Emotions on the surface: Affective speech about the conversations at Kela]. In M.-L. Sorjonen & L. Raevaara (Eds.), *Arjen asiointia. Keskusteluja Kelan tiskin äärellä* (pp. 191-221). Helsinki, Finland: Kotimaisten kielten tutkimuskeskus.

Sorjonen, M.-L. (2006b). Ymmärrystä ja empatiaa: Ammattilainen asiakkaan tuntemusten vastaanottajana [Understanding and empathy: A professional as a recipient of service user's feelings]. In M.-L. Sorjonen & L. Raevaara (Eds.), *Arjen asiointia. Keskusteluja Kelan tiskin äärellä* (pp. 222-240). Helsinki, Finland: Kotimaisten kielten tutkimuskeskus.

Sorjonen, M.-L., & Raevaara, L. (2006). Kuinka päästä alkuun?: Asiointikeskustelun aloittamistavoista [How do I get started?: About the manners for initiating conversation]. In M.-L. Sorjonen & L. Raevaara (Eds.), *Arjen asiointia. Keskusteluja Kelan tiskin äärellä* (pp. 48-85). Helsinki, Finland: Kotimaisten kielten tutkimuskeskus.

The Act on the Restructuring of Local Government and Services [Laki kunta- ja palvelurakenneuudistuksesta]. (169/2007).

The Constitution of Finland [Suomen perustuslaki]. (731/1999).

Tuori, K., & Kotkas, T. (2008). *Sosiaalioikeus* [Social rights]. Helsinki, Finland: WSOY.

United Nations. (1948). *The universal declaration of human rights*. Retrieved from http://www.un.org/en/documents/udhr/index.shtml

Virkki, T. (2010). *Asiakasnäkökulma sosiaalipalvelujen muutokseen [Service users' point of view of the change in social services]*. Retrieved from http://www.thl.fi/thl-client/pdfs/d8fe8bcf-2b6f-4f28-8046-406de45bf9e7

Wilding, P. (1994). Maintaining quality in human services. *Social Policy and Administration, 28*(1), 57–72. doi:10.1111/j.1467-9515.1994.tb00408.x

KEY TERMS AND DEFINITIONS

Education in the Social Welfare Field: Education providing different pathways to social welfare professions

eGovernment: Digital interaction between a government and citizens, businesses or government agencies providing anyone a possibility of communicating and interacting via the Internet utilizing information communication technology (ICT)

eService: Utilizing technology in the delivery of services between service providers, service receivers and the channels (of which Internet is the main channel) of service delivery

Online Consultation: Measures, which provide electronic consultation via the Internet

Social Assistance: Last-resort financial support

Social Rights: Part of human rights that inter alia guarantee social, legal and economic protection along with rights to social security, social and medical assistance, and access to social services

Social Services: Part of social welfare that usually is the duty of the municipality or some other administrative unit or organization to ensure

Chapter 12
Mental Health, Post-Secondary Education, and Information Communications Technology

Jenny Martin
RMIT University, Australia

Elspeth McKay
RMIT University, Australia

ABSTRACT

The primary aim of this chapter is to explore the use of information and communications technology (ICT) in post-secondary education to provide opportunities for students with mental health difficulties to remain engaged in their studies during times of mental illness. Higher incompletion rates are particularly concerning amongst this group. The authors discuss how improved outcomes can be achieved through effective use of ICT. This is particularly important from a human rights perspective so that people diagnosed with mental illness are afforded the same opportunities as other members of the community. Strategies afforded by ICT tools that are essential for supporting students with mental illness to optimise their chances of success in their post-secondary education outcomes are outlined. The authors combine mental health and human-computer interaction (HCI) to argue for the need to design appropriate instructional ICT strategies to support students experiencing mental illness to remain engaged with their studies. ICT has evolved with powerful and unique features, offering special applications such as educational software, eCommerce, and healthcare. Yet, very little is being said about how to streamline these applications as effective HCI environments to enhance mental health and wellbeing. The chapter explores the positive and negative impact of ICT tools on teaching and learning. In considering mental health and post-secondary education, it focuses on human rights issues of access and equity, disclosure, and stigma. Authors suggest that ICT can enable students to remain engaged with their learning in general, while at the same time promote a deep sense of community.

DOI: 10.4018/978-1-4666-1918-0.ch012

INTRODUCTION

All persons with a mental illness, or who are being treated as such persons, shall be treated with humanity and respect for the inherent dignity of the human person… There shall be no discrimination on the grounds of mental illness. UN Principles for the Protection of Persons with Mental Illness GA Resolution 46/119 of 17 December 1991.

People with mental illness are vulnerable to human rights violations in both hospital and community settings. Around the world people experience discrimination due to mental illness that results in the curtailment of opportunities in all aspects of life; most notably in education, employment and housing. The severity and high levels of disability associated with mental illness have led to increased global efforts to address mental health problems, in particular those targeted at prevention. In recent years mental health and wellbeing have been identified as priority areas by the World Health Organisation, the World Bank and government leaders' worldwide (Knapp et al., 2007). This is within the context of a severe shortage of resources, particularly in low and middle income countries (WHO, 2009). Mental health problems have been predicted to be the largest single burden of illness globally within the next two decades (Mathers and Loncar, 2006). Mental health difficulties affect all range of people regardless of age, gender, religion or race, however first onset has been found to be most prevalent in young people. Three quarters of those who develop mental illness, do so between the ages of 16 and 25, an age when most young people are likely to embark on post-secondary education and training programs (Mcgivern et al. 2003; McLean & Andrews, 1999). This chapter explores the human rights of people diagnosed with mental illness in relation to access and equity issues encountered in post secondary education. A main focus is on how Information Communication Technologies can both assist and hinder the recovery process. First mental health, post secondary education and the service delivery context are considered. This is followed by a discussion of the stigma associated with mental illness and the human rights violations that occur through discrimination and disadvantage. A case study reports on research that examined the mental health and well being of students enrolled at a university in Melbourne, Australia and the role of ICT educational tools.

MENTAL HEALTH AND HIGHER EDUCATION

Many individuals who experience mental health difficulties want to undertake postsecondary education (Shankar et al., 2009; Mansbach-Kleinfeld et al., 2007). This aspiration is supported in Conventions, legislation, standards and polices on disability, education and mental health. Australia ratified the United Nations Convention on the Rights of Persons with Disabilities on 17 July 2008. As a result Australia is now one of the 149 signatories to this Convention worldwide. The Convention establishes a legally binding standard that recognizes people with disabilities, including mental illness, as equal and active citizens. This Convention, (in particular Article 4 on Education), requires States to recognise the rights of people with a disability to 'an inclusive education and lifelong learning that will enable them to realise their potential'. Accordingly all people are to be provided with opportunities to reach their full potential, regardless of their disability. A focus of the Convention is on the protection and violation of human rights and how to support people with a disability exercise their rights. In Australia this Convention is supported in Commonwealth legislation in the Disability Discrimination Act 1992, Disability Standards for Education 2005, Australian Vice-Chancellor's Committee Guidelines for Students with a Disability 2006 as well as State mental health legislation and policy.

The Equitable Assessment Arrangements policy and Special Consideration policy, of the university where the case study was undertaken, was designed within this regulatory framework. The Equitable Assessment Arrangements policy provides for pro-active planning so that adjustments can be made to the learning and assessment environment to ensure equity. Special Consideration is a one-off, reactive variation of an assessment due to unexpected or extraordinary circumstances that have affected performance in assessment activities, or prevented them from being undertaken. The granting of equitable assessment arrangements and special consideration is based upon supporting documentation from a qualified practitioner, registered with a recognised body. In the case of special consideration this documentation must demonstrate a severe impact. All Special Consideration submissions are online with no personal contact available with the university's Special Consideration Committee.

This study was undertaken in the State of Victoria with the Mental Health Reform Strategy 2009–2019 (Reform Area 5) identifying 'improved participation in education and training and in the workforce' as a key outcome (p.103).

At the commencement of their studies a student may have a pre-existing mental health condition, or they may experience stress that can trigger a first episode of mental illness. The nature of the studies may generate stress that can lead to mental health difficulties. The incidence of mental health problems amongst university students is steadily increasing with estimates of between 10 to 20 per cent (Collins & Mowbray, 2005). Of particular concern are reports that these students have lower completion rates than all other disability groups (Cavallaro et al, 2005; Moisey, 2004).

The stigma associated with mental illness, and the hidden nature of the disability, constitute powerful barriers to students seeking and receiving assistance (Martin & Oswin 2008). Nevertheless there is increased evidence that students' with mental health problems, who receive appropriate support, are successful in postsecondary education (Mcgivern et al., 2003), experience decreased hospitalisation rates (Isenwater, Lanham & Thornhill, 2002), and increased levels of self confidence, self efficiency and empowerment (Collins, Bybee & Mowbray, 1998).

Stigma

Stigma is a socially constructed mark of disapproval, shame or disgrace that causes significant disadvantage through the curtailment of opportunities. Reidpath et.al (2005) describe stigma as, 'a mark borne by a person judged as unfit for the sharing of social resources, and stigmatisation is a process for controlling community membership or ensuring active social exclusion' (p. 5). Negative impacts on health and wellbeing are experienced by those who are excluded. The effects of stigma have been seen as contributing to an overwhelming sense of fear and isolation for the individual affected with stigma regarded as the most debilitating aspect of mental illness (SANE, 2006; Granello et al., 2005). Erving Goffman's (1974) classic sociological writings on stigma highlight the central feature that the question of acceptance has in the life of the stigmatised individual and the social construction of deviant identities. Jamison (2006) highlights how stigma insinuates itself into policy decisions resulting in institutional discrimination.

A barrier to post-secondary education arises when it is assumed that if student are mentally unwell they should not be attending classes (Martin, 2006). This reflects the dominant view that people must be symptom-free before they can "participate" or be "let in" (Davidson et al., 2004). Students hearing this, receive a double message when they are advised to take time off to recover. Yet if they do so, they may be penalized for not attending or participating in class activities. This absence from the classroom means they are put at risk of failure or exclusion. The result is active social exclusion particularly for those students with persistent and ongoing symptoms of mental illness (Reidpath et al., 2005). Understandably these lost days from class can result in disengagement and lack of continuity with their studies. It may mean they are experiencing an inability to successfully meet study or class attendance requirements. This absence is a major loss for the young person, their family, the institution losing talented students and the broader community. On a personal level, those not studying or working run the risk of social exclusion and a life of ongoing poverty, with this non attendance difficulty compounded by a stigma associated with a diagnosis of mental illness. Productivity loss results in an increased tax burden through government welfare and pensions or payments that are necessary to supplement the lost main income for those diagnosed with mental illness (Shankar et al., 2009). This dilemma increases the financial burdens that are placed on the family at a time when an increased financial independence is expected from the family member suffering the mental illness.

Unfortunately institutional discrimination can occur where some staff and students may hold a view that those with particular mental health diagnoses (such as schizophrenia or personality disorder) are undesirable within a particular discipline or profession (Martin, 2006). This attitude is often covert and can lead to the curtailment of opportunities and make it difficult for students to resist and challenge this form of discrimination particularly given their view may be discredited due to their mental health status at the time. However, if enough people raise concerns of discriminatory practices, and policies and procedures are in place to counter these, discrimination is far less likely to occur.

Disclosure

Students who disclose that they have a mental illness run the risk of being rejected or treated differently with responses varying depending upon the diagnosis. People diagnosed with schizophrenia or antisocial personality disorder are often stereotyped as unpredictable and prone to violence and are viewed more negatively than those diagnosed with anxiety disorders or eating disorders (Granello & Wheaton 2001). It has been found however that negative attitudes often do change if time is taken to get to know the person (Corrigan et al. 2000). In their study of post-secondary students diagnosed with mental illness, McLean and Andrews (1999) found 65 per cent (n=256) of students surveyed indicated that they would not advise others to disclose and many students indicated their regret in having done so. Concealment of a mental health condition can also limit opportunities as a person tries to avoid possible discrimination. Buris (2006) suggests that those who develop strategies to resist and challenge discrimination, 'may actually face less stigma, experience less social harm, and be better able to cope with discrimination. At the same time, they avoid the life-long hidden distress and unhappiness experienced by people who conceal' (p.529). Often, people tend to stereotype a person who is diagnosed with a severe mental illness as someone who is unpredictable and possibly dangerous (Martin, 2006). In accordance with this view, policies and services are often developed by universities that focus on risk management and security rather than duty of care, with it noted that practices vary across different universities and countries. This results in stigma leading to discrimination which in turn causes disadvantage and restricts opportunities.

Figure 1 illustrates mental health pathways that can result in "disempowerment" as a result of stigma from mental illness or "empowerment" when support is provided and stigma is externalised with strategies developed to combat it.

Frequent setbacks and resultant stress can trigger an episode of mental illness or impede recovery. For some people the stigma of mental illness can cause even more negative impacts than the mental illness itself, with disempowerment

Figure 1. Mental health pathways (reproduced from Martin, 2010, p.263)

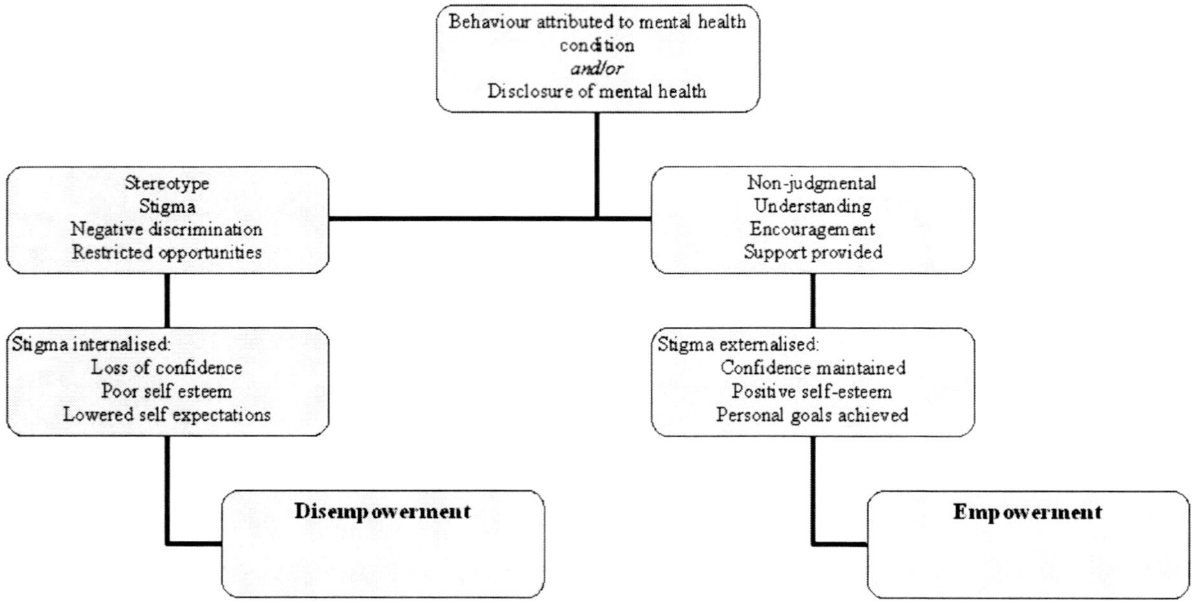

occurring on social, cultural, economic and political levels (Link & Phelan, 2006; Corrigan et al, (2000).

As shown in the disempowerment pathway in Figure 1 a person may internalise these negative responses and experiences, either consciously or subconsciously, resulting in loss of confidence and poor self esteem. Few demands are placed on services with extremely low expectations and grave consequences (Jamison 2006). Pilgrim (2005) sums up the negative impacts of stigma from mental illness; 'The stigmatized person is set apart and they suffer the consequences of the social distance created. The person feels depersonalized, rejected and disempowered' (p.158). However, as indicated in the "empowerment" pathway of Figure 1, there are those who are able to maintain, or regain their confidence and self-esteem, and achieve personal goals. In this pathway the stigma of mental illness is externalised and viewed as a means of oppression. Self expectations are maintained and strategies developed to deal with possible discrimination, resulting in empowerment.

HUMAN RIGHTS DISCOURSES AND MENTAL HEALTH

The United Nations Principles for the Protection of Persons with Mental Illness have guided the development of policy and practice standards in post secondary reflecting a strong commitment to human rights, dignity and empowerment for those experiencing mental health difficulties. However much is left to discretion at a local level; with those diagnosed with mental illness often denied basic human rights that members of the general community take for granted. This chapter explores dominant paradigm shifts in mental health from a human rights perspective, starting with the civil rights movement in the 1960s. During this time a focus was on the rights of full community participation for people who were subject to oppression and discrimination as well as protection of those deemed vulnerable. In the intellectual disability field a focus was on "normalization" for people with disabilities to be able to participate in the community and enjoy the basic rights and civil liberties afforded members of the general population. In mental health the "anti-psychiatry" movement radicalized the debate on the treatment of the mentally ill. Whilst the anti-psychiatry movement was vehemently critical of traditional methods of psychiatric hospitals, psychiatrists continued to insist that the profession was scientific, emphasizing somatic factors within the dominant medical model. Nonetheless the social reforms introduced in the field of mental health may not have been so dramatic in the absence of this anti-psychiatry movement (Martin, 2006). Community health programs developed within a policy framework of "deinstitutionalization" and "normalization" similar to the intellectual disability field. From a human rights perspective deinstitutionalization gave people rights and opportunities to full participation in the community. Historically normalization has two meanings. The first is within a rights discourse and sees deinstitutionalization as a process whereby people live in the community with the same rights and opportunities as afforded to so-called "normal" members of society. The second focuses on change within the person to be able to "fit in" and pass as "normal". This first meaning requires major shifts in community attitudes whereas the second requires individual change and adaptation. The reality is that both are required. Community living is a process that requires adaptation to social norms and values alongside community education and development activities that influence these. Regardless of the intent the successful application of deinstitutionalization is dependent upon the transfer of resources from the closure of the institutions to the community to support people in community living. It also requires major shifts in community attitudes towards mental illness. Unfortunately neither of these has happened to the extent required. The new millennium brought with it a plethora of opportunities. This phenomenon was not lost in the educational technology field. Swept up with this emerging technological enthusiasm, many learning institutions set about implementing ubiquitous online learning policies (Anderson, 2008). There has been scant attention given to investigating the effectiveness of computer aided instruction and mental illness, within universities (Martin et al., 2004). Nor has there been research on how ICT can assist in administrative tasks and engagement.

Recovery

For some people mental illness is a one-off experience from which they fully recover; for others however the experience is recurring and they experience ongoing mental health difficulties. The great majority of mental illnesses are treatable if appropriate care and services are provided. The mental health literature on recovery originated from consumer movements in the United States in the 1980s with a strong focus on the individual. This concept has been developed further in New Zealand in the Mental Health Commission's *Blueprint for Mental Health Services in New Zealand 1998*, to include the individual's social, political, economic and cultural context. The focus is on these broader social contextual factors. The New Zealand model of recovery acknowledges diversity and challenges the dominance of the biomedical model of 'mental illness' that is central to recovery literature in the USA (O'Hagan, 2004:5). A key feature of the New Zealand model that again does not feature in the recovery literature from the USA, is the importance of consumer partnerships at all stages in the design and delivery of mental health services with an increased focus on human rights and advocacy (O'Hagan 2004:10).

In advice to consumers of mental health services in New Zealand, The Mental Health Commission of New Zealand (2002:2) defines recovery as follows:

Recovery means living well in the presence or absence of your mental health problems. It is more than just managing your mental health problem. Recovery also means getting back the things you have lost because of your mental heath problem, such as friends, your home or your job.

Recovery is concerned with quality of life. It is about living well in the presence or absence of symptoms of mental illness. It is about addressing stigma and discrimination and full acceptance and participation in the community. This includes adequate income, access to appropriate and affordable housing, education and employment and leisure activities. It is about being able to participate in the community and engage in daily activities, even though symptoms of mental illness may vary in intensity at different times. It is about 'the kindness of strangers' who will provide opportunities rather than judge, ridicule or discriminate. Ultimately recovery is about acceptance and appreciation of people for who they are and their contribution beyond their mental illness (Martin 2006).

With the advent of deinstitutionalisation people with mental illnesses are expected to integrate into the community. However as Larry Davidson, Associate Professor of Psychiatry at Yale University aptly points out, for many people with mental illnesses, community living is 'a life restricted to what may be considered the psychiatric ghetto of community-based programs' (Davidson, Stayner, Nickou, Styron, Rowe and Chinman, 2004:10). Davidson alerts us to the notion of 'success' as a criterion for people with mental illness to be included in the broader community. By this he means that people need to be seen as well and symptom-free for acceptance and inclusion in education, employment, living independently and developing relationships and friendships with people. Many people are being given double messages. On the one hand they are told that they have a severe long-term illness yet on the other hand they are told to live a normal life in the community – one that is symptom free. While treatment and community supports are available for many people symptoms will persist and the notion of a cure or full recovery is not real (Martin 2006).

A barrier to education is that it is generally assumed that if a person is mentally unwell they should not be attending classes, whether at school, or university. This reflects the dominant view that people must be symptom-free before they can participate or be 'let in' (Davidson, Stayner, Nickou, Styron, Rowe and Chinman, 2004). Thus for many people, education is not an option as they may experience psychotic symptoms several times a day. For others days lost from class will mean lack of engagement and continuity and may mean an inability to successfully complete study requirements.

Central to recovery is 'hope' and the 'active' role taken by the individual in her or his own recovery. The main obstacle to recovery is discrimination. Numerous studies have found that negative stereotypes of people with mental illness lead to discrimination in education, employment, housing and social interactions with others (SANE Australia, 2003; Corrigan, River, London, Wasowski and Campion, 2000; Lyons and Ziviani, 1995; Elliot and Frank, 1990).

Wellbeing

Mental health services today are provided within dominant paradigm of "wellbeing" that has seen a shift from a "disease model" in health to a "wellness model." The World Health Organisation (2009) defines mental health as, 'a state of well-being in which every individual realizes his or her own potential, can cope with the normal stresses of life, can work productively and fruitfully, and is able to make a contribution to her or his community' (p.1). Wellbeing programs are increasingly preferred by policy makers with current health care costs under existing primary care models and projected increases considered unsustainable in the long term (Victorian Department of Human Services 2009; Hassed et. al 2008; WHO, 2007). However, this shift in funding and emphasis, from primary care to general population wellness models, can also be viewed as a further means of stigmatisation of those diagnosed with severe mental illnesses with them deemed 'unworthy of social investment' (Reidpath, et al. 2005, p.1).

The focus of wellbeing models is on general population health promotion and prevention activities such as nutrition, exercise, stress reduction and developing strategies to deal with barriers to wellbeing. The integration of student wellbeing programs in academic programs has resulted in marked improvements in overall student mental health (Hassed et al., 2008). Students are able to access community services or use services provided by the university in Melbourne. In Australia, most universities have counselling, disability support, medical and advocacy services provided by student right's officers in the Student Union. Housing, financial counselling and chaplaincy services are also generally available on campus. All of these services were available on the university campus in Melbourne, where the current study took place.

The main model of mental health service delivery is primary care partnerships in the community with services provided primarily by general practitioners with assistance from other health care workers or counsellors. However only a small minority of people treated for mental health concerns are actually referred on to specialist mental health services with this often for a short term intervention only (Pilgrim, 2005). This may occur in the community or a short term acute hospitalisation, with the person soon returning to the primary carer. Serious concerns have been raised about access to appropriate mental health services. These are particularly in relation to the legislative context, used to determine a person ineligible for treatment by mental health services, if they do not meet the set psychiatric diagnostic criteria. For those deemed eligible for services these can be difficult to access and of varying quality, with this situation exacerbated for those living in rural and remote locations (Mental Health Council, 2005).

ICT, MENTAL HEALTH, AND HIGHER EDUCATION

Models of post-secondary education are based on adult learning principles that require considerable autonomy and resourcefulness from students. The move from secondary school to university can be both exciting and stressful as students learn to adapt to a new learning environment, workload and relationships with both staff and students. Having access to a personal computer is now a necessary educational resource for all post-secondary students in developed countries. It is interesting to note here that the United Nations has declared that Internet access is now a human right (Dadian, 2011). To this end in Australia the present Government has launched their Building the Education Revolution (BER) whereby schools can access funding for infrastructure for computers for each student (Donnelly, 2011). However, the adjustments required with this emerging trend for more learning autonomy are exacerbated for those who are studying away from home and for international students often studying in a new culture and language medium. A person's ability to manage stress and respond to change is a key aspect of mental health adjustment. In these circumstances the human-dimensions (or social context) of human-computer interaction (HCI) come into play (McKay, 2008). In otherwords, the usability of the ICT tools. In the post-secondary education field, these usability issues arise through the numerous benefits derived from ICT tools to enhance student performance in their studies:

- Personal computers and laptops offer mobile computing, which is attractive to students when they need to use a computer in a private setting. The usability issue of the ICT tool relates to the times when a student may need to be absent from the traditional classroom;

- Students can work independently, when isolated from their usual learning environment; (and)
- When a student experiences an episode of mental ill health they may require extra time to complete their study requirements. Easy secondary storage tools such as automated file backups, means the students can easily save their work to retrieve when they are feeling well enough to continue their work.

The Association for Computing Machinery (ACM) was established in 1947, with writings of that era typically adopting the computer science view to explain the inner workings of computer logic/programming etc. Literature that reflects the human-dimensions of HCI has only occurred during the last decade. From this scenario we can see that people building computerized systems have struggled for many years to define the interactive relationships that occur between people and their computers. We have however reached the point where there is no choice. The social networking aspect of our computing is driving a new momentum, which means community informatics now permeate into every part of our educational/working life. (Bradley (2006).

There is little attention in the Information Systems (IS) literature that provides for the differences in people's cognitive wellbeing and computer usage, especially in a post-secondary educational setting. IS designers need to understand the psychological and social context of learners in general and in relation to student mental health. A paradigmatic approach to IS design is needed to achieve the customized learning environment necessary to draw together the inter-disciplinary nature of HCI. For instance, aspects of instructional science, cognitive psychology and educational research contribute to this conceptual framework.

Increasingly, students are able to access course materials and other relevant information for their studies online. It is necessary for educators to facilitate the development of an online learning community with ICT tools that support flexible engagement, yet provide the structure required for students who may be experiencing mental health difficulties to remain engaged (Harris, 2009). A positive example of this is taking a cognitive approach to teaching and learning for students experiencing mental health issues that cause cognitive impairment. Ultimately it is best to discuss with the student what would be the most appropriate way to assist them to remain engaged with their studies during periods of mental illness. While a negative dilemma arises through unmonitored use due to the human right for ubiquitous access.

The use of ICT tools that support student engagement includes the availability of lectures online to provide students with greater flexibility (Anderson, 2008). A key consideration however is not simply provision of information but to acknowledge the human-rights perspective by fostering a learning community that the student has an active participatory role in. Given the availability of quality online course materials, particularly in more recent years, a main challenge is how much classroom activity is required to meet both university and professional standards and requirements. Moreover, consideration is required by instructional systems' developers to engage themselves with the professional health care providers to learn how to develop appropriate instructional strategies that adopt the most appropriate teaching style that best suits the changing and often complex needs of students dealing with mental illness; with suitable (instructional) architecture to support this. This attention to detail requires both a willingness from the (educational) staff member and adequate time and resources on the part of the learning institution's management to do so.

ICT Tools

ICT tools offer increased potential that enhance an individual's innate right to information access through increasing the flexible learning options for students experiencing mental health difficulties during their studies. Access to quality course materials online in visual, audio and print form can aid private study for students who have missed classes as well as those who have attended but possibly missed information due to lapses in concentration.

ICT tools provide a platform for the convergence of technology and community informatics on mental health through the:

- Direct nature of the connectivity;
- Disappearance of barriers between idea and execution;
- Seemingly borderless nature of Internet communications;
- Rising need for computer literacy;
- Immediate distribution of information; (and)
- Multi-dimensional virtual culture afforded by ICT tools.

Web-services by their very nature are a complex mixture of interrelating ICT linkages (Alonso et al., 2004). In today's social networked era, it is often through the wireless ICT tools that people increase their social interactions. Concentrated connectedness is important for mental wellbeing as it affords people the personal space they may require at times when they wish to work alone.

Health and Safety Issues

In the earlier days of computing, some attention was given to the risk factors associated with usage. The most commonly reported were the physical injuries known as repetitive strain injury (RSI) also called cumulative trauma disorder (CTD) and back injury. However the cognitive syndromes took longer to become more obvious (Jacko & Sears, 2007). Computer phobia, the aversion to computer usage, is now treated by psychologists alongside the other phobic disorders (http://www.phobia-fear-release.com/computer-phobia.html). The relationship between the interactive effects of technology, post-secondary education and recovery from a mental illness requires consideration of issues of isolation and borderless participation.

One of the most obvious dangers associated with computer usage is the degree in which the person's computing takes place in isolation from others. Due to the high levels of concentration involved in HCI, people often remove themselves from others to work in a quieter environment. Moreover, we propose that when facing mental health issues and the possible need to 'take time out' from the traditional classroom; it is far too simple to assume that ICT tools will offer the best solution. Instead the online environment should be implemented as a useful adjunct intervention.

There is a type of 'borderless participation' that occurs when people engage in online discussion forums. It has been shown that people's worst behavior often goes unchecked as soon as they are online. This is particularly dangerous in open-ended discussion boards (Wallace, 2001:80). A number of the negative effects of online participation that Wallace identifies include:

- Polarization (through mishandled inter group dynamics);
- Aggression (seen often in the 'flame-wars' that quickly develop when using e-mail); and
- Mistrust (brought on by the anonymity in which people can operate on the Internet).

The use of Virtual Worlds, such as Second Life, can also be problematic particularly for those who are having difficulty distinguishing between reality and fantasy due to mental illness. When offering students access to this type of virtual reality (VR) program (Clark & Kwinn, 2007), care needs to be taken to provide adequate debriefing session that emphasize the differences between the abstract nature of the virtual environment and the real world, acknowledging that for some students this type of learning experience is not appropriate

(Wallace, 2001). Another example of negative impact of ICT tools can be seen in the new iPad camera tools; the camera lens distorts the resulting image to such an extent that it is impossible to discern the real environment. Researchers now know that these emerging VR learning spaces are fraught with dangers (Clark & Kwinn, 2007; McKay, 2008). The uncertainty for the (emotional) safety of this type of ICT environmental tool is due partly to the open ended (cognitive) nature of this imaginary activity. Students with pre-existing cognitive impairment would potentially find this type of learning environment extremely difficult.

In recent years in the rush to implement "sharable content object reference model" (SCORM) compliant programs; many online learning developers have failed to check whether there is any learning that actually occurs (as demonstrated by increased proficiency of the participants) (McKay et al., 2007; Williams, 2004). In cases where checks are made, most attempts fail to use valid assessment measures of the changes in proficiency (Izard, 2004).

CASE STUDY

Method

The purpose of this exploratory study was to generate knowledge about the relatively under researched topic; the mental health of university students. An anonymous on-line survey was sent to all students enrolled in a School, within an Australian university, identified by the university's Disability Liaison Unit as having the highest number of students with mental health difficulties using their services. Students were asked to disclose whether or not they had experienced any mental health difficulties during their studies. Those who had experienced mental health difficulties, that had affected their studies, were then invited to complete the on-line survey. Open and closed questions were asked focusing on the three areas of disclosure, impact on studies and support.

The self-selection process was a significant aspect of the research as it allowed for participation of students who may not have previously declared experiencing mental health difficulties, formally sought assistance or been diagnosed as such. It also meant that students defined their mental health condition rather than selecting from pre-determined categories of "mental illness". The categories identified by the students were compared with those used by mental health services during the data analysis. Previous studies of this nature have surveyed students who have declared a mental illness, and registered for Disability Liaison Unit services. Further broad scale research that provides a brief mental health screening tool to select survey participants would be useful to identify the impacts of different types of mental illness, particularly schizophrenia and personality disorder, on students' education experience and performance.

The survey was posted online for a six week period with a request to participate sent to 1,517 in the School. This method proved effective as students were able to anonymously share their experiences in their own time. A total of 54 students responded – 3.6 percent of the student body. This response rate was consistent with Collins and Mowbray's prevalence estimates of between 10 and 20 per cent.

The comments and suggestions from the students surveyed are presented highlighting both obstacles and opportunities encountered during their studies.

Findings

The self-selection process, and open ended question asking students to provide details of their mental health condition, resulted in the same categories as those used by mental health services in the Diagnostic and Statistical Manual (DSM) of the American Psychiatric Association. Some of these however would be considered physical or intellectual rather than mental health diagnoses. The main conditions were depression (n= 35) and anxiety (n=23). Anxiety included students with eating disorders.

Two students were recorded for both schizophrenia and bi-polar affective disorder. Individual students reported; post traumatic stress disorder, obsessive compulsive disorder, dissociative identity disorder, head injury, Asperger's syndrome, autism and epilepsy. It was only these last four responses that would not normally be classified as mental health conditions by today's standards with it noted however that this was not the case in the not too distant past.

Just over half of the students (n=28) reported multiple conditions with just under half recording a dual diagnosis of depression and anxiety (n=25). The remaining three students reported dual, triple and quad diagnoses. The dual diagnosis was dissociative identity disorder and anxiety. The triple diagnosis was post-traumatic stress disorder, anxiety and depression. The quad diagnosis recorded was Asperger's syndrome, autism, anxiety and obsessive compulsive disorder.

Two students reported physical problems triggered by their mental health condition. One of these reported mental health difficulties with anxiety that resulted in physical problems that caused further and more serious mental health problems with depression. One student's physical condition led to mental health difficulties with anxiety. These student responses illustrated the complex interplay between physical and mental health and the importance of a holistic and collaborative approach to mental health care.

Some students had different diagnoses at different times or more than one diagnosis concurrently. Students reported different responses according to particular diagnoses with a student commenting:

My condition originally was depression and when I was diagnosed with depression I told as many lecturers and tutors as I could but I felt most didn't regard it as a serious problem and often forced me to demonstrate how depression could impact on my studies. I was later diagnosed with anxiety spectrum disorder which some tutors empathized with so they made concessions (ie. not grading me on class participation, not requiring that I speak or contribute if I didn't want to and alternative assessments in the case of oral presentations). Later I was diagnosed with bipolar disorder and told that I most likely had the condition even before starting university.

Some students reported physical problems triggered by their mental health condition. In one instance anxiety resulted in physical problems that caused further and more serious problems with depression. Another student's physical condition led to difficulties with anxiety.

Students reported on a number of areas of their studies that were affected by their mental health condition. Attending classes regularly and participating was difficult for some students with this impacting negatively on grades. Fear of failure when unwell was a concern and negative judgments by teaching staff and fellow students. Disclosing to staff was very uncomfortable with students worried that staff might think they are lazy, telling lies or wanting privileges. A student commented:

Social sciences subjects are very much about interaction and discussion with fellow students. There's lots of group work and class participation is often graded with at least one subject per semester requiring some sort of oral presentation. I had enormous difficulty with attending class mainly due to my anxiety problems. I withdrew and eventually stopped attending classes. I had no contact and my lecturers and tutors assumed I was plain lazy. I ended up failing two years worth of subjects before I managed to get my anxiety under control. Even if I rocked up to class I made sure I was as close to the door as possible, if we were asked to contribute I'd panic and leave the class or stay and attempt to contribute. Afterwards I would hate myself for what I had said and felt that the other students thought I was an idiot so either way, attending Tutorials were very, very difficult.

Mixing with other students was difficult when unwell, with group work particularly challenging. Motivation and concentration were problematic for class attendance and participation with assessment causing significant stress. Some students were fearful of others – both staff and fellow students finding out about their mental health condition resulting in rejection or being judged negatively, misunderstood or treated differently. A student commented:

I'm afraid of being shut out. Like when I became so depressed and anxious and withdrawn, absolutely no-one made an effort to contact me, to give me the opportunity to explain my circumstances. I know they expect us to be responsible adults but adults are not immune from illness. To feel shit about my performance but then be able to comfort myself by telling myself I will get through it, that I have plenty of time to complete whatever assessments I have outstanding and then to receive this insensitive letter (Student Progress) was not just hurtful but disappointing. You do need to 'look-after' your students. I expect that of you.

Confidentiality was a particular concern with disclosure and possible negative impacts on future employment prospects. Some students in vocational degrees worried that if they were 'found out' they may be counseled out of the degree or their employment opportunities would be jeopardized. A student commented:

I have concerns with confidentiality being breached and this impacting on chances for future employment. I feel very uncomfortable telling them because I am worried that they will think I'm lying or that I'm not badly off and just want privileges. I do want them to know though because I want them to know that I do find some things very difficult, especially since 20% of our grades are towards class participation in 3 out of the 4 subjects and I find it very difficult to talk about my opinions in front of the whole class.

Another student commented:

I am too frightened of judgment and stigma to be open about my situation. Certain Departments or School cultures are worse than others. I fear being singled out for different treatment, fear of judgments that my condition in some way precludes my acceptance or suitability for my chosen course/career and ultimately may impact on my results. While many staff espouse openness and valuing diversity in words, their actions and body language appear to me to say something else. Admittedly when vulnerable I look for every tiny minutia of possible judgment or rejection and too often I perceive it in body language, tone of voice, or judgments/statements already made about me without real knowledge of where I am at.

Approaching staff was particularly difficult when unwell with it difficult to describe what was happening and to put forward a convincing and coherent story as described in the following student comment:

When things were really bad, I cut myself off from everyone, even family, so communicating with anyone, staff or otherwise felt very difficult.

Some students felt embarrassed or confused or simply that it was nobody else's business. A student commented:

I haven't formally asked for assistance because I feel confused and afraid that it's all just in my head (I know it is, but that doesn't help!)

Another student commented:

There's definitely a level of not wanting others to know involved. Plus there's the possibility they may ask probing questions which I wouldn't want to answer. I just personally don't like telling the world about these things.

Most of the students in the study had told staff of their mental health problems with staff usually seen as sympathetic and responsive – though not always. The main services used by students were located within the university with assistance from family and friends and outside professionals – particularly general practitioners, psychiatrists, psychologists and nurses, and specialist youth mental health services. A minority of students did not receive any help at all. Most students found the Counseling and Disability services at the University helpful however for some Disability services were not able to assist. Information provided on coping skills provided in different courses and at The Hub, the University's central student administration centre, was considered helpful, as well as support from Student Right's Officers informing students of rights and entitlements and offering advocacy and support. Students commented on using Disability services at the university:

It was very helpful talking to the woman at the Disability Liaison Service, who was very understanding. She got me some extensions, made sure attendance wouldn't be graded, allowed me to sit exams in a smaller room, and also helped me feel that studying while I had depression would be okay.

This next comment on services provided by the Disability Liaison Unit highlights the difficulty in accessing services, particularly if there is no psychiatric or medical diagnosis available:

I was referred on to the DLU (as many students I know with mental problems have been) but I found my meeting with them to be rather traumatic. It feels as though if I want to be treated seriously by the staff at the Disability Liaison Unit then I must rock up in a wheel chair.

Further comments were made on the 'invisibility' of mental illness with a student commenting:

Often it is the person you least imagine to have a mental health condition who in fact may have a serious struggle under the surface. Mental health issues are highly stigmatised, sensationalised, and misunderstood.

Another student offered the following advice to staff:

Be careful of preconceived notions. I know I come across as very confident, together, assertive etc. In many ways these are skills and a mask that I have developed to survive over time. I would say to staff, do not assume ... do not assume... do not assume....

A student commented on support provided by the university's Counseling Service:

The Counseling service was very helpful. They helped to get my assessments altered from essays to multiple choice and short answer questions.

Students valued staff treating them with respect and being non-judgmental, understanding and supportive. Trust was an important consideration and determined whether or not a student felt comfortable to disclose. A proactive approach and follow up for students who had disclosed was important with staff enquiring about their progress and offering assistance if needed. For those who did disclose to a trusted member of staff communicating about their mental health condition was helpful, particularly when this resulted in understanding and assistance. However in some instances even when trusted staff members were identified, students did not approach them believing they did have the power to actually provide any practical assistance.

While students valued a respectful and non-judgmental approach they also wanted assistance provided to support them in their studies. Types of assistance valued by students included access to lectures on-line, altered or choice of assessment tasks, extension of time for submission of assignments. It was important for students to remain connected to the university when unwell. Students found classes that were structured and productive assisted in keeping them engaged with their studies as illustrated in the following comment:

It's important that when I attend, I get a lot out of classes... that lecturers do not waste time and are productive. If I feel they are crucial and I learn heaps my motivation increases. I prefer structured lectures, lectures without interaction (keep this to Tutorials), that way if I'm down I can attend lectures and keep up. Discuss assignments in lectures so I don't miss out. I am not good with Tutorials- having to be with lots of people. Put detailed information on-line on the Learning Hub so a level of correspondence is possible. When I have to attend, for example because of doing an assignment in class, this should be consistent and begin at the start of the semester.

Another student commented on on-line learning resources:

Being able to access lectures on-line and learn independently has been helpful. Classes which place a high degree of importance on attendance were significantly more stressful and harder to achieve in.

Some students found medication assisted with their mental health condition:

Taking the new medication has helped me a lot because I feel less stressed and can focus more on my study. Before I took the medication I didn't find anything helpful because my stress levels were very high.

Others particularly valued support from family and friends and partners, with pets also a source of comfort. Some students relied on their own personal resources as well as regular sleep and exercise. One student found computer games helpful with another finding reducing both drug use and social isolation important for recovery.

CONCLUSION

The study findings are consistent with the literature on recovery and the importance of living well in the presence or absence of signs and symptoms of mental illness. They highlight the complexity of mental health, particularly multiple diagnoses and the interplay between physical and mental health conditions. The invisibility of mental health concerns is an issue, particularly for those students who are experiencing difficulties but do not have a diagnosis. Where a diagnosis is available students experience different responses from staff and support services. This makes it a difficult for students to decide whether or not to disclose their mental health condition. Those who decide to do so are faced with the further dilemma of who they can trust to keep their confidence. Students revealed fears of being 'shut out' or 'not let in' by teachers, peers and employers, particularly those enrolled in vocational courses. However for those who did disclose the great majority received positive support and assistance from the university. Students valued a respectful and non-judgmental approach by staff as well as wanting practical assistance to support them in their studies. This included access to course materials on-line and flexible assessment tasks and timelines. Structured classes, that do not require full attendance and participation, were preferred with ongoing engagement with the university when mentally well and unwell, important for academic success. ICT can be a valuable tool to enhance the learning experience and assist students experiencing mental illness to remain engaged with their studies. Collaborative partnerships between educators and students using ICT to assist students to remain engaged with their studies during periods of mental illness, can promote recovery and lead to improved mental health, educational outcomes and life opportunities.

It is perhaps fair to comment in closing this chapter, that some academic staff may not engage themselves in such matters, as they feel they are not skilled in dealing with mental health issues. However, given that the student is enrolled in their course and as academics, they have a professional 'duty-of-care', which surrounds the student's enrolment; this hesitation must be overcome. As such it needs to be carefully embedded within the educational processes of each learning institution (in particular in the post-secondary education sector) in such a way they can provide appropriate referrals for mental health assistance, if required. To this end, staff development and assurance programs must be devised to assist staff in developing appropriate attitudes and skills relating to mental illness and fostering wellbeing. Helpful conversations by supportive and empathic staff, without specialist knowledge in mental health, are appreciated and lead to positive outcomes (Pilgrim, 2005:99). Empathic conversations such as these are helpful to facilitate a number of issues, including: provide an understanding of how a student's mental health impacts upon their studies, what their rights are, where available assistance is and how to best access these supports if and when required. ICT tools can assist students with mental health issues stay engaged with their studies, however, it is supportive policies and empathic academics/staff that will encourage the student to want to stay engaged and complete their studies.

REFERENCES

Alonso, G., Casati, F., Kuno, H., & Machiraju, V. (2004). *Web services: Concepts, architectures and applications*. Springer.

Anderson, T. (Ed.). (2008). *Theory and practice of online learning*. Athabasca, Canada: Athabasca University. Available from http://www.aupress.ca/index.php/books/120146.

Australia, S. A. N. E. (2003). *Why stigma matters*. Retrieved from www.sane.org/stigmamatter.html

Bradley, G. (2006). *Social and community informatics: Humans on the net*. New York, NY: Routledge, Taylor & Francis.

Burris, S. (2006). Stigma and the Law. *Lancet, 367*, 529–531. doi:10.1016/S0140-6736(06)68185-3

Cavallaro, T., Foley, P., Saunders, J., & Bowman, K. (2005). *People with a disability in vocational education and training*. Adelaide, Australia: National Centre for Vocational Education Research (NCVER).

Clark, C., & Kwinn, A. (2007). *The new virtual classroom: Evidence-based guidelines for synchronous e-learning*. Wiley.

Collins, M., & Mowbray, C. (2005). Higher education ad psychiatric disabilities: National survey of campus disability services. *The American Journal of Orthopsychiatry, 75*, 304–315. doi:10.1037/0002-9432.75.2.304

Corrigan, P., River, L., London, R., Wasowski, K., & Campion, J. (2000). Stigmatizing attributions about mental illness. *Journal of Community Psychology, 28*, 91–102. doi:10.1002/(SICI)1520-6629(200001)28:1<91::AID-JCOP9>3.0.CO;2-M

Dadian, D. (2011). *Internet access is now a human right*. Retrieved from http://blog.powersolution.com/internet-access-is-now-a-human-right/

Davidson, L., Stayner, D., Nickou, C., Styron, T. H., Rowe, M., & Chinman, M. (2004). Simply to be let in. *Ausinetter, 20*(1).

Donnelly, K. (2011). The failed education revolution. *The Drum Opinion*. Retrieved from http://www.abc.net.au/unleashed/43506.html

Elliot, T., & Frank, R. (1990). Social and interpersonal reactions to depression and disability. *Rehabilitation Psychology, 35*, 135–147. doi:10.1037/h0079058

Granello, D., & Wheaton, J. (2001). Attitudes of undergraduate students towards persons with physical disabilities and mental illness. *Journal of Applied Rehabilitation Counseling, 32*(3), 9–17.

Harris, L. (2009). Electronic classroom, electronic community: Designing eLearning environments to foster virtual social networks and student learning. In Martin, J., & Hawkins, L. (Eds.), *Information communication technologies for human services education and delivery: Concepts and cases*. Hershey, PA: IGI Global. doi:10.4018/978-1-60566-735-5.ch006

Hassed, C., Sierpina, V., & Kreitzer, M. (2008). The health enhancement program at Monash University medical school. *EXPLORE: The Journal of Science and Healing, 4*(6), 394–397. doi:10.1016/j.explore.2008.09.008

Isenwater, W., Lanham, W., & Thornhill, H. (2002). The college link program: Evaluation of a supported education initiative in Great Britain. *Psychiatric Rehabilitation Journal, 26*, 43–50. doi:10.2975/26.2002.43.50

Izard, J. (2004). *Impediments to sound use of formative assessment (and actions we should take to improve assessment for learning)*. The Australian Association for Research in Education (AARE). Retrieved from http://www.aare.edu.au/04pap/iza04905.pdf

Jacko, J. A., & Sears, A. (Eds.). (2007). *The human-computer interaction handbook: Fundamentals, evolving technologies and emerging applications (human factors and ergonomics)*. Atlanta, GA: CRC Press.

Jamison, K. R. (2006). The many stigmas of mental illness. *Lancet, 367*, 533–534. doi:10.1016/S0140-6736(06)68187-7

John, D. (2004). Quantifying the impact of equity overlap in VET. In K. Bowman (Ed.), *Equity in vocational education and training*, (pp. 1-18). Adelaide, Australia: National Centre for Vocational Education Research (NCVER).

Link, B., & Phelan, J. (2006). Stigma and its public health implications. *Lancet, 367*, 528–529. doi:10.1016/S0140-6736(06)68184-1

Lyons, M., & Ziviani, J. (1995). Stereotypes, stigma and mental illness: Learning form fieldwork experiences. *The American Journal of Occupational Therapy., 49*, 1002–1008. doi:10.5014/ajot.49.10.1002

Martin, J. (2006). *Mental health practice*. Charnwood, UK: Ginninderra Press.

Martin, J. (2010). Stigma and student mental health. *Higher Education Research & Development, 29*(3), 259–274. doi:10.1080/07294360903470969

Martin, J., McKay, E., & Thomas, T. (2004). Recovery from mental illness: Lifestyle and employment options, in harvesting hope: Across the lifespan, contemporary the MHS in Mental Health Services. In K. Kellehear & M. Teesson (Eds.), *The MHS Conference* (pp. 193 -197). ISBN No: 0-9757653-0-2

Martin, J., & Oswin, F. (2008). Post-secondary education: Opportunities and obstacles for recovery. In K. Kellehear & V. Miller (Eds.), *Looking toward excellence in mental health care in 2020*. New South Wales, Australia: TheMHS.

Mcgivern, D., Pellerito, S., & Mowbray, C. (2003). Barriers to higher education for individuals with psychiatric disabilities. *Psychiatric Rehabilitation Journal*, *26*, 217–231. doi:10.2975/26.2003.217.231

McKay, E. (2008). *The human-dimensions of human-computer interaction: Balancing the HCI equation* (1st ed., *Vol. 3*). Amsterdam, The Netherlands: IOS Press.

McKay, E., Axmann, M., Banjanin, N., & Howat, A. (2007). Towards web-mediated learning reinforcement: Rewards for online mentoring through effective human-computer interaction. Paper presented at the 6th IASTED International Conference on Web-Based Education, March 14-16, Chamonix, France, (pp. 210-215). ISBN: 978-0-88986-650-8

McLean, P., & Andrews, J. (1999). *The learning support needs of students with psychiatric disabilities in Australian post-secondary institutions*. Adelaide, Australia: National Centre for Vocational Education Research (NCVER).

Moisey, S. D. (2004). Students with disabilities in distance education: Characteristics, course enrolment and completion, and support services. *Journal of Distance Education*, *19*, 73–91.

O'Hagan, M. (2004, April). Recovery in New Zealand – Lessons for Australia? *Ausinetter, 20*(1).

Pilgrim, D. (2005). *Key concepts in mental health*. London, UK: Sage Publications.

Reidpath, D., Chan, K., Gifford, S., & Allotey, P. (2005). He hath the French pox: Stigma, social value and social exclusion. *Sociology of Health & Illness*, *27*(4), 468–469. doi:10.1111/j.1467-9566.2005.00452.x

Shankar, J., Martin, J., & McDonald, C. (2009). Emerging areas of practice for mental health social workers: Education and employment. *Australian Social Work*, *62*(1), 28–45. doi:10.1080/03124070802626893

Wallace, P. (2001). *The psychology of the internet*. Cambridge, UK: Cambridge University Press.

Williams, J. R. (2004). *Developing performance support for computer systems: A strategy for maximizing usability and learnability*. Boca Raton, FL: CRC Press.

World Health Organization. (2005). *Mental health information systems: Mental health policy and service guidance package*. Geneva, Switzerland: WHO. ISBN: 92 4 154671 9

World Health Organization. (2009). *What is mental health?* Retrieved from http://www.who.int

Chapter 13
ICTs and Gender-Based Rights

Ana-Cristina Ionescu
Chamber of Commerce and Industry of Romania - CCIR, Romania

ABSTRACT

In this new age, the Internet, the network of networks connected by a complex array of electronic, wireless, and optical technologies extending from the private to the public sector, and from academic to business and governmental organizations, is starting to have increasingly broad social implications, besides the technical ones. Nevertheless, as women and men enter and progress differently into employment and occupations, not all humankind benefits equally from information and communication technologies (ICTs). The question that this chapter addresses is whether women have equal rights and opportunities to access and use ICTs. In this chapter, the author aims to strengthen the idea that in this changing era, new ICTs represent a cardinal instrument for social transformation, enabling and empowering women to become controllers of information.

INTRODUCTION

Reality is merely an illusion, albeit a very persistent one - Albert Einstein

Over time, women have been subject to some of the most brilliant novelists', playwrights', and philosophers' writings. Their vision on women's role within different societies reflects a *status-quo* at a certain moment in history, or expresses a critique of a given system. The various portrayals of women in their writings influenced gender relations, their rights - including access to technologies - and the way they were perceived by societies, such as the interpretation of their image in the media.

In the world of literature, famous fictional heroines whose destinies left a mark and impacted generations, include Edna Pontellier, the main female character in Kate Chopin's "The Awakening", who struggled to find independence; Emma Bovary, the heroine of Gustave Flaubert's "Madame Bovary, the woman full of dreams and romantic notions

DOI: 10.4018/978-1-4666-1918-0.ch013

who was propelled toward adultery and impossible debt by her unfulfilled marriage and died painfully and tragically"; or Leo Tolstoy's "Anna Karenina", one of the greatest tragedies of all time, that portrays a young married woman who has an affair and eventually committed suicide by throwing herself under a train. Among philosophers, Nietzsche, although he appears more welcoming of the feminine than many of his peers, and even though he depicts life and wisdom as two women engaged in a dance, nevertheless refuses "to admit women, qua subjects, as interlocutors into the philosophical conversation" (Froese, 2006, p. 198). Of the playwrights, Tennessee Williams featured women as main characters more often than men (Blackwell, 1970), empathizing with their loss and longing and displacement in a society that hardly had regard for women, and portrayed them as fighters struggling within themselves and with the circumstances surrounding them. Also, Henrik Ibsen's woman character takes care of her life in dire conditions, facing many challenges.

It is imperative to also note here the outstanding achievements of women in fields that traditionally belonged to men, such as science or journalism. In science, examples include Ida Hyde who completed her Ph. D. in 1896 at the University of Heidelberg, becoming the first woman to ever receive the degree for her type of work and, in addition, the first woman ever to conduct research at the Harvard Medical School and the first woman elected to the all-male American Physiological Society; Marie Curie, who received the 1903 Nobel Prize in Physics and became the first woman ever to receive this award, and subsequently also received the Nobel Prize in Chemistry in 1911; Florence Bascom, the first woman and the first female geologist to be awarded a Ph. D. from Johns Hopkins University, even though she could not officially attend classes there as a woman. Florence Bascom also was the first female scientist to be hired at the United States Geological Survey (USGS) in 1896 and became a pioneer of the use of microscopes to study minerals and rocks. Examples of famous women journalists with remarkable contributions over the time include Margaret Fuller (1810-1850), first American female foreign and war correspondent; Nellie Bly (1867-1922), a world-travelling reporter; Alice Dunnigan (1906-1983), a champion of the efforts to end gender segregation; and Ethel Payne (1911-1991), a fearless civil rights reporter. Media initiatives by women include the publication in May 1999, at the initiative of a Scottish journalist, of the world's first virtual women's newspaper, *Worldwoman*, intended to disseminate transnational news written by women to a wide global audience and represented a milestone in promoting gender equality, or the more recent Great Britain-based online journal, International Journal of Gender, Science and Technology, established in 2009. To support freedom of expression and the development of community media, plurality of content and opinion, and the training of media professionals, international organizations like UNESCO have allocated, over the last thirty years, more than US$100 million to 1,200 projects in 140 countries via its International Programme for the Development of Communication (IPDC). Examples of initiatives include support for the Media Institute of South Africa to improve the quality of journalism in post-apartheid South Africa, the deployment of a women's media centre in Cambodia, and the training of the next generation of professional journalists in Mongolia (Souter, 2010).

To set the background on the theme of this chapter, a thorough literature review (with specific focus on the research theme) on ICTs, gender, women's perception in the media and their access to technologies is provided next.

WOMEN AND ICTs

Technology is often understood by people as a gender-neutral technical tool that society can utilize, and not as something that is in itself influenced by society. Yet, the gender-based approach argues that technology is not neutral, but depends on culture. Women's access to technology depends on their allegiance to different social identities such as class, ethnicity, caste, race, or age, which interact with gender.

Today beliefs from the 1990s, according to which computer mediated communication (CMC) is a mere reflection of the social reality (Ebben 1993; Collins-Jarvis, 1995, Herring 1992, 1993, 1994; Ferris 1996), are only true for third world countries untouched by the Internet, where women lack access to basic communication means.

Women's Access to ICTs

The use of ICTs can make essential contributions to reducing poverty, increasing productivity, and stimulating innovation and economic transformation. Technologies provide women with access to critical information that helps them achieve better results and thus better living conditions (Fredriksson, 2011). Yet, gender relations and hence women's access to technologies, are constantly negotiated and the main factors to take into consideration are culture and wealth.

In the undeveloped regions of the world technology has been historically a male preserve. Consequently, women's access to ICTs is controversial and political. The situation is different in the urban areas, where a culture that encourages women to pursue a career and attend higher education, the easy access to information via Internet or mobile phones, and the increasing tendency to adapt to the international trends, shape an optimistic landscape.

The existing power relations in different societies determine the usability of and the access to ICTs. All over the world, the most dramatic situation is encountered in the rural areas, where women have restricted access to ICTs because the basic infrastructure for such technologies is missing and the costs of deployment are high. ICTs in these areas are used almost entirely by the husband, and women, the majority of them illiterate housewives, lack opportunities for training in computer skills. Domestic responsibilities, cultural restrictions on mobility, reduced income, and the lack of relevance to their existence, exclude them, even today, from the information sector.

Patterns of gender segregation apply to the ICT industry as well, because men hold the majority of high-skilled, high value-added jobs, while women are concentrated in the low-skilled, lower value-added jobs like work in call centers. Teleworking, - the home use of telecommunication services that allows employees to work from home - is an example in this regard. Out of the two categories of teleworkers, the well-educated with demanding jobs that necessitate entrepreneurial and specialized skills and the low-level workers who perform tasks like typing or data entry, women are most likely to integrate into the later, the separation being a gendered one (Dodge and Kitchin, 2001). Thereby, women's empowerment in the information society varies depending on how gender relations as a cultural process are being negotiated and contested, in relation to the technology environment. Yet, the situation as such is unacceptable, as hundreds of recent studies on sex and intelligence reviewed by Fine (2010) reveal that there is no scientific evidence for innate biological differences between men and women's minds. In her book "Delusions of Gender: How Our Minds, Society, and Neurosexism Create Difference", Fine (2010) argues that, in fact, cultural and societal beliefs contribute to commonly perceived sex differences. In other words, Fine believes that differences between men and women have less to do with neurological differences and more with our own implicit gender stereotypes, pointing out that thoughts and attitudes often disagree with consciously held beliefs.

Engendering ICT does not refer to a greater use of ICTs by women, but to facilitating women's access to the ICT system by transforming it. Measures in this regard include ICT policies initiated by the government with strong gender perspectives and involvement of civil society in gender equality related issues; considering gender related issues when drafting, implementing, and evaluating ICT projects and policies; and analyzing the differential impact of telecommunications/ICTs on men and women (Gurumurthy, 2004). Mansell and When (1998) point out two different categories of initiatives meant to enhance women's access to the benefits of ICTs: those generated by women themselves in using ICTs as tools of social and economic empowerment, and those taken by national and international organizations to ensure women's access to the benefits of the information society. The Internet has the potential to change women's role in politics on a transnational level, as nowadays they can create, through these new technologies, local and global political networks (Youngs, 2000). The new ICT communication infrastructure facilitates networking in real time and, in this way, women are able to move beyond the patriarchal vision of politics by expressing opinions on websites that tackle their concerns and increase their influence in a field such as international relations, where historically they have been least visible. Furthermore, Youngs (2000) notes that women's access to the Internet has enhanced the creation of new global communities, with a focus on feminist issues, such as violence against women, political, social, and cultural rights, and repression. The so-called *social media* communication channels - like facebook or linkedin - connected the general public with the different public or private institutions, decision making bodies etc. on gender equality topics.

Two major contemporary aspects impact on the spread of the Internet: the availability of personal computers (PCs) and the prevalence of preexisting fixed telephone lines and cable (Rueda-Sabater and Garrity, 2011). Women in the most remote and traditional places are being connected to the world via innovative initiatives. In Afghanistan, in 2010, a mobile phone operator - MTN - enhanced mobile use among women by setting up women-only retail stores. The solution was tailored to the needs of a country where tradition prohibits women from interacting with men unrelated to them. At present, women represent 18 percent of Afghan mobile phone subscribers. In Nigeria, mobile phone use decreased transaction costs and saved time and money for the women running micro-enterprises by cutting out travel, previously necessary to identify buyers and negotiate prices. In the developing world, over 1.5 billion mobile phones are currently in use and the number expected for 2015 is 2.5 billion, as developing nations count for over 80 percent of all new subscriptions worldwide (Fredriksson, 2011).

We deal today with a mix of old and new technologies. Mobile phones are used increasingly to access the Internet. A statistic from June 2009 reveals that in Kenya, for example, 99 percent of all Internet subscribers were at that time accesing the Internet via mobile phones (Fredriksson, 2011).

In a world that constantly redefines its values and principles to balance inequities, technologies need to be easily accessible and meaningful to different segments of populations. The real challenge within this multi-level convergent media reality, which changes the way we create, consume, learn and interact with each other (Jenkins, 2006), is to manage to not leave out audiences unable to keep up with advancements by providing information in formats and languages that they can understand. Technological convergence holds immense potential for the improvement of life and liberty in some ways and can degrade it in others, as the same technology has the potential to be utilized both a weapon of social control and a means of resistance (Rheingold, 2002; United Nations, 2000). Google, for example, has developed sites in 190 domains, with a user interface translated into a total of 130 different languages, from Afrikaans to Zulu. Yet, Google is not the dominant search engine in every country where it exists. In India, Rediff, a Mumbai-based provider of online news, information, communication, entertainment, and shopping services is said to comply better with the needs of the local customers, with tailored services. This is a clear sign that the ICT industry needs to increasingly adopt a location-based approach that involves an in-depth analysis of cultural, legal, and regulatory aspects (Kelly and Blakesley, 2011).

Analyzing the problem of inadequate access to ICTs, Galperin and Mariscal (2007) discuss the need to develop appropriate pro-poor ICT policies within the Latin American and Caribbean context, pointing out that market reforms in this regard have accentuated the social and economic divides, failing to ensure the benefits of the Information Society. The authors discuss the necessity of a policy reform that builds upon the achievements of market liberalization efforts in the region, in accordance with the realities of the digital poverty concept that addresses the multiple dimensions of inadequate levels of access to ICT services by people and organizations, as well as the barriers to their productive use.

FACTS AND FIGURES

The latest Internet usage statistics provided by Internet World Stats on March 31, 2011, and provided in Table 1, highlight that the developing regions of the world - Africa, Asia and Latin America - still have the lowest percent of Internet users out of the total population. Developing countries have only 21.1 Internet users per 100 inhabitants as opposed to 71.6 Internet users per 100 inhabitants in the developed countries. The most severe situation is encountered in Africa, where only 9.6 users exist per 100 inhabitants (United Nations, 2011). Far from making progress in the effort to bridge the digital divide, the statistics listed below highlight significant inequities between continents.

The access to communication, a cardinal tool for social inclusion, is severely affected by poverty in many parts of the globe. Girard (2003) explains that "one third of the world's population has no access to electricity, billions have never made a telephone call, and there are nearly twice as many illiterate adults (98 of them in less-industrialized countries) than there are people online"(p. 8). Referring to efforts made to extend the Internet to less-industrialized areas of the world, Girard (2003) assesses that it is not possible to bridge the digital divide – i.e., to overcome inequities - by providing populations in these areas the same level of services enjoyed in the developed countries. But "connectivity is the tip of the iceberg" (Girard, 2003, p. 8). There are other complex factors that obstruct Internet's expansion to humanity, like illiteracy or language barrier. The dominant language on the Internet is English, and at least 20 percent of the world's

Table 1. World internet users and population stats

World Regions	Population (2010 Est.)	Internet Users Dec. 31, 2000	Internet Users Latest Data	Penetration (%Population)	Growth 2000-2010	Users % of Table
Africa	1,037,524,058	4,514,400	118,609,620	11.4%	2,527.4%	5.7%
Asia	3,879,740,877	114,304,000	922,329,554	23.8%	706.9%	44.0%
Europe	816,426,346	105,096,093	476,213,935	58.3%	353.1%	22.7%
Middle East	216,258,843	3,284,800	68,553,666	31.7%	1,987.0%	3.3%
North America	347,394,870	108,096,800	272,066,000	78.3%	151.7%	13.0%
Latin America/ Caribbean	597,283,165	18,068,919	215,939,400	36.2%	1,037.4%	10.3%
Oceania/ Australia	35,426,995	7,620,480	21,293,830	60.1%	179.4%	1.0%
World Total	6,930,055,154	360,985,492	2,095,006,005	30.2%	480.4%	100.0%

Source: www.Internetworldstats.com

population speaks languages that are hardly encountered on the web, increasing the challenge to provide local, relevant, and contextualized content.

Analyzing the macroeconomic dimension of the sector, usage growth in ICTs has been uneven (Marcelle, 2000). Yet the diffusion rates of ICT goods and services were fast. For example, average compound annual growth rates, corresponding to the 1990 - 1998 period, were 6% for fixed telephones, 52% for mobile subscribers, and 81% for Internet hosts. The number of countries connected to the global network has increased from just over 20 in 1990 to more than 200 in July 1999 (ITU 1999a), and statistics by the Central Intelligence Agency (CIA) indicate that 216 countries were accessing the Internet in 2009.

Freedom of expression is a human right and, in our contemporary society, Internet access itself has become a human right (United Nations, 2011). Yet, much more effort is necessary to help democratize Internet usage and more programs focusing on expanding access in rural areas need to be developed (Arronowitz, 2011).

While countries like Costa-Rica launched initiatives such as the National Program of Educational Informatics to enhance the population's access to ICTs (Villalobos and Monge-González, 2011), the prospects for the many young girls and boys living in less developed regions of the world, far from the Generation C - those connected, communicating, content-centric, computerized, community-oriented, always-clicking consumers born after 1990 (Friedrich, Peterson & Koster, 2011) - are not so bright. The UNESCO statistics below reveal that the access to Internet is still reduced or missing in many schools.

Statistics from a decade ago on the use of ICTs by women (see Table 3) revealed very deep inequalities. While women accounted for 36 per cent of all Internet users in 1999 in Japan, in Africa, Asia and Latin America, the use of new ICTs was limited. The cost of equipment and connectivity was high and adequate policies that would ensure women's participation, education and training in ICTs, to prevent the persistence of the old gender biases, were missing (United Nations, 2000; ILO, 2001).

Recent reports on women and ICTs discuss how having Internet access at home can empower women and influence their participation in society and the labor market. It enhances their access to knowledge and information, improves their skills, especially in the ICT field and helps them to develop careers outside the home (ITU, 2010).

However, despite such advances, inequality between men and women is still significantly high in the less developed countries, which are very often ignored by analyses of development possibilities. Moreover, the existing gap is widened, as most of the reports and studies that tackle these issues are not adapted to the specific features of the undeveloped parts of the world. Consequently, in societies where women have not been traditionally associated with technology, they still face barriers hindering their access to and use of these new technologies. These barriers include poverty and illiteracy, socialization patterns or unequal access to education and training and, hence, lower skills than men. This reveals that even though the new technologies have improved women's standard of living by offering them new opportunities, they may turn into a new element of discrimination and inequality, as many of the tasks performed by women are badly remunerated, call for little training, and the examples of women who managed to reach executive jobs are scarce.

According to a 2010 report by the International Telecommunications Union (ITU), gender equality with respect to ICT access and use has not been achieved. While the differences between men and women using the Internet decreased to less than 10 percent in most countries, men tend to represent a slightly higher share of Internet users, excepting in Honduras, Ireland, New Zealand, Nicaragua, and Thailand, where the percent of women using the Internet is higher than that of

Table 2. Infrastructure (Internet in schools)

	Proportion of schools with Internet access		Proportion of schools with fixed narrowband Internet access (using modem dial-up, ISDN)		Proportion of schools with fixed broadband Internet access (DSL, cable, other fixed broadband)		Ratio of learners-to-computer connected to Internet	
	Total %	**Public%**	**Total %**	**Public%**	**Total %**	**Public %**	**Total %**	**Public%**
Argentina[y]	42,4	28,5	20,7	18,2	21,7	10,2	...	...
Austria[y]	100[8]	100[9]	...	...	...	...	...	...
Bahrain	100	100	-	-	100	100	6	3
Belarus	61,2[4]	61,2	54,3[*,4]	54,3*	6,9*[,4]	6,9*	67[*,4]	67*
Costa Rica	44[4]	44	...	...	...	...	38[4]	38
Dominican Republic	2,3	2,8	...	...	...	...	...	...
Egypt	53,8[4]	53,8	47,4[4]	47,4	6,5[4]	6,5	74	...
Estonia	96,9[1]	97,3[1]	10,7[1]	10,2[1]	86,3[1]	87,1[1]	7[1]	7[1]
Ethiopia	1,6	...	...	...	...	...	...	...
Finland	100	100	14,8	14,8	85,2	85,2	4**	4**
Ghana[z]	.	.	.	.	.	.	.	.
Guate-mala[z]	0,04[4]	0,04	...	...	...	...	132	..
Jordan[z]	79,7	82,5	7,1	6,2	72,6	76,3	...	...
Malaysia	100	100	19,8	20,5	80,1	79,5	...	...
Mauritius	85,5	85,3	5,8	3,1	75	79,1	45	74
Morocco	2,9	1,6	.	.	2,9	1,6	558[4]	558
Norway[z]	100	.	.	.	.	.	...	...
Oman	61,8	...	34,1	...	23,1	...	52**	...
Palestine[z]	23	6,4	...	...	...	...	...	...
Paraguay	7,7	4,6	...	...	...	...	...	...
Poland	...	...	...	...	...	...	12	...
Republic of Korea	100[2]	100[2]	.	.	100[2]	100[3]	6[5]	6[7]
Russian Federation	80[*,10,4]	80[*,10]	36,5[*,10,4]	36,5[*,10]	42,7[*,10,4]	42,7[*,10]	39[4]	39
Senegal	4,8	4,9	...	...	...	...	...	...
Sweden	100	100	-	-	100	100	3	3
Tunisia	80,6	79,3	...	...	...	...	...	...
Uruguay	100	100	...	...	100	100	...	...

Source: UNESCO, 2010.

Notes:

[1] Data for all ISCED level 1-3 general education institutions

[2] The number of educational institutions is 11,760 and the relative size of missing institutions represents 6.6%

[3] The number of public educational institutions is 9,981 and the relative size of missing public institutions is 5.96%

[4] Data refers to public schools only

[5] The learner population for ISCED 1-3 educational institutions is 7,664,185 and the relative size of the learner population for missing institutions is 8.01%

[6] Represent computers installed under Programme GENIE - phase 1

continued on following page

Table 2. Continued

[7] The learner population for ISCED 1-3 public educational institutions is 6,343,675 and the relative size of the learner population for missing public institutions is 7.23%

[8] Data does not include private schools of their own statute as well as schools of the health sector.

[9] Data does not include schools of the health sector

[10] Data includes ISCED 1, 2, 3A

[11] Data refers to learners in schools equipped with computer equipment

[12] The teacher population for ISCED 1-3 educational institutions is 351,102 and the relative proportion of teachers for missing institutions is 4.73%

[13] The teacher population for ISCED 1-3 public educational institutions is 283,029 and the relative proportion of the teachers for missing public institutions is 3.65%

[z] Data are for the school year ending in 2009

[y] Data are for the school year ending in 2007

* National estimate

** UIS Estimate

... Missing data

- Magnitude nil

. Category not applicable

./. Data included under another category

men. The statistics below provide an overview of the present situation around the globe.

VIRTUAL COMMUNITIES

During the twentieth century, information became the hub of the social, political and economic organization of life, which are nowadays "inextricably linked with technology". And, while "gluts of useless information clog the arteries of the Internet", for some it "promises - or threatens - to supplant reality itself" (Lyon, 2005, p. 223).

At the time when the Internet began its growth, media studies started to focus on the mediums of communication - mostly neglected until that time - and their enormous social implications: a virtual world with no limits where all individuals can express their identity and opinion as authors or readers, within an *open communication* (Coate, 1992; Rheingold, 1987, 1990, 1991, 1993; Seabrook, 1997). The Internet era, characterized by diversity of content, rapid transmission of information, and most importantly, interactivity, gave new valences to previously existing technologies. This enabled users - especially women - not only to consume but also to produce information, as in the virtual space many inequities are not so pronounced. The online environment eliminates the *middle men* and *middle women* in social, political and cultural life, flattening social hierarchies and enlarging social freedom and equality. The Internet liberates individuals from the state or corporate controlled apparatuses of information such as television, where women have been depicted as the weaker sex for decades. While the old media dealt with passive recipients that were perceived as a mass, with non-customized messages that did not leave room for individual feedback (Gilder, 1994), the Internet enhances individualism and creativity.

The flourishing of virtual communities, in which women and men all over the world can communicate in a *many-to-many* way, has redefined the concept of place and our traditional understanding of what a community represents in an historical sense. The Internet represents a social platform, where pre-existing community-oriented social and spiritual resources can be reinforced (Baym, 1998; Calhoun, 1998; Castells, 2001; DiMaggio, Hargittai, Neuman, & Robinson, 2001; Doheny-Farina, 1996; Hampton & Wellman, 1999, 2000; Howard, Rainie, & Jones, 2002; Katz & Rice,

Table 3. Women's access to the new ICTs - Developed versus developing regions of the world

	Internet users as % of total population		Women as % of all Internet users
	1997	1999	1999
Sub-Saharan Africa			
South Africa	1.6	3.7	19
South America			
Brazil	0.6	2.1	25
Eastern and South-eastern Asia			
China	< 0.1	0.3	8
Philippines	< 0.1	< 0.1	43
Western Asia			
Bahrain, Jordan, Kuwait, Lebanon, Oman, Qatar, Saudi Arabia and United Arab Emirates	0.4	0.8	4
Eastern Europe			
Croatia	..*	12	42
Czech Republic	1.9	2.6	12
Russian Federation	0.4	0.8	15
Slovakia	5.0	9.5	12
Western Europe			
Belgium	2.3	16	38
Estonia	..*	10	38
France	0.9	12.9	42
Germany	4.7	10.0	35
Ireland	2.9	13.5	31
Italy	0.7	7.9	30
Netherlands	6.0	13.7	13
Spain	3.2	8.7	19
Sweden	21.3	40.9	46
United Kingdom	2.0	18.0	38
Other developed regions			
Australia	6.7	30.5	43
Canada	15.3	25.4	38
Japan	6.3	14.4	36
New Zealand	9.1	15.8	24
United States	19.2	30.7	49

*Two dots (..) indicate that data are not available.
Source: United Nations, 2000.

2002; Neustadtl & Robinson, 2002; Putnam, 2000; Wellman & Gulia, 1999).

The formation of virtual communities is a reaction of the globalized world to the social transformations incurred by the traditional ones, determined by individuals' need to interact (Fernback & Thompson, 1995; Lievrouw, 1998; Shapiro, 1999; Sunstein, 2001), as women, for

*Figure 1. Percentage of Internet users by gender, non-European communities, 2008**

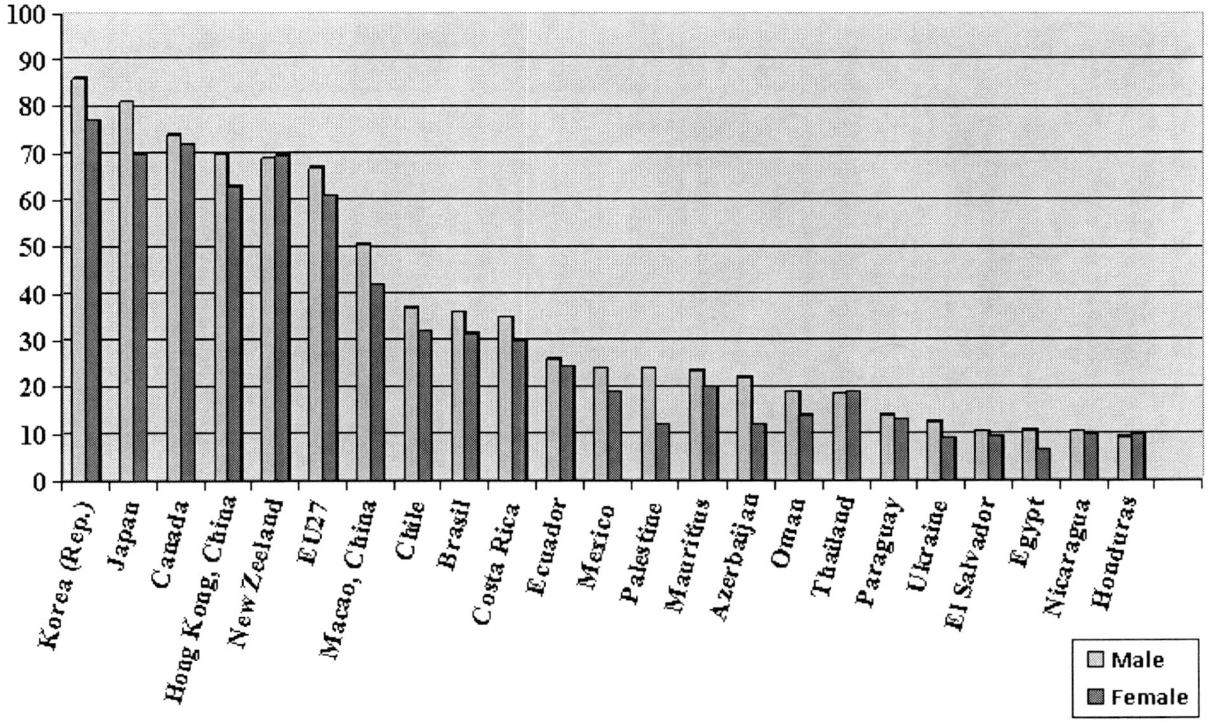

Note: * Or latest available year

Source: ITU (based on Eurostat and national sources), 2010

example, were hardly able to make their voices heard via the old technologies. More critical opinions question the idea of a 'virtual community' and argue that cyberspace can only provide the illusion of a community, i.e. pseudo communities. They consider that computer networks alienate individuals, rather than bringing them together, preventing the formation of social ties (Kiesler, Siegel, & McGuire, 1984; Beninger, 1987; Calhoun, 1991; McClellan, 1994; Parks & Floyd, 1996; Stoll, 1995; Shenk, 1997). Despite these contradictory opinions, I believe that the Internet enhanced women's ability to create their own information and share it online, and in real time, to control the content and distribution channels, and to propagate their messages to large audiences.

In many situations, online social relations are enlivened by the same cultural ideologies found in the geographical space. Cultural identifiers, such as race, gender, and disability enhance exclusion rather than inclusion, as the patriarchal relations are perpetuated online. Women on line are still expected to adopt the same gender roles as in the outer world. Cyberspace contracted the disease of the material world, as "gendered identities [...] are becoming more clearly demarcated through heightened sexism and the creation of women-only spaces" (Dodge & Kitchin, 2001, p. 60).

Diagnoses like Hawthorne & Klein's belief that "[f]or every Feminist issue in the real world, the same issues apply in the cyberworld" (1999, p. 8) make us wonder if women's rights are respected in cyberspace. While literature of the 1990s hardly discussed issues like online harassment (Pollock & Sutton, 1999), today more focus is put on Internet regulations in general and on feminist Internet

*Figure 2. Percentage of Internet users by gender, European countries, 2008**

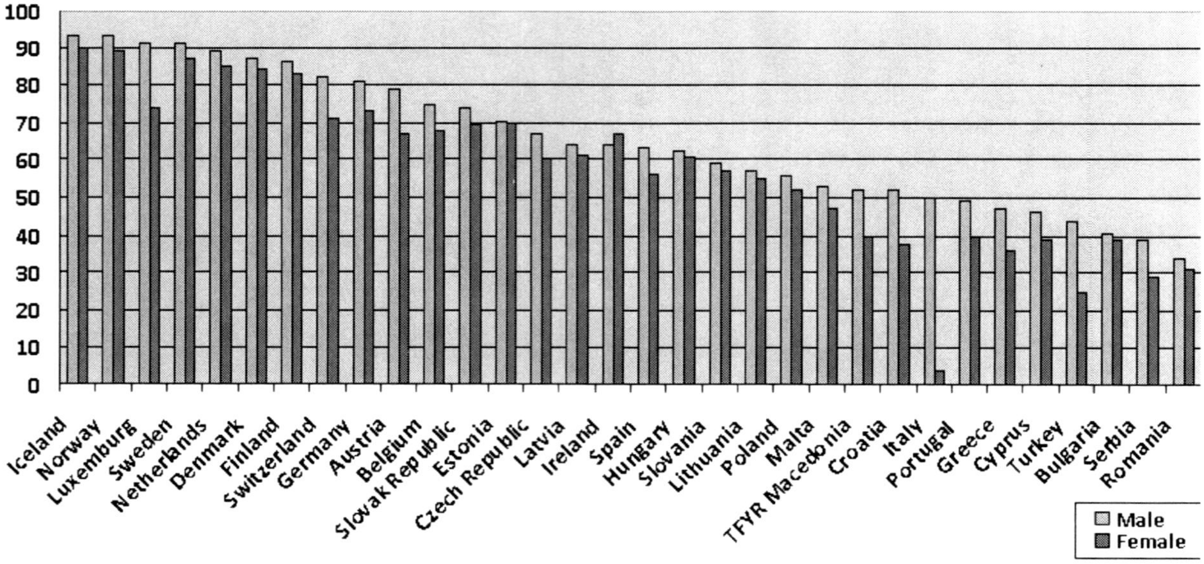

Note: * Or latest available year

Source: ITU (based on Eurostat and national sources), 2010

community regulations in particular, especially issues like identity, anonymity, and open versus closed online networks. Feminist bloggers face problems like anonymous comments, insults, or murder threats, and once their blogs are closed, the URLs are snatched by pornographers (HaggardHarpie blog, 2007). Does online anonymity have positive or negative implications? Kling, Lee, Teich & Frankel (2000) project the Internet and anonymity as inseparable concepts that reinforce each other. They discuss, in this respect, the results of a conference on anonymous communication on the Internet, pointing out that the positive values of anonymous communication (such as investigative journalism, law enforcement, self-help, and personal privacy protection) compensate its negative sides (including hate mail, impersonation, online financial fraud, and the global marketing of prostitution and pornography). However, this is not entirely positive, as the majority of individuals who are victims of gender-based violence (GBV) and in particular sexual violence are women and children, who are more vulnerable to abuse due to their gender, age, and dependence on others (Inter-Agency Standing Committee, 2005). Moreover, anonymity can be considered only to the extent that abusers can be made accountable for their actions. Should online feminist communities be open or closed to others? In a world where feminism is hated because it is considered extreme and against the *status-quo*, regulations are required in matters of access to these communities. Possible solutions to such abuse include a "rules" section, blocking IPs, or screening emails but, still, more dedicated Internet regulations are needed, as a women-only space is not always a safe space (Shugar, 1995). A solution in this regard is provided by Renate Klein (1999) who introduces the concept of feminist CyberEthics - the end to assuming stolen identities, from pretending to have a different gender, a (dis)abled body, or different age or race. In her opinion, respecting such a code of ethics would allow women to survive with their real bodies in cyberspace.

LIBERATING TRANSNATIONAL NETWORKING

The online environment allows women to communicate across cultures, something that previously was challenging or impossible through the main classical channels of male-dominated media. Against the vision according to which the Internet is characterized by a multiplicity of the self (Holmes, 1997) the virtual feminist communities must be an extension of local and embodied experiences. Within these communities - a means for the survival of feminism - the activists can connect online with other like minds to share information, resources, and opinions on issues such as abuse and discrimination that they suffer in the real life patriarchal environment in order to assure (Weiss, 1995; Hawthorne, 1999).

The new ICTs are an important tool for social transformation and gender equality. Electronic networking between women through e-campaigns or e-consultations proved to be one of the most efficient means of communication, in recent years. Among the first and most remarkable initiatives meant to enhance women's access to and use of new ICTs is the Women's Programme of the Association for Progressive Communications - APC, created in 1993. The organization is active in fields like ecology, human rights, feminism, and the protection of minority groups (UNESCO, 1997). As the following examples highlight, the initiative aimed to increase women's participation in CMC so that they can correct gender inequities when designing, implementing, and using new ICTs. In West francophone Africa, Environnement et développement du tiers monde - synérgie genre et développement (ENDA-SYNFEV) promotes electronic communication for women's groups as a tool for action, mostly in areas like health and human rights. In Southern Africa, Women's Net aims to facilitate women's access to resources and information by organizing gender sensitive training programmes and by strengthening the link between projects and organizations. In Asia, the Asian Women's Resource Exchange (AWORC) was established in 1998 to enhance electronic resource-sharing among women's information centres in Asia, to facilitate Internet literacy, and to promote activism among and between individual women and women's organizations. In Latin America, the Area Mujeres (Women's Programme) of the Latin American Information Agency (ALAI) was created in 1989 and carries out lobby and advocacy initiatives on the right to communicate, from a gender perspective. Its success is due to permanent and active dialogue with organizations that share its electronic communication and networking goals (United Nations, 2000).

To determine women and men' participation in CMC and the gender differences between the styles of interaction in men and women, extensive research was dedicated, throughout the years, to understanding the relation between gender and democracy. While early studies suggested that CMC was democratic (Hiltz & Turoff 1978), starting from the 1990s the literature has revealed that CMCs perpetuate gender differences in communication (Herring, 1992; Ebben, 1993; Kramarae & Taylor, 1993; Herring, 1993; Truong, 1993; Herring, 1994; Collins-Jarvis, 1995; Ferris, 1996). Similar to Kiesler, Siegel & McGuire (1984) who assess that virtual communities are less influenced by social norms and pressure in comparison with face-to-face groups, Matheson (1991) argues that CMC users have reduced other-awareness – for example, they demonstrate a more uninhibited behavior and are more resistant to others' ideas. At the same time, she states that CMC increases private self-awareness, as individuals react to available social cues based on their feelings, attitudes, and values. For example, when individuals are informed of the other person's gender, she notes, they have expectations and perceptions that are consistent with gender stereotypes.

Hawthorne and Klein (1999) argue that connectivity gained new valences in the era of cyberfeminism, as cyberfeminists - activists or networkers - "have taken to the Internet with great alacrity"

(p. 6) in order to develop campaigns at both international and local levels. Examples in this regard include online initiatives, such as International Women's Tribune Centre - IWTC (http://www.irc.nl/page/7049), which provides communication, information, education, and organizing support services to women's organizations and community groups working to improve the lives of women, particularly low-income women. The initiatives focus on the Beijing +5 meeting, information access and communication capacity-building, networking and organizational support. Examples include: The Sisterhood Is Global Institute (www.sigi.org), Women's Learning Partnership - WLP (http://www.learningpartnership.org), Women Living Under Muslim Laws (http://www.wluml.org) or The Association for Women's Rights in Development - AWID (http://www.awid.org).

Yet, Herring's early research (1992, 1993, 1994) that examined several academic discussion lists highlighted that women post messages online less frequently than men and, in addition, their messages receive less feedback than those posted by men. In addition to the unequal participation in the online environment, Herring (1993) points out that men and women participate in different discussions, and adopt distinctive communication styles, and the author explains her assumptions by motivating that boys and girls learn sex-appropriate behavior: girls learn to please others and to be nice and thus they perceive verbal aggressiveness as a personal attack, while men perceive it as a part of everyday conversation.

FUTURE PERSPECTIVES

The Internet has revolutionized social and business habits, evolving from a network of computers and information into a network of people, and its changes are far from being over. The available figures about recent Web 2.0 diffusion highlight two aspects. Its spread is outstanding, as the most diffused applications, including wikis, blogs and online social networks have, in only a few years, been adopted by some 20-40% of Internet users. Yet the intensity with which users participate varies. About 3% of European Internet users generate content based on their own creative efforts, about 10% of them provide feedback, comment and review existing content, and 40% are passive consumers of Web 2.0 (European Communities, 2009).

The *World's Women 2010: Trends and Statistics* report (United Nations, 2010) underscores the differences in the status of women and men. Progress regarding gender equality has been made in areas including school enrolment, health, and economic participation. Still, the gender gap remains critical in areas such as decision-making, women's empowerment, and violence against women.

The progress in education - in the literacy status of adult women and men around the world - is slow and uneven, with women still facing many disadvantages and representing two thirds of the world's 774 million adult illiterates, a figure that has not changed over the past two decades. Yet, the report calls for optimism as improvement in access to education will eventually raise literacy levels. Primary enrolment of girls and boys is increasing across the world and trends for less developed regions such as Africa and South-Central Asia are encouraging. However, gender disparities are significant, as from the total of 72 million children being out of school worldwide, 54 per cent are girls. Except for sub-Saharan Africa and Southern and Western Asia, a relevant improvement in women's enrolment is registered in tertiary education, where women's prevalence is higher than men's at a global level. However, the analysis of the various fields of study reveals gender inequalities in tertiary education as women, although predominant in fields like education, health and welfare, social sciences, humanities and art, are severely underrepresented in areas such as science and engineering.

As for poverty, the report points out that, at the household level, the data show that certain types of female-headed households are more likely to be poor than male-headed households of the same type. For example, in Latin America and the Caribbean and the more developed regions, households of lone mothers with children have higher poverty rates than those of lone fathers with children. Women's lack of access to and control over resources limits their development and accentuates their vulnerability to unfavorable social, economic and political evolutions, because they have less cash income than men, particularly in the less developed regions of Africa or Asia. Moreover, relevant proportions of married women in sub-Saharan Africa and Southern Asia have no control over household spending or the spending of their own cash earnings.

Technology in indeed important – not only for women - but escaping from poverty requires knowledge, and knowledge does not arise from technology but from experience and relevant meaningful content, digital or otherwise. Content on rights, responsibilities, and options can be both a prerequisite and catalyst for democracy and gender equality (Girard, 2003; UNESCO, 2005). Women should have access not only to the new technologies, but also to education, research and settings where freedoms can be exercised. The research on Africa and Asia highlights that women have much less disposable income for expenditures related to education and technologies because, according to a report from Zambia, women are generally not engaged in their own economic activities and, in many cases, their husbands prohibit them from earning money (Green and Trevor-Deutsch, 2002).

The inequalities between men and women are accentuated by the difficulties that women encounter in continuing their education. In traditional communities, the access to education is limited and many young girls never attend school or complete their education (United Nations, 2005). Marked differences in this respect between men and women are particularly preeminent in the Arab States, in sub-Saharan Africa, and in South and West Asia, where a woman's access to education is obstructed by customs, local values, and lack of finances or employment (UNESCO, 2005). The same report discussed, on a note of optimism, a promising perspective for the developing world, pointing out that the achievement of knowledge in society is not exclusively within the reach of affluent countries, provided that political will exists. This argument is exemplified by the case of Botswana, a country that achieved far greater advances in education than could have been foreseen from its income level in 1980. Kerala State in India provides another example. Its per capita income is 99 times lower than in the United States but through the quality of its research infrastructure it is largely contributing to making India the eighth nation in the world in terms of science publications (UNESCO, 2005).

Regarding the future of feminism online, the radical activists Renate Klein and Diane Bell (1996) predicted an atmosphere characterized by justice, dignity, and safety from all forms of violence. Cyberfeminism has an essential role, as it will always keep an open eye and react to abuse by critiquing and fighting to change social norms and constructs, with the potential to establish a political identity and unity against the language of exclusion (Wise, 1997). Moreover, cyberfeminism, a trend that transcends time, is "a philosophy which acknowledges, firstly, that there are differences in power between women and men specifically in the digital discourse; and secondly, that CyberFeminists want to change the situation" (p. 2). The solution of the equation lies in the idea of *context:*

How precisely the power differences are played out [...] which elements are highlighted depends on the context. Similarly, the strategies chosen by CyberFeminists to challenge this system depend on the interests and expertise of the women engaged in this work. (Hawthorne and Klein, 1999, p.2)

The promotion of gender equality is crucial for the development of a society. For women to be able to attain true equality of opportunities with men in respect of knowledge, it is essential for them to have access not only to general education but also to an education tailored to the new technologies. Acquiring new technology skills offers women the perspective of financial independence, enhancing them to access fields that are traditionally male dominated. The empowerment of women may be encouraged by cooperative development or microcredit programmes, especially in the developing countries, once they overcome the cultural barriers, prominent especially in the Arab states (UNESCO, 2005).

In an interview given to the U.S. State Department and published in *eJournal USA*, Pink (2006) assesses that the future belongs to people with androgynous minds, which possess both analytical and artistic, empathic abilities. The people with more androgynous minds, reasoning both in a specific *left-brain* masculine way and a *right-brain* feminine way, hold a comparative advantage in today's economy, he explains, as many of the *soft* abilities attributed to women such as empathy and even creativity are, to some extent, more important these days and might concede an advantage to women.

REFERENCES

Association for Progressive Communications (APC). (1995). *Proposal to the Fourth World Conference on Women*. Women's Networking Support Program. Retrieved January 6, 2011, from http://alainet.org/active/1041

Baym, N. (1998). The emergence of online community. In Jones, S. (Ed.), *CyberSociety 2.0: Revisiting computer-mediated communication and community* (pp. 35–68). Thousand Oaks, CA: Sage.

Bell, D., & Klein, R. (1996). Beware: Radical feminists speak, read, write, organise, enjoy life, and never forget. In Bell, D., & Klein, R. (Eds.), *Radically speaking* (pp. XVII–XXX). Melbourne, Australia: Spinifex.

Beninger, J. R. (1987). Personalization of mass media and the growth of pseudo-community. *Communication Research*, *14*, 352–371. doi:10.1177/009365087014003005

Blackwell, L. (1970, March). Tennessee Williams and the predicament of women. *South Atlantic Bulletin*, *35*(2), 9-14. Retrieved January 06, 2011, from http://www.jstor.org/pss/3197002

Calhoun, C. (1991). Indirect relationships and imagined communities: Large-scale social integration and the transformation of everyday life. In Bourdieu, P., & Colemen, J. S. (Eds.), *Social theory for a changing society* (pp. 95–120). Boulder, CO: Westview Press.

Calhoun, C. (1998). Community without propinquity revisited: Communications technology and the transformation of the urban public sphere. *Sociological Inquiry*, *68*(3), 373–397. doi:10.1111/j.1475-682X.1998.tb00474.x

Castells, M. (2001). *The Internet galaxy: Reflections on the Internet, business, and society*. New York, NY: Oxford University Press.

Central Intelligence Agency. (2012). *The world factbook*. Retrieved July 12, 2011, from https://www.cia.gov/library/publications/the-world-factbook/rankorder/2153rank.html#top

Coate, J. (1992). *Cyberspace innkeeping*. Retrieved January 3rd, 2011, from http://protovision.textfiles.com/computers/CYBERSPACE/inkeeping-cyberspace

Collins-Jarvis, L. (1995). *Explaining gender group discrimination in computer-mediated communication: A social identity approach*. Paper presented at the Annual Meeting of the Organization for the Study of Communication, Language, and Gender, Minneapolis, MN.

Conley, M., & Patterson, C. (2000). Communication, human rights and cyberspace. In Hick, S., Halpin, E. F., & Hoskins, E. (Eds.), *Human rights and the internet* (pp. 211–225). New York, NY: Palgrave Macmillan.

DiMaggio, P., Hargittai, E., Neuman, W. R., & Robinson, J. P. (2001). Social implications of the Internet. *Annual Review of Sociology*, *27*(1), 307–336. doi:10.1146/annurev.soc.27.1.307

Dodge, M., & Kitchin, R. (2001). *Mapping cyberspace* (pp. 44–60). New York, NY: Routledge.

Doheny-Farina, S. (1996). *The wired neighborhood*. New Haven, CT: Yale University Press.

Ebben, M. M. (1993). *Women on the Net: An exploratory study of gender dynamics on the soc. women computer network*. Paper presented at the Annual Meeting of the Organization for the Study of Communication, Language, and Gender. Temple, AZ.

European Communities. (2009). *Web 2.0: Where does Europe stand?* Luxembourg: Office for Official Publications of the European Communities.

Fernback, J., & Thompson, B. (1995). *Virtual communities: Abort, retry, failure?* Retrieved January 4, 2011, from http://www.well.com/user/hlr/texts/VCcivil.html

Ferris, S., P. (1996). Women on-line: Cultural and relational aspects of women's communication in on-line discussion groups. *Interpersonal Computing and Technology*, *4*, 29.

Fine, C. (2010). *Delusions of gender: How our minds, society and neurosexism create difference*. New York, NY: W. W. Norton and Company.

Fredriksson, T. (2011). The growing possibilities of information and communication technologies for reducing poverty. In S. Dutta, & I. Mia, (Eds.), *The global information technology report 2010 - 2011. Transformations 2.0,* 10th anniversary edition (pp. 69 - 79). Geneva, Switzerland: World Economic Forum and INSEAD. Retrieved June 17, 2011, from http://reports.weforum.org/global-information-technology-report/content/pdf/wef-gitr-2010-2011.pdf

Friedrich, R., Peterson, M., & Koster, A. (2011). The rise of generation C. *Strategy+Business, 62*. Retrieved March 30, 2011, from http://www.strategy-business.com/article/11110?gko=64e54

Froese, K. (2006). *Nietzsche, Heidegger, and Daoist thought, crossing paths in-between* (pp. 185–219). Albany, NY: State University of New York Press.

Galperin, H., & Mariscal, J. (2007). *Digital poverty. Latin American and Caribbean perspectives*. International Development Research Centre: Practical Action Publishing. Retrieved December 15, 2010, from http://www.idrc.ca/openebooks/342-3/

Gilder, G. (1994). *Life after television*. New York, NY: Norton.

Girard, B. in collaboration with The Friedrich Ebert Stiftung (FES) Geneva Office and Communication for Development Group Extension, Education and Communication Service Research, Extension and Training Division Sustainable Development Department. (2003). *The one to watch. Radio, new ICTs and interactivity* (pp. 1 - 165, 199 - 221). Rome, Italy: Food and Agriculture Organization of The United Nations.

Global Alliance for ICT and Development (GAID). (2009, July). *Information and communication technologies (ICT) in education for development.* White paper. New York, NY: United Nations, Department of Economic and Social Affairs. Retrieved January 3, 2011, from http://www.un-gaid.org/tabid/868/ItemID/1551/language/en-US/Default.aspx

Green, L., & Trevor-Deutsch, L. (2002) *Women and ICTs for open and distance learning: Some experiences and strategies from the Commonwealth.* Vancouver, CA: The Commonwealth of Learning. Retrieved January 2, 2011, from http://www.col.org/SiteCollectionDocuments/women%20and%20ICTs.pdf

Gurumurthy, A. (2004). *Gender and ICTs*. Overview Report. UK: Bridge, Institute of Development Studies (IDS).

HaggardHarpie blog. (2007, May). *Keeping online in line: Online harassment and cyberfeminism. Can radical feminists create an effective online community that furthers feminist aims while remaining relatively free from misogynist harassment?* Retrieved January 6, 2011, from http://haggardharpie.blogspot.com/2007/05/keeping-online-in-line-online.html

Hampton, K. N., & Wellman, B. (1999). Netville online and off-line. Observing and surveying a wired suburb. *The American Behavioral Scientist, 43*(3), 475–492. doi:10.1177/00027649921955290

Hampton, K. N., & Wellman, B. (2000). Examining community in the digital neighborhood. Early results from Canada's wired suburb. In Ishida, T., & Isbister, K. (Eds.), *Digital cities: Technologies, experiences, and future perspectives* (pp. 194–208). Heidelberg, Germany: Springer-Verlag. doi:10.1007/3-540-46422-0_16

Hawthorne, S. (1999). Connectivity: Cultural practice of the powerful or subversion from the margins. In Hawthorne, S., & Klein, R. (Eds.), *Cyberfeminism: Connectivity, critique and creativity* (pp. 125–128). Melbourne, Australia: Spinifex.

Hawthorne, S. (1999). Cyborgs, virtual bodies and organic bodies: Theoretical feminist responses. In Hawthorne, S., & Klein, R. (Eds.), *Cyberfeminism: Connectivity, critique and creativity* (pp. 213–250). Melbourne, Australia: Spinifex.

Hawthorne, S., & Klein, R. (1999). Introduction: Cyberfeminism. In Hawthorne, S., & Klein, R. (Eds.), *Cyberfeminism: Connectivity, critique and creativity* (pp. 1–16). Melbourne, Australia: Spinifex.

Herring, S. C. (1992). *Gender and participation in computer-mediated linguistic discourse*. Paper presented at the Annual Meeting of the Linguistic Society of America, Philadelphia, PA.

Herring, S. C. (1993). Gender and democracy in computer-mediated communication. *Electronic Journal of Communication, 3*(2).

Herring, S. C. (1994). *Gender differences in computer-mediated communication: Bringing familiar baggage to the new frontier*. Keynote talk at American Library Association Annual Convention, Miami, FL.

Hiltz, S. R., & Turoff, M. (1978). *The network nation: Human communication via computer*. Reading, MA: Addison-Wesley.

Holmes, D. (1997). Introduction. In Holmes, D. (Ed.), *Virtual politics: Identity and community in cyberspace* (pp. 1–26). London, UK: Sage Publications.

Howard, P. E. N., Rainie, L., & Jones, S. (2002). Days and nights on the Internet. In Wellman, B., & Haythornthwaite, C. (Eds.), *The Internet in everyday life* (pp. 45–73). Oxford, UK: Blackwell. doi:10.1002/9780470774298.ch1

Inter-Agency Standing Committee. (2005). *Guidelines for gender-based violence interventions in humanitarian settings: Focusing on prevention of and response to sexual violence in emergencies* (Field Test Version). Geneva, Switzerland: Inter-Agency Standing Committee. Retrieved July 2, 2011, from http://www.who.int/hac/techguidance/pht/GBVGuidelines08.28.05.pdf

International Labor Organization – ILO. (2001). *Life at work in the information economy. The World Employment Report*. Geneva, Switzerland: ILO.

International Telecommunication Union. (2010). *Measuring the information society, Version 1.01*. Geneva, Switzerland: ITU.

International Telecommunications Union. (1999). *Challenge to the network - Internet for development*. Geneva, Switzerland: ITU.

International Telecommunications Union. (1999). *Trends in telecommunications reform*. Geneva, Switzerland: ITU.

Internet World Stats. (n.d.). Retrieved June 29, 2011, from http://www.Internetworldstats.com/stats.htm

Jenkins, H. (2006). *Convergence culture: Where old and new media collide* (pp. 1–25). New York, NY: New York University Press.

Katz, J. E., & Rice, R. E. (2002). *Social consequences of internet use: Access, involvement, and interaction*. Cambridge, MA: The MIT Press.

Kelly, J., & Blakesley, N. (2011). Localization 2.0. In S. Dutta, & I. Mia (Eds.), *The global information technology report 2010 – 2011, Transformations 2.0*, 10th Anniversary Edition (pp. 119 - 127). Geneva, Switzerland: World Economic Forum and INSEAD. Retrieved June 17, 2011, from http://reports.weforum.org/global-information-technology-report/content/pdf/wef-gitr-2010-2011.pdf

Kiesler, S., Siegal, J., & McGuire, T. (1984). Social psychological aspects of computer-mediated communication. *The American Psychologist*, *39*(10), 1123–1134. doi:10.1037/0003-066X.39.10.1123

Klein, R. (1999). If I'm a cyborg rather than a goddess will patriarchy go away? In Hawthorne, S., & Klein, R. (Eds.), *Cyberfeminism: Connectivity, critique and creativity* (pp. 185–213). Melbourne, Australia: Spinifex.

Kling, R., Lee, Y., Teich, A., & Frankel, M. S. (2000). Assessing anonymous communication on the Internet: Policy deliberations. In Baird, R. M., Ramsower, R., & Rosenbaum, S. E. (Eds.), *Cyberethics: Social and moral issues in the computer age* (pp. 124–126). New York, NY: Prometheus Books.

Kling, R., Lee, Y., Teich, A., & Frankel, M. S. (2000). Anonymous communication policies for the internet: Results and recommendations of the AAAS Conference. In R. M. Baird, R. Ramsower, & S. E. Rosenbaum (Eds.), *Cyberethics: Social and moral issues in the computer age* (pp. 97 - 99). New York, NY: Prometheus Books.

Kramarae, C., & Taylor, J. (1993). Women and men on electronic networks: A conversation or a monologue? In *Women, information technology, and scholarship* (pp. 52–61). Urbana, IL: Center for Advanced Study, University of Illinois at Urbana-Champaign.

Lievrouw, L. (1998). Our own devices: Heterotopic communication, discourse and culture in information society. *The Information Society*, *14*(2), 83–96. doi:10.1080/019722498128890

Lyon, D. (2005). A sociology of information. In Calhoun, C., Rojek, C., & Turner, B. (Eds.), *The Sage handbook of sociology* (pp. 223–236). London, UK: Sage Publications Ltd.

Mansell, R., & When, U. (1998). Innovative knowledge societies - Consequences of ICT strategies. The benefits, risks, and outcomes. In *Knowledge societies: Information technology for sustainable development* (pp. 241–255). Oxford, UK: Oxford University Press.

Marcelle, G. M. (2000). *Gender, justice and information and communication technologies (ICTs)*. Paper presented at the 44th Session of the Commission on the Status of Women, 28 Feb - 17 March 2000. New York, NY.

Matheson, K. (1991). Social cues in computer-mediated communication: Gender makes a difference. *Computers in Human Behavior*, *7*, 137–145. doi:10.1016/0747-5632(91)90003-J

McClellan, J. (1994, February 13). Netsurfers. *The Observer*.

Moghadam, V. M. (2005). *Globalizing women*. Baltimore, MD: Johns Hopkins University Press.

Parks, M., & Floyd, K. (1996). Making friends in cyberspace. *The Journal of Communication*, *46*, 80–97. doi:10.1111/j.1460-2466.1996.tb01462.x

Pink, D. (2006, February). The changing workplace. An interview with daniel pink. *eJournal USA, The Challenges Of Globalization, 11*(1). U.S. Department Of State. Retrieved January 06, 2011, from http://www.america.gov/publications/ejournalusa/0206.html

Pollock, S., & Sutton, J. (1999). Women click: Feminism and the Internet. In Hawthorne, S., & Klein, R. (Eds.), *Cyberfeminism: Connectivity, critique and creativity* (pp. 42–45). Melbourne, Australia: Spinifex.

Putnam, R. D. (2000). *Bowling alone: The collapse and revival of American community*. New York, NY: Simon and Schuster.

Rheingold, H. (1987, Winter). Virtual communities. *Whole Earth Review*, 78–81.

Rheingold, H. (1990, Summer). Travels in virtual reality. *Whole Earth Review*, 80–88.

Rheingold, H. (1991, Summer). Electronic democracy, the great equalizer. *Whole Earth Review*, 4–8.

Rheingold, H. (1993). Daily life in cyberspace. In *The virtual community: Homesteading on the electronic frontier* (pp. 57–109). Reading, MA: Addison-Wesley.

Rheingold, H. (2002). *Smart mobs: The next social revolution* (pp. 157–182). Cambridge, MA: Perseus Publishing.

Rueda-Sabater, E., & Garrity, J. (2011). The emerging internet economy: Looking a decade ahead. In S. Dutta, & I. Mia, (Eds.), *The global information technology report 2010 – 2011, Transformations 2.0,* 10th Anniversary Edition (pp. 33 - 47). Geneva, Switzerland: World Economic Forum and INSEAD. Retrieved June 17, 2011, from http://reports.weforum.org/global-information-technology-report/content/pdf/wef-gitr-2010-2011.pdf

Seabrook, J. (1997). *Deeper*. New York, NY: Simon & Schuster.

Shapiro, A. L. (1999). *The control revolution: How the internet is putting individuals in charge and changing the world we know*. New York, NY: Public Affairs.

Shenk, D. (1997). *Data smog: Surviving the information glut*. New York, NY: HarperCollins.

Shugar, D. (1995). *Separatism and women's community* (pp. 14–17). University of Nebraska Press.

Souter, D. (2010). *Towards inclusive knowledge societies: A review of UNESCO's action in implementing the WSIS outcomes*. United Nations Educational, Scientific and Cultural Organization (UNESCO), Communication and Information Sector. Retrieved July 6, 2011, from http://unesdoc.unesco.org/images/0018/001878/187832e.pdf.

Stoll, C. (1995). *Silicon snake oil: Second thoughts on the information highway*. New York, NY: Anchor Books.

Stoll, C. (1995, February 27). The Internet? Bah! *Newsweek*. Retrieved January 4, 2011, from http://www.newsweek.com/1995/02/26/the-internetInternet-bah.html

Sunstein, C. R. (2001). *Republic.com*. Princeton, NJ: Princeton University Press.

Truong, H.-A. (1993). *Gender issues in online communication*. Paper presented at a meeting of the Bay Area Women in Telecommunications.

UNESCO. (1997). *World communication report. The media and the challenges of the new technologies*. Paris, France: UNESCO Publishing.

UNESCO. (2000). *World education report*. Paris, France: UNESCO Publishing.

UNESCO. (2005). *World report. Towards knowledge societies*. Paris, France: UNESCO Publishing.

United Nations. (2000). *The world's women trends and statistics*. New York, NY: The United Nations.

United Nations. (2005). *The world's women 2005. Progress in statistics*. New York, NY: The United Nations.

United Nations. (2010). *The world's women 2010 Trends and Statistics*. New York, NY: The United Nations.

United Nations. (2011). *Report of the Special Rapporteur on the promotion and protection of the right to freedom of opinion and expression, Frank La Rue*. The United Nations: Human Rights Council. Retrieved June 18, 2011, from http://documents.latimes.com/un-report-Internet-rights/

Villalobos, V., & Monge-González, R. (2011). Costa Rica's efforts toward an innovation-driven economy: The role of the ICT sector. In S. Dutta, & I. Mia, (Eds.), *The global information technology report 2010 - 2011, Transformations 2.0,* 10th Anniversary Edition (pp. 119 - 127). Geneva, Switzerland: World Economic Forum and INSEAD. Retrieved June 17, 2011, from http://reports.weforum.org/global-information-technology-report/content/pdf/wef-gitr-2010-2011.pdf

Watson, N. (1997). Why we argue about virtual community: A case study of the Phish.net fan community. In Jones, S. G. (Ed.), *Virtual culture* (pp. 102–132). Thousand Oaks, CA: Sage.

Weiss, P. A. (1995). Introduction: Feminist reflections on community. In Weiss, P. A., & Friedman, M. (Eds.), *Feminism and community* (pp. 9–12). Philadelphia, PA: Temple University Press.

Wellman, B., & Gulia, M. (1999). Net surfers don't ride alone: Virtual communities as communities. In Wellman, B. (Ed.), *Networks in the global village* (pp. 331–367). Boulder, CO: Westview Press.

Willis Aronowitz, N. (2011). UN declares internet access a human right. What does this really mean? *Good Magazine*. Retrieved June 26, 2011, from http://www.good.is/post/un-declares-Internet-access-a-human-right-what-does-this-really-mean/

Wise, P. (1997). Always already virtual: Feminist politics in cyberspace. In Holmes, D. (Ed.), *Virtual politics: Identity and community in cyberspace* (pp. 179–197). London, UK: Sage Publications.

Youngs, G. (2000). Internet policies and states. In Kramarae, C., & Spender, D. (Eds.), *Routledge international encyclopedia of women. Global women's issues and knowledge* (pp. 1154–1156). New York, NY: Routledge.

KEY TERMS AND DEFINITIONS

Cyber Feminism: Represents a cyber-community guided by the feminist philosophy and values which aims to enhance feminist interactions and initiatives in the virtual life.

Cyberspace: A global network which reunites IT infrastructures, telecommunications networks and computer processing systems to facilitate individuals a complete social cyber experience characterized by interactivity, ideas exchange and sharing information.

Digital Divide: Describes the inequities between individuals from different parts of the world with respect to their access and use of Information and Communications Technologies (ICTs). The digital divide regards both the disparity in physical access to technologies and the resources, skills and training necessary to generate content on-line. The ICT sector is challenged today to focus not only on technological advances but on enhancing greater access to technologies for disadvantaged populations. The failure to balance hardware availability and Internet access inequities will deepen the already-existing economic gap between individuals around the world.

Gender Equality: Means equal valuing of the roles of women and men within societies. By reducing stereotypes, women and men can equally participate in and benefit the economic, social, cultural and political life.

Gender Stereotypes: Represent over-simple generalizations of the gender attributes, differences, and roles of women and men, which seldom reveal accurate information. When individuals express gender assumptions by default to others regardless of evidence to the contrary, they are perpetuating gender stereotyping. The most common female stereotypic role is that of a loving wife and mother, while the male one projects the husband as the financial provider of the family. These kinds of stereotypes are dangerous as they can negatively affect personal and professional growth.

Human Rights: Represent fundamental civil, political, economic, social and cultural rights that all people are entitled to regardless of nationality, sex, age, national or ethnic origin, race, religion or language. Human rights serve as trans-national norms to protect all individuals from political, legal and social abuses.

ICTs: Information and communications technologies - refer to all communication devices and applications utilized for producing and transmitting information. The ICT sector comprises: radio, television, cellular phones, computer and network hardware and software, satellite systems and the corresponding services and applications. Today, ICTs - especially Web 2.0 - are understood as a time -sharing function that would not only enhance many-to-many communication but also permit users to really benefit from the medium, to migrate from a mere sender-receiver model of communication towards one of interaction.

On-Line Networking: Depicts the set of activities related with generating and developing relationships on-line. The vast and generous cyber premises enhance us to learn about and connect with individuals that we don't have a chance to meet in real life.

Virtual Communities: Aim to reflect the cycle of a face-to-face society by enhancing people with similar interests to converge and unite across large distances through on-line means of interaction like: email, chat and public forms of communications like discussion forums, newsgroups or networking platforms. On-line communities can overcome time, space, class, age and sex to create a society and, focused on social experiences, individuals can experience other cultures and environments, besides of those where they physically live in.

Web 2.0: Associated with web applications - social networking platforms, blogs, wikis or video sharing sites - that facilitate interactive information sharing, interoperability, user-focused infrastructure and networking tools on the World Wide Web. These developments contributed essentially to changing the way women are perceived by the societies traditionally as web 2.0, unlike real life, enabled them to interact in a social media dialogue as creators of content and hence controllers of information within the virtual communities.

Chapter 14
Health Information Technology and Human Rights

Shane O'Hanlon
University of Limerick, Ireland

ABSTRACT

Information technology has the potential to transform healthcare and eradicate many of the inequities seen in the area. However, the use of electronic means to process sensitive health data poses significant risks. Electronic health records have been designed to be more secure than traditional paper records, but there have been notable cases where data has been lost, stolen, or viewed by unauthorised persons. Misuse of health information technology can result in severe violations of human rights. In particular, the right to privacy can be eroded by inappropriate protections, which still exist in some health systems. This chapter describes the rights framework in healthcare, analyses legal provisions for protection of health data, considers why such protections are necessary, outlines examples of rights violations, and proposes future directions.

INTRODUCTION

Of any area, healthcare ought to be a bastion of human rights protection. But there are notable violations in hospitals every day: from overcrowded wards that are devoid of dignity to paternalistic casting aside of patient autonomy. Healthcare is also concerned with the accumulation of some of the largest quantities of data on individuals. This may include very sensitive personal details. Traditionally the majority of health information has been in paper form but there is a trend towards digitisation. This process is expected to produce many improvements in patient care, including better patient safety and quality of care and better access to up-to-date medical information for practitioners. However there are inherent risks involved with this change which need to be

DOI: 10.4018/978-1-4666-1918-0.ch014

foreseen. Maintaining a high level of security is of particular concern as the flow of information increases. It is possible that information may be misused, for example by influencing insurance decisions, or affecting employment prospects. If risks such as these can be managed, then digitisation could be very fruitful. From a consumer point of view, information technology could facilitate access to valuable health data that can help the doctor-patient relationship to blossom. The availability of population level data could help to plan improvements in health services. Better access to healthcare could be achieved by using informatics to provide services according to need. These steps would help to advance healthcare as a human right. However, there is much advocacy to be done in order to achieve this. It is necessary to draw attention to the need for work in this area, with a detailed academic, legal and clinical analysis.

HEALTHCARE: A HUMAN RIGHT?

Whether healthcare is a human right has long been debated. Madden (2002) notes that such claims have either been to a "right to health" or a "right to healthcare". One of the earliest such references was made in the preamble to the 1946 Constitution of the World Health Organisation (WHO) which unequivocally states: "The enjoyment of the highest attainable standard of health is one of the fundamental rights of every human being" (World Health Organization, 1949).The WHO definition of health is comprehensive: "a state of complete physical, mental and social well-being and not merely the absence of disease or infirmity."

Two years later, the Universal Declaration of Human Rights was published. Article 25.1 states: "everyone has the right to a standard of living adequate for the health and well-being of himself and his family, including food, clothing, housing and medical care and necessary social services" (United Nations, 1949). This envisages a right to health as part of a socio-economic aspiration rather than a more quantifiable right to a particular standard of care or health status.

One of the most recently ratified instruments is the Charter of Fundamental Rights of the European Union. When the Treaty of Lisbon was signed in December 2009, the Charter became binding on EU states. It also begins by looking at health mainly from a socio-economic perspective, stating that "every worker has the right to working conditions which respect his or her health" (European Parliament & European Commission, 2001). However Article 35 goes on to say: "Everyone has the right of access to preventive health care and the right to benefit from medical treatment under the conditions established by national laws and practices. A high level of human health protection shall be ensured in the definition and implementation of all Union policies and activities."

The wording emphasises the importance of preventive healthcare, and seems to suggest that there is no recognised right to *health*, but rather a right to *access* to healthcare.

Health Records

Health records have existed at least since Roman times. They began as an aide-memoire and to help document progression between visits. Relatively little had changed about this process up until modern times. Although information technology is taking hold, many physicians still use paper records for their patients' medical details (Ford, 2009). One of the drivers for the change to electronic records was medical negligence litigation. The quality of physicians' handwritten entries has been criticised by the courts (Charatan, 1999). Documentation of clinical activity can be very poor, and there may be little reflection of the decision making process. In addition there is no scope for patients to make their own entries, for example to record their impression of their illness or care. The record has always been physician-centric; being composed, read, and guarded by them. Patient access has traditionally been restricted and they rarely have an opportunity to peruse or correct the entries. All of these factors mean that patients who have been harmed find it difficult to prove their case. Without accurate contemporaneous records, care can never be of the highest standard. Doctors are ethically obliged to maintain accurate, up to date and detailed records. Patients are entitled to demand this. They also have a right to be able to access it – although this operates differently from country to country, and depending on whether a health service is publicly or privately run.

For many years, the doctor was the only person capable of viewing a patient's record. That situation is changing with the advent of electronic records.

Health Information Technology

Over the past 10 years in particular, a revolution has been taking place in healthcare records. Increasing use of health information technology (the Electronic Health Record and its associated tools) has had a huge effect – not only on how medicine is practised, but also on how doctors and patients access medical information.

The aims of electronic health records (EHRs) are to provide a single repository for several different types of records, to increase accessibility, but also to improve security for such a personal document. In sites which still use paper records the old problems associated with this format persist: missing files, illegibility, difficulty locating entries, and large cumbersome charts. With a paper file, there is no capability for it to be used by multiple people simultaneously. Access control is often haphazard, with some ward areas having an unlocked storage trolley within public areas. There is no monitoring system to record who views what pieces of information. And of course, viewing can only take place wherever the chart is located.

The ongoing drive to make all records electronic has gained momentum because of several factors. Benefits have been shown in the areas of patient safety, clinical outcomes and length of stay (Kuperman, 2003). Prescription and dispensing errors have been reduced (Kaushal, 2003). The return on investment can be such that systems pay for themselves as health facilities become more efficient (Wang, 2003). The ability to instantly share records, and gain specialist opinion by telemedicine has changed medical practice (Scalvini, 2011). Coupled with a growing recognition that the patient or service user should be at the centre of the process, there is now a real possibility that EHRs can empower consumers of healthcare.

From a rights perspective such a move is long overdue. It is odd to think that health information technology has been the catalyst to such a significant shift in medical perspective. It demonstrates that technology triggers socio-technical change. What is clear is that the age of medical paternalism is over. The internet has helped to set information free, and healthcare is not immune from this process. But as well as strengthening and offering opportunities to human rights, there are weaknesses and obstacles inherent in the system we are building, and still testing. A sound legal framework is a necessity to protect our health information.

SAFEGUARDS FOR CONFIDENTIALITY OF HEALTH INFORMATION

In 'common law' countries such as the UK, Ireland, Australia and most of the United States, there is a general duty on doctors to respect the confidences of their patient. For example, in the English case of Hunter v Mann (1974), the court stated: "the doctor is under a duty not to disclose, without the consent of the patient, information which he, the doctor, has gained in his professional capacity."

As well as this judge-made law, most jurisdictions have applied legislation which protects personal data, although not necessarily specific restrictions for healthcare data. For example, within the European Union (where EU law supersedes national statutes and even national constitutional law) there are specific measures which have to be implemented by member states. An example is the Data Protection Directive 95/46/EU. This is a general law which protects privacy rights of individuals with respect to their personal data.

Personal data is defined in the Directive as "any information relating to an identified or identifiable natural person ('data subject'); an identifiable person is one who can be identified, directly or indirectly, in particular by reference to an identification number or to one or more factors specific to his physical, physiological, mental, economic, cultural or social identity." The mention of "physiological ... identity" alludes to the use of health data but the measure does not explicitly take the field into account.

There is specific consideration of the human rights impact of breaching confidentiality of health data: "data which are capable by their nature of infringing fundamental freedoms or privacy should not be processed unless the data subject gives his explicit consent ... however, derogations from this prohibition must be explicitly provided for in respect of specific needs, in particular where the processing of these data is carried out for certain health-related purposes by persons subject to a legal obligation of professional secrecy or in the course of legitimate activities by certain associations or foundations the purpose of which is to permit the exercise of fundamental freedoms."

The law protects personal data by regulating its processing, whether by manual or automatic means. Some of the protections include processing data fairly and lawfully, collecting it for specific and legitimate purposes, not allowing it to be used for other purposes, and not keeping it for longer than is necessary. These are all admirable assertions.

Data protection measures can be contrasted with Freedom of Information rules. This legislation, implemented in over 85 countries, usually permits citizens to request documents from government departments or public agencies. It has also made it easier for patients to access their personal health data being held by public healthcare facilities. This two-pronged approach seeks to protect data from those who are not entitled to access it, while clarifying the process for people to view their own data.

THE NEED FOR BETTER PROTECTION FOR HEALTHCARE DATA

As can be seen, the Data Protection measures in operation in the European Union do not deal specifically with the needs of health data. In the US, a federal law known as the Privacy Rule ensures that health information is protected (U.S. Department of Health and Social Services, 2011). In addition, the Security Rule specifies obligations for agencies that store health data electronically. Higher levels of protection are required for sensitive records which may contain details such as sexual orientation, HIV status, mental health diagnoses and previous termination of pregnancy. Despite this, one report by an advocacy group found that in the UK an average of 723 non-clinical staff in each Trust area had access to patients' health records (Big Brother Watch, 2010). Service users have emphasised that this is of importance to them. For example, interviews with patients in general practice demonstrated that they felt that administrative and secretarial staff should not have any access to their record. Some even expressed reservations about doctors who are not directly involved in their care having access (Carman, 1995). There are tensions between who should be able to access health data, and who actually can access it.

An in-depth review of similar studies concluded that patients are unaware of or misunderstand their right to medical confidentiality protections (Sankar, 2003). However such a right is not explicit in most national laws and those pleading it may have to rely on other protections such as the European Convention of Human Rights. The authors of the review found that a significant minority of patients distrust confidentiality protections and some even report that they delay or forgo medical care as a result. This highlights the need for clearer legal provisions, and better educated service users and clinicians. Indeed it has been reported that physicians need to change their attitude towards health information. Doctors have been known to inadvertently reveal personal health information on trains, in lifts and at parties (Siegler, 1982).

Access control is one possible strategy to employ when designing health information technology. For example, administrators may only need to view billing data, while doctors could view the full record. Implementing such a system requires consideration of how access can be restricted. Password control, biometric access and swipe card systems are all in use.

The greater use of health information technology also raises issues of consent. There are widely varying opinions on whether consent is required to digitise pre-existing health information or for health professionals to access electronic records. Paper records are typically opened without consulting with patients. However, in the UK recent experience with the "Summary Care Record" has shown that there was strong protest against permitting electronic records to be viewed without explicit consent.

Case Study: The Summary Care Record

In 2007 the National Health Service in England began uploading patient data to Summary Care Records (SCR) – an electronic record of basic patient information. The initial information included allergies and adverse reactions to drugs. The aim was to ensure that a brief record of important information was available if a patient attended an Accident and Emergency department in any hospital in the country. It was planned to add further information such as discharge summaries and more detailed health care records at a later stage.

At first the NHS decided to create a record for everyone, whether they wished to have one or not. Many advocacy groups and civil liberties organisations felt that this violated patient autonomy and the right to give or withhold consent for such a record. In response to these protests, the NHS announced an 'opt-out' system where patients were allowed a 12 week period in which to state their intention not to participate, after which records were created automatically. Around 4 million care records have now been made. A change in policy resulted in the requirement that clinicians now need to ask a patient for consent to access the SCR at the point of care.

A recent independent evaluation found that the system had yet to deliver significant benefits (Greenhalgh, 2010). Difficulties highlighted included: defining a minimum dataset of key health data, ensuring that the data is accurate and complete, and the need to gain informed consent from 50 million people.

The SCR also included a complementary project known as HealthSpace, where consumers were able to access and modify their own records. The independent evaluation found that there was no evidence of increased patient empowerment, improved health literacy or impact on data quality. This may have been because fewer than 200,000 people opened an account – a far lower response than expected. There has been continued heated debate as to the risks and benefits of the SCR and HealthSpace – rights advocates extol the ability to access one's own record, but bemoan the poor security. Significant opposition remains to further implementation (Anderson, 2010).

There are well founded concerns about allowing health staff to view patient records without appropriate consent. Even more worrying is the possibility that security is insufficient to prevent hacking. In Canada, a 2010 report by the Auditor General of British Columbia on the security of the Clinical Information System in Vancouver found serious weaknesses (Office of the Auditor General, 2010). Sensitive information was accessible to thousands of users as controls were not put in place. Hacking and extraction of information was found to be possible, and could occur even without the health authority's knowledge. There was no suitable access control or monitoring of what data had been viewed or copied. Already in 2009 there had been a report of a virus causing an EHR breach affecting several thousand patient records (HealthcareITNews, 2009). In this context it becomes questionable whether there really exists a right to privacy with electronic records, and how far it can be relied upon.

THE RIGHT TO PRIVACY OF ONE'S HEALTH INFORMATION

It has long been recognised that there is an obligation on healthcare staff not to reveal private health information. It is now clear that there is also a positive obligation to take steps to ensure that confidential information is not disclosed. For example, in the NHS the authorities had to appoint a Caldicott guardian whose role it is to safeguard the protection of confidential information. The higher degree of protection derived from the positive obligation emphasises that protective measures must be more than simply passive systems – it is incumbent on health services to do as much as possible to actively protect private health information. This was recognised by the European Court of Human Rights in the landmark case of I. v. Finland.

Case Study: I. v. Finland (European Court of Human Rights Case)

I. v. Finland (ECHR, 2008) concerned a complaint that there was access of personal medical records by unauthorised hospital staff. The applicant was a nurse who had been found to be HIV positive. The European Court of Human Rights upheld the applicant's argument that her medical data were not adequately secured against unauthorised access at the material time (para. 46). The Court stated that "the mere fact that the domestic legislation provided the applicant with an opportunity to claim compensation for damages caused by an alleged unlawful disclosure of personal data was not sufficient to protect her private life. What is required in this connection is practical and effective protection to exclude any possibility of unauthorised access occurring in the first place. Such protection was not given here" (para. 47). The respondent State (Finland) had "failed in its positive obligation under Article 8 § 1 of the Convention to ensure respect for the applicant's private life" (para. 48). There had therefore been a violation of Article 8 of the Convention (para. 49).

The judgment places a clear onus on parties to the Convention to have adequate protection to exclude unauthorised access. In countries such as the UK the European Convention of Human Rights has been incorporated into national law leading to a legal obligation to comply. The UK Human Rights Act 1998 allows someone to sue a public authority for damages where their convention rights have been breached.

PRIVACY AND OTHER RIGHTS

As with all human rights, there is a hierarchy which comes into play when setting privacy alongside other apparent rights. The following two cases represent notable and contrasting examples of how the right to privacy can be set against other competing rights such as public interest.

Case A

In December 2009, a television news report disclosed that the Irish Minister for Finance had cancer of the pancreas. This diagnosis had been recently received by the Minister but not publicly revealed. The broadcaster felt that it was in the national interest that the public be aware of this, as there was a continuing financial crisis. It was argued that the Minister's ability to deal with this might be affected by his illness.

However, the Minister did not approve of the publication of such a personal diagnosis without his agreement, and there was widespread criticism by the general public (Daily Telegraph, 2011). The announcement had been made only a day after Christmas. A later investigation by the Broadcasting Authority of Ireland found that the broadcast had not contravened guidelines and was indeed in the public interest. No action was taken against the broadcaster, or those who had access to the Minister's medical records, and no investigation was undertaken.

Case B

In 1995, soon after the death of French President Francois Mitterrand, his personal physician published a book detailing his diagnosis of prostate cancer and his treatment. This diagnosis had been concealed from the French public for over a decade. Days after the book's publication a Paris judge banned further distribution and instructed the seizure of all remaining copies. She based her judgment on a person's absolute right to privacy and declared that the book was "a particularly grave intrusion into the intimacy of family private life" (Dorozynski, 1996). Mitterrand's family pressed charges and the doctor was sentenced to 4 months in prison for breach of professional secrecy. The book was later permitted to be released.

These cases represent similar breaches of privacy but with radically different responses. The French judge noted that privacy is "absolute". In Ireland there is still no specific legislation which protects patients when their health information is breached, or punishes wrongdoers. Case A demonstrates that the media appear to be able to decide what information can be disclosed in the public interest, and argue the merits later. The assertion by the media that a cancer diagnosis may affect job performance is questionable – would it have been appropriate to act in a similar fashion if the diagnosis was erectile dysfunction, or asthma? In Z v Finland (ECHR, 1997), the European Court of Human Rights suggested that some types of medical information were more sensitive than others, and that the competing rights need to be stronger to allow disclosure. But it is far from clear who should make these decisions. Other judicial comments such as that of Lady Hale in the English case of Campbell v MGN (UKHL, 2004) add to the ambiguity: "Not every statement about a person's health will carry the badge of confidentiality or risk doing harm to that person's physical or moral integrity. The privacy interest in the fact that a public figure has a cold or a broken leg is unlikely to be strong enough to justify restricting the press's freedom to report it. What harm could it possibly do?" Despite this, it is clear that any disclosure potentially represents an erosion of the right to privacy, which may be justiciable under Article 8 of the ECHR.

The EU Data Protection Directive also considers disclosure in the public interest, but in a slightly different context:

"Member States must also be authorised, when justified by grounds of important public interest, to derogate from the prohibition on processing sensitive categories of data where important reasons of public interest so justify in areas such as public health and social protection - especially in order to ensure the quality and cost-effectiveness of the procedures used for settling claims for benefits and services in the health insurance system - scientific research and government statistics; whereas it is incumbent on them, however, to provide specific and suitable safeguards so as to protect the fundamental rights and the privacy of individuals."

This is mainly of interest for insurance claims, which can certainly contain sensitive personal health information and may be open to privacy abuses. This was clearly recognised in the United States, where the Health Insurance Portability and Accountability Act (HIPAA) sets out civil and criminal penalties for misuse or misappropriation of health information, with fines of up to $250,000 or up to 10 years in prison. Such severe penalties do not exist in many other jurisdictions, suggesting that a right to privacy of health information has not yet translated into firm legal protection.

PERSONAL ACCESS TO HEALTH DATA

The corollary of improving security is that the information flow should be improved to consumers of health services. The idea that a patient owns their own data is gaining acceptance. There is growing rights advocacy in the area and patients are becoming more adept at calling for access to their information, and the ability to control who accesses it and when. Disappointingly, the law appears to be lagging behind. In the contentious case of R v Department of Health ex p Source Informatics Ltd (All ER, 2000), the English Court of Appeal rejected the argument that a patient owns the information about themselves. In jurisdictions which have implemented Freedom of Information legislation, this ensures that patients can request copies of their record, but this may be rejected if there is a fear that disclosure could harm them. Private healthcare providers are not subject to this law. The Data Protection Directive states that "Member States may, in the interest of the data subject or so as to protect the rights and freedoms of others, restrict rights of access and information; whereas they may, for example, specify that access to medical data may be obtained only through a health professional". Thus access remains difficult, and this is particularly the case when medical negligence is alleged where court discovery may have to be ordered before access is granted.

There have been notable efforts, including the HealthSpace project mentioned above, although this had a poor uptake, possibility for technical reasons (Greenhalgh, 2010). The US health system Kaiser Permanente has had more success with its HealthConnect Online portal. Patient access to the secure messaging feature was associated with significantly reduced rates of primary care office visits and telephone contacts (Garrido, 2005). Other versions of personal health records have been introduced by private companies such as Microsoft and Google, although the latter has since withdrawn their service (Google, 2011). The drive behind such 'personal health records' is to empower consumers of healthcare and to help them manage their own health. Further work is necessary to convince health professionals of the benefits of appropriate information transparency, and to fully engage consumers.

RESEARCH AND SECONDARY USE OF DATA

Research involving personal health data has been performed for many years. There have been several international agreements which aimed to ensure tight regulation of research, particularly in light of human rights abuses perpetrated by Nazi doctors. The Nuremberg code, the Declaration of Helsinki and the Council of Europe's Convention for the Protection of Human Rights and Dignity of the Human Being with regard to the Application of Biology and Medicine all provide guidance on the principals of ethical research.

In addition, the development of Research Ethics Committees has added to the protection for patients and volunteers who enter trials. Proposed trials are now discussed by a multidisciplinary group who consider any ethical implications raised. Informed consent by participants in research is vital, and there must be adequate explanation of what the research consists of. Assurances that the participant can leave at any time without affecting normal patient care are also standard.

Unfortunately there is a lack of consensus regarding some of the measures provided for. Recent revisions of the Declaration of Helsinki have not been accepted by the US Food And Drug Administration (Goodyear, 2009). Another issue is whether consent needs to be obtained from patients to use their data in research, if it is anonymised. Denmark and Austria allow research on secondary uses of patient data without the need for prior consent, if the national data protection office approves of it. Other jurisdictions vary, with some requiring explicit consent. The UK and Ireland recommend consent where possible when using personal health information, but where this is impractical or burdensome then anonymised data should be employed.

In recent times there has been more emphasis placed on service users' opinions, and calls for greater explanation of what research entails. In one survey, two thirds of a public sample were unwilling to allow general practitioners (GPs) to decide when researchers could access identifiable personal health information. However almost 90% reported that they would agree to ongoing consent arrangements which would eliminate the need to obtain patient approval each time (Buckley, 2011). These findings accord with a similar study which noted that patients worried about lack of respect for their data, and lack of control over the process. Unauthorised access to data by external agencies is a common fear.

FUTURE RESEARCH DIRECTIONS

Health IT for Better Care

It is important to remember that several notable benefits to patient care have been demonstrated by employing information technology in healthcare. Despite the risks, great strides have been made – for example telemedicine now permits better monitoring of chronic diseases at home (Anker, 2011). Digital x-rays and scans are instantly reported on, facilitating rapid decision making, and can be viewed from anywhere. Electronic prescribing has improved patient safety and reduced adverse reactions (Kaushal, 2003). Ongoing research is likely to open up new areas of opportunity. One such example is the possibility for ambient assisted living systems to empower older people to live independently in their own home for a longer period of time. Investment in such technology may have a positive effect on patients' rights – but caution is required, and adequate usability testing of health information systems should be advocated for. For example, the traditional doctor-patient relationship is being replaced by a triadic doctor-computer-patient relationship (Pearce, 2011). It is necessary to ensure that the patient is not displaced from the centre of the consultation. Also, as with surgery or drugs, there is a risk of adverse events with technology. There is a real need to establish a regulatory framework for health information technology so that poor outcomes are avoided.

Health IT to Improve Rights Education

There have been reports of clinicians that have inappropriately discussed patients, or posted photographs on social networks such as Facebook (MacDonald, 2010). The concept of online professionalism is only just being recognised, but such sites may permit gross breaches of rights in rare cases. Fortunately the Internet and other forms of information technology also offer the possibility to complement traditional teaching and can be used to inform medical students. Existing cases serve as useful teaching material, and e-learning is a practical means of accessing large numbers of students in a cost effective way.

Health IT in the Developing World

In countries where human rights have not achieved their due level of recognition, health IT could be implemented to roll out nationwide health programmes. The prospect of a unique health identifier means that tracking displaced peoples is possible. In conflict areas, health IT could be used to improve care provision and allow expert opinion to be sought from distant sites, using telemedicine (Patterson, 2007).

The Need for More Research

Despite the concept of health information technology being proposed as a panacea for our healthcare needs from as far back as 1969, much work remains to be done. Important questions remain, such as

- Can health information technology be successfully used on a widespread basis to improve human rights?
- Will a level of security be achievable where rights breaches are not possible?
- Will health information technology aid the recognition of human rights in healthcare?

This is a rapidly changing area, and the future is exciting and full of potential. But we need to ensure that human rights remain firmly on the agenda as these developments come on stream.

CONCLUSION

With the great changes of the past decade or more in healthcare, health information technology has undergone significant development. Many noble and valuable interventions have been introduced and there has been a proliferation of work in the area. But there is limited recognition of the effect that such development has had on human rights. While there is potential to improve consumer access to personal health data and educational information, there also exists a very dangerous possibility that gross violations of privacy can occur, as health providers move to electronic storage of data. The fact that poor levels of protection have been found up to the present illustrates that more advocacy is required. Clinicians, developers, patients and rights advocates all have a role to play in ensuring that the future sees a safe rollout of protective measures. It would be a great pity if the recent gains were to be reversed by significant adverse events which could undermine the potential of information technology to transform healthcare for the benefit of all.

REFERENCES

Anderson, R. (2010). Do summary care records have the potential to do more harm than good? Yes. *British Medical Journal*, *340*, c3020. doi:10.1136/bmj.c3020

Anker, S. D., Koehler, F., & Abraham, W. T. (2011). Telemedicine and remote management of patients with heart failure. *Lancet*, *378*(9792), 731–739. doi:10.1016/S0140-6736(11)61229-4

Big Brother Watch. (2010). *Broken records*. Retrieved August 24th, 2011, from http://www.bigbrotherwatch.org.uk/brokenrecords.pdf

Buckley, B., Murphy, A. W., & MacFarlane, A. E. (2011). Public attitudes to the use in research of personal health information from general practitioners' records: a survey of the Irish general public. *Journal of Medical Ethics*, *37*, 50–55. doi:10.1136/jme.2010.037903

Campbell v MGN. (2004). UKHL 22, 157.

Carman, D., & Britten, N. (1995). Confidentiality of medical records: the patient's perspective. *The British Journal of General Practice*, *45*(398), 485–488.

Charatan, F. (1999). Family compensated for death after illegible prescription. *British Medical Journal*, *319*, 1456. doi:10.1136/bmj.319.7223.1456

Daily Telegraph. (2011). *Obituary: Brian Lenihan*. Retrieved August 24th, 2011, from http://www.telegraph.co.uk/news/obituaries/8569027/Brian-Lenihan.html

Dorozynski, A. (1996). Mitterrand's doctor stands trial for breach of secrecy. *British Medical Journal*, *312*(7046), 1559. doi:10.1136/bmj.312.7046.1559

European Parliament & European Commission. (2001). *Charter of fundamental rights of the European Union. Office for Official Publications of the European Communities*. Retrieved August 24th, 2011, from http://www.europarl.eu.int/charter/

Ford, E. W., Menachemi, N., Peterson, L. T., & Huerta, T. R. (2009). Resistance is futile: But it is slowing the pace of EHR adoption nonetheless? *Journal of the American Informatics Association*, *16*, 274–281. doi:10.1197/jamia.M3042

Garrido, T., Jamieson, L., Zhou, Y., Wiesenthal, A., & Liang, L. (2005). Effect of electronic health records in ambulatory care: Retrospective, serial, cross sectional study. *British Medical Journal*, *330*(7491), 581. doi:10.1136/bmj.330.7491.581

Goodyear, M., Lemmens, T., Sprumont, D., & Tangwa, G. B. (2009). The FDA and the declaration of Helsinki: A new rule seems to be more about imperialism than harmonisation. *British Medical Journal*, *338*, 1157–1158.

Google. (2011). *An update on Google Health and Google Powermeter*. Retrieved from http://googleblog.blogspot.com/2011/06/update-on-google-health-and-google.html

Greenhalgh, T., Hinder, S., Stramer, K., Bratan, T., & Russell, J. (2010). Adoption, non-adoption, and abandonment of a personal electronic health record: Case study of HealthSpace. *British Medical Journal*, *341*, c5814. doi:10.1136/bmj.c5814

Greenhalgh, T., Stramer, K., Bratan, T., Byrne, E., Russell, J., & Hinder, S. (2010). *The devil's in the detail: Final report of the independent evaluation of the Summary Care Record and HealthSpace programmes*. London, UK: University College London.

HealthcareITNews. (2009). *Virus blamed for HER breach*. Retrieved August 24th, 2011, from http://www.healthcareitnews.com/news/virus-blamed-ehr-breach-canada

Hunter v Mann, QB 772. (1972).

I. v. Finland. (2008). ECHR Judgment of 17 July 2008, Application No. 20511/03

Kaushal, R., Shojania, K. G., & Bates, D. W. (2003). Effects of computerized physician order entry and clinical decision support systems on medication safety: A systematic review. *Archives of Internal Medicine*, *163*, 1409–1416. doi:10.1001/archinte.163.12.1409

Kuperman, G. J., & Gibson, R. F. (2003). Computer physician order entry: Benefits, costs, and issues. *Annals of Internal Medicine*, *139*(1), 31–39.

MacDonald, J., Sohn, S., & Ellis, P. (2010). Privacy, professionalism and Facebook: A dilemma for young doctors. *Medical Education*, *44*(8), 805–813. doi:10.1111/j.1365-2923.2010.03720.x

Madden, D. (2002). *Medicine, ethics and the law*. Butterworths.

Office of the Auditor General. (2010). *The PARIS system for community care services: Access and security.* Office of the Auditor General of British Columbia (Report ; 2009/2010: 7)

Patterson, V., Swinfen, P., Swinfen, R., Azzo, E., Taha, H., & Wootton, R. (2007). Supporting hospital doctors in the Middle East by email telemedicine: something the industrialized world can do to help. *Journal of Medical Internet Research*, *9*(4), e30. doi:10.2196/jmir.9.4.e30

Pearce, C., Arnold, M., Phillips, C., Trumble, S., & Dwan, K. (2011). The patient and the computer in the primary care consultation. *Journal of the American Medical Informatics Association*, *18*(2), 138–142. doi:10.1136/jamia.2010.006486

R v Department of Health ex p Source Informatics Ltd. (2000). 1 All ER 786.

Robling, M. R., Hood, K., Houston, H., Pill, R., Fay, J., & Evans, H. M. (2004). Public attitudes towards the use of primary care patient record data in medical research without consent: A qualitative study. *Journal of Medical Ethics*, *30*, 104–109. doi:10.1136/jme.2003.005157

Sankar, P., Mora, S., Merz, J. F., & Jones, N. L. (2003). Patient perspectives of medical confidentiality. *Journal of General Internal Medicine*, *18*, 659–669. doi:10.1046/j.1525-1497.2003.20823.x

Scalvini, S., Rivadossi, F., Comini, L., Muiesan, M. L., & Glisenti, F. (2011). Telemedicine: The role of specialist second opinion for GPs in the care of hypertensive patients. *Blood Pressure*, *20*(3), 158–165. doi:10.3109/08037051.2010.542646

Siegler, M. (1982). Sounding boards. Confidentiality in medicine--A decrepit concept. *The New England Journal of Medicine*, *307*(24), 1518–1521. doi:10.1056/NEJM198212093072411

United Nations General Assembly. (1949). *Universal declaration of human rights*. Washington, DC: US Government Printing Office.

US Department of Health and Social Services. (2011). *Health information privacy.* Retrieved August 24th, 2011, from http://www.hhs.gov/ocr/privacy/hipaa/understanding/consumers/index.html

Wang, S. J. (2003). A cost–benefit analysis of electronic medical records in primary care. *The American Journal of Medicine*, *114*(5), 397–403. doi:10.1016/S0002-9343(03)00057-3

World Health Organization. (1949). *Constitution: Signed at the International Health Conference, New York, 22 July 1946.* Geneva, Switzerland: Author.

Z. v. Finland. (1996). ECHR Judgment of 25 February 1997, Application No. 9/1996/627/811

Conclusion

The importance of communication to the protection and the enjoyment of human rights is highlighted in the 2000 book, *Human Rights and the Internet* (Hick et al, 2000). Its efficacy has always had resonance with human rights campaigners and defenders, long before 'new' ICTs came into widespread use. Indeed this is exemplified by the iconic human rights organisation Amnesty International who marked their 50th anniversary in 2011 by conducting an 'old fashioned' letter writing campaign. As the Director of Amnesty International UK Kate Allen explained, "our original founding idea, of writing either to authorities that are abusing human rights or to people who are on the receiving end of that, can still be massively powerful" (Kappala-Ramsamy, 2011).

The chapters in this book provide evidence of the significance of communications – and information - for human rights in today's world. In exploring a range of contexts, both geographical and political, the authors provide positive and negative examples of their impact. However, whilst there is evidence of innovative adoption of ICTs in support of human rights, communications structures and information flows within the human rights community continue to reflect local political and socio-economic contexts, as well as global patterns of inequality and hegemony. ICTs are not – or never will be – the key driving force in the human rights community. But they can still be a powerful enabler of freedom and development.

In terms of opportunity, current trends follow a rich history of predecessors who have adopted and adapted mechanisms to use information and ICTs in their work. In drawing this book to a conclusion it is worth reflecting on the origins of some of this use of information and ICTs for human rights, as this provides not only a distant vision of the past but also the opportunity to understand how we devise our future strategies.

THE PIONEERS OF INFORMATION AND ICTs IN HUMAN RIGHTS – A VERY SHORT HISTORY

It is possible to start a review of the history of information use in support of human rights at many points. However, since this conclusion does not attempt to be definitive in terms of historical overview, we limit ourselves to providing a glimpse at the world as it unfolded from the late 1960s. This was an important time in terms of today's ICTs. Tools like the computer mouse, teleconferencing and email that are now commonplace were being demonstrated for the first time. And in 1969, Arpanet, the early research-oriented prototype of the Internet, was introduced.

In the period from the 1950s to the 1980s there was an exponential growth in the number of human rights organisation internationally - from approximately 38 in the 1950s to around 14,500 by 1984 (Pal and Alexander, 1998). This was undoubtedly a reaction to the then newly established United Nations and the enactment of the various human rights conventions. One such organisation was Amnesty International, who from their origins in 1961, understood and used information and communication to shine a light on abuses of human rights. For Amnesty the use of information as a campaigning and advocacy tool was central to protecting human rights, and it established the ground rules for their work and that of others. Credibility became a key to success, and information quality was therefore critical.

Metzl (1996) provides a clear account of expectations for information usage by human rights NGO's such as Amnesty International:

....accurate and timely information is an indispensable tool and an essential precondition for effective and responsive action and the promotion of human rights ...

The importance of timely, accurate, and verified information, communicated in an appropriate format, became a vital element of human rights action, and remains so to this day. Inaccurate or misleading information can shatter a human rights organisation's credibility, and once discredited their validity is difficult to regain. Even more importantly it leaves those subject to abuse, and the human rights defenders acting on their behalf, more vulnerable.

Martin Ennals, the first General Secretary of Amnesty International from 1968 -1980 recognised the significance of these values. He was a key participant in the creation of the Human Rights Information and Documentation Systems, International (HURIDOCS), as well as being the organisation's first President. HURIDOCS was formed following a meeting of key human rights organisations in Paris in 1979. The meeting participants noted that ICTs were being used by commercial companies and government agencies, and as HURIDOCS themselves now note, they saw that the community of non-governmental human rights organisations needed to familiarise themselves with these tools. If this was done collaboratively, resources could be pooled. (HURIDOCS, 2011a)

Ennals articulated the then thinking on information and technology as follows:

The rapid increase of interest in human rights coincides with the rapid development of information technology. Unless a common and universal system of communication is evolved, valuable information will be wasted, existing international machinery will not function, and implementation not monitored. (HURIDOCS, 2011b)

For three decades HURIDOCS has been a vital resource in providing tools and training to the rest of the human rights community. They have created thesauri and evidence systems, and built knowledge and capacity of frontline campaigners and defenders. Today they continue their role as an international NGO helping human rights organisations use information technologies and documentation methods to maximise the impact of their advocacy work.

As we can see in the chapters of this book, the vital nature of information, its communication, and the role it plays in advocacy, campaigning, recording abuses, defending victims, and holding perpetrators of human right violations to account remains paramount.

DRAWING CONCLUSIONS FROM THE CHAPTERS

One of the consistent messages in the first section of this book is the paradoxical nature of the use of ICTs for human rights. The authors provide evidence of the potential for both positive application and counter-balancing threats. Ultimately they indicate the need for care and critical engagement. The development, application and functionality of technology present opportunities to advance change in the political, economic, and social spheres of society. However these carry threats to economic well-being, social structure, freedom of speech and privacy. To try to counteract these, awareness of the positive and negative implications of technology is vital, as are opportunities for appropriation by civil society and the human rights community.

A number of the early chapters consider the role of corporations in the delivery of human rights, and in general they recognise that there are strengths and opportunities to be gained from their role in defending human rights. However Bowe et al. consider the consequences of providing such technology and the threat this may present to users, particularly young users within repressive states. Like the authors of the other two chapters in the opening section, their contribution highlights the question of balance and accountability in the use of technology. As new platforms and applications are adopted and appropriated, and the next generation of activists becomes engaged, it is vitally important to keep these in mind.

In their conclusions Dueck and Rempel consider the opposing paradoxes of digital utopia and dystopia, with promises of a wonderland or of chaos. They make the point that at the very least, organisations and their leaders must proceed with caution in today's technology wonderland. Their advice is reminiscent of the words of Brian Loader, who in his 1997 book, *The Governance of Cyberspace*, warned that we "avoid the hyperbole of both the utopian exhortations of the cyber-libertarians and the dystopian prophecies of the digital luddites" (Loader, 1997, p.ix).

Bowe et al. also draw attention to the need for sober assessment of the opportunities and risks posed by political organising via the Internet. Several chapters reflect the importance of this for human rights defenders and activists. Notley and Hankey demonstrate that while it is not possible to remove digital risks completely for human rights defenders, there are supports available to help them identify and address these risks. Other contributions, such as Douai's account of how YouTube videos elevate discussion of police corruption and human rights abuse to the public agenda, or Harrison's description of how statistical analysis of raw data can be used to shed light on mass atrocities, also demonstrate that creative solutions are being developed for and by the human rights movement using available technologies.

These trends show that the human rights community has, with the help of private sector companies, donors and specialist NGOs, appropriated ICTs for their effective use. Notwithstanding Weber's salutary reminder (in chapter 2) that economic inequalities need to be overcome for civil society to take proper advantage of the opportunities presented by ICTs, this bodes well for the future of human rights activism and advocacy.

In addition to the rich base of practitioner expertise driving the use of ICTs in support of human rights, there is now a growing academic discourse in the area. We are pleased to be able to bring these together in this book, and to contribute to further cycles of learning based on experiential insights. However, whilst patterns of ICT use and misuse are now becoming established vis-à-vis political rights and civil liberties, the trends and consequences relating to economic, social and cultural rights are more subtle and less well understood. According to Article 2 of the International Covenant on Economic, Social and Cultural Rights (ICESCR), state parties must undertake to take steps to the maximum of their available resources to achieve the full realisation of rights for everyone. These rights include the right to work, fair pay, adequate housing, social security, an adequate standard of living (including food, clothing and housing), education, the highest attainable standard of physical and mental health, and the right to take part in cultural life. But while everyone is entitled to these rights without discrimination, existing social and economic structures inevitably play a role. Technological innovations tend to reinforce existing social disparities, as was noted by Pippa Norris in her 2001 book on the digital divide (Norris, 2001). So while ICTs may improve access to services like education and healthcare for some, they do not do so for everyone.

Cristina Ionescu notes in chapter 13 that the existing power relations in different societies determine the extent to which ICTs can be accessed and used. Women all over the world have restricted access, especially in rural areas where the basic infrastructure is missing and the costs of deployment are high. In such areas ICTs tend to be used almost entirely by the men. Women are excluded because of a lack of opportunities for training in computer skills, domestic responsibilities, cultural restrictions on mobility, reduced income, or the lack of relevance to their existence.

The application of a human rights perspective to the use of ICTs in areas like education and mental health (Martin and McKay) and social service provision (Strömberg-Jakka) highlight a range of other issues, including cultural background, language, stigma and disclosure of personal information. Both of these chapters are set in countries that are politically stable and economically well-developed, in which individuals enjoy a high degree of freedom and social justice. They demonstrate that ICTs are not a panacea for problems of disadvantage, even in environments where technological access barriers have largely been removed. Indeed the potential of ICTs to eradicate inequities can sometimes even lead to violations of other human rights such as the right to privacy, as outlined by O'Hanlon (healthcare, chapter 14) and Rodrigues Filho (e-government, chapter 6). Such unintended consequences must be addressed at policy level by taking steps to minimise the gap between human rights standards and reality in relation to the enjoyment of human rights. One way for states to achieve this is through the development and use of appropriate human rights impact assessment (HRIA) tools. These are already used to measure the impact of policies, programmes, projects and interventions on human rights in a variety of settings including development projects, the activities of multinational corporations, trade agreements, and the activities of public authorities (Harrison, 2011). HRIAs include assessment of activities which directly and intentionally aim at changing a human rights situation as well as activities which may have unintended human rights consequences. They can assess activities that have happened in the past (ex post) as well as planned future activities (ex ante), and for this reason they are ideally suited to the evaluation of existing ICT policies and programmes, and the development of new ones.

The availability of applicable human rights impact assessment instruments to assess ICT policies would help to ensure that states not only secure the protection of human rights but also refrain from violating them – a point emphasised by Weber in chapter 2. They would also provide civil society with mechanisms, including context-specific indicators, to perform meaningful, evidence-based assessments of policy. Such assessments could lead to a deeper understanding of how ICT policies and programmes – including infrastructure investments and services deployment - impact on human rights in practice.

Finally, it is clear from the chapters in this book that research and development is still only at an early stage in terms of human rights and ICTs. Several areas requiring further work were identified – for example the enactment of policies to force technology companies to comply with their human rights commitments (Bowe et al.); studying the advantages and disadvantages of e-government in relation to human rights and democracy (Rodrigues Filho); assessing the efficiency of crowdsourcing in human rights monitoring (Heinzelman & Meier); and understanding how technology can be used to improve human rights in specific areas like healthcare (O'Hanlon). We hope from an academic perspective that the funding and resources required are made available over the coming years to address the many challenges already identified.

What of the Future?

In the introduction to this book we noted that the ubiquitous nature of ICTs means that government policies, private sector investment and civil society innovation can all impact on human rights, and that this trend will continue with both positive and negative consequences. However it is always difficult to predict the events that will shape such trends. Could we have envisaged the appalling 2001 attack on the Twin Towers of the World Trade Centre in New York that sparked the U.S. lead "war on terror"? Or could we with any certainty have predicted the 'Arab Spring' and the role that technology would play in it?

There are some things that we can predict however. It remains likely that oppressive regimes will continue to exist, as will torture, disappearances, false imprisonment and ongoing threats to freedom of speech and privacy. Poverty will not be eradicated in the near future, and denials of economic, social and cultural rights will continue to create inequality and suffering.

The world of technology and ICTs is a fast-changing and dynamic one. There are illustrations throughout this book of new and emerging applications and approaches that ten or even five years ago were still in their infancy. Human rights organisations and activists have always been early adapters of technology (Brophy and Halpin, 1999), with pioneers like Amnesty International and HURIDICS taking a lead in the past. Today the access to ICTs is perhaps easier for many people, notwithstanding the digital divide, economic and educational deprivation and the malign acts of some states in denying access. As a result, organisations, activists and even ordinary citizens can now use interactive and instant communications media to try to hold rights violators to account in real-time, or very nearly real-time.

As Web 3.0 become reality it brings with it opportunity for greater use of data in accessible and available formats for human rights activists. Key enablers are a maturing infrastructure for integrating Web data resources and the increased use of and support for the languages developed by the World Wide Web Consortium (W3C) according to Hendler (2009), who notes that

The base of Web 3.0 applications resides in the Resource Description Framework (RDF) for providing a means to link data from multiple websites or databases. With the SPARQL query language, a SQL-like standard for querying RDF data, applications can use native graph-based RDF stores and extract RDF data from traditional databases (Hendler, 2009)

One of the keys to leveraging this technology in any domain is what information scientists refer to as an ontology. This is the representation of knowledge as a set of concepts within a domain, and the relationships between them. The languages that allow meaning to be introduced can infer relationships and bring together information accurately, thereby allowing the integration of data from more than one source in a useable and effective way. For the human rights community, the opportunity to obtain data in such a way and to distribute it effectively have the potential to be of great benefit, if the challenges identified by Dueck and Rempel in chapter 1 can be overcome.

Beyond Web 3.0 which is really only emerging, there is talk of Web 4.0. With this we can expect information to be sent to a cloud, located in some unknown part of the world where it will be analyzed, filtered and responded to as needed. And we can look forward to increased real-time integration between individuals and the virtual worlds and objects they interact with (Kambil, 2008). These developments have the potential to be of even greater benefit to civil society whose real-world actions are curtailed by oppressive regimes. But they will also almost certainly be used by governments and corporations for purposes of manipulation and control.

Castells (2011) presents a stark analysis of the threat presented by current possibilities:

The expansion of Internet networks and the development of the Web 2.0 and Web 3.0 offer extraordinary business opportunities for the implementation of the strategy I call the commodification of freedom: enclosing the commons of free communication and selling people access to global communication networks in exchange for surrendering their privacy and becoming advertising targets (Castells, 2011, p. 782)

If we return to the thoughts expressed in the early chapters of this book (Dueck and Rempel, Weber, and Bowe, et al.) we can see the reasons for the concerns expressed and the warnings to be vigilant. Echoing the need for the technology to be accountable and accounted for, Ekine (2010) argues in *SMS Uprisings: Mobile Activism in Africa* that the technologies described

...do not follow the traditional development model, where technology tends to be shaped by the economic forces that created it. Instead the social change model is driven by the forces of people's local needs and is therefore more able to respond quickly and appropriately to specific events and political change. (Ekine, 2010)

The social change model is one that should sit comfortably with human rights activists and NGOs as early adopters and adapters of new technologies. For them it ensures that the new and exciting applications that are developed to support the protection and enjoyment of human rights are appropriate to their needs.

Moving beyond the technology, it is important to look at one of the most significant agendas for human rights, the UN Millennium Development Goals (MDGs). These provide a road map to address many of the major elements of structural violence within the world. However while there is acknowledged progress in some areas, the United Nations state in their own MDG Report of 2011:

Although many countries have demonstrated that progress is possible, efforts need to be intensified. They must also target the hardest to reach: the poorest of the poor and those disadvantaged because of their sex, age, ethnicity or disability. Disparities in progress between urban and rural areas remain daunting. (United Nations, 2011, p. 4)

There is a point of view that not only are the MDGs not achieving the required change, but that they are not even fit for purpose. Vandemoortele (2009) points out, for example, that instead of the MDGs targets being missed they are in fact missing the point.

The global MDG canon has not yet accepted that growing disparities within countries are the main reason why the world will miss the 2015 targets. Cognitive dissonance seems to prevail regarding growing inequalities. Instead, the global discourse has been dominated by a money-metric and donor-centric interpretation of the global targets. It has not yet started to mind the disparity gap. (Vandemoortele, 2009)

Against this background what can we expect of ICTs in addressing the continued inhumanity and the ongoing abuses of human rights? The trends evidenced in this book indicate that there is both grounds for optimism in the role that technology can play in addressing human rights abuses and violations, but also that there are dangers and difficulties. The early advice of Dueck and Rempel, which is echoed in different ways in other chapters, advises us that technology can be of benefit but that we must ensure it is used with care. We must also hold to account others who might use it or abuse it to deny human rights. Borrowing from Charles Dickens it might be said that the world of human rights is a little like the introduction to his work; *A Tale of Two Cities*:

It was the best of times, it was the worst of times, it was the age of wisdom, it was the age of foolishness, it was the epoch of belief, it was the epoch of incredulity, it was the season of Light, it was the season of Darkness, it was the spring of hope, it was the winter of despair, we had everything before us, we had nothing before us, we were all going direct to Heaven, we were all going direct the other way- in short, the period was so far like the present period, that some of its noisiest authorities insisted on its being received, for good or for evil, in the superlative degree of comparison only. (Dickens, 1859)

Whatever the future brings, it will be the responsibility of those who defend and campaign for human rights to be the noisiest authorities. As the rapid development of ICTs continues, there is a responsibility on everyone to ensure that they enhance human dignity rather than diminish it. The human rights community, which will always be an active stakeholder in ICT policies and possibilities, must ensure that this is so.

Edward F. Halpin
Leeds Metropolitan University, UK

John Lannon
University of Limerick, Ireland

REFERENCES

Brophy, P., & Halpin, E. F. (1999). Through the Net to freedom. *Journal of Information Science*, *25*(5), 351–364. doi:10.1177/016555159902500502

Castells, M. A. (2011). Network theory of power. *International Journal of Communication, 5*, 773–787. Retrieved December 23, 2011, from http://ascnetworksnetwork.org/wp-content/uploads/2010/02/IJoC-Network-Theory-2011-Castells.pdf

Dickens, C. (1859). *A tale of two cities*. Retrieved December 22, 2011, from http://www.literature.org/authors/dickens-charles/two-cities/book-01/chapter-01.html.

Ekine, S. (Ed.). (2010). *SMS uprising: Mobile activism in Africa*. Cape Town, South Africa: Pambazuka Press.

Harrison, J. (2011). Human rights measurement: Reflections on the current practice and future potential of human rights impact assessment. *Journal of Human Rights Practice*, *3*(2), 162–187. doi:10.1093/jhuman/hur011

Hendler, J. (2009). *Web 3.0 emerging*. Retrieved December, 23 2011, from http://ieeexplore.ieee.org/stamp/stamp.jsp?tp=&arnumber=4755170

Hick, S., Halpin, E. F., & Hoskins, E. (Eds.). (2000). *Human rights and the Internet*. Houndmills, UK: MacMillan Press Ltd.

HURIDOCS. (2011a). *Our history*. Retrieved December 19, 2011, from http://www.huridocs.org/our-history/

HURIDOCS. (2011b). *Vision, mission and goals*. Retrieved December 19, 2011 from http://www.huridocs.org/mission-vision-and-goals/

Kambil, A. (2008). What is your Web 5.0 strategy? *The Journal of Business Strategy*, *29*(6), 56–58. doi:10.1108/02756660810917255

Kappala-Ramsamy, G. (2011, 27 November). Amnesty: Why the pen is mightier than the sword. *The Guardian*. Retrieved December 27, 2011, from http://www.guardian.co.uk/world/2011/nov/27/amnesty-international-50-write-rights

Loader, B. J. (Ed.). (1997). *The governance of cyberspace: Politics, technology, and restructuring*. London, UK: Routledge. doi:10.4324/9780203360408

Metzl, J. (1996). Information technology and human rights. *Human Rights Quarterly*, *18*, 705–746. doi:10.1353/hrq.1996.0045

Norris, P. (2001). *Digital divide: Civic engagement, information poverty, and the Internet worldwide*. Cambridge, UK: Cambridge University Press.

Pal, L., & Alexander, C. J. (1998). *Digital democracy*. Toronto, Canada: Oxford University Press United Nations. (2011). *The millennium development goals report 2011*. Retrieved December 23, 2011, from http://www.un.org/millenniumgoals/11_MDG%20Report_EN.pdf

Vandemoortele, J. (2009). The MDG conundrum: Meeting the targets without missing the point. *Development Policy Review*, *27*(4), 355–371. doi:10.1111/j.1467-7679.2009.00451.x

Compilation of References

Abdel Dayem, M. (2009, Summer). Attempting to silence Iran's 'Weblogistan.' *Nieman Reports,* 42-44.

Abdo, L. (2007, November 12). *Morocco's 'video sniper' sparks a new trend.* Mennassat.com. Retrieved October 30, 2009, from http://www.menassat.com/?q=en/news-articles/2107-moroccos-video-sniper-sparks-new-trend

Abraham, S. (2011a, 30th June). *Do you want to be watched?* Retrieved July 4, 2011, from http://www.cis-india.org/advocacy/igov/blog/want-to-be-watched/

Abraham, S. (2011b, 16th June). *Privacy and security can co-exist.* Retrieved July 4, 2011, from http://india-today.intoday.in/site/story/privacy-and-security-can-co-exist/1/142179.html/

ACM Committee on Computers and Public Policy. (2011). *The risks digest: Forum on the risks to the public in computers and related systems.* Retrieved from October 20, 2011 from http://catless.ncl.ac.uk/Risks/

Aday, S., Farrell, H., Lynch, M., Sides, J., Kelly, J., & Zuckerman, E. (2010). *Blogs and bullets: New media in contentious politics.* Report from an event at US Institute of Peace and George Washington University's Institute for Public Diplomacy and Global Communication. Retrieved August 11, 2011, from http://www.usip.org/events/blogs-and-bullets-evaluating-the-impact-new-media-conflict

Aitchison, J. (1996). *International thesaurus of refugee terminology.* New York, NY: United Nations.

Akpan, P. I. (2003). Basic-needs to globalization: Are ICTs the missing link? *Information Technology for Development, 10,* 261–274. doi:10.1002/itdj.1590100405

Alfaro, V. (2009). Digital activism in the virtual public sphere, from silence and disruption to cyberactivisms 2.0. In *Proceedings of the WebSci '09: Society On-Line,* 18-20 March 2009, Athens, Greece. Retrieved August 21, 2011, from http://journal.webscience.org/174/

Al-Malky, R. (2007). Blogging for reform: The case of Egypt. *Arab Media and Society, 1.* Retrieved May 10, 2009, from http://www.arabmediasociety.com/articles/downloads/20070312143716_AMS1_Rania_Al_Malky.pdf

Alonso, G., Casati, F., Kuno, H., & Machiraju, V. (2004). *Web services: Concepts, architectures and applications.* Springer.

American Association for the Advancement of Science. (2000). *Political killings in Kosova/Kosovo, March-June 1999: A cooperative report by the Central and East European Law Initiative at the American Bar Association and the Science and Human Rights Program of the American Association for the Advancement of Science.* Washington, DC: Author.

Amnesty International. (2000). *Updated list of Amnesty International keywords.* London, UK: Amnesty International. AI Index: DOC 20/01/00. Internal document.

Amoretti, F. (2007). International organizations' ICTs policies: E-democracy and e-government for political development. *Review of Policy Research, 24*(4), 331–344. doi:10.1111/j.1541-1338.2007.00286.x

Anderson, K. (2007, January 12). YouTube exposes torture in Egypt. *The Guardian.* Retrieved June 5, 2010, from http://www.guardian.co.uk/news/blog/2007/jan/12/youtubeexposes1

Anderson, T. (Ed.). (2008). *Theory and practice of online learning*. Athabasca, Canada: Athabasca University. Available from http://www.aupress.ca/index.php/books/120146.

Anderson, R. (2010). Do summary care records have the potential to do more harm than good? Yes. *British Medical Journal*, *340*, c3020. doi:10.1136/bmj.c3020

Anker, S. D., Koehler, F., & Abraham, W. T. (2011). Telemedicine and remote management of patients with heart failure. *Lancet*, *378*(9792), 731–739. doi:10.1016/S0140-6736(11)61229-4

Arocena, R., & Senker, P. (2003). Technology, inequality, and underdevelopment: The case of Latin America. *Science, Technology & Human Values*, *28*(15), 15–33. doi:10.1177/0162243902238493

Article 29 Data Protection Working Party. (2009, December 1). *The future of privacy: Joint contribution to the consultation of the European Commission on the legal framework for the fundamental right to protection of personal data*. Retrieved from http://ec.europa.eu/justice/policies/privacy/news/docs/pr_01_12_09_en.pdf

Association for Progressive Communications (APC). (1995). *Proposal to the Fourth World Conference on Women*. Women's Networking Support Program. Retrieved January 6, 2011, from http://alainet.org/active/1041

Australia, S. A. N. E. (2003). *Why stigma matters*. Retrieved from www.sane.org/stigmamatter.html

Azimi, N. (2007, February 19). Blogging against torture. *The Nation*. Retrieved June 12, 2010, from http://www.thenation.com/article/bloggers-against-torture?page=0,2

Baber, Z. (2005). The unintended consequences of technological policy: The Internet and civil society in Singapore. In Baber, Z. (Ed.), *Cyberasia: The Internet and society in Asia* (pp. 57–74). Leiden, The Netherlands: Brill.

Backer, L. C. (2002). Global panopticism: States, corporations and the governance of monitoring regimes. *Indiana Journal of Global Legal Studies*, *15*(1). Retrieved October 11, 2010, from http://papers.ssrn.com/sol3/papers.cfm?abstract_id=1081242

Baehr, P. R. (1999). *Human rights: Universality in practice*. Basingstoke, UK: Palgrave Macmillan.

Bagdikian, B. H. (1992). *The media monopoly*. Boston, MA: Beacon Press.

Balancing Act. (2008). Web2.0 technology to help the Truth and Reconciliation Commission in Liberia. *Balancing Act*, *398*. Retrieved February 9, 2011, from http://www.balancingact-africa.com/news/en/issue-no-398/web-and-mobile-data/web20-technology-to/en

Ball, P. (1996). *Who did what to whom? Planning and implementing a large scale human rights data project*. Washington, DC: American Association for the Advancement of Science.

Ball, P. (1999). *Policy or panic? The flight of ethnic Albanians from Kosovo*. Washington, DC: American Association for the Advancement of Science.

Ball, P. (2000). *Refugee flow patterns in Kosovo, March-May 1999. American Association for the Advancement of Science, Science and Human Rights Program*. Washington, DC: American Association for the Advancement of Science.

Ball, P. (2001). Making the case: The role of statistics in human rights reporting. *Statistical Journal of the United Nations Economic Commission for Europe*, *18*(2-3), 163–174.

Ball, P., & Asher, J. (2002). Statistics and Slobodan. *Chance*, *15*(4), 17–25.

Ball, P., Cifuentes, R., Dueck, J., Gregory, R., Salcedo, D., & Saldarriago, C. (1994). *A definition of database design standards for human rights agencies*. Washington, DC: American Association for the Advancement of Science.

Ball, P., Girouard, M., & Chapman, A. (1997). Information Technology, information management, and human rights: A response to Metzl. *Human Rights Quarterly*, *19*(4), 836–859. doi:10.1353/hrq.1997.0035

Ball, P., Spirer, H., & Spirer, L. (Eds.). (2000). *Making the case: Investigating large scale human rights violations using information systems and data analysis*. Washington, DC: American Association for the Advancement of Science.

Ball, P., Tabeau, E., & Verwimp, P. (2007). *The Bosnian book of the dead: Assessment of the database (Full Report). Households in Conflict Network Research Design Note 5*. Brighton, UK: Institute of Development Studies, University of Sussex.

Banisar, D. (2006). The right to information in the age of information. In Jørgensen, R. F. (Ed.), *Human rights in the global information society* (pp. 73–89). Cambridge, MA: The MIT Press.

Barahona, C., & Levy, S. (2003). *How to generate statistics and influence policy using participatory methods in research: Reflections on work in Malawi 1999-2002*. Institute of Development Studies.

Barboza, D. (2010, August 13). New China search engine will be state-controlled. *New York Times*. Retrieved from http://www.nytimes.com/2010/08/14/technology/internet/14search.html

Barns, E. (2010, November 26). Mystery surrounds cyber missile that crippled Iran's nuclear weapons ambitions. *Fox News*. Retrieved from http://www.foxnews.com/scitech/2010/11/26/secret-agent-crippled-irans-nuclear-ambitions/

Baym, N. (1998). The emergence of online community. In Jones, S. (Ed.), *CyberSociety 2.0: Revisiting computer-mediated communication and community* (pp. 35–68). Thousand Oaks, CA: Sage.

BBC. (2010a). *Google releases censorship tools*. Retrieved July 1, 2011, from http://www.bbc.co.uk/news/technology-11380677/

BBC. (2010b, 8 October 2010). *United Arab Emirates will not ban Blackberries*. Retrieved June 16, 2011, from http://www.bbc.co.uk/news/technology-11499755/

Becker, L. B., Vlad, T., & Nusser, N. (2007). An evaluation of press freedom indicators. *International Communication Gazette*, *69*, 5–28. doi:10.1177/1748048507072774

Bell, D., & Klein, R. (1996). Beware: Radical feminists speak, read, write, organise, enjoy life, and never forget. In Bell, D., & Klein, R. (Eds.), *Radically speaking* (pp. XVII–XXX). Melbourne, Australia: Spinifex.

Beninger, J. R. (1987). Personalization of mass media and the growth of pseudo-community. *Communication Research*, *14*, 352–371. doi:10.1177/009365087014003005

Benkler, Y. (2006). *The wealth of networks: How social production transforms markets and freedom*. Yale University Press.

Bennett, W. L. (2003). Communicating global activism: Strengths and vulnerabilities of networked politics. *Information Communication and Society*, *6*(2), 143–168. doi:10.1080/1369118032000093860a

Berners-Lee, T. (1997). *Realising the full potential of the Web*. Retrieved October 11, 2011, from http://www.w3.org/1998/02/Potential.html

Berners-Lee, T. (1998). *What the semantic web can represent*. Retrieved October 20, 2011, from http://www.w3.org/DesignIssues/RDFnot.html

Best, M. L., Smyth, T. N., & Serrano-Baquero, D. (2009). *Designing for and with diaspora: A case study of work for the Truth and Reconciliation Commission of Liberia*. Paper presented in the Extended Abstracts of the ACM Conference on Human Factors in Computing Systems (CHI 2009), April 4-9, Boston, MA.

Big Brother Watch. (2010). *Broken records*. Retrieved August 24th, 2011, from http://www.bigbrotherwatch.org.uk/brokenrecords.pdf

Bi, J. (2001). The Internet revolution in China: The significance for traditional forms of communist control. *International Journal (Toronto, Ont.)*, *56*, 421–441. doi:10.2307/40203576

Bimber, B. (1998). The internet and political transformation: populism, community, and accelerated pluralism. *Polity*, *31*(1), 133–160. doi:10.2307/3235370

BlackBoxVoting.Org. (2007). Diebold's *PROCOMP subsidiary awarded largest order in Diebold history*. Retrieved October 11, 2010, from http://www.bbvforums.org/cgi-bin/forums/board-profile.cgi?action=rate&topic=70328&page=46799&post=33641

Blackwell, L. (1970, March). Tennessee Williams and the predicament of women. *South Atlantic Bulletin*, *35*(2), 9-14. Retrieved January 06, 2011, from http://www.jstor.org/pss/3197002

Block, D. (2001). *Broadcast and archive: Human rights documentation in the early digital age*. A paper presented at the Florida State University Conference on Human Rights, November, 1-3.

Bonneau, J., & Anderson, J. (2009, 20-22nd July, 2009). *Prying data out of a social network*. Paper presented at the 2009 Conference on Advances in Social Network Analysis and Mining, Athens, Greece. Retrieved June 1, 2011, from http://www.cl.cam.ac.uk/~jra40/publications/2009-ASONAM-prying-data.pdf/

Boyle, M., & Schmierbach, M. (2009). Media use and protest: The role of mainstream and alternative media use in predicting traditional and protest participation. *Communication Quarterly*, *57*(1), 1–17. doi:10.1080/01463370802662424

Bradley, G. (2006). *Social and community informatics: Humans on the net*. New York, NY: Routledge, Taylor & Francis.

Bragues, G. (2007). *Wiki-philosophizing in a marketplace of ideas: Evaluating Wikipedia's entries on seven great minds*. SSRN eLibrary. Retrieved from http://papers.ssrn.com/sol3/papers.cfm?abstract_id=978177

Brannagan, C. A. (2009). Corporate complicity in international humans rights violations: The tort of negligence as a civil remedy in Canadian courts. *Peace and Conflict Review*, *3*(2), 1–23.

Breindl, Y. (2010). Internet-based protest in European policymaking: The case of digital activism. *International Journal of E-Politics*, *1*(1), 57–72. doi:10.4018/jep.2010102204

British Broadcasting Corporation (BBC). (2007, January 10). *"Torture" victim jailed in Egypt*. Retrieved July 5, 2010, from http://news.bbc.co.uk/2/hi/6249027.stm

Brophy, P., & Halpin, E. (1999). Through the net to freedom: Information, the Internet and human rights. *Journal of Information Science*, *25*(5), 351–364. doi:10.1177/016555159902500502

Brown, A., & Grant, G. (2008). *Is it ICT "for development" or "in developing countries"? Exposing the duality of the ICT and development research agenda*. First Annual Workshop, ESCP-EAP University, Paris (13 October 2008).

Brunazo, F., & Cortiz, M. A. (2006). *Fraudes e defesas no voto eletronico*. São Paulo, Brazil: All-Print-Editora.

B'Tselem. (2008). *Activity report*. Retrieved from http://www.btselem.org/english/about_btselem/2008_Activity_Report.asp

Buckley, B., Murphy, A. W., & MacFarlane, A. E. (2011). Public attitudes to the use in research of personal health information from general practitioners' records: a survey of the Irish general public. *Journal of Medical Ethics*, *37*, 50–55. doi:10.1136/jme.2010.037903

Burgess, J., & Green, J. (2009). *YouTube: Online video and participatory culture*. Cambridge, UK: Polity Press.

Burris, S. (2006). Stigma and the Law. *Lancet*, *367*, 529–531. doi:10.1016/S0140-6736(06)68185-3

Butler, E. (2010). *Firesheep*. Retrieved October 20, 2011, from http://codebutler.com/firesheep

Caccia, I. (1993). *Human rights thesaurus*. Ottawa, Canada: Human Rights Research and Education Centre and Human Rights Internet.

Calhoun, C. (1991). Indirect relationships and imagined communities: Large-scale social integration and the transformation of everyday life. In Bourdieu, P., & Colemen, J. S. (Eds.), *Social theory for a changing society* (pp. 95–120). Boulder, CO: Westview Press.

Calhoun, C. (1998). Community without propinquity revisited: Communications technology and the transformation of the urban public sphere. *Sociological Inquiry*, *68*(3), 373–397. doi:10.1111/j.1475-682X.1998.tb00474.x

Caltech/MIT Study. (2001). *Residual votes attributable to technology – An assessment of the reliability of existing voting equipment*. Caltech/MIT Voting Technology Project. Retrieved from http://www.hss.caltech.edu/~voting/CalTech_MIT_Report_Version2.pdf

Campbell v MGN. (2004). UKHL 22, 157.

Carlsson, U. (2003). *The rise and fall of NWICO – And then? From a vision of international regulation to a reality of multilevel governance*. Paper presented at the EURICOM Colloquium, Information Society: Visions and Governance, 5-7 May 2003, Venice, Italy. Retrieved from http://www.bfsf.it/wsis/cosa%20dietro%20al%20 nuovo %20ordine.pdf

Carman, D., & Britten, N. (1995). Confidentiality of medical records: the patient's perspective. *The British Journal of General Practice*, *45*(398), 485–488.

Carroll, L. (1865). *Alice's adventures in Wonderland.* Retrieved October 20, 2011, from Project Gutenberg http://www.gutenberg.org/files/11/11-h/11-h.htm

Carroll, L. (1871). *Through the looking glass, and what Alice found there.* Retrieved October 20, 2011, from Project Gutenberg http://www.gutenberg.org/ebooks/12

Castells, M. (1997). An introduction to the information age. *City*, *7*, 6–16. doi:10.1080/13604819708900050

Castells, M. (2001). *The Internet galaxy: Reflections on the Internet, business, and society*. New York, NY: Oxford University Press.

Cavallaro, T., Foley, P., Saunders, J., & Bowman, K. (2005). *People with a disability in vocational education and training*. Adelaide, Australia: National Centre for Vocational Education Research (NCVER).

Cecez-Kecmanovic, D. (2001). *Critical research in information systems: The question of methodology.* Retrieved from http://is2.lse.ac.uk/asp/aspecis/20070023.pdf

Central Intelligence Agency. (2012). *The world factbook.* Retrieved July 12, 2011, from https://www.cia.gov/library/publications/the-world-factbook/rankorder/2153rank.html#top

Centre of Municipality Information. (2009). *Population censuses*. Retrieved from www.kunnat.net/attachment.asp?path=1;29;374;36984;148786;149482;150319.

Chakravartty, P. (2007). Governance without politics: Civil society, development and the postcolonial state. *International Journal of Communication*, *1*, 297–317.

Chapman, A. R., & Ball, P. (2001). The truth of truth commissions: Comparative lessons from Haiti, South Africa, and Guatemala. *Human Rights Quarterly*, *23*(4), 1–42. doi:10.1353/hrq.2001.0005

Charatan, F. (1999). Family compensated for death after illegible prescription. *British Medical Journal*, *319*, 1456. doi:10.1136/bmj.319.7223.1456

Charny, N. (2006, April 20). Chinese partner censors Skype text messages. *PCmag.com.* Retrieved from http://www.pcmag.com/article2/0,2817,1951637,00.asp

Chaves, H. (1989) *Confidentiality of information*. Paper presented at the Conference Human Rights Violations and Standard Formats: Towards Compatibility in Recording and Transferring Information, Utrecht, Netherlands.

Cheung, A., & Weber, R. H. (2008). Internet governance and the responsibility of ISPs. *Wisconsin International Law Journal*, *26*, 403–477.

CIA World Factbook. (2011). Retrieved from https://www.cia.gov/library/publications/the-world-factbook/

Cibelli, K., Hoover, A., & Krüger, J. (2009). *Descriptive statistics from statements to the Liberian truth and reconciliation commission. A Report by the Human Rights Data Analysis Group at Benetech and Annex to the Final Report of the Truth and Reconciliation Commission of Liberia*. Palo Alto, CA: Benetech.

Clark, C., & Kwinn, A. (2007). *The new virtual classroom: Evidence-based guidelines for synchronous e-learning*. Wiley.

Clark, J. D., & Nuno, S. T. (2006). Linking the Web and the street: Internet-based 'dotcauses' and the 'anti-globalization' movement. *World Development*, *34*(1), 50–74. doi:10.1016/j.worlddev.2005.09.001

Clay Shirky on institutions vs. collaboration on TED. (2005). Retrieved from http://www.ted.com/talks/clay_shirky_on_institutions_versus_collaboration.html

Clayton, M. (2011, January 3). Stuxnet attack on Iran nuclear program came about a year ago, report says. *Christian Science Monitor.* Retrieved from http://www.csmonitor.com/USA/2011/0103/Stuxnet-attack-on-Iran-nuclear-program-came-about-a-year-ago-report-says

Clinton, H. R. (2010, January 21). *Speech on Internet freedom*. Retrieved from http://www.state.gov/secretary/rm/2010/01/135519.htm

Coate, J. (1992). *Cyberspace innkeeping*. Retrieved January 3rd, 2011, from http://protovision.textfiles.com/computers/CYBERSPACE/inkeeping-cyberspace

Codesria, & Amnesty International. (2000). *Ukweli: Monitoring and documenting human rights violations in Africa: A handbook*. Amsterdam, the Netherlands: Council for the Development of Social Science Research in Africa, Amnesty International, African Books Collective (distributor).

Colley, A. (2007, March 6). States still hold out on YouTube. *Australian*. Retrieved from http://www.theaustralian.com.au/australian-it/states-still-hold-out-on-youtube/story-e6frgamx-1111113102808

Collins-Jarvis, L. (1995). *Explaining gender group discrimination in computer-mediated communication: A social identity approach*. Paper presented at the Annual Meeting of the Organization for the Study of Communication, Language, and Gender, Minneapolis, MN.

Collins, M., & Mowbray, C. (2005). Higher education ad psychiatric disabilities: National survey of campus disability services. *The American Journal of Orthopsychiatry*, *75*, 304–315. doi:10.1037/0002-9432.75.2.304

Colvin, M. (2010, September 30). Taking the twit out of Twitter and finding value. *The Punch: Australia's Best Conversation*. Retrieved December 14, 2010, from http://www.thepunch.com.au/articles/taking-the-twit-out-of-twitter-and-finding-value/

Committee to Protect Journalists. (2011, April 11). *More journalists held in Libya; blogger jailed in Egypt.* Retrieved from http://www.cpj.org/2011/04/more-journalists-held-in-libya-blogger-jailed-in-e.php

Concordia University President's Conference Series. (2009). *Bibliography*. Retrieved October 11, 2011, from http://www.concordia.ca/presidentsconferences/every-breath-you-take/bibliography/

Conley, M., & Patterson, C. (2000). Communication, human rights and cyberspace. In Hick, S., Halpin, E. F., & Hoskins, E. (Eds.), *Human rights and the internet* (pp. 211–225). New York, NY: Palgrave Macmillan.

Cordela, A. (2007). E-government: Towards the e-bureaucratic form? *Journal of Information Technology*, *22*, 265–274. doi:10.1057/palgrave.jit.2000105

Corrigan, P., River, L., London, R., Wasowski, K., & Campion, J. (2000). Stigmatizing attributions about mental illness. *Journal of Community Psychology*, *28*, 91–102. doi:10.1002/(SICI)1520-6629(200001)28:1<91::AID-JCOP9>3.0.CO;2-M

Cowie, J. (2011). Egypt leaves the Internet. *Renesys Blog*. Retrieved from http://www.renesys.com/blog/2011/01/egypt-leaves-the-internet.shtml

Crawford, K., & Lumby, C. (2011). *The adaptive moment: A fresh approach to convergent media in Australia*. The University of New South Wales. Retrieved July 1, 2011, from http://www.apo.org.au/node/24734/

Cross, N., & Jarvis, H. (2000). *New information technology applied to genocide research: The Cambodian genocide program*. Graduate School of Library and Information Science, Simmons College. Retrieved December 10, 2010, from http://web.simmons.edu/~chen/nit/NIT'98/98-019-Cross_Jarvis.html

Custard, H. A. (2008). The Internet and global civil society: Communication and representation within transnational advocacy networks. *Global Media Journal: Mediterranean Edition*, *3*(2), 1–11.

Dadian, D. (2011). *Internet access is now a human right*. Retrieved from http://blog.powersolution.com/internet-access-is-now-a-human-right/

Daily Telegraph. (2011). *Obituary: Brian Lenihan*. Retrieved August 24th, 2011, from http://www.telegraph.co.uk/news/obituaries/8569027/Brian-Lenihan.html

Dann, G. E., & Haddow, N. (2008). Just doing business or doing just business: Google, Microsoft, Yahoo! And the business of censoring China's Internet. *Journal of Business Ethics*, *79*, 219–234. doi:10.1007/s10551-007-9373-9

Davidson, L., Stayner, D., Nickou, C., Styron, T. H., Rowe, M., & Chinman, M. (2004). Simply to be let in. *Ausinetter, 20*(1).

Dayem, M. A., & Mahoney, R. (2010, February 16). *Human rights coverage spreads, despite government pushback*. The Committee to Protect Journalists, February 16, 2010. Retrieved June 10, 2010, from http://cpj.org/2010/02/human-rights-coverage-spreads.php

De Waal, M. (2010, December 10th 2010). The WikiLeaks effect - An end to free speech that radically offends? Retrieved June 1, 2011, from http://www.thedailymaverick.co.za/article/2010-12-10-the-wikileaks-effect-an-end-to-free-speech-that-radically-offends/

de Witte, B. (2005). The trajectory of fundamental social rights in the European Union. In de Búrca, G., & de Witte, B. (Eds.), *Social rights in Europe* (pp. 153–168). New York, NY: Oxford University Press. doi:10.1093/acprof:oso/9780199287994.003.0008

Deibert, R. J., Palfrey, J. G., Rohozinski, R., & Zittrain, J. (Eds.). (2008). *Access denied: The practice and policy of global internet filtering*. Cambridge, MA: The MIT Press.

Deibert, R. J., & Rohozinski, R. (2010). Risking security: Policies and paradoxes of cyberspace security. *International Political Sociology*, *4*, 15–32. doi:10.1111/j.1749-5687.2009.00088.x

Deibert, R., Palfrey, J., Rohozinski, R., & Zittrain, J. (Eds.). (2010). *Access controlled: The shaping of power, rights, and rule in cyberspace*. Cambridge, MA: MIT Press.

Deibert, R., & Rohozinski, R. (2010b). Risking security: Policies and paradoxes of cyberspace security. *International Political Sociology*, *4*, 15–32. doi:10.1111/j.1749-5687.2009.00088.x

Denham, E. (2009). *Report of findings into the complaint filed by the Canadian Internet Policy and Public Interest Clinic (CIPPIC) against Facebook Inc. under the Personal Information Protection and Electronic Documents Act*. Privacy Commissioner of Canada. Retrieved October 1, 2011, from http://www.priv.gc.ca/cf-dc/2009/2009_2008_0716_e.cfm/

Diamond, L. (2010). Liberation technology. *Journal of Democracy*, *21*(3), 69–83. doi:10.1353/jod.0.0190

DiMaggio, P., Hargittai, E., Neuman, W. R., & Robinson, J. P. (2001). Social implications of the Internet. *Annual Review of Sociology*, *27*(1), 307–336. doi:10.1146/annurev.soc.27.1.307

Dodge, M., & Kitchin, R. (2001). *Mapping cyberspace* (pp. 44–60). New York, NY: Routledge.

Doheny-Farina, S. (1996). *The wired neighborhood*. New Haven, CT: Yale University Press.

Donnelly, K. (2011). The failed education revolution. *The Drum Opinion*. Retrieved from http://www.abc.net.au/unleashed/43506.html

Dorozynski, A. (1996). Mitterrand's doctor stands trial for breach of secrecy. *British Medical Journal*, *312*(7046), 1559. doi:10.1136/bmj.312.7046.1559

Douai, A. (2009). Offline politics in the Arab blogosphere: Trends and prospects in Morocco. In Russell, A., & Echchaibi, N. (Eds.), *International blogging: Identity, politics, and networked publics*. New York, NY: Peter Lang.

Driscoll, M. (2007). Comment: Will YouTube sail into the DMCA's safe harbor or sink for Internet piracy? *The John Marshall Review of Intellectual Property Law*, 550. Retrieved June 2, 2010, from http://www.jmripl.com/Publications/Vol6/Issue3/Driscoll.pdf

Drummond, D. (January 12, 2010). A new approach to China. *Official Google Blog*. Retrieved from http://googleblog.blogspot.com/2010/01/new-approach-to-china.html

Dueck, J., Guzman, M., & Verstappen, B. (1993). *HURIDOCS events standard formats: A tool for documenting human rights violations*. Oslo, Norway: HURIDOCS.

Dueck, J., Guzman, M., & Verstappen, B. (2001a). *Micro-thesauri: A tool for documenting human rights violations*. Versoix, Switzerland: HURIDOCS.

Dueck, J., & Noval, A. M. (1993). *HURIDOCS events standard formats: Supporting documents*. Oslo, Norway: HURIDOCS.

Dunleavy, P., & Hood, C. (1994). From old public administration to new public management. *Public Public Money and Management*, *14*(3), 9–16.

Dunn, A. (2010). *Public as politician? The improvised hierarchies of participatory influence of the April 6th Youth Movement Facebook group*. Presented at the New Media/Alternative Politics Conference, Centre for Research in Arts, Social Sciences, and History, University of Cambridge.

Dutton, W. H., Dopatka, A., Hills, M., Law, G., & Nash, V. (2010). *Freedom of connection – Freedom of expression: The changing legal and regulatory ecology shaping the Internet*. Report prepared for UNESCO's Division for Freedom of Expression, Democracy and Peace.

Ebben, M. M. (1993). *Women on the Net: An exploratory study of gender dynamics on the soc.women computer network*. Paper presented at the Annual Meeting of the Organization for the Study of Communication, Language, and Gender. Temple, AZ.

Electronic Frontier Foundation. (2011). *Well-meaning "Privacy Bill of Rights" wouldn't stop online tracking*. Retrieved June 1, 2011, from https://www.eff.org/deeplinks/2011/04/well-meaning-privacy-bill-rights-could-codify/

Elkus, A. (November, 2009). Reflecting on Iran, social media, and change. *HuffPost World*. Retrieved October 4, 2011, from http://www.huffingtonpost.com/adam-elkus/reflecting-on-iran-social_b_355448.html

Elliot, T., & Frank, R. (1990). Social and interpersonal reactions to depression and disability. *Rehabilitation Psychology*, *35*, 135–147. doi:10.1037/h0079058

Ellis, S. (2006). *The mask of anarchy: The destruction of Liberia and the religious dimension of an African civil war*. New York, NY: New York University Press.

El-Naggar, M. (2010, June 25). Beating death in Egypt ignites protests over police brutality. *McClatchy Newspapers*. Retrieved June 30, 2010, from http://www.mcclatchydc.com/2010/06/25/96572/beating-death-in-egypt-ignites.html

Encyclopaedia Britannica. (n.d.). *Britannica online encyclopedia*. Retrieved December 17, 2010, from http://www.britannica.com/EBchecked/topic/186618/Encyclopaedia-Britannica

Endeshaw, A. (2004). Internet regulation in China: The never-ending cat and mouse game. *Information & Communications Technology Law*, *13*, 41–57. doi:10.1080/1360083042000190634

Eng, P. (1998, September/October). A new kind of cyberwar. *Columbia Journalism Review*, 20–21.

Etling, B., Kelly, J., Faris, R., & Palfrey, J. (2009). *Mapping the Arabic blogosphere: Politics, culture, and dissent*. Published by the Berkman Center for Internet and Society at Harvard University.

European Commission. (1999). *eEurope: An information society for all: A communication on a commission initiative for the special European Council of Lisbon, 23 and 24 March 2000*. Retrieved from http://www.support-eam.org/waec/docs/mod01/COM(1999)_687_eEurope_initiative_en.pdf

European Commission. (2002a). *eEurope 2005: An information society for all: An action plan to be presented in view of the Sevilla European Council, 21/22 June 2002*. Retrieved from http://eur-lex.europa.eu/LexUriServ/LexUriServ.do?uri=COM:2002:0263:FIN:EN:PDF

European Commission. (2002b). *eEurope 2005: Executive summary*. Retrieved from http://ec.europa.eu/information_society/eeurope/2002/news_library/documents/eeurope2005/execsum_en.pdf

European Commission. (2003). *eEurope 2002 final report*. Retrieved from http://eurlex.europa.eu/LexUriServ/site/en/com/2003/com2003_0066en01.pdf

European Commission. (2006a). *i2010 eGovernment action plan – Accelerating eGovernment in Europe for the benefit of all*. Retrieved from http://europa.eu/legislation_summaries/information_society/l24226j_en.htm

European Commission. (2008). *Vienna "e-inclusion" Ministerial Conference conclusion*. Retrieved from http://ec.europa.eu/information_society/events/e-inclusion/2008/doc/conclusions.pdf

European Commission. (2010a). *E-government usage by individuals by gender*.

European Commission. (2010b). *Europe's digital competitiveness report*. Retrieved from http://ec.europa.eu/digital-agenda

European Commisson. (2006b). *The Riga Ministerial Declaration on eInclusion*. Retrieved from http://ec.europa.eu/information_society/events/ict_riga_2006/doc/declaration_riga.pdf

European Communities. (2009). *Web 2.0: Where does Europe stand?* Luxembourg: Office for Official Publications of the European Communities.

European Parliament & European Commission. (2001). *Charter of fundamental rights of the European Union. Office for Official Publications of the European Communities*. Retrieved August 24th, 2011, from http://www.europarl.eu.int/charter/

European Parliament. (2010). *Information and Communications Technologies and Human Rights. Directorate-General for External Policies of the Union. (EXPO/B/DROI/2009/24, PE 410.207, June 2010)*. Brussels, Belgium: European Parliament.

Ezra, H., & Kempinski, Y. (2010, August 18). *First ever: Zionist Wikipedia editing course*. Israel National News. Retrieved November 18, 2010, from http://www.israelnationalnews.com/News/News.aspx/139189

Fabre, C. (2005). Social rights in European constitutions. In de Búrca, G., & de Witte, B. (Eds.), *Social rights in Europe* (pp. 15–28). New York, NY: Oxford University Press. doi:10.1093/acprof:oso/9780199287994.003.0002

Fahmi, W. S. (2009). Bloggers' street movement and the right to the city. (Re)claiming Cairo's real and virtual 'spaces of freedom.'. *Environment and Urbanization*, *21*(1), 89–107. doi:10.1177/0956247809103006

Faris, D. (2009). The end of the beginning: The failure of April 6th and the future of electronic activism in Egypt. *Arab Media & Society, 9.*

Fathi, M. (2009, June 23). In a death seen around the world, a symbol of Iranian protests. *New York Times*. Retrieved from http://www.nytimes.com/2009/06/23/world/middleeast/23neda.html

Feigenbaum, L. (2009). *The 2009 Semantic Web landscape.* Retrieved October 20, 2011, from http://www.slideshare.net/LeeFeigenbaum/semantic-web-landscape-2009

Fernback, J., & Thompson, B. (1995). *Virtual communities: Abort, retry, failure?* Retrieved January 4, 2011, from http://www.well.com/user/hlr/texts/VCcivil.html

Ferris, S., P. (1996). Women on-line: Cultural and relational aspects of women's communication in on-line discussion groups. *Interpersonal Computing and Technology*, *4*, 29.

Figliola, P. M., Nakamura, K. H., Addis, C. L., & Lum, T. (2010). *U.S. initiatives to promote global Internet freedom: Issues, policy, and technology*. Washington, DC: Congressional Research Service.

Fine, C. (2010). *Delusions of gender: How our minds, society and neurosexism create difference*. New York, NY: W. W. Norton and Company.

Fleming, S. (2002). Information and communication technologies (ICTs) and democracy development in the South: Potential and current reality. *The Electronic Journal of Information Systems in Developing Countries*, *10*(3), 1–10.

Ford, E. W., Menachemi, N., Peterson, L. T., & Huerta, T. R. (2009). Resistance is futile: But it is slowing the pace of EHR adoption nonetheless? *Journal of the American Informatics Association*, *16*, 274–281. doi:10.1197/jamia.M3042

Fors, M., & Moreno, A. (2002). The benefits and obstacles of implementing ICTs strategies for development from bottom-up approach. *Aslib Proceedings*, *54*(3), 198–206. doi:10.1108/00012530210441746

Foth, M., & Hearn, G. N. (2007). Networked individualism of urban residents: Discovering the communicative ecology in inner-city apartment buildings. *Information Communication and Society*, *10*(5), 749–772. doi:10.1080/13691180701658095

Fredriksson, T. (2011). The growing possibilities of information and communication technologies for reducing poverty. In S. Dutta, & I. Mia, (Eds.), *The global information technology report 2010 - 2011. Transformations 2.0,* 10th anniversary edition (pp. 69 - 79). Geneva, Switzerland: World Economic Forum and INSEAD. Retrieved June 17, 2011, from http://reports.weforum.org/global-information-technology-report/content/pdf/wef-gitr-2010-2011.pdf

Freedman, E., Shafer, R., & Antonova, A. (2010). Two decades of repression: The persistence of authoritarian controls on the mass media in Central Asia. *Central Asia and the Caucasus*, *11*(4), 94–110.

Friedrich, R., Peterson, M., & Koster, A. (2011). The rise of generation C. *Strategy+Business, 62*. Retrieved March 30, 2011, from http://www.strategy-business.com/article/11110?gko=64e54

Froese, K. (2006). *Nietzsche, Heidegger, and Daoist thought, crossing paths in-between* (pp. 185–219). Albany, NY: State University of New York Press.

Frontalini, J. (1990). Advantages of using standard formats. *HURIDOCS News*, *9*, 20–25.

Galperin, H., & Mariscal, J. (2007). *Digital poverty. Latin American and Caribbean perspectives*. International Development Research Centre: Practical Action Publishing. Retrieved December 15, 2010, from http://www.idrc.ca/openebooks/342-3/

Garrido, T., Jamieson, L., Zhou, Y., Wiesenthal, A., & Liang, L. (2005). Effect of electronic health records in ambulatory care: Retrospective, serial, cross sectional study. *British Medical Journal*, *330*(7491), 581. doi:10.1136/bmj.330.7491.581

Gartner. (2010). *Gartner says IT end-user spending in Brazil will reach $ 101.3 billion in 2010*. Press release. Retrieved October 10, 2010, from http://www.gartner.com/it/page.jsp?id=1435720

Garvie, J. (2007). Trading free speech. *Index on Censorship*, 42–50.

Gatto, A. (2011). *Multinational enterprises and human rights: Obligations under EU law and international law*. Cheltenham, UK: Edward Elgar Publishing Limited.

Geneva Declaration of Principles. (2003, December 12). *WSIS-03/GENEVA/DOC/4-E*. Retrieved from http://www.itu.int/wsis/docs/geneva/official/dop.html

Geneva Plan of Action. (2003, December 12). *WSIS-03/GENEVA/DOC/5-E*. Retrieved from http://www.itu.int/wsis/docs/geneva/official/poa.html

George, C. (2009). *Coercion unmasked: The counter-hegemonic impact of new media activism in Singapore*. Paper presented at the annual meeting of the International Communication Association, Chicago, IL.

George, A. L. (2009). Quantitative and qualitative approaches to content analysis. In Krippendorff, K., & Bock, M. A. (Eds.), *The content analysis reader* (pp. 144–155). Los Angeles, CA: Sage.

George, C. (2003). The Internet and the narrow tailoring dilemma for "Asian" democracies. *Communication Review*, *6*, 247–268. doi:10.1080/10714420390226270.002

Giddens, A. (1985). *The nation-state and violence*. Cambridge, UK: Polity Press.

Gilder, G. (1994). *Life after television*. New York, NY: Norton.

Giles, J. (2005). Internet encyclopaedias go head to head. *Nature*, *438*(7070), 900–901. doi:10.1038/438900a

Gillmor, D. (2011) Egypt's communications "kill switch." *Salon*. Retrieved from http://www.salon.com/technology/dan_gillmor/2011/01/28/egypt_kill_switch

Gingrich, N. (2009). *Has bureaucratic dictatorship arrived?* Retrieved October 11, 2010, from http://www.washingtonexaminer.com/opinion/columns/Has-bureaucratic-dictatorship-arrived_-8648572-79001702.html

Girard, B. in collaboration with The Friedrich Ebert Stiftung (FES) Geneva Office and Communication for Development Group Extension, Education and Communication Service Research, Extension and Training Division Sustainable Development Department. (2003). *The one to watch. Radio, new ICTs and interactivity* (pp. 1 - 165, 199 - 221). Rome, Italy: Food and Agriculture Organization of The United Nations.

Global Alliance for ICT and Development (GAID). (2009, July). *Information and communication technologies (ICT) in education for development*. White paper. New York, NY: United Nations, Department of Economic and Social Affairs. Retrieved January 3, 2011, from http://www.un-gaid.org/tabid/868/ItemID/1551/language/en-US/Default.aspx

Global Network Initiative. (2010). *Inaugural report 2010*. Retrieved from http://www.globalnetworkinitiative.org/cms/uploads/1/GNI_annual_report_2010.pdf

Global Voices Online. (2007, November 6). Egypt: Final chapter of a torture case. *Global Voices Online*. Retrieved June 2, 2010, from http://globalvoicesonline.org/2007/11/06/egypt-final-chapter-of-a-torture-case/

Goldkuhl, G. (2007). What does it mean to serve the citizen in e-services? *International Journal of Public Information Systems*, *3*(3), 135–159.

Goodyear, M., Lemmens, T., Sprumont, D., & Tangwa, G. B. (2009). The FDA and the declaration of Helsinki: A new rule seems to be more about imperialism than harmonisation. *British Medical Journal*, *338*, 1157–1158.

Google. (2010). *Google transparency report*. Retrieved from http://www.google.com/transparencyreport/governmentrequests/

Google. (2010). *Transparency report*. Retrieved June 1, 2011, from http://www.google.com/transparencyreport/governmentrequests/

Google. (2011). *An update on Google Health and Google Powermeter*. Retrieved from http://googleblog.blogspot.com/2011/06/update-on-google-health-and-google.html

Grabowicz, P. (2011). *Databases, data visualizations and map mashups: The Transition to digital journalism*. Retrieved November 1, 2011, from http://multimedia.journalism.berkeley.edu/tutorials/digital-transform/databases/

Granello, D., & Wheaton, J. (2001). Attitudes of undergraduate students towards persons with physical disabilities and mental illness. *Journal of Applied Rehabilitation Counseling*, *32*(3), 9–17.

Green, L., & Trevor-Deutsch, L. (2002) *Women and ICTs for open and distance learning: Some experiences and strategies from the Commonwealth*. Vancouver, CA: The Commonwealth of Learning. Retrieved January 2, 2011, from http://www.col.org/SiteCollectionDocuments/women%20and%20ICTs.pdf

Greenhalgh, T., Hinder, S., Stramer, K., Bratan, T., & Russell, J. (2010). Adoption, non-adoption, and abandonment of a personal electronic health record: Case study of HealthSpace. *British Medical Journal*, *341*, c5814. doi:10.1136/bmj.c5814

Greenhalgh, T., Stramer, K., Bratan, T., Byrne, E., Russell, J., & Hinder, S. (2010). *The devil's in the detail: Final report of the independent evaluation of the Summary Care Record and HealthSpace programmes*. London, UK: University College London.

Gregory, S. (2011). *The ethical engagements of human rights social media*. Retrieved May 11, 2011, from http://blog.witness.org/2010/11/the-ethical-engagements-of-human-rights-social-media/

Gregory, S. personal communication, December 18, 2010

Gregory, S. (2006). Transnational storytelling: Human rights, WITNESS, and video advocacy. *American Anthropologist*, *108*(1), 195–204. doi:10.1525/aa.2006.108.1.195

Gregory, S. (2010). Cameras everywhere: Ubiquitous video documentation of human rights, new forms of video advocacy, and considerations of safety, security, dignity and consent. *Journal of Human Rights Practice*, *2*(2), 191–207. doi:10.1093/jhuman/huq002

Grudgings, S. (2010). *Scandals dominate Brazil campaign as votes nears*. Retrieved September 14, 2010, from http://af.reuters.com/article/worldNews/idAFTRE68D5LJ20100914

Guinchat, C., & Minou, M. (1983). *General introduction to the techniques of information and documentation work*. Paris, France: United Nations Educational, Scientific and Cultural Organization.

Gupta, A. (2011, June 30th). *Analysis of the Privacy Bill, 2011*. Retrieved July 1, 2011, from http://www.iltb.net/2011/06/analysis-of-the-privacy-bill-2011/

Gurumurthy, A. (2004). *Gender and ICTs*. Overview Report. UK: Bridge, Institute of Development Studies (IDS).

Gutwirth, S. (2007). Biometrics between opacity and transparency. *Annali dell'Istituto Superiore di Sanita*, *43*(1), 61–65.

Guzman, M., & Verstappen, B. (1998). International Conference on Computerised Documentation of Human Rights Events: Mexico City, 11-13 November, 1998. *HURIDOCS News*, *22*, 11-17.

Guzman, D. R., Guberek, T., Shapiro, G. M., & Zador, P. (2009). *Studying millions of rescued documents: Sampling plan at the Guatemalan National Police Archive (GNPA). JSM Proceedings, Survey Research Methods Section*. Alexandria, VA: American Statistical Association.

Hachigian, N., & Wu, L. (2003). *The information revolution in Asia*. Santa Monica, CA: RAND.

HaggardHarpie blog. (2007, May). *Keeping online in line: Online harassment and cyberfeminism. Can radical feminists create an effective online community that furthers feminist aims while remaining relatively free from misogynist harassment?* Retrieved January 6, 2011, from http://haggardharpie.blogspot.com/2007/05/keeping-online-in-line-online.html

Hall, C., Slembrouck, S., & Sarangi, S. (2006). *Language practices in social work: Categorisation and accountability in child welfare*. London, UK: Routledge.

Hamdy, N. (2008). Building capabilities of Egyptian journalist in preparation for media in transition. *Journal of Arab and Muslim Media Research, 1*, 215–243. doi:10.1386/jammr.1.3.215_1

Hamdy, N. (2009). Arab citizen journalism in action: Challenging mainstream media, authorities and media laws. *Westminster Papers in Communication and Culture, 6*, 92–112.

Hamel, J. (2010). ICT4D and the human development and capabilities approach: The potentials of information and communication technology. *Human Development Research Paper Series, 37,* 1-77. Retrieved August 11, 2011, from http://ideas.repec.org/p/hdr/papers/hdrp-2010-37.html

Hampton, K. N., & Wellman, B. (1999). Netville online and off-line. Observing and surveying a wired suburb. *The American Behavioral Scientist, 43*(3), 475–492. doi:10.1177/00027649921955290

Hampton, K. N., & Wellman, B. (2000). Examining community in the digital neighborhood. Early results from Canada's wired suburb. In Ishida, T., & Isbister, K. (Eds.), *Digital cities: Technologies, experiences, and future perspectives* (pp. 194–208). Heidelberg, Germany: Springer-Verlag. doi:10.1007/3-540-46422-0_16

Hansen, S. A. (2000). *Thesaurus of economic, social, and cultural rights: Terminology and potential violations*. Washington, DC: American Association for the Advancement of Science and HURIDOCS.

Hardaker, D. (2008). *Putting the genie back in the bottle: Ruling regimes and the new media in the Arab world.* Lowy Institute for International Policy.

Harris, L. (2009). Electronic classroom, electronic community: Designing eLearning environments to foster virtual social networks and student learning. In Martin, J., & Hawkins, L. (Eds.), *Information communication technologies for human services education and delivery: Concepts and cases*. Hershey, PA: IGI Global. doi:10.4018/978-1-60566-735-5.ch006

Hassed, C., Sierpina, V., & Kreitzer, M. (2008). The health enhancement program at Monash University medical school. *EXPLORE: The Journal of Science and Healing, 4*(6), 394–397. doi:10.1016/j.explore.2008.09.008

Hawthorne, S. (1999). Connectivity: Cultural practice of the powerful or subversion from the margins. In Hawthorne, S., & Klein, R. (Eds.), *Cyberfeminism: Connectivity, critique and creativity* (pp. 125–128). Melbourne, Australia: Spinifex.

Hawthorne, S. (1999). Cyborgs, virtual bodies and organic bodies: Theoretical feminist responses. In Hawthorne, S., & Klein, R. (Eds.), *Cyberfeminism: Connectivity, critique and creativity* (pp. 213–250). Melbourne, Australia: Spinifex.

Hawthorne, S., & Klein, R. (1999). Introduction: Cyberfeminism. In Hawthorne, S., & Klein, R. (Eds.), *Cyberfeminism: Connectivity, critique and creativity* (pp. 1–16). Melbourne, Australia: Spinifex.

Hayner, P. (2007). *Negotiating peace in Liberia: Preserving the possibility of justice*. Geneva, Switzerland: Centre for Humanitarian Dialogue.

Hayner, P. (2011). *Unspeakable truths: Transitional justice and the challenge of truth commissions*. New York, NY: Routledge.

HealthcareITNews. (2009). *Virus blamed for HER breach*. Retrieved August 24th, 2011, from http://www.healthcareitnews.com/news/virus-blamed-ehr-breach-canada

Hedebro, G. (1982). *Communication and social change in developing nations – A critical view*. Iowa State University Press.

Heinonen, H.-M. (2009). *Byrokraatti vai asiakaspalvelija?: Kelan virkailijan toimintatavat ja roolit Yhteyskeskuksessa palvelukulttuurin muutosten keskellä* [Bureaucrat of customer servant?: The role and conduct of officials in Kela's customer contact centre over the course of a transition in the service culture]. Helsinki, Finland: Kela.

Herring, S. C. (1992). *Gender and participation in computer-mediated linguistic discourse*. Paper presented at the Annual Meeting of the Linguistic Society of America, Philadelphia, PA.

Herring, S. C. (1993). Gender and democracy in computer-mediated communication. *Electronic Journal of Communication, 3*(2).

Herring, S. C. (1994). *Gender differences in computer-mediated communication: Bringing familiar baggage to the new frontier*. Keynote talk at American Library Association Annual Convention, Miami, FL.

Herrmann, S. (2009, June 16), Social media in Iran. *BBC News*. Retrieved from http://www.bbc.co.uk/blogs/theeditors/2009/06/social_media_in_iran.html

Hick, S., Halpin, E. F., & Hoskins, E. (Eds.). (2000). *Human rights and Internet*. Basingstoke, UK: Macmillan.

Hildebrandt, M. (2009). Profiling and the rule of law. *Identity in the Information Society*, *1*(1), 55–70. doi:10.1007/s12394-008-0003-1

Hiltz, S. R., & Turoff, M. (1978). *The network nation: Human communication via computer*. Reading, MA: Addison-Wesley.

Holmes, D. (1997). Introduction. In Holmes, D. (Ed.), *Virtual politics: Identity and community in cyberspace* (pp. 1–26). London, UK: Sage Publications.

Hood, C. (1995). The "new public management" in the 1980s: Variations on a theme. *Accounting, Organizations and Society*, *20*(2/3), 93–109. doi:10.1016/0361-3682(93)E0001-W

Hoover, A. G. (2010). Learning the hard way at the ICTY: Statistical evidence of human rights violations in an adversarial information environment. In Smeulers, A. (Ed.), *Collective violence and international criminal justice: An interdisciplinary approach*. Antwerp, Belgium: Intersentia.

Howard, P. E. N., Rainie, L., & Jones, S. (2002). Days and nights on the Internet. In Wellman, B., & Haythornthwaite, C. (Eds.), *The Internet in everyday life* (pp. 45–73). Oxford, UK: Blackwell. doi:10.1002/9780470774298.ch1

Howard, P. N. (2010). *The digital origins of dictatorship and democracy: Information Technology and political Islam*. Oxford University Press. doi:10.1093/acprof:oso/9780199736416.001.0001

Howe, J. (2009). *Crowdsourcing: Why the power of the crowd is driving the future of business*. New York, NY: Three Rivers Press.

Howland, T. (2008). How El Rescate, a small nongovernmental organization, contributed to the transformation of the human rights situation in El Salvador. *Human Rights Quarterly*, *30*(3), 703–705. doi:10.1353/hrq.0.0019

Human Rights Committee. (2010). *Draft general comment No. 34* (Upon completion of the first reading by the Human Rights Community). (CCPR/C/GC/34/CRP.5). Retrieved from http://www.aidh.org/ONU_GE/Comite_DH/Images/Projet.pdf

Human Rights Council. (2009, March 20). *Promotion and protection of all human rights, civil, political, economic, social and cultural rights, including the right to development*. Retrieved from http://www.un.org/disabilities/default.asp?id=1477

Human Rights Watch (HRW). (2006, December 22). *Egypt: Hold police accountable for torture*. Human Rights Watch. Retrieved May 12, 2010 from http://www.hrw.org/english/docs/2006/12/23/egypt14924.htm

Human Rights Watch (HRW). (2010, January 24). *World report 2010: Abusers target human rights messengers*. Human Rights Watch. Retrieved August 12, 2010, from http://www.hrw.org/en/news/2010/01/24/world-report-2010-abusers-target-human-rights-messengers

Human Rights Watch. (2006). *China report*. Retrieved from http://www.hrw.org/english/docs/2006/01/18/china12270.htm

Human Rights Watch. (2009). *Brazil: Prosecute dictatorship-era abuses. Landmark international decision provides powerful push for accountability*. Retrieved October 25, 2010, from http://www.hrw.org/en/news/2009/04/14/brazil-prosecute-dictatorship-era-abuses

Hunter v Mann, QB 772. (1972).

HURIDOCS. (1990). Human rights violations and standard formats: towards compatibility in recording and transferring information. *HURIDOCS News*, *9*, 38.

I. v. Finland. (2008). ECHR Judgment of 17 July 2008, Application No. 20511/03

Ibahrine, M. (2008). Mobile communication and sociopolitical change in the Arab world. In Katz, J. (Ed.), *Handbook of mobile communication studies*. Cambridge, MA: The MIT Press.

Inter-Agency Standing Committee. (2005). *Guidelines for gender-based violence interventions in humanitarian settings: Focusing on prevention of and response to sexual violence in emergencies* (Field Test Version). Geneva, Switzerland: Inter-Agency Standing Committee. Retrieved July 2, 2011, from http://www.who.int/hac/techguidance/pht/GBVGuidelines08.28.05.pdf

International Labor Organization – ILO. (2001). *Life at work in the information economy. The World Employment Report*. Geneva, Switzerland: ILO.

International Telecommunication Union. (2010). *Measuring the information society, Version 1.01*. Geneva, Switzerland: ITU.

International Telecommunications Union. (1999). *Challenge to the network - Internet for development*. Geneva, Switzerland: ITU.

International Telecommunications Union. (1999). *Trends in telecommunications reform*. Geneva, Switzerland: ITU.

Internet WorldStats. (n.d.). Retrieved June 29, 2011, from http://www.Internetworldstats.com/stats.htm

Isenwater, W., Lanham, W., & Thornhill, H. (2002). The college link program: Evaluation of a supported education initiative in Great Britain. *Psychiatric Rehabilitation Journal*, *26*, 43–50. doi:10.2975/26.2002.43.50

Ishani, M. (2011). The hopeful network. *Foreign Policy*. Retrieved from http://www.foreignpolicy.com/articles/2011/02/07/the_hopeful_network

Ishay, R. M. (2008). *The history of human rights: From ancient times to the globalization era* (2nd ed.). Berkeley, CA: University of California Press.

Isherwood, T. (2008). A new direction or more of the same? Political blogging in Egypt. *Arab Media and Society*, *6*.

Izard, J. (2004). *Impediments to sound use of formative assessment (and actions we should take to improve assessment for learning)*. The Australian Association for Research in Education (AARE). Retrieved from http://www.aare.edu.au/04pap/iza04905.pdf

Jacko, J. A., & Sears, A. (Eds.). (2007). *The human-computer interaction handbook: Fundamentals, evolving technologies and emerging applications (human factors and ergonomics)*. Atlanta, GA: CRC Press.

Jamison, K. R. (2006). The many stigmas of mental illness. *Lancet*, *367*, 533–534. doi:10.1016/S0140-6736(06)68187-7

Jardin, X. (2007). Future web: Exporting censorship. *Index on Censorship*, •••, 80.

Jelin, E. (1994). The politics of memory: The human rights movement and the construction of democracy in Argentina. *Latin American Perspectives*, *81*(4:2), 38-58. Retrieved October 1, 2011 from http://www.latinamericanstudies.org/argentina/human-rights.pdf

Jenkins, H. (2006). *Convergence culture: Where old and new media collide* (pp. 1–25). New York, NY: New York University Press.

Jiang, S. (2010). China blanks Nobel Peace Prize searches. *CNN*. Retrieved from http://www.cnn.com/2010/WORLD/asiapcf/10/08/china.internet/index.html.

John, D. (2004). Quantifying the impact of equity overlap in VET. In K. Bowman (Ed.), *Equity in vocational education and training*, (pp. 1-18). Adelaide, Australia: National Centre for Vocational Education Research (NCVER).

Johnson, B. (2011) How Egypt switched off the internet. *GigaOm*. Retrieved from http://gigaom.com/2011/01/28/how-egypt-switched-off-the-internet/

Jones, M. (2011). *The human cost of the social media revolution*. Amnesty International. Retrieved May 11, 2011, from http://www.amnesty.org.au/features/comments/25268/

Jorgensen, R. F. (2006). *Human rights in the global information society*. Cambridge, MA: The MIT Press.

Jørgensen, R. F. (2006). The right to express oneself and to seek information. In Jørgensen, R. F. (Ed.), *Human rights in the global information society* (pp. 53–72). Cambridge, MA: The MIT Press.

Joyce, M. (2010). *Digital activism decoded: The new mechanics of change*. International Debate Education Association. Retrieved from http://www.meta-activism.org/book/

Juhila, K. (2009). Sosiaalityön selontekovelvollisuus. [Accountability in social work]. *Janus*, *17*(4), 296–312.

Kalathil, S., & Boas, T. (2003). Open networks, closed regimes: The impact of the Internet on authoritarian rule. *First Monday, 8*(1). Retrieved May 12, 2010, from http://firstmonday.org/htbin/cgiwrap/bin/ojs/index.php/fm/article/view/1027/948

Karjalainen, J., Hiilamo, H., & Raivio, H. (2003). *Harkinta toimeentulotuessa: Toimeentulotuen muutosten arvioinnin väliraportti* [Discretion in social assistance: The interim report of the evaluation of the changes in social assistance]. Helsinki, Finland: Stakes.

Kaskisaari, M., Tammelin, M., Hirvonen, J., Hämeenaho, P., Ilmarinen, K., & Vartiainen, A. (2010). *Kuntalaisten arvioita sosiaalipalveluista: ParasSos-tutkimus Keski-Suomen yhdeksän kunnan alueella. [Residents' assessments of social services: ParasSos study in Central Finland, of nine municipalities in the region].* Helsinki, Finland: Terveyden ja hyvinvoinnin laitos.

Katz, J. E., & Rice, R. E. (2002). *Social consequences of internet use: Access, involvement, and interaction.* Cambridge, MA: The MIT Press.

Kauppinen, T. M., & Raivio, H. (2007). *Toimeentulotuen uusien asiakkaiden jonotilanne 2007* [The queues of new applicants in social assistance 2007]. Helsinki, Finland: Stakes.

Kaushal, R., Shojania, K. G., & Bates, D. W. (2003). Effects of computerized physician order entry and clinical decision support systems on medication safety: A systematic review. *Archives of Internal Medicine, 163*, 1409–1416. doi:10.1001/archinte.163.12.1409

Keck, M. E. (1998). *Activists beyond borders: Advocacy networks in international politics.* Cornell University Press.

Keck, M. E., & Sikkink, K. (1998). *Activists beyond borders: Advocacy networks in international politics.* Ithaca, NY: Cornell University Press.

Kelly, J., & Blakesley, N. (2011). Localization 2.0. In S. Dutta, & I. Mia (Eds.), *The global information technology report 2010–2011, Transformations 2.0,* 10th Anniversary Edition (pp. 119 - 127). Geneva, Switzerland: World Economic Forum and INSEAD. Retrieved June 17, 2011, from http://reports.weforum.org/global-information-technology-report/content/pdf/wef-gitr-2010-2011.pdf

Kelly, J., & Etling, B. (2008). *Mapping Iran's online public: Politics and culture in the Persian blogosphere.* Retrieved from http://cyber.law.harvard.edu/publications/2008/Mapping_Irans_Online_Public

Kerchen, N. (2009). The welfare system of Luxembourg. From past dependency to the European approach. In Schubert, K., Hegelich, S., & Bazant, U. (Eds.), *The handbook of European welfare systems* (pp. 310–327). London, UK: Routledge.

Kerry, J. (2011). *Proposed Commercial Bill of Privacy Rights.* Retrieved July 1, 2011, from http://kerry.senate.gov/work/issues/issue/?id=74638d00-002c-4f5e-9709-1cb51c6759e6&CFID=79733731&CFTOKEN=26547080/

Kessler, G. (2011, October 16). *An overview of cryptography.* Retrieved October 20, 2011, from http://www.garykessler.net/library/crypto.html

Khaled, M. (2009). *An Egyptian blogger crosses red lines.* Committee for the Protection of Journalists. Retrieved August 11, 2011, from http://www.cpj.org/blog/2009/10/an-egyptian blogger-crosses red lines.php

Khamis, S., & Vaughn, K. (2011). Cyberactivism in the Egyptian revolution: How civic engagement and citizen journalism tilted the balance. *Arab Media & Society, 13.* Retrieved from http://www.arabmediasociety.com/?article=769

Kia, A. A. (2008). Iranian youth online: Identity between traditional and modern lifestyles. *3CM. Journal of Community, Citizen's and Third Sector Media and Communication, 4*, 28–36.

Kiesler, S., Siegal, J., & McGuire, T. (1984). Social psychological aspects of computer-mediated communication. *The American Psychologist, 39*(10), 1123–1134. doi:10.1037/0003-066X.39.10.1123

Klein, H. (2006). The right to participation and the information society. In Jørgensen, R. F. (Ed.), *Human rights in the global information society* (pp. 185–196). Cambridge, MA: The MIT Press.

Klein, H. K., & Myers, M. D. (1999). A set of principles for conducting and evaluating interpretive field studies in information systems. *Management Information Systems Quarterly, 23*(1), 67–94. doi:10.2307/249410

Klein, R. (1999). If I'm a cyborg rather than a goddess will patriarchy go away? In Hawthorne, S., & Klein, R. (Eds.), *Cyberfeminism: Connectivity, critique and creativity* (pp. 185–213). Melbourne, Australia: Spinifex.

Kling, R., Lee, Y., Teich, A., & Frankel, M. S. (2000). Anonymous communication policies for the internet: Results and recommendations of the AAAS Conference. In R. M. Baird, R. Ramsower, & S. E. Rosenbaum (Eds.), *Cyberethics: Social and moral issues in the computer age* (pp. 97 - 99). New York, NY: Prometheus Books.

Klinger, J., & Silva, R. (2010). *Combining found data and surveys to measure casualties. Human rights data analysis group*. Palo Alto, CA: Benetech.

Kling, R., Lee, Y., Teich, A., & Frankel, M. S. (2000). Assessing anonymous communication on the Internet: Policy deliberations. In Baird, R. M., Ramsower, R., & Rosenbaum, S. E. (Eds.), *Cyberethics: Social and moral issues in the computer age* (pp. 124–126). New York, NY: Prometheus Books.

Knowles, E. (Ed.). (2006). *A dictionary of phrase and fable*. Oxford University Press. Retrieved October 1, 2011, from http://www.oxfordreference.com/views/ENTRY.html?subview=Main&entry=t214.e7762

Kovach, B., & Rosenstiel, T. (2007). *The elements of journalism*. New York, NY: Three Rivers Press.

Kramarae, C., & Taylor, J. (1993). Women and men on electronic networks: A conversation or a monologue? In *Women, information technology, and scholarship* (pp. 52–61). Urbana, IL: Center for Advanced Study, University of Illinois at Urbana-Champaign.

Kuivalainen, S. (2004). *A comparative study on last resort social assistance schemes in six European Countries*. Helsinki, Finland: Stakes.

Kulikova, S. V., & Perlmutter, D. D. (2011). Blogging down the dictator? The Kyrgyz revolution and *Samizdat* websites. In Freedman, E., & Shafer, R. (Eds.), *After the czars and Commissars: Journalism in authoritarian post-Soviet Central Asia* (pp. 263–286). East Lansing, MI: Michigan State University Press. doi:10.1177/1748048507072777

Kuperman, G. J., & Gibson, R. F. (2003). Computer physician order entry: Benefits, costs, and issues. *Annals of Internal Medicine*, *139*(1), 31–39.

Kushner, A. (n.d.). *Crowdsourcing: The trailer*. Retrieved from http://crowdsourcing.typepad.com/cs/2008/07/crowdsourcing-t.html

La Rue, F. (2011). *Report of the Special Rapporteur on the promotion and protection of the right to freedom of opinion and expression*. Retrieved from http://www2.ohchr.org/english/bodies/hrcouncil/docs/17session/A.HRC.17.27_en.pdf

Laaksonen, K. (2006). Mitä mieltä asiakkaat ovat Kelan lomakkeista? [What do the service users think about the application forms of The Social Insurance Institution of Finland?]. In M-L Sorjonen & L. Raevaara (Eds.), *Arjen asiointia. Keskusteluja Kelan tiskin äärellä* (pp. 35-47). Helsinki, Finland: Kotimaisten kielten tutkimuskeskus.

Lai, O. K. (2004). Differential e-mobilization and cyberspace in East Asian economies: Contours of emerging cyber-activism and (anti)democratic regimes in the information society. In Abbott, J. P. (Ed.), *The political economy of the Internet in Asia and the Pacific: Digital divides, economic competiveness, and security challenges* (pp. 33–56). Westport, CT: Praeger.

Land, M. B. (2009). Peer producing human rights. *New York Law School Legal Studies, Research Paper Series 09/10 #12*, 1-25.

Landler, M., & Stelter, B. (2009, June 16). Washington taps into a potent new force in diplomacy. *New York Times*. Retrieved from http://www.nytimes.com/2009/06/17/world/middleeast/17media.html

Lannon, J. (2010). The role of information and communications technologies in human rights monitoring and advocacy. In Martin, J., & Hawkins, L. (Eds.), *Information communication technologies for human services education and delivery: Concepts and cases* (pp. 184–200). doi:10.4018/978-1-60566-735-5.ch012

Lee, T. (2004). Emulating Singapore: Towards a model for Internet regulation in Asia. In Gan, S., Gomez, J., & Johannen, U. (Eds.), *Asian cyberactivism: Freedom of expression and media censorship* (pp. 162–199). Bangkok, Thailand: Friedrich Naumann Foundation.

Ley, M. (2009). DBLP - Some lessons learned. *Proceedings of the VLDB Endowment,* Vol. 2, (pp. 1493-1500). Retrieved October 20, 2011 from http://www.vldb.org/pvldb/2/vldb09-98.pdf.

Lievrouw, L. (1998). Our own devices: Heterotopic communication, discourse and culture in information society. *The Information Society*, *14*(2), 83–96. doi:10.1080/019722498128890

Lima, V. A. (2010). *Os escândulos políticos midiáticos*. Observatório da Imprensa. Retrieved from http://www.observatoriodaimprensa.com.br/artigos.asp?cod=607JDB002

Line, F. (2010). *United Arab Emirates: Young activists arrested for organising peaceful protest via BlackBerry*. Retrieved December 10th, 2010, from http://www.frontlinedefenders.org/node/12818/

Link, B., & Phelan, J. (2006). Stigma and its public health implications. *Lancet*, *367*, 528–529. doi:10.1016/S0140-6736(06)68184-1

Li, S. (2010). The online public space and popular ethos in China. *Media Culture & Society*, *32*, 63–83. doi:10.1177/0163443709350098

Lodge, J. (2007). Freedom, security and justice: The thin end of the wedge for biometrics? *Annali dell'Istituto Superiore di Sanita*, *43*(1), 20–26.

Lunn, B. (2010, April 27). *Does Facebook Open Graph help or hinder the Web of trust?* Retrieved October 20, 2010, from http://semanticweb.com/does-facebook-open-graph-help-or-hinder-the-web-of-trust_b595

Lyle, G., & Ng, Y. (2011). *WITNESS media archive cataloging manual section 1*. Retreived October 1, 2011, from http://www.witness.org/sites/default/files/downloads/witness_catalogingmanual_2011aug_sect1.pdf

Lynch, J. (2010). *Applying for citizenship? U.S. Citizenship and Immigration Wants to Be Your "friend*." Retrieved January 10th, 2011, from https://www.eff.org/deeplinks/2010/10/applying-citizenship-u-s-citizenship-and/

Lynch, M. (2007). Blogging the new Arab public. *Arab Media & Society*, *1*, 1–30. Retrieved May 10, 2009, from http://www.arabmediasociety.com/?article=10

Lyon, D. (2005). A sociology of information. In Calhoun, C., Rojek, C., & Turner, B. (Eds.), *The Sage handbook of sociology* (pp. 223–236). London, UK: Sage Publications Ltd.

Lyons, M., & Ziviani, J. (1995). Stereotypes, stigma and mental illness: Learning form fieldwork experiences. *The American Journal of Occupational Therapy.*, *49*, 1002–1008. doi:10.5014/ajot.49.10.1002

MacDonald, J., Sohn, S., & Ellis, P. (2010). Privacy, professionalism and Facebook: A dilemma for young doctors. *Medical Education*, *44*(8), 805–813. doi:10.1111/j.1365-2923.2010.03720.x

MacKinnon, R. (2005, June 17). Screenshots of Censorship. *RConversation Blog*. Retrieved from http://rconversation.blogs.com/rconversation/2005/06/screenshots_of_.html

Maclay, C. M. (2010). Protecting privacy and expression online: Can the Global Network Initiative embrace the character of the Net? In Deibert, R., Palfrey, J., Rohozinski, R., & Zittrain, J. (Eds.), *Access controlled: The shaping of power, rights, and rule in cyberspace* (pp. 87–108). Cambridge, MA: MIT Press.

Madden, D. (2002). *Medicine, ethics and the law*. Butterworths.

Maneschy, O. (2000). Fraude eletronica nas eleições. *Jus Navigandi, Teresina, 5*(45). Retrieved from http://jus.uol.com.br/revista/texto/1552/fraude-eletronica-nas-eleicoes

Mansell, R., & Nordenstreng, K. (2006). Great media and communication debates: WSIS and the MacBride report. *Information Technologies and International Development*, *3*(4), 15–36. doi:10.1162/itid.2007.3.4.15

Mansell, R., & When, U. (1998). Innovative knowledge societies - Consequences of ICT strategies. The benefits, risks, and outcomes. In *Knowledge societies: Information technology for sustainable development* (pp. 241–255). Oxford, UK: Oxford University Press.

Marcelle, G. M. (2000). *Gender, justice and information and communication technologies (ICTs)*. Paper presented at the 44th Session of the Commission on the Status of Women, 28 Feb - 17 March 2000. New York, NY.

Marshall, T. H. (1950). *Citizenship and social class*. Cambridge, MA: The University Press.

Martin, J., & Oswin, F. (2008). Post-secondary education: Opportunities and obstacles for recovery. In K. Kellehear & V. Miller (Eds.), *Looking toward excellence in mental health care in 2020*. New South Wales, Australia: TheMHS.

Martin, J., McKay, E., & Thomas, T. (2004). Recovery from mental illness: Lifestyle and employment options, in harvesting hope: Across the lifespan, contemporary the MHS in Mental Health Services. In K. Kellehear & M. Teesson (Eds.), *The MHS Conference* (pp. 193 -197). ISBN No: 0-9757653-0-2

Martin, J. (2006). *Mental health practice*. Charnwood, UK: Ginninderra Press.

Martin, J. (2010). Stigma and student mental health. *Higher Education Research & Development*, *29*(3), 259–274. doi:10.1080/07294360903470969

Matheson, K. (1991). Social cues in computer-mediated communication: Gender makes a difference. *Computers in Human Behavior*, *7*, 137–145. doi:10.1016/0747-5632(91)90003-J

Maturana, H., & Varela, F. (1980). *Autopoiesis and cognition: The realization of the living*. Dordrecht, The Netherlands: Reidel Publishing Company.

McClellan, J. (1994, February 13). Netsurfers. *The Observer*.

Mcgivern, D., Pellerito, S., & Mowbray, C. (2003). Barriers to higher education for individuals with psychiatric disabilities. *Psychiatric Rehabilitation Journal*, *26*, 217–231. doi:10.2975/26.2003.217.231

McKay, E., Axmann, M., Banjanin, N., & Howat, A. (2007). Towards web-mediated learning reinforcement: Rewards for online mentoring through effective human-computer interaction. Paper presented at the 6th IASTED International Conference on Web-Based Education, March 14-16, Chamonix, France, (pp. 210-215). ISBN: 978-0-88986-650-8

McKay, E. (2008). *The human-dimensions of human-computer interaction: Balancing the HCI equation* (1st ed., *Vol. 3*). Amsterdam, The Netherlands: IOS Press.

McLagan, M. (2006). Introduction: Making human rights claims public. *American Anthropologist*, *108*(1), 191–195. doi:10.1525/aa.2006.108.1.191

McLaughlin, S. M. (2003). The use of the Internet for political action by non-state dissident actors in the Middle East. *First Monday*, *8*(11). Retrieved October 10, 2009, from http://131.193.153.231/www/issues/issue8_11/mclaughlin/index.html

McLean, P., & Andrews, J. (1999). *The learning support needs of students with psychiatric disabilities in Australian post-secondary institutions*. Adelaide, Australia: National Centre for Vocational Education Research (NCVER).

Mehanna, O. (2008). *Internet and the Egyptian public sphere*. Presented at CODESRIA General Assembly.

Meier, P. (2010a, April 8). *Wag the dog, or how falsifying crowdsourced data can be a pain*. Retrieved December 20, 2010, from http://irevolution.wordpress.com/2010/04/08/wag-the-dog/

Meier, P. (2010b, September 19). Analyzing the veracity of tweets during a major crisis. *iRevolution*. Retrieved January 12, 2011, from http://irevolution.wordpress.com/2010/09/19/veracity-of-tweets-during-a-major-crisis/

Meier, P. (2010c, September 22). *Calling 911: What humanitarians can learn from 50 years of crowdsourcing*. Retrieved January 12, 2011, from http://irevolution.wordpress.com/2010/09/22/911-system/

Metzl, J. F. (1996). Information technology and human rights. *Human Rights Quarterly*, *18*(4), 705–746. doi:10.1353/hrq.1996.0045

Metzl, J. F. (1997). Metzl response to Ball, Girouard, and Chapman. *Human Rights Quarterly*, *19*(4), 860–863. doi:10.1353/hrq.1997.0041

Minas, R., & Stenberg, S.-T. (2000). Telefonmottagningen – Socialtjänstens dörrvakt. [Telephone Reception – Social Services´ Gatekeepers]. In A. Puide (Ed.), *Socialbidrag i forskning och praktik* (pp. 205-223). Göteborg, Sweden: Centrum för utvärdering av socialt arbete och Förlagshuset Gothia AB.

Minikon, P., & Shepler, S. (2009). Documenting human rights abuses among the diaspora: Lessons learned from the Liberian Truth and Reconciliation Commission. In Shawki, N., & Cox, M. (Eds.), *Negotiating sovereignty and human rights: Actors and issues in contemporary human rights politics* (pp. 141–158). Farnham, UK: Ashgate Publishing.

MISSOC. EU's Mutual Information System on Social Protection. (2010). *Guaranteed minimum resources.* Retrieved December 5, 2010, from http://ec.europa.eu/employment_social/missoc/db/public/compareTables.do?lang=en

Moghadam, V. M. (2005). *Globalizing women.* Baltimore, MD: Johns Hopkins University Press.

Moisey, S. D. (2004). Students with disabilities in distance education: Characteristics, course enrolment and completion, and support services. *Journal of Distance Education, 19*, 73–91.

Moody, R., Bekkers, V., Edwards, A., & Beunders, H. (2008). *Micro-mobilization, political resonance and the role of new and old media: Towards a conceptual framework.* Paper presented at the PSA Conference 2008. Retrieved August 11, 2011, from http://www.psa.ac.uk/journals/pdf/5/2008/Moody1.pdf

Moore, M. (2010, April 29). The world's most influential leaders (Luiz Inacio Lula da Silva. The 2010 Time 100). *Time.* Retrieved April 29, 2010, from http://www.time.com/time/specials/packages/article/0,28804,1984685_1984864_1984866,00.html

Moore, A. (1998). Intangible property: Privacy, power, and information control. *American Philosophical Quarterly, 35*, 365–378.

Morillon, L., & Julliard, J. (2010). *Enemies of the Internet: Web 2.0 versus control 2.0.* Reporters Without Borders. Retrieved from http://www.rsf.org/ennemis.html

Morillon, L., & Julliard, J. (2010). *Web 2.0 versus Control 2.0.* Reporters Without Borders. Retrieved October 4, 2011, from http://en.rsf.org/web-2-0-versus-control-2-0-18-03-2010,36697

Morozov, E. (2009). *From the "told you so" department.* Retrieved June 1, 2011, from http://neteffect.foreignpolicy.com/posts/2009/12/03/from_the_told_you_so_department/

Morozov, E. (September 16th, 2010). The Great Internet Freedom Fraud: How Haystack endangered the Iranian dissidents it was supposed to protect. *Slate.* Retrieved June 1, 2011, from http://www.slate.com/id/2267262/

Morozov, E. (2011). *The Net delusion: The dark side of Internet freedom.* New York, NY: Public Affairs.

Murphy, T., & Cuinn, Ó, G. (2010). Works in progress: New technologies and the European Court of Human Rights. *Human Rights Law Review, 10*, 601–638. doi:10.1093/hrlr/ngq038

Muuri, A. (2006). Sosiaalipalvelut 2004 – Väestön mielipiteitä ja asiakkaiden palvelukokemuksia. [Social services 2004 – Public opinions and service experiences] In Kautto, M. (Ed.), *Suomalaisten hyvinvointi 2006* (pp. 204–235). Helsinki, Finland: Stakes.

Muuri, A. (2008). *Sosiaalipalveluja kaikille ja kaiken ikää?: Tutkimus suomalaisten mielipiteistä ja kokemuksista sosiaalipalveluista sekä niiden suhteesta legitimiteettiin* [Social welfare services for all, at every age?: Opinions of the Finnish public on, and its experiences of, social welfare services, and their relation to legitimacy]. Helsinki, Finland: Stakes.

Nasseri, L. (2010, November 29). Ahmadinejad confirms several Iran centrifuges affected by computer virus. *Bloomberg.* Retrieved from http://www.bloomberg.com/news/2010-11-29/ahmadinejad-confirms-several-iran-centrifuges-affected-by-computer-virus.html

Neistat, A. personal communication, December 7, 2010

Neumayer, C., & Raffl, C. (2011). *Facebook for protest? The value of social software for political activism in the anti-FARC rallies.* In DigiActive Research Series, December 2008. Retrieved August 11, 2011, from http://www.digiactive.org/research/facebook-for-protest-the-value-of-social-software-for-political-activism-in-the-anti-farc-rallies/

Neumayer, C., Raffl, C., & Bichler, R. (2009). Politics and social software: Recommendations for inclusive ICTs. In Riha, D., & Maj, A. (Eds.), *The real and the virtual: Critical issues in cybercultures* (pp. 183–191). Oxford, UK: Interdisciplinary Press.

Newman, J. (2000). Beyond new public management: Modernizing public services. In Clarke, J., Gewirtz, S., & Mclaughlin, E. (Eds.), *New managerialism, new welfare?* (pp. 45–61). London, UK: Sage Publications.

Newman, J., & Vidler, E. (2006). Discriminating customers, responsible patients, empowered users: Consumerism and the modernisation of health care. *Journal of Social Policy, 35*(2), 193–209. doi:10.1017/S0047279405009487

Niiranen, V. (2002). Asiakkaan osallistuminen tukee kansalaisuutta sosiaalityössäkin. [Service user's participation supports citizenship in social work] In Juhila, K., Forsberg, H., & Roivainen, I. (Eds.), *Marginaalit ja sosiaalityö* (pp. 63–80). Jyväskylä, Finland: Sophi.

Nolan, J. M. (2009). The China dilemma: Internet censorship and corporate responsibility. *Asian Journal of Comparative Law, 4*, 1–28. doi:10.2202/1932-0205.1160

Norden, L. (2006). *The machinery of democracy: Protecting elections in an electronic world*. New York, NY: The Brennan Center of the NYU School of Law.

O'Hagan, M. (2004, April). Recovery in New Zealand – Lessons for Australia? *Ausinetter, 20*(1).

O'Brien, D. (2010, January 15th). *Haystack vs how the internet works.* Retrieved June 1, 2011, from http://www.oblomovka.com/wp/2010/09/14/haystack-vs-how-the-internet-works/

OECD. (2001). *The new economy – Beyond the hype*. Retrieved from http://www.oecd.org/dataoecd/2/26/2380634.pdf

OECD. (2003). *ICT and economic growth – Evidence from OECD countries, industries and firms*. Retrieved from http://www.labs-associados.org/docs/OCDE_TIC.PDF

Office of the Auditor General. (2010). *The PARIS system for community care services: Access and security.* Office of the Auditor General of British Columbia (Report ; 2009/2010: 7)

Office of the Privacy Commissioner of Canada. (2010). *Information related to the Privacy Act*. Retrieved December 4, 2011, from http://www.priv.gc.ca/legislation/02_07_01_01_e.cfm

Office of the United Nations High Commissioner for Human Rights. (2008). *Human rights, terrorism and counter-terrorism, fact sheet No. 32*. Retrieved October 21, 2011, from http://www.ohchr.org/Documents/Publications/Factsheet32EN.pdf

Ogura, T. (2006). Electronic government and surveillance-oriented society. In Lyon, D. (Ed.), *Theorizing surveillance – The panopticon and beyond*. Devon, UK: Willan Publishing.

ONHCR. (n.d.). *Special Rapporteur on the situation of Human Rights Defenders*. Office for the United Nations High Commissioner for Human Rights. Retrieved July 14, 2011, from http://www2.ohchr.org/english/issues/defenders/who.htm

OpenNet Initiative. (2005, April 15). *Special report: Kyrgyzstan, election monitoring in Kyrgyzstan.* Retrieved from http://opennet.net/special/kg/

Organisation for Economic Co-operation and Development. (1998). *Macrothesaurus for information processing in the field of economic and social development*. Paris, France: Organisation for Economic Co-operation and Development.

Orlikowski, W. J., & Baroudi, J. J. (1991). Studying information technology in organizations. Research approaches and assumptions. *Information Systems Research, 2*(1), 1–28. doi:10.1287/isre.2.1.1

Osborn, M. (2008). Fuelling the flames: Rumour and politics in Kibera. *Journal of Eastern African Studies, 2*(2), 315–327. doi:10.1080/17531050802094836

Padovani, C., & Nordenstreng, K. (2005, December). From NWICO to WSIS: Another world information and communication order? *Global Media and Communication, 1*(3), 264–272. Retrieved from http//www.ufa.fi/jour/laitos/From_NWICO_to_WSIS.pdf-doi:10.1177/1742766505058123

Palen, L., Vieweg, S., Liu, S. B., & Hughes, A. L. (2009). Crisis in a networked world. *Social Science Computer Review, 27*(4), 467. doi:10.1177/0894439309332302

Parks, M., & Floyd, K. (1996). Making friends in cyberspace. *The Journal of Communication*, *46*, 80–97. doi:10.1111/j.1460-2466.1996.tb01462.x

Patra, R., Pal, J., & Nedevschi, S. (2009). ICTD State of the Union: Where have we reached and where are we headed? *ICTD '09, Proceedings of the Third International Conference on Information and Communication Technologies and Development*, (pp. 357-365). Piscataway, NJ: IEEE Press.

Patterson, V., Swinfen, P., Swinfen, R., Azzo, E., Taha, H., & Wootton, R. (2007). Supporting hospital doctors in the Middle East by email telemedicine: something the industrialized world can do to help. *Journal of Medical Internet Research*, *9*(4), e30. doi:10.2196/jmir.9.4.e30

Paul, I. (2010, May 6). Facebook privacy complaint: A complete breakdown. *PC World*. Retrieved June 10, 2010, from http://www.pcworld.com/article/195756/facebook_privacy_complaint_a_complete_breakdown.html

PayPal. (2010, 28th June). *PayPal statement regarding WikiLeaks*. Retrieved June 1, 2011, from https://www.thepaypalblog.com/2010/12/paypal-statement-regarding-wikileaks/

Pearce, C., Arnold, M., Phillips, C., Trumble, S., & Dwan, K. (2011). The patient and the computer in the primary care consultation. *Journal of the American Medical Informatics Association*, *18*(2), 138–142. doi:10.1136/jamia.2010.006486

Pelsinger, S. (2010). Liberia's long tail: How Web 2.0 is changing and challenging truth commissions. *Human Rights Law Review*, *10*(4), 730–748. doi:10.1093/hrlr/ngq036

Pilgrim, D. (2005). *Key concepts in mental health*. London, UK: Sage Publications.

Pilieci, V. (2010). *New ePassports flawed, security expert warns; ID chips easily copied, researcher says. The Ottawa Citizen*, A1. Retrieved October 20, 2011 from http://search.proquest.com/docview/241360594?accountid=32724

Pink, D. (2006, February). The changing workplace. An interview with daniel pink. *eJournal USA, The Challenges Of Globalization, 11*(1). U.S. Department Of State. Retrieved January 06, 2011, from http://www.america.gov/publications/ejournalusa/0206.html

Pintak, L. (2008). *The role of the media as watch dogs, agenda setters and gatekeepers in Arab states*. Paper presented in "The Role of the News Media in the Governance Reform Agenda," Harvard World Bank Workshop, 29 31st May 2008. Retrieved May 5, 2010, from http://www.hks.harvard.edu/fs/pnorris/Conference/Conference%20papers/Pintak%20Arab%20Media.pdf

Pollock, S., & Sutton, J. (1999). Women click: Feminism and the Internet. In Hawthorne, S., & Klein, R. (Eds.), *Cyberfeminism: Connectivity, critique and creativity* (pp. 42–45). Melbourne, Australia: Spinifex.

Prensky, M. (2001). Digital natives, digital immigrants. *Horizon*, 9.

Price, M. E., Guberek, T., Guzman, D. R., Zador, P., & Shapiro, G. M. (2009). A statistical analysis of the Guatemalan National Police archive: Searching for documentation of human rights abuses. In Proceedings, J. S. M. (Ed.), *Survey Research Methods Section*. Alexandria, VA: American Statistical Association.

Privacy Rights Clearinghouse. (2011). *Chronology of data breaches: Security breaches 2005 – present*. Retrieved December 4, 2011, from https://www.privacyrights.org/data-breach

Putnam, R. D. (2000). *Bowling alone: The collapse and revival of American community*. New York, NY: Simon and Schuster.

Quinn, A. (2010, 6th February, 2011). US weighs security after 'serious' Google allegation *Reuters*. Retrieved June 1, 2011, from http://www.msnbc.msn.com/id/43253703/ns/technology_and_science-security/t/us-weighs-security-after-serious-google-allegation/

Quirk, P. W. (2009, June 17). Iran's Twitter revolution. *Foreign Policy in Focus*. Retrieved from http://www.fpif.org/articles/irans_twitter_revolution

R v Department of Health ex p Source Informatics Ltd. (2000). 1 All ER 786.

Raffl, C., Fuchs, C., Hofkirchner, W., & Schafranek, M. (2008). The Web as techno-social system. The emergence of Web 3.0. In Trappl, R. (Ed.), *Cybernetics and Systems 2008* (pp. 604–609). Vienna: Austrian Society for Cybernetic Studies.

Rakha, M. (2009). *Egypt: Bad boys who do not moderate blog comments*. Global Voices Online. Retrieved August 11, 2011, from from http://globalvoicesonline.org/2009/09/09/egypt□bad□boys-who-do-not-moderate□blog□comments/

Ramonas, A. (2011). Leahy introduces bill to update digital privacy law. Retrieved May 20th, 2011, Retrieved June 1, 2011, from http://www.mainjustice.com/2011/05/17/leahy-introduces-bill-to-update-digital-privacy-law/

Raoof, R. (2009). *Egypt: Egyptian government utilizes electronic media*. Global Voices Online. Retrieved August 11, 2011, from http://advocacy.globalvoicesonline.org/2009/08/12/egyptian-government-utilizes-electronic-media/

Raoof, R. (2010). *Egypt security department to monitor Facebook and support government*. Global Voices Online. Retrieved August 11, 2011, from http://advocacy.globalvoicesonline.org/2010/08/29/egypt-security-department-to-monito-facebook-and-support-the-government/

Raoof, R. (Creator). (2010). *Illustration for using online tools & digital devices between detainees & FDEP on 6 April 2010* (Image). Retrieved December 12, 2010, from http://www.flickr.com/photos/ramyraoof/4537322405/

Raymond, E. S. (2000). *Homesteading the Noosphere*. Retrieved October 20, 2011, from http://catb.org/~esr/writings /homesteading/homesteading/

Raymond, E. (2001). *The cathedral and the bazaar: Musings on Linux and open source by an accidental revolutionary* (Rev. ed.). Sebastopol, CA: O'Reilly.

Raynes-Goldie, K. (2011). *Digitally mediated surveillance, privacy and social network sites*. Retrieved October 11, 2011, from http://www.digitallymediatedsurveillance.ca/wp-content/uploads/2011/04/Raynes-Goldie-Digitally_mediated_surveillance_privacy_and_social_network_sites.pdf

Reidpath, D., Chan, K., Gifford, S., & Allotey, P. (2005). He hath the French pox: Stigma, social value and social exclusion. *Sociology of Health & Illness*, *27*(4), 468–469. doi:10.1111/j.1467-9566.2005.00452.x

Report, H. (2008). *Two to three years: Data mashups*. The New Media Consortium. Retrieved November 1, 2011, from http://wp.nmc.org/horizon2008/chapters/data-mashups/

RFIDWorld.ca. (2010). IT expert in Britain warns that Canadian RFID E-passports not secure enough. *RFID-World Canada*. Retrieved on October 11, 2011, from http://www.rfidworld.ca/it-expert-in-britain-warns-that-canadian-rfid-e-passports-not-secure-enough/116

Rheingold, H. (1987, Winter). Virtual communities. *Whole Earth Review*, 78–81.

Rheingold, H. (1990, Summer). Travels in virtual reality. *Whole Earth Review*, 80–88.

Rheingold, H. (1991, Summer). Electronic democracy, the great equalizer. *Whole Earth Review*, 4–8.

Rheingold, H. (1993). Daily life in cyberspace. In *The virtual community: Homesteading on the electronic frontier* (pp. 57–109). Reading, MA: Addison-Wesley.

Rheingold, H. (2002). *Smart mobs: The next social revolution* (pp. 157–182). Cambridge, MA: Perseus Publishing.

Risse, T. (2000). Let's argue! Communicative action in world politics. *International Organization*, *54*(1). doi:10.1162/002081800551109

Roberts, J. J. (2011, 12th July, 2011). A new law-enforcement tool: Facebook searches. *Reuters*. Retrieved June 1, 2011, from http://newsandinsight.thomsonreuters.com/Legal/News/2011/07_-_July/A_new_law-enforcement_tool__Facebook_searches/

Robinson, B. (2010). Web mashups put transparency to the test. *Federal Computer Week*. Retrieved November 1, 2011, from http://fcw.com/articles/2010/01/11/feat-mashups-test-transparency.aspx

Robling, M. R., Hood, K., Houston, H., Pill, R., Fay, J., & Evans, H. M. (2004). Public attitudes towards the use of primary care patient record data in medical research without consent: A qualitative study. *Journal of Medical Ethics*, *30*, 104–109. doi:10.1136/jme.2003.005157

Rodrigues Filho, J. (2010). E-government in Brazil – Reinforcing dominant institutions or reducing citizenship? In Reddick, C. (Ed.), *Politics, democracy and e-government: Participation and service delivery*. Hershey, PA: IGI Global. doi:10.4018/978-1-61520-933-0.ch021

Rodrigues Filho, J., & Gomes, N. P. (2008). E-voting in Brazil – Exacerbating alienation and the digital divide. In Santap, S. M. (Ed.), *E-democracy – Concepts and practices*. India: IFCAI Books.

Rodrigues Filho, J., & Gomes, N. P. (2010). E-health in Brazil: Less care for the poor? In Pease, C., Cooper, M., & Gururajan, R. (Eds.), *Biomedical knowledge management: Infrastructures and processes for e-health systems*. Hershey, PA: IGI Global. doi:10.4018/978-1-60566-266-4.ch017

Ron, J., Ramos, H., & Rodgers, K. (2005). Transnational information politics: NGO human rights reporting, 1986–2000. *International Studies Quarterly*, *49*(3), 557–588. doi:10.1111/j.1468-2478.2005.00377.x

Rosneau, J. M. (2002). The drama of human rights in a turbulent, globalized world. In Brysk, A. (Ed.), *Globalization and human rights*. Berkley, CA: University of California Press.

Roth, K. (2010). The abusers' reaction: Intensifying attacks on human rights defenders, organizations, and institutions. *Human Rights Watch World Report 2010*. Retrieved May 11, 2011, from http://www.hrw.org/en/node/87544

Rowan, D. (2011). Behind the scenes of wired UK magazine's personalized covers. *Wired Magazine*. Retrieved October 21, 2011, from http://www.wired.com/epicenter/2011/02/behind-the-scenes-of-wired-uk-magazines-personalized-covers/

Rubin, A., & Babbie, E. R. (2008). *Research methods for social work* (6th ed.). Belmont, CA: Wadsworth/Thomson Learning.

Rueda-Sabater, E., & Garrity, J. (2011). The emerging internet economy: Looking a decade ahead. In S. Dutta, & I. Mia, (Eds.), *The global information technology report 2010 – 2011, Transformations 2.0,* 10th Anniversary Edition (pp. 33 - 47). Geneva, Switzerland: World Economic Forum and INSEAD. Retrieved June 17, 2011, from http://reports.weforum.org/global-information-technology-report/content/pdf/wef-gitr-2010-2011.pdf

Rutherford, R. (2000). Internet activism: NGOs and the Mine Ban Treaty. *International Journal on Grey Literature*, *1*(3), 99–106. doi:10.1108/14666180010345528

Sakr, N. (2010). News, transparency and the effectiveness of reporting from inside Arab dictatorships. *International Communication Gazette*, *72*, 35–50. doi:10.1177/1748048509350337

Sankar, P., Mora, S., Merz, J. F., & Jones, N. L. (2003). Patient perspectives of medical confidentiality. *Journal of General Internal Medicine*, *18*, 659–669. doi:10.1046/j.1525-1497.2003.20823.x

Scalvini, S., Rivadossi, F., Comini, L., Muiesan, M. L., & Glisenti, F. (2011). Telemedicine: The role of specialist second opinion for GPs in the care of hypertensive patients. *Blood Pressure*, *20*(3), 158–165. doi:10.3109/08037051.2010.542646

Scott, S., & Burns, J. F. (2010, January 8th, 2011). U.S. subpoenas Twitter over WikiLeaks supporters. *New York Times*. Retrieved January 1, 2011, from https://www.nytimes.com/2011/01/09/world/ 09wiki.html?_r=1/

Scott, A., & Street, J. (2001). From media politics to e-protest? The use of popular culture and new media in parties and social movements. In Webster, F. (Ed.), *Culture and politics in the information age: A new politics?* London, UK: Routledge.

Seabrook, J. (1997). *Deeper*. New York, NY: Simon & Schuster.

Seib, P. (Ed.). (2007). *New media and the new Middle East*. New York, NY: Palgrave Macmillan. doi:10.1057/9780230605602

Shankar, J., Martin, J., & McDonald, C. (2009). Emerging areas of practice for mental health social workers: Education and employment. *Australian Social Work*, *62*(1), 28–45. doi:10.1080/03124070802626893

Shapiro, S. M. (2009, January 22). Revolution, Facebook-style. *New York Times*. Retrieved from http://www.nytimes.com/2009/01/25/magazine/25bloggers-t.html

Shapiro, A. L. (1999). *The control revolution: How the internet is putting individuals in charge and changing the world we know*. New York, NY: Public Affairs.

Shapiro, G. M., Guzman, D. R., Zador, P., Guberek, T., Price, M. E., & Lum, K. (2009). Weighting for the Guatemalan National Police Archive Sample: Unusual Challenges and Problems. In Proceedings, J. S. M. (Ed.), *Survey Research Methods Section*. Alexandria, VA: American Statistical Association.

Shenk, D. (1997). *Data smog: Surviving the information glut*. New York, NY: HarperCollins.

Shiels, M. (2010, December 30). Cyber-sabotage and espionage top 2011 security fears. *BBC*. Retrieved from http://www.bbc.co.uk/news/technology-12056594

Shugar, D. (1995). *Separatism and women's community* (pp. 14–17). University of Nebraska Press.

Shuguang, Z. (2008). Notes on the net. *Index on Censorship*, 90–96.

Siegler, M. (1982). Sounding boards. Confidentiality in medicine--A decrepit concept. *The New England Journal of Medicine*, *307*(24), 1518–1521. doi:10.1056/NEJM198212093072411

Silva, R., & Ball, P. (2005). On the use of sample surveys and multiple systems estimations in assessing large-scale human rights violations: Recent experiences from Timor-Leste. *Proceedings of the Social Statistics Section – Joint Statistical Meetings*. Alexandria, VA: American Statistical Association.

Silva, R., & Ball, P. (2006). *The demography of large-scale human rights atrocities: Integrating demographic and statistical analysis into post-conflict historical clarification in Timor-Leste*. Paper presented at the 2006 meetings of the Population Association of America. Silver Spring, MD: Population Association of America.

Silva, R., & Ball, P. (2006). *The profile of human rights violations in Timor-Leste, 1974-1999. A report by the Benetech Human Rights Data Analysis Group to the Commission on Reception, Truth and Reconciliation*. Palo Alto, CA: Benetech.

Silva, R., & Ball, P. (2007). The demography of conflict-related mortality in Timor-Leste (1974-1999): Empirical quantitative measurement of civilian killings, disappearances & famine-related deaths. In Asher, J., Banks, D., & Scheuren, F. (Eds.), *Statistical methods for human rights*. New York, NY: Springer. doi:10.1007/978-0-387-72837-7_6

Singel, R. (2011a, January 10th, 2011). Twitter's response to WikiLeaks subpoena should be the industry standard. *Wired Magazine*. Retrieved March 1, from http://www.wired.com/threatlevel/2011/01/twitter/

Singel, R. (2011b, 13th May, 2011). Dropbox lied to users about data security, complaint to FTC alleges. *Wired Magazine*. Retrieved October 1, from http://wired.com/threatlevel/2011/05/dropbox-ftp

Smyth, T. N., Etherton, J., & Best, M. L. (2010). *MOSES: Exploring new ground in media and post-conflict reconciliation*. Paper presented at the ACM Conference on Human Factors in Computing Systems (CHI 2010), April 10-15, Atlanta, GA.

Social Assistance Act [Laki toimeentulotuesta]. (1412/1997).

Soghoian, C. (2009). *An open letter to Google's CEO, Eric Schidt*. Retrieved October 1, 2011, from http://cloudprivacy.net/letter

Soliani, A., & Galvao, A. (2010). Brazil to boost security at tax agency after leaks. *Bloomberg Businessweek*. Retrieved November 12, 2010, from http://www.businessweek.com/news/2010-09-14/brazil-to-boost-security-at-tax-agency-after-leaks.html

Somma, N. M. (2009). How strong are strong ties? The conditional effectiveness of strong ties in protest recruitment attempts. *Sociological Perspectives*, *52*(3), 289–308. doi:10.1525/sop.2009.52.3.289

Sorjonen, M.-L. (2006a). Tunteet pinnassa: Affektista puhetta Kelan asioinneista [Emotions on the surface: Affective speech about the conversations at Kela]. In M.-L. Sorjonen & L. Raevaara (Eds.), *Arjen asiointia. Keskusteluja Kelan tiskin äärellä* (pp. 191-221). Helsinki, Finland: Kotimaisten kielten tutkimuskeskus.

Sorjonen, M.-L. (2006b). Ymmärrystä ja empatiaa: Ammattilainen asiakkaan tuntemusten vastaanottajana [Understanding and empathy: A professional as a recipient of service user's feelings]. In M.-L. Sorjonen & L. Raevaara (Eds.), *Arjen asiointia. Keskusteluja Kelan tiskin äärellä* (pp. 222-240). Helsinki, Finland: Kotimaisten kielten tutkimuskeskus.

Sorjonen, M.-L., & Raevaara, L. (2006). Kuinka päästä alkuun?: Asiointikeskustelun aloittamistavoista [How do I get started?: About the manners for initiating conversation]. In M.-L. Sorjonen & L. Raevaara (Eds.), *Arjen asiointia. Keskusteluja Kelan tiskin äärellä* (pp. 48-85). Helsinki, Finland: Kotimaisten kielten tutkimuskeskus.

Sorrentino, M. (2010). The challenges of e-government evaluation. In D'Atri, A., & Saccà, D. (Eds.), *Information systems: People, organizations, institutions, and technologies*. Berlin, Germany: Springer Physica-Verlag.

Sorrentino, M., Naggi, R., & Agostini, P. L. (2009). In Wimmer, M. A. (Eds.). Lecture Notes in Computer Science: *Vol. 5693*. *E-government implementation evaluation: Opening the black box*. Berlin, Germany: Springer-Verlag.

Souter, D. (2010). *Towards inclusive knowledge societies: A review of UNESCO's action in implementing the WSIS outcomes*. United Nations Educational, Scientific and Cultural Organization (UNESCO), Communication and Information Sector. Retrieved July 6, 2011, from http://unesdoc.unesco.org/images/0018/001878/187832e.pdf.

Sparks, C. (2005). Civil society as contested concept: Media and political transformation in Eastern Central Europe. In Hackett, R., & Shao, Y. (Eds.), *Democratizing global media: One world, many struggles* (pp. 37–56). Boulder, CO: Rowan & Littlefield.

Spence, R., & Smith, M. (2009). *Information and communication technologies, human development, growth and poverty reduction: A background paper*. Retrieved from http://www.idrc.ca/uploads/user-S/12412058391HF2_Background_Paper_28-04-09.pdf

Srinivasa, S. (July 29, 2010). *BlackBerry agrees to address India's security concerns, says ministry*. Retrieved May 1, 2011, from http://www.ibtimes.com/articles/39418/20100729/blackberry-security-india-india-concerns-on-blackberry.htm/

Stahl, B. C. (2008). *Information systems – Critical perspectives*. London, UK: Routledge Taylor and Francis Group.

Stanyer, J., & Davidson, S. (2009). *The Internet and the visibility of oppression in non-democratic states: The online exposure of human rights violations and other repressive acts*. Paper prepared for the 2009 Annual Meeting of the International Communication Association Conference, Chicago, IL, May 20-25, 2009.

Steinberg, J. (2010a). Liberia's experiment with transitional justice. *African Affairs*, *109*(434), 135–144. doi:10.1093/afraf/adp085

Steinberg, J. (2010b). A truth commission goes abroad: Liberian transitional justice in New York. *African Affairs*, *110*(439), 1–19.

Stoll, C. (1995, February 27). The Internet? Bah! *Newsweek*. Retrieved January 4, 2011, from http://www.newsweek.com/1995/02/26/the-internetInternet-bah.html

Stoll, C. (1995). *Silicon snake oil: Second thoughts on the information highway*. New York, NY: Anchor Books.

Stormorken, B., & Zwaak, L. (1998). *Human rights terminology in international law: A thesaurus*. Dordrecht, The Netherlands: Martinus Nijhoff Publishers.

Sullivan, A. (2009, June 13). The revolution will be twittered. *The Atlantic*. Retrieved from http://www.theatlantic.com/daily-dish/archive/2009/06/the-revolution-will-be-twittered/200478/

Sunstein, C. R. (2001). *Republic.com*. Princeton, NJ: Princeton University Press.

Surowiecki, J. (2005). *The wisdom of crowds* (1st ed.). New York, NY: Anchor Books.

Survival International. (2010, October 22). *Indonesian government admits its soldiers tortured Papuans*. Retrieved December 21, 2010, from http://www.survivalinternational.org/news/6610

Sussman, L. R. (1989, October). What the North wants from UNESCO: Mediator and catalyst.*Sources*, *8*, 13.

Svensson, P. (2010). WikiLeaks website kicked off Amazon's servers. *Yahoo Finance, 2011*. Retrieved from http://finance.yahoo.com/news/WikiLeaks-website-kicked-off-apf-2762807500.html?x=0/

Swaine, J. (2008, August 11). Georgia: Russia 'conducting cyber war.' *The Telegraph*. Retrieved from http://www.telegraph.co.uk/news/worldnews/europe/georgia/2539157/Georgia-Russia-conducting-cyber-war.html

Syal, R. (2009, February 1). 17,000 asylum seekers' files lost. *The Guardian*. Retrieved October 22, 2011, from http://www.guardian.co.uk/uk/2009/feb/01/refugees-asylum

Tableu Software. (2010, December 2nd 2010). *Why we removed the WikiLeaks visualizations*. Retrieved February 1, 2011, from http://www.tableausoftware.com/about/blog/2010/12/why-we-removed-wikileaks-visualizations?page=7/

Tactical Technology Collective. (2009). *10 tactics for turning information into action*. India: Tactical Technology Collective. Retrieved June 1, 2011, from http://www.informationactivism.org/

Tactical Technology Collective. (2010, unpublished). *Digital security at the grassroots: Vulnerabilities of rights advocates and independent journalists through using information and communications technologies.*

Tapscott, D., & Williams, A. D. (2010). *Macrowikinomics: Rebooting business and the world*. Portfolio Hardcover.

The Act on the Restructuring of Local Government and Services [Laki kunta- ja palvelurakenneuudistuksesta]. (169/2007).

The Advocates for Human Rights. (2009). *A house with two rooms: Final report of the Truth and Reconciliation Commission of Liberia Diaspora Project*. Retrieved February 9, 2011, from http://www.theadvocatesforhumanrights.org/Final_Report.html

The Constitution of Finland [Suomen perustuslaki]. (731/1999).

The Daily Show with Jon Stewart. (2009, June 16). *Irandecision 2009 - CNN's unverified material*. Retrieved from http://www.thedailyshow.com/watch/tue-june-16-2009/irandecision-2009---cnn-s-unverified-material

The Economist. (2010, October 3). Grumpy on the stump: America's views. *The Economist.*

The Truth and Reconciliation Commission of Liberia. (2009). *Volume II: Consolidated final report*. Retrieved February 9, 2011, from http://www.trcofliberia.org/reports/final/volume-two_layout-1.pdf

Thomas, C. (2006). An empirical examination of Wikipedia's credibility. *First Monday*, *11*(11).

Times, N. Y. (2010, December 26th, 2010). Banks and WikiLeaks. *New York Times*. Retrieved 01st June 2011, from https://www.nytimes.com/2010/12/26/opinion/26sun3.html?_r=1

Times, W. (2009, June 16). *Iran's Twitter revolution*. Retrieved from http://www.washingtontimes.com/news/2009/jun/16/irans-twitter-revolution/

Transparency Maroc. (2009). *Revue de pressehebdomadaire n°56. Transparency Maroc: Observatoire de la Corruption*, January 2009. Retrieved June 10, 2010, from http://transparencymaroc.ma/uploads/revue/42.pdf

Truong, H.-A. (1993). *Gender issues in online communication*. Paper presented at a meeting of the Bay Area Women in Telecommunications.

Tunis Agenda for the Information Society. (2005, November 18). *WSIS-05/TUNIS/DOC/6*(Rev. 1)-E. Retrieved from http://www.itu.int/wsis/docs2/tunis/off/6rev1.html

Tunis Commitment. (2005, November 18). *WSIS-05/TUNIS/DOC/7-E*. Retrieved from http://www.itu.int/wsis/docs2/tunis/off/7.html

Tuori, K., & Kotkas, T. (2008). *Sosiaalioikeus* [Social rights]. Helsinki, Finland: WSOY.

Twitter (June, 2009). *Down time rescheduled*. Retrieved from http://blog.twitter.com/2009/06/down-time-rescheduled.html

U.S. State Department. (2010a). *2009 human rights report: Egypt*. Retrieved from http://www.state.gov/g/drl/rls/hrrpt/2009/nea/136067.htm

U.S. State Department. (2010b). *2009 human rights report: Singapore*. Retrieved from http://www.state.gov/g/drl/rls/hrrpt/2009/eap/136008.htm

U.S. State Department. (2011). *2010 human rights report: Iran*. Retrieved from http://www.state.gov/g/drl/rls/hrrpt/2010/nea/154461.htm

UN Human Rights Council. (2010, January 7). *UN expert concludes that Sri Lankan video is authentic, calls for an independent war crimes investigation.* Retrieved from http://www.reliefweb.int/rw/rwb.nsf/db900SID/EGUA-7ZGQCB?OpenDocument

UN. (2004). *UN global e-government readiness report. Towards access for opportunity*. Publication No: UN-PAN/200/11.

UNESCO. (1997). *World communication report. The media and the challenges of the new technologies*. Paris, France: UNESCO Publishing.

UNESCO. (2000). *World education report*. Paris, France: UNESCO Publishing.

UNESCO. (2005). *World report. Towards knowledge societies*. Paris, France: UNESCO Publishing.

United Nations Economic and Social Council. (2009, December 21). *Committee on Economic, Social and Cultural Rights, Forty-third Session, General comment No. 21* (E/C.12/GC/21).

United Nations Educational, Scientific and Cultural Organization. (1980). *Many voices one world.* Report of the MacBride Commission. Paris, France: Author. Retrieved from http://unesdoc.unesco.org/images/0004/000400/040066eb.pdf

United Nations Educational, Scientific and Cultural Organization. (1995). *UNESCO thesaurus: A structured list of descriptors for indexing and retrieving literature in the fields of education, science, social and human science, culture, communication and information*. Paris, France: UNESCO Publishing.

United Nations General Assembly. (1949). *Universal declaration of human rights*. Washington, DC: US Government Printing Office.

United Nations. (1948). *The universal declaration of human rights*. Retrieved from http://www.un.org/en/documents/udhr/index.shtml

United Nations. (1948). *Universal declaration of human rights.* Retrieved June 1, 2011, from http://www.un.org/en/documents/udhr/

United Nations. (1986). *Declaration on the right to development*, Res. 41/128, Retrieved from http://www.un.org/documents/ga/res/41/a41r128.htm

United Nations. (2000). *The world's women trends and statistics*. New York, NY: The United Nations.

United Nations. (2005). *The world's women 2005. Progress in statistics*. New York, NY: The United Nations.

United Nations. (2010). *The world's women 2010 Trends and Statistics*. New York, NY: The United Nations.

United Nations. (2011). *Report of the Special Rapporteur on the promotion and protection of the right to freedom of opinion and expression, Frank La Rue*. The United Nations: Human Rights Council. Retrieved June 18, 2011, from http://documents.latimes.com/un-report-Internet-rights/

Urquhart, C. (2007, March 4).Why torture is routine in Egypt. *The Toronto Star*. Retrieved July 5, 2010, from http://www.thestar.com/news/article/188036

US Department of Health and Social Services. (2011). *Health information privacy.* Retrieved August 24th, 2011, from http://www.hhs.gov/ocr/privacy/hipaa/understanding/consumers/index.html

Van Dijk, J., & Hacker, K. (2000). *The digital divide as a complex and dynamic phenomenon.* Paper presented at the Annual Conference of the International Communication Association, Acapulco, Mexico.

Van Laer, J., & Van Aelst, P. (2009). Cyber-protest and civil society: The Internet and action repertoires in social movements. In Jewkes, Y., & Yar, M. (Eds.), *Handbook on Internet crime* (pp. 230–254). Willan Publishing.

van Zoonen, L., Vis, F., & Mihelj, S. (2010). Performing citizenship on YouTube: Activism, satire and online debate around the anti-Islam video *Fitna. Critical Discourse Studies*, *7*(4), 249–262. doi:10.1080/17405904.2010.511831

Villalobos, V., & Monge-González, R. (2011). Costa Rica's efforts toward an innovation-driven economy: The role of the ICT sector. In S. Dutta, & I. Mia, (Eds.), *The global information technology report 2010 - 2011, Transformations 2.0,* 10th Anniversary Edition (pp. 119 - 127). Geneva, Switzerland: World Economic Forum and INSEAD. Retrieved June 17, 2011, from http://reports.weforum.org/global-information-technology-report/content/pdf/wef-gitr-2010-2011.pdf

Virkki, T. (2010). *Asiakasnäkökulma sosiaalipalvelujen muutokseen [Service users' point of view of the change in social services].* Retrieved from http://www.thl.fi/thl-client/pdfs/d8fe8bcf-2b6f-4f28-8046-406de45bf9e7

Wall Street Journal. (2010). *Dictionary.com.* Retrieved May 12th, 2011, from http://blogs.wsj.com/wtk/2010/07/30/dictionaryreferencecom/

Wall Street Journal. (2010). *What they know.* Retrieved June 1, 2011, from http://online.wsj.com/public/page/what-they-know-digital-privacy.html

Wallace, P. (2001). *The psychology of the internet.* Cambridge, UK: Cambridge University Press.

Wan, C. D. (2009). The Shi Tao case: Its development in mainland China. *Journal of Contemporary China, 18*, 517–539. doi:10.1080/10670560903033836

Wang, S. J. (2003). A cost–benefit analysis of electronic medical records in primary care. *The American Journal of Medicine, 114*(5), 397–403. doi:10.1016/S0002-9343(03)00057-3

Watson, N. (1997). Why we argue about virtual community: A case study of the Phish.net fan community. In Jones, S. G. (Ed.), *Virtual culture* (pp. 102–132). Thousand Oaks, CA: Sage.

Weber, R. H. (2004). From "many voices one world" to "information society". *Computer und Recht International*, 97-104.

Weber, R. H. (2010a). *Regulatory framework for mobile financial services.* In National Forum on Mobile Applications for Inclusive Growth and Sustainable Development. Delhi. Retrieved from http://www.mgovworld.org/libra/mbanking/papers

Weber, I., & Jia, L. (2007). Internet and self-regulation in China: The cultural logic of controlled commodification. *Media Culture & Society, 29*, 772–789. doi:10.1177/0163443707080536

Weber, R. H. (2010b). Digital trade in WTO-law – Taking stock and looking ahead. *Asian Journal of WTO & International Health Law and Policy, 5*, 1–25.

Weber, R. H., & Grosz, M. (2009). Governments' interventions into the real economy under WTO law revisited: New tendencies of governmental support of the automobile industry. *Journal of World Trade, 43*, 969–1013.

Weber, R. H., & Menoud, V. (2008). *The information society and the digital divide – Legal strategies to finance global access.* Zurich, Switzerland: Schulthess.

Weinberger, S. (October 15, 2010). US government monitoring social networking sites. *AOL News*. Retrieved June 1, 2011, from http://www.aolnews.com/2010/10/15/homeland-security-monitoring-social-networking-sites/

Weiss, P. A. (1995). Introduction: Feminist reflections on community. In Weiss, P. A., & Friedman, M. (Eds.), *Feminism and community* (pp. 9–12). Philadelphia, PA: Temple University Press.

Wellman, B., & Gulia, M. (1999). Net surfers don't ride alone: Virtual communities as communities. In Wellman, B. (Ed.), *Networks in the global village* (pp. 331–367). Boulder, CO: Westview Press.

Weyker, S. (2002). The ironies of information technology. In Brysk, A. (Ed.), *Globalization and human rights.* Berkley, CA: University of California Press.

Wiebelhaus-Brahm, E. (2010). A volunteer's perspective on the Liberian Truth and Reconciliation Commission Diaspora Project. *Journal of Human Rights Practice, 2*(3), 386–400. doi:10.1093/jhuman/huq010

Wikipedia. (n.d.). *Wikipedia, the free encyclopedia.* Retrieved November 16, 2010, from http://en.wikipedia.org/wiki/Wikipedia

Wilding, P. (1994). Maintaining quality in human services. *Social Policy and Administration, 28*(1), 57–72. doi:10.1111/j.1467-9515.1994.tb00408.x

Williams, J. R. (2004). *Developing performance support for computer systems: A strategy for maximizing usability and learnability*. Boca Raton, FL: CRC Press.

Willis Aronowitz, N. (2011). UN declares internet access a human right. What does this really mean? *Good Magazine*. Retrieved June 26, 2011, from http://www.good.is/post/un-declares-Internet-access-a-human-right-what-does-this-really-mean/

Winfield, B. H., & Peng, Z. (2005). Market or party controls? Chinese media in transition. *International Journal for Communication Studies*, *67*, 255–270.

Wise, P. (1997). Always already virtual: Feminist politics in cyberspace. In Holmes, D. (Ed.), *Virtual politics: Identity and community in cyberspace* (pp. 179–197). London, UK: Sage Publications.

World Bank. (1997). *World development report 1997: The state in a changing world*. Washington, DC: World Bank.

World Bank. (2002). *Information and communication technologies: A World Bank group strategy*. Washington, DC: World Bank.

World Health Organization. (1949). *Constitution: Signed at the International Health Conference, New York, 22 July 1946*. Geneva, Switzerland: Author.

World Health Organization. (2005). *Mental health information systems: Mental health policy and service guidance package*. Geneva, Switzerland: WHO. ISBN: 92 4 154671 9

World Health Organization. (2009). *What is mental health?* Retrieved from http://www.who.int

YNET. (2010, August 28). The battle for Wikipedia: Palestinians counter Israeli editing group. *Ynetnews*. Retrieved November 18, 2010, from http://www.ynetnews.com/articles/0,7340,L-3944937,00.html

Young, L. A., & Park, R. (2009). Engaging diasporas in truth commissions: Lessons from the Liberia Truth and Reconciliation Commission Diaspora Project. *International Journal of Transitional Justice*, *3*(3), 341–361. doi:10.1093/ijtj/ijp021

Youngs, G. (2000). Internet policies and states. In Kramarae, C., & Spender, D. (Eds.), *Routledge international encyclopedia of women. Global women's issues and knowledge* (pp. 1154–1156). New York, NY: Routledge.

Z. v. Finland. (1996). ECHR Judgment of 25 February 1997, Application No. 9/1996/627/811

Zetter, K. (2009, 1st December, 2009). Yahoo, Verizon: Our spy capabilities would 'shock', 'confuse' consumers. *Wired*. Retrieved October 1, 2001, from http://wired.com/thratlevel/2009/12/wiretap-prices

Ziraoui, Y., & Alaoui, M. S. (2009, October 14). Sur la piste du sniper de Targuist. *TelQuel*. Retrieved June 12, 2010, from http://www.telquel-online.com/292/couverture_292.shtml

About the Contributors

John Lannon holds an MA in Peace and Development Studies from the University of Limerick, Ireland, and has completed a PhD in Information Systems Usage in the Human Rights Movement at Leeds Metropolitan University, UK. He worked in software systems design, development, and project management for over a decade and a half, and now provides information management and ICT-related expertise to the non-profit sector. He is also a Lecturer and Researcher with the Centre for Information and Knowledge Management at the University of Limerick. John has been involved in human rights activism for over 20 years and is a founding member of Shannonwatch, an Irish-based organization of peace and human rights activists (www.shannonwatch.org).

Edward F. Halpin (Professor) works for the Faculty of Health & Social Sciences at Leeds Metropolitan University. He is also associated with the Faculty of Arts, Environment and Technology, leading the Social Informatics theme in their research. For his PhD he studied "The use of ICT and Information for Human and Child Rights" and has a long record of working on human rights information and ICT, including work as an expert for the European Parliament Scientific and Technical Options Assessment Unit (STOA). Edward is currently the Chair of the Geneva-based international NGO *Human Rights Information and Documentation Systems, International* (HURIDOCS) who help human rights organisation use information technologies and documentation methods to maximise the impact of their advocacy work. Professor Halpin has published widely, particularly with John Lannon, and co-edited the book "Human Rights and the Internet" with Hick and Hoskins in 2000.

* * *

Robin Blom is a Doctoral student in the Media and Information Studies program and a teaching assistant for the School of Journalism at Michigan State University. He earned his Bachelor's degree in Journalism at the Hogeschool van Utrecht, The Netherlands, and a Master's degree in Journalism and Mass Communication at Point Park University, Pittsburgh, Pennsylvania. Blom has also been a news reporter for several national and regional newspapers in The Netherlands, predominantly focusing on local governmental affairs, crime, culture, and media. He has also participated in investigations for the Innocence Institute of Point Park University. His research and teaching areas are, but not limited to, media bias (perceptions), agenda setting and framing, and the influence of news media on civic engagement and the marketplace of ideas.

Brian J. Bowe is a visiting Journalism Professor at Grand Valley State University and a Doctoral student in Michigan State University's Media and Information Studies program. He earned his Bachelor's degree in Journalism and a Master's degree in Communications at Grand Valley State. His research interests include new media and press freedom, framing, agenda setting, and media coverage of Muslims. He began his career at daily newspapers in Michigan and New Hampshire, and his byline has appeared in many regional and national publications. Bowe was the first editor of the online incarnation of CREEM Magazine, and he co-edited the anthology *CREEM: America's Only Rock 'n' Roll Magazine* (2007, Harper/Collins). He is also the author or co-author of five books, including young adult biographies of rock bands Judas Priest, the Ramones, and the Clash.

Aziz Douai (Dr.) is an Assistant Professor of Communication at the University of Ontario Institute of Technology, Canada. His research focuses on new media and activism, Arab media and democracy, global media and international conflict, among other areas of international communications. Dr. Douai's publications have appeared in *The Journal of International Communication, The Global Media Journal, First Monday, The Journal of Arab & Muslim Media Research, Arab Reform Bulletin,* and *The Westminster Papers in Communication and Culture.* His forthcoming article, "Commenting in the Online Arab public Sphere: Debating the Swiss Minaret Ban and the 'Ground Zero' Mosque Online," will appear in *The Journal of Computer Mediated Communication.*

Judith Dueck, Adjunct Professor, The University of Winnipeg Global College, has contributed to innovative human rights projects as a director, researcher, consultant, board member, and educator. She was the Director: Research, Content & Scholarship for the Canadian Museum for Human Rights. She is a HURIDOCS International Advisory Council member and an advisor/trainer for ILGA–Europe. Judith is the author of a book on censorship (Award of Merit, University of Manitoba), co-author of 4 practical books on human rights documentation, key HURISEARCH contributor, and author of chapters in 2 human rights books published by University of Pennsylvania Press. She is an international presenter on information access, technology, education, and human rights. She has trained peacekeepers and international NGOs; consulted for the OSCE; has been an Amnesty Canada Board member; and was Al Haq's administrative director (West Bank branch, ICJ).

Alix Dunn works primarily as a co-founder of the engine room, an organization that investigates and supports the use of technology in advocacy. She moved to Cairo, Egypt in 2009 to conduct research on the role of new technologies, especially Facebook, in emerging pro-democracy movements. In addition to this research, she led media and technology strategy for the largest Arab human rights NGO, the Cairo Institute for Human Rights Studies (CIHRS). She is also a consultant on strategy and security for digital human rights campaigns, working with MobileActive.org as their Egypt training coordinator. Dunn holds a Master's degree in Media Studies from the University of Oslo and a Bachelor's degree from Colorado College.

Eric Freedman is an Associate Professor in Michigan State University's School of Journalism and Associate Dean of International Studies and Programs. Freedman is a winner of the Pulitzer Prize for reporting. He is a former Fulbright senior scholar in Uzbekistan and has conducted training workshops for professional journalists in Central Asia sponsored by the U.S. State Department, Internews, Freedom

House, and other organizations. He has led MSU journalism study abroad programs in Australia and the British Isles. Freedman's research interests include press rights and journalistic practices in Central Asia and media coverage of international environmental issues. He is the author or co-author of eight books, including *After the Czars and Commissars: Journalism in Authoritarian Post Soviet Central Asia* (2011, Michigan State University Press). Freedman earned a Bachelor's degree in government from Cornell University, a Master's degree in resource development from Michigan State University, and a law degree from New York University.

Stephanie Hankey has been working to help human rights and social justice advocates to creatively use digital technologies since 1998. First as a programme officer at the Open Society Institute's Information Program and then as the Executive Director of Tactical Tech, an organisation she co-founded in 2003. At Tactical Tech she has worked to advance *information activism*, to defend online freedom of expression, and to promote the artful use of information for campaigning worldwide. Over the past eight years she has built Tactical Tech into the leading international organisation helping advocates to utilise technology in their work. Stephanie has a Master's degree from the Royal College of Art in London, BA Hons from Manchester Metropolitan University and a certificate in campaigning and lobbying from NCVO. She is the co-author of an upcoming book "Visual Persuaders: Activism and the Artful Presentation of Evidence".

Ann Harrison is the Communications Director of Benetech (http://www.benetech.org/), a non-profit technology company based in Palo Alto, California. She documents the work of the Benetech Human Rights Data Analysis Group (HRDAG) (http://www.hrdag.org/), which analyzes the patterns and magnitude of large-scale human rights violations. Harrison also works with the Benetech Martus project (http://www.martus.org/), which develops software that allows human rights groups to protect sensitive information. A journalist and photographer, Harrison has written about human rights data analysis projects in Liberia, Colombia, Chad, and Guatemala. Harrison earned an M.S. in Science Reporting from the Columbia University Graduate School of Journalism.

Jessica Heinzelman is a freelance ICT strategist and provides assistance to NGOs that wish to leverage Internet and communication technologies to gather data that can be used for decision-making and direct response. She is Board Chair of Sisi Ni Amani - Kenya, a Kenyan NGO that empowers community peacebuilders with training and an SMS-based communication system that enables localized and customized civic education, civic engagement and conflict early warning and response. Additionally, Jessica coordinates the Verification Team for the Standby Task Force, a virtual community of online volunteers that provides support to organizations in compiling, verifying and analyzing geospatial information in crisis situations. Jessica has a Master's from the Fletcher School of Law & Diplomacy focusing on Conflict Resolution and Communications and a Fellowship from Harvard University's Program on Negotiation.

Ana-Cristina Ionescu is Head of Foreign Affairs within the Chamber of Commerce and Industry of Romania (CCIR). She holds a BA in Communication and Public Relations from the National School of Political and Administrative Studies and a MS in International Business Studies from the Economical Studies Academy in Bucharest, Romania. She spent the last 7 years working in the European Chamber System as Head of Foreign Affairs, Head of Protocol, Deputy Director of a chamber practices division, head of a training center, and Public Relations specialist within the CCIR which is nationwide promoter of sustainable economic development in Romania. Her fields of interest are public affairs, social sciences, chambers systems, corporate social responsibility - CSR for small and medium enterprises - SMEs, gender equality, information and communication technologies (ICTs), innovation, and innovative entrepreneurship. Her writings include chapters on the importance of CSR and innovation for SMEs, ICTs, gender, and cyber identity.

Jennifer Martin (Dr.) is an Associate Professor of Social Work at RMIT University in Melbourne, Australia, and a reviewer for numerous professional journals and conferences in social work, mental health and ICT, and health and human services. She designed the "human computer interaction spiral" grounded in learning theory and reflexive practice as well as empowerment models in mental health. Current research is in innovative use of information communication technology in learning and teaching to enhance student mental health and well being. Her main areas of teaching, research, and practice are mental health, conflict management and mediation, social work, and the law. She is actively involved in social work and human rights for people experiencing stigma and discrimination due to mental illness, particularly in educational and workplace settings. Her partnership with Associate Professor Elspeth McKay over the years has combined mental health, human rights, and ICT.

Elspeth McKay is an Associate Professor of Information Systems (IS) at the RMIT University, School of Business IT and Logistics, Melbourne, Australia. She is passionate about designing effective e-Learning resources for the education sector and industry training/reskilling programmes, including investigations of how individuals interpret text and graphics within Web-mediated learning environments. She has designed e-Learning tools implemented through rich internet applications, including: ARPS – an advanced repurposing pilot system, COGNIWARE – a multi-modal e-Learning framework, GEMS – a global eMuseum System, eWRAP – Electronic work readiness awareness programme, EASY – Educational/academic (skills) screening for the young, offering enhanced accessibility through touch screen technologies. Over the last decade, Dr. McKay has published extensively in the research fields of HCI and educational technology. In recognition of her contribution to the professional practice of IS research, she was elected as a Fellow of the Australian Computer Society (FACS). Elspeth and Jennifer Martin have developed a long standing collaborative partnership with 15 joint journal papers and conference publications.

Patrick Meier (PhD) is an internationally recognized thought leader on the application of new technologies for crisis early warning, humanitarian response, human rights, and civil resistance. He currently serves as Director of Crisis Mapping at Ushahidi—a non-profit technology company voted by MIT's Technology Review as one of the 50 most innovative companies in the world alongside Facebook, Google and Twitter. He previously co-founded the International Network of Crisis Mappers and co-directed Harvard University's Program on Crisis Mapping and Early Warning. In addition, Patrick has consulted for major international organizations including the UN, OSCE, OECD, and the World Bank on numerous cutting-edge projects in Africa, Asia, and Europe over the past 10 years. He is also a distinguished scholar, holding a PhD from The Fletcher School, a Doctoral Fellowship from Stanford University, and an MA from Columbia University.

Tanya Notley has been working as a new media practitioner and researcher since 1998. During that time she has worked in Australia, the UK, Nepal, Thailand, India, and Sri Lanka with tertiary education bodies, the third sector, international development agencies, and with many community-based organisations. As the Info-activism Program Lead at Tactical Technology Collective Tanya most recently led the successful film project "10 Tactics for Turning Information into Action" (http://www.informationactivism.org/), which documents and supports the effective use of information and technology for rights advocacy. In 2008 Tanya completed her PhD in the Creative Industries Faculty at Queensland University of Technology. Her PhD study examines the ways internet use changes the way young people participate in society. Tanya has a Master's Degree in Social Change and Development and a Degree in Communication and Media, both from the University of Newcastle, Australia.

Shane O'Hanlon (Dr.) teaches Health Informatics at the Graduate Entry Medical School, University of Limerick, in Ireland. He graduated with a degree in Medicine in 2003. He also holds an MSc in Health Informatics, a Bachelor's Degree in Law, and a Certificate in Human Rights. He has published in the area of human rights in healthcare, and has presented on health informatics at national and international conferences. As a student, he undertook volunteer work in Malawi, and at Dachau and Ravensbrueck Concentration Camp memorial sites. He currently works as a clinician in Geriatric Medicine & Rehabilitation, and a Clinical Fellow in Medicine at University Hospital Limerick.

Michael Rempel is a Software Developer and architect of software systems ranging from real estate and government regulatory projects, to industrial automation and control systems. He has maintained a lifelong interest in human rights matters, with active participation in many education, aid, and relief projects. He has an unbending focus on deep understanding of difficult problems and their meanings, coupled with a tireless commitment to finding workable solutions. Michael has authored several articles and technical White Papers for industry. He is also a multimedia producer with credits on several CDs, videos, and a few movies. He was a Pipeline Data Architect for the movie Avatar. Most recently Michael spent a year as Data Architect for the Canadian Museum for Human Rights.

José Rodrigues Filho is an Associate Professor of Management Information Systems at the Universidade Federal da Paraíba, Brazil. He was Takemi Fellow at Harvard University and completed his Postdoctoral studies at the Johns Hopkins University School of Public Health, and his Doctoral studies at the University of Manchester, England. He was visiting Professor at Acadia University (Canada), and Associate Professor at the Universidade Federal de Pernambuco, Brazil. His areas of interests include management information systems, and information management (especially health information, nursing information, and hospital information systems), in addition to e-government and e-voting.

Minna Strömberg-Jakka is a Doctoral candidate at the University of Turku's Faculty of Social Sciences. She holds an M. Soc. Sc. in social work and is preparing her Ph.D. thesis on electronic services in social work and social services. Her past endeavors include the evaluation of marginalized youth in EU funded projects, welfare research, and research and work with suburban projects. As a social worker she has strived to develop social services. Ms. Strömberg-Jakka has mentored university students completing their practical training, taught at three Finnish universities, and acted as a consultant for the national project on information technology in social services. She has also lectured at various national meetings and the seminar of European Resource Centre for Research in Social Work. She is the author of several professional and scientific publications and a co-editor of a book on the challenges of social work in Finland (2012). Currently, she serves as the secretary of The Finnish Society of Social Work Research.

Rolf H. Weber is ordinary Professor for Civil, Commercial, and European Law at the University of Zurich, Switzerland, and a Visiting Professor at the University of Hong Kong. His main fields of research are Internet and information technology law, international business law, media law, competition law, and international financial law. Rolf is also director of the European Law Institute and the Center for Information and Communication Law at the University of Zurich. Since 2008 he has been a member of the Steering Committee of the Global Internet Governance Academic Network (GigaNet), and of the European Dialogue on Internet Governance (EuroDIG). Since 2009 he has also been a member of the High-level Panel of Advisers of the Global Alliance for Information and Communication Technologies and Development (GAID). Besides this, he is engaged as an attorney-at-law and as a member of the editorial board of several Swiss and international legal periodicals and serves as expert for several international and national organizations in his wide-spread fields of research.

Eric Wiebelhaus-Brahm is currently Director of Professional Development in International Affairs and Lecturer in Political Science and International Affairs at Florida State University. His research focuses on the evaluation of transitional justice tools, DDR processes, and on labor and welfare issues in emerging economies. His most recent book, *Truth Commissions and Transitional Societies,* was published by Routledge in 2010. Eric is also the author of several book chapters and his articles have appeared in journals such as the *International Journal of Transitional Justice*, *Journal of Human Rights*, and *International Studies Perspectives*. He served as a volunteer with the Liberian Truth and Reconciliation Commission's Diaspora Project between 2007 and 2009. Previously, he has held positions at DePaul University's International Human Rights Law Institute, AON Hewitt, and UNLV. Eric earned his Ph.D. in Political Science from the University of Colorado at Boulder.

Christopher Wilson has supported the coordination of freedom of expression advocates, and consulted international and national organisations on the use of ICTs to disseminate information and build local partnerships. He currently manages communications for the UNDP Global Programme on Governance Assessments, supporting country efforts to make processes of governance assessment inclusive and governance data actionable. Christopher holds a Master's degree in International Human Rights Law from the University of Oslo's Law Faculty, and a Bachelor's degree in Rhetoric from University of California Berkeley.

Index

A

American Association for the Advancement of Science (AAAS) 145-146, 148, 151
American Convention on Human Rights (ACHR) 25
Amnesty International 2-3, 14, 17, 19, 49, 58, 114, 124-125, 136-137
Arab Spring 14, 57, 100, 120, 159
autopoiesis 104, 119
awareness raising media 157

B

biometric identification 86-87, 94
biometrics voting 94
botnets 40, 55
broadcast indeterminacy 116
Building the Education Revolution (BER) 203

C

censorship 27
choice-oriented service 182
citizen journalism 53, 63
Commercial Bill of Privacy Rights 158, 173
computer mediated communication (CMC) 216
computer phobia 205
constitutional democracy 91
content filtering software 27
contingency 104
crowdsourcing 113, 123-126, 128-138
cumulative trauma disorder (CTD) 205
cyber activists 67
cyber-dissidents 42, 46
cyberfeminism 225, 227, 230-232
cyber movements 101
cyber-utopians 51
cyberwar 48, 52
CycL 9

D

dark networks 158
data protection 26, 28, 33, 238, 241-243
deep packet inspection 27
denial of service attacks 27, 55
detention response 109, 113
Diaspora Project 72-82, 84
digital activism 100-105, 116-121
digital advocacy 100, 105-106
digital broadcast 110-111, 113-115
digital divide 21, 32-33, 35, 55, 98, 191, 218, 233
digital documentation 112
digital privacy rights 159, 170-171
digital surveillance 92, 158, 161, 163
DNS tempering 27
dot-causes 101

E

eCommerce 196
e-government 86-87, 89-92, 96-99, 179, 192-193, 195
e-health 92-93, 99
electric shock torture 144
Electronic Frontier Foundation 158, 163, 172
electronic health records (EHRs) 237
electronic surveillance 86-87, 158
Equitable Assessment Arrangements policy 198
e-services 177-179, 193
European Convention on Human Rights (ECHR) 25
e-voting 86-87, 92-96, 98

F

face-to-face trainings 111
freedom of expression 21, 25, 28, 31, 33, 44, 48-49, 54, 86, 157-160, 167-169, 171, 215, 219
Front to Defend Egyptian Protesters (FDEP) 100, 106, 116

G

gendarme 60-64, 66-67
gender equality 86, 215, 217, 219, 225-227, 234
gender stereotypes 216, 225, 234
geolocation filtering 27
Global Network Initiative (GNI) 49

H

hashtags 105, 113
Haystack debacle 168
health information technology 235, 237, 239, 243-244
human-computer interaction (HCI) 196, 203
human interactivity 1, 8
human rights 1-23, 25-34, 36-39, 41, 45, 47, 49-51, 53, 55, 57-61, 63-76, 79-81, 83-84, 86-88, 91-96, 98, 100-101, 103, 106, 113-114, 118-119, 123-175, 177-179, 181, 192, 195-197, 200-201, 225, 229, 233-241, 243-244, 246
human rights abuse 10, 69, 95
Human Rights Data Analysis Group (HRDAG) 139-140, 156
Human Rights Defenders 20, 25, 157, 159-171, 173, 175
Human Rights Information and Documentation Systems International (HURIDOCS) 3
human rights monitoring 119, 123-125, 129-132, 135-136
human rights reporting 71, 123-124, 130, 136, 154
human rights violations 17-19, 37, 55, 57, 60-61, 63, 67-68, 71, 73-75, 81, 91, 131, 137, 139-142, 144-151, 153-155, 197
Human Rights Watch 14, 20, 47, 53, 55, 58, 60, 70, 91, 98, 114, 125-126, 156
hybrid communication 111
hybridity 105

I

ICT tools 196, 203-206, 211
IDOL (Intelligent Data Operating Layer) 10
informed public 111-113
Inter-American Commission on Human Rights (IACHR) 144
International Covenant on Civil and Political Rights (ICCPR) 25
International Criminal Tribunal for the Former Yugoslavia (ICTY) 148, 151
International Labour Organization (ILO) 144
International Telecommunications Union (ITU) 22, 24, 34, 219
Internet and mobile telephony surveillance 158
Internet censorship 39, 48, 54
Internet intermediaries 159
interpretivist approach 92
IP address filtering 27

K

Kefaya 60
knowledge-based society 21, 25

L

liberation technologies 101
Liberian Truth and Reconciliation Commission (LTRC) 72
Linus's Law 133

M

Mashups 8, 18, 20
Mass Media Declaration 23
mental health 196-213, 238
Mental Illness
    and human rights 200
    disclosure 199
    recovery 201
    stigma 198
metamoderation 133
microblogging 107
MObile Story Exchange System (MOSES) 80
multiple systems estimation (MSE) 131, 141, 145-147, 149, 156

N

netactivists 59
New Public Management (NPM) 90
New World Information and Communication Order (NWICO) 21

O

online consultation 178, 181, 185-186, 188-192, 195
online propaganda 106

P

peer verification 133-134, 136
people-centred development 88
police brutality 58, 60-67, 70, 162

Privacy Ombudsmen 158
protest documentation 109, 111-112, 115-116

R

Radio Frequency Identifier tags (RFID) 4
Receitagate 87, 94
Recovery of Historical Memory (REMHI) Project 152
repetitive strain injury (RSI) 205
repressitarian regimes 49-50
resistance networks 158
right to development 21-22, 26, 29, 31-32, 34, 99

S

Semantic Web technology 6, 9
SIVAM 93
Skype 29, 38-39, 52, 163
Slashdot 133
social assistance 177-181, 183-195
social media 1, 14-15, 18-19, 37-38, 41, 43, 47, 50-51, 53, 58-59, 103, 106-107, 109, 112-113, 120, 134, 159, 164, 217, 234
social networking sites (SNS) 59
social rights 22, 29-30, 33, 177-179, 181, 184, 192-193, 195
social services 178-180, 182, 187, 189, 191, 193-195, 236, 238, 246
Special Consideration policy 198
subjective right 180
Summary Care Record 239, 245
SwiftRiver 134

T

Tactical Technology Collective 157, 160-163, 166, 169, 172, 174
Teleworking 216
trade barriers 22, 29-30
transitional justice 72, 74-76, 79-80, 83-84
Truth and Reconciliation Commission (TRC) 81

U

Universal Declaration of Human Rights 141, 159, 169, 174, 179, 195, 236, 246
URL filtering 27

V

virtual communities 221-222, 225, 229, 232-234

W

Web of Trust 12, 19
wellbeing models 203
Who Did What To Whom (WDWTM) 143, 156
Women and ICTs 215, 219, 230
World Health Organisation (WHO) 236
World Summit of the Information Society (WSIS) 21

Y

YouTube effect 63-64

CPSIA information can be obtained at www.ICGtesting.com
Printed in the USA
BVOW051755311012

304278BV00006B/12/P

9 781466 619180